Domestic and International Banking

M.K. Lewis

and

K.T. Davis

The MIT Press
Cambridge, Massachusetts

First MIT Press edition, 1987

This book was set in Times Roman by Dataset, Oxford, and printed and bound by A. Wheaton & Co. Ltd., Exeter, in Great Britain.

Library of Congress Cataloging-in-Publication Data

Lewis, Mervyn
Domestic and international banking.

Bibliography: p.
Includes index.
1. Banks and banking. 2. Banks and banking, International. I. Davis, Kevin. II. Title.
HG 1586.L39 1986 332.1 87–2962
ISBN 0–262–12126–3

Contents

Preface

A recent survey of the theory of banking by Santomero (1984) showed there to be a well-developed literature of how banks operate in traditional deposit-taking and lending operations — those activities roughly corresponding to what we call retail banking. But the survey touched little on three other aspects of banking. One, the subject of a separate survey article in the same journal (Aliber 1984), but treated in a quite different manner, is the spread of banking beyond domestic markets, especially in the Eurocurrency markets. A second is the related growth of wholesale banking. Third, there is the movement by banks into a range of off-balance sheet business, including 'securitised' lending. It is our aim both to describe and explain these developments, and to provide an account of them which is integrated with the analysis of traditional banking practices.

Our starting point in the book is the essential similarity between the activities of most financial institutions. Whether called banks, insurance companies, savings institutions or securities firms, financial institutions are providing information services of various kinds and are dealing in, underwriting, and managing risks as part of their normal operations. Despite these common threads, a distinct literature has grown up for the different types of financial activity. This book attempts to draw some parallels between the different disciplines: in particular, between banking and insurance, arguing that many banking operations can be looked upon as insurance-type services. This comparison provides a frame of reference for our analysis of the similarities and differences between retail, wholesale and international banking, and the on- and off-balance sheet activities of banks.

While the major thrust of the book is analytical (although non-mathematical), illustrations are given of banking practices in the United Kingdom, the United States and also Australia, the countries with which we have some familiarity (and, in fact, chapters of the book were drafted in all three). Many of the ideas in the book have their origins in the early 1980s in the research studies which we prepared as consultants to the Australian Financial System Inquiry, and of research undertaken by one of us while a Visiting Scholar at the Bank of England.

Wherever possible, we have tried to ensure that the tables and text are carried through to 1985 or 1986, but the longer-than-anticipated gestation period has made us all too aware that the pace of change in banking markets is rapid, as other institutions enter into activities that were long the province of banks, and as banks diversify into services previously left to non-banking firms. Methods of effecting payments are undergoing considerable change under the impact of new technology and competitive pressures, while recent events underline that the safety of the banking and payments system remains a lively topic. We wished to include discussion of these matters in the book, and indeed they follow on naturally from our theme of the similar functions performed by financial institutions.

Thus the book falls into three parts. Four chapters at the beginning deal with intermediation generally, and the principles and practices of retail and wholesale banking in particular. Four chapters at the end examine international and multinational banking and banks' international securities operations. In between, three chapters look in turn at bank safety and depositor protection, payments systems, and the structure of banking markets and diversification by banks.

We have benefited considerably from reading the works of others who have written at length on issues necessarily discussed much more briefly here, and have endeavoured to acknowledge their contribution in the bibliography. Officials at the Bank of England, Bank for International Settlements, Morgan Guaranty Trust Company of New York and the Federal Reserve Bank of Chicago kindly assisted with data for some of the tables. Mr J.S. Alworth of the BIS in addition provided most valuable comments. Heather Prior and Margaret Uylaki helped with the preparation of the tables for Chapters 8 and 9. Carole Hawthorn and Vicky Garton very willingly typed the manuscript and endured the many alterations. Finally, we thank our publishers. Robert Bolick and his team at MIT Press gave us many useful suggestions and comments. Philip Allan deserves special thanks, both for his patience and for his confidence that the book would eventually be completed.

Mervyn K. Lewis
Kevin T. Davis

July 1987

1

Modern Banking

1.1 Changing Patterns of Banking

In his classic work, *Modern Banking*, R.S. Sayers noted a tendency for banking systems around the world, despite some national differences, to gravitate towards a common pattern. That pattern had first taken shape in Britain in the second half of the nineteenth century. But it had done so after nearly half a century of structural change which saw the decline of bi-metallism and the establishment of the gold standard, a switch from note issue towards the use of cheque deposits and, finally, the formation of limited liability banks which transformed banks from small, regional country partnerships into major national and international institutions. Thereafter, in terms of structure, practices and technology, banking apparently remained largely unchanged until the 1960s. As late as 1967, in the seventh and final edition of *Modern Banking*, Sayers could record that the 'ordinary business of banking' had been practised for generations, and that the shape of British banking had been settled for more than a century.

In many respects the business of banking is little changed today. Despite oft-repeated predictions of a transition to a cashless society, well over three quarters of the volume of transactions in the United States and Britain are still made with cash.[1] Dispensing notes and coin to customers for use in cash payments remains a function of banks. In Britain and the United States, and in many other countries, most remaining payments are made by cheque. Much of the ordinary business of banking thus continues to be the provision of payments services, involving the transfer of ownership of bank deposits from one account to another. In their other activities, banks still provide deposit facilities to customers and advance credit by means of overdrafts and loans, by the discounting of bills, and by trade finance.

In other respects, however, the business of banking has been dramatically altered over the past 20 years, as exemplified by the rise of wholesale banking, liability management, multinational banking, Eurobanking, the Asian currency market, international banking facilities, rollover credits, multiple currency loans, 'securitised' lending, collaterised mortgages, note

DIB-A*

issuance facilities, interest rate and currency options and swaps, and financial futures. Credit cards, debit cards, automated teller machines, cash management accounts, electronic fund transfers, point of sale terminals are also part of this worldwide process of change which began in the 1960s, has been sustained over two decades, and continues to re-shape the nature of banking and financial markets. It would seem that structural change in banking and financial markets is once again a major element. Against this backdrop of adjustment, a re-examination of the business of banking is timely.

The Sources of Change

The immediate question raised by the preceding observations about structural change is: why? Are banks performing different economic functions, or have they simply adopted new ways of doing the same job? What factors have prompted either a change in role or a change in the method of performing that role?

A straightforward answer to the second of these questions is, we believe, not possible, since the changes of the past two decades reflect (in varying degrees) a number of different influences. One such is a change in the 'real' sector of the economy leading to demands for new types of financial services. One explanation for the phenomenon of multinational banking (see Chapter 8, s.5) is of this kind, the argument being that the growth of multinational business corporations prompted bankers to follow suit. Similarly, syndicated lending (see Chapter 10, s.4) can be seen as a market response to demands for large-scale loans which are individually beyond the scope of a single financier.

A second influence in the process of change has been that of improvements in technology. The growth of electronic funds transfer systems and plastic card-using devices has been the most obvious effect of the computer revolution, but the influences go much deeper than that. Many of the financial assets on offer today, such as money market mutual funds, require continuous calculation of the value of the portfolio backing them and an ability to compute instantaneously the value of the asset for withdrawal purposes. Without modern computing technology the costs involved in producing such assets could be prohibitive.

Technological advances can, by reducing costs, give individuals and business firms direct access to some previously inaccessible markets and thereby obviate the need for financiers to offer certain services. Various ways in which this can occur may be noted. Lowered transactions costs, enabling primary securities to be issued more cheaply in smaller denominations, curtail the scope for intermediaries to perform 'size intermediation'. Similarly, risk diversification may be feasible even for small-sized portfolios. Finally, improved information flows make it easier for individuals to undertake their own portfolio management, and for credit-rating agencies to supplant the loan assessments made by financial intermediaries.

Technological advances and subsequent innovations have also led to the creation of new markets. Futures, forward, options, secondary mortgage markets have burgeoned in recent years, expanding the range of portfolio strategies open to financial intermediaries. In the face of such new opportunities, the appearance of banking was sure to change, although we argue that the essential functions performed by banks have not greatly altered (see Chapters 4, s.6 and 10, s.2).

A third influence, which should not be underrated, is that of financial liberalisation or deregulation, together with the responses by financial firms to existing regulations in a changing economic environment. The inflation of the 1970s, for example, with its effects on nominal interest rates, altered the impact of interest rate ceilings and other regulations, thereby increasing the payoff to innovations designed to bypass such regulations. More recently, and in some degree often in response to the declining effectiveness of regulations, governments worldwide have embarked on a course of financial liberalisation, extending the range of activities permitted to banks and allowing other, non-bank, financial institutions access to banking markets.

The influences identified above tend to depict structural change in banking as being prompted by forces external to the financial sector (technological advance, attitudes to regulation, changes in the type of financial services demanded). While that is a large part of the story, it is important not to forget the role of innovation and change emanating from within the financial system as a consequence of the ongoing competitive struggle. Indeed, distinguishing the relative roles of factors within and without the financial sector is extremely difficult. For example, parts of the deregulatory process often represent an *ex post* validation of activities supposedly prohibited to, but in fact undertaken by, financiers.

Despite the ongoing changes in style and structure of financial markets, it is worth making a point at this stage which underlies the whole of this book. In the face of international variations in financial structures, legislation and traditions, banks can best be examined by recognition of the functions they perform. Those functions, largely unchanged over time, can be listed briefly (to be expanded upon in later chapters) as the provision of payments services, information and intermediation services of various kinds and risk-sharing services. The emphasis upon each may vary, as may the way of providing those services, but it is in the role of banks as providers of those services that a common ground can be found between apparently differing national, as well as past and present, banking systems.

The Traditional Structure

As a way of introducing some of the themes of this book we look first at the structure of banking as seen by Sayers in the 1960s and then at the changes which have occurred since. The pattern of banking which Sayers saw as having universal applicability had three features. First, banking in a majority of developed countries was highly *concentrated*. British banking, which Sayers used as his principal example, was dominated by the London clearing banks, each with a large number of branches fanning out from London. But the same pattern could be seen in Paris, Frankfurt, Tokyo, and many other financial centres, which saw a wide network of banks, grouped around the chief trading city of the country concerned. And in most countries, the typical commercial bank was a very large institution having many branches scattered all over the country. The chief exception to his story was the US banking system, with its many thousands of individual or 'unit' banks, geographically spread and having local traditions and practices.

Second, banking was *national*, and was becoming increasingly so. For much of the nineteenth century, large parts of the world obtained banking services from the major centres like London, Amsterdam or Paris, or from banks with origins in those large financial centres. But gradually the pattern in which each country developed its own structure of banks and financial institutions was established, leading Sayers to write that 'banking organisation does not easily straddle national frontiers' so that 'the banking business of the world is organised in the main on national lines' (Sayers 1967, p. 16).

Nevertheless, despite the organisation of banking along mainly national lines, the principles of banking appeared to have universality and to be *relatively settled*. Sayers' contention was that the business of banking and the structure of the banking system in Britain had been unchanged for a century. The tendency for the banking system in most other countries to take on a similar shape, and for banks to be fewer and larger and of the branch-banking type, pointed to some advantages of large-scale organisation, of general applicability. Reinforcing these economic forces were those of habit and custom. Sayers observed:

> . . . bankers think in much the same way the world over. They get into the same habits, they adopt the same attitudes to their customers, and they react in much the same way to changes in the economic climate. The principles of banking therefore have world-wide validity, and what is said of English bankers and the working of the English system can often be said with almost equal truth of other countries. (ibid., p. 16)

His claim was, of course, immediately qualified to allow for the major exception of the United States. Differences of law and history lent a distinctive character to the US banking system. The dominance of unit banks, the role played by an active interbank market in deposits and reserves, and the co-operative lending practices which developed, set the US system apart from other banking systems.

On all these counts — the settled structure of banking and banking principles, the high concentration of banking, the national organisation of banking and the separate practices in US banking — things are different today.

The Nature of Change: A Balance Sheet Perspective

Tables 1.1 and 1.2 document some of the changes reflected in the domestic balance sheets of British and US banks. By 'domestic' in this context is meant the banking business undertaken in the home country in local currency. This is to draw a distinction between lending and borrowing which is denominated in foreign currencies (for example, British banks in London in Eurocurrency activities taking deposits and making loans in US dollars) and banking undertaken by the banks in overseas countries (such as foreign branches of US banks). That is, much (but certainly not all) of international banking is excluded. One reflection of the changes which have occurred is that in Sayers' time this distinction did not need to be made.

For Britain, comparison with earlier years is made most readily by concentrating on the balance sheets of the six London clearing banks (Barclays, Lloyds, Midland, National Westminster, William and Glyns, Coutts) which dominate the English payments system. The data presented in Table 1.1 enable comparisons over the years 1920 to 1985. In the pre-war years the clearers' distribution of assets followed what seemed to be a fairly constant pattern. W. Manning Dacey (1951) stylised the asset composition as follows:

	As % of deposits
Cash	10
Money market assets	6
Bills	14
Securities and investments	20–25
Loans and advances	45–50

During the war years the banks filled their portfolios with government securities and, with the constraints upon lending in the early post-war years, the dominance of government debt continued. Around 1950, with less than 30 per cent of deposits in loans and advances to the private sector and with over 60 per cent of deposits held directly or indirectly in government debt, the role of the banking sector had changed significantly from its traditional one. Instead of interposing themselves between depositors on one side of the balance sheet, and a large array of business and personal borrowers on the other side, the banks were essentially custodians of savings (like the old Post Office Savings Bank) allowing depositors to avoid the inconvenience of having to hold government securities themselves. By the 1960s the banks had resumed their traditional role, and their balance sheets had taken on a more traditional appearance. Indeed, in broad outline, the 1960s balance sheets replicated the 1920s pattern — in line with Sayers' suggestion of an unchanged structure.

Yet a marked change had begun to take place in British banking during the 1960s with the development of 'wholesale' funds markets. As banks began

Table 1.1 Major Balance Sheet Items in Sterling of London Clearing Banks 1920–1985* (expressed as percentage of total sterling deposits)

Year	*Current deposits*	*Deposit accounts*	*'Wholesale' deposits***	*Cash balances*	*Money market*	*Bills discounted*	*Securities & investments*	*Loans & advances*
1920	63.8	36.2	—	11.0	5.8	15.1	21.4	48.4
1930	51.1	48.9	—	10.7	7.8	14.2	14.3	51.8
1940	60.7	39.3	—	10.7	5.9	14.8	26.6	38.1
1950	66.2	33.8	—	8.3	9.1	21.6	25.0	26.7
1960	58.1	41.9	—	8.1	7.8	15.9	19.4	43.2
1966	52.8	47.2	—	8.1	10.7	12.1	12.1	50.5
1976	31.6	26.9	41.5	3.4	26.7	5.5	9.2	57.6
1980	27.8	28.1	44.1	2.7	30.0	4.0	6.8	63.5
1985	23.8	12.7	63.5	1.5	26.7	2.3	5.4	69.4

Sources: Sheppard (1971); Committee of London Clearing Banks (1985) *Abstract of Banking Statistics*.

Notes: *From 1976, data are for Clearing Bank Groups, i.e. parent banks and banking subsidiaries.
**'Wholesale' deposits comprise large value deposits raised from other banks (interbank deposits), commercial enterprises and overseas residents, and by the issue of certificates of deposit (CDs). They are calculated as the difference between all sterling deposits and 'retail deposits', where the latter consist of ordinary cheque accounts, high interest personal current accounts, and 7-day notice deposit accounts (time deposits) raised through the branch network.

Table 1.2 Major Balance Sheet Items of Domestic Offices of US Commercial Banks, 1914–1985*

	% of total domestic deposits			*% of total domestic assets*					
	Demand deposits	*Time deposits*	*CDs*	*Deposits*	*Cash items*	*Interbank balances*	*Reserves*	*Securities & investments*	*Loans*
1914	85.2	14.8	—	72.6	9.4	10.2	2.3	18.2	56.1
1920	74.4	25.6	—	73.4	6.9	4.8	5.3	18.1	59.3
1930	63.4	36.6	—	79.8	7.6	5.3	5.3	23.7	51.4
1934	70.7	32.5	—	84.5	6.3	7.9	10.2	40.2	30.0
1934	67.5	32.5	—	84.0	5.9	9.0	8.8	39.1	31.5
1940	75.2	24.8	—	89.7	5.8	11.6	19.8	34.2	26.0
1950	76.2	23.8	—	92.0	7.0	6.3	10.5	43.9	31.1
1960	68.0	32.0	—	89.3	8.4	5.2	6.5	31.6	46.0
1970	51.2	43.4	5.4	83.7	8.1	3.9	4.0	25.5	54.5
1980	36.4	42.1	21.5	77.4	6.6	3.2	2.0	25.7	55.4
1983	25.4	55.2	19.4	75.6	5.2	1.8	1.2	25.7	56.3
1985	25.2	56.1	18.7	75.7	n.a.	1.6	1.2	23.4	59.2

Sources: Board of Governors of the Federal Reserve System, *Banking and Monetary Statistics 1914–1941, 1941–1970*; Federal Reserve Bulletins, April 1981, June 1984 and January 1987, Table 4.22.

Note: *1914–1934 data refer to member banks, 1934–1985 to insured banks. Time deposits in 1983 and 1985 comprise savings accounts and time deposits of less than $100,000. Included in CDs (certificates of deposit) are brokered deposits and time deposits of $100,000 or more.

to participate in those markets and make loans with the funds they borrowed, there came the growth of *wholesale banking* – the first major break from the established pattern of banking. Here we introduce a distinction which forms the basis for much of this book: that between retail and wholesale banking. When Sayers and other earlier writers talked about 'banking' and the 'ordinary business of banking', they were referring to what is now termed *retail banking*. This is the type of banking conducted on High Street/Main Street and in the suburbs by cheque-paying banks, dealing with households and small- to medium-sized firms. 'Wholesale banking' is the term used for transactions between banks and large customers (corporate and government) involving large sums (deposits in hundreds of thousands and loans in millions of dollars or pounds). We also use the term 'wholesale' to embrace transactions which the banks conduct with each other via interbank markets separate from customers — what might be termed 'true' wholesaling in the language of the distributive trades.

Wholesale banking was not unknown 20 or 30 years ago. Something akin to wholesale banking in its present form was being conducted by the merchant banks (or accepting houses) in London. Before the War, Wall Street money centre banks (such as Bankers Trust, Chase Manhattan, Chemical, City Bank, Manufacturers Hanover, Marine Midland, Morgan Guaranty, Irving Trust) were mainly, if not entirely, wholesale banks, concentrating on lending to big businesses in New York City and other large centres. Since then, there has been a greater emphasis upon retail banking, although in recent years some banks, like Bankers Trust Company, have withdrawn from retail operations to concentrate upon wholesale banking. New York has also had its Wall Street investment banking houses, specialising in securities business, and widening corporate access to markets. But legislative barriers in the US, and lending controls along with self-imposed constraints ('internal' barriers) in Britain, kept commercial banks separate and prevented their participation or even direct competition.

In Britain the internal barriers broke down in the late 1960s, and the lending controls were lifted in 1971. With the clearers' entry to wholesale banking their balance sheets have taken on a different character. On the asset side, holdings of cash, bills and securities have declined. Money market assets, of which three quarters are interbank, and loans and advances, dominate. In the pre-war years it was considered remarkable that two of the clearing banks briefly had advances-to-deposits ratios of 60 per cent. Now the banks in aggregate have an advances ratio of about 70 per cent. Moreover, much of the increased lending is in the form of medium-term loans, not the traditional short-term self-liquidating paper. On the deposits side, funds drawn from the wholesale markets have, in recent years, contributed over 60 per cent of deposits, attesting to the development of what is known as the *liability management* revolution amongst banks. Rather than holding cash reserves and other liquid assets to meet unexpected contingencies — the practice of 'asset management' — the banks have recently aimed to manage liabilities and 'buy in' (i.e. borrow) funds when needed from the markets for interbank deposits, large-sized time deposits and certificates of deposit.

Similar trends can be seen in the United States. Table 1.2 gives details of the balance sheets of US commercial banks from 1914 to 1985. As in the UK, there have been wide swings in the banks' loan portfolios. During the war and early post-war years, US banks were also large holders of government debt, but have since brought loan ratios back to historical levels. At the same time, there has also been a switch from asset to liability management. Holdings of cash, reserves and interbank balances have declined sharply, while banks have relied upon funds 'bought in' from the wholesale markets. Certificates of deposit (CDs) issued by US banks now constitute about one fifth of deposits. There has also been an increased reliance upon non-deposit liabilities, in the form of repurchase agreements ('repos') and bought Federal funds drawn from the wholesale markets, to finance their asset holdings. These funds, and other such borrowed amounts, accounted for 11 per cent of assets at the end of 1985 (see Chapter 4, s.7 for further discussion).

The figures shown in Table 1.2 are balance sheet aggregates for all US banks in their domestic operations. In considering the trend to liability management and wholesale banking, a distinction needs to be drawn between large money centre (or money market) banks, regional banks, and small, local banks. The large banks, like the UK clearing banks, rely extensively on funds drawn from wholesale sources, but the position is different for the other banks, as Stigum (1983, p.117) observes:

> . . . a money market bank has the option of buying huge sums of money in the Fed funds, repo, CD and Euromarkets; and money market banks liberally exercise this option. A typical money market bank may finance over 60% of its assets with money bought in these markets. The corresponding position for a regional bank would be 30 to 40%, and for a small bank, 0%.

Thus we observe, in both countries, a large increase in bank lending, a reduction in cash reserves, a decline in demand and current deposits, and an increased reliance by banks upon markets, especially for wholesale funds. These common trends give rise to some common problems. With banks in the US and UK now placing over 70 per cent of deposits in loans and advances, risks are much higher than in the years when deposits were invested predominantly in government securities and, moreover, yields on those assets changed little. Much of the lending is medium-term and associated with the rise of wholesale funding. In both countries over three quarters of deposits now bear interest, and increasingly those interest rates fluctuate with market rates of interest, increasing the chance of a sudden loss of earnings should market rates rise and loan rates not follow. This in turn has accelerated the switch to variable rate lending contracts or 'flexi-rate' loans.

On their deposit instruments, banks have customarily offered payment-related services of various kinds — for example, transferability by cheque, convertibility into cash — with depository or safekeeping facilities. In order to compete in the wholesale markets, banks developed certificates of deposit for which they themselves provided no payments services. Instead, transferability or encashability came from the secondary markets in which the instruments could be traded. The same phenomenon on the asset side (illustrated by the secondary mortgage markets) involves banks originating loans and then selling the resulting securities in the market place.

The Nature of Change: An Off-Balance Sheet Perspective

Perhaps the most significant, and least well-documented, recent development in banking has been the rapid expansion of the 'off-balance sheet' activities of banks, some traditional, but many new. Four types of such activity can be distinguished. The first goes under the heading of commitments, a long-standing example of which is unused overdraft facilities and a more recent example of which is note issuance facilities (NIFs). In both cases the bank may be called upon to advance funds and acquire a credit exposure at some future date. A second set of activities, partly reflecting, partly encouraging the growth of direct financing markets, is that of bank provision of guarantees to customers wishing to borrow in such markets. Bankers' acceptances of commercial bills or time drafts are another traditional example of such an activity. By 'accepting' a bill or draft drawn by a borrower financing, say, the shipment of goods, the bank effectively substitutes its own credit rating for that of the borrowing firm, turning the debt of the firm into the equivalent of a cashier's cheque payable at a future date, and making it as saleable as any top-grade IOU in the market. This generates fee income for the bank and, so long as the acceptance is not 'discounted' and held by the accepting bank, leaves it with an 'off-balance sheet' exposure.[2] A third set reflects the growth of various markets in foreign exchange, interest rate and stock market forward contracts into which banks enter. Finally, banks (where allowed to do so) may engage in merchant and investment banking activities like securities underwriting, again fee-yielding, but involving the incurring of risks. These developments (more details of which can be found in Chapter 4) have blurred the distinctions which previously existed between the business of banks and other institutions like investment banks, and between banking and financial markets generally, and are often referred to as the 'marketisation' of banking.

The Nature of Change: An Industry Perspective

The 'marketisation' of banking finds reflection in the industrial structure of banking.[3] On first appearance, banking looks as concentrated as in Sayers' time (see Table 1.3). Mergers have reduced the number of large commercial

Table 1.3 Structure of Banking in Various Countries, 1977

Country	*Number of institutions*	*Concentration*
Australia	13 commercial banks	3 largest with 60% of assets 7 largest with nearly 90%
Austria	19 commercial banks	4 largest account for just under 90%
	7 regional banks	3 largest with just over 80%
Belgium	87 commercial banks	3 largest with more than 75%
Canada	11 chartered banks	2 largest with just under 45% 5 largest over 90%
Finland	750 banks	5 largest account for the bulk of deposits and lending
West Germany	263 commercial banks	6 largest with 44%
Netherlands	74 commercial banks	2 largest have 66%
Norway	26 commercial banks	5 largest with more than 70%
Sweden	14 commercial banks	3 largest with 75%
	188 savings banks	15 largest with 52%
Switzerland	441 commercial banks	3 largest with 45%
United Kingdom	372 commercial banks	6 largest with 47% of sterling deposits
United States*	13,669 insured commercial banks	5 largest with 13% of domestic assets 20 largest with 26% of domestic assets 330 largest with 57% of domestic assets

Source: OECD (1980) *Costs and Margins in Banking*, Paris.
Note: *1972 figures.

banks in England, Scotland, Belgium and the Netherlands. As a result, banking remains concentrated in most of Europe and in Canada, Australia, New Zealand and South Africa. Yet, paradoxically it would seem, in many of these countries there has been a large increase in the number of banks. In the UK, for example, the number of banks has increased from 125 in the late 1950s to 648 at the end of 1983. The apparent paradox is resolved by the distinction between retail and wholesale banking.

Retail banking was, and remains, highly concentrated in all countries other than the United States. However, 'non-bank' competitors, such as credit unions, savings institutions and building societies, have effectively filled the void left by the merged banks, and their existence and growth as providers of banking-type services make it difficult to define rigorously the relevant market and thus measure concentration. Even in the United States, a low level of concentration defined for the national market disguises a much higher degree of concentration within regional markets.

Wholesale banking, by contrast and, as we explain later, by virtue of its interaction with securities and funds markets, has taken on a 'large numbers' form. Many of the 'new' entrants to banking are branches or offshoots of banks based elsewhere. Here we come to the second major break from the earlier pattern: the *internationalisation* of banking.

Sayers, we recall, described a banking system which did not straddle national frontiers and, despite employing common ideas and attitudes, was organised along national lines. Retail banking is still highly national in its organisation despite the spread in recent years of a common technology of cash dispensers, debit cards, and electronic fund transfers. By contrast, wholesale banking is international in its operation, and straddles the various national money markets.

The most publicised aspect of international banking is the large-scale syndicated loans to both developed and less developed countries. But, on a day-to-day basis, in the management of liquid assets and their liability raising (i.e. 'funding'), banks arbitrage between the various international financial centres and between the major international currencies. Funding may come from domestic sources or from the Eurocurrency markets. Lending may be in domestic or in foreign currency, to local or to foreign borrowers. Off-balance sheet activities by international banks blur the distinctions between international bond and international loan markets. These various operations have been major vehicles for the integration of capital markets and currency markets worldwide.

While for the purposes of our analysis it is convenient at times to treat wholesale banking and international banking separately, much of the recent growth of both has gone hand in hand. International banking is retail as well as wholesale. Wholesale banking is domestic as well as international, with the two developing along similar lines.

The Nature of Change: Institutional Practices

With the internationalisation of banking, the gap between banking practices in the United States and Europe has narrowed. London has been a focus for many developments, with an influx of US banks to the City bringing about a transatlantic fertilisation of ideas. Innovations such as loan syndications, interbank funds markets, rollover credits and floating rate loans now form the backbone of wholesale banking around the world, and reflect the melding of US and British/European banking practices, exported throughout the world by the growth of Eurocurrency banking and banks' participation in international banking. In the process, financial centres have grown or emerged to challenge the traditional duopoly of London and New York. Tokyo now deserves to rank on an equal footing with New York and London. Strong financial centres have developed in continental Europe, Canada, Southeast Asia, and the Middle East.

Wholesale banking practices have spread not only geographically, but have filtered through to the retail end. Term lending by means of rollover credits on a flexi-rate or 'prime-plus' basis is now commonplace in banks' lending to small and medium-sized customers. Yet in most other ways the retail and wholesale sectors remained segmented until the late 1970s.

Personal customers continued to be offered the customary chequing deposit at zero interest, or time and savings deposits, at regulated rates, while corporations and those with large sums at their disposal received market rates of interest on certificates of deposit and negotiated wholesale accounts. Inflation and high and variable interest rates, facilitated by computer technology, changed all that. As market and market-related deposit rates rose to record levels, the regulated rates did not follow and a gap was created between retail and wholesale interest rates which was too large not to be filled.

In the United States, Britain, and in other countries, like Australia, market innovations called money market mutual funds (US), money market accounts (UK), and cash management trusts (Australia) were created to arbitrage the size differences which separated the retail and wholesale segments of the capital market. These market devices enabled retail depositors to take advantage of the higher rates paid on wholesale funds by aggregating the small amounts into parcels large enough for access to the wholesale sector, selling depositors, or unitholders, shares in the pooled portfolio. By offering ready encashment of units or by allowing funds encashed to be transferred into a 'cash management account' against which cheques could be written, the devices tied limited transactions services with market rates of interest.

The funds were a spectacular success. In the competitive and regulatory flux which followed in the early 1980s, banks introduced new deposit instruments which replicate many of the features of the funds. Other institutions have followed suit. Money market deposit accounts in the US and high-interest cheque accounts in the UK pay market-related deposit rates in return for limited cheque-writing facilities, bringing about an unbundling of transactions and depository services. The result is a new pattern of retail banking, marked by competition and the diversification of services, along with the application of computer technology.[4]

Two developments seem especially portentous. First, the banks' monopoly of the cheque transfer system in both the US and the UK has been removed. Other depository institutions, such as building societies, savings banks, savings and loan associations and credit unions, now provide transactions services. In the UK, transactions services are also offered by unit trusts and merchant banks. In the US, cheque facilities can be obtained from some insurance companies, finance houses, securities firms and retailers. There has thus been a blurring of lines between banks and other financial institutions and the creation of 'universal' financial institutions, variously called financial conglomerates, financial department stores or financial supermarkets.

Second, with money market mutual funds and securities firms now offering cheque-writing facilities, there has been an important change in the character of payments services. Until this innovation, payments were made by exchanging notes and coin directly or by transferring notes and coin indirectly, in the form of bank deposits, which are guaranteed claims to fixed amounts of notes and coin. Now, for the first time, millions of Americans can, in effect, write cheques against portfolios of securities, the value of which fluctuates daily, albeit within a narrow range.

In some eyes we are witnessing with this development the beginning of a revolution in financial practices. If cheques can be written against portfolios of securities, why not against portfolios of shares and other assets? Building on the prescient views of Fischer Black in 1970, a number of writers hold out the vision of a world in which banks as we know them will disappear and be replaced by markets and market-based institutions like mutual funds.[5] As futures markets and options markets develop, so will the need for financial intermediaries diminish. Thanks to modern technology, markets may increasingly allow individuals, as they do large corporations, the ability to bypass banks and other financial intermediaries when conducting their day-to-day transactions.

We mention this to illustrate that the theory of money and banking is also far from being in a settled state. An examination of modern banking must start by re-examining the fundamentals of banking theory, of why banks and financial intermediaries exist at all, before moving on to the wholesale and international characteristics of banking. There is also a marked imbalance in the literature. While retail banking, at least in its traditional form, is well covered and so, to a lesser extent, is international banking, there is virtually no literature on wholesale banking *per se*, nor on its relationship to the other categories. Analysis of the newer forms of off-balance sheet business is in its infancy. In the analysis below we sometimes find it helpful to argue by analogy with the theory and practice of insurance as a way of integrating some of these strands. We shall now outline some of the major issues.

1.2 Outline of the Analysis

Banks are financial firms and, like all firms, exist because of economies of size and because of the gains which arise from internalising certain activities within an organisation rather than relying on market transactions. We do not produce motor vehicles in our own toolsheds because there are economies of specialisation and large-scale production which give firms producing cars a considerable cost advantage. By the same token, automobile manufacturers do not typically produce all components of their product within the firm, nor supply long-term after-sales service as part of a motoring package. So it is with financial services: financial firms provide packages of financial services which individuals find too costly to search out, produce, and monitor by themselves. The questions then to be asked are: what is it that banks produce? What are the scale economies upon which their existence rests? What determines the degree of internalisation of activities and thus the product range?

At the most general level, banks are institutions which combine various types of transactions services with financial intermediation. A study of banking must therefore embrace: the nature of payment systems and banks' contributions to them; the nature of financial intermediation; and why it is that banks combine transactions services with these intermediary or 'middle-man' activities.

For Britain and the United States, three types of transactions services are generally provided by banks. First, banks stand ready to convert deposits into notes and coin in convenient amounts, and at various locales, to enable holders of deposits to undertake transactions in cash. Second, they operate an accounting and organisational framework by which ownership of wealth in the form of bank deposits is transferred by bookkeeping entries as a means of settling debts. Third, banks exchange cash and deposits denominated in the unit of account of one country into notes and coin and deposits of other countries. As noted, banks are not alone in providing these transactions services, and there is the question, considered in Chapter 6, to what extent other providers — savings banks, building societies and credit unions — are effectively banks.

Since transactions services could be provided separately by specialised service companies, as is the case with giro transactions and credit cards, there is the further question of why it is that banks combine money transmission with financial intermediation and typically price the two jointly, the latter indicating preference by many customers for packaged pricing arrangements. We approach the question in Chapter 3 from two directions, suggesting on the one hand reasons, in terms of the collection and usage of information, why firms producing transactions services may be able to offer a cheaper product by joint production, and on the other hand why firms acting as financial intermediaries tend to evolve into providers of transactions services.

As financial intermediaries, operating both on- and off-balance sheet, banks interpose themselves between borrowers and lenders of funds, but the nature of the borrowers and lenders and the ways in which banks interpose themselves can vary markedly over time. We have already drawn attention to the large postwar increase in loans and advances as banks switched from government finance to business and personal lending. At the international level the changes have been even more dramatic, as banks took over from bond and equity markets the role of financing economic development and payments imbalances between countries.

Shifts like these in underlying imbalances between borrowers and lenders and in the preferences of both groups can occur, and, as tailors of financial services, matching the wishes of both, banks must adapt. But so also can the ways in which banks undertake intermediation be adapted. The joint rise of medium-term lending and wholesale banking is one example; another is the advent of inflation and the switch to variable-rate lending. As financing requirements have altered, so the intermediary services of banks have adapted with them, and our aim is to put these developments into perspective.

Intermediary services can be regarded as of two basic kinds. One is a *brokerage function*, as represented by the activities of brokers and market operators, processing and supplying information — but it is part and parcel of all intermediation by institutions. Brokers bring together borrowers and lenders in different parts of the country or in different parts of the world or in different walks of life, but in doing so do not greatly alter the terms and conditions of particular securities which the parties exchange. In effect, brokerage firms exist because of their ability to reduce market 'imperfections', such as search, information and transaction costs, which exist in the markets for particular financial assets. Indeed, without such institutions, the markets might not exist — if the anticipated size of such costs is sufficiently large. In this respect, the existence of brokers will alter the relative use of different types of securities, as well as the overall magnitude of financing.

The other kind of service is provided by institutions which do qualitatively alter the securities in which they deal, issuing claims against themselves which differ from the assets they acquire. The difference could be as little as one of size intermediation, such as providing many depositors with a share of a large asset (or spreading one depositor's funds between many borrowers). Or it might be as large as purchasing equity-type assets and issuing debt-type liabilities. Such *portfolio transformation* is carried out by most intermediaries, normally along with brokerage functions. Mutual funds (known as unit trusts in the UK), insurance companies, banks and depository institutions all fall into this category. Where they differ is in the nature of the transformation undertaken and in the nature of the protection or guarantees which are offered. By pooling together a large number of company shares or a large number of real estate properties, mutual funds provide protection against loss should one of the assets fall in value. Insurance companies protect against losses to 'assets' (broadly interpreted) arising from other contingencies, such as premature death, fire, burglary. Banks and depository institutions offer their customers protection against the possibility of being short of funds.

Somewhere in between the brokerage and asset transformation activities of financial firms (and blurring the distinction between the two) are various off-balance sheet activities of financiers such as the issuing of guarantees and underwriting of security issues. Once largely the preserve of accepting houses, merchant banks and investment banks, commercial banks and other financiers have in recent years begun to play a major role. For a fee, such institutions provide the 'insurance' necessary to facilitate direct financing. Guarantees, such as bill acceptances, reduce the default risk attached to such bills, by virtue of the accepting banks' good reputation. The reduction in the interest rate risk premium attached to the bill (for which the drawer of the bill pays a fee to the bank) represents a type of 'insurance premium' paid indirectly by the purchaser of the bill to the bank. In a similar implicit vein underwriting fees can be seen as premia for 'insurance' against the market not absorbing a security issue at the hoped-for price.

With portfolio transformation it is also instructive to regard the activities as a form of insurance. The intermediary can be thought of as buying securities issued by borrowers of funds and then offering them to lenders of funds with an insurance policy added. Costs of servicing the policy are recovered from the interest rate differential and service charges. In the case of banks, insurance is provided against the contingency that depositors have unexpected needs for cash, with banks providing a guarantee that deposits can be withdrawn on demand or at short notice, in full or in part, at a fixed price in terms of the unit of account. In short, banks provide liquidity insurance to their depositors.

An analogous argument can be made to indicate how banks also provide insurance-type services to their borrowers. The intermediary, we visualise, accepts liquid deposits from lenders and offers them to a borrower with an assurance added. The guarantee, in effect, is that the intermediary will provide substitute deposits, on agreed terms, should lenders demand their funds before the borrower's need for them has ended. The nature of the protection afforded will, for example, depend upon whether the loan contract is fixed or flexi-rate, and, again, costs of servicing the policy are reflected in the interest rate differential (between loans and deposits) and in service charges.

In general, then, banks can be viewed as providing a package of information and risk-sharing (insurance) services to their customers via their intermediation activities. And in doing so, they (bank owners) also take on part of the risk involved. How they structure their activities and devise appropriate contracts so as to manage this risk and increase their income is a large part of the subject matter of this book.

By means of the analogy with insurance, we endeavour to throw a different light upon the nature of traditional retail banking, wholesale banking, international banking, and the new forces of competition in retail financial markets.

Almost all insurance arrangements are based on the holding of reserves. Individuals could themselves lay up a fund to cover, say, ill health and car accidents, and many in fact do so. Others prefer to purchase insurance, leaving the insurer to accumulate and manage the funds. They do so because the intermediary is able to pool reserves more economically, taking advantage of the fact that not all accidents occur at the same time. So it is with banks. Not all depositors want cash at the same time, nor do all loans fail, allowing economies of scale in reserve holdings and capital resources.

In both cases there is pooling of individual risks so that the law of large numbers can operate, as in the case of motor car insurance and retail banking, where the numbers of customers served by individual companies run into thousands and millions. Wholesale bankers have a small number of large customers and cannot readily operate on the law of large numbers. The same is true of insurers underwriting risks which are large relative to their capital resources. Amongst insurers the solution is a complex industry network of risk-pooling arrangements and options contracts involving co-insurance and re-insurance treaties. We argue that wholesale banks employ similar procedures to spread their risks. They adopt interbank arrangements which are tantamount to formal and informal risk spreading with other banks and they also employ a number of balance sheet options to maintain flexible investment strategies. By virtue of the arrangements, banks act as efficient organisers of risk-bearing services. But risk spreading means that the risks are shared, converting individual risk into an explicit systems risk and creating a need for collective monitoring arrangements.

Much of international banking is wholesale, and our starting point is that similar practices and similar arguments apply. Yet, available evidence is sparse. A recent OECD report[6] observed that there is virtually no evidence on the extent to which balance sheet structures in international banking mirror those in national banking. Opinions also differ. Some have argued that in international operations, especially Eurobanking, the brokerage function dominates the asset transformation role. In essence, their view is that the banks undertake currency transformation but do not basically alter the character or the maturity of the securities concerned. After presenting some evidence on these matters, we go on to look at what are, in all accounts, some of the distinctive features of international banking. One is the extent to which banking services have been externally produced in the Eurocurrency markets; much international bank lending has been undertaken by what are in effect 'duty-free' banks. A second characteristic is the amount of interbank business, which makes up perhaps three quarters of the total, and a third is the protracted repayment of bank loans by the less-developed countries.

With respect to this third characteristic, the analogy with insurance again provides a different viewpoint. Insurers have long pondered over the question of how to distinguish between insurable and uninsurable risks; and the risks of international loans may have much in common with natural disaster insurance. For disasters, the law of large numbers breaks down not only for individual insurers but for the system as a whole. Use of the standard risk-sharing arrangements helps but still leaves individual firms and the system as a whole with risks which they are ill equipped to bear. Nevertheless, in the final analysis, insurance is concerned with the best allocation of risk bearing in the prevailing circumstances. Current attempts to deal with international bank loans need to be judged in that light.

Finally, when looking at the new competitive forces in retail banking, we can again gain some insights from the insurance literature. Some of the recent cross-industry invasions by banks, depository institutions, insurance companies and other institutions into each others' 'patches' reflect the fact that most financial intermediaries can and do offer financial security to customers in a variety of ways. Because of this common element there is a basic similarity between financial services, and the products can be fashioned to compete with others at the margin.

But there is also a well-established theoretical proposition in the literature on risk and insurance: that, in a world of complete financial and commodity markets embracing futures and options, there would be no role for insurance and intermediaries offering risk-sharing services; indeed, without transactions costs, information costs, indivisibilities and frictions of any kind, there would not be a role for *any* financial intermediaries. We are a long way from such a world, despite the rapid development of futures markets and options markets in recent years, and the lowering of transactions and information costs due to advances in computer technology. Nevertheless, economies of scale in the processing of information and portfolio management, upon which the existence of intermediaries rests, are neither continuous nor unchanging, depending upon the state of technology and the range of markets. Nor, for that matter, is the optimal degree of internalisation of activities within the financial firm or the appropriate range of products produced by any one firm. In the face of developments in computer technology and information processing, we do not expect the business of banking to remain invariant.

Notes

1. Accurate information on the use of cash is difficult to obtain. Estimates made by Humphrey (1984) suggest that cash transactions in the United States might represent 73 per cent of all transactions by number; but Humphrey admits that the estimate is 'very approximate' (p.6). These estimates are reported in Table 6.1 in Chapter 6. For the United Kingdom, the International Bank Research Organization estimated that, in 1981, payments in cash accounted for 88 per cent of the number of all transactions of £1 or more and 78 per cent of all transactions of £3 or more. The importance of cash for payments by households is evident also when the value of payments is considered. Data based on a survey in 1981 of 10,000 adults living in Britain indicate that 50 per cent of the value of transactions over £3 were in cash (Trundle 1982).
2. The recent growth of bankers' acceptances in the USA is examined in Jensen and Parkinson (1986).
3. A detailed analysis of the comparative structure of banking in the early 1980s is contained in Wilson (1986).
4. These developments are examined in Carter, Chiplin and Lewis (1986).
5. Black (1970), Fama (1983), and Greenfield and Yeager (1983).
6. Pecchioli (1983).

2

Financial Intermediaries and Financial Assets

2.1 Intermediary Services: An Introduction

Financial intermediaries are merely firms which produce financial services. But, having said this, it must be admitted that their activities raise definitional problems which distinguish them from other types of firms, and foremost among these difficulties is that of determining what is produced.

A number of approaches can be found in the academic literature. One, advocated by Sealey and Lindley (1977), looks upon loans as the end product. The financial firm uses deposits merely as an input to produce a flow of services to its debtors, represented by the volume of loans. A directly opposite approach, which is also implicit in the usual textbook story of credit creation, sees deposits produced as an output of the act of making loans (Pesek 1970; Towey 1974). Empirical studies of scale economies in the industry (see Chapter 7) usually follow one or other of these approaches, although some are amalgams of both.[1]

Despite these differences, there is agreement that financial institutions are part of the service economy and that they produce a flow of services to their customers. This characteristic finds reflection in the methods used in the national income accounts to measure the financial sector's contribution to national production. In essence, the value of this output is measured by the gap between interest paid by borrowers and interest paid to depositors (along with any fees received, net of purchases of intermediate goods). That interest differential is seen as the value placed by the market on services provided by financial firms for which, however, they do not levy explicit fees.[2]

This, in turn, leads to the question of why it is that many financial firms, like banks, exempt their customers from paying fees and charges for services, at the expense of offering higher interest to depositors. A history of regulations (such as the longstanding prohibition of interest payments upon demand deposits in the USA) and cartels (like that operated by the British clearing banks from the 1930s through to 1971) encouraged such practices and plays a role still in shaping industry norms. But there are also problems of joint production and joint consumption to be solved in moving to alternative pricing arrangements. Financial firms usually supply a range of diverse services and the costs of providing them can be divided between product lines and customers only in arbitrary ways. Payments services, for example, involve banks and other institutions in jointly servicing two customers, one being the payer and the other the recipient, utilising a clearings infrastructure provided cooperatively. Intermediation services (borrowing and lending) require an act of joint consumption by the loan and deposit customers. It is for such reasons that we adopt the view of the financial firm as a collection of contracts (between it and its customers) with the provision of services arising from differences in the characteristics of contracts entered into with depositors and borrowers.

Given these characteristics, it is perhaps not surprising to find that a number of national income accounting conventions have been used for allocating the output of financial firms between various customers. One convention (found, for example, in the USA before 1947 and in Australia until 1973) was to avoid the problem by treating banks as akin to government, providing general services to the community. An alternative (found in the United Nations pre-1968 methodology and in the current US approach) is to treat bank output as services to depositors, and allocate it to bank customers according to their share in deposits. A third alternative (the current United Nations methodology) treats the output as services to borrowers, allocating it according to the share of various sectors as borrowers from financial institutions.

Despite these differences, the national accounting approaches do recognise that the provision of financial services requires institutions to use real resources and their owners to supply factor inputs. Often, analyses of banking focus exclusively upon the features of the balance sheet without reference to the income–expenditure flows associated with creating and maintaining a particular balance sheet structure.[3] Perhaps the most obvious of these 'real resource' inputs are the buildings, staff and equipment employed by the financial sector. Less obvious are such intangibles as the 'knowledge capital' built up by years of serving particular customers and evaluating their past performance. Information gained from such lasting relationships is valuable for lending business. It is also an important ingredient in the story of the growth of multinational banking (see Chapter 8). Central to all banking operations, both 'on' and 'off' balance sheet, are the entrepreneurial qualities of bank owners and their willingness to take risks. The way in which banks facilitate the undertaking of risky activities (such as long-term investment projects) by assuming risks themselves, and the way in which they adopt strategies to ameliorate those risks, are major topics of this book. The relative importance of these factors of production naturally depends upon the type of activity undertaken by a particular financial firm.

Intermediation between borrowers and lenders of funds is the central process of financial markets (see Carter, Chiplin and Lewis 1986) and can occur in a great many ways, as will be explained when we examine different intermediary types (in this chapter) and different forms of banking (in following chapters). But at the outset of the discussion it may be helpful to distinguish two different types of intermediation, while recognising that most intermediaries do both and that there are many shades in between. One is a 'distributive' or 'brokerage' function whereby the economic role of the intermediary is to facilitate the transfer of ownership of existing financial assets. While supplying information and specialised advice, the intermediaries do not create new financial securities nor do they alter the basic characteristics of those securities in which they transact.[4]

Most financial intermediaries, however, do more than act as brokers or agents in the transmission of funds between borrowers and lenders. They issue contracts which, in various ways, modify the attributes of the financial securities which pass between the borrower and lender. In the clearest example of this transformation, intermediaries acquire securities with particular characteristics from borrowers and offer entirely different types of securities to lenders, both types of contracts differing in nature from what might have arisen in a direct arrangement between the borrower and lender. The resulting changes in the *primary* securities (those offered by borrowers) and differences between them and the *secondary* securities offered by the financial intermediary to lenders (with regard to characteristics such as marketability, transferability, capital certainty, convenience, maturity, contract enforcement costs, etc.) represent the services provided by such financial firms. Inputs of labour and capital are needed to carry out such a transformation, along with the creation and assumption of certain risks by the financial firm itself.

As a result of these activities, there is a vast array of financial products on offer, but most of the services involved are directed, in one way or another, towards satisfying three basic financial needs of households and firms. These are:

1. Payment services, which provide means of paying for and acquiring goods and services.
2. Consumption transformation, which enables the purchase of goods to be rearranged over time. For example, households can defer spending to later periods, firms can undertake investment now.
3. Financial security, which ensures the continuance of consumption and investment expenditure in the face of changed economic circumstances, as may arise from ill health, accidents to life or property, unemployment, exchange rate and interest rate variations, etc.

It is possible to conceive of households and firms meeting these needs without the assistance of financial institutions, but there are widely divergent paradigms about the nature of a world without financial institutions and the subsequent reasons for and benefits from the existence of financial firms in the world as we know it. Some envisage such a world to be financially primitive, others see it as a highly sophisticated and technologically advanced state.

2.2 Stages of Intermediation

In this section we outline a number of hypothetical 'states' so as to illustrate the reasons for 'introducing' intermediation. This is followed in the later sections by an outline of certain intermediary types operating in the US and the UK.[5]

The first paradigm is the portrait presented in most of the traditional texts on money and banking of primitive financial arrangements: how primitive depends on the range of financial assets available. At the most basic, we might envisage an economy without 'money', that is, paper money issued by governments, and without any other financial assets.

Absence of Financial Assets

In the absence of money, the economy would face the inefficiencies and uncertainties of *barter* exchanges. A long chain of complex and uncertain exchanges would be needed for people to convert their initial endowments of goods and labour services into the preferred consumption bundles. One good (for example gold or silver) might be chosen to serve as a unit of account, so as to reduce the vast number of calculations involved in a set of relative prices, and this commodity might also be used for exchanges. The gains are obvious, but there are resource costs to the society as a whole in holding, adding to and maintaining the stocks of the commodity (i.e. costs of mining and storing gold).

Introduction of paper money overcomes the inefficiencies and uncertainties of barter exchanges at potentially a much lower social cost, because the resource costs of commodity money can be avoided.[6] As compared with barter, use of paper money involves more exchanges: a direct exchange of good A for good B is replaced by the switch of good A into money and then money into good B. But the indirect monetary exchange is more convenient, since the two parts can occur at different times. It is also more certain, there being a greater probability of not being able to carry out the direct exchange at the expected terms than with the monetary transactions (Hahn 1982, p.25).

Introducing paper money also breaks the nexus between savings and investment decisions. Previously, households could save, but only by undertaking investment in real goods (including the commodity used for exchanges). Others could not invest beyond their current savings because there was no means of borrowing. Money loosens this constraint to the extent that saving can occur by accumulating money balances, and investment take place by running down holdings of previously accumulated money balances.

Direct Financing

By allowing for borrowing and lending, the constraints upon savings and investment can be more comprehensively lifted. Ultimate borrowers issue new financial assets ('primary securities') and these are purchased directly by the ultimate lenders, either in face-to-face negotiations or by participating in marketplaces. Borrowers can invest beyond their present resources by incurring debt, allowing a division of labour between investors and savers. Lenders are encouraged to save by the widened menu of assets. Before, a household could save in two ways: either by holding commodities, the value of which on disposal is uncertain in terms of the medium of exchange, or by holding paper money which is certain in money value but bears no interest. Financial assets offer a middle choice, giving an interest return yet having resale value in the financial markets.

Nevertheless, there are unexploited gains for financial intermediaries inherent in the nature of financial assets. These are, by definition, promises to deliver at some future date. The value of one to a potential lender will depend upon the perceived character of the individual issuing the promise (as regards honesty, unwarranted optimism about future prospects, etc.), together with expectations of how future events may influence the worth of that promise. In addition, lenders have preferences as to what is to be delivered, how the amount is to be calculated, time of delivery, and so on, which typically do not coincide with those of potential borrowers.

For direct financing to take place there must be a meeting between a lender and borrower whose preferences overlap, thereby providing some common ground upon which negotiations as to the precise form of the contract can take place. And unless such a meeting occurs by accident, there will be *search and/or transaction costs* involved in obtaining information about, and in meeting and negotiating with, potential other parties to a contract. These costs will be built into the minimum (maximum) interest rate acceptable to lenders (borrowers) or will affect other contract terms demanded, so reducing the range of mutually acceptable contracts.

One reason is initial differences in the *preferred habitats* of borrowers and lenders. Borrowers undertaking investment may wish to borrow for relatively long terms so as to pace out the repayments with the flow of expected returns from the project, issuing long-term debentures or mortgages. Other borrowers may be so uncertain about future income and costs from the project that they prefer to borrow in a form which does not commit them to specific repayments, issuing shares and equity claims. By lending funds, the saver is indicating a willingness to give up some present goods and services in return for a larger amount of goods in the future. But there are a great many uncertainties in life, and the saver may wish to retain discretion as to when the future consumption takes place; but he is limited to trading in the sort of security which the borrower issues. Some compromise must be struck, but at a cost which may inhibit many potential lenders and borrowers from entering the market.

These difficulties with direct financing relate to the nature of what is to be delivered, when, and on what terms. Of at least as great an importance is the problem of assessing the inherent value of the promise to deliver. Two types of difficulty arise when there is a separation of savings from the accumulation of wealth.[7] First, there is the *ex ante* problem of imperfect information whereby lenders are unable to assess the future prospects of a borrower accurately, particularly when some borrowers may have an incentive to paint an overly-optimistic picture of the future. *Adverse selection* can occur when an asymmetry in information costs exists due to the lenders' inability to observe the attributes of borrowers and the contingencies under which they operate.[8] Second, there is an *ex post* problem of monitoring the actions of the borrower for consistency with the terms of the contract, and ensuring that any failure to meet the delivery promise is for genuine reasons. *Moral hazard* refers to the problems which may flow from the inability of lenders to ascertain and exercise control over the behaviour of borrowers.[9] Finally, should the borrower be unable to meet the commitments as promised, a solution must be worked out between the borrower and lender. This also requires much information since a 'workout' is most likely to be successful if it is tailormade realistically to the borrower's business prospects and capacity to repay.

Such information difficulties create, as an immediate consequence, the problems of designing financial contracts which, once entered into, give both parties the appropriate incentives with respect to the other's welfare. They can inhibit ways in which differences between borrower and lender preferences can be overcome, for example with regard to maturity. Secondary markets for long-term securities, which would reduce the maturity constraint imposed on a lender, are impeded by the costs which arise because potential buyers are unable to assess accurately the underlying worth of the assets on offer. These markets must also cope with the 'moral hazards', due to actions which may be taken by the borrower to escape from fulfilment of the obligation or from the reduced incentive to perform up to expectations. (Such hazards can arise in secondary markets for mortgages and other loans in the context of maintaining appropriate incentives for initiators of loans to screen and manage adequately loans which they do not subsequently hold as assets – see Chapter 4, s.7.) Similarly, borrowers are inhibited from entering a sequence of short-term contracts because duplication of information gathering costs by successive lenders can increase the effective borrowing costs. Also, risks of obtaining reasonable future loan accommodation may arise if the information gathering process still leaves large uncertainties.

Information Services of Intermediaries

In these circumstances, there are clearly-defined roles for financial institutions to play. A niche exists for middlemen, brokers or operators in the markets for financial contracts who can bring together borrowers and lenders at lower costs than would otherwise be the case and to facilitate the transfer of ownership of existing financial assets. They provide and process information and evaluate credit risks, thereby saving on resources used in search and information gathering. These activities do not involve the creation of new financial assets by the firms, nor do they alter the form of the contracts.

We can envisage information services being provided in a number of ways. Intermediaries could function solely like an introduction agency or marriage bureau, relying for their existence upon running a centralised information pool. This obviates the need for potential market participants, whose demand for or supply of credit has some degree of flexibility in timing, to be in the same location at the same time in order to be aware of the existence of the other potential party to the loan contract. Potential borrowers and lenders would willingly pay amounts for access to the pool which reflect the associated reduction in search and transactions costs and which, if the institution is to be viable, cover the costs of creating and maintaining the pool.

Providing a listing service of potential borrowers and lenders is, of course, a far cry from intermediation as we generally recognise it. Somewhat closer to intermediation proper would be the situation where the institution utilises the specialised information acquired in the course of its listing activities to advise customers as to suitable partners to a loan contract or perhaps even act as an agent in selecting partners (computer dating!). Further reductions in transactions costs are clearly available, and it is unusual for such institutions not to proceed to this type of activity.

Loan brokers and investment bankers provide financial services to corporate enterprises which are in many respects akin to the second type of function. Investment management advisers do so in personal financial markets. An example of the 'marriage bureau' role is provided by the London Enterprise Agency, which acts as a clearing house bringing together would-be backers and seekers of small-scale venture capital. The agency publishes a bulletin which gives details of proposals from individuals seeking funds and provides a venue for introducing (but not advising) the parties. Its formation was prompted by an apparent information/equity gap from conventional capital-raising sources, due to the fixed costs of evaluating a company (in the order of £15,000–£20,000) and then monitoring its performance (£5,000 per annum). The agency may have reduced the former, but other monitoring costs remain high (see Binks and Coyne 1986).

Clearly, if search, transactions, monitoring and enforcement costs are largely invariant to the scale of transaction, and if potential borrowers and lenders are large in number, markedly heterogeneous in relevant characteristics and possessing diverse tastes, the task of matching may remain costly even with a degree of centralisation. Borrowers may want longer-term loans than lenders are willing to contemplate, may want larger loans than any individual lender can provide, or be unable to assure lenders of their creditworthiness.

Portfolio Transformation Services

Scope thus exists for financial intermediaries, acting as principals, to bridge the gap between the types of financial assets that lenders prefer to acquire and the forms of debt that borrowers want to issue, where the two do not match up in size, duration or in other respects. The most important way that intermediaries do so is by 'debt substitution', the substitution of the intermediary's own liabilities for those of the ultimate borrowers. This activity can take a number of forms, but we envisage it at two levels.

At the first level, the one contract involved in direct financing is replaced by contracts of the intermediary upon the primary lender and of the primary borrower upon the intermediary, but with relatively little change in terms and conditions involved. By this means the process of gathering information and monitoring the investments is also centralised, but in addition to reducing transactions and search costs, this substitution alters the pattern of claims and therefore reduces the risk to lenders, if only by means of the pooling process. Further, by allowing lenders to have a claim upon the one entity (the intermediary) instead of a heterogeneous collection of claims on other individuals, there is greater scope for a secondary market to develop. The activities of mutual funds (unit trusts) fall into this category. So also do bankers' acceptances not held by the accepting bank and other similar 'off' balance sheet activities where the only change is the substitution in the market place of a banker's liability and reputation for that of the drawer of a commercial bill or security.

At the second level, intermediaries issue contracts to lenders which differ fundamentally from those which are issued to borrowers. In this way the intermediary lender may be better able to solve the information and incentive problems inherent in the separation of borrower from lender, using privileged information for credit evaluation and enforcing loan compliance and specialising in 'workout' problems for individual borrowers. Where the borrowers' assets acquired by the intermediary are highly information and incentive specific, the process of converting them into liquid claims from the viewpoint of lenders is termed the 'creation of liquidity', in contrast to the distribution of liquidity at the first level of transformation distinguished above. While it is useful at this juncture to maintain a clear distinction between the two 'levels' of transformation services, we note, for later reference, that guarantees and other 'off' balance sheet activities of banks have blurred the two distinctions. In particular, the guarantees and assurances provided have gone a long way to imparting to primary securities the degree of 'liquidity' which has customarily been associated with secondary securities (see Chapter 4, section 6). Since liquidity production is such an important feature of intermediaries' activities, a brief digression on the meaning and definition of liquidity is warranted.

The Nature of Liquidity

When comparing the nature of the liabilities issued by certain institutions with the type of assets held it is often said that the institutions have imparted *liquidity*, that is, the indirect or secondary securities which they issue are more liquid than the primary securities which they purchase. Unfortunately, although the term is a popular one, it is also an amorphous one, since liquidity is a catch-all term based on a number of properties of assets: marketability, reversibility, divisibility, and capital certainty.[10]

Marketability relates to the ease and speed with which the value of an asset can be realised. By 'value' is meant the maximum amount of cash that could be obtained by selling or otherwise liquidating the asset at that particular time, under the most favourable conditions. Cash is fully marketable since realisation is defined in terms of cash. Savings deposits can be fully realised as soon as the depositor gets to the branch or ATM of an institution or after the term of notice elapses. Listed shares can be sold at current value as soon as the broker is notified and effects the sale. For shares in private companies or real assets such as houses, where the characteristics are highly specific, time must be taken to search out and negotiate with potential buyers.

Reversibility refers to the discrepancy in value between the contemporaneous acquisition and realisation of an asset. Suppose that an asset is acquired and then immediately sold. Reversibility is measured by the realised amount relative to the contemporaneous acquisition price. For new cars, sold after driving out of the showroom, the difference is considerable. For cash, there is no difference, save for the negligible time and effort involved. The extent of the discrepancy depends on transactions costs broadly interpreted as brokerage, commission, insurance, time and effort, information uncertainties, and so on.

Divisibility is reflected in the smallest unit in which transactions in the asset concerned can occur. Cash is for most purposes fully divisible although this is not true of individual denominations, such as a $1,000 note. At the other end of the scale, money market paper sold in minimum denominations or job lots is not divisible.

Capital certainty is the extent to which an asset's future value in terms of cash can be predicted at future dates. Cash and deposits which are guaranteed as redeemable in terms of cash are fully predictable, so long as there is no risk of the institution defaulting on the promise. Shares have imperfect capital certainty since stock market valuations in general and the fortune of particular firms can change. Government bonds are predictable at issue and on redemption; in between their value can fluctuate due to interest rate variations. Note that capital certainty is defined here in terms of cash. In terms of predictability in real terms, the ordering above could be reversed.

Assets which are highly marketable, highly divisible, highly reversible and are capital certain can be referred to as 'liquid'. But because 'liquidity' represents this collection of characteristics which may be present in varying degrees in various assets, the liquidity of an asset is not a measurable characteristic. Moreover, liquidity lies very much in the eye of the beholder, since it reflects in part assessments of future conditions in the market for that asset. Thus, the perceived liquidity of an asset may reflect an expectation of government policies aimed at stabilising yields and that asset price, or a belief that not all holders will want to dispose of the asset simultaneously. If government policies change or bank runs occur (for example) the perceived liquidity of bonds or bank deposits may turn out to be misconceived.

The Rationale for Intermediaries: A Summary

The ability of institutions to create liquidity and undertake other portfolio transformation activities reflects two fundamental factors. On the one hand, there is the divergence between borrower and lender preferences as to contract terms and the costs of direct financing, which create a space for intermediaries to fill. By taking on certain activities such as information gathering and monitoring of borrowers, and accepting risks associated with asset transformation, intermediaries provide services to their customers. But, on the other hand, the contracts they enter into with customers must also assure customers that the intermediary's activities are, with 'delegated monitoring', consistent with their welfare. The lender to an intermediary, for example, is still confronted with the (albeit altered) problem of imperfect information and monitoring enforcement costs. In short, there are enhanced choices and informational advantages when people delegate the selection and management of portfolios to financial intermediaries, but the intermediaries must themselves be monitored.[11] Intermediaries must design attractive contracts in response to these twin forces of customer preferences and customer concern, and they must overcome associated costs and risks.

This, then, is the essence of the traditional story of the social functions of financial intermediaries. They are seen as a 'step up' from market-based arrangements. In the modern analysis of the theory of finance, financial intermediaries still carry out the same activities. But, taking the opposite tack, they are seen to be a 'step down' from a system of direct financing via markets. Indeed, far from improving matters, financial intermediaries under some circumstances can misinform and distort the workings of the system.[12]

The Complete Markets Paradigm

To reach such conclusions, a very different world of markets is visualised. It is one in which there are negligible transactions and information costs and a complete set of spot, futures, and options markets, embracing all commodities and all contingencies, as in the Arrow–Debreu general equilibrium model.[13] Futures markets deal in contracts to future spot transactions: for example, an agreement to buy or sell a given quantity of an asset at a specified date. With the Arrow–Debreu framework, individuals are able to borrow by selling goods now for delivery at a future date and lend by buying goods now for future delivery. Investors can buy inputs of labour and materials and finance the purchases by selling today the outputs for future delivery. In the absence of transactions costs and uncertainty, direct barter exchanges make more sense than direct exchanges via money as a means of making payments.

There is no uncertainty because of the markets for contingent claims. Options markets, for example, deal in contracts which give purchasers the right to undertake future transactions; that is, a purchaser secures (by paying a fee for the contract) the right to buy or sell a certain amount of an asset at an agreed price at some future date or over some specified time period, but is not obliged to take up the option. Under present-day conditions, such contracts give their holders insurance against future contingencies such as the possibility of a major price decline in a particular asset. But options could conceivably be written to cover almost any contingency. In the extreme, as Tobin (1984) imagines:

> Such a market, for example, would enable me to contract now for an umbrella on the day of the Harvard–Yale football game in 1990 if it is raining that day and if a Republican is in the White House. In exchange I could sell a promise to give an economics lecture in New York City in 1994 if I am still in good health and the unemployment rate exceeds 8 per cent.

By such means households would obtain financial security against various economic hazards. By participating on both sides of the markets, it is the households, and not intermediaries, who would bear all risks, according to their tastes for risk bearing.

We need hardly observe that very few markets of this type in fact exist, in large part because of the extensive costs of operating and enforcing contracts made in such markets. Because of this 'market failure', financial intermediaries enter the story, as it were, by the back door and, moreover, for reasons much the same as those in the old story: that is, to reduce search, monitoring and transactions costs by acting as middlemen, and to provide savers with greater safety and financial security than they can obtain from their own portfolios without access to markets for contingent claims.[14]

Despite this common ground, the modern view provides us with a very different conception of the evolution of the financial system and the purpose of financial intermediaries. In the traditional view, financial intermediaries represent the final stage in the evolution of the financial system:

> The financial development of our country can be thought of as a rather steady progression from the cruder to the more sophisticated techniques for solving a common economic problem, with the colonial governments' paper money issues at one end and modern intermediative techniques at the other. (Gurley 1961)

By contrast, in the new view, financial intermediaries must be seen as no more than a transitory phase in the evolutionary path to a full set of Arrow–Debreu markets.

What is more, advances in computer technology and the associated decline in transactions costs may fast be pushing the financial system in that direction. Banks and other financial intermediaries are turning loan business over to markets and moving off-balance sheet in their activities, both domestically and in international business. Futures markets and options markets are burgeoning, and individuals are using them increasingly. Not so long ago futures markets were confined to agricultural goods, raw materials and metals. Now they cover foreign exchange, interest rate and financial assets, and also groupings of financial assets, for there are futures contracts on stock market indexes such as *Standard & Poor's 500*, options on stock indexes, and options contracts on futures contracts on stock indexes. There is even the ability to gamble or invest directly in US inflation by means of the Consumer Price Index futures contract traded in the New York Coffee, Sugar and Cocoa Exchange. In the United States, the volume of transactions in all futures increased from less than 4 million contracts in 1960 to over 50 million in 1978 (Burns 1979). Since then financial futures have shown explosive growth. Trading in interest rates futures on Treasury bonds in Chicago alone has expanded from 3 million contracts in 1978 to 41 million contracts in 1985. Also in the United States, computer technology has 'revived' a form of 'barter' by allowing people to write cheques against portfolios of securities.[15] For these reasons, the Arrow–Debreu paradigm may be seen as providing a guide to the direction of current and future trends in financial systems.

While recognising these insights, it must also be said that financial markets, on this interpretation, have a long way to go. There are good reasons why futures markets are likely to fall well short of theoretical ideals. Contracts are written now at set prices, but most goods and services are far from constant over time in terms of the quality of the services provided and in production technologies, creating problems of specification and moral hazard. Partly for these reasons, the probability of default is higher than for spot transactions and the contracts are more difficult to enforce. Markets for options face even more difficulties, limiting the extent to which markets can allow individuals to protect themselves.

We also doubt whether people really want to effect payments by the exchange of non-monetary assets, that is, by 'barter'. In the absence of futures markets there is uncertainty about the (particularly asset) prices at which future consumption will occur. For relatively short time horizons there may be greater uncertainty about relative commodity price movements than about the money price of commodities, so that people wish to write fixed money contracts and to store purchasing power in forms which are constant in money terms. Market securities do not provide such guarantees, but banks and many other financial intermediaries do so in their deposit contracts, despite the fact that the deposits are backed by those same market securities.[16]

Later, we shall examine how banks are able to offer these guarantees. For the moment, having established that financial intermediaries have a niche to fill, we shall look at the function of several broad classes of intermediaries: mutual funds (unit trusts), money market funds, savings institutions and insurance companies. We shall find that the similarities are more striking than the differences, and will summarise the common elements in the final section.

2.3 Pooled Investment Funds

Both mutual funds, or open-ended investment companies (the American name), and unit trusts (the British name) are legal constructions which permit the 'pooling of a large number of small unequal amounts of money belonging to different individuals in a common fund to be invested by skilled managers'.[17] Pooled investments can take a variety of forms, exemplified in the confusion which continues to arise in British discussion between unit trusts and investment trusts. The latter involve an investment vehicle with share capital fixed in amount and are referred to in the US as a 'closed-ended investment company'. British unit trusts are the equivalent of the American 'open-ended mutual funds' and issue new units or shares every time they receive additional money from subscribers.

The most common form of closed-ended fund is a company which uses the funds provided by shareholders to 'invest' in the shares (stocks) of other companies. Despite a fixed share capital, 'gearing up' of ordinary shares by borrowing is possible, thereby making the risk–expected return combination facing shareholders different from that of the asset portfolio. Consequently, because of gearing and the forces of supply and demand for the closed-ended investment companies' fixed stock of shares, the market price of closed-ended funds' shares can be greatly above or below the market value of the underlying share portfolio. This cannot happen with open-ended funds, because gearing is prohibited by charter and the number of units or shares is not fixed. Being open-ended, the supply of units, i.e. capital, can be increased or decreased according to demand. If unitholders wish to dispose of all or some of their units, the manager of the fund can simply cancel the units and sell off the corresponding assets. Accordingly, the market value or price of the units will, within set limits, vary directly with the market value of the securities represented by those units.

Pooled investment funds began in Britain in 1868 with the formation of the Foreign and Colonial Government Trust, an open-ended trust. Because of legal difficulties, this and other funds were converted eleven years later to closed-ended investment companies, and they remained the sole form of pooled fund in Britain until 1931. It was not until 1985 that open-ended funds in Britain overtook the closed-ended funds in terms of size. At the end of 1985, assets managed by open-ended funds had a market value of £20,307 million, as compared with the market value of £18,385 million for the closed-ended investment companies.[18] In the USA, the open-ended trusts dominate the industry, due in part to the salutary demonstration in the 1930s of the ability of gearing to accentuate downward movements, but in the main to a reflection of the aggressive promotion of open-ended funds by advertising and direct selling methods — an option denied the closed-ended funds.[19] In the mid-1960s, open-ended mutual funds were five times larger than the closed-ended investment companies and that difference in size has probably widened since then.[20] It is the open-ended funds upon which we shall now concentrate.

By allowing individuals to purchase a share of a managed portfolio, mutual funds perform a number of functions which we group under three headings. First, there is what we have called the 'brokerage' function, in which information is processed and collected for resale. Left to their own devices, people would need to gather information about the various securities, assess the inherent risks, devote time to monitor and evaluate new information on an ongoing basis, and then undertake all the administration involved in making alterations to the composition of their portfolio. The fund arrangement centralises the collection and the processing of the information, and the administrative chores. Subscribers acquire the information and professional investment management at a price — the management fee — but are left to assess the ability of the managers of the various funds.

Second, diversification is made possible by the size of the fund. This is the factor which prompted the formation of the first British pooled fund in 1868, its prospectus making clear that the purpose was 'to secure for the investor a degree of diversification in his investment portfolio which a single individual is unable to obtain unless he is extremely wealthy'.[21]

Third, units can be readily encashed, and open-ended funds are more liquid than direct shareholdings. This comes about partly from the lower variability of the market value of a well-diversified portfolio, but mainly from the nature of fund arrangements. All pooled funds are, of course, owned by the unit-holders, but they are held in trust and invested in the name of the trustee (normally a bank or insurance company), such investment being performed, for a fee, by the management company. Under the trustees' supervision, the job of the manager is to invest and administer the funds, advertise and promote the units, and conduct a market in the units. This market is a distinctive feature of mutual funds.

Creation and cancellation of units by asset sales and purchases involve costs (stockbroking, duties, etc.) which can be avoided. One way of avoiding these costs would be to hold, in the asset portfolio, a buffer of liquid assets, and charge purchasers and sellers of units transactions fees which reflect the reduced return on the overall portfolio. An alternative is for a third party (a 'market maker') to arbitrage between buyers and sellers at different times, purchasing and selling units at prices where the spread reflects the savings on asset transactions costs. The manager, operating on his own account, is obviously well placed to perform this role.

Thus, in the USA, one shareholder in a mutual fund is able to redeem his or her shares while another is acquiring newly issued shares in the same fund. No portfolio transactions need be executed by the fund to accomplish this change of ownership. As would a depository institution, the fund simply records a transfer in the ownership of its liabilities. In addition, cash holdings are used to absorb net redemptions of shares or to supplement a low level of net sales. At the end of 1985, open-ended investment companies in the USA held cash and liquid assets at 2.8 per cent of total assets. The savings in costs which result can be illustrated by the situation in the UK.

Government regulations covering the operation of open-ended funds in the UK determine the maximum permitted offer price and the minimum permitted bid price and thus the maximum margin available to the manager. These are based on charges that stockbrokers would make to buy and sell the underlying shares in the fund, allowable service charges for the manager, along with stamp duties, and so on. The maximum margin varies from fund to fund, according to the trust deed, and normally is around 13 per cent. Managers are usually able to operate with a dealing margin of about 6–7 per cent.

Consequently, by running a market in the units, the management company greatly reduces the costs of buying and selling units, so enhancing their liquidity. This involves a marked change in the role of the management company. When acting as investment manager, the company is making decisions which can give rise to risks of gains or losses, but these are passed on fully on an agency basis to the unit-holders. As a market maker the company is bearing similar risks, but as a principal on its own account.

2.4 Money Market Mutual Funds

Whereas mutual funds had their origins in Britain in the nineteenth century, and were well established in the US by the 1930s, money market mutual funds are of very recent origin. Introduced in the US in 1970, they remained virtually unused until 1978. Since then their growth has been spectacular and, at the end of 1982, they were far larger than conventional mutual funds with assets under management of $207 billion compared with the $90 billion of conventional funds. By the end of 1985, this relative position had altered. Conventional mutual funds had grown to $283 billion, while the money funds had relatively stagnated with $208 billion of funds under management. This has been replicated in a number of other countries, notably Canada and Australia. In all three countries the money funds are a textbook example of how quickly financial institutions can evolve to fill a gap in the financial structure, and they illustrate Kindleberger's (1983) dictum that 'necessity is the mother of institutions'.

The particular gap filled differs from that which gave rise to standard mutual funds, which pool mainly equities and long-term fixed interest securities. For them the basic idea was to create a size sufficiently large for risk diversification to operate. Pooling in the case of the money funds is not for that reason, since the pooled funds are placed mainly in short-term 'prime' paper. This paper is issued only in large denominations ($1 million minimum) and without pooling the investment would clearly be beyond the resources of most individuals. Thus the funds undertake a *size intermediation*, enabling individuals to aggregate their resources in order to take advantage of the higher interest rates available on large job lots. The regulation of interest rates on small job lots through depository institutions provides part of the rationale for their explosive growth, although the reductions in the costs of continually valuing such assets (as is necessary for withdrawal on demand) afforded by modern technology also play an important role.

While the legal structure of money market funds is basically the same as that of open-ended mutual funds, terms and conditions are fashioned to reflect the niche they were designed to fill, in particular to take account of the short-term revolving character of liquid funds for which the bid–offer spread of conventional mutual funds would be inappropriate.

Investors are invited by prospectus to take up units in the trust, which describes the range of assets in which funds may be placed, together with the fees (including any up-front initial joining commission) and expenses which may be charged. The net income from the money fund is distributed fully at intervals to unit-holders simply by dividing this net income by the number of units. Thus they are in the US terminology 'no-load' funds.

From the customer's viewpoint the great initial appeal of the funds lay in the high interest rates, relative to those offered by depository institutions in the early 1980s, combined with the low minimum subscription ($1,000 or even less), ready redeemability (same day or 24 hours' notice) and low riskiness. The relative interest advantage has been eliminated by new deposit instruments introduced by depository institutions in 1982 to compete with the money market funds, but the features of the money funds remain. Interest rates are simply market rates minus a small management fee, divided between the fund management company (the investment adviser) to cover portfolio management and dealing costs and professional management fees, and its parent sponsoring company (the distributor) to cover selling costs and direct personal services provided to unit-holders. Both income and expenses are calculated daily, and dividends are declared and reinvested daily, so that the redemption value is known daily and can be published in the financial press. Since the funds collected together are invested in diversified pools of large denomination money market instruments such as Treasury bills, commercial paper and negotiable CDs, all with relatively short maturities (with the average maturity of the portfolio normally ranging from 30 to 60 days) and negligible default risk, they offer a low-risk investment.

In practice the valuation methods adopted by funds can create an element of risk for unit-holders which in principle should not exist. By valuing assets at face value rather than market prices and paying withdrawals by customers at a unit price based on the former value, losses can be made when withdrawals force asset sales at market prices below face value. The remaining customers bear the resulting loss. However, for funds holding government and prime securities, and especially with such short average maturities, the rise in rates would need to be of crisis proportions to prevent unit-holders from at least recovering their principal. Thus Merrill Lynch record in their prospectuses:

> It is anticipated that the net asset value will remain constant at $1.00 per share.

Yet they add the rider:

> There can be no assurance that the objectives of the Money Market Fund will be realised.[22]

Some of the Cash Management Trusts, as they are called in Australia, go further and issue a guarantee that, should the market value of units fall below one dollar, the sponsoring company will redeem the units at parity. Because the capital resources of the sponsors are small relative to the size of the trusts' portfolio it is widely assumed that the backing for the guarantee comes, indirectly, from the sponsors' overseas parents — namely, US banks.[23] In offering such a promise the trusts are acting more in the manner of a bank or depository institution than a mutual fund, as we shall see in the next section. Moreover, in basing the promise upon the backing of a parent, the trusts are not unlike depository institutions which rely on the support of a central bank or a government-run deposit insurance fund.

Before looking at the activities of depository institutions, we must comment on the money market mutual funds from the viewpoint of the sponsoring companies. For sponsors of funds, fees charged provide a gross annual income of around $600,000 per $100 million of mutual funds out of which operating costs — brokerage, handling costs, redemption costs, advertising, etc. — must be met. Since 140 of the 330 money market mutual funds on offer in the United States at the beginning of 1985 had funds of less than $100 million, it is obvious that the management of funds has not been a large profit centre for the sponsors (although many control several funds). Industry sources report that some funds with $1 billion of assets produce little profit.

Many sponsors seek to tie the fund(s) to other financial services, and so defray costs across other product lines. A large number of brokerage and other firms offers cash management accounts (CMAs)[24] which combine the features of money market mutual funds and traditional margin accounts. These allow for withdrawal of funds by cheque, although there is often a lower limit to the denomination of the cheque drawn (usually $500). More sophisticated variants are blossoming in which a controlling cash management account is linked with several special purpose money funds. Automatic sweeping arrangements, handled with the assistance of modern computer technology, switch balances to and from the cash account and the funds. To the cash account or brokerage account is tied an automatic overdraft privilege, a cheque book enabling cheques to be issued against a conventional commercial bank, and a credit card, which might also be used in automatic teller machines at various banks and other locations. In this way, funds move automatically into or out of conventional transactions balances to mutual funds paying market rates of return. Cheques are written, in effect, against portfolios of securities, so monetising them for transactions purposes.

From the viewpoint of the evolution of financial systems generally, as well as in the US, the importance of the money market mutual funds and the cash management systems, and their equivalents in other countries, is difficult to overstate. Across the whole spectrum, the 'higher level' financial intermediaries have, by the pressure of competition, been forced to rethink and alter the financial services they provide. Banks have been forced to recast the ways in which they have historically bundled together transactions and depository services. A merging of wholesale and retail banking practices has been hastened. Savings institutions have now followed the example of the money funds, and, like banks, bundle together transactions and depository services. Insurance institutions have altered their traditional bundling of insurance and savings facilities.[25]

In order to appreciate these developments we need to look first at how the 'higher level' intermediaries operate. As retail intermediaries, banks share many features with savings institutions and insurance companies. Before looking into the activities of 'banks', we shall examine savings institutions and insurance institutions.

2.5 Savings Institutions

Savings and loans associations, mutual savings banks, building societies and credit unions share a number of features, despite their different origins.

Savings banks, with beginnings dating back to a crofter's cottage in Ruthwell, Scotland, in 1810, are the oldest of the institutions. Their development proceeded from a gap on the deposit side. Founders of many of the early savings banks were concerned to provide an outlet for the savings of the working man and encourage thrift. Building societies, savings and loan associations and credit unions provide examples of gap filling from the loan side. In most countries, their origins can be traced to poorly developed loan markets — for housing finance and personal loans — which provided scope for viable intermediation.

These different origins continue to shape the present-day balance sheets, which are compared in Table 2.1 as at the end of 1985. Building societies in the UK, and savings and loan associations in the US, have a larger proportion of assets in mortgage loans and mortgage-backed securities (80 per cent and 72 per cent respectively) than do the US mutual savings banks (50 per cent). US credit unions have much larger portfolios of consumer loans (55 per cent of assets) than the other savings institutions in the US (4 per cent for the associations and 8 per cent for the savings banks).

But the institutions also have many elements in common. First, most liabilities take the form of *deposits* whereby the gathering of funds is facilitated, and the attractiveness of the liabilities enhanced, by the ability of customers to make small-scale deposits and withdrawals upon savings

Table 2.1 Distribution of Assets of Selected Savings Institutions at end 1985 (% of Total Assets)

	USA			*UK*
	Savings and Loan Associations	*Mutual Savings Banks*	*Credit Unions*	*Building Societies*
Mortgage loans	61.3	50.4	6.9	80.3
Mortgage-backed securities	10.4	n.a.	n.a.	–
Consumer loans	4.2	8.0	55.2	–
Commercial and industrial loans	1.6	n.a.	–	–
Cash bank deposits and government securities	5.2	17.7	26.4	18.2
Corporate bonds and investments	8.1	16.7	6.0	–
Fixed assets	1.3	0.9	n.a.	1.0
Other assets	7.9	6.3	5.5	0.5
TOTAL	100.0	100.0	100.0	100.0
Value of assets (m.)	$1,072,100	$218,800	$137,200	£121,239

Sources: Savings Institutions Source Books, 1968; *Flow of Funds Accounts, Financial Assets and Liabilities, 1962–1985,* Building Society Fact Book, 1986.

accounts with the intermediary. In the US, savings and time accounts still make up 79 per cent of the liabilities of savings and loan associations, 91 per cent of liabilities of mutual savings banks and 91 per cent of liabilities of credit unions. For these institutions, chequing accounts still comprise only about 3 per cent of assets. Second, no depositor has an account which could be regarded as of significant size relative to the intermediary's total deposit liabilities. Third, the asset portfolio is, on average, of longer maturity than the liability portfolio. Fourth, the asset portfolio contains a reserve of highly liquid assets (cash, deposits at call with other intermediaries, etc.) in addition to *earning assets* such as mortgages, securities, and so on. Nevertheless, earning assets still make up the great bulk of assets — between 80 to 90 per cent in the case of US savings institutions and UK building societies. Fifth, these earning assets mostly consist of a large number of small claims (relative to total assets) on different households or firms which in most cases are individually not marketable.

Viewing their activities as a whole, we see that savings institutions are typically significant producers of liquidity, as indicated by the differences listed above between their asset and liability portfolios. Compared, for example, to mutual funds, the gap between the two sides of their balance sheet is wider in terms of the attributes which make up 'liquidity'. Many, perhaps most, of their earning assets are individually highly illiquid. Mortgages are not individually marketable; they are irreversible and not divisible, and are also capital uncertain. Portfolios of mortgages have been rendered more capital-certain by private and government insurance, and more marketable, reversible and divisible by virtue of schemes whereby individual mortgages are packaged together, claims against the pool created, and secondary marketing of them takes place — essentially, mutual funds of mortgages (see Chapter 4, section 7). But not all mortgages and loans are so packaged, pooled and insured, and thus the contrast remains with the other side of the balance sheet, where deposits are frequently readily realisable, reversible and divisible, and the institution provides a guarantee that at future dates the deposit can be exchanged dollar for dollar, or pound for pound, into cash.

Even more so than mutual funds, the savings institutions undertake a brokerage function, allowing depositors to save on the information and transactions costs involved in searching out and evaluating potential borrowers. On the loan side, the savings institutions act like mortgage bankers and finance companies. Mortgage bankers specialise in the making and administration of mortgage loans. Finance companies specialise in instalment credit, personal loans and leasing. Mortgage banks (in the US) and finance companies (in the US and UK) are 'one-sided' retail institutions, in the sense that their liabilities come entirely from wholesale sources. They borrow in large lots, providing retail services on the loan side only. Savings institutions are 'retailers' on the deposit side as well as on the loan side, although in both the UK and US they are drawing more upon the wholesale deposit markets.

Like mutual funds, savings institutions pool together a large number of assets and thus derive the benefits of risk diversification. But their activities differ in two respects. First, the savings institutions may be able to get a spillover effect from their deposit business to their loan portfolio. In the course of monitoring the deposit business of customers, the institutions build up a profile as to a customer's ability to repay loans. This interrelationship may even be formalised into an implicit intertemporal contract, as with building societies in the UK and savings institutions in Australia, in which a period of years as a depositor qualifies a customer for immediate access to mortgage finance. Consequently, safe and risky borrowers can (to some extent) be identified and loan contracts written which reflect these characteristics. The institution is able to provide depositors with claims on a portfolio of loans which have lower *individual* default risk (with the same expected return) than those loans which lenders would have chosen individually. Intermediation by savings institutions does not involve a third party being interposed between the *same* group of lenders and borrowers.

Nevertheless, despite pooling and selection procedures, some asset risk must remain. Unlike mutual funds, savings institutions do not pass on the residual risk to all holders of their liabilities. Depositors are given a guarantee of repayment of principal at full money value, along with interest. Unlike the money market mutual funds, the institutions do not have prime, short-term assets to help make good the promise. The undiversified risk of uninsured mortgages and loans held on the balance sheet or on-sold with a guarantee by the institution falls upon shareholders and debtors (including possibly depositors). In order to shield depositors from declines in the value of asset holdings, sufficient capital resources must be held to make good the promise. Determination of a sufficient level of capital resources is referred to in the literature as the *capital adequacy decision*.

Savings institutions also promise to repay deposits on demand or at the expiration of a term of notice. Like the managers of open-ended investment companies, the institutions effectively conduct a market in deposit claims. Unlike mutual funds, the asset portfolios which back the claims are not all marketable, and many assets could be sold off at short notice only at considerable capital loss. Thus, when 'cancelling units', the deposit manager must ensure that illiquid assets do not have to be sold off. In order to insure against this contingency, the deposit manager must ensure that there are sufficient holdings in the portfolio of cash and near-cash assets which can be drawn down. But such holdings reduce the earnings of the overall portfolio and the returns which can be paid to depositors and shareholders. Reconciliation of these objectives forms the basis of the *reserve asset decision*.

How savings institutions are seen to go about determining the best holding of capital resources and reserve assets is examined in the next chapter where we shall look at the theory of retail banking. Retail banks are basically savings-type institutions which bundle these services together with payment facilities, and we shall pick up the main issues in Chapter 3.

2.6 Insurance Institutions[26]

At the most general level, insurance institutions are much like other financial institutions. Savings institutions take in funds, called deposits, invest them in securities and loans to earn interest, and then repay depositors. Insurance companies take in funds, called premiums, invest them in securities to generate investment income, and then pay out to policy-holders. Yet insurance institutions are frequently put into a different compartment from other institutions: the element of insurance they provide is seen as making them special. We argue in this section that insurance institutions have much in common with the institutions that we have already examined, that is, savings institutions and mutual funds. This slant reflects our starting point in this chapter. In section 2.7 we shall go on to develop the argument outlined in Chapter 1 by starting from the opposite tack: that banks and other financial intermediaries can be looked upon as sellers of insurance-type services.

Insurance companies issue financial contracts which give their customers protection in the event of various contingencies capable of causing financial loss (such as premature death, robbery, fire, accidents, injury, ill health). We shall first consider the operations of life insurance companies.

Life Insurance

Life offices could offer financial security against death by means of one-year contracts, with annual premiums rising sharply in line with the age of the life covered and the increasing likelihood of dying. Although it is possible to buy *term insurance* (or temporary life insurance) on this basis, this is not the usual way in which life insurance policies operate.

Under the standard form of term life insurance policy, a contract period of a number of years' duration is specified and a constant annual premium is determined. If the person whose life is the subject of cover then dies during the contract period, and if the various other terms of the contract have been complied with, the insurer pays out the sum specified in the contract, and no further premiums are payable. If at the end of the contract period the relevant person is still alive, the obligations of the insurer simply end.

The fact that a constant annual premium is being levied when the likelihood of a claim arising on the policy is in fact increasing from one year to the next means that, during the early years of the contract, premium monies are being paid in excess of what would have been necessary to secure the same cover under one-year term policies for those years. The insurer then holds these 'excess' premiums on behalf of the insured until the later years of the contract when the premiums paid are falling short of what would be required under one-year term policies. In effect, then, the insurer is providing the insured with two distinct sets of services: death cover over the contract period via a sequence of one-year term policies (each with its own appropriate premium rate); and a 'premium-equalisation' service, consisting of the management of a balance of pre-paid premiums on behalf of the insured.

Under a *whole-of-life* policy, the contract period is not a specified number of years: it is the remaining lifetime of the person whose life is the subject of the cover. A constant annual premium rate is again the norm. The difference between this type of contract and the standard type of term contract is essentially one of degree, since very long-term contracts (say 120 years) are effectively whole-of-life policies. But this difference of degree is a basic change. In most other classes of insurance, there are some policies on which the relevant insurers do incur claims and there are some on which they do not. In a whole-of-life contract, both the insurer and the insured know with certainty that sooner or later a claim must arise.

If we ignore for the moment the complications of the costs of administration, investment income on funds held, and the insurer's surplus (or profit), we can say that the premium rate on a whole-of-life policy must be set such that, in the case of the person who lives for exactly the mean expected number of years from the year of having his (or her) life become the subject of cover, the aggregate of premiums paid must exactly equal the sum specified as payable at death (the 'sum insured'). With a person who lives longer (less) than the relevant mean expectation, the aggregate premiums paid exceed (fall short of) the sum insured. For the person whose lifetime exactly matches the relevant mean expectation, payment by the insurer of the sum insured is tantamount to a simple refunding of premiums, and the relevant policy has acted as a vehicle for saving. A stream of constant annual premiums has been handed over to the insurer through a number of years. The insurer has held these funds on behalf of the insured and, on a particular day when the sum has reached a predetermined figure, has made repayment of the accumulated balance. The analogy with a highly self-disciplined 'target saver' building up a time deposit in a savings bank and eventually, on a planned day, closing the account, is apparent.

A pool of such whole-of-life policies serves an insurance function *and* a saving function. By the time the last of these contracts expires, the insurer will have paid out the sum insured on each and every policy. In the early years, when few claims are being made, the insurer must be accumulating the funds necessary for coping with the more rapid flow of claims in later years. The funds held are, in effect, an aggregate of a set of 'prepaid premium deposits' – one deposit per policy still in force. The insurer manages these deposits and simultaneously provides each insured with death cover.

Under an *endowment insurance* contract, the sum insured becomes payable *either* with the death of the person, if this happens during the contract period, *or* at the conclusion of the contract. These policies consequently also provide both death cover and a vehicle for saving. When the contracts commence, the mean expectation of life of the person is usually greater than the contract period, and the bulk of claims takes place at maturity. The saving element is accentuated and for the insurer it means that a still greater proportion of the premiums charged must be set aside in special funds held on behalf of those insured.

Annuities also require the insurer to hold 'time deposit' type funds. In the simplest type of annuity contract the insurer agrees to pay a fixed sum per year, from the starting date of the contract until the death of the person, in return for a single lump-sum premium, paid in advance. Abstracting again from administration costs etc., we can say that the premium set on such a contract must be such that, for the 'average' person, the annual payments received from the insurer must exactly equal the lump-sum premium paid. The contract boils down to a gradual refunding of the lump-sum premium, and the annuity has served simply as a vehicle for *dissaving*. With a pool of annuity policies, the insurer is providing people with two flows of services: insurance cover and the management of 'dissavings account' funds.[27]

To summarise, then: for term policies the insurer holds prepaid premiums on behalf of those insured. With whole-of-life policies the same principle applies, but on a larger scale. Endowment insurance policies require the insurer to manage an accumulating balance of the insured's savings. Annuities require the insurer to manage a decumulating balance of the annuitants' savings. The other standard types of life insurance contract in existence can be regarded as outgrowths of these four key types, and all in one way or another bundle together life cover with a substantial 'savings bank' type facility. In order to provide interest on the 'time deposits', life insurance companies hold assets of various kinds. In the US, these assets are predominantly fixed interest rate bonds and securities, basically long-term; such securities accounted for 78 per cent of assets in 1985 (see Table 2.2).

Thus the US life insurance offices, in providing portfolio management services, operate much along the lines of savings banks, acquiring long-term mortgages, bonds and government securities and issuing time deposit facilities providing a guaranteed rate of interest. Of course, unlike ordinary savings accounts, the savings facilities offered by life insurance offices are not designed to be realised readily, except at substantial cost. Under the pricing arrangements adopted by the companies, 'administration' expenses (mainly commissions to the sales force) are front-end-loaded against initial premiums, so that surrender values are zero for most of the first two years. Thus the 'time deposits' of life offices have capital certainty, but not the attributes of marketability and reversibility. Nevertheless, life offices do provide for policy-holders' liquidity needs in another way, by issuing options in the form of standby credit facilities. These enable policy-holders to borrow against policy liabilities, often at guaranteed fixed rates of interest.

During the late 1970s and early 1980s life policies, not surprisingly, came

Table 2.2 Distribution of Assets of Life Insurance Companies at end of 1985

Type of asset	*US life companies (% of total)*	*UK life companies (% of total)*
Government securities	15.0	25.3
Corporate securities:		
bonds	36.0	3.8
stocks	9.4	48.3
Mortgages	20.8	1.9
Real estate	3.5	15.5
Policy loans	6.6	0.6
Miscellaneous	8.7	4.6

Sources: American Council of Life Insurance *Life Insurance Fact Book*, 1986, p. 17; *Financial Statistics*, January 1987, Table 7.13, HMSO.

Notes: 1. UK 'corporate stocks' include unit trusts.
2. UK 'real estate' includes only land, property and ground rents in UK.
3. UK assets are valued at market values; US bonds at amortised values.

under the same pressures as the time and savings deposits of the savings institutions when market interest rates soared, at times up to levels of 20 per cent per annum. Both the savings institutions and the life offices had inherited portfolios of bonds and mortgages providing income at the interest rate levels of 10 years before. Both were unable to compete with the yields on market instruments and the yields on money market mutual funds which followed market trends. Time and savings deposits at savings institutions were withdrawn. Life insurance policies were cashed in and policy-holders exercised options to borrow at guaranteed and, by then, low fixed interest rates. On new business, many people themselves effectively 'unbundled' the death cover and savings element of life insurance polices. Thus an intended whole-of-life policy was replaced by a term insurance contract written with an insurer and a 'savings account' held with a money market mutual fund.

In response to these competitive pressures, some US life offices have introduced new types of policies. *Universal life* is a repackaged variant of whole-of-life policies, but with in-house unbundling of death cover and the savings facility, and an ability to alter the two components with flexibility. It is still no cheaper to cash in policies, but premium payments can be halted in the face of unexpected needs for cash. New computer technology is deployed to 'customise' these facilities to an individual's preferences and needs. *Variable life*, however, is a quite different arrangement, pioneered by British insurers. *Unit-linked* or *investment-linked* policies, as they are called in Britain, were introduced in the 1960s and have become very popular there. In 1985 these policies accounted for 27 per cent of new yearly premiums and 94 per cent of single premium income in the UK. The existence of these policies accounts for the markedly different asset structure of life insurance companies in the UK as compared with US counterparts, as shown in Table 2.2.

Instead of bundling together death cover and a savings-type account, the unit-linked or investment-linked policies package the insurance cover with a unit trust (mutual fund) or a special management fund. Premiums are collected over the length of the contract and a determined minimum death benefit may be guaranteed (based upon an assumed but very modest rate of return on assets). A part of the premiums goes to pay for the insurer's expenses and another part can be regarded as going to the minimum life cover in the way described above. The balance, rather than being invested in the normal life insurance fund, is used to buy units (shares) in a mutual fund or in one of the office's special funds consisting, say, of common stocks. Both funds contain assets which can be expected to increase in nominal value year by year and thus provide a hedge against inflation. When the policy matures or the person dies, all units credited to the policy are sold, with the value of the proceeds depending upon the growth of performance in the interim of the underlying fund or investment pool.

Provision for switching between funds is a feature of the British 'policies'. An office may provide a policyholder with a choice of, say, six different funds. There may be a specialised equities fund, a property fund for real estate investments, a fund of international shares, a fund of money market deposits (essentially a money market mutual fund), and a fund of longer-term fixed interest securities. In addition, the policyholder may be able to opt for a managed portfolio in which the money is allocated between the other funds at the investment manager's discretion. More valuably, the saver is allowed to allocate not just new premiums but the whole of the accumulated value of capital from one fund to another. Frequently, one switch every policy year is free of charge. For additional switches the charge is low, perhaps between half to one per cent of the funds invested, well below brokerage and commission costs. The companies are able to offer this flexibility to savers by conducting their own capital market, selling the units purchased from one saver to another saver switching into that fund. Again, this is based on the mutual fund arrangement.

General Insurance

General insurers are in no sense savings institutions or providers of other forms of wealth accumulation. But the basis of almost all insurance is the accumulation of a fund of assets from which uncertain losses can be met. For general insurers such a fund comes about in a number of ways. One is that premiums are paid to the insurance company in advance of the risks insured against. Out of the premium the company pays commission, management expenses, taxes and losses. At any point of time it will hold a portfolio of policies on which its liability has not expired but for which it has received the premium. The premium held against future expenses and losses, called the 'provision for unexpired risks' or 'provision for unearned premiums', is invested. If premiums are increasing over time, this provision and, in turn, the company's investments, will also increase. Second, not all losses are paid in cash immediately they occur, because it often takes time to assess the extent of the loss. Where legal liabilities are involved, as in third party insurance, legal proceedings may not be held for two or three years or more after the accident. In the meantime, the insurance company invests an amount equal to its estimate of the eventual award. Finally, the company will need to keep at least some minimum level of reserves as security against unexpected losses or unfavourable developments in the insurance market.

With this pool of assets, insurers are able to generate 'investment income' which they can use to reduce the premiums charged to policyholders. Following the high interest rates since the mid-1970s, interest income has been a major source of earnings for general insurers. In many countries, insurers have been writing new business at a 'loss' because they are able to take the premiums and invest them at high interest rates until the claims come due. Insurers' profits have come more from their skills at portfolio management than in their assessment of insurable risk. This trend has been commented upon in industry circles and has been dubbed 'cash flow underwriting' to distinguish it from historic patterns.

This distinction is unwarranted: the investment of premium income and the generation of income from funds held which can be defrayed against underwriting charges is in fact the essence of standard principles. People and firms facing economic losses of various kinds could lay up their own reserves, and for many forms of potential loss (health, litigation, housing repairs) do undertake self-insurance. But in many other cases they prefer to buy insurance contracts, covering specific contingencies, leaving the accumulation and the investment of the reserves to the insurance institution. By this arrangement, people are able to get the benefit of the economies in size in risk pooling and portfolio management which the institution is able to reap. Thus 'insurance cover' and the 'management of funds' are joint products, and in this respect the distinction implicit in the description 'cash flow underwriting' is a misleading one.

One other way in which general insurance arrangements can be seen as akin to intermediation arises from noting that the contingency in question may occur prior to the individual having had time to lay up sufficient reserves. The need to borrow then imposes costs upon the individual. General insurance, in effect, provides the individual with an automatic loan should the contingency occur, with (voluntary, but likely) repayments taking the form of subsequent premiums for future cover. The analogy should not be pushed too far, but the insurance contract can be interpreted as a package of a savings and credit facility (with a return and cost dependent upon the occurrence of the contingency) and a risk-sharing arrangement.

As we shall see in the next chapter, this bundling principle also underlies the reason why banks typically provide both transactions and intermediation services. In the same way that insurers are able to lend profitably funds left with them to defray underwriting expenses, banks do likewise with balances which arise as a byproduct of payment arrangements.

2.7 Intermediary Services: A Summary

Lenders of funds can always accumulate wealth by holding primary securities, that is, mortgages, debentures, common stock, commercial paper, issued by borrowers of funds. In most developed countries, a shrinking proportion do so (although the 'perfect markets paradigm' and the evolution of technology imply that this need not continue). Instead, they have accumulated wealth 'indirectly' in the forms of claims against financial intermediaries, delegating to them decisions about the allocation of savings to various ends. Take, for example, the situation in the US from 1971–1983. Of new funds raised by non-financial enterprises in domestic credit markets, only 10 per cent came directly from other domestic non-financial entities and households; some funds came from foreigners (7 per cent). Financial intermediaries accounted for 80 per cent of funds advanced via credit (see Table 2.3).

In the preceding sections we have examined a number of reasons why a financial contract exchanged directly between the lender and borrower of funds might be replaced by one between the intermediary and lender on one hand and the intermediary and borrower on the other. We have also described briefly the workings of some major classes of institution. We shall now try to draw together some of those threads before proceeding to focus more directly upon banks in the next two chapters.

Lenders of funds look to intermediaries to provide the information and brokerage services involved in effecting financial contracts. They also want intermediaries to help them manage the risks of financing. One such risk is *asset risk*. Assets backing an issue of common stocks may prove to be worthless or decline markedly in value. Borrowers may be tardy in repaying

Table 2.3 Takeup of New Funds Raised in US Financial Markets by Non-Financial Sector, 1951–1983 (% of total)

	Foreigners	*Government*	*Persons*	*Financial institutions*	*Total*
1951–1960	2.9	2.1	18.0	77.0	100
1961–1970	2.6	2.3	4.7	90.4	100
1971–1980	7.4	3.1	11.1	78.4	100
1981–1983	5.6	2.9	10.5	81.0	100

Source: B.M. Friedman (1984).

loans, may default or defraud the lender. Another is *liquidity risk*. While funds are tied up in long-term loans, spending opportunities and consumption needs may present themselves which encourage the lender to sell all or part of the funds lent.

Indirect financing via financial intermediaries well suits borrowers, too. Direct placement of the securities with the intermediary saves on the costs involved in entering markets. Fama (1985) notes that equity and debenture financing requires the provision of much public information which is both costly and unwelcome to many small enterprises. They prefer to give one institution access to the information on a confidential basis.

Because of indivisibilities of size, borrowers are generally unable to provide by themselves the risk diversification sought by lenders, although some multinationals and conglomerates do conduct their own internal capital market and provide a substantial diversification of risks to holders of their claims. Nor, generally, are borrowers well placed to meet lenders' liquidity risks, and are thereby saved the costs and uncertainties of frequent refinancing at unknown terms. They also have their own liquidity problems to look after. Overdraft facilities and standby credits provide liquidity services to borrowers.

Thus financial intermediaries provide information services and financial security on both sides of the balance sheet. They are able to meet the demands for financial security by taking advantage of economies of scale in portfolio management. So long as there exists imperfect correlation in the fate of the different investments, the fact of having a large and diversified range of assets allows risks of default to be pooled and reduced. Diversification of risks *within* the financial firm is valuable when information about enterprises is difficult and costly to obtain via public channels. Similarly, pooling a large number of independent requirements for cash withdrawal enables depository institutions to economise on the reserve backing for liabilities and unutilised lending commitments. One comes from the size and character of the assets they hold, the other from the number and form of their liabilities.

Together, the two enable intermediaries to issue contracts to both borrowers and lenders which differ from those which would be exchanged under direct financing. For example, savers buying mutual fund shares obtain from the investment company a single contract with built-in diversification which replaces the numerous contracts represented by the individual securities. Other intermediaries issue, in place of the primary securities, contracts with options which can be exercised in various contingencies. One example is the options contract issued by savings institutions which allows depositors to make a claim on demand or after giving notice in the event of depositors experiencing a shortage of cash. Another example is that of insurance companies which allow policyholders to make a claim in the event of a burglary or an accident.

Intermediaries as Insurers

Following on from this last example, there is a clear parallel between the options contracts issued by a broad class of intermediaries and insurance companies. This analogy can be taken further. We can visualise financial intermediaries purchasing primary securities from borrowers and reselling them to lenders of funds with an insurance policy added. The insurance premium is covered in the bid–offer spread.[28] Thus mutual funds buy shares, pool them to diversify risks, and then resell them in the total, diversified portfolio. A form of 'insurance' is provided in this way against the risk that one share falls in price. If the service is valued, the margin between bid and offer prices on units will enable the investment companies to cover expenses and earn profits. Savings institutions offer depositors insurance against the risk that they may be short of cash for undertaking transactions. Concurrently, they offer to borrowers insurance against having to refinance a long-term loan at unknown (or unspecified) interest rates.

Risks may be managed by financial intermediaries in a number of ways. First, intermediaries may *reduce or diversify risks*, as we have discussed above with mutual funds. Second, intermediaries may *shift risk*, either on to the parties with whom they contract, i.e. borrowers or lenders, or on to markets. Third, intermediaries may *bear risk* by issuing guarantees or insurance policies of various kinds. Finally, intermediaries may use some *combination* of these strategies.

These distinctions are important to bear in mind when we consider the operation of intermediaries. Let us return again to the activities of mutual funds. When an investment manager of a fund is administering the fund on an agency basis and is also not underwriting the offering, the investment company has no need for the holding of cash and liquid assets, nor for equity capital. Liquidity needs of shareholders can be met by cancelling their units and selling off the underlying stocks. Asset risk of primary securities is pooled, diversified and thus reduced, but the residual, undiversified risk in the total portfolio is passed on fully to holders of shares in the fund. Substitution of a single contract allows the manager to make a market in the units of shareholders, buying them on a principal basis for later sale: that is, speculating on the course of stock prices. When the fund is expanding, the manager takes units on to his 'book' and sells them to new shareholders if and when they are demanded. When the fund is contracting, the manager repurchases the units for later resale or cancellation. In both cases, holding profits or losses can be made while the units are on the manager's 'book' (i.e. stock of units). By standing ready to meet withdrawals, the fund manager must hold sufficient cash and near cash to pay out shareholders. There must be sufficient capital reserves so that shareholders in the fund are protected from the manager's dealing losses.

So it is with other intermediaries. Savings institutions, for example, stand ready to repurchase deposits on demand, but at a fixed price — what Pesek and Saving (1967) called the 'fixed repurchase clause'. In order to meet deposit withdrawals, the institutions must hold cash and near cash assets. Since depositors are assured of repurchase at full capital value plus interest, none of the undiversified asset risk is passed on to depositors. Capital reserves must be held to shield depositors from portfolio losses and thus make good the insurance provision.

Asset risk and withdrawal risk are not the only risks which intermediaries manage: 'contingent liabilities risk' and 'interest rate risk' are the other main risks. Asset risk arises because of the characteristics of the contracts on the assets side of the balance sheet. Withdrawal risk comes from the characteristics of the contracts on the liabilities side of the balance sheet. *Contingent liabilities risk* comes from the off-balance sheet activities of intermediaries when they issue options and guarantees additional to those which appear on the balance sheet. Thus merchant banks in the UK 'accept', that is, guarantee bills of exchange, promising to pay the bill should the issuer of the bill default. Investment banks in the US underwrite issues of shares and debentures. These risks generate need for equity and also liquid assets, which are also needed for coping with mismatches in the duration, size and timing of the contracts on the two sides of the balance sheet. In the case of depository institutions, if each fixed remuneration deposit contract written were twinned with a fixed rate asset contract written at the same time, for the same amount and for the same duration, there would be no *interest rate risk* (although, if asset returns failed to cover deposit interest and the costs of intermediation, there could be a loss).

There are two main on-balance sheet activities of intermediaries which can lead to exposure on relative interest rates. (Off-balance sheet exposures can come from interest rate futures, options, caps and swaps, but these contracts can also offset balance sheet exposures). On-balance sheet exposure is exemplified by the activities of finance companies in the US and UK. Both conduct size intermediation which is the direct opposite of that of mutual funds (unit trusts). Mutual funds collect a large number of small savings and pool them together into a large investible fund. Finance companies borrow bulk from wholesale sources and parcel these funds out into smaller loans for instalment credit, leasing and factoring finance. Since an intermediary of this type 'breaks lots', it cannot match each loan with a deposit raising, even if they are of the same duration. It therefore funds in advance at discrete intervals, maintaining a cash inventory which is drawn down and replenished over time as loans are approved. The intermediary is vulnerable to fluctuations in loan demands which leave it either with surplus liquid funds and a reduced return on the asset portfolio (in the case of declining demand) or with emergency borrowings (in the case of unexpectedly high demand). As Deshmukh, Greenbaum and Kanatas (1983) note, the quantity uncertainty translates into an interest rate risk.

The other, more familiar, case is where, to accommodate differences in preferences between borrowers and lenders, the intermediary issues liabilities which are of shorter duration than assets. Future deposit raisings (fundings) over the duration of the loan may be at interest rates which, in comparison with the fixed loan rate, result in losses. This is the circumstance which confronted US savings and loan associations in the early 1980s. Following the lifting of interest rate ceilings, associations were encouraged by competitive pressures to offer deposit rates which exceeded the return from their asset portfolio. In 1982, deposit rates averaged 11.03 per cent, while assets yielded 10.64 per cent, the latter reflecting mortgages on their books earning fixed rates negotiated in earlier years.

Intermediaries like the savings and loan associations have historically borne interest rate risk, relying on a spread between deposit and loan rates sufficiently large to cover changes in likely funding costs. Views about what is possible and likely in financial markets have altered markedly in recent years, and intermediaries have aimed to reduce their interest rate exposures. They can do so by shifting the risk to other parties. For example, they can hedge the risk in markets for interest rate futures or by conducting interest rate swaps. At a price, the risk can be transferred to someone else. To give another example, they can shift the risk onto their borrowers, by revisions to loan contracts. A loan contract may contain a provision entitling the lending institution to adjust the loan rate periodically, according to some agreed formula. Alternatively, as is more usual, the intermediary may shift some of the risk onto its borrowers (for example, at interest adjustment dates) and bear the residual itself (in between such adjustments). Most variable or flexi-rate loan schemes are of this form.

Banks have taken such arrangements as far as any institutions, especially in wholesale operations, and we defer further discussion to the following chapters. One observation can, however, be made at this stage. In examining arrangements for shifting risk it is necessary, as in the literature of taxation, to examine the final incidence of the risk, not just the initial distribution. Banks in their international lending operations have discovered the importance of this distinction.

Notes

1. Many of these studies do, however, attempt to convert such stock variables into flow measures of output.
2. See Arndt (1984) for a recent discussion, and Davis (1986) for an analysis of how interest rate deregulation has affected these national income accounting conventions.
3. The dichotomy between 'real resource' and 'portfolio' models of the banking firms was highlighted by Baltensperger (1980) in his review of theories of the banking firms.
4. A distinction needs to be drawn between 'pure' brokers and dealers. Brokers are intermediaries who bring together buyers and sellers for a commission, providing

informational services without assuming risk (such as a 'best efforts' transaction of an investment bank in which the issuer of the securities bears all the risks). Dealers act as principals, buying and selling financial assets which they themselves hold in their 'books', making a profit from the margin between buying and selling prices. Such market-making enhances the marketability of the securities and moves us closer to the second type of intermediation. This distinction between agent and market making arises when we examine the operations of the investment managers of mutual funds.

5. Our emphasis in those sections is upon the functional characteristics of the institutions concerned. Readers seeking a detailed account of the workings of US financial institutions are referred to Stigum (1983) and Edmister (1986), while Bain (1981) and Revell (1973) provide analyses of UK financial institutions. For information about the financial institutions in Australia, the other country to which reference is made on occasion, see Lewis and Wallace (1985).
6. For these benefits to be realised, the social savings must be balanced against the 'resource costs' of a paper money system in terms of the potential of a fiduciary standard to impose inflation costs and economic instability upon the community (Friedman 1986).
7. For early accounts of these difficulties, see Keynes (1936, p.144), who drew a distinction between borrowers' risks and lenders' risks, and Stigler (1967), who posed the issues in terms of information costs — costs of acquiring knowledge of borrowers and overseeing their performance during the course of the loan.
8. This is the type of market imperfection analysed by Leland and Pyle (1977) as a basis for intermediation.
9. Imperfections of this sort as a basis for intermediation are analysed by Diamond (1984).
10. These characteristics are discussed more fully in Moore (1968).
11. In this respect, Diamond (1984) makes an interesting point. Viewing an intermediary as a coalition of monitoring agents, he argues that customers' costs of monitoring the intermediary (called the 'delegation costs') diminish as the intermediary diversifies across borrowers. The Diamond model is extended to embrace continuing banker–customer relationships by Haubrich (1986).
12. See, for example, McCulloch (1981).
13. It is called such to acknowledge the original work of Arrow and Debreu (1954). A comprehensive account is contained in Arrow and Hahn (1971).
14. This conclusion can be restated in terms of the Modigliani and Miller (1958) theorem that in the setting of perfect capital markets, with no transactions costs and with every agent completely informed and honest about his environment, institutional structure has no effect on pure risk sharing and financial and economic coordination.
15. The 'barter' description is borrowed from Greenfield and Yeager (1983) in that many of the assets underlying money market mutual funds, against which cheques can be written, are indirect claims against real assets.
16. There is also a practical consideration why the practice of writing cheques against portfolios of securities has not become widespread. Since the cheque would be considered a sale of shares, a capital gain would likely result, triggering a tax liability. Bank deposits, and for all practical purposes money funds also, are payable at par, so that no such problem arises for cheques written on them.
17. Stutchbury (1964, p. 5). The British description of 'unit trust' is not to be confused with the American unit investment trusts, which are 'second-degree' investment companies selling shares of an open-ended investment fund on an instalment basis, or with the American trust funds of the type commonly known as Massachusetts business trusts, described in Edmister (1986, p.272).

18. *Financial Statistics*, January 1987, Tables 7.11 and 7.12.
19. One of the constraints for closed-ended investment companies is that they, like other publicly-quoted companies, are unable to invite people to buy their shares through advertising, except for new issues.
20. Data for the 1960s comes from Goldsmith (1968).
21. Stutchbury (1964, p. 2).
22. These quotations and other details are based on the prospectuses issued by Merrill Lynch, Pierce, Fenner and Smith Incorporated ('Merrill Lynch') for their CMA Money Fund, CMA Government Securities Fund and CMA Tax-Exempt Fund.
23. See Scott and Wallace (1985).
24. 'Cash management account' is a registered proprietary name patented by Merrill Lynch. But accounts with broadly equivalent features are offered by other fund managers, e.g. by Travelers' 'Capital-T account' and by American Express.
25. Developments in the US and UK are surveyed in Carter, Chiplin and Lewis (1986), while parallel developments in Australia are examined in Lewis and Wallace (1985). Examinations of the US experience can be found in Kane (1984) and of the UK experience in Llewellyn (1985).
26. This section draws extensively upon Covick and Lewis (1985).
27. Note that the insurance cover being provided here is not cover against the risk of premature death, it is cover against the risk of unanticipated longevity. It is, therefore, *life-cover* in the literal sense, and not death-cover as in other classes of 'life insurance'.
28. Here we borrow from the earlier insights of Arrow (1970, Ch. 5), Arrow and Hahn (1971, Ch. 14) and Scitovsky (1969, Ch. 3).

3

Principles of Retail Banking

3.1 Retail Banking

Retail banking refers to the provision of services to individuals and small businesses where the financial institutions are dealing in large volumes of low-value transactions. This is in contrast to wholesale banking where the customers are large, often multinational companies, governments or governmental enterprises, and the institutions deal in large-valued transactions, usually in small volumes.

In practice, it is difficult to identify *purely* retail banks, limiting themselves to the tapping of retail deposit markets and lending only in retail loan markets. US banks are probably more retail than most. In terms of numbers, many are 'family' or 'small business' orientated. Some do little commercial banking. Almost 20 per cent of US commercial banks have 5 per cent or less of their assets in loans to businesses, and nearly one half have less than 20 per cent of assets in commercial loans. But the great bulk of banking assets in the United States is controlled by the big 'money centre' banks with substantial wholesale books. British clearing banks, Canadian chartered banks and Australian trading banks all combine retail and wholesale activities under the one financial organisation. In some cases, funds may be gathered from retail deposit markets, but used to finance wholesale as well as retail lending. Other institutions, such as finance companies, do the reverse.

Perhaps the closest to retail-only establishments are the savings institutions, but even here US savings banks and savings and loan associations are moving into commercial lending (albeit on a limited scale), while UK building societies are tapping wholesale deposit markets. Trustee savings banks in the UK have already become fully-fledged retail and wholesale bankers.

Nevertheless, it is helpful to begin discussion by examining a stylised set of accounts for a purely retail bank. By doing so, a number of principles of retail banking can be derived, based upon the structure of those accounts and the problems and opportunities they create for such an intermediary. Even where retail and wholesale activities are integrated, these principles remain relevant to the overall business of banking, albeit in a modified form (as explained later). And one question which must be addressed is why retail activities are so typically combined with wholesale business. That question and its companion — why wholesalers have until recently eschewed expanding into retail activities — are taken up in a later section.

The Structure of a Retail Bank

Table 3.1 provides us with the elements of a picture of a retail bank in terms of a stylised balance sheet and profit and loss account. Off-balance sheet business is usually less important for retail banks. In the US, for example, the 27 big money-centre banks, each with assets greater than $10 billion, held 75 per cent of standby letters of credit, 67 per cent of commercial letters of credit, 61 per cent of loan commitments, and 97 per cent of positions arising from foreign exchange transactions, as at end December 1985 (Chessen 1986). Discussion of most, and especially the newer, forms of off-balance sheet activities is deferred to Chapter 4, s.6.

Looking first at the balance sheet, a number of aspects are relevant:

Table 3.1

Balance Sheet

Assets		*Liabilities*	
Cash reserves:		Deposits:	
Required	R	customer 1	D_1
Excess	E	⋮	⋮
		customer N	D_N
Total	C	Total	D
Marketable securities	G	Other borrowings	B
Advances:		Shareholders' equity	E
customer 1	A_1		
⋮	⋮		
customer M	A_M		
Total	A		
Physical capital	K		

Profit and Loss Account

Income	*Expenditure*
Interest earnings	Operating expenses
Fees and charges	Interest paid
	Profit (transferred to shareholders' funds)

1. There are many depositors (N is large) none of whom have a deposit (or set of deposits) which is large relative to the total (D).
2. Many different types of deposits may exist: at call, fixed term, required notice of withdrawal, transferable by cheque or another instrument.
3. There are many borrowers (M is large) none of whom has a loan advanced which is large relative to the total (A).
4. Advances and loans outstanding to various customers will mature at various dates, may have interest rates fixed or variable over the life of the loan, are typically non-marketable, have an average maturity longer than that of deposits, and are of larger average size than deposits.
5. Holdings of cash (or at call deposits at the Central Bank or other institutions) are in excess of those required by regulation.
6. A portfolio of marketable securities, such as government debt, may be held (and may often be required by regulation).
7. Buildings, offices, premises and equipment are usually a significant part of the balance sheet (although they may be leased instead).
8. Borrowings from other institutions may, from time to time, comprise some part of total liabilities (but very much less than in wholesale banking).
9. Banks are able to operate with a high degree of leverage, that is, shareholders' equity capital (including provisions for bad and doubtful debts) is a relatively small proportion of total liabilities. Equity in some cases reflects a corporate body and in others reflects a mutual or cooperative body. In the latter case, much of that sum may be reserves accumulated as the result of past 'profits', raising complex questions about the ownership of such reserves.

The allocation of a portion of the profits to reserves and shareholders' equity, thereby causing that component of the balance sheet to grow over time, is one of the links between the balance sheet and the income–expenditure statement. Other links come from expenditure in maintaining the associated balance sheet structure and flow of services to customers, and from the income flow representing customer payments (as interest or fees) for services provided, either directly as reflected in various asset characteristics, or indirectly as services available to customers of the institution. Looking at the stylised profit and loss statement in greater depth:

1. Fees and charges have typically been small relative to interest earnings.
2. Fees and charges do not usually cover non-interest expenses.
3. Labour costs comprise a larger part of expenses than in the case of wholesale banking.

4. The interest rate margin (between interest earned and interest paid) is normally larger than for wholesale banking.
5. A significant proportion of expenses is associated with the provision of payments services.

In addition to these balance sheet and income–expenditure characteristics, 'retail' often pertains as well to the organisation of the business, with the services provided through large networks of branches. Thus, for statistical purposes, the Bank of England defines 'retail banks' as having either extensive branch networks in the United Kingdom or as participating directly in a UK clearing system. A feature of the production of financial services is that it requires interaction between the institution and the customer and, in the past at least, that has meant a physical 'bricks and mortar' presence in the customer's region of domicile or employment. Achievement of size then needs multiple branches or offices to overcome the limits imposed by a physical catchment area. Again the contrast is with wholesale banking where business is conducted at head office or in offshore centres.

In this chapter we shall concentrate upon the balance sheet characteristics of retail banking, leaving until later the real resource issues of the technology or infrastructure of intermediation. Although the two issues are not independent (and in that later discussion we shall identify some of the interdependencies), focusing upon balance sheet activities enables us to identify some general principles of retail banking which have, as already noted, some parallels with insurance. In both instances, a major problem is the establishment of a sufficiently large area over which the general principles of risk management can be applied. In retail banking, the 'law of large numbers' provides the key. In other circumstances, different arrangements and balance sheet structures are required which wholesale banking and international insurance markets illustrate. This will be explained in the next chapter.

Like the institutions examined in Chapter 2, banks both process information and manage risks. The risks managed by banks are those which also face those institutions, namely:

(i) **Withdrawal risk.** Like savings institutions, banks issue deposits which can be converted into cash on demand (current accounts or demand deposits) or on expiration of a term of notice (time deposits), despite having a longer term asset portfolio.

(ii) **Asset risk.** Banks pool assets and loans which are not capital certain, yet provide depositors with the assurance of redemption at full face value.

(iii) **Interest rate risk.** Banks bear some or all of the interest rate risk in maintaining a loan inventory in their funding operations, which arises when returns on assets and liabilities change differently for the same change in market interest rates.

(iv) **Contingent liabilities risk.** Banks issue guarantees and options contracts in off-balance sheet operations.

(v) **Operations risk.** As in any business, fraud, theft, excessive operating costs as a result of poor management also create risks for the viability of the bank.

(vi) **Conglomerate risk.** Where retail banks are part of a wider corporate group, interdependencies between group members may link their fates, introducing risks of cross-infection from the activities of the others.

In addition, some special factors are in operation. Banks in retail operations combine intermediary services with the operation of a chequing system for the transfer of ownership of banks' deposits. The transfer of deposits to accounts at other banks creates an additional, indeed the prime, source of deposit variability. Banks offer other payment services (such as transfer by direct debit, wire transfer, overseas remittances) which result also in transfers of deposits. Banks also provide for the liquidity needs of customers by issuing contingent claims in the form of overdraft facilities, standby credit facilities, lines and forward commitments to make loans. These are all means by which banks ensure that customers have access to an agreed amount of credit, sometimes at a predetermined interest rate, sometimes for a fee, but with take-up at the customer's volition. In the UK, as at October 1986, 45 per cent of outstanding sterling loans by London clearing banks to companies were by means of overdraft. As at August 1986, 80 per cent of short-term and 71 per cent of long-term commercial and industrial loans made by US banks were under loan commitments.[1] Upon usage of the facility the bank is faced with a loss of cash or bankers' deposits constituting an additional drain on reserves.

So far we have skirted around the issue of how to define banks. For reasons explained in the following section we do not think it is possible to give a definite answer. Nor do we think that it is important to do so in the present context, for the principles of risk management are common to a number of institutions, whatever they are called. Thus we say that banks are institutions which combine transactions services with intermediation, and go on to examine why this is the case.

3.2 Why Do Banks Combine Transactions and Intermediary Services?

The integration of transactions and intermediary services could (and indeed did) arise in a number of ways. Specialist payments service institutions could evolve into intermediaries;[2] while, from the opposite tack, 'pure' intermediaries could add payments services to their list of activities, as has happened in recent years in the case of savings institutions. In the first case, joint production arises from methods of producing 'accounting money' which open up opportunities for profitable intermediation. From the alternative perspective, successful retail intermediation leads to deposit-type claims which are suitable for use as money and the provision of payments services.

The reasons for joint production of payment and intermediation services are rooted in the workings of a monetary economy — in particular, in the interconnections between the medium of exchange and the store of value functions of money under current institutional and social conventions. As will be explained in Chapter 6, these conventions are undergoing change rapidly, but at the moment intending buyers of goods and services must offer money, or a credible promise to deliver money in the near future, in order to be able to effect a transaction. Imperfect information about the extent to which other parties will be able to honour credit obligations and collection costs has so far prevented the widespread use of 'trade credit' in day-to-day transactions. What has evolved is a system of government-issued paper money and, linked to it, a limited range of claims on certain classes of institutions (e.g. bank deposits) which are accepted in transactions. The institutional arrangements needed to ensure that such claims are generally acceptable in exchange and that payments services are provided at minimum cost give rise to the scope for profitable intermediation.

When accepting a payments instrument such as a cheque, the recipient incurs the risk that either ultimate payment will not take place or that it will involve long lags in collection. Providers of payments services, such as banks, could overcome this impediment to acceptance by guaranteeing payment and assuming the risk themselves. Indeed, some payment services providers, such as those issuing credit cards, have gone that route and, in Europe and the UK, banks' cheque guarantee cards perform a similar role. Elsewhere, banks have eschewed this 'instantaneous overdraft' option, requiring instead that customers maintain a credit balance if cheques written against an account are to be honoured. By imposing penalties (mainly taking the form of reputational costs) on customers who flout this requirement, banks endeavour to assure cheque recipients that they are simply accepting a more convenient means of payment and not in fact extending risky credit to the cheque writer. Payment via claims on a bank dominates payment via trade credit or IOUs because banks possess advantages in enforcing contracts.

But why are cheques preferred to cash? Obvious benefits come from the greater convenience and safety, but the cost of operating the bank payments system must somehow be recovered. Consider, for example, the case where banks hold 100 per cent reserves of currency so that the cost of operating the bank payments system must be met by charges upon users. In such a system, banks would hold a positive inventory of currency, for the reason outlined below.

In a monetary economy decisions to sell and decisions to buy are separated in time since money enables individuals to delay transactions by selling goods and services for generalised purchasing power which can be exercised later. This means that money must serve as a store of purchasing power 'in which the seller holds the proceeds in the interim between sale and subsequent purchase or from which the buyer can extract the general purchasing power with which he pays for what he buys.' (Friedman and Schwartz 1970, p.106). The means of payment function of money and the store of value function necessarily overlap.

Because of this 'buffer stock' role of money,[3] balances held in cheque accounts rise and fall with the ebb and flow of transactions. On average, each customer will hold a positive balance when banks do not offer full overdraft facilities and because it is too costly to make currency deposits coincide with each writing of a cheque. Of course, the opportunity to lend surplus funds and receive interest limits the size of such balances that an individual wants to hold. To bank customers, the balances held represent funds which cannot profitably be lent out because of transactions requirements.

To the bank, however, the aggregation of these balances does represent an opportunity for profitable lending activities. Provided that additions to and withdrawals from customer accounts are random, the bank's currency holdings will not deviate greatly from the average value. Rather than make interest-free loans to the issuer of fiat money, banks have an incentive to exchange part of their currency holdings for interest-bearing assets. Intermediation thus emerges as a byproduct of payments services because of the possibility (and profitability) of fractional reserve banking.

When calculating the charges made to their customers for payments services, banks have relied heavily upon the worth to them of these funds, 'cross-subsidising' costs of the payments system with the income which they earn on the interest-free balances left with them. How much they have utilised this process can be appreciated from evidence submitted to the British Prices Commission in 1978. This showed that 50–60 per cent of the operating costs of the London clearing banks was due to money transmission services, and that in 1977 the banks relied upon the interest margin to cover 75 per cent of those costs.[4]

We emphasise, for later discussion in Chapter 6, that this 'cross-subsidisation' is not an inherent feature of all payments systems. It is really a consequence of the entry price, in the form of a non-interest-bearing positive account balance, charged by banks. (In the same way, the portfolio management services of insurers come about largely because premiums are collected in advance.) Consequently, it is often argued that, under competitive conditions and freedom from regulation, banks and other institutions will be forced to eliminate cross-subsidisation arrangements, paying market interest rates on transactions accounts and pricing transactions services at their marginal costs of production. But this merely begs the question of what is the 'product'. Many customers may regard cash withdrawal facilities, cheque transfers and the holding of funds temporarily in a bank deposit as joint products. Accordingly, they prefer to pay for a service package as a whole, rather than for each component separately.[5] When these psychic costs are combined with the institutions' own accounting costs, complete unbundling may not be cost-effective. It is, presumably, for these sorts of reasons that banks and savings institutions do not levy an explicit charge for each deposit or withdrawal (so as to cover the costs of providing teller facilities) and pay a higher yield on the account balance.

If anything, cross-subsidisation reduces the amount of intermediation undertaken jointly with provision of payments services via transactions accounts. Customers have an incentive to hold minimal transactions balances so as to use subsidised transactions services and transfer idle balances to higher-yielding accounts. Where services and charges are unbundled that incentive is reduced, but even in the absence of such changes payments institutions possess advantages in competing for intermediation business through their provision of non-transactions accounts.

One such advantage stems from the existence of travelling and inconvenience costs which makes it simpler for customers to centralise their financial business with one institution — provided, of course, that doing so does not mean too great an exposure to risk of default. Since depositor protection schemes encompass both transactions and non-transactions deposits, that condition has generally been met. In practice, though, the cost savings from centralising business probably are of minor importance when compared with the role of banker–customer relations developed through an ongoing business relationship. This works in two ways.

The first aspect is that banks obtain informational advantages because they are their customers' bookkeepers: this enables them to be efficient lenders. In comparison with other providers of finance, banks have one very great advantage in that they are in touch with borrowers' and many would-be borrowers' transactions and have many opportunities for informal contacts with customers. If customers route most transactions through their accounts, information is gained enabling a profile to be built up of a customer's suitability for credit and ability to repay loans. But the information gained is not of a type which can be packaged and resold to others. In these circumstances, the institution can best capture the benefits by undertaking intermediation, lending on the basis of its specialised information (Leland and Pyle 1977). Once the loan is made, the transactions account becomes a continuing source of credit information, enabling banks to monitor the use made of funds advanced and to identify problem loans. These 'spillovers' from banks' provision of payment services to their lending business may enable banks to select a portfolio comprising claims which have a lower *individual* default risk, but with the same expected return, than those loans which depositors would have otherwise chosen either when acting as direct lenders of funds or as indirect lenders via other institutions.

A second aspect of the banker–customer relationship is the benefit it provides for potential borrowers who are also depositors. Because bankers are thus better able to assess credit risks, potential creditworthy borrowers have less to fear from suffering credit rationing because of imperfect information. Their deposit history provides the information banks require to sort out good from bad risks. In fact, the surer access to bank loan financing is only a part of the story. It has also been suggested, for example by Fama (1985), that banks' known skills at loan monitoring may serve as a 'good housekeeping award' in financial markets generally. Renewals of loans may signal to other lenders that the firms are still creditworthy, enabling the firms to gain cheaper access to other sources of finance. For this service, the organisations may be prepared to negotiate and renegotiate forward loan commitments and pay the commitment fees involved.

It is in large part because of such benefits that other intermediaries have sought access to the payments system. In the USA, credit unions, savings associations and savings banks all now allow 'cheques' to be drawn on them: the 'cheques' being in fact share drafts or negotiable orders of withdrawals (NOWs) with a slightly different legal status. The experience in other nations is varied, sometimes reflecting legislation, but also reflecting economic forces. For example, customer–firm relationships can be fostered in other ways, such as the common bonds of membership in a credit union. Similarly, through agency arrangements with members of the payments system, customers can be given the convenience of access to transactions services without significant involvement on the part of the intermediary.

While the competitive threat of payments institutions taking intermediation business partly explains the expansion by savings institutions into payments services, an important factor in this process is that the characteristics of their deposit liabilities are well suited to serve as payments media. Payments services generate a desire for instruments which (i) serve as a medium of exchange, enabling consumers to acquire goods; (ii) serve as a medium of payment, to effect payment of the goods acquired; and (iii) since purchases and sales are not synchronised, act as a temporary store of purchasing power. A chequing deposit with a bank may perform all three functions. But the functions can also be 'unbundled' and carried out by separate vehicles. Thus a credit card issued by Visa/Barclaycard, Mastercard/Access, or American Express may serve as a medium of exchange enabling the individual to obtain the goods. A bank cheque deposit may still be used for the actual payment, but funds serving as the temporary abode of purchasing power in between receipt of income and payment for goods may be held with other intermediaries.

Because intermediaries such as savings institutions exist to reconcile differences in the preferred habitats of savers and investors, they normally 'create liquidity', that is, issue claims which are more marketable, reversible, divisible, and capital-certain than the claims they acquire. Savers do not want to specify too closely the timing of future consumption because of the many accidents and uncertainties of life. Most wish to keep part of their assets readily withdrawable. Over the time span in which many households make decisions, the balance between uncertainty in terms of real purchasing power and transactions costs is most effectively resolved by financial contracts which guarantee redeemability in full in terms of money.

Also relevant to an explanation of why deposit-type contracts dominate retail intermediation is the existence of imperfect information which contributes towards the formation of intermediaries. To the extent that individual lenders are unable, before or after the event, to assess whether a borrower can meet loan obligations, similar problems can be expected to persist with regard to their assessment of the profitability of an intermediary which finances such a borrower. The inability of suppliers of funds to observe the returns on banks' investments militates against the issue of liabilities with pay-offs contingent upon those returns. Instead, the circumstances are conducive to intermediaries offering deposit-type liabilities which are not contingent upon the outcome of the intermediary's investment decisions (except where insolvency occurs).

Such deposit claims are well suited to serve as a temporary abode of purchasing power. But in order to issue call deposits successfully the institution must convince depositors that it can meet encashment demands. If the institution succeeds in instilling this confidence in depositors, it has gone a long way, as an indirect consequence of intermediation, towards creating a claim which can serve not just as a store of value but as a medium of exchange and payment. Once the confidence exists, no one feels it necessary actually to take the step of converting the claim into 'money'. It becomes money. We accept share drafts drawn on Great Lakes Credit Union, for example, because they have been accepted in the past and others will accept them from us in return, even if we know nothing whatsoever of the institution concerned. This is simply the exercise of consumer sovereignty, in that whatever is considered as good as money thereby becomes money. This was the case historically with private paper money, government paper money, and bank cheque facilities. It seems the case now with savings institutions.

3.3 Portfolio Management

As earlier comments have made clear, intermediaries must make decisions about the appropriate use of physical resources (land, labour, capital and materials) as well as about an appropriate balance sheet structure. In retail intermediation, these decisions have a high degree of interdependence since achieving a particular balance sheet structure involves expenditure, often substantial, on physical resources. When providing payments services to households in a particular region and obtaining access to their loanable funds, banks usually require a physical presence in the region. Similarly, physical resources are involved in assessing the creditworthiness of retail loan applicants and in monitoring and collecting loan repayments. In both cases, it is worth noting, technology is changing the type of activity and costs involved. Physical presence may now be achieved by automatic teller machines which can accommodate many of a customer's needs. Applications by customers for credit cards afford a one-off assessment of creditworthiness which substitutes for a gradual accumulation of information over time. Access to credit rating services enables intermediaries to 'buy in' information about the suitability of potential borrowers, rather than utilising their own resources directly.

Despite this general interdependence between the portfolio and 'resource costs', changes in labour costs and technology seem unlikely to influence the day-to-day composition of a bank's asset portfolio. On the liabilities side, there is always some trade-off between interest rates and expenditures on services, but variations in the latter are unlikely to be effective in the short run. It is thus usual to examine the balance sheet without explicit reference to physical resources. The appropriate size of capital reserves (shareholders' equity) is treated similarly.

In terms of the balance sheet a number of issues stand out. Banks (more precisely, their owners) subject themselves to risk, in the sense of uncertainty of the return on funds invested. Asset transformation is, in effect, a risk-sharing arrangement between the intermediary and its suppliers of funds conditioned by how much the contracts issued to lenders differ from those made with borrowers with respect to matters like maturity and interest rates. In principle, both interest rate and maturity transformation risks are possible outcomes of a single decision made by the intermediary about what implicit forward contracts to enter into with customers. The range of contracts and outcomes is large. Forward contracts may specify a fixed quantity and price (term deposits, for example) and range through to situations where no forward commitments are implied (current deposits, overnight loans). In between, implied forward contracts might involve a fixed quantity but price-contingent upon the market conditions which eventuate (fixed term, variable rate loans), or involve an option over quantity for one or other party (early repayment by borrowers, immediate repayment of an outstanding overdraft).

In practice, a small set of combinations dominates actual experience, and the absence of most of the other possibilities is easily explained by their unsuitability as risk-sharing devices.[6] In what follows we examine the rationale and effects of those particular combinations.

Maturity Transformation and Interest Rate Risk

Mismatching of contracts by maturity is a feature of most intermediation and this forms the basis for the models of 'interest rate uncertainty' of Niehans (1978, Chapter 9) and Niehans and Hewson (1976). In terms of the forward contracts approach, fixed price, fixed quantity forward contracts are written on one side of the balance sheet (long-term loans for example), but not on the other (e.g. deposits at call).

Where the fixed price liabilities have a longer maturity than assets, the intermediary is faced with the necessity to reinvest funds which become available when assets mature. Uncertainty exists because of the difficulty, in the absence of hedging on futures markets, of foretelling the yield which will be received on those reinvested funds relative to the costs in the form of interest and expenses of carrying the liability portfolio. Conversely, in the much more common case — upon which we focus below — of positive maturity transformation, a situation when assets have a longer maturity than liabilities, there is a need for the intermediary to refinance its asset holdings by the issue of new liabilities. Risk arises from the uncertainty surrounding the interest rate which will need to be paid to attract funds or, alternatively, from the need to sell (liquidate) assets at an uncertain market price, if refinancing is not to be pursued.

The incentive for banks to take on such risks arises from the potential profits available from maturity transformation when yields in markets of different maturity exhibit differences. Suppose that a *term premium* exists in which longer-term rates, r_L, exceed short-term rates, r_S. A potential for profitable intermediation involving positive maturity transformation is apparent. By borrowing short at a rate of r_S and lending long at r_L, a potential return of $r_L - r_S$ per dollar of funds intermediated is available, provided that the short rate, r_S, remains unchanged. Then, the implicit forward contracts involved in long-term loans turn out to be profitable in the light of 'spot' market developments. Alternatively, though, the potential for loss is apparent (as many US thrift institutions discovered during the 1970s).[7] This risk will be the greater the larger is the variability in the short-term interest rates needed to maintain a particular deposit level. Conversely, the existence of a secondary market in which long-term assets can be sold (albeit at a loss) provides an escape route for moderating losses, provided that yields in the asset and deposit markets are not perfectly correlated.

But we must ask why it is that long-term rates exceed short-term rates. Perhaps other transactors are expecting short-term rates next period to be higher by an amount which just compensates for the current long-term rate. Thus, over two years, say, the holding of two one-year securities is expected by those other transactors to give the same return as the holding of one two-year security. In this case, by 'riding the yield curve' and raising deposits for a shorter period than asset holdings, the bank is backing its judgment as being superior to that of other market participants. The bank believes that interest rates are going to rise by less than is reflected in the current term structure of interest rates.

Otherwise, a bank which undertakes this maturity transformation is relying upon yield differences between maturities which cannot be attributed to expectations. A number of explanations have been offered for what Hicks (1946) described as a 'constitutional weakness' at the long end of the markets for loanable funds. One is the liquidity preference of lenders, and the

'Keynesian' interpretation of interest rates as the price for sacrificing liquidity suggests that the longest-term securities should always yield the greatest return. Looked at from the viewpoint of borrowers, they are seeking hedges, or insurance, against the consequences of changes in interest rates over the length of a long-term contract. Lenders require compensation for providing borrowers with this insurance in the form of a premium for holding longs.

If liquidity preference is a factor contributing to an upward-sloping yield curve, the activities of banks in transforming short-term deposits into long-term loans should moderate that effect. Were there, for example, no costs incurred in this transformation, so that banks viewed long- and short-term loans as equivalent, the liquidity premium would disappear. In practice, of course, banks incur the costs of undertaking positive maturity transformation, one sort being the costs of intermediation *per se*. The other comes from the risk of having an open forward position on the liabilities side of the balance sheet combined with a fixed price forward commitment on the asset side, which increases with the degree of maturity transformation. These commitments can be 'bought off' by sales of the assets in secondary markets, but the variability of asset prices (and thus the risks of doing so) increases with term to maturity.[8]

Were maturity transformation of one short-term deposit into one longer-term asset the only activity undertaken by an intermediary, its portfolio management would involve deciding at what point the increases in expected profit from increased maturity transformation (assuming a positively sloped yield curve) cease to outweigh the extra uncertainty of outcome thereby created. The answer, not unexpectedly, depends upon the attitude to risk of the intermediary's owners, the term premium, the intermediary's expectation of future yields, and the resource cost of intermediation.

In practice, the nature of the risk borne by retail intermediaries can be transformed by institutional practices. Perhaps the most important way is the adoption of flexi-rate loans, whereby the interest rate is adjusted periodically in some manner in response to market developments.[9] Rather than entering implicit forward contracts specifying fixed price and quantity, a price contingent upon spot market developments is specified. As might be expected, the incentive to develop such contracts is higher in situations where no secondary market is available in which fixed price forward contracts can be 'bought off'.

Variable-rate loan arrangements may be formal, as for example is often the case in wholesale markets where the interest rate charged is linked to some overall market indicator rate, or informal, as for example in some retail markets where variations in the yield may be at the lender's discretion or negotiated between borrower and lender. In similar vein, the timing of adjustments may be formal, at prespecified dates, or informal. Because interest rates on loans are usually adjusted less frequently than deposit rates change, banks are not completely absolved from interest rate risk due to maturity mismatching. In addition, where variable loan and deposit rates are market-determined, the bank still incurs risk to the extent that loan and deposit rates are imperfectly correlated.

Compared with making equivalent loans at fixed-interest rates, the variable-rate loan should involve a lower average yield, reflecting the passing on of much of the interest rate risk to the borrower. How much lower commencing interest rates on variable-rate loans will be is hard to judge. Apart from the influence of expectations of future rates, it should be remembered that loan returns are a combination of contract rates and default losses. Contract rates on loans and deposits can be expected to be highly correlated in the case of variable-rate loans. While interest rate risk is transferred from the bank to the borrower, this transfer alters the ability of the borrower to meet the remaining contractual repayment obligations: increasing this ability when yields drop and reducing it when yields increase. Consequently, flexi-rate loans at the same initial interest rate as fixed-rate loans and equivalent in all other respects can be expected to involve a higher default risk. The risk to the intermediary from rising interest rates is transformed in nature rather than removed.

Most banks undertake some combination of fixed- and variable-rate financing, but it is normal, as we shall discuss in the next chapter, for loan contract rates to be revised at set intervals (called interest rate periods). Banks are thus insulated from interest rate risk (but not default and funding risks) across interest rate periods. Within interest rate periods, the loan rate is effectively fixed, and banks bear interest rate risk from liabilities of shorter duration than the interest rate period. When liabilities are at call, the interest rate needed to maintain the deposit stock constant is, in effect, varying continuously, as indicated by the variability in the deposit stock arising from withdrawals and deposits when the interest rate is held constant. Because such variations are largely self-correcting, it is often cheaper for the bank to accept the quantity variation rather than adjusting and readjusting deposit interest rates. To adopt such a strategy successfully requires a particular balance sheet structure, and it is this that we shall examine now, deferring until later a discussion of the conditions under which it is preferable to a policy of more or less continuous interest rate variation on deposits, as is implied by 'liability management'.

3.4 Management of Reserve Assets

Where deposits can be withdrawn at call or transferred by cheque, banks must cope with the inflows and outflows of balances. At existing interest rates, the amount of deposits supplied tomorrow may vary from that supplied today, either temporarily because of a purely stochastic element, or permanently in reflection of a change in interest rates which alters the relative attractiveness of those deposits. A similar uncertainty may surround outstanding loans when borrowers can draw upon unused overdraft facilities and lending commitments. We shall now examine how a bank can structure its balance sheet and minimise the costs of these events. An early account (Madden 1959) highlighted the time dimension of the problem and the importance of bankers taking into account the whole balance sheet structure (pp.31–33):

> . . . look at the deposit you may have in a bank. If you stop a moment to think about it, this money really consists of different slices, so to speak. Part of it will be drawn down for lunches this week, another part is money building toward payment next week of monthly bills, and part may be building up toward transfer to a savings account in a month or two to finance a trip. The idea of money having, as it were, a time dimension is fundamental in banking.
>
> All of a bank's deposits can be sliced up in just the same way. Some are going to be withdrawn tomorrow, some the next day, some next week, and next month, and next year. The bank has an idea from experience of what proportion of its total deposits is to be withdrawn daily, while at the same time it receives more new deposits each day. But of course your bank has no way of knowing when and how you or any other particular depositor may be planning to draw out your dollar of deposits . . .
>
> . . . Of course, the time character of loans is important as well. A . . . bank may have some one-day, two-day, or one-week loans backed by securities traded in the short-term money market . . . Then there are loans to customers — short-term loans to finance cars, TV sets, business inventories, office equipment; medium-term loans of two to five years to finance plant expansion outlays; and long-term mortgages that may run in maturities up to twenty years. Funds in loans are not so easily withdrawn quickly as funds in investments, and the bank must try to space loan maturities to match demands for cash, loan renewals, and new loan applications.
>
> . . . Because much of commercial banks' deposits may be withdrawn by check, such banks, uniquely among financial institutions, find practically the whole of their deposits legally withdrawable either on demand or on a few days' notice, and they must provide for unexpected drains even if they may be guided only by rough rules of thumb . . . [A bank] must invest its money in some way to earn interest, to be sure, because it must meet the heavy expenses of salaries, expensive buildings, manifold services performed for its customers; and must make a profit for its stockholders. But it must also keep constantly in mind that some of its deposits are today's drain of funds, some tomorrow's, the next day's, and so on. As the bankers themselves say it, a banker must try to 'ladder' the maturities of his holding of assets to give an adequate flow of cash to meet drains on his deposit liabilities.

This 'maturity laddering approach' to liquidity needs remains of importance in banking today. Stigum and Branch (1983), for example, describe the 'liquidity indexes' constructed by many US money market banks, which weight assets and liabilities according to maturity and compare the mismatched position. In the UK, the maturity laddering idea finds reflection in the requirement for banks when reporting to the Bank of England to place assets and liabilities into maturity bands so as to enable the Bank to assess a bank's liquidity on prudential grounds (see Chapter 5). But where the *raison d'être* of the institution is to marry long-term demands for loans with short-term deposits, there are limits as to how far this principle can be followed. This fact, combined with the uncertain maturity of deposits and drawdown of loans, means that a banker must look to other ways of coping with the possibility of substantial outflows of balances. In retail banking especially these strategies involve the holding of cash and liquid assets and diversifying the customer base for deposit liabilities and unused credit lines. Because the issues posed by uncertain loan take-ups are essentially the same as those posed by deposit variability, we shall concentrate upon the latter.

Two modes of behaviour can be adopted in the face of deposit variability. At one end of the spectrum, the entire burden of adjustment can be levied upon quantities. Interest rates on deposits can be held constant and the scale of the asset portfolio varied in line with the quantity of deposits forthcoming at that rate. Deposit rate setting behaviour and random deposit supplies form the basis of the Klein model (1971). In contrast, by adjusting interest rates paid so as to induce a quantity of deposits equal to the pre-existing stock of assets, all the burden of adjustment can be placed upon prices. Quantity setting and random deposit rates form the basis of the Pyle model (1971).

Between these two polar positions lie a variety of possible responses, the relative appeal of which will depend upon the structure of the bank's balance sheet, the nature of its deposit market, and thus the responsiveness of its deposit flows. In principle, a 'two-stage' decision-making process can be visualised. For each balance sheet structure the bank must determine the profit-maximising mixture of price and quantity responses to deposit fluctuations. Then, given these profit estimates and its estimates about the future variability of deposits, it must pick the balance sheet structure which will best achieve its objectives.

In recent years, there has been an apparent tendency for retail banks and other intermediaries to alter the nature of their portfolio behaviour from the end of the spectrum involving quantity responses towards behaviour based more upon price responses. Adopting the commonly used terminology, the tendency has been to move away from 'reserve asset management' towards 'liability management' policies. The reasons for this trend are complex. Factors cited in the literature include deregulation, growth of interbank markets, volatility in deposit flows, interest rate variability and competition for deposits, but there is the difficulty of sorting out exogenous from induced elements. What can be said is that the trend to liability management began in wholesale banking and hence discussion is deferred until Chapter 4. We concentrate now upon models of *reserve asset management*.

Certainly the oldest, and perhaps the most well-known, approach to the analysis of reserve asset (or liquidity) management is that pioneered by Edgeworth (1888) and found in more recent works by Baltensperger (1972, 1980) and Niehans (1978). In this model, pure quantity adjustment is assumed. Deposit interest rates are taken as unchanging, either by choice or as a result of regulation, over the decision-making period. Within that period, the level of deposits may change because of random inflows or outflows of funds.

Inflows of deposits over the period are added to holdings of cash and liquid assets. Outflows require the rundown of cash and sale of the liquid assets. An inventory of cash and liquid assets thus serves as a buffer stock to shield the illiquid loan portfolio from unexpected variations in deposit flows. Accordingly, the principles of inventory theory are used to determine the 'optimal' stock of reserve assets. We shall first look at the analysis with cash reserves, and then at choice with cash and liquid assets.

Cash Reserves

Using inventory theory, the expected marginal costs of reserve holdings are balanced against the benefits. Since reserve assets (i.e. cash and bankers' free reserves) earn no interest, the opportunity cost of each dollar (pound) of funds held in reserves is the loan rate of interest. Benefits come from reducing the likelihood of net outflows exceeding reserves, thereby reducing either potentially costly asset liquidations or enforced borrowings at penalty rates. Consequently, the marginal benefit of the *R*th dollar (pound) of reserves is equal to the probability that net outflows of at least *R* dollars (pounds) will occur, multiplied by the cost per dollar (pound) of asset liquidation and/or penalty borrowing.

Algebraically, the desired level of reserves must satisfy:

$$i_p.\text{Prob}\left(\frac{W}{D} > \frac{R^*}{D}\right) = i_a \tag{3.1}$$

where

i_p = marginal cost of penalty borrowing/asset liquidation
i_a = yield on other assets (e.g. loans)
W = size of outflow
D = size of deposits
R^* = desired reserve holdings

In (3.1), the left-hand side represents the marginal benefits from reserve holdings and the right-hand side gives the marginal opportunity costs. If the LHS of (3.1) exceeds the RHS, the bank finds it profitable to add to reserve holdings. If the LHS is less than the RHS, reserve holdings are reduced. By such adjustments, the bank is visualised as reaching its preferred reserve holding.

If we examine (3.1), the determinants of a bank's desired reserve ratio, R^*/D, can be fairly easily noted. First, the greater the variability of the deposit stock due to inflows and outflows, the greater will be R^*/D.[10] Second, increases in the opportunity cost of reserves (i_a) induce a lower cash reserve ratio and, third, increases in the penalty costs increase the desired reserve ratio.

These results have intuitive appeal (and practical relevance), but it is worth examining the structure of the model which gives rise to them in more detail. In particular, it should be noted that the model assumes that inflows of deposits during the decision period cannot be used to earn interest. It is this imposed asymmetry between the effects of inflows and outflows which provides the model's results. Suppose instead that a perfect interbank market in cash reserves exists so that banks receiving deposits can lend the resulting cash in this market at rate i_p and those experiencing withdrawals can borrow at the same rate. Provided that the expected value of net withdrawals is zero, risk-neutral banks (another assumption of the model) have no incentive to hold positive reserves. Reserve gains or losses simply determine the bank's net position in the interbank cash markets. As Niehans (1978) notes: 'the Edgeworth type models of banking are indeed based on market imperfections' (p.177, note 10) although, even with a perfect interbank market, similar results would appear to result from an assumption of risk aversion on the part of banks. The proviso that no net withdrawals are expected ignores system-wide influences upon deposit flows in the banking system. Interbank funding cannot be relied upon if there is a shortage of funds in the system as a whole.

Cash and Liquid Assets

More generally, we can think of assets being grouped into a number of categories, starting with cash giving no interest return but having no liquidation costs and ranging through assets bearing an increasing return but having higher liquidation costs. In the following example, we focus upon three categories: cash, government securities (i.e. Treasury bills and bonds) and advances (loans). Thus deposits can be allocated between cash (C) with zero yield and zero liquidation cost, government securities (G) with yield $i_G > 0$ and per dollar liquidation cost $p > 0$, and advances (A) with yield $i_A (> i_G)$ and liquidation cost of $q (> p)$. If $F(X)$ represents the probability of deposit outflows in the period being less than X, the marginal benefit from the last dollar of cash held is given by $p(1-F(C))$, which represents the expected saving of liquidation costs (which might otherwise be incurred if that dollar were held as government securities). In that expression, $(1-F(C))$ represents the probability of outflows exceeding cash holding (C) and thus the incurrence of liquidation costs of p on that dollar. A bank will then choose C so as to equate this marginal benefit with the marginal cost of holding cash, given by the interest rate i_G foregone. Thus the model is based on a dependency which has cash holdings depending upon i_G, but not i_A. Similar considerations (of balancing marginal costs and benefits) apply in regard to the decision of how to allocate the remainder of the portfolio between G and A.

Formally, the optimum portfolio allocation is given by the solutions to the equations:

$$p\,[1-F(C)] = i_G \tag{3.2}$$
$$(q-p)\,[1-F(C+G)] = i_A - i_G \tag{3.3}$$
$$A = D-C-G \tag{3.4}$$

the first of which has been interpreted above. The second equation (3.3), which has a similar interpretation, indicates that government securities (in addition to cash) should be held up to the point at which the expected saving of liquidation costs (of advances) equals the interest yield foregone. The third equation (3.4) is simply the balance sheet constraint, ignoring equity capital.

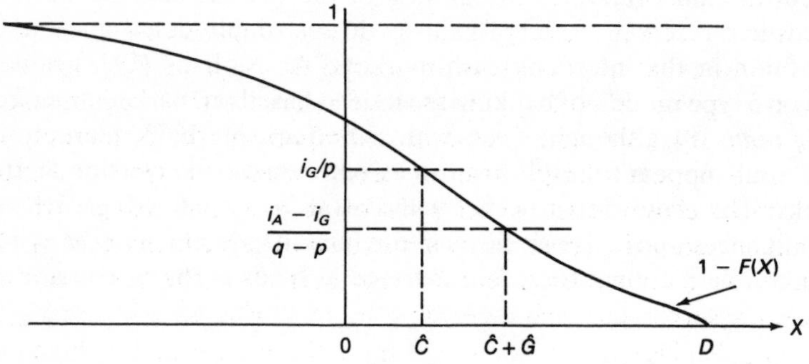

Figure 3.1

Figure 3.1 illustrates these results. The curve $(1-F(X))$ indicates the probability of a total deposit outflow in excess of X. Optimal cash holdings are given by $\hat{C}$ where this curve takes on the value i_G/p and the optimal holdings of cash plus government securities $(\hat{C}+\hat{G})$ where it has the value $(i_A-i_G)/(q-p)$. Government security holdings thus equal the gap between $(C+G)$ and C and advances equal the gap between D and $(\hat{C}+\hat{G})$.

Several intuitively appealing results follow from the equations above. First, an increase in the yield on 'less liquid' assets (those with higher liquidation cost) will reduce the holding of liquid assets. *Ceteris paribus*, the cash (or liquid assets) ratio (to deposits) can be expected to move inversely with the opportunity cost of cash holdings given by the *level of interest rates*. Second, an increase in *liquidation* costs will encourage a shift into more liquid, lower-yielding assets. Liquidation costs, we note, reflect the institution's valuation of the cost of the potential variability of returns from the various assets should they be sold before maturity. In some cases, such as with non-marketable private securities, this may reflect the risk of default if loans have to be called in. Alternatively, where borrowings from the authorities at penalty rates of interest are undertaken, the effective yield on securities used as collateral is reduced. Finally, with respect to *deposit variability*, the holding of liquid assets will be greater, the more volatile is the level of deposits. (In terms of Figure 3.1 this corresponds to an anticlockwise rotation of the curve labelled $(1-F(X))$ around its intersection with the vertical axis.)[11]

Because liquidation costs and deposit variability necessitate the holding of cash and liquid assets, and thus reduce the expected profits of banks, their presence can be expected to encourage the development of institutional arrangements which reduce these costs. One such development is a *secondary market* for assets similar to those which have grown recently for mortgage, auto and credit card loans in the USA. These operate, in effect, by having an institution create a negotiable security backed by, say, mortgages sold or pledged to it by an intermediary, which the intermediary can then sell to supplement its cash reserves.

Another institutional arrangement is an *interbank market* for deposits. Deposit variability at one bank is in most cases mirrored by offsetting variations in deposits at other banks. Under reserve asset management, all banks will hold large cash reserves. Some will experience large cash outflows, while others experience large offsetting cash inflows. Scope for mutually beneficial trades clearly exists in the form of an interbank market whereby those banks experiencing cash inflows make short-term loans at a market-determined rate to those experiencing cash outflows. The latter can hold smaller cash reserves and avoid possibly more costly sales of assets. The former group also benefits by holding lower cash reserves and by being able to obtain a return on temporary surplus funds.

These arrangements require cooperation between banks. In the absence of this cooperation, or the ingenuity to devise the system and expend the resources needed to maintain them, there is an alternative way by which a bank can lower the costs of reserve management. This is by taking advantage of any economies of scale in reserve holdings to reduce deposit variability.

Economies of Scale in Reserve Management

Economies of scale in reserve management exist if the possibility of outflows exceeding any given proportion of deposits declines as the size of deposits increases. Whether this is so depends upon what is meant by the 'size' of deposits. If an increase in deposits is due to an increase in the monetary value of the same number of accounts, scale economies are unlikely. But if the increase is accompanied by an increase in the number of independently acting depositors then, by the 'law of large numbers', a reduction in the variance of total outflows can be expected (Baltensperger 1972).

This result hinges upon the assumed independence of depositors' actions. Provided independence exists, the variance of total outflows (relative to total deposits) will be less than the average variance of outflows from each account. Intuitively, the outflows from one account may be accompanied by inflows to another account, and the likelihood of this event increases as the number of accounts increases. Formally, and assuming that all deposits are identical and depositors act independently, the variance of the withdrawals/deposit ratio is given by:

$$\text{var}\left(\frac{(W)}{(D)}\right) = \frac{1}{n}\,\text{var}\left(\frac{(w)}{(d)}\right) \tag{3.5}$$

where n is the number of deposit accounts and w/d is the withdrawals/deposit ratio of the representative account.

Thus, as n increases, var(W/D) falls, which corresponds to a clockwise rotation of the curve [1–$F(X)$] in Figure 3.1 and reduction in the optimal reserve ratio. In fact, if the distribution of withdrawals is assumed to be normal (with mean zero), more specific results can be derived. Then, condition (3.5) leads to the result that:

$$\frac{R^*}{D} = b\sqrt{\text{var}\left(\frac{W}{D}\right)}$$

$$= \frac{bx}{\sqrt{n}} \tag{3.6}$$

where x is the standard deviation of the withdrawals/deposit ratio of the representative account and b is a function of the two interest rates i_p and i_a. The desired reserve ratio declines with the increase in the number of accounts; indeed, in the limit the ratio approaches zero as the number of depositors increases.

Scale economies in reserve management derive from the actuarial principle of risk pooling, in this case from pooling independent risks of deposit withdrawals. These risks can be reduced by pooling only if one depositor's decision to withdraw deposits is largely independent of the decisions made by others. The history of banking is littered with circumstances in which that assumption broke down. In modern terminology 'the demand deposit contract has an undesirable equilibrium (a bank run) in which all depositors panic and withdraw immediately' (Diamond and Dybvig 1983). Once a 'run' begins, nothing less than 100 per cent reserves may suffice. How these circumstances can be averted, and the consequences ameliorated, forms the basis of collective arrangements for the prudential supervision of banks (see Chapter 5).

Note also that the pooling principle summarised in (3.5) is a general one. It says nothing about the organisation used to achieve the scale economies. That is, the pooling can be within the firm or across firms. With interbank markets and other such cooperative arrangements, the pooling occurs *outside* the firm via the market transactions. In the case of a large firm or a branch network, the pooling occurs *within* the firm. A branch network can be thought of as an *intra-bank* market. As we shall see, this distinction is the same as that which underlies the difference between retail and wholesale banking practices.

Size economies in reserve management may contribute towards a more concentrated banking sector, which is a point that Sayers noted years ago in his book *Modern Banking* (see Chapter 1). As an empirical matter, it is the case that banking in most developed countries is concentrated, with a small number of large, multi-branch banks dominating the payments mechanism. The exception is the United States (see Table 1.3).

These figures are subject to a number of interpretations. Has the existence of correspondent and interbank balances in the USA obviated the need for branch banking systems, or have the interbank arrangements merely reduced what would otherwise have been high costs of reserve management? Does the longstanding concentration in banking in Europe reflect the existence of historical and institutional factors inhibiting interbank links, or have such links been made unnecessary by the spread of branch banking? Sayers was in no doubt as to which interpretation he favoured:

> . . . A comparison between unit banking and branch banking is essentially a comparison between small-scale and large-scale operation. The large concern — the branch bank — secures certain economies of large-scale production. The economy of reserves is of enormous importance for, as we have seen above, the maintenance of adequate reserves is absolutely vital to the banker. The large bank can afford to hold a lower cash reserve in each office, for one office can draw on another — by transferring assets or by borrowing — far more readily than can one unit bank draw on another unit bank in the same way. The system of correspondent banks modifies the disadvantage here of the unit bank, but only slightly, for deposits with a correspondent bank are relatively unremunerative. The cheapness of doing remittance business (the sending of money from one place to another for clients) is much increased by the convenience of the branch system, for inter-office indebtedness can be far more easily adjusted. The correspondent system enables the bank to offer the client service comparable with that afforded by the branch but not at as low cost. (*Modern Banking*, 1st edn, p.23)

The modern view would seem to favour the opposite interpretation. We noted, when discussing (3.1) above, that reserves would not be needed at all if a perfect interbank funds market existed. When such a market operates, 'diversification across maturities will have no value in helping the bank handle cash flows' (Black 1975). The issue is whether the 'market' can be internalised more cheaply than it can be externalised.

Scale economies in reserve management alone are unlikely to have contributed to the concentration shown in Table 1.3. Sayers referred also to 'the spreading of risks geographically' and to the 'minimisation of the "bad debts" that are incurred in the business of lending to customers' which comes from having a varied business 'in terms of industries and trades'. The first factor he mentioned is of relevance for the spread of multinational banking (Chapter 8), and we shall now look at the second factor.

3.5 Management of Asset Risk

Lending by banks is a risky business. Keynes (1936, p.144) drew a distinction between borrower's risk, arising from the variability of outcome of the projects in which funds are being invested, and lender's risk, due to the problems of adverse selection and moral hazard referred to in the previous chapter. Lenders may be less well informed than borrowers about the contingencies under which borrowers operate, and be unable to control subsequent actions of borrowers to take advantage of the situation and escape fulfilment of their obligation. These factors generate uncertainty about the extent and speed of repayment of principal and interest, and thus give rise to credit risk in bank lending. Bankers must exercise discretion not only in maintaining a distribution of liquidity in assets — as examined above — but in deciding upon proper borrowers.

Credit officers must seek to identify entrepreneurial risk, and mitigate adverse selection and the moral hazards. Here the banker will be concerned both with evaluating the worth of the project and the capacity of the borrower to repay the debt within an acceptable period, using personal knowledge and past records to assess the character and financial acumen of the client. An important consideration will be the extent of 'insider equity', signalling the degree to which proprietors are prepared to back their own ventures. Banks will seek to exercise control over borrowers (or the management) by writing restrictive covenants into the credit agreement. They will also seek 'insurance' against unforeseen developments in the form of security against the loan. This collateral may take the form of a title over shareholders' personal assets, the pledge of company assets such as property, accounts receivable or inventories, or (as used in the UK) a floating charge over all of the company's assets. Banks may be able to enforce repayment of loans in other ways, such as the implied threat of withholding future financing and by the exemplary effect of a few foreclosures on other borrowers.

We emphasised earlier the ability of banks to reduce the riskiness of individual loans by means of improved information due to what is in effect an informational 'economy of scope' when lending is combined with the provision of payments services. An additional implication of the points in the previous paragraph is that banks may be able to reduce individual loan risks as well by designing and enforcing incentive-compatible loan contracts, so improving the prospects of loans being repaid.[12] The banker is also well placed, by virtue of his knowledge of a customer's business, to tailor-make a 'workout' which takes cognisance of the borrower's financial and trading position.

Nevertheless, loan risks remain. Serious trading reverses, alterations to management, new technology, changes in fashion, additional competitors, downturns in the economy, variations in exchange rates or energy prices can all diminish the prospects of repayment and the value of assets held as collateral. A bank engaging in liquidity production must be able to convince depositors that, despite having an asset portfolio composed of (at least partly) risky assets, its deposit liabilities can be redeemed at full value. In the absence of government guarantees, this is achieved by the institution's buffer stock of shareholders' funds which absorbs losses on the income account such as those due to default on loans or capital losses on unanticipated security sales. (For cooperative institutions a similar function is achieved by members' funds accrued from past surpluses.)

Consider a bank with given assets yielding a flow of net returns, X. Let A indicate the market value of assets. Equity capital can be thought of as being held for three reasons. One is to prevent insolvency: a loss (interest payments (iD) greater than receipts (X)) which is larger than the institution's shareholders' equity (E), i.e.

$$iD-X>E \tag{3.7}$$

results in insolvency. Since $E=A-D$ (where A is total assets and here incorporates fixed capital assets), we have:

$$(A+X)-(1+i)D<0 \tag{3.8}$$

that is, end-of-period assets ($A+X$) are less than end-of-period debt ($D(1+i)$). Debt holders can force the firm into receivership and there are substantial resource costs involved. Second, depositors also face potential losses from the institution's unprofitability, since they bear the excess of losses over the firm's equity capital. They could themselves avert this risk by spreading deposits across many institutions, but this creates costs to them. By undertaking the diversification for them, and shouldering part of the risk, large intermediaries save depositors this effort. Third, loan losses may provoke withdrawals of deposits. Equity is needed to maintain confidence in the bank and hence to reduce withdrawal risks.

As with the reserve asset decision, it is possible to conceive of an 'optimal' equity/assets or equities/liabilities ratio under the assumption that operating losses which reduce shareholders' funds involve the intermediary in costs. The higher the equity ratio, the lower is the probability that such costs will be incurred. At the same time, however, the expected rate of return on shareholders' funds (net of such costs) will be lowered. The optimal equity ratio will be positively related to the degree of variability of its operating profits/losses. (These matters are taken up in Chapter 5 where we discuss depositor protection.)

Since the variability of operating profits/losses reflects the outcome of individual loans and investments, the law of large numbers again assures us that an increase in the number of such loans will (provided that their outcomes are not perfectly positively correlated) reduce the relative variability of the outcome. Suppose that the flow of net returns from assets, W, has a density function of $f(W)$. If this function is normally distributed depending upon the number of loans or security types, it can be shown that the standard deviation of W is given by:

$$\sigma W = \frac{cA}{\sqrt{m}} \tag{3.9}$$

where m refers to the number of loans etc. outstanding and c is a constant. In this case, analogously with the reserve ratio:

$$E^* = \frac{\mathrm{dcA}}{\sqrt{m}} \quad or \quad \frac{E^*}{A} = \frac{dc}{\sqrt{m}} \tag{3.10}$$

where d is the desired level of risk. Increases in the size of an intermediary which take the form of an increase in the number of independent loans will lower the optimal equity/deposit ratio for a given extent of risk and thus increase the expected rate of return on shareholders' funds. (Alternatively, in terms of Modigliani and Miller's 1958 analysis, the institution moves into a lower risk class.)

A number of implications of this result need to be emphasised. First, application of the 'law of large numbers' to the loan portfolio does not alter the average default experience. Loans and investments can be characterised in terms of their expected mean rate of return and the variability of possible returns about the expected mean. Pooling of loans reduces risk in the sense that the variability of losses approaches zero, and actual defaults approach those that can be anticipated, as m, the number of independently defaulting borrowers included in the group, increases.[13]

Second, the economies of size to be had depend upon the number of loans, investments, and so on, of particular categories, not the dollar value of the balance sheet. Thus a small bank with 100 × \$10,000 loans may be just as diversified as a larger bank with 100 × \$100,000 loans. This is a point we take up below when considering wholesale business. But the critical factor giving risk diversification is the independent fates of the investments. Here the spread of business across different industries, the geographical spread of business, and the division between retail and wholesale activities are of significance.

Consequently, third, a loan's riskiness to a bank cannot be judged in isolation, but must be determined by how it relates to the other assets with which it is combined in the portfolio. The nature of the covariance of returns is an important consideration when we come, later, to consider the desire of banks to spread internationally for portfolio diversification. We shall take up this point again when we consider international banking. But we note that the benefits to a bank of diversifying independent risk must to some extent be balanced against its skills in information production and contract design, discussed earlier, which may be enhanced by specialising in particular types of loans and by confining operations to a limited geographical region.[14]

In the next chapter we shall look at wholesale banking, and in particular at how it differs from the activities described in this chapter.

Notes

1. *Federal Reserve Bulletin*, December 1986, Table 4.23.
2. At a conceptual level, a bank issuing demand deposits and subject to a 100 per cent reserve requirement (à la Friedman 1960) would be a specialist payments service provider. Weakening the reserve requirement provides scope for intermediation. At an historical level, Newlyn and Bootle (1978) argue that the transition from goldsmiths to banks in seventeenth-century Britain involved a similar process. As described by Newlyn and Bootle, the goldsmiths did not replace pre-existing direct financing by making loans upon gold deposited with them. By and large, the deposits with the goldsmiths were not amounts that otherwise would have been lent by their owners to primary borrowers. Rather, they were deposited with the goldsmiths primarily because the goldsmiths provided a better and cheaper alternative to self-storage. The payments services provided by goldsmiths were then supplemented by intermediation services when the goldsmiths adopted a fractional reserve strategy.
3. See Laidler (1984).
4. Revell (1983).
5. Startz (1979) provides some relevant information on the relative responsiveness of 'implicit' and 'explicit' interest rates to market conditions which is consistent with the argument in the text.
6. For example, consider an intermediary which enters fixed-price forward contracts with both depositors and lenders and which gives both of those groups the option to withdraw from the contract. Any movement in interest rates would cause one or other party to opt out, leaving the intermediary in a loss-making position.
7. See Carron (1982).
8. It is an interesting speculation as to whether growth in intermediation can help explain the behaviour of the yield curve over time. Experience after 1930 in the United States and other countries seems to provide clear support for liquidity preference type ideas. The following facts stylise the US experience. In the 42 years from 1931 to 1972 there were 37 years in which the yield curve sloped upwards. During the other five years the yield curve was, on average, approximately horizontal. Experience before and after these years was different. With the higher and more variable interest rates ruling after 1972, the preponderance of ascending yield curves has gone. During the 12 years from 1972, upward-sloping curves were in evidence, on average, in only five years, with five years of downward-sloping curves and two years of approximately horizontal curves. Experience before the 1930s provides even more of a contrast. From 1901 to 1930, the yield curve sloped upwards, on average, in only one year. There were 17 years of downward-sloping curves and 12 years with the yield curve horizontal.
9. Santomero (1983) provides a formal analysis of fixed and variable interest rate loan financing.

10. This reflects an increase in the probability of W/D exceeding any given value and a need for an increase in R^*/D to preserve the equality (3.1).
11. It is also possible to introduce reserve ratio requirements into the model. Since such reserves are not available to meet deposit outflows (or at most only partially available), banks will still hold excess cash reserves. Changes in the reserve ratio will lead to an across-the-board change in holdings of other assets.
12. In this respect, recent analyses of Swary and Udell (1985) and Sofianos (1985) are of interest. Swary and Udell argue the importance of bank collateral in enhancing the flow of information to a bank, while Sofianos emphasises the role of banks in imposing penalties upon defaulting borrowers.
13. For a general analysis of mean and variance analysis in the context of portfolios containing large numbers of securities, see Markowitz (1959, Ch.5). An excellent recent account of the selection of bank loan portfolios is given by Flannery (1985).
14. See Flannery (1985) and Bernanke and Gertler (1986).

4

Wholesale Banking

4.1 Origins of Wholesale Banking

It is often difficult to date the beginnings of a new idea. But the concept of wholesale banking, at least in the UK, can be dated to a paper written by Professor J.R.S. Revell (1968), calling attention to:

> the growth of an entirely new banking system, with a method of operation quite different from that of the deposit banks as described in the textbooks. The Americans would describe the business of the banks as 'wholesale banking', contrasting it with the 'retail banking' undertaken by deposit banks. (p.422)

He identified a number of distinguishing characteristics, the first of which was the mix of domestic currency and foreign currency business:

> Of the total deposits of the secondary banking system at the end of 1966 over 60 per cent came from overseas residents, and 56 per cent of total deposits was in currencies other than sterling. Of total advances over 70 per cent was to overseas residents, and roughly the same proportion was in currencies other than sterling. Although international business thus accounts for more than half of all the assets and liabilities of secondary banks, their domestic business is by no means negligible. (p.424)

Second, there was the size of deposit and loan business, and the implications for costs which flowed from that feature:

> The other feature of both deposits and advances is that the units are large. For many banks in the secondary system the minimum unit for a sterling deposit is £50,000, and the minimum tends to be larger for other currency deposits. Hardly any of the banks would look at the offer of a deposit of less than £10,000. For advances the unit is typically larger still, and £500,000 would be regarded as the norm by many banks, with advances occasionally running into millions of pounds. (pp.425/6)
>
> Such large deposits and advances are very cheap to process. Secondary bankers can conduct their business with few of the expensive clerical procedures that face the deposit banker, there is no need for a widespread branch network and the number of staff is small, consisting largely of specialists. (p.426)

> For all these reasons the banks in the secondary system are low-cost institutions, operating with narrow margins between borrowing and lending rates. There are no agreements as to the rates to be paid and charged, and the system is highly competitive. (p.426)

Third, there was the nature of advances:

> Of the advances, both in sterling and in other currencies, only a small part is of the overdraft type common to deposit banking in this country. The remaining loans take a variety of forms because secondary bankers pride themselves on being able to find a 'tailor-made' solution to each financing problem. One common feature is that loans are nearly all for a definite period, with or without provision for repayment by instalments, and we shall lump them all together under the generic description of 'term loans'. With advances it is . . . common . . . to have a variable interest rate. (p.425)

And finally:

> The growth of the secondary banking system which we have been describing is closely bound up with the development of the London market for deposits and loans in currencies other than sterling — the 'Euro-dollar market'. It has also been dependent on the newer parallel money markets in sterling . . . secondary banking as we have described it could not exist without an active inter-bank market. (p.428)

Professor Revell used the phrase 'secondary banking system' because in 1968 there were two banking systems operating in Britain. One was a retail (or primary) banking system, conducted by the clearing banks and the small deposit banks, dealing with households and small- to medium-sized firms. The other was a wholesale (or secondary) banking system operated by the other banks. They dealt in large sums with large companies and public authorities, having a relatively small number of customers on both sides of the balance sheets. Wholesale banking was subdivided into foreign currency (Euromarket) business and domestic wholesale business, but the two grew up together as the banks serviced the domestic as well as international needs of multinational corporations and transferred staff and skills developed in the Euromarkets into domestic operations. However, the retail and wholesale systems were then separated by practices and regulatory controls.

It is now the case that we can no longer identify purely retail banks and purely wholesale banks. Reforms to monetary controls in 1971 and 1980, and a new Banking Act in 1979, have resulted in a similar regulatory treatment for all banks.[1] At the same time, from 1971, the retail banks were encouraged to imitate the practices of the secondary banks and they entered into domestic wholesale and foreign currency business. All British banks are now multiproduct firms, operating simultaneously in the different markets and producing different kinds of services. Moreover, the division between retail and wholesale has been broken down by what is termed 'intermediate' business, as some companies move between the two markets in response to credit needs. Nevertheless, the old secondary banks are to be found far more towards the wholesale end — indeed, most are still almost entirely wholesale; and vice versa for the old retail-only banks. These differences are explored in section 4.3 to give a statistical profile of the respective balance sheets.

Broadly speaking, the other characteristics of wholesale banking mentioned by Revell remain, namely, the interbank and 'parallel' funds markets and variable rate lending. Because of inflation, though, the money value of minimum transactions has increased. For sterling wholesale business, deposits of £250,000 would now be the more usual minimum value (Cooper 1984). On Eurocurrency business, $500,000 should be seen to be the minimum deal, with most transactions between $5 million and $10 million. For advances, £500,000 on domestic and $1 million on Eurocurrency business would be the respective minimums.[2]

While much of our data on wholesale banking is drawn from the UK, there are world-wide similarities in the characteristics of wholesale banking. The reason for this is quite simple. Much of the stimulus for the development of wholesale banking in London came from the influx of US banks in the late 1950s and the 1960s, bringing with them techniques which had long been part of the US scene. Indeed, we noted in Chapter 1 that the retail–wholesale division was a feature of US banking pre-war, with the Wall Street money market banks being predominantly wholesale banks. The techniques of US banks were merged with features of the British scene, refined in Eurocurrency operations, and exported back to the USA. As new Eurocurrency markets developed in other countries, so the practices pioneered in London by US and British banks spread worldwide.

Three such practices can be identified as forming the basis of wholesale banking in a large number of centres, namely:

(i) the existence of interbank markets in domestic and foreign currencies;
(ii) the issuing of domestic and foreign currency certificates of deposit;
(iii) lending by means of term loans (rollover credits) at variable rates of interest.

Here we shall focus upon their origins (particularly in the UK context) and, because Eurocurrency operations will be examined later, we shall concentrate upon the domestic wholesale aspects. This will provide us with a basis for examining the economic functions of wholesale banking in sections 4.2–4.4.

Interbank Markets

Interbank lendings and borrowings have their (recent) origins in Great Britain and France in the eighteenth and nineteenth centuries, in the relationship between the country banker and either the London agent or Paris correspondent, as the case may be. With the growth of branch banking those relationships declined in importance in Europe, and ceased altogether in Britain. Indeed, it became an article of faith amongst British banks (and in countries like Australia which for a long time adopted British banking arrangements) that banks did not borrow from and lend to each other. This 'self-imposed inhibition', as Einzig (1971) called it, is surprising in view of the importance of the officially-supported discount market. The clearing banks lent surplus funds to the discount houses, which met subsequent withdrawals by attracting surplus funds from another bank. Thus interbank borrowing and lending occurred indirectly through the agency of the discount houses. Yet, so strong was the inhibition against direct dealings between banks that, when interbank dealings did actually begin in foreign currencies around the late 1950s, deposits were described as being 'given' and 'taken', not 'lent' and 'borrowed'.

Meanwhile, in the United States, interbank transactions in the form of correspondent relationships and via the federal funds market assumed considerable importance. *Correspondent relationships*, as in Britain and France in the last century, allow US banks to overcome geographical impediments to cheque clearing and the flow of funds. A bank in a small country town has a correspondent bank in a neighbouring city, while the city banks in turn have their own correspondent links with major city banks in New York or Chicago. The system enables cheques to be cleared more readily, both within and across state boundaries. It also permits banks to make use of surplus funds. As was shown in Table 1.2, such interbank balances accounted for nearly 12 per cent of deposits in the 1940s, but they have declined in importance relative to federal funds ever since.

In the *federal funds market*, institutions with immediately available funds lend them to other institutions, mainly on an overnight basis. The 'market', as is the case with most wholesale funds markets, consists of a loosely structured telephone network by which the major participants are connected. Its origins date back to the 1920s when New York banks began to lend and borrow unanticipated excess or deficient balances held at the Federal Reserve, and this practice quickly spread to other parts of the country. Transactions declined during the depression years, but picked up in the 1960s as banks increasingly used the market as an alternative to correspondent relationships. Since then, regulatory and other developments have transformed the market from one based on balances of member banks to one involving virtually all depository institutions, along with other non-banking participants.

Nevertheless, the market is effectively segmented into a primary market between the large banks, and other institutions are involved indirectly through a money centre correspondent. Within the primary market, there exists a 'tiering' of rates, ranging from large money centre banks to large regional and domestically operating foreign banks down to medium-sized regionals and agencies of foreign banks (Allen and Saunders 1986). In the case of transactions between member banks (i.e. banks which are members of the Federal Reserve System), the lending bank increases its asset category 'Federal funds sold', while the borrowing bank increases its nonreservable liability 'Federal funds sold', with the Federal Reserve debiting the lending bank's account and crediting the borrowing bank's account. A similar set of balance sheet entries marks transactions between member and non-member correspondents. Small banks are generally net sellers of funds, whereas large banks are almost always net buyers of funds although they may sell on particular days (especially reserve settlement day) in the course of evening up reserve positions (see Melton 1985).

The US bankers brought habits fashioned in correspondent relationships and the federal funds market with them to London in the late 1950s and encouraged a revival in the practice of interbank dealings, especially in US dollars. The rapid growth of the dollar interbank market also inspired the systematic development of an interbank market in the local currency.[3] Many foreign banks operating in London had established links with multinational corporations for loan business but they lacked a local deposit base to supply them with funds. Other banks were better able to accumulate deposits but sometimes lacked immediate lending opportunities. It was another instance of 'necessity being the mother of institutions' (Kindleberger 1983b).

However, institutions may shape, as well as be shaped by, banking practices. The interbank markets which developed in London are much more than a kind of federal funds market transplanted overseas, both in character and in importance. Federal funds sold are about 5 per cent of the assets of the weekly reporting banks in the USA. In London, interbank deposits constitute about 70 per cent of total Eurocurrency liabilities and about 35 per cent of sterling 'wholesale' liabilities. In the USA, federal funds are lent and borrowed overnight mainly, and hardly ever for periods longer than a fortnight. In the two (domestic and foreign currency) London interbank markets, funds are lent (and borrowed) for periods as long as five years. (However, most interbank funds have a maturity of three months or less.) These striking comparisons suggest that interbank dealings play quite a different role in 'pure' wholesale banking operations. In addition to spreading or distributing surplus funds between the banks, we argue (in section 4.4 below) that the interbank and related funds market are an important source of liquidity to the banks. We also suggest that the markets may serve as an informal mechanism for risk sharing in lending operations.

Certificates of Deposit[4]

The markets for certificates of deposit (CDs) in Britain are a direct transplant of the markets in the USA which began in 1961 when First National City Bank of New York (now Citibank) issued CDs. From the viewpoint of an issuing bank, a CD is merely a time deposit with a fixed maturity date. From the purchaser's viewpoint, there are two further features: negotiability and the secondary market. Since the certificates are payable to bearer, their ownership can be transferred prior to the redemption date. Simultaneously with the first issue in 1961, a major securities dealer, Discount Corporation of New York, announced that it would make a market in certificates of $100,000 or larger on a yield-to-maturity basis; other dealers soon followed suit. A secondary market was essential to reduce the effective maturity from the legislated minimum of 30 days, although dealers' spreads in the market limit trading to maturities well in excess of seven days.

CDs now contribute about 20 per cent of deposit funds of US commercial banks (see Table 1.2 in Ch.1). US banks, when raising funds in their London operations, also rely upon CDs extensively: they raise 35 per cent of their non-sterling funds and around 20 per cent of sterling deposits by means of issues of CDs. But CDs have proven less popular amongst the other UK-based banks. Overall, 16 per cent of non-sterling deposits and only 6 per cent of sterling deposits are contributed by CDs.

A possible explanation as to why CDs are used less for deposit raising in sterling business is suggested by Harrington (1987). CDs in America are issued in two ways. One is nationally, in pieces of $1 million or more through dealers, which also make an active secondary market in the certificates.[5] However, currently there are only about 20 large domestic banks whose CDs have a deep secondary market (Stigum 1983). The other method is direct placement by the bank's own sales force to the bank's own clients, tailored to customers' requirements. For banks whose paper is excluded from the national market, the CD acquired by customers is not highly marketable. But, should funding needs arise, the holder can use the CD as collateral for obtaining a bank loan. In the UK, banks have preferred instead to issue wholesale time deposits to individual customers. Issue costs to the bank are less, while customers can obtain the 'marketability' characteristic by utilising overdraft facilities (not necessarily with the wholesale banker).

Rollover Credits

It is doubtful whether the growth of wholesale financing in the 1970s would have been sustained without the invention of rollover 'credits' or loans. With such a large proportion of their funds interbank or drawn from funds markets, some at relatively short maturities, the banks' interest costs rose and fell in line with the path of interest rates generally. A need arose to adjust interest earnings on assets in line with market trends. But when undertaking other than very short-term lending to industry, the banks looked for documentation and regular repayments to generate a flow of income along the lines of the American term loans. These had always been made at fixed rates of interest. The British (more correctly, Scottish) system of lending by overdraft gave the banks the flexibility they sought to adjust interest rates, but the loans were short-term or, when allowed to drift into more or less permanent lending, the repayment was largely at the customer's convenience, creating liquidity problems. Thus neither the American nor the British tradition held the solution.

Rollover credits represented a cross-fertilisation of ideas and demonstrated the adaptability of banking techniques to financing needs. They combined the interest rate flexibility of British overdrafts with the legal formality of US medium-length term loans. Instead of fixing the interest rate for the entire duration of the loan, the rate is fixed for intervals of time (normally 3 or 6 months) and adjusted at those intervals to the constantly changing market rates on deposits. In the UK, the normal formula for determining the interest rate is:

Loan rate = LIBOR + Spread

LIBOR stands for London InterBank Offer Rate. It is the dominant rate at which banks are willing to make loans to each other on interbank deals for terms corresponding to the interest rate adjustment interval of the loan (e.g. 6 months money). LIBOR varies daily according to market fluctuations. By contrast, the spread is the margin which the bank adds on to this base rate to cover the costs and risks of intermediation. Usually the spread is fixed for the term of the loan. The term 'rollover credit' comes about because the loan or credit is automatically renewed on terms modified by the formula given above over a number of intervals as determined in the contract. That is, the loan is 'rolled over' from one interest period to another at a floating rate until maturity.

The principle underlying rollover credits has now been adopted very widely in banking and, like so many of the innovations which began in wholesale banking, has spread to retail banking, blurring the lines between the two. In UK banking, almost all loans to business in domestic currency are on a flexi-rate basis. Large (wholesale) loans are tied to LIBOR, as above. Middle-sized and small loans are tied to base rate (prime rate), but an increasing proportion of the former are now being linked to interbank rates. In the United States, most commercial and industrial (C&I) loans are now made on a floating-rate basis. As at August 1986, 81 per cent of long-term C&I loans (average maturity 57 months) and 31 per cent of short-term C&I loans (average maturity 4 months) were floating rate.[6] A variety of base rates are used. The prime rate (sometimes referred to as a bank's 'basic' or 'reference' rate) is the most commonly used rate. But, as in London, use is also made of base rates tied to money market funding costs such as the federal funds rate or the 90-day certificate of deposit rate, although some loans are tied to foreign money market rates such as LIBOR for dollars. Broadly similar arrangements are followed for wholesale-type loans made by banks and wholesale financiers in a large number of other countries.

4.2 Matching and Liquidity Distribution

When Professor Revell first drew British attention to the concept of wholesale banking, he also went on to sketch out the basis of its operations in terms of the principle of 'matching':

> Just as liquidity is the basic principle of deposit banking, so matching is the basic principle of secondary banking. (p.428)
>
> . . . It is, of course, an age-old principle of banking but it is only in the last few years that it has come into play in British banking with the advent of large deposits and advances, fixed for definite periods and expressed in a number of different currencies. A completely matched balance sheet is one in which for every deposit of a certain amount and in a certain currency maturing on a certain day there is an asset of the same amount and in the same currency maturing on the same day. Provided nobody defaults, it is a self-liquidating balance sheet. (p.427–8)

Matching corresponds to the 'maturity laddering approach' described in the previous chapter. There we noted its limited applicability to retail banking. Significantly, Revell was careful to point out that matching was far from being the whole story of wholesale banking:

> In practice few secondary bankers have a completely matched position. Because of the narrow margins in this kind of banking, there is very little profit in just 'putting business through', and most secondary bankers aim to increase their profits by having assets somewhat longer than deposits because yields rise with maturity. Nearly all secondary bankers also take a view on future interest rates and exchange rates although some do so far more than others.
>
> . . . some banks will be more closely matched than others, but equally some banks in the secondary system are rather scornful of the principle of matching, describing it as 'broking' (as opposed to banking) . . . (p.428)

Later, we shall show that these comments have proved to be perceptive. For the moment we shall stay with the concept of matching, for it forms the basis of the major theory of wholesale banking — the 'liquidity distribution' theory — in which it is hypothesised that wholesale banks are pure 'brokers' or distributors of liquid assets. This is an argument advanced for the foreign currency business of wholesale banks in London and the other Eurocentres, notably by Niehans and Hewson (1976), Freedman (1977), Niehans (1978), Weston (1980) and Niehans (1984). The possible importance of the distribution function of banking for domestic markets is mentioned in Benston and Smith (1976) and Baltensperger (1980).

In earlier chapters we drew a distinction between the role of financial institutions as producers of liquidity and their function as brokers or middlemen. Most institutions combine both activities to a certain extent. In the former capacity, the institutions use factors of production to transform primary securities into technically different products. In the other capacity they are using factors of production to facilitate the exchange of technically unchanged products. They spread or distribute liquidity, without producing it. As applied to wholesale banks, the liquidity distribution theory does not deny that liquidity production ever occurs. It merely supposes that in wholesale banking the brokerage function is dominant.

Liquidity distribution could take place 'off-balance sheet' by financial firms engaged in distributive techniques which match up borrowers and lenders. But it is the 'on-balance sheet' business upon which we focus. Wholesale banks are assumed to balance or 'match' the maturity structure of their liabilities and assets, in the sense that loans of a particular maturity are financed by deposits of the same maturity. As an example, a liability portfolio of three-month certificates of deposit may be used to support an asset holding of three-month commercial bills.

Because the bank is matching maturities of liabilities and assets, it has no need for reserves to meet liquidity needs. Accordingly the opportunity does not arise for scale economies in reserve asset management (see Chapter 3, section 4) to account for the bank's existence. Since there may be little difference between assets and liabilities in terms of risk characteristics there may be only limited potential for scale economies from risk diversification (see Chapter 3, section 5) to justify the bank's existence either.

Instead, brokerage activities can be seen as improving the operation of the market for liquid financial assets. For middlemen to exist there must be some impediments to the functioning of a direct market between borrowers and lenders. Such impediments can take the form of information and transactions costs for both borrowers and lenders which lead to a divergence between the effective interest rates paid and received in direct transactions. Such costs take the form of uncertainty about creditworthiness, costs of acquiring information about possible outlets and sources of funds, and other resources expended in making transactions. Firms engaged in the function of liquidity distribution have their *raison d'être* in reducing the costs which otherwise exist in credit markets and distributing funds at a margin that is lower than in direct dealings. Through specialisation, information is acquired which enables the firm to offer and charge interest rates preferable to the effective rates (net of transactions costs) otherwise available.

To illustrate these issues, suppose that in the absence of banks there is either an intercompany market for wholesale funds or a commercial paper market. Firms solicit loans directly from each other, if necessary through a market broker, or issue and purchase commercial bills or promissory notes. The supply of funds from lenders (l) is:

$$F_l = F_l(r_l) \tag{4.1}$$

where r_l is the interest return to lenders, net of transactions costs. The demand for funds by borrowers (b) is a function of the total cost of loans; that is, the interest cost plus transactions costs, namely:

$$F_b = F_b(r_b) \tag{4.2}$$

Most of the costs of transacting are common to borrower and lender alike. Included are brokerage fees, search costs (costs of searching for lenders to finance loans or borrowers of sufficient credit standing), costs of communications, and the costs of recording information and administering accounts. Lenders face the additional cost of obtaining information about borrowers and assessing their creditworthiness. In total, the costs drive a wedge between the net interest return received by lenders and the total cost paid by borrowers, even though the transacted interest rate to each pair of lenders and borrowers must be equal. Denoting the market clearing interest rate under competitive conditions as r, the net interest return on the last loan transacted is:

$$r_l = r - t_l \tag{4.3}$$

where t_l is the marginal transactions costs of lenders; and the cost to borrowers of the last loan concluded is:

$$r_b = r + t_b \tag{4.4}$$

where t_b is the marginal transactions costs incurred by borrowers. Thus:

$$r_b - r_l = t_b + t_l \tag{4.5}$$

In equilibrium, the interest rate differential between the cost to the borrower and the return to the lender reflects the sum of their marginal transactions costs.

Financial intermediaries in general, and wholesale banks in particular, may possess a comparative advantage in processing loan transactions, acquiring information about borrowers and monitoring bills of exchange and such market instruments, for four reasons. First, banks may be able to achieve economies of scale as a consequence of specialising in lending and borrowing. Knowledge acquired and routines followed in dealing with one loan can be used for subsequent loans. Second, banks can establish a reputation for discretion when dealing with investigations about the creditworthiness of borrowers. They may, in consequence, be able to obtain information at a lower cost than others. Third, banks may be able to reduce the costs associated with search by widening the area over which search occurs. Finally, even in wholesale business, loan sizes exceed deposit sizes so that coordination and monitoring costs are reduced by 'size intermediation'.

For these reasons, banks may be able to work with transactions costs lower than those previously ruling in the intercompany market. Ignoring any costs of dealing with banks, they are able to enter the market so long as their transactions costs are less than the sum of t_b and t_l. With competition, r_b would tend to fall and r_l rise as funds are channelled from lenders to borrowers at lower cost and thus more efficiently when routed through the banks. From (4.1) and (4.2) we should expect the entry of banks to be accompanied over time by an expansion of borrowings and lendings even if the overall (average) level of interest rates were unaltered.

These results are illustrated in Figure 4.1 where the solid lines represent loan demand and loan supply curves in the absence of transactions costs (L_{dt}, L_{st}), and the broken lines reflect the presence of transactions costs involved in direct financing which shift the demand and supply curves vertically by the amount of those costs. At equilibrium, when only direct financing exists, at quantity A and interest rate r, the net yield to lenders is $r_l = r - t_l$, the cost to borrowers $r_b = r + t_b$. Where intermediation involves average costs less than $(t_b + t_l)$ so that the spread between r_b and r_l is reduced (and customers avoid transactions costs) the amount of financing increases towards B.

Should the cost of direct transactions between borrowers and lenders be large, while that between banks is low, the funds may pass from ultimate lenders to ultimate borrowers via a number of banks. The existence of economies of specialisation could enable some banks to specialise in tapping lenders, allowing other banks to specialise in lending. This is the position illustrated schematically in Figure 4.2. In the sterling interbank market, British banks in aggregate have tended to be net suppliers of sterling funds to the overseas banks. In Canada, the Canadian banks channel Canadian dollar funds to affiliates of foreign banks operating in Canada. In foreign currency operations in London, the US banks perform a similar role and channel dollar funds to British banks for on-lending.

As described, the sole reason for the entry of banks lies in their ability to distribute funds at a cost that is lower than in direct dealings. By assumption, the banks balance the maturity of their liabilities and assets, and both sides of the balance sheet contain claims of the same type. Banks exchange securities without really changing their basic characteristics. In particular, the interest rate margin that banks work with does *not* reflect the market's evaluation of

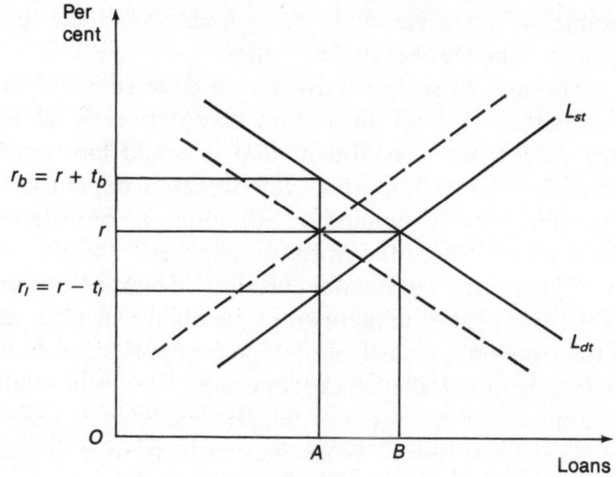

Figure 4.1

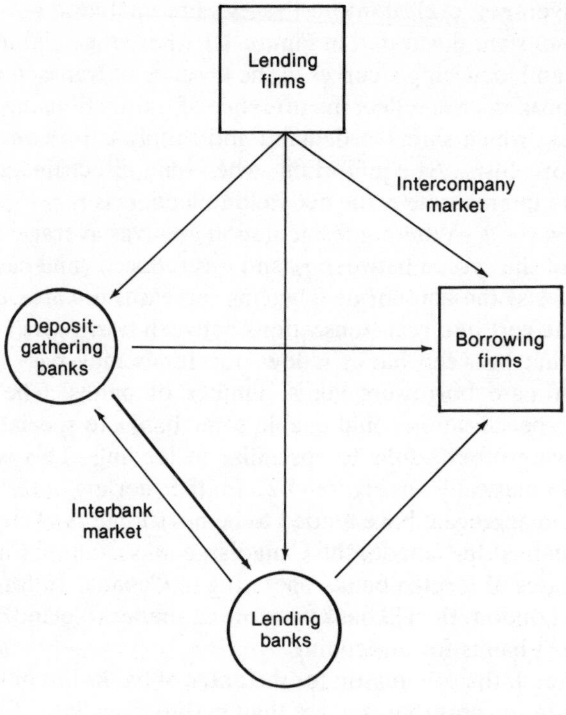

Figure 4.2 Hypothetical Structure of Wholesale Funds Markets

the 'liquidity' of banks' liabilities (or assets), since the banks do not undertake maturity transformation. It follows that, in this view, the basis of banks' existence is the cost of transactions in credit markets and their ability to generate economies of scale *vis- à-vis* direct financing in the real resources used for information and 'brokerage' activities.[7]

Whether economies of scale persist over a large range of intermediary sizes is another matter. A large institution may derive an advantage from being willing to accept funds, confident that it would have somewhere to place them profitably. How important this effect is depends, as with the reserve management case examined in Chapter 3, on the institutional structure of the market. Where the firms are engaged in largely independent operations, a stochastic effect of greater certainty of larger firms being able to match borrower and lender may operate, enabling institutions to avert uncertainty in the frequency of arrival of deposit supplies and loan demands. But if an active interbank/parallel market operates, wholesale dealing consists of an operator armed with a battery of telephones, telexes, monitor panels, and automatic dealing systems. Scale may consist of a large wholesale establishment adding more dealers and communications equipment, replicating what several smaller establishments could do, yet increasing coordination costs. This may explain why a large number of banks (648 at the end of 1983) is able to participate in the wholesale funds markets in London (and other centres).

There is also the question of whether a scale effect applies to the equity ratio, deriving from the intermediary's substitution of claims on itself for direct claims on ultimate borrowers. Since the identity of the issuer of a claim is important to those assessing its safety, the arguments outlined earlier regarding the effects of a diversified asset portfolio on the 'riskiness' of the intermediary seem relevant. Provided that increases in size are associated with increased numbers of independent loans, the intermediary will be able to operate with a lower equity/deposit ratio, to the advantage of its shareholders.

Two factors work against this scale effect assuming significance. First, the large dollar values of individual transactions militate against the application of stochastic principles, a point taken up in section 4.4. Second, many of the assets dealt with in wholesale markets are already diversified. They are the claims of large multinational firms whose activities are diversified across many forms of economic activity. The additional diversification which a bank provides in terms of pooling several multinationals may be small. Greater diversification is likely to come from combining retail and wholesale activities (see section 4.7). Other than that, there is the title of 'bank' and the expectation that, if it is large enough the monetary authorities will not let it fail — the 'safety in numbers' argument considered in Chapter 5.

There are grounds for querying the comparative advantage of banks in wholesale funds markets in other respects. New York money market banks, for example, have long operated as information processing plants, accumulating financial data about thousands of businesses in the form of newspaper clippings, balance sheets and income data which are filed away for future use. This public information is supplemented by the bank's own experience with the firms as borrowers. But, in contrast with retail banking, much of the banking history of large corporations also becomes public information, if only because the banker's own decisions are more readily observable. Thus much at least of the information acquired by the banks is available to credit-rating agencies and to other transactors in the market.

A recent phenomenon is the growth of 'in-house banking' amongst large enterprises. British Petroleum, the world's largest exporter, has an 'in-house bank', so also does Volvo.[8] These conduct group treasury operations, trade foreign exchange, and arrange the direct placements of funds in securities markets. Large 'investors' such as insurance companies and pension funds can deal in securities markets without the intermediation of banks. Corporations can bypass borrowing from banks by issuing their own commercial paper. In 1986, 1,450 US companies issued commercial paper rated by credit agencies. Admittedly, all issuers of commercial paper, even the largest finance companies, back their issues with credit lines from banks should it be difficult to sell new paper or pay off maturing paper. Without such credit lines, the issuers would have difficulty persuading fund managers and others to take up the paper. Also, about 400 of the commercial paper programmes are rated by the credit agencies on the basis of bank guarantees, thus utilising the bank's rather than the company's credit standing. Thus banks have an important role in the market. Nevertheless, by comparison, fewer than 350 companies sold commercial paper through dealer programmes in 1960. While these developments hold considerable portent for the role of banks, it is important also to place matters in their historical context. The US commercial paper market is the oldest of US money markets, with a history dating back a century or more, and in 1920, we may observe, 4,395 US firms sold commercial paper through dealers.[9]

This recent rebirth in securities issues by firms is part of a more general trend towards 'securitisation', in which banks are involved in the processing of financing the form of 'off-balance sheet' activities such as guarantees and credit backups rather than as deposit-takers and loan-makers. Before looking into these issues, we need to be sure about the basis of wholesale banking. Liquidity distribution based on information and transactions costs is undoubtedly one facet of wholesale banking, but is it the sole, or even the major, characteristic of wholesale banking? The model outlined above carries the testable prediction that wholesale bankers will have a relatively matched balance sheet with respect to their total business, interbank transactions *and* their non-bank customer business, and we shall now provide some evidence on these points using UK data.

4.3 Balance Sheets of Wholesale Banks

Empirical evidence of the balance sheet structure of wholesale banks is hampered both by the paucity of data on the maturity profile of banks' assets and liabilities and by the difficulty of identifying purely wholesale banks. Our data of maturities are drawn from banks operating in the UK but, as noted earlier, there is no longer the sharp division between the primary and secondary banking sectors. All banks in the UK are to some extent multiproduct; nevertheless, the division between retail/domestic, wholesale/foreign currency (i.e. Eurocurrency) does differ amongst the categories of banks.

For our purposes we shall divide the banks, as at the end of 1983, into three groups:

(a) *Retail banks*, numbering 22 banks in all. These comprise the six London clearing banks, the three Scottish clearing banks, the four Northern Ireland banks, four Trustee banks and five other (minor) banks. These banks form the basis of the payments mechanism and have an extensive network of branches and agencies in the UK. Three quarters of their business is in sterling and one quarter in foreign currency.

(b) *British non-retail banks*, numbering 300 in all. They specialise in merchant banking or wholesale banking activities. The merchant banks proper are the accepting houses, which have traditionally financed commerce and international trade via the 'accepting' of bills. Their activities are now much broader than this and they are involved in money market activities and lending to industry, as are the specialised subsidiaries of the clearing banks and the UK registered banks with predominantly overseas business. Also forming part of this grouping are the discount houses which are pure wholesalers in short-term securities. Overall, 37 per cent of this grouping's business is in sterling and 63 per cent in foreign currency.

(c) *Overseas banks*, 326 in all. These are the branches, subsidiaries and joint ventures (consortia) of banks owned and registered overseas, that is, American banks, Japanese banks, EEC banks, British Commonwealth and other overseas banks. Like most of the British non-retail banks, these banks have few branches in the UK and have little involvement in the payments system. In fact, only 9 per cent of their business is in sterling, the rest being in foreign currency, with US dollar business dominant.

Our data on the maturities of assets and liabilities are drawn from two samples. One, presented in Table 4.1, is a comprehensive survey of banks in category (b) above, made in 1980. The second, given in Table 4.2, is of data published recently by the Bank of England for all three categories of banks, as at the end of January 1987. Both present a snapshot of the maturity profiles of the aggregate balance sheets on particular days, whereby assets and liabilities are placed into 'maturity ladders'.

Table 4.1 presents the sterling and foreign currency business of selected British banks engaged mainly in wholesale business. From discussions with members of the banking community, it would seem that the data are reasonably representative of the wholesale balance sheets of many other banks in London. Assets and liabilities are classified according to the remaining period to maturity.

The total sterling balance sheet of the banks is not 'matched'. There is an excess of liabilities (L) over assets (A) at the short end of the scale, and conversely at the long end. When the relatively matched interbank position of the banks selected is netted out to reveal the business with the non-bank sector, a much greater extent of maturity mismatching is evident. With non-bank customers, 61 per cent of liabilities mature either on demand or at 7 *days'* or less notice, while 33 per cent of assets had a residual maturity of 3 or more *years*.

A very similar pattern is revealed in the banks' foreign currency (Eurobanking) operations. Interbank business is again relatively matched and it contributes much more to the overall foreign currency balance sheet. Nevertheless, even the total balance sheet is mismatched. Assets and

Table 4.1 Maturity Analysis of British Non-Retail Banks in Sterling and Foreign Currencies by Class of Business, as at February 1980 (%)

	STERLING BUSINESS						FOREIGN CURRENCY BUSINESS					
	Total		*Bank*		*Non-Bank*		*Total*		*Bank*		*Non-Bank*	
	A	L	A	L	A	L	A	L	A	L	A	L
Sight	17.67	24.38	28.74	16.83	10.52	30.76	18.28	22.50	22.25	18.37	10.88	39.84
1–7 days	9.61	21.61	14.14	10.96	6.68	30.62						
8 days–1 month	12.39	19.35	19.67	21.36	7.68	17.65	12.41	19.31	16.38	19.26	5.25	19.51
1–3 months	14.04	20.55	18.69	32.82	11.04	10.17	18.24	29.92	24.22	31.87	7.10	21.73
3–6 months	7.81	6.94	9.92	10.71	6.45	3.74	11.55	19.33	15.12	21.23	4.89	11.34
6 months–1 year	7.33	3.71	6.39	5.16	7.94	2.48	7.53	6.28	8.07	6.82	6.53	4.51
1–3 years	10.50	2.13	1.96	1.79	16.00	2.43	1.94	1.58	5.86	1.61	17.54	1.45
3–5 years	8.56	1.09	0.37	0.32	13.84	1.73	21.97	1.08	8.10	0.84	47.80	1.62
5 years +	12.09	0.25	0.10	0.05	19.83	0.41						
Total	100.00	100.00	100.00	100.00	100.00	100.00	100.00	100.00	100.00	100.00	100.00	100.00

Notes: A = Assets
L = Liabilities

Sources: Bank of England, *Sterling Business Analysed by Maturity and Sector*, March 1987; Bank of England, *Maturity Analysis by Sector of Liabilities and Claims in Foreign Currencies*, March 1987.

Table 4.2 Maturity Analysis of Sterling and Foreign Currency Business with Non-Bank Customers of Retail and Wholesale Banks in Britain, as at end January, 1987 (%)

	STERLING BUSINESS						FOREIGN CURRENCY BUSINESS			
	Retail banks		*British non-retail banks*		*Overseas banks*		*All banks*		*British banks*	
	A	L	A	L	A	L	A	L	A	L
0–7 days	3.54	83.51	13.98	52.83	12.64	41.29	11.96	38.15	11.11	47.95
8 days–1 month	3.49	7.89	3.09	18.74	12.75	21.97	11.00	23.97	8.20	20.70
1–3 months	6.18	6.28	6.27	15.61	15.35	20.88	13.71	18.15	10.21	17.19
3–6 months	5.01	1.00	6.19	4.36	5.69	5.16	9.33	6.87	7.86	6.71
6 months–1 year	5.91	0.67	10.42	4.70	7.20	4.03	6.09	2.68	6.61	2.29
1–3 years	10.21	0.24	18.11	1.83	12.65	2.37	13.11	2.02	15.20	1.74
3 years +	65.68	0.41	41.94	1.93	33.72	4.30	34.80	8.16	40.81	3.42
Total	100.00	100.00	100.00	100.00	100.00	100.00	100.00	100.00	100.00	100.00

Sources: As for Table 4.1.

liabilities with non-bank parties are again mismatched to a considerable extent, with 40 per cent of liabilities maturing in 7 days or less and nearly half of assets longer than 3 years.

What is also revealed is a considerable similarity between the mismatched positions in sterling and in foreign currencies. There are some differences. The banks have more of their sterling liabilities at the short end than is the case with foreign currencies, but hold more short-term claims in sterling. Another balancing factor is that less sterling assets are at the long end (three years or more) than is the case with foreign currency assets. But, overall, the extent of mismatching is very similar. This is perhaps not surprising, for wholesale banking developed in domestic markets as the practices followed in the Eurodollar market spilled over into sterling business.

These impressions can be brought up to date with the 1987 data, based on a wider number of banks. In broad details, the picture provided differs little from that sketched out above. To avoid repetition, we focus upon the non-bank business in Table 4.2, and use the opportunity to present a comparison between the maturity analysis of the 'retail' and 'wholesale' banks. Amongst the various categories of wholesale banks, in both sterling and foreign currency business, the extent and similarity of the mismatching of wholesale balance sheet categories is again notable. The only major difference comes when we compare the wholesale banks and the retail banks. The retail banks have an even more mismatched balance sheet (both in total and with non-bank customers) than the wholesale bankers and this reinforces the point we made in the last chapter about the difficulty which banks have in matching the 'laddering' of maturity of liabilities with that of assets in their dealings with non-bank customers.

There are, however, a number of difficulties which arise because of the way maturities are classified in the tables. In general, the most 'pessimistic' view is taken, and this presents problems of interpretation in three main areas. First, the maturity of deposits is defined in terms of the earliest possible repayment date. Thus a deposit at call which may stay with a wholesale bank for six months is called a 'sight' deposit. However, this is no different from the situation facing a retail intermediary. Many demand deposits or savings deposits also sit around for years. Unless the institution, whether wholesale or retail, can identify with certainty which deposits will sit and which will not, there remains a risk that the customer might exercise the option of withdrawal and the 'sight' classification seems appropriate.

A second possible problem comes from the existence of overdrafts. Repayment is at the customer's choosing, and may be next week or in 10 years' time. Overdrafts are all lumped into the longest maturity asset category, possibly overstating the extent of maturity mismatching. A large number of advances made by overdraft does, in fact, seem to be a more or less permanent source of finance to the customer (as one of the authors can confirm). Moreover, the contingent liabilities of the unused overdraft limits are ignored in the figures. If there is an overstatement of maturity mismatching, it is important in magnitude only for the retail banks. We note that, if overdrafts are taken out, the maturity of the retail banks' assets is very similar to that of the wholesale banks.

Finally, there is the more controversial issue of the treatment of rollover credits. Based on the sample in Table 4.1, nearly one half of the sterling assets of 'wholesale banking business' consists of loans. About one half of these loans is nominally for terms in excess of one year, some of them well in excess of five years, renegotiated ('rolled over') on a three- or six-monthly basis at variable interest rates. These are classified according to the period remaining to the ultimate maturity date of the loan and not to the next rollover date.

It is argued, notably by Niehans and Hewson (1976) and Niehans (1984), that use of the final date of maturity grossly overstates the extent of maturity transformation undertaken in wholesale banking, and especially Eurocurrency banking. Indeed, it is the burden of their 'liquidity distribution' theory to argue that there is *no* maturity transformation undertaken. Legally, the bank is not compelled to renew the credit (there is normally an escape clause) or, if it does renew, it may be completely confident of obtaining the deposits and so it is argued that ' the rollover period is more relevant than the commitment period. A five-year loan with a three-month rollover is more like a succession of three-month loans than a five-year loan.' (Niehans 1984, p.190).

In examining this proposition, let us first query the argument that renewal may not occur, by noting the views of Einzig (1973):

> As a general rule lenders have no option to demand early repayment except in special (changes in) circumstances. If lenders had the right to demand early repayment borrowers would lose the advantage derived from medium-term borrowing. Debtors might be called upon to repay their debts at a time when they might find it difficult or impossible to raise the necessary cash, or when they might only be able to do so on less favourable terms . . . If the practice of giving lenders the option to recall their credits were widespread it would go a long way towards discouraging borrowers from availing themselves of rollover credit facilities owing to the uncertainty to which they would be exposed. (pp.54–55)

In practice, virtually all rollover loans are renewed automatically, and a bank which regularly refuses to do so 'would soon go out of business', to quote one banker. Some banks now question whether inclusion of a 'changes in circumstances' (escape) clause is really necessary. It is the expectation of renewal which induces the borrower to pay a premium ('spread') over 3- or 6-month funds. If the repayment provisions are applied, the borrower has obtained very little from the spread. On our interpretation, rollover credits can command a margin over six-month funds (a margin which is the basis of banks' earnings) because of the near certainty, or at least very high probability, that the loan will not have to be repaid during the period of commitment. Borrowers are prepared to pay a premium to obtain this 'insurance' policy. From their viewpoint, the rollover credit must be preferable to a 6-month loan. Looked at from the bank's viewpoint, loans have a default risk which is built into the spread. Consequently, the question which must be asked of each banker is whether he is carrying the default risk on a rollover loan for 6 months, that is, to the next renewal date, or for five years. We contend the latter.

At the risk of labouring the point, two further comments are made on the rollover classification question, for it does seem vital to the manner in which wholesale banking is viewed. The first concerns the implication for the maturity transformation undertaken by retail banks. An increasing proportion of retail loans is being made on a rollover basis. On the Niehans and Hewson view, a greatly lessened extent of maturity transformation is implied by what is merely a switch in lending techniques from a fixed to variable rate basis. Consider also the loan portfolio of the London clearing banks. As well as undertaking many rollover loans, one half of the banks' advances is by way of overdraft. In principle, an overdraft is repayable on demand and the interest rate can be altered daily. In effect, for an overdraft the 'rollover period' is one day or less, and under the Niehans and Hewson view it should presumably be classified as assets at call. We seem to be led to the position that the clearing banks do not undertake, and never have undertaken, maturity transformation.

Finally, even if we go along with the rollover view for wholesale banking and reclassify most loans as assets with, say, a 6-month maturity, we are still left with the fact that wholesale bankers in aggregate are undertaking maturity transformation. This is because over 90 per cent of liabilities to non-bank customers mature in *less* than 6 months. Moreover, over 50 per cent of liabilities have a maturity of seven days or less (with half of those in sterling business being at call).

So as not to be misunderstood, we acknowledge that the matching and liquidity distribution activities highlighted by Niehans and Hewson are facets of wholesale banking, especially in Eurocurrency operations. We have argued as much in section 4.2 above and we shall expound it further in Chapter 9 when we look at international banking. However, liquidity distribution is seen by us as being some distance from the whole story.

At this juncture we may note that no comparable data exist for the United States, breaking down maturities of assets and liabilities according to the category of bank and customer. Some overall estimates have, however, been made by economists at the Federal Reserve Bank of Chicago, and kindly made available to the authors. These give data of maturity mismatches as at June 1984 for a sample of all US banks for their total balance sheet position. The estimates show, as in the UK, an excess of liabilities (L) maturing in 6 months or less over assets (A) maturing in the same band. The measure of the maturity gap used is $(A - L)/A$ and thus we can see that, for maturities of 3 months or less, the excess of liabilities over assets expressed as a percentage of assets averaged 31 per cent for the sample:

Maturity Band	*(A − L)/A*
0– 3 months	−0.31
3– 6 months	−0.02
6–12 months	+0.03
1– 5 years	+0.20
5 years +	+0.10

Conversely, assets exceeded liabilities for maturities in excess of 6 months. These estimates, we emphasise, embrace both retail and wholesale banks, and both interbank and non-bank business.

To summarise on the data we have presented above for the UK, and our interpretation of them, we draw two conclusions. First, there is a remarkable similarity in the degree of maturity mismatching between foreign currency and domestic currency (sterling) business. We may be entitled to speak of characteristics of 'wholesale' intermediation, whether carried out in Eurocurrencies or in domestic currencies. The two may effectively constitute a single market for international wholesale intermediation.

Second, we maintain that banks in wholesale markets *are* undertaking considerable maturity transformation, although probably to a lesser extent than in retail banking. But it is the burden of the argument in the next section to establish that the major contrast with retail banking is not so much in the extent of the transformation, as in the manner by which it is performed.

4.4 Liquidity Production in Wholesale Banking[10]

Let us begin by restating our major conclusions to date. Based on the evidence in the previous section, banks in wholesale operations are involved in the production of liquidity, including a substantial transformation of customers' short-term funds into long-term loans, much as in retail banking. This is the case in both domestic wholesale banking and in international (Eurocurrency) wholesale banking.

Wholesale banks are creating liquidity by virtue of the 'insurance'-type policies which they write. They provide the majority of depositors with the assurance that deposits can be withdrawn at short notice, despite holding assets of much longer maturity. They give customers the assurance that sums deposited with them can be redeemed at full value, while themselves holding assets which fluctuate in redemption value. They assure borrowers that loans will not have to be repaid within the period over which the funds are committed. Borrowers are protected against interest rates on their loans fluctuating daily, despite variations each day in the banks' cost of funds. These assurances are essentially the same as those in the contracts which retail banks issue.

In previous chapters we argued that retail banks are able to meet their contractural commitments by adopting the classic principles of insurance. Insurance is based around the holding of reserves, and insurers owe their existence to economies of scale in reserve holding due to the law of large numbers. So it is with retail banks. Similar principles can be used to determine the size of cash and liquid asset holdings needed to cover the risks of deposit withdrawals. Each depositor wants the option of conversion into cash on demand but has no idea when the need may arise. When a large number of such options is combined, regularities emerge which impart a stability to cash needs and enable the bank to balance finely the returns from investment against the costs of running out of reserves. Similar actuarial principles enable retail banks to determine the holding of capital reserves and shield depositors from the risks of defaulting loans. Not all loans fail or for the same reasons, and by combining a large number with independent fates the retail bank can pool risks economically. When diversifying across independent risks of default and of deposit variability, the principle of the law of large numbers is simple: the larger the better.

These stochastic elements cannot be applied so readily in wholesale banking. Whereas retail banks have a large number of little accounts, wholesale banks typically have a small number of big customers. How 'large' is 'large' in retail banking, and what is 'small' in wholesale banking? For the retail banks in Britain, the number of accounts runs in terms of millions. Consider the figures for 1983 (the most recently available for all of the groups):

	No. of accounts
6 London clearing banks	38.0 million
3 Scottish clearing banks	4.7 million
4 Trustee savings banks	13.0 million
Yorkshire Bank	1.9 million
National Giro Bank	1.3 million
Cooperative Bank	1.2 million

No comparative figures exist for the wholesale banks, but some rough estimates can be made from the amount of deposits. Table 4.3 gives details at the end of 1983 of the number of UK-based banks engaged predominantly in wholesale finance, the deposits of the various classes of banks and, by division, the average value of deposits per bank. Remembering that the minimum-sized *transaction* is £½ million and that the average is typically £5m. to £10m. or more, it is clear that many banks engaged in wholesale banking in London must have deposits numbering only double or triple figures (Harrington 1987). Hill Samuel, the accepting house with the largest clientele, had 147 corporate clients in 1987.[11]

If the usual 'insurance' principles of liquidity production are to be applied, banks would have to be very large indeed and there would be marked tendencies to concentration. A significant proportion of international banking worldwide is in fact undertaken by very large Japanese and US banks, but smaller banks survive in the international and domestic wholesale

Table 4.3 Average Size of Foreign Currency and Sterling Deposits of UK-Based Banks, December 1983 (£m.)

	No. of institutions	*Foreign currency deposits*	*Average deposits per bank*	*Sterling deposits*	*Average deposits per bank*
Accepting houses	36	12,604	350	8,415	234
Other British banks	241	45,909	190	26,634	110
Consortium banks	23	13,883	604	1,642	71
American banks	63	93,532	1,485	8,418	134
Japanese banks	25	107,434	4,297	4,657	186
Other overseas banks	228	118,082	518	17,280	76

Source: Bank of England Quarterly Bulletin, March 1984.

markets. A few may do so by combining a small international wholesale/domestic wholesale book with a larger retail base, but many are specialist wholesalers. Matching of maturities and currencies offers them a protection, but maturity mismatching seems to be the rule. How are loans of five or more *years* to be matched with deposits of 7 *days'* maturity? How can the risks of large loan losses be diversified?

Essentially the same problems face insurance companies in general insurance business. Theirs is an industry marked by fierce competition and relatively free entry. With a large number of firms, none of which have a very large share of a national or regional market, risks are often large relative to the resources of the firms. Risks from natural disaster insurance, marine insurance for tankers, or aeroplane insurance are examples. Individual firms are unable to get the full benefits of the 'pooling of risks' from amongst their own policyholders, in the same way that wholesale bankers cannot get sufficient risk diversification from their own balance sheet. In the insurance industry, the solution is *coinsurance* and *reinsurance*.

An individual insurance company cannot maintain reserves which will cover the most extreme losses, or even minor losses from events like earthquakes. Reserves would either be excessive relative to current premiums or simply beyond the capacity of the company to create. In these circumstances a number of companies group together to form a pool. Pooling occurs in two main ways. With *coinsurance*, the insurance is split between one or more companies so that a contract exists between the policyholder and each coinsurer. In the event of the claim, each coinsurer pays out directly its share of the loss (Carter 1979). Insurance of a large oil refining plant or an oil platform would be handled in this way.

With *reinsurance*, each of the coinsurers may then cede (i.e. transfer or 'reinsure') part of its share of the risk to another insurance company. Alternatively, with smaller risks, the policyholder may insure with one insurer alone (the underwriter), which then cedes some part (perhaps even the major part) to other insurance companies, that is, to the reinsurers. They may in turn reinsure part of their risk with other companies, and so on. In all cases, the reinsurance contract is issued by one insurance company, the reinsurer, to another insurance company, the ceding company or the direct underwriter. When a claim is made, the insured is paid out by the underwriter(s), which then makes claims against the reinsurers. Reinsurance is an international business, and contracts are spread worldwide. Arrangements are also complex, with treaty arrangements of various kinds and proportional cover or excess of loss cover being the major types obtained. These details need not concern us.

Pooling by coinsurance and reinsurance has two main purposes. It spreads individual risks that are too big for even the largest insurance companies, and allows small companies to write more business than their own reserves or capital could safely support. It is an institutional response by private markets to otherwise uninsurable risks and to the bankruptcy which a large loss would impose on the individual firm. Because companies have reinsurance arrangements to protect themselves against catastrophes or unusual risk accumulations, and since their claims against the reinsurers can be collected within a few days, the underwriters do not feel the need to hold large amounts of liquid assets.

Note that the insurance principle of risk pooling and scale economies in reserve holdings is a general one, and is in no way invalidated by reinsurance arrangements. In fact, the reverse is the case. Coinsurance and reinsurance arrangements are needed to create a unit or pool which is large enough for the principle to apply. With small (i.e. 'retail') insurance risks, such as motor vehicle insurance or personal accidents, pooling often occurs within the firm. For large ('wholesale') risks, risk pooling occurs outside the firm but within the insurance market.

This is the position in aggregate, viewed in terms of the risks which are being insured. Looked at from the individual firms' viewpoint, the transformation can be expressed differently. Reinsurance provides a 'size intermediation' function. The complex network of ceding and reinsurance has the objective of breaking up large risks into shares or participations which are, in the end, individually small enough to be encompassed and pooled with other participations in an individual firm's portfolio.

Our contention is that the position with respect to wholesale banking is analogous. Institutional mechanisms have been established in private banking markets which enable risk spreading and liquidity production to occur in wholesale banking. These institutional responses involve loan syndication, the interbank market, and the development of balance sheet options.

Loan Syndication

Syndicates enable banks to spread loan risks. By avoiding too much exposure to individual borrowers and by means of the participations, banks can undertake lending to a wider range of firms than they would be able to do individually. As with so many other innovations in wholesale banking, the development of syndicates was inspired by the influx of American banks to London.

Syndication of loans has long been part of the US banking scene. Elsewhere the tradition has been for the bank making a loan to do so fully from its own lending resources. But with the preponderance of unit banks in the USA, and prohibition upon expansion by branching, and with loans to single customers limited to a percentage of a lending bank's capital, the banks frequently syndicate loans. As at August 1986, 15 per cent of the large long-term floating rate commercial loans and 26 per cent of floating rate construction loans of US banks surveyed by the Federal Reserve were participation loans. The loans in question are usually term loans because the formal repayment arrangements and the three- to ten-year periods which characterise this type of lending make it suitable for spreading over a number of cooperating banks. In this way the banks contribute jointly to the provision of the funds and share in the repayments, generally under an organising lead bank. This was the technique refined in wholesale banking in London.

Methods of syndication in London vary considerably, from the informal through to arrangements involving extensive documentation. To illustrate (Einzig 1973):

> The unpublicised credits usually assume the form of letters of credit in which the maximum amount, the maximum period, and the terms on which the interest rate is subject to adjustment, are set out. The borrower has often the option to draw upon the credit in instalments as and when he requires the money. The lending banks may envisage the possibility of subsequently granting participation to other banks in the transaction. (p.22)

> An alternative way of arranging rollover credits is for the borrowing firm or institution or authority to issue notes and sell them to a managing bank or a consortium of managing banks, which in turn sells them to a syndicate of banks and other financial institutions. Each one of them takes over a relatively small amount which it would be able to keep in its own portfolio or would be able to place with its own customers, so that no public issue would be necessary. (p.23)

> Occasionally rollover credits assume the form of promissory notes, which are one-name papers bought from the borrowers and placed by the managing banks with the syndicates or lenders. (p.24)

> Another alternative procedure is the conclusion of an agreement by the managing banks with the borrower; in this case photocopies of the contract are circulated among potential members of the syndicate: or a Placing Memorandum containing the essential terms may be circulated. In many instances the managing banks issue Participation Certificates which are underwritten, in the

> same way as Euro-bonds, by a syndicate consisting of some dozens of banks and other dealers or institutional investors. Their number is anything up to 50, or even higher. (p.23)

This is an early account of the themes and variations on themes which are possible. Since then the last-mentioned, particularly in Eurocurrency operations, has become almost an art form. Individual loans run into billions of dollars, and syndication has become increasingly complex. Instead of the manager and a dozen or so participating banks as in US domestic markets, there are lead managers, co-managers, clubs of managers, agents, underwriters and as many as 150 participating banks. The 'tombstone' announcements found in international and national financial papers provide publicity of such arrangements once deals have been completed.

These large syndications, accompanied by documentation prepared by armies of lawyers and bearing as many signatures as King Charles's Death Warrant,[12] are needed and, in view of the costs of administration, are economically viable only by virtue of the vast size of the loans. These are akin to coinsurance contracts. In domestic wholesale business, the less formal arrangements prevail, which are more akin in their flexibility to reinsurance treaties. Lending by means of letters of credit, notes and US-style participations marks, for instance, the activities of wholesale banks in the UK, such as the accepting houses, and the wholesale financiers (merchant banks) in Australia.

We are able to gain a picture of the participations in both domestic wholesale and foreign currency business from evidence which the UK accepting houses (merchant banks) submitted to the Wilson Committee. Table 4.4 is based on that evidence and summarises some aspects of the syndicated credits for which the accepting houses act as managers. A number of features stand out. Most (52 per cent) participations in sterling are to domestic firms in the private sector, whereas 57 per cent of the foreign currency credits are to overseas governments or public utilities. In both cases, however, the majority of loans are for initial maturities in excess of five years. When the accepting houses act as managers they retain very little of the overall risk on their own balance sheets (on average 7 per cent). Rather more (12 per cent) is kept for sterling participations reflecting the smaller size of the loans and the smaller number of participants. The remaining risk is spread across a wide category of banks. With sterling syndications, the other participants are all banks which operate in London, although not all are British banks. In the case of Eurocurrency operations, the participants are spread more widely and the accepting houses look beyond London banks (or UK balance sheets) for one third of amounts contributed to the pools.

Like coinsurance and reinsurance arrangements, participations are an institutional device for spreading around the loan business which is too large an individual exposure for a single bank to assume. Consider a loan, L, which is of such a size that no single bank can bear the credit risk. If n participating

Table 4.4 Analysis of Syndicated Credits Managed by UK Accepting Houses, January 1977 (£m.)

	Amounts Outstanding		
LENDER	*Sterling*	*Foreign Currency*	*Total*
Own participations	255	297	551
Participations of other accepting houses	355	38	393
Participations of British banks	1,149	1,121	2,270
Participations of UK-based overseas banks	402	1,181	1,538
Participations of overseas banks	4	2,736	2,740
	2,165	5,373	7,538
ANALYSIS OF BORROWERS			
UK private sector	1,129	812	1,941
UK public sector	207	316	523
Overseas private sector	371	1,169	1,541
Overseas public sector	458	3,076	3,533
	2,165	5,373	7,538
ORIGINAL PERIOD OF CREDITS	*0–2 yrs*	*2–5 yrs*	*Over 5 years*
Sterling	667	446	1,373
Currency	233	1,288	3,880

Source: Committee to Review the Functioning of Financial Institutions (1978) Vol. 5, p.51, HMSO.

banks can be found, the loan can be broken down into n participations, l_i, where:

$$L = \sum_{i=l}^{n} l_i$$

and each l_i is a certain percentage share of L. Each of the l_i are fully dependent on each other and objectively have the same risk characteristics. But to an individual bank, the idiosyncratic risk is not important. What matters is the subjective risk in terms of the covariance of the participation with other loans in the bank's portfolio, and thus its contribution to the perceived riskiness of the bank's portfolio. With each bank carrying the partial risk, l_i, the whole risk can be borne. Benefits flow to the borrowers. If syndicates were not formed, borrowers would have to negotiate much smaller loans with a number of different banks. The managing banks carry out this task more conveniently and cheaply.

Interbank Markets

Syndications of loans must be seen primarily as a device for managing default risks, but wholesale banks must also manage 'liquidity' risks. Matching of maturities does not occur either in terms of the principal involved or in terms of interest flows. Repayment arrangements on rollover credits, for example, cover a wide gamut. They may allow for one lump sum at maturity date, several instalments at dates fixed in the contract, or options to repay the whole or part of the credit after the lapse of some minimum period of time. Borrowers are also provided with options in the form of substantial credit facilities (i.e. lines and commitments). For example, in January 1977 the undrawn loan facilities held by borrowers of the UK accepting houses amounted to 14 per cent of foreign currency and 76 per cent of sterling loans outstanding. At the same time, two thirds of borrowers held in effect guarantees that funds advanced by means of credits would be renewed virtually automatically over five years. On the liabilities side of the balance sheet, 32 per cent of their non-bank customers held options allowing their funds to be withdrawn on demand. A further 38 per cent held the option of withdrawing balances after 1–7 days' notice. In all, 68 per cent of non-bank customers were issued by the banks with the option of redemption in full within a week. These option contracts define the extent of liquidity production by the wholesale bankers.

One response of the wholesale banks is to hold balance sheet options of their own, but in addition the interbank deposit markets in a number of ways serve a special function in mitigating the risks of liquidity transformation. A major function of interbank funds is to enable banks to cope with the lumpiness of wholesale-sized deposits and loans, and plug up holes in the balance sheet. Loans are lumpy and, because of the front-end participation fees, banks do not want to turn away good loan business; yet they cannot rely upon an equally lumpy deposit turning up in the near future. In Revell's words (Revell 1968):

> If he has arranged to make a loan of £1 million for one year, it is most unlikely that his customers will of their own accord come forward with the offer of deposits to that amount and with a maturity that he can accept as matching the loan — at least he cannot rely on this happening within the next two or three days. Instead the secondary banker turns to the inter-bank market for the deposits he needs to support the loan. His chances of success are many times greater than if he relied on his own customers because all that is required is that somewhere in the secondary banking system deposits shall have been placed with the banks that have no immediate lending business in prospect. (p.430)

The same is the case with deposits. They do not arrive in 'marginal' amounts that can be turned away, so they are lent out to other banks.

Interbank markets may also allow the opportunity for informal risk and maturity sharing arrangements to occur. Consider two hypothetical examples:

(i) Wholesale Bank *A* receives a large deposit. It seeks out some non-bank customers, and lends on the rest to Bank *B* via the interbank market. Bank *B* in turn lends out some to non-bank customers and the rest to Bank *C*, etc.

(ii) Wholesale Bank *X* is approached for a medium-term loan by a non-bank customer on a 6-month rollover basis. On the interbank funds borrowed, Bank *X* may want to go as long as possible, but beyond 3 months is difficult (see Table 4.1). It thus bids for 3-month interbank funds. Bank *Y* supplies a 3-month interbank loan, itself accepting 1-month money from Bank *Z* which has received a call deposit from a customer.

The first transaction can be seen as a form of informal risk bearing. Given the normal maturity of deposits, Bank *A* is subject to the risk that the deposit may be withdrawn at short notice. In this case the risk is spread across a number of banks. As when reinsurance arrangements exist, a 'claim' by the customer against his option of withdrawal is met in part by the bank drawing upon its 'contracts' with the other banks.

In the second example another type of informal risk sharing is illustrated: that of loan risks. The interbank claims held by banks *Z* and *Y* are 'backed' by the rollover loan which Bank *X* has made to its customer. Because the customer's loan has default risk, so does the interbank loan, though to a lesser (limited) extent because of pooling. In principle, at least, the two banks should be assessing the riskiness of Bank *X*'s asset portfolio and, unlike non-bank customers, ought to be in a position to do so. Interest rates on interbank transactions are to some extent 'tiered' into quality classes. The margin levied by the lending bank is in effect a premium paid by the borrowing bank for insurance against the default risk shared, the lending bank being at the same time the insurer.[13]

A further dimension to the interbank market is also illustrated in the second example. This is the market's possible role in maturity transformation. The difference in maturity between a customer's deposit at one end and a loan of several years may be broken up into several steps carried out by different banks. In retail banking, one bank will have the demand deposit and the three-year loan. That is, the transformation is undertaken fully within the bank which accepts the deposits. In wholesale banking, funds may be channelled from ultimate lenders to ultimate borrowers through several banks. In the process, what begins as short-term deposits is transformed into loans of several years' maturity. Each bank is mismatched, but not to a great extent, and no one bank is left with a large share of the transformation process.

Thus there is a role for the interbank market to perform which is additional to its liquidity distribution function. This is in facilitating and also 'masking' the overall degree of maturity transformation inherent in non-bank business, to which banks owe their social function.

Through a chain of individual banks which each undertake 'small' amounts of positive maturity transformation, significant maturity transformation between non-bank deposits at the start of the chain, and loans to non-banks at the end of the chain, can occur. Moreover, the statistical effect of interbank transactions is to mask the extent of maturity transformation undertaken between non-bank lenders and borrowers.[14] In this way, a bank's total balance sheet is less maturity mismatched than is its position with non-bank customers, allowing the bank to structure its maturity ladder so as to accord more closely with the matching principle noted earlier.

Balance Sheet Options

In order to deal with residual 'liquidity' risks (which cannot be diversified away into regularities by the law of large numbers as in retail banking) wholesale bankers hold balance sheet options. Myers (1977) and Mayers and Smith (1982) have made the observation that many current activities of firms can be viewed as a form of investment designed to create implicit options contracts of value to the firm. In this respect, wholesale banks have generated a number of balance sheet options to cope with the uncertain demand for funds arising from withdrawals of short-term deposits, draw-downs of lines and loan commitments, and variations in loan repayments. We group the options under two headings.

One is *liability management*, which has been defined as 'financial institutions . . . rely(ing) . . . on instruments bearing market-related interest rates in funding their activities'.[15] In the USA, these instruments include certificates of deposits and Federal funds bought. Amongst UK banks, the instruments are interbank borrowings, certificates of deposits and wholesale time deposits. These, and the markets in which they are traded, were discussed in section 4.1. More generally, the practice of liability management involves varying the interest rate paid on deposits to attract the desired quantity of total liabilities.

Whether, and in what form, liability management is attractive will hinge crucially on the nature of the markets for funds from which existing deposits are drawn. If, for example, the interest rate on all deposits must be increased in line with the rate paid to attract new deposits, the marginal cost of those funds will be extremely high. The appeal of liability management will be enhanced if particular markets exist in which the intermediary is effectively a price taker, able to obtain whatever volume is required at the market rate without, individually, exerting a significant effect on the rate.

For many banks and other financial institutions this condition is met by the interbank markets in London, and the banks have come to look to the markets as the first line of defence, replacing maturing and withdrawn deposits with new interbank borrowings. As we noted in Chapter 3, section 4, with a near-perfect interbank funds market it would be unprofitable to hold reserves and practice reserve asset management. If the market imperfection prompting reserve holding comes from fixed costs of transacting, liability management is most likely to be used in wholesale banking in which the fixed costs can be spread over large volumes.

But this merely begs the question of how the funds markets came to be established. We have said that the interbank market and the growth of liability management should be seen as mutually interacting phenomena. The markets developed in response to banks' needs, then in turn encouraged new techniques of funds management, creating a need for more extensive facilities. In addition, the 'needs' served by the wholesale funds market are many. As well as providing an alternative to asset management to cover banks' liquidity risks, the interbank market, in particular, permitted:

(i) foreign banks to tap domestic deposit sources;
(ii) specialisation in developing skills in particular forms of lending and fund raising;
(iii) banks to plug gaps in their balance sheets arising from the lumpiness of deposits and loans;
(iv) the development of informal risk-sharing arrangements.

It should also be noted that interbank markets are not perfect and that banks are not pure price takers. There is some 'tiering' for quality, and a bank's ranking can alter with its exposure in the markets. Rationing is normal, in the sense that banks set limits on loans to other banks beyond which they will not lend at any price. Consequently, banks face funding risks, in that there is uncertainty about quantity as well as price. In order to keep their borrowing options open, banks want to ensure an unsatisfied demand for their paper and trade on both sides of the market so as to be seen as a lender as well as a borrower. A continued presence is also valuable for widening future borrowing strategies. Shaw (1978) reports that banks sometimes make deposits and borrow them back again at a (short-term) loss so as to retain borrowing options for the future.[16]

As a second line of defence, as it were, banks have institutionalised options on the assets side of the balance sheet. The contingencies form part of what is known as the *securitisation*, or *marketisation*, of assets, especially loans. The term 'securitisation' embraces two major trends in financing in recent years. One is the apparent switch away from bank intermediation to direct financing via capital markets. The other is the transformation of previously illiquid assets like loans into marketable instruments (Gardener 1986). It is the latter meaning to which we refer here, and in wholesale banking the contingencies take on a variety of forms such as:

(a) Participation certificates which, issued as part of a syndicate, can often be resold to the issuing banks. A clause to this effect may be included.

(b) A managing bank retaining participation certificates may issue them subsequent to the granting of the credit, thus carrying a smaller part of the loan to maturity.

(c) A bank may include in a loan contract an option requiring the borrower upon request to draw the equivalent sum of commercial bills. This permits the bank to substitute a marketable security (the bill) for the loan.[17]

Securitisation of lending and liability management practices have now spread to retail banking, as we note in section 4.7 below.

Retail and Wholesale Banking Compared

Summarising the various points raised in this section, the major contrast between wholesale and retail banking is not so much in the extent of liquidity production, for wholesale banks are undertaking maturity transformation and thus producing liquidity services for non-bank customers. Rather, the contrast comes from the manner in which the liquidity creation occurs.

In retail markets, institutions themselves provide for their own safety by utilising the law of large numbers to determine the size of reserves needed to 'insure' against the risks of withdrawal (illiquidity) and to determine the amount of equity capital needed to 'insure' against default of loans (insolvency). Wholesale banks cannot operate so readily on the same stochastic principles.

Instead, banks in wholesale operations operate the equivalent of 'reinsurance' arrangements, establishing formal and informal syndicates to spread loan risks. Liquidity risks are handled by means of 'options' on their balance sheets in the form of liability management practices and the securitisation of assets. The existence of the interbank market performs a 'fiction' which allows liquidity creation to occur in wholesale banking.

By virtue of these collective devices, no one bank is left with a large share of the maturity transformation and liquidity creation process. Each bank is mismatched, but not to any great extent. In retail operations, the transformation is undertaken fully by the bank which accepts the deposits. In wholesale markets, some or all of the transformation is undertaken by the system.

The collective arrangements provided by banks are far from costless. Decision rules must be formulated in syndicates, documentation prepared, and banks have to monitor their interbank exposures. But banks are presumably able to organise and police these exposures more cheaply than customers could do themselves. In the absence of the interbank network, borrowers would have to spread their business over a number of banks. By performing this function for the customers, the banks act as arrangers of risk-bearing services.

As in retail banking, confidence is crucial for these risk-sharing arrangements; perhaps more so, because the backing for deposits is 'command' over funds from the wholesale funding markets. There must be confidence on the part of banks that the funds can be commanded, and confidence by depositors that the funds will be commanded. This is one aspect of the riskiness of wholesale intermediation which will be examined in the next two sections.

4.5 On-Balance Sheet Risks

Because of the different 'production techniques' employed in wholesale banking, some differences exist with respect to the two major risks which banks face. In this section we summarise the asset and liquidity risks from the 'on'-balance sheet business. The following section looks at 'off'-balance sheet activities and risks. A further discussion of both will be found in Chapter 5.

Asset and Liquidity Risks

The special factors come from the collective arrangements by which wholesale banks parcel out loan risks and divide up the maturity transformation. Interbank markets, we argue, contribute to both ends. Because of the peculiar way in which maturity transformation is undertaken in wholesale markets, via the interbank market, there is the chain risk that a few defaulting loans can rebound through the whole banking system.

Interbank markets can generate more fundamental risks. Whereas an individual bank may deem it prudent to limit the share of its advances placed with a particular customer, funds placed 'interbank' may eventually end up with that customer. Loan risks are backed not just by the capital of the lending bank, but also indirectly by the capital of the banks which agree to lend to it. This results in a sharing of risks. By granting a loan to a limited liability banking or financial company, the debtholder is supplying the shareholders with an option (put) to default as an implied part of the loan transaction: shareholders can 'put' the firm's assets onto the debtholders by defaulting on the loan. In principle, the margin ('tiering') levied by the lending bank should be seen as 'insurance' premium for the shared risk but, in practice, interbank lending is often 'brokered' by specialist operators, and the identity (and riskiness) of the counterparty is not revealed until after the transaction is negotiated.

In these ways, 'out of sight' may mean 'out of mind', encouraging excessive risk taking. In retail banking, the individual bank accepting a demand deposit and making a long-term loan to a customer knows that it is sacrificing liquidity and bearing risk, and demands an appropriate premium. When the process is shared among a group informally via interbank transactions the extent of risk bearing may be masked:

> The interbank market may conceal from an individual bank the degree of transformation being undertaken by banks in aggregate . . . An active interbank market may therefore increase the scope for behaviour which seems prudent at the level of the individual bank, but seems less so when the whole picture is examined. (Ellis 1981, p.359)

Syndicates divide up loan risks in more formal and identifiable ways, making explicit each bank's contribution to the total risk. As with coinsurance arrangements, the basic objective is to create a pool which is large enough for the standard stochastic principles of insurance to operate. But with some syndicated credits, especially those to overseas governments, the question must be asked whether the pools are large enough relative to the overall risk. We shall take up this question later.

Liquidity risk is shared amongst the banks by interbank dealings and liability management policies. By these dealings, banks which gain excess reserves lend to those which are short of funds, and in this way the holding of reserves is obviated. Wholesale bankers in Britain have virtually moved to a cashless society: their holding of excess cash and Bank of England deposits is practically zero (for the accepting houses 0.09 per cent). But this does not diminish the importance of control of base money or the role of lender of last resort *vis-à-vis* a world of reserve asset management. Just as *all* banks cannot run down their holdings of cash, not *all* banks can borrow from each other at the same time. Liability management allows banks to 'run but not hide' from system-wide drains of funds. There is a 'prisoner's dilemma' and, being a zero-sum game, competitive bids merely worsen matters (Smith 1982). The role of a lender of last resort may be heightened under wholesale banking.

Interest Rate and Funding Risks

Wholesale bankers pioneered arrangements by which interest rate risks are passed on fully to borrowers at rollover dates based directly upon funding costs (e.g. LIBOR and CD rates), making the rollover credit a 'cost-plus' contract. Contracts of this nature are sometimes used in the construction industry, but are commonly employed in military purchases of new technology, when the government compensates the supplier for all costs plus an agreed profit margin. As Arrow (1970) has noted, a cost-plus contract can be visualised as a fixed-price (i.e. rate) contract combined with an insurance contract by which the purchaser reimburses the supplier for unexpected costs. In the case of military purchases, it is thought to be an appropriate distribution of risk bearing. The risk is shifted to the agency best able to bear it.

Whether this insurance arrangement can be held to be appropriate for loan contracts depends on the risk-bearing capacity of the borrowers. Some argue that banks are more efficient bearers of risk than their customers, since they are better able to shift it to futures markets and are thus abrogating their responsibilities (Kaufman 1983; Hess 1984). Others argue that flexi-rate loans 'provide a rough protection to both debtors and creditors' (Tobin 1984). In terms of Raviv's (1979) model of optimal insurance, the shifting of costs would be justified if the borrower were less risk-averse than lending banks. For borrowers with incomes which are negatively correlated with rising interest rates, the arrangement can be questioned (Arvan and Brueckner 1985). What is undeniable is that the nature of the risk to the bank is changed more than shifted, since loan default risks are increased. Moreover, the defaults no longer have independent fates, rebounding onto the banks. Immediate benefits to the banks may be offset by write-offs of loans in later periods. This is an important consideration in international wholesale business.

In between the dates when interest rates are adjusted, an 'interest rate risk' is borne since banks generally rely on borrowings much shorter than the rollover period and face a profits squeeze over the intervening period until loan rates are renegotiated. There is an 'earnings risk' over the period of the loan if increases in operating costs erode the fixed margin above LIBOR which the bank is charging for loans. But the most important risk facing the bank is a 'funding risk'. All liquidity creation by banks is illusory and rests on confidence. Grunewald and Pollock (1985) argue that, unlike the stock market which 'prices' risk and operates over a continuum, the money market is a rationing market and reacts discontinuously to risk. Once some perceived risk threshold is passed, funds simply dry up and cannot be had for any price. Either a bank is thought to be sound and can borrow at the market rate, or it cannot borrow at all. If their argument is correct, it goes a long way towards explaining why recent bank runs have originated in wholesale markets and have snowballed so rapidly.

4.6 Off-Balance Sheet Activities and Risks

Recent years have seen a tremendous growth in banks' off-balance sheet items (see Table 4.5 which shows off-balance sheet business of US banks since 1980). The 'off'-balance sheet description reflects that the activities involve contingent commitments not captured as assets or liabilities under conventional accounting procedures. A loan enters as an asset on a bank's balance sheet, whereas a promise to make a loan is a contingent liability: it is an obligation to provide funds should the contingency be realised and does not appear on the balance sheet until after that occurrence. For this reason 'off-balance sheet' banking is sometimes referred to as 'invisible banking' or 'assetless banking'.

A variety of activities are embraced by the off-balance sheet description, many of which are far from new. They can be grouped under four headings, given below, and the individual items identified are summarised in Table 4.6.

Table 4.5 Off-Balance Sheet Activities of US Banks, 1980–1986 ($ bn.)

Year-End	*Capital*	*Loan commitments*	*Standby letters of credit*	*Commercial letters of credit*	*Foreign exchange transactions*
1980	108	n.a.	47	20	177
1981	118	n.a.	72	20	189
1982	129	n.a.	100	17	215
1983	141	432	120	30	464
1984	154	496	146	30	584
1985	170	531	175	29	735
1986*	179	567	189	28	995

Source: Chessen (1986) and Federal Deposit Insurance Corporation.
Note: * End September 1986.

Commitments

In the activities under this heading, a bank has committed itself to advancing funds and acquiring a credit exposure at some future date. In some cases, there may be a predetermined date when the option to borrow must be exercised. In others, the bank will only be called upon to advance funds when other parties have refused to do so (e.g. note issuance facilities). Finally, there are the looser commitments where a bank has agreed a facility, but has the right to withdraw it in certain circumstances (such as overdrafts). Some leading examples of commitments are:

1. unused overdrafts and credit lines
2. revolving lines of credit
3. note issuance facilities (NIFs)
4. repurchase agreements ('repos')

Guarantees

These are the more traditional off-balance-sheet exposures, where a bank has underwritten the obligations of a third party and currently stands behind the risk. Default by a counterparty on whose behalf a guarantee has been written may trigger an immediate loss or, more usually, will result in the bank acquiring a substandard claim. Examples of the types of exposure falling under this heading are:

5. asset sales with recourse
6. acceptances
7. standby letters of credit
8. commercial letters of credit

Table 4.6 Glossary of Some 'Off-Balance Sheet' Activities

1. **Unused overdrafts and credit lines**. A borrowing facility opened up by a bank in favour of another bank or customer, which is subject to review.
2. **Revolving lines of credit.** An unconditional commitment to lend when the borrower makes a request under the facility.
3. **Note Issuance Facilities** (NIFs) and **Revolving Underwriting Facilities** (RUFs). An arrangement whereby a borrower may draw down funds up to a prescribed limit over an extended period by repeated issues to the market of, for example, three- or six-month promissory notes. If at any time the notes cannot be placed in the market at a minimum price, a group of underwriters undertakes to buy them at a prescribed price. The contingent risk to banks arises from their role as underwriters of such issues.
4. **Repurchase agreements** ('repos'). An arrangement whereby a bank sells a loan, security or fixed asset to a third party with a commitment to repurchase the asset after a certain time, or in the event of a certain contingency.
5. **Asset sales with recourse.** An arrangement whereby a bank sells a loan or other asset to a third party, but retains an obligation to assume the credit risk if the borrower defaults or the value of the asset otherwise deteriorates.
6. **Acceptances.** An obligation by a bank to pay on maturity the face value of a draft or bill of exchange, normally covering the sale of goods.
7. **Standby letters of credit.** An obligation on the part of the bank to a designated beneficiary to perform or provide compensation under the terms of the underlying contracts to which they refer, should the bank's customers fail to do so.
8. **Commercial letters of credit.** A letter of credit guaranteeing payment by the issuing or opening bank in favour of an exporter against presentation of shipping and other documents.
9. **Forward foreign exchange transactions.** A contract to pay and receive specified amounts of one currency for another at a future date at a predetermined exchange rate. Default by one party prior to maturity exposes the other to an exchange risk.
10. **Currency futures.** These are contracts traded on exchanges for the delivery of a standardised amount of foreign currency at some future date. The price for the foreign currency is agreed on the day the contract is bought or sold. As with forward contracts, gains or losses are incurred as a result of subsequent currency fluctuations.
11. **Currency options.** An option contract allows the holder to exchange (or equally to choose not to exchange) a specific amount of one currency for another at a predetermined rate during some period in the future. For the institution writing the option the risk lies in its exposure to movements in the exchange rate between the two currencies (a market risk). For a bank buying an option the risk lies in the ability of the counterparty to perform (a credit risk).
12. **Interest rate options.** Similar to currency options. The buyer has the right (but not the obligation) to lock into a predetermined interest rate during some period in the future. The writer is exposed to interest rate movements, the buyer to counterparty default.
13. **Interest rate caps and collars.** An institution guarantees the maximum rate (cap) or maximum and minimum rate (collar) on floating rate loans.
14. **Interest rate and currency swaps.** In a currency swap two parties contract to exchange the cash flows – of equal net present value – of specific assets or liabilities which are expressed in different currencies. In the classic ('plain vanilla') interest rate swap two parties contract to exchange interest service payments (and sometimes principal service payments) on the same amount of indebtedness of the

same maturity and with the same payment dates – one providing fixed interest rate payments in return for variable rate payments from the other, and vice versa. The risks to banks arise from taking on positions by entering into such swaps and from the possibility that default by a counterparty will open up unexpected or unanticipated foreign exchange or interest rate exposures during the life of the swap.

15. **Securities underwriting.** The underwriter undertakes to take up the whole or a pre-agreed part of a capital market issue at a predetermined price. The major risk is that the underwriter will be unable to place the paper at the issue price or better because of an unfavourable movement in prices, an unforeseen political or economic event, a misjudgement of the market price, or a sudden deterioration in the perceived credit quality of the issuer.

Source: Bank for International Settlements (1986a).

Foreign Exchange and Interest-Rate-Related Transactions

These items are essentially interest rate and foreign exchange rate agreements, in most cases binding on both parties, but in some cases exercisable at one party's discretion (such as options). With the exception of currency swaps, no exchange of principal is generally involved. Where the transaction is unhedged, the bank is exposed to movements in interest rates or exchange rates. Whether the transaction is unhedged (designed deliberately to open up an exposure) or hedged (to neutralise a position exposure), the bank is vulnerable to the creditworthiness of the counterparty (the ability to carry out its side of the contract). Examples of transactions are:

9. forward foreign exchange transactions
10. currency futures
11. currency options
12. interest rate options
13. interest rate caps
14. interest rate and currency swaps

Other Activities

Banks manage portfolios and trust funds on behalf of clients and act as agents or brokers for insurance companies. A major exposure for banks outside the US comes from the banks' involvement in investment banking and merchant banking activities, including the organisation of mergers and securities issues associated with leveraged buyouts, and also:

15. securities underwriting

Such activities, entered into because of the fee income which they produce, may take these many different forms, but nevertheless bring out more closely than traditional bank activities the parallels between banking and insurance developed in this and earlier chapters. Many of the fees received by banks for such activities can be interpreted as premia paid by customers for insurance against particular financial risks.

A number of fee-generating activities can be identified which ameliorate financial risks incurred by bank customers and impose risks on banks. Not all are new. The establishment of an overdraft limit, for example, earns banks a commitment fee and affords the customer protection against liquidity risks; but it exposes the bank to offsetting liquidity risk, which it is better able to bear. This example, however, is probably more appropriately associated with retail banking. At the wholesale end of the market, insurance against liquidity risk might be provided by note issuance facilities and discount commitments, whereby banks agree to accept short-term paper of their customers and can manage the resulting liquidity risk via an ability to rediscount the paper in the market.

Banks also insure against, and incur, asset risk through activities such as bill acceptances and standby letters of credit. In both cases banks essentially guarantee payment of a customer's liability to a holder of its debt should the customer default on the debt.[18] Fees charged to the customer reflect the benefits of the lower interest rate required by the market on the customer's paper once a bank guarantee of payment is attached. Although the initial incidence of the fee is on the bank's customer (the borrower), the ultimate effect of lower yield is equivalent to the holder of risky (higher-yielding) paper paying a premium to the bank, in terms of foregone interest, for insurance against default. This is precisely equivalent to a depositor accepting an insurance policy from a bank in lieu of uninsured income on primary securities.

Other activities can involve banks in interest rate risk. Underwriting activities, although more associated with investment banking, are an example. Similarly, loan commitments can lead to interest rate exposure. Where the commitment is on a fixed-rate basis, the risk is obvious. Even where the commitment is on a variable-rate basis, but at a fixed premium on some market yield, banks face the risk of changes in the funding conditions they encounter (due to, for example, changes in their credit rating).

At the risk of violating established accounting conventions, Table 4.7 represents our attempt to provide a structure for analysing the effect of off-balance sheet activities of banks. The items in the on-balance sheet part of the table need no explanation. 'Below the line' in the off-balance sheet component are a number of examples of such activities.

In interpreting the table, two points warrant emphasis. First, many of the items below the line have a probabilistic element, like the on-balance sheet items. In the same way that the option held by depositors to withdraw deposits may not be exercised, the contingent liability of unused overdraft limits may never involve any actual on-balance sheet consequences: the holder of the limit may never draw upon it. Should the holder do so, effects arise on-balance sheet which are easily depicted in this framework. On-

Table 4.7 Claims and Contingent Claims

	On-Balance Sheet	
	Assets	*Liabilities*
	Loans Cash reserves	Deposits Equity
	Off-Balance Sheet	
Contingent liabilities	Loans yet to be drawn down	(Unused overdrafts)
	Potential loans to (debt of) customers	(Standby letters of credit)
	Interest to be received from other party in swap	(Interest to be paid to other party in swap)
	Cash receipt from holder of forward contract	(Foreign currency delivery required under forward contract)
	Securities to be delivered	(Underwriting of security issue)
Contingent assets	(Unused lines of credit at other banks)	Potential debt to other banks

balance sheet loans increase and cash reserves decline, while off-balance sheet, unused overdrafts decline and loans yet to be drawn also decline. In this example, the off-balance sheet item involves a liquidity risk the magnitude of which depends upon the probability of the contingency being realised. Thus one part of the analysis of off-balance sheet activities involves the likelihood of these being transferred into on-balance sheet amounts.

The second aspect of the table and of the analysis of off-balance sheet activities concerns the effect which such transfers have upon the on-balance sheet part of the table. To illustrate, consider the second off-balance sheet item of standby letters of credit which are contingent liabilities of the bank. Should the bank's customer (whose debt to a third party has been guaranteed by the bank through the letter) default, the bank is called upon for payment and finds cash reserves reduced. The on-balance sheet counterpart to this item is an increase in loans outstanding (to the customer) while off-balance sheet, the contingent liability 'standby letters of credit' falls, as does the corresponding item 'potential loan to customer' — which has become an actual loan. So far, this is little different from the example of use of overdraft limits, but it is possible that the involuntary loan made to the bank's customer is, in fact, worthless. (The use of the standby letter may have been brought about by the customer's insolvency.) In such circumstances, an appropriate depiction of the on-balance sheet changes would involve the decline in cash being accompanied by a decline in equity (or net worth of the bank) with no change in loans outstanding. The contingent liability involved is an asset risk to the bank.

That banks are able, and willing, to take on these risks reflects a number of factors. The motive is the fee income generated which can be substantial. Citicorp, for example, derived 35 per cent of its revenue in 1984 from fees. But how can banks provide these guarantees and 'insurance' facilities sufficiently cheaply to make them attractive?

An important consideration is cost. Consider the case of bankers acceptances in the USA. An importer seeking to finance a shipment of goods could borrow the funds by means of a bank loan, which the bank could fund by issuing, say, a CD to a depositor. By accepting the bill of exchange instead, and adding its own credit rating to that of the borrower, the bank turns the debt of the merchant into a prime marketable instrument which can be purchased in place of the CD by the potential depositor. Thus the same effect has been achieved — a deposit and loan equivalent — but, unlike the CD, the bankers acceptance is free of the deposit insurance levy and eligible acceptances are exempt from reserve requirements, making them a cheaper source of funds than deposits (Jensen and Parkinson 1986). Similar cost considerations led UK banks to switch to acceptance financing in the 1970s to avoid the cost of supplementary special deposits (i.e. reserve requirements) imposed on liability raising (see Artis and Lewis 1981, Chapter 6).

As to why it is a bank which conducts this business, the answers are essentially the same as those explaining traditional intermediation, since the same functions are being performed (Lewis 1987b). That is, banks are specialists in both evaluating and diversifying the risks. Where banks insure against asset risk by providing guarantees, they are exploiting opportunities arising from imperfect information. Banks are better able to assess the risks of particular borrowers than are potential lenders, and the higher credit standing of banks makes their guarantee a valuable commodity. Consequently, the risk premium which would be required by the market for certain borrowers is greater than the fees charged to them by banks.

Banks may also be better able to bear liquidity risk. Access to the interbank market is one obvious source of such an advantage, as can be a superior ability to rediscount customers' paper. Finally, any interest rate risk can also be ameliorated in various ways. At a price, the banks are able to shift the interest rate risk of loan commitments onto futures markets. This is a case of optimal risk bearing, whereby risks are shifted to those willing to bear them. In 1984, 40 per cent of large US banks offering this service hedged their forward loan contracts in the futures markets for interest rates. (These markets are similar to currency futures, except that the contracts are for delivery of standardised amounts of securities like Treasury bills, bonds or bank CDs.) By holding a futures contract which mirrors the forward loan, losses on the loan commitment can be offset by the gains on the futures contract. Use of the hedge means that the bank foregoes the possibility of future profits, but gains from the origination and servicing fees. This type of hedging is beginning to filter through to retail markets.

In addition to those advantages which banks possess through imperfect information, and so forth, two other factors motivating off-balance sheet activities warrant mention. First, banks may derive diversification gains from mixing off-balance sheet activities with more traditional activities. By unbundling transactions, other parties may be able to acquire some of the risk, promoting a better spread of risk sharing generally. This is an important consideration in the case of mortgage loans, considered below. Second, off-balance sheet activities and associated risks enable banks to achieve dramatic increases in leverage — as measured using conventional balance sheet quantities. Such activities can thus enable banks to escape regulatory barriers to increased leverage imposed by deposit insurers, prudential supervisors, and so on, and thwart their intentions of limiting bank risk exposure. This important issue is taken up in Chapter 5.

4.7 Merging of Wholesale and Retail Banking

While some institutions continue to specialise in wholesale banking or in retail banking, there is no longer a completely separate wholesale banking system, nor a completely separate retail system. Most large banks, at least in their global operations, combine a retail/domestic wholesale/international balance sheet. Smaller banks generally add a wholesale book to their retail operations; or vice versa. There are benefits from pooling loan risks of different characteristics, of offsetting withdrawal risks of lumpy wholesale deposits against retail deposits made relatively predictable by the 'law of large numbers', and from conducting size intermediation between retail and wholesale markets to exploit any yield differences which arise.

Floating Rate Loans

More generally, most of the basics of wholesale banking have spread to the retail area. Flexi-rate loans are now universal. In the UK, virtually all (99 per cent) loans to business, large and small, are on a variable-rate basis. Smaller loans have been linked to base rate (i.e. 'prime') but an increasing proportion are being tied to LIBOR. In the United States, floating rate loans are no longer confined to wholesale-sized operations; as at August 1986, 55 per cent of small C&I loans ($1,000–$24,000) were made on a flexi-rate basis.

Liability Management

Liability management techniques, developed in the wholesale markets in London and amongst large New York banks, have widened the options open to all banks in adjusting to deposit and loan variability. In the UK, all 'retail' banks regularly tap the wholesale fund markets, and so do institutions such as the building societies. Adding wholesale liabilities to a retail operation may enable the institutions to have a more diversified liabilities structure, both in terms of maturity and customer characteristics. Access to wholesale funds is also advantageous to the retail institutions both because funds can be raised more quickly than from retail sources and because additional funds can be raised without having to raise rates across the board on existing, as well as new, deposits.

Once the province of large banks, the US federal funds market is now used by banks of all sizes, although small banks have virtually no access to the federal funds market as buyers of funds. There has been a wider use of repurchase agreements ('repos'), which are short-term 'sales' of securities, with an agreed 'repurchase', providing the banks with temporary borrowings (secured against the securities). The seller 'borrows' the value of the securities under the RP and 'repays' the funds a few days or weeks later by repurchasing the securities.

These funding sources can offer cost advantages to individual banks additional to the flexibility and 'marginal money' attributes. Federal funds bought, and repo money, are technically borrowings and not deposits, so there is no deposit insurance premium paid on the funds. Federal funds bought are not subject to reserve requirements, since the reserve requirements are met by the bank that accepted the original deposit on-sold as federal funds. The same is the case for repo borrowings, which are exempt from reserve requirements if the collateral consists of government or federal agency securities (Stigum 1983).

Some writers argue that there has been a more or less permanent change in banks' behaviour, in which asset management has been eschewed for liability management (Goodhart 1984). It is argued (for example, by Budzeika 1980) that the transition came about as banks ran out of the excess cash and government securities built up during the war years. Asset management in the form of sales of government securities had in any case become more costly as withdrawal of the authorities' interest rate peg raised liquidation costs. Liability management filled the void.

Funding Strategies

More generally, however, we should be talking of 'funds management', with asset and liability management as special cases. An individual bank needing funds can enter the money markets both by selling assets and by issuing liabilities. It can react in a variety of ways: by bidding for interbank funds, disposing of bills or bonds or commercial paper, selling CDs, running down holdings of call money, and so on. The route actually chosen will be the one most profitable to the bank (although whether these are long-run or short-run profits remains an open question).

Funds management is of importance to banks because they operate in certain markets in the short run as price setters, accepting whatever quantity of those assets or liabilities eventuate in their balance sheets. Underlying this behaviour is a recognition that random self-reversing fluctuations in the demand or supply of a particular financial asset do occur and that accepting these quantity variations may be less costly than trying to prevent them. Demand deposits are a prime candidate, especially when the averaging process inherent in large numbers makes the stochastic element relatively small and predictable. Loans also have a short-run stochastic element, due to changes in customers' usage of overdraft limits, credit lines and commitments.

Over longer periods of time, banks can undertake alterations to the structure of retail deposit rates, adjust the pricing and amount of depository services, and cut back or expand credit lines, so as to induce a desired balance sheet structure. But, for very short-run funding policies, deposits and loans can be treated as the exogenous elements, so that changes in their difference necessitate adjustments in other balance sheet components. This is illustrated in Table 4.8 by converting a simplified balance sheet into a sources and uses of funds statement.[19]

Items on the sources side of the funds statement must be adjusted (endogenously) to meet the imbalances which arise between deposits and outstanding loans. In the face of a loss of deposits and/or draw-down of lending commitments, banks have the choice of running down free reserves, selling off government securities, issuing new CDs, buying in (or selling off) interbank funds, and selling assets on repurchase agreements.

Which of these options (or mix thereof) they choose depends upon the conditions in those markets and expectations about future funding needs. Where, for instance, a need for funds is seen as very short-run, running down

Table 4.8 Simplified Flow of Funds Statement*

Uses of funds	*Sources of funds*
Net increase in loans minus deposits	Decrease in net free reserves (bankers' balances)
	Decrease in government securities (gilts and bills)
	Increase in certificates of deposits
	Increase in federal funds bought (sterling interbank borrowings)
	Increase in repurchase agreements

*For a US bank. Items in square brackets are UK equivalents.

free reserves or borrowing interbank overnight may be the courses adopted, because of their easy reversibility. Where there is less certainty that the immediate future will see inflows of funds, issues of CDs or sales of government securities may occur. In both of these markets banks can be assumed to be price takers, so that these courses of action represent alternatives. Fama (1985) presents a model in which, in response to periods of high demand for loans, banks sell CDs and run down government security holdings. When loan demands are low (*vis-à-vis* deposits), banks withdraw from the CD market and build up security holdings. Other factors will, however, complicate the process. Banks issuing CDs perceive a need to have a continuing presence in the market, so as to maintain their names on fund managers' approved banking lists (money market funds are the major buyers of CDs). Also, expectations about future interest rate movements and potential capital gains or losses on security holdings will influence the bank's funding strategy.

As this last factor suggests, short-term funds management is interrelated with longer-term portfolio management. Fundamental to that interrelationship is the existence of secondary markets in certain assets whereby portfolio decisions, even if made with a longer term perspective, can easily be reversed or adjusted. The rapid development in the 1980s of secondary markets for a wide range of assets is beginning to revolutionise the portfolio behaviour of banks.

Secondary Loan Markets

Banks in Australia have for many years adopted some of the 'securitisation' methods in their retail operations developed originally in wholesale banking. Middle-sized loans (around $50,000) to firms are frequently made by discounting a firm's commercial bill or by means of a loan along with an option for a bill to be issued. The bills are broken up and then sold to deposit customers in smaller parcels (say $10,000 or more) for terms preferred by them. Both the 'loan' and the 'time deposit' go off-balance sheet.

But it is in the United States that the idea of the securitisation of loans has been developed to a considerable degree of sophistication. In the face of shifts in deposit supplies, balance sheet options of US banks now include the ability to sell off part of the loan portfolio prior to maturity.

The technique is best known in the case of home mortgages held by banks and savings institutions, for which a well-developed secondary market allows the buying, selling and trading of existing mortgage loans and mortgage-backed securities. Investors can buy whole loans, participations, or a variety of mortgage-backed securities. In the case of participations, the holder acquires an interest in an underlying pool of mortgages on which payments received are 'passed through' to the investor. Thus they do not alter the cash flow characteristics of the underlying individual mortgages. Collaterised mortgage obligations (CMOs) do so, by splitting up the cash flow in varying ways between investors. More generally, issuers of mortgage-backed securities create marketable instruments so that the ultimate lenders (those holding these instruments) can change without the need for any transfer of the mortgages themselves.

These developments are important for funds management in that an option now exists for mortgage lenders to sell off part of their loan portfolio should a need for liquidity arise. At the same time, the range of marketable securities available to other financial institutions is increased. They can, for example, acquire mortgage-backed securities as part of their asset portfolio and thus diversify the risk characteristics of their balance sheet at low cost.

There has been a veritable explosion of similar arrangements by which financial contracts are unbundled (so as to retain some elements and pass on others) and by which secondary markets are able to develop in previously unmarketable assets. Essentially the same unbundling principle is followed with STRIPS, which strip a pool of Treasury bonds into interest coupons and principals, repackaging and selling off each cash flow separately. Interest rate swaps are another example by which interest repayments on loans are unbundled from the principal, thereby allowing one borrower to trade ('swap') a variable rate of interest for a counterparty's fixed rate of interest (see Ch. 10, s. 2). Secondary marketing of assets by collaterisation has now developed for small business loans, auto loans ('CARS', i.e. collaterised automobile receivables), credit card loans ('CARDS', i.e. certificates of amortising revolving debts) and computer leases.[20]

A number of aspects of secondary loan markets warrant mention. The first is that their development provides scope for specialisation and separation of the tasks of loan originating, credit insurance, management and long-term financing. The second is that secondary markets can influence the nature of loan contracts written by mortgage originators. Whereas a long-term fixed interest rate loan is generally unsuitable for a retail intermediary's portfolio, it is potentially more suitable as backing for a mortgage-backed security than many variable-rate loans. Knowing that interest rate risk can be passed on to the market reduces the disincentive to issue fixed-rate mortgage loans.

In all the securitisation arrangements, there is a principal/agent problem to be solved, which gives rise to the need to design contracts with appropriate incentives. Knowledge that a loan is to be packaged and sold off to other institutions may diminish the originator's keenness to select good lending risks. In some cases, the default risk can be shifted to a third party which agrees to insure the loans in the pool. But otherwise, the buyer needs to be convinced that the originator has done a good job.[21] Often this requirement means that the originator must retain some part of the risk. One is by the issue of guarantees of 'sales with recourse' contracts by the originator (see the previous section). Another is by 'incentive pricing', whereby the seller puts part of the service fee 'on the line'. Or, alternatively, the originating and loan servicing fees may be based on a specified default rate, with 'kick-backs' should the actual experience prove to be better.

This remains an area where, at the time of writing, change is rapid and much experimentation is occurring, posing many worries for regulators. Off-balance sheet operations are frequently prompted by a desire by regulated institutions to free up equity by avoiding minimum capital requirements levied on balance sheet risks. But, where the business goes off-balance sheet backed by a guarantee as to credit risk, there is no 'real' saving on equity, since no risk has in fact been given up. There are clear implications for bank safety from the growth of such business, and we shall now look at some of these issues.

Notes

1. For a recent account, see Lewis and Chiplin (1985).
2. An idea of the average size for US dollar advances can be gained from the average size of large (i.e. $1 million or more) commercial and industrial (C&I) loans by money centre banks in the USA. As at August 1986, short-term loans averaged $9.6 million, while long-term loans averaged $6.1 million. Note that these are the averages for 'wholesale' loans in the United States.
3. Einzig points out that the first interbank transactions in fact occurred between branches of Commonwealth banks operating in London, but the example of the dollar market led to their large-scale operation.
4. Details of the markets are given in Einzig (1971), Hadjimichalakis (1982) and Harrington (1987).
5. In recent years a market has developed for brokered CDs, in which large CDs are broken into amounts of $100,000 or less so that they qualify for deposit insurance, but this is basically a retail market (see Konstas 1986).
6. *Federal Reserve Bulletin*, December 1986, Table 4.23.
7. Diamond (1984), for example, emphasises the role of delegated monitoring by depositors to banks in response to imperfect information and shows that the benefits of intermediation from this source accrue only when more than one depositor exists per borrower.
8. Wriston (1986).
9. Selden (1963). Information of US commercial paper programmes is from Feeney (1986).
10. Many of the arguments presented here were outlined earlier in Lewis (1980a, 1980b), Artis and Lewis (1981) and Davis and Lewis (1982b, 1982c).
11. Crawford's Directory of City Connections, 1987 edition.
12. The description is Einzig's. King Charles I of England, after losing the civil war, was sentenced to death on 27 January 1649 'as a tyrant, traitor, murderer and public enemy'. The death warrant was signed by 59 commissioners of the court, after some persuasion (Cook and Wroughton 1980).
13. The analogy is borrowed from Arrow (1970, Ch. 5).
14. In aggregate, interbank assets and liabilities must be perfectly matched, since each such asset is a liability of another bank in the aggregate. (In Tables 4.1 and 4.2 mismatching occurs because the sample of banks with which accounts are presented differs from the population of banks for which transactions are recorded.) To illustrate, let **x** be the average period to maturity (apm) of both interbank loans and deposits. Let **A** and **D** be the apm of loans to and deposits from non-banks and let w and $1 - w$ be the shares of the interbank and non-bank

business. Then, the apm of total loans ($\mathbf{A}'$) and total deposits ($\mathbf{D}'$) are given by

$$\mathbf{A}' = w\mathbf{x} + (1 - w)\mathbf{A}$$
$$\mathbf{D}' = w\mathbf{x} + (1 - w)\mathbf{D}$$

and overall maturity transformation, measured by ($\mathbf{A}' - \mathbf{D}'$), equals

$$\mathbf{A}' - \mathbf{D}' = (1 - w)(\mathbf{A} - \mathbf{D})$$

Because $w \leqslant 1$, overall maturity transformation is less than that for business with non-bank customers.

15. The Bank for International Settlements (BIS), Fifty-third Annual Report, June 1983, p.50.
16. See also Ellis (1981).
17. Merchant banks in Australia use this technique. See Scott and Wallace (1985).
18. Note, however, that there is a legal distinction in the USA between guarantees and acceptances, in that nationally chartered banks are prohibited from issuing 'guarantees'. Standby letters of credit are also an instrument form peculiar to the USA due to the inability of banks to extend guarantees.
19. In presenting this statement we ignore such things as changes in asset valuations, interest income, owners' equity, etc.
20. For a recent survey, see Pavel (1986).
21. In the case of variable-rate loans, where (as in the UK) the originating institution retains some control over the frequency and amount by which interest rates are adjusted, the buyer must be convinced that the seller will continue to act in the buyer's interest. On the other hand, if the buyer also acquires some control over how rates and other terms and conditions are changed, the original customer may have some cause for concern. These problems have proved difficult to circumvent in the development of secondary mortgage markets in the UK (see Wright 1986).

5

Bank Safety and Depositor Protection

5.1 The Causes of Concern

The history of banking is replete with cases of individual bank failures and general banking crises, and the reader is referred to Charles Kindleberger's book *Manias, Panics and Crashes* for a detailed, and thoroughly entertaining, account. By far the most famous episode was during the depression years in the USA where, in the four years 1930–33, 9,096 bank suspensions occurred, imposing losses on depositors, shareholders and creditors of $2.5 billion, and bringing about a sharp contraction in the money supply.[1] Coming on the heels of bank failures in Austria and Germany, and a run to gold which spread from Austria to Germany and then to Britain, the emphasis of banking policy worldwide thereafter switched to ensuring bank safety.

For a long time after the 1930s, the problem of bank failures seemed to have gone away. A cluster of events in the mid-1970s and mid-1980s has altered that perception. The year 1974 saw the failure of Bankhaus Herstatt (Germany), Franklin National Bank (USA), at the time of the failure the 12th largest bank in the USA,[2] and the 'secondary banking crisis' in Britain, whereby the failure of several 'fringe banks' reverberated through the British financial system until it looked like threatening, at one juncture, the largest insurance company and one of the clearing banks. So as to ameliorate that crisis, a 'lifeboat' support scheme was organised by the Bank of England:[3] interestingly, for students of history, a virtual repetition of its response to the 'Baring crisis' of 1890. In 1984 there were failures, and regulatory takeovers, of Johnson Matthey Bankers (UK) and, notably, Continental Illinois Bank (USA), followed the next year by runs on thrift institutions in Ohio and Maryland. The years 1984–1985 also saw the collapse of Denmark's seventh largest bank, the rescue of Ireland's largest bank following losses by its insurance subsidiary, and the first bank failures in Canada for 52 years.[4]

While the containment of such failures can be cited as evidence of the effectiveness of government 'safety nets' for banking and depository institutions (Volcker 1985), some extraordinary measures were taken to do so. For instance, consider the case of Continental Illinois. In order to prevent the contagion effects (observable in stock market prices) from spreading to the deposits of other banks, federal authorities in the USA effectively nationalised the bank, guaranteed all creditors and depositors (insured or not) of the holding company, and publicly stated for the first time that regulators would prevent any failure amongst the 11 largest banking organisations in the United States.[5] These actions have enhanced already existing concerns about the appropriate pricing and the extent of support, whether by explicit schemes to protect depositors at retail intermediaries or by implicit guarantees to large banks with international depositors and creditors.

Events like those listed above have undoubtedly stimulated a resurgence of interest in bank safety and depositor protection, but in addition a number of other developments in banking markets have played a role. Broadly speaking, instability in banking can arise on the asset side of banks' balance sheets (bad loans), on the liability side (deposit withdrawals), from off-balance sheet activities (including failures of related organisations), or from some combination of these three. Deregulation of financial markets has contributed to risks in a number of ways. Greater competition and earnings pressures in traditional lines of business seem to have 'shifted the focus of bank policies away from concerns with safety and toward greater risk-taking in a quest for larger profits' (Volcker 1985). The range of activities permitted to banks has generally been expanded. Diversification can work to reduce risk, but the intent (if not always the effect) of regulation has typically been to constrain bank activities to relatively low-risk areas. Interest rate ceilings in the past, for example, were often justified as preventing competition between banks from bidding up deposit rates to such levels that banks and depository institutions had to search out riskier investments.

Deregulation and changes in the underlying economic environment have altered the nature of the markets in which banks operate. Greater flexibility of interest rates and exchange rates alters, and is likely to have increased, the risks confronting financial institutions. Rapid swings in energy and agricultural prices in the 1980s have exposed banks with large portfolios of loans to these sectors. World recession, along with interest rate and oil price movements, has altered the repayment prospects of loans made to developing countries (see Chapter 10).

In addition, interbank markets and the shift to liability management have increased the direct links between the fortunes of individual banks. Continental Illinois, a largely wholesale bank, was an extreme case, but not wholly atypical of other large money centre banks. As at December 1983, it had assets of \$42.1 billion (making it the eighth largest US bank), which were three quarters financed by liabilities bearing interest rates sensitive to market movements. Continental relied extensively upon large short-term deposits, including domestic interbank deposits (about 16 per cent) and foreign interbank deposits (40 per cent), so that the great bulk of deposits was uninsured.[6] Earnings of Continental were affected by rising interest rates and by write-downs on foreign and energy loans, and it was clearly vulnerable to any faltering of confidence amongst uninsured depositors. It has been estimated by the Federal Deposit Insurance Corporation (FDIC) that 179 banks had uninsured deposits with Continental of amounts greater than half of their total equity, so that its failure would have seriously jeopardised them.[7]

Not surprisingly, there has been a renewed interest in the study of financial instability and banking theory, and several economists have constructed models of the banking system in which bank runs emerge as an outcome of market reactions (Diamond and Dybvig 1983, Bryant 1981, Taylor and O'Connell 1985). There has also been an interest in alternative banking systems, for not all economists accept that governments need to be involved in bank rescues. Recent studies by White (1984), Rolnick and Weber (1985) and Vaubel (1984) of free banking in Scotland (1800–1845) and the USA (1837–1863) attempt to demonstrate that the conventional wisdom about the instability of a free banking system is historically unfounded. Even the US experience in the 1930s, which underpins much of that conventional wisdom, has been reinterpreted by some as evidence of the effects of inappropriate regulation, rather than of uncontrolled banking (Kareken 1983). Most of the proposals to reform deposit protection in the USA recommend shifting some (and, in a few cases, *all*) of the risk from governments to private markets — either to depositors, bank shareholders, or private sector insurers (see below).

Most countries have government schemes for depositor protection and the oversight of bank activities. The US banking failures in the early 1930s prompted the inception there of deposit insurance schemes for both banks and the savings institutions. Broadly similar schemes can be found operating in Canada, Germany, India and Japan, to name a few examples.[8] In fact, though, explicit deposit insurance schemes along American lines are found in a minority of countries. Other countries, such as Australia, France, Italy, Switzerland, rely on other methods, ranging through government ownership of banks, government supervision and explicit or implicit government support on an *ad hoc* basis. Even in the United States, deposit insurance is only part of the story. The government 'safety net' there comprises three safety mechanisms: deposit insurance (now predominantly federal); lender-of-last-resort facilities via the 'discount window' of the Federal Reserve system provided to nearly 40,000 banks, savings institutions and credit unions, which offer transactions facilities; and the examination and supervision of bank capital, lending limits and their range of activities by federal and state regulatory authorities[9] designed to detect 'problem' banks and encourage corrective action.

In order to assess the relative merits and justification for these schemes, we shall first reconsider the nature of the risks in banking without regulation.

The business of banking involves the taking of various risks, aspects of which have been spelt out in previous chapters. A number of questions form the basis for our subsequent discussion. Will bankers, acting out of self-interest, structure their activities so that, in 'normal times', banking is not a risky business? (By this we mean that the probability of bank insolvency and thus of depositors not being fully repaid is low.) Are there characteristics of banking which make 'abnormal times' (in which prudent bankers find insolvency threatening) a commonplace? Should failures of banks be viewed with more alarm than failures of firms in other industries?

5.2 The Prudence of Bankers

Bank depositors can find themselves at risk of loss from the activities of two types of bankers. First, there are 'fly-by-night' operators with no intention of repaying borrowed funds. Second, there are honest operators whose activities involve a degree of risk and therefore create a probability greater than zero that insolvency will arise. Whether fly-by-night operators are potentially more numerous in banking than in other industries requiring external funding is not a question which, as far as we are aware, has been addressed in the banking literature. Certainly, fraud by bank officers and staff has been a major cause of bank failures in the USA. Fraud and other irregularities were the most frequently cited causes of bank failures between 1865 and 1931, and accounted for about two thirds of failures between 1959 and 1971 and also from 1980 to mid-1983. Loans to business associates were the most common form of fraudulent activity (Benston and Kaufman 1986).

Our focus, however, is upon the question of whether honest bankers (and their staff) are likely to be prudent, in the sense of structuring their affairs so that the probability of depositors not being repaid in full is very low. In addition, there is the question of whether depositors are fully aware or 'informed' of the risks taken by banks. For the moment, we shall defer the 'consumer protection' issue and focus upon the risks. Consider the simplified bank balance sheet below:

Assets	*Liabilities*
Earning assets (A)	Deposits (D)
Reserves (R)	Shareholder equity (E)

Contingent claims

The 'off-balance sheet' contingent claims have been described in some detail in Chapter 4, section 5. There are four characteristics which can put depositors' funds at risk. First, there is the inherent riskiness of the set of earning assets chosen by the bank. These risks reflect default possibilities and/or variability in the market price of those assets at some expected selling date. Second, there are the additional risks created by the composition of the asset portfolio as between earning assets and reserves. As outlined in Chapter 3, holding a low reserves/earning assets ratio may lead to liquidation costs if deposit outflows are large and unexpected sales of assets are required.[10] Third, the division of the entire asset portfolio risk between depositors and shareholders is influenced by the deposits/equity ratio, indicating the extent of 'gearing' of the bank.[11] Other things being equal, the lower this ratio, the more likely it is that the promised returns to depositors can be met out of the uncertain value of the asset portfolio. A fourth source of risk must also be considered. As outlined in the previous chapter, 'off-balance sheet' activities of banks create risks, and these have grown in importance in recent years. In addition, the novelty and other characteristics of these activities mean that measurement and management of the associated risk exposure is in its infancy. Finally, to these financial characteristics we should add variations in net operating costs as a potential drain on the bank's resources and a source of risk affecting the ability to honour deposit obligations.

This listing indicates the two fundamental ways in which bankers can generate risk. At one level, they can engage in 'risky business', that is, make loans to high-risk customers, mismatch the currency denominations of assets and liabilities, undertake extensive maturity mismatching, or hold few liquid reserves. At a second level, the bank's capital structure determines the extent to which these risks are passed on to customers rather than borne by the bank's owners.

Any tendency for a bank's owners or managers to adopt a balance sheet structure which increases deposit risk should, at least in principle, lead to depositors demanding higher promised interest rates in compensation. Algebraically, the contracted interest rate on deposits, i_b, will need to be an increasing function of the riskiness of deposits (σ_D^2):

$$i_D = f(\sigma_D^2), f_1 > 0$$

while deposit riskiness in turn depends upon the overall riskiness of the bank's business (σ_B^2) and the deposit/equity ratio (D/E). This gives:

$$i_D = f(\sigma_B^2, D/E), f_1 > 0, f_2 < 0$$

In the absence of prohibiting regulation we might expect to see different banks offering (in effect) deposits of differing risk, depending upon what their owners perceive as the most desirable balance sheet structure.[12]

Some banks may engage in risky business, paying higher interest rates than competitors, except to the extent that they maintain in compensation a deposit/equity ratio sufficiently lower so as to reduce the risk falling on depositors. Banks of the same risk class may adopt different deposit/equity ratios, thereby offering deposits of differing risk and being forced to pay different interest rates. (These arguments suppose that depositors monitor bank risk and can distinguish between a higher rate due to risk and one due to greater efficiency.)

Governments have rarely tried to give to banks much flexibility in adopting balance sheet structures and activities which generate a range of deposit risks. As a consequence of deposit insurance and bank supervision, bank deposits are widely perceived by the public to be of low risk. Would this be the case without the regulation? Are there forces at work which would cause bankers to be prudent and to ensure that deposits issued are (virtually) risk-free?

Judging by the lessons of history, the answer would appear to be in the negative: bank failures were a feature of banking systems prior to government regulation. Some observers, notably Kareken and Wallace (1978), dispute that conclusion. To them, banking failures in the past were not so much the result of free banking as of inappropriate regulations blunting the market mechanisms which would place limits upon the prudence of bankers. They contend that the lender-of-last-resort role of the Federal Reserve System induced depositors to regard bank deposits as risk-free. That in turn gave the owners of banks an incentive to adopt much riskier portfolios. In the absence of the Federal Reserve System, risk-averse depositors would have demanded risk premia on deposits sufficiently high to have prevented bank owners from pursuing such a strategy.

Two studies (Kareken and Wallace 1978, and Dothen and Williams 1980) go further and contend that an unregulated banking industry would be 'risk-free' in that profit-maximising bankers would voluntarily choose an asset portfolio and deposit/equity ratio which would involve no risk of insolvency and depositor loss. To suppose this implies that banks have control over some special factor which provides a continuing source of profits and that the firms' owners have a low rate of time discount. Pursuit of short-run profits which resulted in bankruptcy would destroy the valuable asset, and they are led instead to adopt behaviour which would enhance long-run profits. Banks may in practice possess some unique rent-providing asset such as monopoly rights to payments service provision, but it is far from clear that this is a natural concomitant to an unregulated banking industry.

A risk-free strategy by banks does seem an unlikely result for competitive markets because banks owe their existence, in part, to being efficient diversifiers and processors of risk which customers delegate to them. Nevertheless, it is possible to conceive of low deposit-risk strategies arising under alternative institutional arrangements. White (1984) notes that the low failure rate during the free banking era in Scotland was associated with the unlimited liability of bank owners. With the entire wealth of bank owners at risk, their incentive to run risks was low. To some extent, the absence of financial crises in Scotland may have been due to the ability of the Scottish bankers to shift reserve pressures to London. Goodhart (1985) points out that Scottish banks were always able to turn to the Bank of England as lender of last resort. Also, for the historical experience to have relevance for modern banking firms, for which there exists a possible separation of ownership from control, equity holders must be able to control the risk-taking activities of bank management. Unlimited personal liability, we also note, has not made all Lloyd's insurance underwriters adopt low-risk strategies.

Arguments for free banking rely on bank customers having the necessary information to pick and choose amongst banks according to risk, and to extract correct risk premia. If freedom from risk is valued sufficiently, market forces will lead some bankers to position themselves at that end of the risk spectrum, and vice versa if risk is not highly prized. But part of the rationale for bank intermediation lies in the existence of *imperfect* information. Banks have a special role as 'inside lenders' (Fama 1985) based on specialised information about borrowers, so that it is difficult, if not impossible, for outsiders to assess accurately the riskiness of a bank's portfolio. Specialised risk-assessing agencies exist, but their services are far from cheap and at present they report on only the larger banks. Crude indicators likely to be used by people, such as 'size' and 'safety in numbers', may be judged as inimical to competition and likely to give rise to a concentrated structure of banking. Only where banks hold 100 per cent cash reserves will their deposits be, and be seen to be, risk-free. If banks undertake the socially valuable activity of intermediation, even prudent bankers, structuring their activities to ensure risk-free deposits in normal times, may be unable to guard against the consequences of a bank run (abnormal times). In what follows, we draw on the arguments of Diamond and Dybvig (1983) and Bryant (1981) to demonstrate the potential fragility of the banking system.

5.3 Bank Runs and Failures

One observed characteristic of banking systems, in the absence of a perceived guarantee of deposit safety, is the vulnerability of individual banks to 'runs' and the contagious nature of the 'run' mentality. Re-examination of past financial crises points to a variety of origins. Instability in the macroeconomy arising from wars, technological change, and swings in investment expenditures is seen to be a prime source of shocks to the financial system (Eichengreen and Portes 1986). Real sector disturbances can be magnified by 'overtrading' and the underpricing of risk by financial institutions, leading to a shakeout when perceptions of the risks are revised (Kindleberger 1978; Minsky 1975 and 1984). A common thread running through most explanations is the potential which exists for shocks to the financial system, whatever the source, to be converted into a run on individual banks and to spread like a contagion to other banks due to the combination of incomplete knowledge and the nature of bank contracts. Indeed, in an environment of imperfect information, a bank run is seen to be a logical outcome of a free banking sector, given the usual form of the deposit contract.

To see this, consider a bank which produces liquidity and which, if depositor confidence exists, is a viable enterprise. With banks so highly geared, the value obtained at any time from liquidating the asset portfolio by calling in loans and realising assets at distress prices is likely to be less than total deposit liabilities. Should the bank have to be wound up, depositors would receive less than 100 per cent compensation: what Benston and Kaufman (1986) call a 'fire-sale insolvency'. Any depositor fearing such an eventuality can withdraw funds at their face value under the 'first come — first served — fixed price' rule of deposit contracts. By staying with the bank, a depositor cannot earn more than the contracted rate of interest (except for goodwill), but can lose. Any worry that the bank cannot maintain the par value for deposits (as is likely if forced to meet all obligations quickly) makes it sensible for individual depositors to attempt to withdraw funds at the agreed price immediately.

To put the argument slightly differently, the deposit of funds in an institution providing liquidity services relies upon a particular form of behaviour from other depositors. Specifically, a demand deposit contract provides investment in illiquid assets packaged together with 'insurance' for the depositor that liquidity is available if required. That insurance package is viable only if some small fraction of depositors demands liquidity. In the normal run of events it will be possible to estimate that fraction and provide for liquidity needs. However, while one's demand for liquidity will depend normally on external factors (the normal hazards of life), it may also be prompted by concerns about the behaviour of other depositors and solvency of the bank. Should a change in the behaviour of other customers be expected to occur, it becomes sensible to withdraw funds. The change in behaviour (actual or expected) of withdrawing depositors imposes an externality on the others, since any costs of liquidating a part of the asset portfolio to meet withdrawals are met by the remaining depositors rather than by those withdrawing funds. To avoid that externality, customers join the run, thereby aggravating the problem for the remaining depositors.

Similar arguments provide an explanation for contagion (the tendency for a run at one bank to inspire runs elsewhere). Depositors have only imperfect information about a bank's safety. Observing difficulties at one bank, they are unable to assess whether the problem is specific to that bank or common to a wider set of financial institutions. They may reassess the soundness of other banks or simply fear, for whatever reason, that the run may catch hold. For many depositors it may be cheaper to observe the behaviour of those thought to be 'in the know' than to monitor the bank directly, so that large depositors may exert a 'demonstration effect' on other depositors. In these circumstances, an immediate withdrawal of funds makes good individual sense. Fears become self-justifying, for the preconditions for the run spreading are thereby established.

This susceptibility of an unregulated banking system to swings in depositor confidence provides a major rationale for government intervention, either to prevent 'unnecessary' failures or to oversee bank failures.

Depositors as a group do not gain if bank assets are sold off in a hurry. Their interests would be better served if the bank were to be taken over on their behalf and deposits paid out as assets mature or are disposed of in more favourable circumstances. That, in essence, is what happens when central banks and government agencies take over failing institutions.

Bank runs and crises are not zero-sum games where some players gain at the expense of others, but involve substantial social costs. These costs go beyond the losses to depositors, shareholders and creditors of part of their wealth. While banks are closed and wind-up proceedings take place, depositors lose the liquidity associated with their deposits, and this can be expected to impinge on their expenditure plans.[13] Business borrowers, engaged in illiquid production activities, find their businesses threatened by the need to make earlier-than-expected repayments of loans, or take out replacement loans in an unfavourable economic climate. Bernanke (1983) has recently emphasised the role of such disruptions in credit markets in explaining the severity of the Great Depression in the USA.

In addition, banks evolve partly to overcome informational deficiencies which otherwise exist in financial markets. Their success in doing so rests upon knowledge capital and banker–client relationships built up over a number of years. Bank failures involve the destruction (or, at least, depreciation) of those valued private and social assets. Some borrowers at failed institutions will incur significant costs in demonstrating or establishing a reputation sufficient to obtain loan accommodation at other banks. Where bank failures result from a malfunctioning of the banking system rather than any inherent poor performance of the bank in question, there are benefits from measures to avoid these costs.

These 'social costs' arguments often get interwoven with others advocating government intervention to ensure bank safety. One is on grounds of efficiency. Only government agencies may be able to get confidential access to the proprietary information upon which an accurate assessment of bank safety relies. Or, given the widespread use of bank deposits, it may simply be less costly for one agency to undertake risk rating than for each depositor and creditor to do so (Mayer 1986). Perhaps the most common argument is that the principle of *caveat emptor* — 'let the buyer beware' — should not apply for those individuals who are unable adequately to assess the safety of depository institutions. They gain considerable benefit from having at least part of their wealth in a risk-free form, and only federal governments may be able to provide them with a credible guarantee in nominal terms. Such considerations appear to underlie the upper limit on the size of insured deposits in many schemes, the view being that those with larger wealth are better able to undertake themselves, or buy in the information needed for risk assessment. Whether this is an appropriate policy is one of the issues to which we now turn.

5.4 The Methods and Problems of Providing Depositor Protection

When a government takes responsibility for deposit protection, it faces problems familiar to any guarantor. Either the activities of the bank must be constrained in such a way that default is unlikely to occur, or the competitive advantage given to banks and the existence of moral hazard (the incentive for bank owners, with depositors' encouragement, to exploit the guarantee by undertaking riskier activities) must somehow be offset. These problems are not peculiar to government schemes, and we shall also look at methods which do not involve governments.

(a) Self-Insurance

Our discussion in Chapter 3 emphasised the importance of 'self-insurance' activities by individual banking firms designed to limit their exposure to risk. Diversification of loan portfolios, maintenance of adequate capital reserves and the holding of reserves of liquid assets are all part of such a strategy. However, the nature of such activities is precisely that they provide insurance against 'normal risks'. Any attempt to self-insure against abnormal risks like a bank run would involve foregoing normally profitable activities to hold large amounts of liquid assets. The forces of competition can be expected to preclude this outcome. During good times, risk-taking banking enterprises would 'free-ride' on the reputation of the sound bankers, while the conservative bankers would lose market share without any expectation of regaining during bad times the business lost in the good years (Goodhart 1985).

Some forms of insurance specifically designed for crisis situations may be possible. However, given the costs should a bank run be allowed to continue, such measures must involve ways of stopping the run. An obvious possibility is for the 'redeemability on demand' characteristic of deposits to be made optional at the decision of the bank.[14] In effect, banks take out insurance by buying an option contract from their depositors. Alternatively, banks may unilaterally take action which involves reneging on contracts with customers but manages to halt the crisis. 'Closing the doors' allows time for the run mentality to subside and for an orderly sale of assets to occur: but whether it works efficiently is another matter.

The option to suspend deposit convertibility is thus a way of reducing the dire consequences and the likelihood of runs. If it is known by depositors that suspension will occur whenever outflows would otherwise threaten bank solvency, and if the promised returns from maintaining funds in the account exceed those of panic withdrawal, incentive to join in a run is reduced. Yet, the existence of that option and, more particularly, its exercise by the bank, imposes costs on depositors in the form of unwanted and unpredictable losses of liquidity. Thus, even though this was the solution commonly used by banks confronted by runs in earlier times, it is not one which receives much support currently (see, however, Diamond and Dybvig 1983).

(b) *Industry Support and Private Insurance*

In Chapter 4 we noted how interbank arrangements provide insurance against risks in normal times and, equally, it might be asked whether similar arrangements could be formulated for abnormal times. Two possibilities spring to mind. The first involves the existence of a formal contributory deposit insurance scheme run by the industry, or by some private organisation. The second involves no formal insurance scheme, but the agreement by members of the industry to provide mutual support for co-members in difficulties — perhaps, as suggested by one author (Ely 1985), by formal cross-guarantees like those used in the Lloyd's insurance market in London.

Both approaches have been tried in various places and at various times. We have already mentioned the 'lifeboat' rescue of fringe banks in the UK by the clearing banks and the Bank of England in 1973, and its similarities to the rescue operation during the Baring Crisis of 1890. In the USA, clearing house associations emerged as private market lenders of last resort in the years before the establishment of the Federal Reserve System (Timberlake 1984; Gorton 1984). A special role was played by the New York money market banks. Due to the correspondent system, by which banks in the regional centres held bankers' balances with the money market banks, reserve pressures around the country centralised in New York, and the reserves of the money market banks served as the fulcrum for the stability of the system as a whole. The New York Clearing House was originally instituted in 1853 to facilitate cheque clearing, but soon evolved into acting in addition as an organiser of liquidity support. During crises, loans were made to member banks by the issue of clearing house certificates which other members agreed to accept in place of currency. This released currency, which would otherwise have been tied up for interbank clearing to meet depositors' withdrawals, and effectively augmented the supply of reserves. At other times, the Clearing House suspended the convertibility of deposits into currency at par, allowing currency to trade at a premium relative to deposits, so imposing a penalty on those wishing to encash deposits (Cleveland and Huertas 1985).

There are fewer examples of private insurance schemes for banks, although Benston (1983) notes the existence of deposit guarantee schemes by mutual agreement among banks in Indiana in 1834, Ohio in 1845 and Iowa in 1858. Such schemes are more common amongst savings institutions. For example, an industry-wide deposit guarantee scheme exists amongst building societies in the UK. As we argue below, one major difficulty which faces private insurance is illustrated by the failure of the deposit insurance scheme for Ohio savings and loan associations in 1985.

A problem common to both the insurance and the rescue schemes is that of preventing 'moral hazard': rules are needed to prevent members from exploiting the schemes by 'sailing closer to the wind'. Reluctance by banks to disclose details of their activities to their competitors poses obvious difficulties in devising and enforcing a set of rules. Since the rules are unlikely to satisfy all, some banks will want to opt out of the scheme. The reasons for doing so might be quite appropriate (big, low-risk institutions assessing the costs and benefits and opting for self-insurance) or may reflect a free-rider problem, if non-members of the group can capture some of the benefits of increased public perception of bank safety. Mutual support schemes require cooperative behaviour among participants, encouraging cartel-type arrangements regarding pricing and other aspects of behaviour (as has happened in Hong Kong, which does not have a central bank and has had regular runs on banks). Another problem is the danger that membership of the club may be barred to newcomers and thus be used as an industry entry barrier. Supervision by some regulatory body seems desirable to prevent such practices.

Speed is of the essence when arranging rescue groups. Naturally, each potential member will prefer to minimise its role and exposure to risk. If the institution being rescued is judged to be insolvent, the rescuers will be unwilling to provide full recompense, out of their own pockets, to depositors. If the issue is primarily one of illiquidity, withdrawals from the institution at risk are likely to turn up as deposits at the rescuing institutions. Then, loans from the latter to the former can offset the crisis. Yet, should the rescue fail, the loans expose the rescuers to loss. To go on lending may ensure the safety of pre-existing loans (but may not), while to deny a further loan will most likely result in default on the existing ones. The incentive to opt out of the rescue team if one is not concerned about contagion is fairly clear. These difficulties point to the need for a team leader, able to exert moral authority over chisellers and capable of making the snap judgements needed in such circumstances. A central bank seems ideally suited for this role. It may be noted that, after the panic of 1907 in the United States, bankers perceived the need for a bankers' bank to assume the liquidity support operations performed by the loan committee of the New York Clearing House. From these plans resulted the Federal Reserve System, created in 1913.

Industry-based deposit insurance schemes also face a number of problems. One is 'adverse selection', where those who are good risks self-insure and only the poor risks remain in the scheme. The effect of this on premia and the viability of the scheme can be significant. Second, the problem of assessing relative risks, benefits and contributions to be made by institutions of varying size is considerable. Contributions made by a large institution may easily cover the failure of a small one, but the latter's contributions may add virtually nothing to the coverage of the former. Setting a premium structure which entices all potential contributors to join is a well-known problem of voluntary insurance schemes.

The third problem of an industry-based deposit insurance scheme is perhaps the greatest and reflects the difficulties involved in setting premia. Insuring against complete industry-wide failure is impossible, and practical considerations like the maximum viable premia rates to attract members imply that the insurance scheme will be able to cover a certain level of risk, but no more. Thus the insurance scheme itself is open to failure if a claim exceeds its net worth, necessitating an additional layer of confidence. This was the experience of the Ohio Deposit Guarantee Fund for savings associations in 1985.

Although the Ohio savings and loan insurance scheme was state government rather than privately run, the problems encountered are instructive. Briefly, a largish member of the industry (Home State Savings Bank) failed, and the claim upon the insurance scheme was sufficient to deplete the fund's reserves and leave it without immediate resources to protect other industry members. A run upon other members then occurred, because of the perceived reduction in the safety of their deposit liabilities, which led to a mandatory 3-day 'banking holiday' for all Ohio insured savings institutions, and the transfer of responsibility for insurance to federal authorities.[15]

Questions have been raised about the adequacy of even federal deposit insurance in the USA. The $4.5 billion provided by the Federal Deposit Insurance Corporation to rescue Continental Illinois Bank represented 27 per cent of its funds. While insured depositors are backed by the 'full faith and credit of the United States', this Congressional support does not necessarily flow onto uninsured depositors.

(c) Reforming Banking

Bank runs arise because banks issue call or very short-term deposit liabilities, guaranteed at par value, against an illiquid and risky asset portfolio. Were the nature of bank activities or bank contracts to change, the problem of runs might disappear. Several suggestions to reform banking along those lines can be, and have been, made. These proposals involve government initiative. Whether such changes would emerge naturally if governments removed the existing regulatory structure is a question not discussed here in detail — but we doubt that they would.

One possibility recently canvassed by Tobin (1985), but most popularly associated with Friedman (1960) and with a lineage dating back to Chicago economists in the 1930s (see Hart 1935), is that of requiring banks to hold 100 per cent cash reserves. Such an approach would quite clearly remove the problem by making banks run-proof, but at the risk of discarding the baby with the bathwater, for banks would be precluded from engaging in intermediation and would need to rely on safe-keeping and the provision of transactions services to attract deposits. Tobin admits the possibility of firms undertaking both activities separately (with the hypothecation of specific assets to honouring means of payments accounts), but the implications of such a proposal are still wide-ranging. For example, they involve the possibility of marked changes in the role of monetary policy. Also, any efficiency gains which come from jointly producing payments and intermediation services are eschewed.

An alternative possibility comes under a number of descriptions: 'mutual fund banking', 'unit trust banking' or 'marking deposits to market' (Giddy 1985; Kareken 1986; McCulloch 1986). Basically, the idea is that banks operate as mutual funds, valuing and redeeming deposits according to the current market value of their asset portfolio (which could be more or less than face value). Were this feasible, it is argued, the source of bank runs would be removed.

In order to assess the merits of such a suggestion, it is instructive to contrast it with 100 per cent reserve banking. The latter (100 per cent reserves) involves a separation of the means of payment function from the function of intermediation, but keeps the means of payment and medium of account functions together. The alternative (mutual funds) approach separates the means of payment and medium of account functions (since transactions balances have a floating exchange value in terms of cash), but apparently does not preclude combining payments and intermediation activities. In practice, however, a separation of payments from traditional intermediation activities is largely implied. For mutual funds accounts to be acceptable as transactions accounts, relatively low price variability is likely to be required (see Chapter 6). To ensure little price variability, backing in the form of liquid marketable assets must be held, in sharp contrast to traditional bank advances to individuals and firms for which no deep secondary markets exist. In this sense, the mutual funds payments account approach has a similar consequence to that of the 100 per cent reserves approach. Indeed, if money market mutual funds provide the appropriate model for mutual fund banking, they are equivalent to 100 per cent reserve banking, but with reserves held in Treasury bills or notes rather than as cash.

While mutual fund-type arrangements have grown markedly in popularity (see Chapter 2), they are not a suitable form of intermediation in all circumstances. Where overcoming imperfect information is a crucial part of the intermediary's role, and proprietary information prevents 'marketisation' of the asset portfolio, deposit-style contracts appear to be the likely outcome of the intermediation process. Because of this, and the economies of combining payments and intermediation services, it is not clear that an unregulated financial sector would lead to a payments system based on mutual fund accounts.

Nor are we convinced that mutual fund banking would render the industry truly invulnerable to runs, as is argued by its proponents:

> There is nothing strange in a bank promising to pay what it may not be able to pay. Save only for the Treasury, all issuers of fixed-coupon obligations do that; and lenders are willing to accept the gambles, implicit in such obligations . . .
>
> If the owner of a transactions account balance can never get more than a proportionate share of his bank's assets, then he (or she) has no incentive to ever be, as it were, first in line. Whether the owner of such a balance converts to currency is thus independent of what he expects other owners will do. So the probability of a bank run is zero. (Kareken 1986, p.41)

> Traditionally, transaction deposits are denominated as a fixed number of currency units, while the assets corresponding to these deposits are mostly finite-term securities or commercial loans . . . if there is a run on the banking system as a whole, the banks' scramble for funds could conceivably drive interest rates up and asset prices down to the point at which the banks are actually insolvent simply because of depositor fears that they might fail . . .
>
> . . . the money market mutual fund (MMMF) is a recent market innovation that completely solves this inherent instability problem of the payments system. . . . MMMFs, like all mutual funds, are run proof since their obligations to their investors are simply pro rata shares in the current market value of the fund's portfolio. To the extent that depositors/investors line up at the front door to take their money out, the rate of return to depositing new funds will increase, and new depositors/investors will line up at the back door to put their money in. (McCulloch 1986)

For mutual funds comprising short-term, low-risk assets like Treasury bills, there are clear limits to the downside risk. When the portfolios are long-term assets, or there are large amounts of assets like commercial paper for which secondary markets do not exist, an incentive to 'beat the market' in the face of an expected price decline would seem to remain. Thus, so long as maturity transformation and liquidity production are undertaken, the risk of runs would remain. Only when unit holders are sure that the pattern of asset dispositions which follow withdrawals cannot reduce the per unit value of the remaining asset portfolio will there be no incentive to join in the withdrawals. Strict limits on asset portfolio composition and divestment policies are thus required, and there is no guarantee that these would emerge voluntarily.

The possibility that legislation be passed to require transactions accounts to operate like mutual funds is not one we consider seriously. The points outlined above, and also in Chapter 6, suggest that the alternatives prevail. Moreover, in the present context (as is also the case with 100 per cent reserve banking) the problems of runs and crises extends beyond transactions accounts. The run on Continental Illinois Bank began with holders of short-term time deposits, not holders of transactions accounts. Nevertheless, a greater significance, and perhaps greater vulnerability, may attach to failure of participants in the payments system, if only because of the very high turnover of many cheque accounts.

(d) Prudential Supervision and Regulation

The first type of government-based approach we consider is that found in varying forms in the UK,[16] Australia and other countries. A complex net of formal regulations and informal arrangements exists which is designed to prevent bank failure and, if necessary, pick up the pieces.

These schemes have a number of common features. First, bank activities are constrained to prevent an excessive risk of insolvency (for example, banks are precluded from investing in certain assets, like shares). Second, minimum liquidity constraints are imposed. Third, lender-of-last-resort facilities are available from the central bank to meet liquidity crises. Fourth, entry into banking is subject to licensing requirements, with the aim of excluding improper entrants. Fifth, banks' deposit liabilities are either formally guaranteed or, as is more usual, public perception that this is so is not vigorously disabused. Finally, problems surrounding the viability of any bank are handled in *ad hoc* ways depending on the magnitude and source of the problem: official takeover and replacement of management, arrangement of a takeover, implicit subsidy via low interest loans, are all possible measures.

The problems associated with such schemes are well known. Large amounts of resources are tied up in bank supervision — examining, reporting, and so on — although at least some of these replace private sector expenditures on monitoring bank status. Regulation may stymie competition and initiative between banks and the guarantee of safety may enable inefficient institutions to survive. Supervisors may be no better at foreseeing particular risks than individual bankers, as appears to have been the case with the international debt crisis at the start of the 1980s. Accordingly, the regulators become to some extent 'captured' by their tacit consent to the activities.

A fourth problem warrants greater elaboration. Schemes to protect depositors necessarily confer benefits upon both depositors and the owners of institutions whose claims are guaranteed. Central banks argue that they protect depositors, not banks, but the fact remains that the institutions are able to attract deposits at a cost lower than that faced by otherwise comparable but 'risky' institutions. Competition between the guaranteed institutions may cause some of these benefits to be passed on to customers, but bank owners seem likely to reap some of the gains by virtue of the competitive advantage over those institutions not covered by the scheme.

In principle, governments could impose charges upon the guaranteed institutions sufficient to just offset these benefits. But this is not enough. Because schemes to protect depositors reduce the risk of contagion, they have an element of public good provision about them. That is, the total cost of running the scheme is less than the aggregate benefits endowed upon participants. Again, an appropriate set of charges could expropriate the benefits conferred on owners, but determining and charging the appropriate levy is a task which is rarely undertaken. What has eventuated is a set of implicit charges by way of regulations specific to guaranteed institutions, which have the effect of somewhat reducing their competitive advantage. Rarely have either banks or their non-guaranteed competitors regarded the outcome as a 'fair' one.

(e) Deposit Insurance

In previous chapters we have found it helpful to regard the deposit, loan and off-balance sheet business of banks as forms of insurance, with banks writing what are essentially insurance contracts of various types with their customers. Continuing this analogy, schemes to protect depositors can be viewed as forms of reinsurance. When that protection takes the form of deposit insurance, the reinsurance is readily apparent.

Banks' insurance of customers' liquidity needs, we have noted, has a special characteristic in that confidence, as well as the natural hazards of life, governs the firms' exposure. Pooling of deposit withdrawals can work only if one depositor's decision to withdraw deposits is largely independent of the decision made by others, and that is the case only so long as depositors are fully confident that their cash needs will be met.

'Reinsurance' of deposits with government-sponsored insurance funds also has a special feature. Unlike conventional insurance, the main aim is not so much to recompense people after the loss of deposits, but to maintain confidence in banks so that they can continue with their 'normal' business. As such, deposit insurance is more akin to a guarantee, similar to what banks themselves issue to their customers in the form of standby letters of credit (see Chapter 4, section 5).

These differences suggest some caution in arguing by way of analogy with conventional forms of insurance. Nevertheless, there are some useful parallels which can be drawn in terms of the 'actuarial fairness' of premia and 'moral hazard'.

Since deposit insurance schemes involve explicit payments by participants in the form of insurance premia, they may avoid some of the problems of unfair competition associated with the schemes discussed in the previous section, which guarantee banks but levy only implicit premia in the form of prudential regulation. Insurance premia set to cover expected payouts may seem to be 'actuarially fair', but the public good aspect of the lowered risks of contagion means that actuarial calculations do not match the aggregate of benefits. However, as long as membership of the insurance fund is open to competing institutions, this economic benefit is not a major problem.

Greater problems arise from the existence of moral hazard, which is common to most forms of insurance. In standard types of insurance, the problem of moral hazard is handled in a number of ways:

1. **Premia varied in relation to risk** — for example, no-claim discounts for 'safe' drivers, and higher health insurance rates for smokers.
2. **Limiting coverage** — the insured bears some part of the claim loss, as is frequently incorporated in medical, liability and property insurance.
3. **Coinsurance or partial insurance** — the risk is shared with other parties, as is common in marine, property and some other types of insurance.
4. **Risk reduction activities** — monitoring and imposing bounds upon behaviour so as to reduce the frequency or severity of loss, as, for example, insurers requiring the installation of fire protection equipment and the use of safety equipment by workers.

These all have their analogues in deposit insurance, and appear either in actual schemes or in proposed revisions to US deposit insurance, canvassed by the Working Group of the Cabinet Council on Economic Affairs (1985) and by a number of authors in special issues of the *Journal of Business* (January 1986) and the *Journal of Banking and Finance* (June 1986).

Variable Rate Premia An insurer charging the same premium rates for compulsory health insurance would bring about a redistribution from the healthy to the sick, and provide little incentive for individuals to adopt 'healthy' habits. Critics of the current fixed rate assessment for US federal deposit insurance ($\frac{1}{12}$ of 1 per cent of total domestic deposits, with a subsequent rebate) argue that much the same effects can be observed in US banking. Healthy banks are bearing the cost of the depletion of the insurance funds — described colourfully by one writer (Ely 1985) as 'the cross-subsidisation of crap shooters by sound, prudent bankers'. There are few disincentives to risk taking. Individual taxpayers bear too little of the cost of bail-outs to monitor bank risk. Depositors merely need to ascertain whether or not they are insured to feel safe and, along with shareholders, benefit from greater risk taking. Constant premium rates, it is said, enable bank owners (with depositors' connivance) to play 'heads the bank wins, tails the insurance agency loses' (Benston and Kaufman 1986). Such an assessment, we note below, is a little simplistic, but certainly a consensus seems to be emerging within the USA in favour of some move towards the levying of risk-related insurance premia as a way of altering the incentive structure.

There is less consensus, however, on how to summarise banking risk in terms of an objective measure which would form the basis for risk assessment.[17] Use of regulatory CAMEL ratings would likely strain the relationship between banker and examiner and make bankers less willing to provide confidential and sensitive information. CAMEL is the check list used in the USA by federal bank examiners, namely, capital adequacy, asset quality, management quality, earnings, and liquidity, with each component rated on a scale from 1 ('strong') to 5 ('unsatisfactory'). A major difficulty is that of objectively scaling management quality, and especially the ability of credit officers, by careful or unwise selection of loans, to alter the inherent riskiness of an asset portfolio.

In a system comprising 20,000 banks and savings institutions subject to government insurance, the criteria used would need to be spelt out clearly and objectively. CAMEL ratings, for example, are subjective, and this means that premia based on them would not be determined uniformly. But there are hazards with objective criteria if the insurer's method of risk determination is known to participants. The existence of political and administrative costs makes it unlikely that the criteria would be revised frequently. Consequently, the effect of penalising the taking of risks by banks into known, identified avenues of riskiness may be to encourage them to seek out newer, and thus relatively underpriced, areas of risk (Goodman and Shaffer 1983). This substitution process is readily observable in the potentially more flexible application of prudential supervision.

It seems unlikely, in practice, that the higher premia levied upon 'riskier' institutions would be large enough fully to discourage risk taking in the identified areas, in which case the possible side effects assume greater significance. Amongst the 'problem' banks will be some endeavouring to reconstruct themselves after experiencing temporary difficulties, due perhaps to the ups and downs of the business cycle. Application of higher insurance premia will merely add to those difficulties, and increase the chance of insolvency, without altering behaviour. Proposals to publish the insurance 'listings' would merely make insolvency more certain, counteracting to some extent one of the major objectives of deposit insurance — that of macroeconomic and financial stability.[18]

Limited Coverage Upper limits on coverage, or partial coverage, in ordinary insurance both limit the potential losses of the insurer and, by enforcing a degree of self-insurance, encourage better monitoring by those insured of the cost and frequency of claims. Deposits in the USA are insured fully up to $100,000. By contrast, in the UK, deposits are 75 per cent insured up to a maximum value of deposits of £10,000. Depositors in the UK should react to the possibility of this 'haircut' by monitoring more carefully the riskiness of banking institutions, as compared with their US counterparts. In practice, the lower *de jure* coverage merely increases the extent of the *de facto* insurance. There would be a public outrage if the Bank of England allowed one of the *major* banks or depository institutions to fail (whether there would be in the case of a minor institution is less clear). Most customers and staff of the major clearing banks, we contend, are unaware even of the existence of a deposit insurance fund, let alone its limited coverage. The perception of the general public is that banks are made 'safe' by the Bank of England, and any attempt to shake that faith would lead to greater financial instability.

Admittedly, the unstated premise of *de facto* insurance in the UK is less secure in the case of large, wholesale depositors who deal with the smaller specialised banking firms, but whenever the insurance coverage has been put to the test, as in 1974 and 1984, the Bank of England has come to the party despite avowals that matters will be different next time. Pressure of events in the USA, as well, has seen the extension of *de facto* insurance to uninsured depositors, even though there is an active market 'brokering' large deposits into insured ($100,000) lots for retail customers. Proposals to impose a limited 'haircut' on uninsured depositors, as a way of instilling a market discipline upon bankers, seem unlikely to alter this situation. Uninsured depositors would merely 'run' earlier and thereby induce compensating implicit guarantees from the authorities.

Coinsurance Coinsurance is a risk-sharing device, designed also to alter the incentive structure. In the context of deposit insurance, coinsurance can take on a variety of forms. Higher capital ratios, in particular, are seen as shielding deposits, and thus insurance funds, from the effects of bank insolvency, and at the same time inducing equityholders to observe and discipline risk taking by management. Ratios of equity capital to total bank assets have generally declined in both the UK and the US during this century (see Table 5.1). Bank regulators in a number of countries have moved in recent years to raise capital ratios maintained by banks. US regulators currently require all banks to maintain a minimum level of primary capital to total assets of 5.5 per cent, and a minimum level of total capital to assets of 6 per cent.[19] But the Cabinet Office Working Party suggested that levels of 8 to 10 per cent might be more appropriate.

In some eyes, this emphasis upon capital is misplaced:

> Recent history shows that illiquidity rather than lack of capital *per se* is a primary cause of a bank's economic insolvency. (Crouhy and Galai 1986)

And there is the conclusion of the President of the Federal Reserve Bank of Cleveland in the wake of the Ohio savings and loan crisis of 1985:

> My most lasting impression of the crisis is how quickly depositors' confidence plummeted at the privately insured institutions. The Federal Reserve Bank and commercial banks shipped currency to institutions that were experiencing heavy withdrawals, but cash alone was not enough to restore confidence. The further public confidence fell, the more difficult the problem became to solve. Without depositors' confidence, even the best-capitalised financial institution can be severely affected. (Federal Reserve Bank of Cleveland Annual Report 1985)

At best, the protection afforded by capital is to some extent illusory. Additional capital can protect deposits from loss only if it is held in 'safe' assets (and there is no fraud). In fact, capital is distributed across the asset portfolio. Algebraically, capital is the difference between the market value of assets and the value of deposit (and other) liabilities. Since depositors are promised repayment in fixed nominal sums, loan losses and other declines in

Table 5.1 Equity Capital to Total Assets Ratios of UK and US Banks, 1880–1985

	*UK banks**	*US banks†*
1880	16.8	n.a.
1900	12.0	n.a.
1914	8.7	18.3
1930	7.2	14.2
1940	5.2	9.1
1950	2.7	6.7
1966	5.3	7.8
1980	5.9	6.8
1985	4.6	6.9

Source: as for Tables 1.1 and 1.2.
Notes: *UK deposit banks 1880–1966; UK clearing bank groups, 1980 and 1985.
†All member banks.

the market value of assets are reflected dollar for dollar or pound for pound in a reduced value of capital. In this respect, 'equity is therefore not a shield for depositors, but rather a reflection of the status and economic situation of the bank' (Crouhy and Galai 1986).

Whether 5, 10 or 50 per cent capital ratios are appropriate cannot be ascertained *a priori*; it depends upon the nature of the asset portfolio — in particular, its distribution across asset types and the nature of loan risks. This is the rationale for risk-related *capital adequacy requirements*, which are guidelines used by regulators to assess an institution's capital holdings against the risks of its asset and liability structure.

The Bank of England moved to such a risk–asset capital ratio assessment in 1980 with assets ranked according to risk on a scale from 0 to 2.0. The measure includes a weighting for certain contingent liabilities, since widened to include note issuance facilities in 1985 and a higher weighting for non-bank acceptances in 1983.[20] Use of risk-related capital ratios in the United States dates back to the 1950s with the formula developed by the Federal Reserve Bank of New York (the 'New York Formula') and the Form for Analyzing Bank Capital (Form 'ABC') of the Board of Governors of the Federal Reserve System. However, US regulatory authorities shifted away from the risk–asset capital ratio approach in 1981 when the focus switched to minimum ratios of capital to assets. The federal regulatory agencies have since looked to return to risk-related capital guidelines, partly because of the growth of off-balance sheet risk exposures by banks to avoid the current minimum capital requirements.[21] It hardly needs to be said that the weights used in the risk-related adequacy approach are arbitrary, and that there can be, and are, substantial differences in the risk characteristics of assets within particular categories accorded equal risk weighting.

Increasingly, banks are being allowed to augment equity capital by including loan stock in the form of *subordinated debt* as a part of total capital. At the end of 1985, UK clearing bank groups had loan stock amounting to 3.3 per cent of total assets, bringing total capital resources (equity plus loan stock) to 7.9 per cent of total assets. This debt is long-term, invariably with an initial maturity in excess of five years and occasionally irredeemable and, in the case of UK banks, issued in a variety of currencies, such as sterling, US dollars, Deutschmarks and Swiss francs.[22] The subordinate status means that the claims of holders are secondary to those of depositors and creditors. In the event of losses by the bank, the claims of depositors remain secure until those of equityholders and debtholders are fully written off to meet the losses. Issuing the loan stock in currencies other than that used for equity claims is designed to enable the banks, albeit in a limited way, to gear capital backing to the currency composition of deposits, thus providing holders of foreign currency deposits with a buffer against variations in exchange rates which might widen the gap between the value of deposit claims in one currency and equity capital in another (Wesson 1985).

As well as providing, in these ways, an additional cushion for deposits, both in domestic and foreign currencies, subordinated debt is seen as a way of exerting market discipline upon banks. In contrast to deposits, the claims are long-term and cannot be withdrawn at short notice. Unlike equityholders, holders of the debt do not share in the 'upside' gains from increased risk, but are concerned with the institutions' ability to service the debt. They are thus seen to be a conservative influence upon management. Against these advantages, however, must be set the greater risk which comes when a bank has extra leverage and more contractual interest rate commitments. Unless subordinated debt is refinanced at regular intervals, the market discipline seems at best indirect. More frequent refloating of subordinated debt makes it closer to uninsured deposits, with attendant risks of financial instability.

One form of risk sharing comes from the costs imposed upon bank management by bank failure. Government takeover or reconstruction normally results in existing top management losing its jobs and other staff being tainted in terms of future employment prospects. This is why it is incorrect to say that present arrangements provide no disincentives to risk taking. Again, this effect can cut both ways, since management of a troubled bank facing certain job loss may be inclined to 'roll the dice'. Commenting on developments in the 1980s, the Chairman of the Board of Governors of the Federal Reserve System observed:

> From the standpoint of managers or owners, the chance of failure of the institution was already large, and should sizeable losses rather than gains materialise, depositors would, in any event, be protected, in whole or in part, by deposit insurance. (Volcker 1985)

Monitoring Behaviour As in conventional insurance, insurers of deposits have a stake in ensuring that the behaviour of the insured institutions does not add to the insurance risks. Given the difficulties inherent in altering institutional behaviour by means of risk-sensitive premia, by limiting coverage and by coinsurance, it is hardly surprising to find that those countries which have introduced deposit insurance schemes have much the same paraphernalia of regulatory controls as other countries. Capital adequacy requirements, minimum liquidity ratios, maximum foreign exchange exposure positions, 'risky-asset' limits are common to a number of banking systems. Supervision remains necessary under deposit insurance to prevent (or try to prevent) fraudulent behaviour and to ensure that insured institutions abide by the terms of the 'reinsurance contract' as regards the taking of risks. The insurance levy is simply a way of charging for this public 'service'.

Looked at from an alternative angle, regulatory interference by the insurer can be regarded as a risk-related scale of *implicit* insurance premia, as outlined by Buser, Chen and Kane (1981). Focusing upon the choice between deposits and bank equity they argue that, for a given scale of activities (assets), the optimal deposit level of an uninsured bank involves balancing the benefits of leverage against the costs of bankruptcy. When interest payments are tax-deductible, banks can gain tax savings by substituting debt for equity in their liabilities structure. But as deposits increase, so do the expected costs of bankruptcy; beyond some point, the value of the bank is reduced. In Figure 5.1, the value of the uninsured bank for varying deposit levels (and thus deposits/equity ratios) is indicated by V and the value-maximising level of bank deposits by D^o, entailing (presumably) some probability of

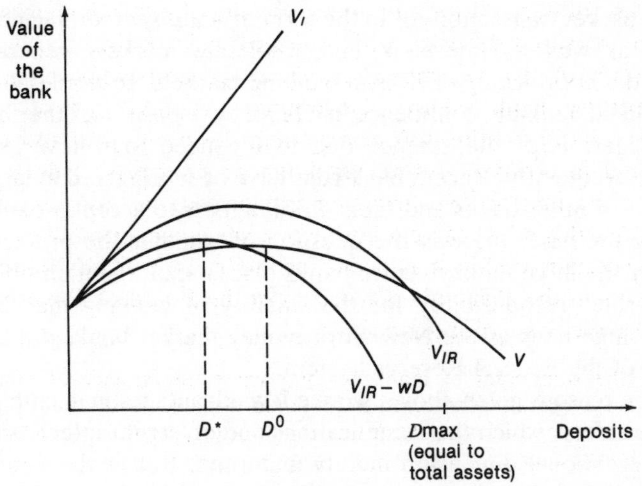

Figure 5.1 The Bank Capital Decision (Buser, Chen and Kane 1981)

bankruptcy. Deposit insurance, by offsetting the effect of bankruptcy costs, leads to the value of the bank increasing with the level of deposits, as indicated by V_I, and encouraging (in the absence of risk-related insurance charges) a tendency to a zero equity position and high default probabilities. However, where regulatory interference per dollar of deposits increases with the level of balance-sheet riskiness, and thus imposes administrative costs upon the bank, the value of the bank will be depicted by a curve such as V_{IR}. If, further, a flat-rate insurance premium of w per dollar of deposits is charged, $V_{IR} - wD$ will represent the value of the bank, leading to an optimal balance sheet structure at deposit level D^*. Of course, the problem for the insuring agency is to find the appropriate forms and level of regulatory interference and flat-rate premia which, in the absence of explicit risk-related charges, yield the preferred outcome at least social cost. To this end, the prescribing of capital adequacy ratios, satisfaction of which keeps regulatory interference at lower levels, has some obvious merits.

In general, deposit insurance schemes seem likely to operate best when there are many contributing banks, of relatively equal significance, so as to achieve the desired pooling of risks. Where there is only a handful of large multi-branch banks, the system is less appropriate. When the banking industry ranges between 'giants' and 'tiddlers' which may have vastly different inherent riskiness, it is difficult to levy insurance contributions which are both actuarially appropriate and perceived as fair by the participants.

This unfairness is accentuated when certain banks, by virtue of their role in the financial system, are 'too big to be allowed to fail'. In the USA, these are the large money centre banks with extensive wholesale and international books, which lead-manage loan syndicates for correspondents, and which have large off-balance sheet exposures with other banks, either as counterparties in market transactions or in the form of standby credit facilities. These activities, as well as interbank and wholesale markets generally, have increased the interlocking of risks in banking markets. In wholesale banking, as indeed in all banking, confidence in a bank by depositors, other banks, and fund managers is of the essence due to the need to rollover short-term borrowings frequently. Recent bank runs have been triggered in large part by the distrust of other banks and their unwillingness to accept a bank's paper. This being the case, there is the question of whether the protected status enjoyed by the large money centre banks places upon them an obligation to assume greater responsibility for the stability of banking markets, acting along the same lines as the New York money market banks did before the formation of the Federal Reserve System.

For the reasons given above, we see few advantages in a 'club' approach to banking safety, which the complications and divergent interests presented by the international dimension merely underline. But at the same time we appreciate that explicit deposit insurance schemes of the type which operates in the USA lose much of their appeal if failures of large banks are not countenanced by regulatory authorities. This, as we have said, appears to be the case in the UK where (at least as far as the large clearing banks are involved) the explicit insurance of small deposits is largely unnecessary, since all depositors (we suggest) view their deposits as being *de facto* government guaranteed. Extending explicit insurance to all deposits, levying an insurance surcharge on large institutions, requiring divestment into smaller institutions — these are among the options which have been canvassed to get around the difficulties presented by large banks and large depositors,[23] but each seems unsatisfactory on either equity or efficiency grounds. Ultimately, regulation and supervision on a significant scale seem a necessary concomitant to prevention of financial crises.

(f) Off-Balance Sheet Activities and Risk Measurement

Any attempt to set deposit insurance premia or capital adequacy standards which reflect the 'riskiness' of bank activities is going to encounter difficulties. The information asymmetries which induce much of banking intermediation mean that outsiders have at best imperfect knowledge of the specific risks of any one bank's business. General rules can be developed drawing upon observable indicators of risk exposure (such as the distribution of the asset portfolio across types of borrowers, maturity mismatching, liquidity ratios, etc.) and less objective factors (such as the banks' earnings record, demonstrated management capability, etc.), but the correlation of such indicators with individual bank risk exposure is bound to be less than perfect.

More generally, the use of information about particular bank activities to impose charges or capital requirements on banks can be expected to encourage them to look to other non-monitored activities in order to weaken the force of the imposts. Such regulatory avoidance behaviour provides part of the explanation for the growth of off-balance sheet activities of banks (but only part), and these activities have created even greater problems for bank supervisors attempting to measure banks' risk exposure.

One difficulty created by off-balance sheet activities stems from their relative novelty and thus the absence of an historical record against which to judge the risk exposure involved. Even where an historical experience exists, market practices can alter. Standby letters of credit which take the form of performance bonds are rarely called upon, suggesting that they involve a limited risk exposure. However, until now their use has apparently been mainly restricted to businesses of high credit standing, making past experience a limited guide to future riskiness as such practices become more widespread. Not only are the individual risks of particular activities open to question, but their correlations with returns on traditional activities, and thus contribution to overall portfolio risk, are not well established. A second difficulty arises from deficiencies in accounting information provided on off-balance sheet activities under current conventions and regulations.

Regulators have not ignored, but also have not solved, these problems. For example, contingent claims feature in the statistical returns which the Bank of England requires for examining UK banks' liquidity position and capital adequacy. These returns formed the basis for the examination of the maturity profile of bank assets and liabilities which was provided in Chapter 4. Use of this information for the assessment of liquidity needs is based on the maturity ladder approach referred to in Chapter 3. Each bank forecasts cash flows in various maturity bands (the two key bands being of 0 to 7 days, and 8 days to 1 month), taking into account not only the likely rundown of deposits and assets, but also the use made of commitments to make loans and financing options available to the bank, such as standby lines of credit.[24] We have noted already that the Bank of England's evaluation of a bank's capital adequacy, involving the calculation of a risk-related capital-to-assets ratio, includes certain contingent liabilities in the formula.

An international committee of central banks and bank supervisors met in 1985 under the chairmanship of Mr Sam Cross of the Federal Reserve Bank of New York (the Cross Report)[25] to attempt to elaborate the risks of various off-balance sheet activities. Such was the importance accorded to the exercise, despite the difficulties involved, that the Bank of England and the US federal regulatory agencies (the Board of Governors of the Federal Reserve, the Office of the Comptroller of the Currency, and the FDIC) later met and were able to agree, in January 1987, upon a joint approach to the assessment of capital adequacy embracing off-balance sheet risks: the so-called 'convergence accord'.[26]

Their proposal is similar in many respects to that currently in use in the UK and to the framework which the US regulatory authorities had themselves agreed upon early in 1986. Thus the accord is in terms of a risk-related approach in which it is proposed that credit risk be measured by means of a hierarchy of risk weights, classified, broadly, according to the nature of the obligor and the maturity of the claim. Both on- and off-balance sheet risks are to be captured. It is intended to calculate for each bank a ratio of primary capital to total risk weighted 'assets', with a common minimum ratio to be published and to apply in both countries. A minimum level may be set for each institution, but this would be confidential. There are five risk weight categories proposed: 0%, 10%, 25%, 50%, and 100%, so that the old UK weights of 150% and 200% no longer apply. Banks' holdings of short-term and long-term domestic government securities are given risk weights of 10 and 25 per cent respectively, reflecting not that these claims have credit risk, but that banks may have an interest rate exposure when holding them. This is, by admission, a crude measure, and there is evidence of arbitrariness when the risk weighting is extended to the off-balance sheet items.

A wide range of off-balance sheet items is included, covering acceptances, standby letters of credit, guarantees, commercial letters of credit, asset sales with recourse, interest rate and currency swaps, foreign exchange and options contracts. Capital backing under the proposals would be needed to cover the 'credit equivalent amount'. This is calculated by first determining the value of the contract, based on what it would be worth if sold, and then making an estimate of the potential future credit exposure by applying an arbitrary conversion factor. To illustrate, commercial letters of credit and performance bonds are judged to be of a lesser risk than acceptances and credit-related standby letters of credit, and so have a credit conversion factor of 50 per cent, as compared with 100 per cent on the latter. Thus the deemed credit risk equivalent of a commercial letter of credit of $10 million would be $5 million which in turn would be weighted according to obligor and in some cases maturity, and added along with the assets to the denominator of the risk ratio measure. Measurement of credit exposures on interest rate and currency swaps poses special problems because the potential credit risks involved depend upon the juxtaposition of interest rates and exchange rates over time, and differ for a portfolio of swaps in comparison with individual deals. The treatment of swaps was the subject of a supplementary proposal issued in March 1987.[27]

Despite the difficulties inherent in the exercise, the Bank of England and the US supervisory authorities intend to introduce the new system later in 1987 after a period of consultation with banks and other interested parties. The initiative is not intended to be simply an Anglo-American accord, and the proponents hope that it will give a lead towards the international harmonisation of bank prudential regulation (see Chapter 11 below).

Conclusion

The worldwide deregulation of banking markets, combined with concerns arising from the international debt crisis, has brought the issue of bank safety into the forefront of recent discussion. Insurance schemes, of the American kind, have (in part) turned out to be a fiction as the authorities have proved unwilling to let even uninsured depositors absorb losses. The rescue of Continental Illinois is a case in point. Moreover, the experience of the 1980s indicates how much supervision and regulation would be necessary to prevent bank failure.

The difficulty confronting regulatory authorities is essentially that some part of the monetary system (especially that related to the payment system) needs to be made run-proof, while at the same time scope is allowed for appropriate risk taking in other areas. Deciding on an appropriate division may be possible, but the spread of institutions across the whole spectrum of activities creates practical difficulties for any attempt at segmentation. In following chapters, we shall examine some of the implications of widened entry to the payments system, and of the diversification of banks into 'non-banking' activities.

Notes

1. Friedman and Schwartz (1963), p.351.
2. See Spero (1980).
3. Reid (1982) gives details of this experience.
4. Working Group of the Cabinet Council on Economic Affairs (1985).
5. Swary (1985).
6. Saunders (1986).
7. Swary (1985).
8. See McCarthy (1980).
9. The regulatory structure in the United States is examined by Carron (1984). See also Board of Governors of the Federal Reserve System (1984).
10. It is worth noting, for future reference, that such deposit outflows create an unequal distribution of risk between early deposit withdrawers and late withdrawers.
11. This ratio will also influence the likely size of deposit outflows relative to the total portfolio size and thus the optimal ratio of reserves to assets.
12. We assume that bankruptcy costs, taxes and other market imperfections do not make the deposit/equity ratio a matter of indifference to bank owners. At some point increases in D/E start to reduce the expected gains to bank owners.
13. An emphasis in studies of consumption behaviour has been put upon the role of liquidity constraints to explain apparent anomalies in consumption behaviour relative to the predictions of life cycle theories.
14. For some cooperative financial institutions (e.g. credit unions in Australia), share liabilities need not be available on demand, but normally are and are marketed as being so.
15. Federal Reserve Bank of Cleveland Annual Report, 1985.
16. Although the UK has a deposit insurance scheme, its coverage is relatively slight and, we argue, the approach taken to depositor safety places much greater emphasis upon prudential supervision etc. than upon the characteristics of the insurance scheme.
17. Hirschhorn (1986) and Murton (1986) survey the literature and issues concerning risk-related insurance schemes.
18. In terms of macroeconomic stability, Goodman and Santomero (1986) argue that risk-related premia would rise in recessions, leading to a procyclical contraction of bank lending.
19. Primary capital consists of common stock, perpetual preferred stock, surplus, undistributed profits, contingency and other capital reserves, mandatory convertible instruments, loan loss reserves, and minority interest in equity accounts of subsidiaries less goodwill. Secondary capital, which is included in total capital, includes limited-life preferred stock, bank-subordinated notes and debentures, and unsecured long-term debt of the parent company and nonbank subsidiaries.
20. The Bank of England considers that the gearing ratio, relating liabilities (or deposits) to capital resources, either gross or net of premises and infrastructure, is adequate for public information, but that the risk/asset ratio measure is needed for its prudential supervision. In the current approach, all assets are given an arbitrary risk weighting relative to the value of 1.0 for loans to the UK private sector. Weights range from zero for cash assets to 2.0 for property and property loans. A weighting is also applied to certain contingent liabilities, ranging from a zero weighting for overdrafts, 0.5 for revolving underwriting facilities, through to 1.0 for nonbank acceptances. Capital resources (on a gross basis) are then divided by risk-weighted assets and contingent liabilities to give the risk/asset ratio.
21. The history of capital adequacy arrangements in the USA, and current proposals

for risk-related measures developed by the Board of Governors of the Federal Reserve System, the Office of the Comptroller of the Currency and the FDIC, are examined by Carroll, Kalambokidis, and Kise (1986).

22. For UK banks' loan stock to qualify for inclusion as capital for application of the Bank of England's risk/asset capital ratio, the initial maturity of the debt has to be five years or more. Such loan stock can count as capital resources in the assessment up to a maximum of one third of the capital base net of goodwill.
23. Working Group of the Cabinet Council on Economic Affairs (1985).
24. The Bank's approach is outlined in *The Measurement of Liquidity* (1982). As we observed in earlier chapters, the maturity ladder approach is far from precise, due to the uncertain maturity of deposits and lending commitments. Consequently, a bank must look to its holding of cash and liquid assets and the diversification of its deposit base, as we argued in earlier discussion. For a practical banker's assessment which emphasises these three elements (maturity laddering, cash reserves and deposit diversification), see Close (1987) and Wesson (1985). For a US perspective on these issues, see Stigum and Branch (1983, Chapter 8).
25. BIS (1986).
26. 'Agreed proposal of the United States Federal Banking Supervisory Authorities and the Bank of England on primary capital and capital adequacy assessment', *Bank of England Quarterly Bulletin*, February 1987.
27. Board of Governors of the Federal Reserve System/Bank of England, 'Potential credit exposure on interest rate and foreign exchange-related transactions', March 1987.

6

Payments Services

6.1 Payments Systems

In Chapter 2, we defined banks simply as institutions which combine payments services with intermediation, and suggested reasons why both activities are combined. In the past, there has been a relatively clear-cut division between the operators of non-cash payments services (banks) and other financial institutions (non-bank financial intermediaries, or NFIs). That is no longer the case. Regulatory changes have adapted to the new economic and technological pressures so as to remove many of the legal prohibitions upon the participation of non-banks in clearing systems. In the USA, savings institutions are now allowed to offer transferable deposits, use Federal Reserve clearing facilities, and receive liquidity support via the 'discount window'. Nearly 40,000 institutions in the USA now offer transactions accounts and contribute towards the money supply. In some other countries, such as Australia, prohibitions still remain, but they can be circumvented by agency arrangements. In the UK, building societies offer cheque-writing facilities also by means of cooperative ventures.

Technological change has lowered entry barriers to the provision of payments services, and is also altering the nature of those services as electronic signals become increasingly more efficient *vis-à-vis* paper signals (cheques) as a means of initiating and undertaking the accounting entries which constitute the non-cash payments system. If only for this reason, regulatory change was inevitable, as developments such as electronic funds transfer systems (EFTS) alter the social costs of, and benefits from, regulations. But another influence should be noted. The provision of payments services, along with any special protection afforded transactions balances, gives a competitive advantage to the institutions supplying payments services when they are marketing other financial services. Previously, regulators tried to perform a delicate balancing act whereby constraints upon other activities offset the benefits flowing from restricted access to the payments mechanism. The worldwide trend to allow the providers of payments services to diversify into other forms of intermediation activities carries with it an obligation to re-assess the merits of regulatory barriers to entry to the payments system.

In what follows we shall examine cash and non-cash payments systems before considering some of the issues which are generally raised about entry to the payments system industry and the appropriate regulatory framework.

Cash and Non-Cash Payments Alternatives

Money and banking texts explain how changes in payments systems evolve from barter, through commodity money to fiat money and beyond, with social savings in information and transactions costs and in the freeing up of resources tied up in commodity money. Chapter 2 looked at some of these points and we commence the story here at the later stages of the evolutionary cycle, focusing upon the incentives that the private sector has to replace fiat money partially with other stores of value and means of exchange.[1]

Use of currency as a means of exchange and store of purchasing power involves the user in holding costs (interest foregone, storage costs) and in relatively low costs of effecting transactions. Intermediaries reduce the holdings costs through providing currency storage and dispensing facilities, but this has the effect of raising transactions costs by increasing the number of transactions coming from the withdrawal of cash, the exchange of cash, and the redeposit of cash. The answer is to short-circuit the withdrawal and redeposit of cash by the exchange of claims to cash; for example, by using cheques for payments. Transactions costs are reduced because the costs of effecting and recording the change in ownership of claims is low and the payer can avoid the withdrawal of cash.[2]

For non-cash alternatives to be successful in supplanting cash as the means of payment in certain transactions, a number of conditions must be met. First, the asset exchanged must be acceptable to the recipient as a store of value, or convertible at low cost into a preferred form. If bank deposits are to be used as a means of payment, cooperation among banks is needed to establish a clearing and settlements system so as to minimise convertibility costs and increase acceptability. Second, unlike cash, acquiring a claim to cash involves accepting a risk of default either because the claim offered is fraudulent (the 'dud' cheque) or because the entity upon which the claim is drawn is unable to honour the obligation. Where exchange and settlement of claims does not take place instantaneously, use of non-cash payments instruments thus introduces an element of risk into the exchange and payments process. Some method of limiting this risk is called for if the cash payments system is to be supplemented (at least in part) by non-cash alternatives.

Measures to reduce cost and risk are of benefit to both banks and their customers. White (1984) argues that self-interest by banks in order to keep down costs can lead to the development of an interbank clearing house. But without such facilities the costs and risks involved in realising a claim upon a distant bank would likely be so great as to prevent the widespread use of cheques. In this respect it can be argued, seemingly paradoxically, that cooperation between banks is needed before competition can begin (Hopton 1983). Concern about 'dud' cheques will also limit the cheque habit. One solution is for banks to guarantee the cheques of their customers up to a certain amount, as is done by UK banks for amounts up to £50 for domestic cheques (for bearers of guarantee cards) and up to £100 on Eurocheques, despite the belief of one US commentator (De Vany 1984) that such a system is unworkable.[3] Banks gain from the widened use of cheques, and they also have a 'reputation capital' to maintain, since their standing suffers if their customers write large numbers of bad cheques. There is still the risk of bank failure, and this provides one reason for schemes to prevent bank insolvencies. These again benefit both bank and customer alike.

The two issues of cost and risk are the crucial elements in any non-cash payments system, and account for the continued use of cash for the vast majority of transactions. For Britain, it has been estimated that around 60 billion cash payments are made each year as compared with only 4 billion payments by non-cash means (Bankers Clearing House 1984). Table 6.1 shows that cash payments are estimated to comprise 73 per cent of the numbers of transactions undertaken in the USA in 1983, but less than 2 per cent in terms of value. Whereas the average value of payments made by cheque is estimated to be $910, the average value of transactions made by using cash is $25. Transfers made by electronic means were for very much larger average amounts. The relative importance of the different methods will depend upon the structure of the payments system under consideration. In turn, the structure of payments systems will reflect the influences of technology as well as government intervention and regulation. In order to assess how recent changes in technology are affecting the risk and cost characteristics of payments systems, and to understand more fully the

Table 6.1 Comparison of Payment Methods in the USA, 1983

Method	*Number of transactions (millions)*	*Value of transactions ($ trillions)*	*Value per transaction ($)*
Cash	112,000	2.8	25
Cheques	40,000	36.0	910
Electronic transfers			
via automated clearing houses	400	0.7	1,800
Wire transfers	57	142.0	2,500,000

Source: Humphrey (1984)

rationale for changes in public policy towards the payments system, we shall now examine the characteristics of the major systems.

Characteristics of Non-Cash Payments Systems

A payments system is a mechanism by which (i) ownership of claims is transferred, (ii) conversion of those claims into a preferred form is arranged, and (iii) consequent exchanges of assets are made between the issuers of claims in settlement of debts incurred. For the moment, we shall ignore the question of what type of claims might be transferred and focus upon the nature of the mechanisms and institutional arrangements involved in the transfer and settlement process.

Table 6.2 reveals marked international differences in the relative contribution of various types of non-cash payments. The cheque system dominates in the USA, Canada, France, Italy, Australia (not shown) and, to a lesser extent, in the UK where a giro system run by the Post Office is well established. Amongst the other European countries shown in the table, credit transfers made by means of giro systems play an important role. Japan and West Germany stand out in terms of the importance of electronic fund transfer systems.

These different systems are explained below, but the distinction made in the table between debit and credit transfers needs first to be clarified. A cheque is initiated into the payments system by the creditor and circulates within the clearing system as an order to debit the account of the debtor with the paying bank. It is thus a means of making a debit transfer. By contrast, a

Table 6.2 International Comparison of Non-Cash Payments, 1983 (per cent of number of transactions)

<table>
<tr><th rowspan="2">Country</th><th rowspan="2">Cheques (paper debits)</th><th rowspan="2">Giro (paper credits)</th><th colspan="2">Electronic</th><th rowspan="2">Transactions per inhabitant per year</th></tr>
<tr><th>debit transfers</th><th>credit transfers</th></tr>
<tr><td>Belgium</td><td>47</td><td>41</td><td>5</td><td>7</td><td>34</td></tr>
<tr><td>Canada</td><td>97</td><td>—</td><td>3</td><td>—</td><td>88</td></tr>
<tr><td>France</td><td>84</td><td>2</td><td>6</td><td>8</td><td>86</td></tr>
<tr><td>West Germany</td><td>11</td><td>34</td><td>32</td><td>23</td><td>85</td></tr>
<tr><td>Italy</td><td>86</td><td>10</td><td>1</td><td>3</td><td>13</td></tr>
<tr><td>Japan</td><td>24</td><td>2</td><td>73</td><td>1</td><td>15</td></tr>
<tr><td>Netherlands</td><td>22</td><td>41</td><td>16</td><td>21</td><td>85</td></tr>
<tr><td>Switzerland</td><td>11</td><td>54</td><td>1</td><td>34</td><td>94</td></tr>
<tr><td>United Kingdom</td><td>68</td><td>13</td><td>7</td><td>12</td><td>67</td></tr>
<tr><td>United States</td><td>99</td><td>—</td><td colspan="2">1</td><td>159</td></tr>
</table>

Source: Mitchell (1986).

giro payment is initiated by the debtor, and circulates within the system as an order to credit the account of the creditor with the collecting bank. It is thus a means of making a credit transfer. Debit and credit transfers can be made by means of magnetic tape and electronic signals as well as by the circulation of pieces of paper.

1. The Cheque Payments System

Figure 6.1 illustrates the nature of the transactions involved in a payment made by individual *A*, writing a cheque drawn on his account with bank *X* (the paying bank), to individual *B* who deposits it with bank *Y* (the collecting bank). As explained above, the transaction is a *debit* transaction since it is initiated by a request (by *B*) to debit the other individual's account.

The numbers alongside various transactions indicate the order in which they occur, with *B* (the creditor) first receiving the cheque, then depositing it at bank *Y* which transmits the cheque to bank *X* which debits *A*'s account and authorises (clears) the transaction. (However, *A* is normally notified of the transaction much later, by means of a monthly or regular statement.) The remaining two transactions have not been numbered since institutional practices vary. Credit to *B*'s account might not be given until the cheque has been cleared, that is, until step 4 has been completed. Alternatively, an immediate credit might be given (for purposes of calculating interest), but conditional upon step 4 being completed, so that the funds are not available to the creditor to draw upon until clearing occurs. Similarly, the transfer of assets (settlement) between banks *X* and *Y* depends on institutional arrangements but normally occurs after clearing. In addition, obvious savings are made by settling on a net basis (the outcome of all cheques written and deposited by both banks' customers) each day (or some other appropriate period).

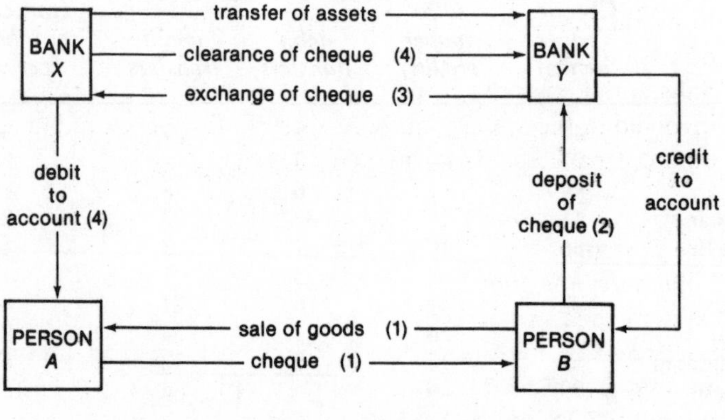

Figure 6.1 The Cheque Payments System

The mechanics by which cheques are exchanged between banks and settlement effected vary between countries. In nations with concentrated branch banking systems (UK, Australia), the banks jointly operate a clearing house and settle by cheques drawn on accounts at the central bank. A certain proportion of cheques deposited at any branch will be drawn on another branch of the same bank. Such 'on us' transactions are cleared within the bank and no settlement is needed. Even in the apparently less concentrated US banking system, it is estimated that as many as 12 billion (30 per cent) of the 40 billion cheques written in 1983 were 'on us' items, deposited at the same bank upon which they were drawn. This is probably much the same percentage of 'on us' items as in the UK (Bankers Clearing House 1984). Of the remaining 28 billion cheques, 13 billion (33 per cent) were deposited at one of the 48 cheque-clearing centres maintained by the Federal Reserve System. These facilities arrange the clearance, crediting the deposit account of the payee's institution and later debiting the account of the payor's institution. The remaining 15 billion cheques (37 per cent) were processed by private clearing houses and via correspondent links (Humphrey 1984). In the latter case larger banks act as clearing agents for smaller banks. A small bank will pass on all cheques it receives (other than 'on us') to a large bank to arrange clearing, and the large bank accepts from other banks cheques drawn on the small bank. The net outcome of these transactions is then credited or debited to an account held by the small bank at the large bank for this purpose. The complex cheque-clearing system in the USA results in each cheque being handled on average by 2.4 banks (Bankers Clearing House 1984).

This brief outline of the cheque payments system raises a number of issues to be taken up later. Here we simply note that:

(a) Lags in the operation of the system introduce the risk that ultimate transfers of wealth may not eventuate.

(b) Similar lags can create 'float' being extended by the banking system to its customers whereby credit may be given to them prior to the offsetting debit being made.

(c) Substantial costs are incurred in the transfer and handling of paper involved in the system, and these costs must be shared in some way amongst participants in the system.

2. The Giro System

Figure 6.2 illustrates the transactions involved when payment is made by use of a Giro system such as is commonly used in Europe. The transaction is a *credit* transaction since it is initiated by *A* (the debtor) making a request to the paying bank that a credit be made to another individual's account.

The undoubted merit of the Giro system is the simplicity that results from the unidirectional flow of paper and information. Consequently, many

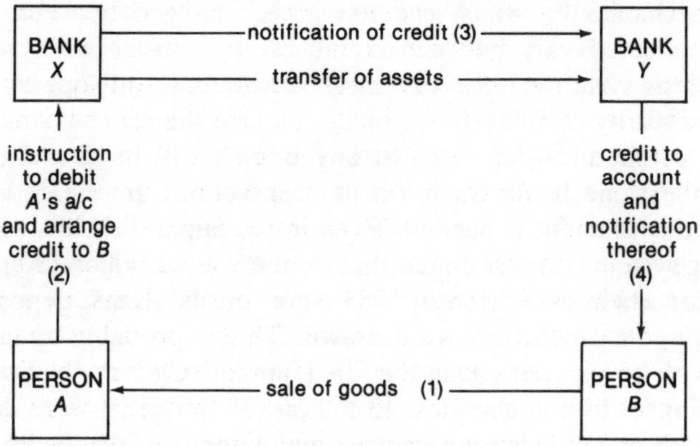

Figure 6.2 The Giro Payments System

of the costs incurred in the cheque system are avoided. Additionally, because the transactions involve an initial debit and subsequent credits to accounts, the default risk is reduced once the transactions begin. The drawback of the Giro system is, however, readily apparent. It relies upon the debtor (purchaser) initiating the transaction. The creditor thus loses control over the implementation of the payment which the debtor has an obvious incentive to delay and is uncertain about receiving payment until notification is given. Consequently, Giro transactions are not suitable for a large number of transactions where the seller of goods has no way of influencing the purchaser's actions, and there may be a greater use of cash for day-to-day transactions in comparison with countries which use cheques. The Giro system is particularly suitable for payments where the goods are supplied in advance of payment on a regular basis. Payments to public utilities for electricity, gas and water are obvious examples. There are advantages in notifying the seller of a listing of the various payments and credits rather than each being the subject of a separate transaction. This commonality in many payments can be exploited in the bill-paying services offered by some banks, building societies and credit unions, which effectively substitute a credit for a debit transfer.

3. Automated Clearing House (ACH) Systems

In view of the cost savings available with credit transfers it is only to be expected that, where feasible, they have been integrated into the infrastructure set up to run the cheque payments system. Direct crediting of pay or government benefits to bank accounts is now relatively commonplace and achieved through automated clearing house systems. By means of, say, the delivery of magnetic tape, an employer is able to provide the clearing house (via his bank) with instructions to credit each of his employees' accounts at their various banks with their salary and debit the total to his account. In contrast to the alternatives of payment in cash or by cheque, the savings (at least to the employer) can be considerable.

Automatic clearing houses were introduced in most major centres during the 1970s, the notable exception being Canada where the functions of an ACH are carried out by the data processing centres within the large chartered banks through the direct exchange of magnetic tapes. In the UK, there is only one ACH, the Bankers' Automated Clearing Services (BACS), which accepts files of transactions on magnetic tape, cassette tape, diskettes and switched telephone networks. West Germany, France and the USA, by contrast, each have numerous automated clearing houses. Although there are some private ACHs in the USA, in particular that operated in New York by the New York Clearing House Association, the great bulk of transactions (95 per cent) is routed through the 35 ACHs run by the Federal Reserve System under service contracts with local ACH associations. Government transactions accounted for about 60 per cent of total ACH volume in the USA during 1984. These provide for the direct crediting to customers' accounts of recurrent payments such as government and military salaries, pensions and social security payments. ACHs also enable the debiting of customers' accounts for regular payments such as mortgage repayments, insurance and utility bills.

4. Electronic Funds Transfer (EFT) Systems

Each of the preceding systems differs in the way in which messages are sent to initiate and effect the transfers of ownership of assets required to achieve payment. Both the cheque and Giro systems utilise paper-based messages. The ACH utilises information provided predominantly by way of a computer tape which contains payment instructions.

Recent developments in information technology have made feasible (and operative) payments systems whereby messages to effect payments can be sent via electronic impulses along telecommunications networks. Figure 6.3 provides an illustration of the operations of an EFT system using point-of-sale (POS) terminals. Other means by which messages could be initiated are by terminals located in the home, as in home banking, or by means of ATMs (automatic teller machines) located at a branch, place of work or elsewhere. The evolution of EFTPOS, ATM and home banking networks in the United States and a number of other countries is surveyed by Felgran and Ferguson (1986).

Considering the EFTPOS system illustrated in Figure 6.3, at the point of sale person *A* can initiate a debit transfer which is relayed, virtually instantaneously, to his bank, *X*, for verification and which, if approved, leads to a credit to *B*'s account at bank *Y*. Individual *B* is notified of the credit and the sale can thus be completed. At some stage, bank *X* transfers ownership of assets to bank *Y* to complete the transaction.

This simplified account of EFTPOS ignores a myriad of logistical issues.

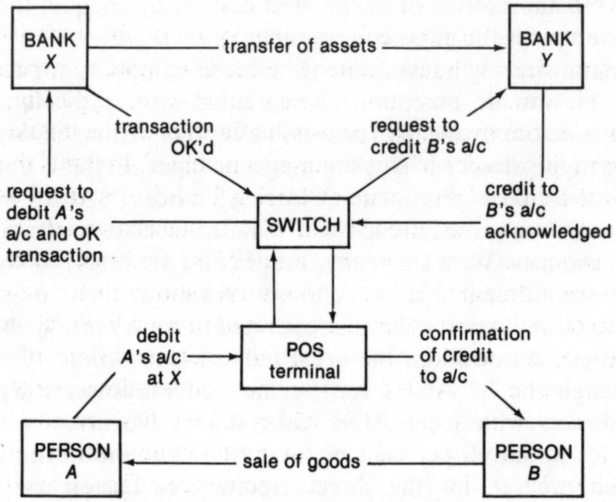

Figure 6.3 The EFTPOS Payments System

Counterfeit cheques, for example, have their counterpart in unauthorised individuals initiating messages to debit *A*'s account. Current safeguards involve the use of a personalised plastic card to access the system, together with entry of a secret personal identification number (PIN number) to verify the identity of the transactor. Technological considerations may dictate whether the system is 'on-line' or 'off-line' for certain sorts of transactions, and how the computer at the switch (where messages are directed to the appropriate source) interacts with computers at the banks.

Once the logistical issues are settled, the distinctive features of the system emerge. First, the equivalent of the bouncing cheque does not exist, since point-of-sale verification and debiting of the asset balance of the payer occurs simultaneously with the crediting. Second, instantaneous credits and debits to accounts remove the float which usually arises in the cheque payments system. Third, unless settlement between banks *X* and *Y* also occurs simultaneously, default risks can still persist in the system. Finally, there are a number of issues which depend upon who owns the equipment (POS terminals) and the network, and the conditions set for use by non-owners. The switch/network could be owned and operated by a specialist company independent of the institutions involved. Alternatively, it could be under the control of some of the participants. Similarly, terminals could be owned by the retailer, a bank, or by an independent supplier. In all cases, the access for card holders of other institutions, costing and charges for use, and the availability of the equipment are matters to be determined, and about which it must be asked whether private decisions will lead to maximum social benefit.

5. Wire Transfers

A further component of non-cash payment systems which merits attention is that of wire transfers, whereby (much like the Giro system) a transfer of funds takes place via instructions sent by telegraphic wire. Typically, this type of transaction is concentrated at the wholesale end of the market where the demand for rapid transfer of the large sums involved warrants the extra costs.

One of the oldest leased wire systems is Fedwire, which was established in the United States soon after World War I, but has greatly expanded and altered in sophistication since the mid-1970s. Fedwire links all Federal Reserve System offices and allows depository institutions to transfer funds for their own account that arise from purchases or sales of Federal funds, to move balances at correspondent banks, and to effect transfers of balances for business customers. It is also important for the working of the government securities market, enabling a bank selling a Treasury security to 'deliver' it electronically to another bank, whose reserve account is simultaneously debited while that of the selling bank is credited. This is possible because, since 1976, the marketable federal debt is represented by 'book-entry' securities rather than engraved pieces of paper, and member banks hold the securities as book entry accounts in the Federal Reserve Bank computers.

About one half of the 8,500 institutions which use Fedwire rely on telephones or telexes to initiate transactions, while the remainder — which includes the high-volume users — are connected 'on line', with the individual bank's computer linked by wire to the computer at its district Federal Reserve Bank. That computer is in turn linked to the Federal Reserve System's central computer in Virginia, which 'switches' messages between the various districts.

Such 'on line' links form the basis of the other important wire transfer system in the United States, called CHIPS (Clearing House Interbank Payment System), established in 1970 primarily to handle interbank money transfers in New York connected with international transactions.[4] Each of the 130-odd participating institutions (two thirds of which are foreign banks) are linked directly by leased telephone lines to the central CHIPS computer, through which payment messages can be received and sent. About 90 per cent of CHIPS volume is international, and the great bulk of interbank transfers due to Eurodollar transactions is handled by CHIPS. The reason why Eurocurrency clearances occur in New York will become apparent when we consider the nature of Eurocurrency claims (see Chapter 9, p.277).

The volume and value of the transfers routed by wire transfers is considerable. On an average day, Fedwire handles 150,000 transfers and CHIPS handles around 100,000 message (Smoot 1985). In the case of CHAPS (Clearing House Automated Payments System), which is the wire transfer system in the UK for the electronic transfer of sterling payments between banks, the average value per payment in 1984 was just under £700,000. For wire transfers in the USA in 1983, the average value was $2,500,000 (see Table 6.1).

Because settlement between banks does not normally take place simultaneously with the wire transfer, these systems also involve risks resulting from the significant *daylight overdrafts* of payment banks. An overdraft comes about when more funds are electronically transferred out of an account than have been transferred in, a position which may not be rectified until end-of-day settlement occurs. The vast turnover of deposits at the large money market banks means that the within-day exposures are of staggering dimensions, as Stigum (1983) illustrates:

> The average demand deposit at one major New York bank turns over 7,000 times a year! Noted an officer of this bank, which has an institutional — as opposed to retail — client base, 'I pay and receive on an average day $145 billion. The assets of my institution are $55 billion. I roll those assets every 2½ hours, and I roll the bank's capital 70 times a day — roughly every 10 minutes. Operations of this size mean that I must at times experience large extremes in my net debit or credit positions at CHIPS and at the Fed. There is no way we can regulate the flow of these payments so everyone stays in balance so long as so many payments are made on the basis of such small balances.' (p.585)

The risks resulting from these intraday imbalances are generally recognised as one of the major concerns for the stability of modern payments systems. They were brought home to participants when a computer malfunction at the Bank of New York in November 1985 meant that electronic deliveries of securities to it by other banks were unmatched by sales of securities by that bank to them. This resulted in the bank running up a daylight overdraft of $23 billion at the Federal Reserve Bank of New York, which was double the assets of the bank and 23 times larger than its capital reserves. Interest on the overnight loan which the bank obtained from the Federal Reserve Bank of New York via the 'discount window' amounted to $5 million![5]

6. Credit Cards

Credit cards are the final type of transactions media which we discuss. From a modest start in the USA in 1950 with the Diners Club card, they have spread to all parts of the globe. Credit cards are now used regularly by 52 per cent of US households, according to a Survey of Currency and Transactions Account usage commissioned by the Board of Governors of the Federal Reserve System in 1984.[6] Nevertheless, credit cards account for a relatively modest share of household expenditures. The survey referred to above revealed that the families made 36 per cent of expenditures by cash and money order, 57 per cent by cheques, and 6 per cent by credit card.[7]

Table 6.1 and the other figures cited earlier did not include credit cards because, strictly speaking, they do not form part of the payments system. Credit cards are a means of exchange, not of payment. Ultimate payment by the card user occurs at (say) the end of the month when a cheque is written or a bank account is debited to settle the outstanding balance. In that respect, credit cards are akin to trade credit for the users, and a substitute for credit long extended by retailers to customers. However, to the seller of goods, sales made to credit card users have similarities to those made to cheque writers. Costs and fees may differ, but credit card sales vouchers can be effectively credited to the merchant's bank account in a similar manner to cheques received. Because the voucher is a claim on the credit card company or card-issuing bank, the risk of non-payment is lower.

In the way that most are currently structured, credit card systems can be thought of as similar to the cheque payments system. Paper (i.e. vouchers) flows in a similar direction, the major difference being the timing of transactions and liabilities incurred along the way. The card holder/voucher writer is given short-term credit (a short-term loan or long-term float) by the card-issuing body between the immediate unconditional credit to the merchant involved and delayed collection of value from the card holder. The combination of float to card holders and more or less immediate reimbursement to stores is thought to be one factor inhibiting the greater use of EFTPOS systems, in which float is absent.

6.2 The Pricing of Payments Services

This brief outline of non-cash payment systems indicates some of the costs associated with their operation. Sophisticated (and expensive) electronic equipment is needed for EFTPOS systems while the cheque system, although using a different technology, also relies upon complex sorting and decoding equipment. The use of labour (tellers accepting cheques, and so on) should also not be forgotten.

The nature of these costs varies markedly, depending upon the types of system under consideration. For EFTPOS systems there are large fixed costs associated with the infrastructure and relatively low variable costs. For the cheque system, there are fixed costs but the variable costs are of greater significance. (US data suggest a cost per transaction in the order of 68 cents per cheque.[8]) Two features of these costs should be noted. First, they bear little or no relationship to the value of the transaction being undertaken. It is the transaction itself which creates costs (although other costs are incurred through account-keeping and monitoring expenses, etc.). Second, the transaction involves crediting one account and debiting another, and thus comprises a joint service to two individuals with costs spread between at least two banks.

Recoupment of these costs by banks has in the past followed a fairly common procedure. Either by convention, or because of legal prohibition, banks paid zero interest on cheque accounts and would not honour cheques on overdrawn accounts (unless a pre-arranged, and sometimes charged for, overdraft limit or loan commitment had been established). Consequently, users of the cheque payments system found it necessary to maintain a positive minimum, and average, account balance. Subject to maintaining appropriate reserves, these balances were available to banks to invest in earning assets, with the resulting income helping to defray the costs of operating the system. Explicit charges on cheque account customers, either as a periodic account-keeping fee or a per transaction charge, were avoided or at least kept well below the cost recoupment level. Savings institutions also provided cash withdrawal, cheque clearance and encashment services at low cost.

To the extent that such arrangements persist today, it would seem that payments services are a product for which customers do not like to pay much, or at least are accustomed not to pay much, and thus they resist changes in the status quo. 'Implicit interest' (the remission of service charges) to cheque account customers can have practical advantages over the payment of explicit interest on balances in cheque accounts. Rarely is implicit interest subject to tax (unlike explicit interest), so that customers on high marginal tax rates may prefer the former to the latter. But tax distortion aside (and there are limits to the amount of service charge remissions practicable), explicit interest should be preferred by customers, in the same way that any cash payment is superior to a payment in kind. Payment of implicit, rather than explicit, interest can also distort the usage which customers make of the cheque payments system, as a number of economists from Harry Johnson (1968) onwards have argued.

Unless carefully structured, schemes which involve the payment of implicit interest lead to cross-subsidisation between customers. Those customers who are holders of large average account balances subsidise the large-volume cheque writers, creating a number of inefficiencies. One is the incentive to hold small account balances and write a large number of small-value cheques. Anyone who has stood in a supermarket checkout queue in the USA or UK and watched cheques being written for small sums can easily comprehend the inefficiency. Often the costs of handling and processing the cheque exceed its face value. Certainly, the resource costs to society of using cheques for small-value transactions exceed those of using currency, and the absence of activity charges fosters an inefficient use of the chequing system in these circumstances.[9]

In addition, the cross-subsidisation between customers can have deleterious effects on the profits of those running the payments system. Low account balances and high-volume cheque writing bring about low interest earnings and high costs. The challenge for banks has been to devise schemes which deliver implicit interest in a way that mitigates these effects. One common practice is remissions of account-keeping fees linked to the size of account balances. This encourages higher account balances but does not reduce incentives to cheque writing. Activity (per transaction) charges do that, but not completely if some subsidy element is involved. Innovative schemes can, however, produce some preferable results. In Australia, banks have utilised activity charges which come into effect only when the number of transactions exceeds a specified number per quarter. Because the charges then apply to all transactions made, a strong incentive exists not to exceed the 'trigger' number of transactions. In effect, cheque writing is subsidised (the charges do not cover costs), but an extra charge is levied on large-volume cheque writers.

As deregulation of banking proceeds, it must be asked whether such partial solutions will be replaced by the payment of explicit market-related interest rates on account balances and the charging of cost-related fees for cheque writing and account management. That, at least, has been the assumption of many analysts of unregulated banking (for example, Black 1970; Fama 1980). For several reasons, however, we are not convinced that payments services and portfolio management services are so easily segregated and separately priced, or that banks will want to go fully down that road.

Two reasons revolve around the jointness in consumption and jointness in production characteristics. Jointness in production creates difficulties, although not insurmountable ones, in allocating joint costs as between cheque transfers, cash withdrawals, cashed cheques, and so on, and distinguishing them from other banking activities. But provision of payments services also involves a joint service to payer and payee (and most often involves cooperation with another bank). Suppose that it is possible to divide the costs of a cheque transaction appropriately between payer and payee. This costing will encourage payers to use cheques (rather than cash) for payments in excess of some amount (x) and payees to prefer payment by cheque (rather than cash) for amounts greater than, say, y. However, unless x and y coincide (and there is no reason to expect this) a conflict over the preferred payments media will exist over a range of payment values. The method of resolving this conflict and the implications for payments pricing policies cannot be considered here, but the point established is that the simple textbook rule for pricing is inappropriate.

Further, payments services and intermediation services are, to some extent, a package. Although the components of the package can be priced separately, it may not be optimal to do so. The act of pricing itself (designing, levying, collecting charges) involves some costs and customers may prefer the benefits of a package price to separate charges for each component.

The third reason is, perhaps, the most compelling. There are grounds for suspecting that the payments system is a decreasing cost industry. With electronic funds transfer systems, in particular, there are large fixed costs and low marginal costs of effecting transactions. (The situation with the cheque transfer system is less clear-cut.) In industries with decreasing costs, such as the public utilities, optimal pricing strategies are far from simple: a marginal cost pricing rule leaves fixed costs adrift and average cost pricing will result in consumption exceeding, or falling short of, levels dictated by social resource costs. One possible solution involves a two-part tariff; that is, to charge a lump sum entry fee to consumers (to defray the fixed component of costs) and set the per unit or transaction cost at or near marginal cost (so as to encourage efficient use by consumers).[10] If the lump sum component can be made to differ between consumers to reflect differences in their valuation of the product, so much the better. (Individuals with little desire for the product will completely eschew it if the lump sum charge is too high, and thus contribute nothing towards meeting the fixed cost element.)

This pricing rule enables us to cast present arrangements in a more favourable light. One entry fee comes from fixed fees for account keeping. But a more subtle form of 'entry fee' exists. By requiring that accounts always remain in credit, banks induce customers to maintain a positive average account balance. Interest foregone on those balances acts much like an entrance charge. Moreover, the size of this entry fee is likely to exhibit some degree of positive correlation with customers' valuations of the product. This is because the average account balance necessary to honour the zero minimum balance requirement will tend to increase with the volume (more precisely, value) of transactions undertaken per period.

These arguments suggest that the practice of banks' 'cross-subsidising' transactions via interest earnings on zero (or low) interest transactions accounts may persist under deregulation. The practice constitutes one, albeit rough and ready, way of implementing an efficient pricing system. Competition undoubtedly limits the range of 'cross-subsidising' arrangements feasible, but neither precludes the arrangement nor implies that it is inappropriate.

6.3 Entry to the Payments System: Risks and Costs

Public policy may be interested in entry conditions to the payments system, the impact of risks upon the mechanism of exchange, and whether cost conditions encourage a concentrated industry structure. Many attitudes to these issues can be traced to how one responds to one simple question: can provision of payments services be an activity separate or separable from provision of other financial services? Were the answer yes, the payments services industry could be analysed in its own right, and regulation framed without reference to other financial services. An affirmative answer is implicit in the influential models of unregulated banking of Black (1970) and Fama (1980) which have viewed banks as providing two distinct functions: portfolio management and provision of payments services.[11] These models envisage a world in which there are no transactions costs between banks and their customers. Once transactions costs are allowed for, the separation they assume between payments and other services does not come about naturally.

Let us suppose, to begin with, that payments services are provided by an entity which is completely independent of the banks whose deposits serve as the means of exchange.[12] The payments operator could produce cheque books (or other payments instruments) which are used to authorise debiting of customers' bank accounts, collect cheques received by payees, arrange debiting and crediting of appropriate accounts at the relevant banks, arrange settlement between banks, and charge fees to customers for these services. In effect, the firm acts as an agent for individuals and allows banks to provide call deposits, which are also used for payments services, without the need for the banks to get involved in payments activities.

The fact that such a dichotomous system has not evolved could be the result of accidents of history, but more likely reflects the existence of advantages from integrating the two activities. Some of these are readily appreciated. Bank offices established for the collection of deposits can be used for the collection and processing of cheques. Also, the dichotomous system involves an extra layer of short-term credit, and risk (as payments are processed via the agent), which is not needed in a bank-operated payments system. EFTS seem more suited to a separate system, although again an integrated arrangement involving provision of payments services by the suppliers of transferable deposits seems most likely.

But to appreciate further why separation is unlikely, we return to a dichotomous system and imagine that the independent operator decides (on the basis of certain criteria and fees) that deposits at a particular group of institutions will be transferable through the system and thus serve as the means of exchange. Ignoring the question of what criteria might be adopted (which would depend on the technology in place and the settlement risks), we go on to ask whether those institutions 'hooked up' to the system are advantaged when providing other financial services. This question can be posed in another way. Assuming customers were paying fees which covered the costs of the payments operator, would those institutions be willing to pay an additional fee for joining the system? Since customers are paying separately for the costs of payments services, this would result only if they derived some external advantage in the provision and marketing of their services.

Our view (and this is an empirical matter open to dispute) is that, because of transactions costs associated with personal financial management, the institutions concerned do gain from participation. Payments made by customers do not fully reflect the benefits they receive (there is 'consumer surplus'), even if at the margin additional benefits equal additional costs. Some customers benefit from being able to conduct 'one-stop shopping' and thus gain in terms of convenience and lessened travelling costs, as compared with the situation where their non-payments-system business is undertaken by firms which do not participate in the system. Customers' ability to combine the two is a competitive advantage to the participating institutions.

In the past, this competitive advantage has been muted by factors such as the regulation of bank interest rates, the 'tax' effect of reserve requirements, and restrictions on banks' ability to enter into other areas of financing. Despite these handicaps, bank holding companies have prospered. Removal of the restrictions suggests a strong argument for policies to promote freer entry into the payments system in order to prevent banks from waging unfair competition in other areas of intermediation. We advocate 'policies', since reliance on the market may not be sufficient. A payments system requires cooperation between institutions competing among themselves and with others for deposit business. It is far from obvious that members of the payments 'club' will decide to adopt an open-door policy towards newcomers, while establishing an alternative 'club' may not be viable.[13]

Until recently, national policies have generally not encouraged entry to the payments system. Indeed, regulatory barriers to entry have been commonplace, although in some countries (for example, the USA) licences have not been difficult to acquire. Various explanations can be advanced for the restrictions upon entry. Regulators may have been 'captured' by the existing 'club' and persuaded to apply policies of benefit to them. It may have been a tacit acceptance that economies of scale in the payments system would limit the number of providers anyway.[14] Thirdly, policymakers may have been concerned to limit risks in the payments system.

Risks in the Payments System

In debit transfer systems, there are two sorts of risk which need to be distinguished. One (deposit risk) is the risk that funds on deposit become valueless because of insolvency of the bank. The other (payments risk) comes from the existence of lags in the payments system, during which time the paying bank may become insolvent, settlement not occur, and thus the payments instruments be rendered valueless. Schemes to protect depositors (examined in the previous chapter) clearly remove both deposit risk and payments risk. But we need to be clear as to whether the objective is one of protecting deposits *qua* deposits, or because they happen to be the assets for which claims are being transferred through the clearing system, so that making deposits safe is a way of eliminating payments risk. Any misgivings about the safety of bank deposits reduces the acceptability of the payment instruments and impedes the mechanism of monetary exchanges.

In our view, the issue of deposit protection does go beyond the safety of transactions balances. Much recent financial instability and 'runs' have not involved just the transactions accounts (see Chapter 5). Also, the macro-economic consequences of sudden reductions in the liquidity of funds are not confined to balances which can legally be transferred, but extend to those funds which the public intends to use for expenditures in the near future.[15]

It is neither practical nor desirable to guarantee all financial assets, however. Some part of the financial system, especially that related to the payments system, needs safety proofing. But, at the same time, there must be scope for risk taking in other areas. A large number of institutions now combine payments services with intermediation of various kinds. Since intermediation is inherently risky, there is the question of whether this risk matters for the safety of the payments system. A number of authors, notably Fama (1980), argue that it does not matter; that any asset, regardless of its risk characteristics, could be used as a means of exchange without indicating any concerns about the use of risky payments media on the smooth functioning of the payments system.

Their argument turns on the nature of the payments system in operation. In current debit transfer systems, deposit risk and payments risk are necessarily intertwined by virtue of the lags in settlement and clearing. Consider, for example, a hypothetical scheme in which such lags exist and deposits at risky institutions are used as payments media, while recipients of payments instruments are protected from loss so as to ensure confidence and the smooth functioning of the payments system. Is such a risk-free payments system which provides for the transfer of risky assets viable? The answer is undoubtedly 'no' when clearing and settlement lags exist, because a severe moral hazard problem is apparent. Any holder of deposits who finds that his bank has become insolvent has an incentive to issue backdated cheques and others who, as recipients of payments intruments, are protected from loss have no reason not to accept them. *De facto* protection of the risky assets used in the payments system would thus exist.

In contrast, where no lags (including settlement) exist in the payments system, the nature of the assets regarded by individuals as a means of payment is irrelevant to the functioning of the payments system. The fact that deposits or other assets held by a payer are risky does not impinge upon a payee. If funds are there, they are instantaneously and unconditionally transferred into the preferred form. Should sufficient funds not be available for transfer, the transaction can be truncated at that point, or settled in cash, as occurs when a retailer fails to obtain authorisation to draw upon a cardholder's predetermined credit card line. But, as lags do exist in present-day debit transfer systems, prevention of deposit risk of participants may be a sensible strategy for ameliorating payments risk.

The point made in the prior paragraph needs to be borne in mind as payments technologies alter, although the 'perfect' technology implicit in arguments such as those of Fama is not yet with us. Many of the lags in clearance and settlement have been reduced: with EFTPOS instant verification of the counterparty's creditworthiness is possible. But, unless instantaneous settlement also takes place, payments system risk still occurs and the interbank extensions of short-term credit which are involved intertwine the fortunes of payments system participants. There are also ways of reducing the risks which remain in the other systems other than by guaranteeing all deposits. For recipients of cheques, the risk of the paying institutions going into insolvency prior to settlement is generally secondary to the risk of accepting a 'dud' cheque. That risk can be reduced by cheque guarantee cards, on the grounds that banks should be better able to assess those risks than are third parties. For banks, the greater risks come at the clearing/

settlement stage, where lags even of a few hours can create significant extensions of short-term credit (daylight overdrafts, for example) and thus link the fortunes of participants — domestic and international — in the payments system. The case of the Bank of New York, referred to earlier, drew attention to the importance of 'back office' operations for bank safety, as Mr Corrigan, President of the Federal Reserve Bank of New York, noted:

> Operating the payments system is not limited to pushing paper or to computer blips — as important as these processes are — but fundamentally entails continuous extensions of credit and hundreds of credit decisions a day. The back office must be incorporated into the front office.
>
> *Federal Reserve Bulletin,* February 1986.

> The day-to-day operation of the large-dollar payments entails very sizeable amounts of credit exposure by all participants — including the Federal Reserve Banks — to a wide array of institutions in every part of the world. The amount and incidence of such exposure varies from one institution to another and is generally confined to relatively short periods of time, but the hard fact of the matter is that linkages created by the large-dollar payments systems are such that a serious credit problem at any of the large users of the systems has the potential to disrupt the system as a whole.
>
> Federal Reserve Bank of New York, Annual Report 1986.

Costs of the Payments System

Changes in technology are also altering the nature of costs associated with payments system. A general view has long prevailed that economies of scale exist in the provision of payments services. But the implications of assessing that view are difficult. A cost function for the payments industry should probably incorporate as arguments at least the number of transactions (N) and the number of participating institutions (I) so that total cost C is given by:

$$C = f(N, I, Z)$$

where Z is a vector of other relevant variables such as the number of accounts (transactors) and prices of factors of production. The notion that there are relatively large fixed costs associated with running a payments system (in recent years the computer hardware, networks, and so on) and low marginal costs per transaction would be reflected by declining average costs, that is, by:

$$\frac{\partial C}{\partial N} < \frac{C}{N}$$

Even if correct, this implies nothing about the relationship between C and I, such as whether costs increase, decrease or are unaffected by the number of participating institutions.

To consider this, imagine the effect of breaking up one of the major UK clearing banks into a (large) number of unit banks (that is, each branch becomes a separate entity). The number of accounting transactions, namely debits and credits to individual accounts at different branches/banks, is unaffected. But, whereas previously many cheques received at the branch were drawn on other branches of the same bank and thus cleared internally, now most cheques will be drawn on a different bank. The number of 'on us' transactions falls, and a greater proportion of business is pushed through the interbank clearing house. Whether this is more expensive than the previous situation is a matter for conjecture. The internalisation of interbranch clearing as the first stage in a two-stage clearing process may be less costly (as well as less risky) than a one-stage clearing process between all branches/unit banks under some technologies. But virtually no evidence exists on this matter, at least for banks with thousands of branches, and recent advances in technology may make the historical record of limited relevance for current times.[16]

Nor can the evidence be used to predict events in a deregulated world. As noted earlier, regulation of interest rates on bank deposits encouraged the provision of subsidised services (such as payments services) and possible 'overuse' of the bank payments system and lower holdings of bank deposits. Given these constraints, banks would adopt certain cost-minimising technologies. These may not be relevant to a deregulated environment, in which a lower turnover to deposit ratio would be likely to result in a different cost–output relationship.[17] The question of economies of scale in banking is considered further in the next chapter.

6.4 The Means of Payment

The payments system is merely an accounting procedure by which transfers of ownership of certain assets are carried out in settlement of debts incurred. In concluding this discussion of payments systems, we return to the question deferred earlier of what types of asset might serve this purpose. In effect we might ask, as many before have done, 'what is money?'

Money has usually been defined as those assets performing the functions (i.e. having the characteristics) of a unit of account, a means of payment and store of value or (in Milton Friedman's terminology) a temporary abode of purchasing power. Recent analyses of financial systems by Fama (1980), Black (1970) and Greenfield and Yeager (1983) have in effect questioned whether these characteristics are necessarily complementary. Put differently, is the concept of money as defined above a useful one in analysing the financial system?

Fama (1980) envisages a world in which payments instruments could be drawn on mutual funds accounts which, unlike deposits, have a fluctuating value in terms of the unit of account. In a world where there are no information deficiencies, no transactions costs and no lags in clearing and settlement, that possibility is indeed viable. There would be no necessary nexus between those assets serving as the unit of account and those serving as a means of payment. All assets could serve equally well as a means of payment since recipients of a payments instrument could immediately and costlessly arrange to convert it into a preferred asset of known value.

In practice, information deficiencies, transactions costs and lags limit both the range of assets which serve as a means of payment and the form of payments instruments. In the 'perfect' world, a payments instrument could be an order to transfer a certain number of particular assets (say, 10 shares in company *X*) or to transfer particular assets of a given value in terms of the unit of account. In that world the two instructions would be equivalent. In any other world, however, the recipient would view the two instruments differently and (we believe) would prefer the instrument specifying transfer of ownership of assets of given value in terms of the unit of account. Payments instruments, in our view, will continue to be of the form 'pay the bearer *x* dollars'.

The homogeneity of payments instruments does not, however, preclude a heterogeneity of accounts upon which payments instruments are drawn. In principle, there is no reason why cheques could not be drawn upon a mutual fund, upon an account of shares in company *X* managed by a stockbroker who participates in the payments system, or upon an account of holdings of a particular government security at a government stock registry office, as well as upon a 'standard' deposit account. The difference, in effect, is that, in the former cases, the payments instrument carries with it an explicit instruction to the account manager to dispose of particular assets to the specified value. Writing cheques upon a standard deposit account where the value of the account is known *ex ante* (assuming no default risk) does not expose the cheque writer to a risk that the underlying assets may have fallen in value at that time (or increased just prior to extra assets being paid into the account). By providing transactions deposits fixed in value in terms of the unit of account, banks enable the holder to undertake transactions without at the same time having to worry about portfolio management. The alternative scenario would see the purchaser of a commodity having to ascertain upon which account to issue a payments order, on the basis of which asset was at that time the most highly priced. Similarly, recipients of payments instruments would have to ascertain which account at that moment was the most profitable place to lodge those funds.

The fact that deposit-type accounts enable individuals to separate transactions and payments decisions from portfolio management decisions does not, of course, rule out the possibility that other types of accounts might sometimes be preferred as the means of payment. Banks and other depository institutions which 'insure' customers against those portfolio risks do so by taking them onto their own books. To protect themselves, they must take actions to alter their gearing and the composition of their assets (discussed in earlier chapters of this book). These may be of sufficient magnitude to lower the relative yield on deposit accounts by enough to make other payments accounts preferable, despite the latter's fluctuating value. To an extent that has already happened, and in some countries (such as the United States) individuals now write cheques upon money market mutual fund accounts. The interest rate available and the fact that the value of the account is based upon an averaging of the institution's stock of both older and newer assets (which moderates fluctuations in the account's value relative to current market fluctuations) are important factors in this respect. Admittedly, the asset involved (shares in the fund) is not a perfect substitute for the asset serving as the unit of account (the value of the former is not predetermined in terms of the latter), but that does not stop it acting as a means of payment. Without deposit insurance and other schemes to protect depositors, the numbers wanting to use money market funds might well be larger.[18] Nevertheless, the range of assets suitable for pooling in money market funds and using for transactions seems relatively small (at the moment, short-term government securities and high-grade corporate paper).

Conceivably, advances in technology which reduce information deficiencies, transactions costs, and so on, may broaden the range of assets viewed by customers as suitable for use as means of payments. It must then be asked whether money as we know it, and monetary control, will disappear. In large part, that depends upon the type of settlement arrangements. Ultimately, the transfer of value from one institution to another as a result of payment settlement made between them involves the one in selling certain assets and the other in buying certain (quite possibly different) assets. Use of a common means of settlement (such as deposits at a central bank) will facilitate matters. Even providers of non-deposit payments services would find it desirable to hold such a settlement medium so as to avoid excessive buying and selling of assets underlying their accounts at possibly adverse prices. Provided that such a settlements medium exists (and has no close substitutes), control of it should enable some measure of control over the stock of payments assets.

Notes

1. We do not take up the question of whether government fiat money could or should be replaced by private issue of currency. As Tobin (1985) notes, the difficult legal questions associated with defining certain assets as appropriate for expunging debt and tax liabilities provide a strong case for government-supplied currency.
2. Two implications of this analysis are worth noting. First, technological change may see some resurgence of cash rather than the emergence of a cashless society if the costs of dispensing and depositing cash etc. are reduced by low-cost automatic teller machines/cash dispensing machines. Second, the bulk of the benefits of lower transactions costs from use of cheques accrues to the writer of the cheque since the recipient still has to deposit cheques to initiate the clearing and settlement process. The recipient additionally incurs a risk of eventual non-payment if the cheque bounces. The implications of these factors for the pricing of payments services are considered in section 6.2 below.

3. De Vany argues that 'banks cannot guarantee all their clients' checks without creating a severe misincentive problem'. An upper limit of £50 per cheque reduces this incentive (to £1,250 for a normal-sized cheque book), but nevertheless frauds in 1983 amounted to £23.1 million.
4. Other wire transfer systems operating in the USA are Cashwire and CHESS, but the volumes handled are small compared with Fedwire and CHIPS (see Humphrey 1984, Smoot 1985, and Stevens 1984).
5. *Federal Reserve Bulletin,* February 1986, pp.117–125. A major difference between Fedwire and CHIPS comes about because the settlement risk for Fedwire payments is borne by the Federal Reserve Banks, since, once a transfer has been accepted and acknowledged, it is guaranteed. Consequently, the recipient institution is shielded in the event of sender failure. Settlement risk in Cashwire is absorbed by the 180 participating banks, while it is shared with the customers of participating banks in CHIPS (see Stevens 1984).
6. *Federal Reserve Bulletin*, February 1986, pp.87–108.
7. A recent survey amongst European countries revealed a relatively low usage of credit cards as compared with cash, cheque or giro, even for transactions such as meals in restaurants and purchases of consumer durables, as reported in *The Economist*, 6 December 1986.
8. Humphrey (1984), Table 2.
9. Humphrey (1984) provides a figure of 7 cents as the social cost per cash transaction.
10. Dornbusch and Fischer (1984). Thus telephone companies may charge an annual rental along with a per call costing.
11. Their argument is different from that of Tobin (1985) who notes a basic dilemma because current systems involve competition among financial intermediaries entangled with provision of transactions media. He suggests a legal separation between the two.
12. Fischer (1983) considers this possibility.
13. Both in the UK and in Australia the existing bank owners of the respective clearing houses have recently set entry fees for potential new members. In those circumstances the quesiton at issue is the determination of a 'fair' entry price.
14. Johnson (1968), for example, suggests that 'presumably . . . there are significant economies of scale . . . which . . . on the payments side at least, may indicate the social desirability of operating the banking business as a public utility.'
15. The point is made by Mayer (1986), but its origins can be traced to the Radcliffe Committee (1959) and its emphasis upon 'liquidity' rather than the volume of money.
16. Humphrey (1984) argues that US data suggest that economies of scale in retail payments activities only exist for small commercial banks.
17. An additional effect which arises if deregulation leads to higher deposit holdings and lower transactions value as predicted by Johnson (1968) is that the distribution of net outflows relative to deposits (see Chapter 3) will have smaller variance, and the need for reserves is correspondingly reduced.
18. The attractiveness of money market funds is governed by the alignment of money markets to those of depository institutions. The comments in Note 16 to Chapter 2 should also be considered.

7

Issues in Banking Structure

7.1 Institutional Differences

Previous chapters have focused upon the intermediation activities of banks and put to one side the questions of what (if anything) distinguishes banks from other financial firms and what factors determine the industrial structure of the banking and financial industry. Significant country-by-country differences in the way banking is organised suggest that a number of diverse influences are at work. Sayers (1967), we recall, contrasted the unit banking system of the USA with the preponderance elsewhere of branch banking along English lines. A recent analysis (Wilson 1986) has added 'hybrid banking systems', in countries like France, India, Austria, Belgium, Holland, West Germany and Switzerland, which fall between and combine features of the US pattern and that in Britain and other Commonwealth countries. Banking in the Scandinavian countries is seen as having characteristics which provide yet another distinctive category. In fact, the impact of history and national regulations has resulted in some unique features in every country.

In most countries, a difference exists between banks and non-bank financial institutions (NFIs) by virtue of government licensing (or chartering) of certain firms to operate as 'banks' under the conditions of governing legislation. The UK Banking Act of 1979 provides for a two-tiered licensing of qualifying financial institutions as either banks or deposit-taking institutions (DTIs), only the former being able to use the label of 'bank'.[1] In the USA, commercial bank charters have been issued by both national and state governments since the mid-nineteenth century. But legal distinctions do not help much in identifying the fundamental characteristics of a bank. There are significant differences across countries in the range of activities reserved for the holders of banking licences. Within nations there seems often to be little other than the official label which distinguishes banks from other financial firms.

Lord Denning remarked, in a celebrated judgment before the House of Lords in 1966, that 'like many other beings, a banker is easier to recognise than to define'.[2] Even recognition has become more difficult. Savings institutions offer payments services, and banks encroach into areas once the preserve of NFIs. Where NFIs have been prevented by legislation from providing transactions directly, they have done so by utilising legal loopholes (as savings banks and credit unions in the USA did with NOW accounts and share drafts) or by offering third-party cheque writing (building societies and credit unions in Australia). In the USA, investment banks and securities companies are now major providers of 'banking' services, such as cheque and transactions accounts, eroding the Glass-Steagall Act of 1933 which has separated investment banking from commercial banking in America. Another longstanding feature of the US financial system, the separation of 'banking' from 'commerce', has been breached by means of the 'non-bank bank' loophole (see below).

Banks, for their part, have sought to evade restrictions upon their undertaking of non-bank activities through the vehicle of subsidiary or affiliated companies. Holding company structures enable one financial 'group' to encompass both bank and non-bank institutions. Thus in Australia, banking groups typically involve a trading bank and savings bank, finance company and merchant banking subsidiaries. In the UK, an even broader range of activities, including insurance broking and underwriting, mutual funds management, and securities broking is undertaken by banks via the holding company arrangement (see Table 7.1 on p.200). By contrast, strict legal limitations are placed on the activities which can be undertaken by bank holding companies in the USA.

Changes in financial legislation have partly responded to, and partly facilitated, the blurring of distinctions between banks and other financial institutions. The 1980 Depository Institutions Deregulation and Monetary Control Act in the USA required the Federal Reserve System to provide its various facilities to depository institutions other than commercial banks in return for the imposition of reserve requirements on transactions accounts at those institutions. Despite this similar regulatory treatment, the separate legal classifications between institutions called 'banks' and other depository institutions have been retained (as is also the case in the UK).[3]

The rationale for keeping separate licensing or chartering of banks is presumably that banks perform certain functions which give them a special role in the economic system. Six factors might form the basis for differences between banks and other financial institutions:

1. **Liability characteristics**. Financial intermediaries create a multitude of liabilities, differing in terms of maturity, capital certainty, default risk, and a myriad of other characteristics. Maturity is important because, in the absence of 'perfect' capital markets (so that borrowing against existing assets involves extra costs), having funds 'at term' rather than 'at call' constrains a wealthholder's flexibility to adapt to changing circumstances. Capital certainty refers to the degree of risk exposure to

movements in asset markets. Deposit liabilities provide an *ex ante* specification of their future nominal value (but leave the real value uncertain). Mutual fund liabilities, by contrast, determine the future nominal value *ex post* and thus expose holders fully to developments in certain asset markets. But safety also embraces the third characteristic, that of freedom from default risk. Concern about the safety of deposits has prompted much of bank regulation, largely because depository institutions find it difficult to honour their *ex ante* nominal guarantee. Government backing for this guarantee may make the institutions concerned 'special'.

2. **Asset characteristics**. The primary securities which intermediaries purchase vary markedly in characteristics such as size, maturity, default risk and marketability. Intermediaries differ further in the extent to which they 'acquire' or 'create' the assets they hold. Mutual funds deal in existing securities with pre-determined characteristics, whereas depository institutions also create new financial instruments (such as loans) tailored to the individual needs and characteristics of the borrower.
3. **The nature of intermediation**. The difference in asset holdings between mutual funds and depository institutions noted above evidences a difference in the type of intermediation undertaken. Liquid liabilities can be created out of marketable securities (mutual funds) or non-marketable assets (banks). Intermediation can also involve size transformation, maturity transformation, risk transformation, and so on.
4. **Joint provision of other services**. Intermediaries provide services other than intermediation. Payments services are an obvious example. (We have avoided describing this as a characteristic of particular liabilities – although there is an obvious overlap. One reason for doing so is that payments services, under the overdraft system of lending, are also provided in significant volume to borrowers from such intermediaries.) A second example is the joint provision of protection and intermediation services by life offices.
5. **Special relationships with the authority**. Some institutions (banks) have had privileged access to central bank liquidity support, exclusive rights to provide certain services (agents for government securities), and government guarantees of safety, and have also been subject to various constraints on their activities. But there is a circularity here. Our objective is to identify possible peculiarities which can justify distinctive regulatory treatment, and the existence of regulation itself hardly qualifies.
6. **Financial structure**. The final factor we identify as relevant could be termed a derived difference. Because of some of the aforementioned differences, a particular set of institutions may have a place of special

significance in the interrelationships which exist within the financial sector.

Several of these factors have been singled out in various analyses which focus upon bank and non-bank differences. Fama (1985), we recall from Chapter 4, asked why banks in the USA, although subject to a reserve requirement 'tax', are able to compete favourably with untaxed competitors in wholesale deposit markets. His answer focused upon the second factor in terms of the special nature of bank assets, which he refers to as 'inside debt' of the borrowers. Bank loans and credit lines can command a premium because they carry a built-in seal of approval from the bank as to the borrower's creditworthiness (much like a premium credit card). Sayers (1967), in contrast, after noting that 'there is no fixed barrier between what is and what is not banking business' (p.174), indicated a preference for the first and fourth of the factors listed above: 'The modern distinguishing feature of banks is due primarily to the efficiency of the clearing system they have developed, but it has its roots deeply in the command they have achieved over public confidence' (p.176). In Chapter 5 we examined the arguments of Kareken (1986) and McCulloch (1986) who look to solve the problem of banks' safety and the excessive reliance of banks on government insurance funds by having banks 'mark deposits to market' and become 'mutual funds banks'. They presumably see the present special significance of banks as stemming from the third and fifth factors; that is, the nature of banks' intermediation and their access to the public safety net.

US legislators ignored Lord Denning's remarks when amending the Bank Holding Company Act in 1970 and defined a bank as an organisation which '(1) accepts deposits that the depositor has a legal right to withdraw on demand, and (2) engages in the business of making commercial loans'. That duality has been the source of the 'non-bank bank' loophole, referred to above, since entities that offer only one or the other service can operate as banks, yet avoid the legal constraints imposed upon bank holding companies.[4] In seeking a basis for regulatory reform, Mr Corrigan, who is currently President of the Federal Reserve Bank of New York, has sought to enunciate the special characteristics of banks (Corrigan 1982 and 1986). These are: the 'issue of transactions accounts' (item 1), acting as a 'transmission belt for monetary policy' (item 6), and 'the backup source of liquidity for all other institutions and markets'. Banks' central position in financial markets, however, comes about because, on the asset side, they give entrée to firms and entities which 'do not enjoy stand-alone direct access to the securities markets' (items 3, 4). Their capacity to act as the source of backup liquidity depends on the 'high degree of public confidence', itself contingent on the 'quality of banks' assets' (item 2), and their unique access to the 'public safety net' (item 5). Thus, on close inspection, all the factors we have suggested as being of possible significance figure in his schema.

One of the essential characteristics of banks — their role in the transmission of monetary policy — features in money and banking textbooks, in which banks are special because they create credit. Tobin (1963) and Guttentag and Lindsay (1968) have addressed the question whether banks amongst financial institutions have a special ability to create credit and thus are more important for the conduct of monetary policy. Tobin identifies the fifth factor above (regulation) as the basis for banks having a 'widow's cruse', in comparison with NFIs. Guttentag and Lindsay focus upon peculiarities in the structure of the financial sector (the sixth factor). We shall examine this specific question before returning to more general issues.

7.2 Bank and Non-Bank Claims

Modern financial systems cannot be thought of as a simple structure in which primary lenders place funds with an intermediary who passes them on directly to a primary borrower. Our analysis of wholesale banking in Chapter 4 indicated how a complex chain of financial claims might exist between primary lenders and borrowers. At the retail level, liquid reserves of an intermediary may be held, not as base money, but as deposits with another intermediary. Thus state banks in the USA choose to hold reserves with member banks, savings institutions hold reserves at banks, Eurodollar banks hold reserves with New York banks, and so on. A balance sheet for the financial sector would show a large volume and diversity of intermediary claims. (Even prior to intermediaries gaining funds from primary lenders, investment advisors and brokers can play a significant role.)

The issue under consideration can be framed in two questions. Is there some specific financial system structure which gives a particular group of intermediaries a special ability to create credit? If such a system exists, what factors account for its existence?

The first of these questions was addressed by Guttentag and Lindsay who argued that, because of a 'layering' of reserve assets implied by the nature of the (US) financial system, banks as a group had a greater capacity than NFIs to create credit. As the same points resurface in debates about Eurocurrency credit creation (see Chapter 9), it is worthwhile devoting some time to them.

Imagine that 'level one' intermediaries (banks) hold base money, i.e. vault cash and balances at the central bank, as reserves, and that 'level two' intermediaries (NFIs) hold bank deposits as reserves. Then, when cheques written against bank loan accounts are deposited with NFIs, banks experience no loss of reserves. Because NFIs hold bank deposits as reserves, customers withdrawing funds from bank accounts to place them with NFIs alter only the ownership (and not total) of bank deposits.

But no such indestructibility exists for the NFIs. Some (large) part of their lending will flow into deposits at banks and thus involve the NFIs in losing reserves to the banks. Transfers by customers from NFI deposit

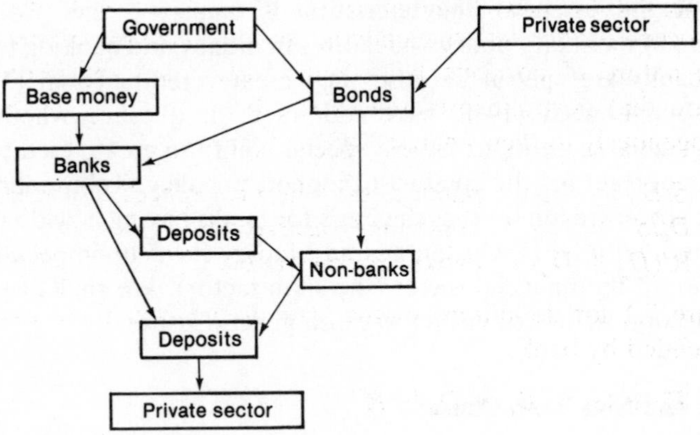

Balance Sheets

Private Sector: *Assets*	Private Sector: *Liabilities*	Banks: *Assets*	Banks: *Liabilities*
Bank deposits (D_p)	Bonds issued to banks (P_b)	Private bonds (P_b)	Deposits of private sector (D_p)
Non-bank deposits (S)	Bonds issued to non-banks (P_a)	Govt. bonds (G_b)	Deposits of non-banks (D_a)
		Base money (R)	

Non-Banks

Assets	*Liabilities*
Private bonds (P_a)	Deposits of private sector (S)
Govt. bonds (G_a)	
Bank deposits (D_a)	

Figure 7.1

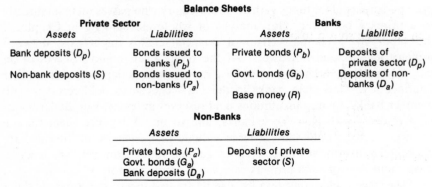

accounts to bank deposits reduce NFI deposits, but only change the ownership of bank deposits. This greater 'indestructibility' of bank deposits gives banks a significantly greater credit-creating capacity.

This argument can be formalised with the aid of Figure 7.1. That figure identifies four sectors: government, banks, NFIs and the private sector; and it identifies three types of financial assets: base money, bonds issued by either the government or the private sector (where 'bonds' is a synonym for loans to that sector) and deposits issued by either banks or NFIs. The arrows in the figure run from the issuer to the holder. The simplified balance sheets establish the notation. As drawn, that figure, and the associated balance sheets, incorporates three major assumptions. The first, which is unnecessary but simplifies the analysis, is that the private non-financial sector holds no base money (i.e. cash). The second, again purely a simplification, is that there is no direct financing between transactors in the private sector. The third, which is critical, is that a *layering* of financial claims exists in which only banks hold base money as reserves. A three-tiered financial structure exists consisting of the authorities, the banks and the NFIs, with each of the latter groups using the monetary liabilities of the previous one as reserves.

To proceed further with the analysis, specific assumptions must be made about the nature of portfolio behaviour. Those made by Guttentag and Lindsay are that portfolio preferences can be represented as fixed ratios (given exogenously to their analysis) of the form:

$K = S/D_p$	public's portfolio preferences
$\alpha = D_a/S$	non-banks' reserve ratio
$\beta = R/(D_p + D_a)$	banks' reserve ratio

(See Figure 7.1 for definitions of the symbols.) Given these assumptions, credit extended by banks:

$$C_b = P_b + G_b = D_p + D_a - R$$

and by non-banks:

$$C_a = P_a + G_a = S - D_a$$

can easily be shown to be:

$$C_b = R\left(\frac{1}{\beta} - 1\right)$$

$$C_a = \frac{R(1 - \alpha)K}{\beta(1 + \alpha)K}$$

and total credit:

$$C_t = C_b + C_a = \frac{R(1 + K)}{\beta(1 + \alpha)K} - R$$

Changes in bank and non-bank reserve ratios (β and α respectively) will clearly produce substantially different effects upon total credit.[5] Similarly, exogenous changes in the public's preferences between bank and non-bank liabilities (as indicated by K) would affect the total volume of credit extended in the economy (increases in K would increase C_t). These results also stem from the special feature noted above: neither the public's portfolio preferences (indicated by K) nor the non-bank's reserve ratio (indicated by α) affect bank credit, whereas the bank reserve ratio β, as well as α and K, affect non-bank credit. Bank deposits and bank credit appear to be immune to the competition of NFIs.

The explanation for the differential effects of reserve ratio changes is readily apparent from Figure 7.1. Suppose banks attempt to reduce their reserve ratio (β) by purchasing bonds from (i.e. making loans to) the private sector, offering new bank deposits in return. Even when the private sector transfers part of these funds into non-bank deposits (to restore K to its desired value), the banking sector experiences no offsetting reduction in deposits due to the use of bank deposits as reserves by the non-banks. Merely the ownership of bank deposits is changed and, in this example, bank deposits increase one for one with bank credit extended until the lower reserve ratio is achieved via deposit expansion. NFI liabilities also increase in line with the banking sector's expansion (because K is assumed to be constant), as does credit extended by the NFIs.

A reduction in the NFIs' reserve ratio (α) gives rise to a very different result. When non-banks purchase bonds, their liabilities do not increase one for one with the credit they have extended. For each $\$(1 + 1/K)$ of bonds bought, NFI liabilities increase by \$1, the public's holdings of bank deposits increase by $\$1/K$ and NFI reserves fall by $\$1/K$. The lower NFI reserve ratio is achieved in part by an expansion of liabilities and in part by reduced reserve holdings, this leakage of reserves limiting the credit-creating capacity of NFIs as compared with banks. Since the ownership, but not the total, of bank deposits is changed, credit extended by the banking sector is unaffected.

Assumptions made about cash holdings and portfolio behaviour are critical to these results. Introducing cash holdings by either the public or by NFIs removes the indestructibility of bank deposits and thus moderates (or even removes) the differential credit-creating ability of banks. Portfolio preferences must also be such that they can be represented by treating the various assets and liabilities as being held in fixed proportions to each other.

For many practical issues of monetary analysis, these assumptions are often not greatly wide of the mark, and the Guttentag–Lindsay results have frequently been helpful in understanding phenomena of relevance to monetary policy formulation.[6] However, these results do not demonstrate that banks are *inherently* different. For that question, it is necessary to ask why layering occurs and, given its existence, what implications follow for how portfolio preferences are specified.

The risk return, maturity characteristics of deposit liabilities issued by financial intermediaries depend upon the nature of the assets held by them, their capital structure, and the real resource costs involved in providing services such as liquidity insurance. When layering occurs, the different reserve assets held by 'level 1' and 'level 2' intermediaries imply, *ceteris paribus*, that the characteristics of their asset portfolios differ. Consequently, their deposits ought to be dissimilar; or, if not, their capital structures must vary, the remainder of their asset portfolios must vary, or different real resource costs must be involved in their intermediation. Any distinct deposit characteristics need to be recognised in specifying portfolio preferences. Alternatively, account must be taken of the other adjustments needed to keep deposit characteristics identical. The Guttentag–Lindsay approach ignores these considerations and leads to inconsistent results.

The nature of the inconsistency is best seen from considering the effects of an arbitrary switch in depositors' holdings from 'level 1' to 'level 2' intermediary deposits, which are assumed identical. In the Guttentag–Lindsay approach this increases the demand for primary assets used by borrowers since total credit granted (primary securities purchased) by intermediaries increases. But the characteristics of secondary assets available to wealth holders (as deposits or equity in intermediaries) will derive from and reflect the characteristics of primary assets supplied by borrowers. In the switch hypothesised here, there is no change in the demand for derived characteristics (of deposits) but, nevertheless, it has led to a change in the demand for underlying primary asset characteristics. Given the 'technological' link between primary and derived characteristics, something is missing from the story.

That omission can be rectified by acknowledging that deposits have different characteristics, so that a switch in depositors' preferences corresponds to a shift in their preferences for asset characteristics. There is, then, nothing remarkable about a change occurring in the demand for primary securities. Alternatively, if deposit characteristics are to be kept constant and equal, the adjustments to asset portfolios, equity or real resources necessary to ensure this will impinge upon the demand for primary assets. These adjustments should completely mitigate the effect upon primary asset demand resulting from the assumption of layering. The Guttentag–Lindsay model employs a partial equilibrium approach where a general equilibrium approach is called for. (The Guttentag–Lindsay world is the textbook credit creation one of fixed interest rates, elastic capital leverage, and persistent demands for intermediary loans.)

Our conclusion is that banks and NFIs are not *inherently* different because of layering. Layering may be accompanied by differences in credit-creating capacity, but it is not the underlying cause of these differences. Any such differences arise for two reasons. One is because the institutions' intermediation activities are different in terms of the sorts of factors listed in the previous section. (Thus US state banks and NFIs differ in certain respects from money centre banks, retail intermediaries differ from wholesale ones, nationally-based banks differ from international banks.) The other reason is that the existence of government regulation has severed the links between primary and secondary asset characteristics. (Thus, the liabilities of money centre banks which are 'too large to be allowed to fail' are viewed by other institutions as being as good as cash, introducing layering.)

7.3 Regulatory Distinctions

Financial regulation as seen today (or seen being dismantled today) reflects a variety of concerns about the functioning of the financial system. One is the apparent vulnerability of banking and financial systems to crisis and panic. Second, the financial system is seen by many as playing an important role in business cycles and the determination of macroeconomic activity. Third, an aversion to undue concentration of economic and financial power often finds specific expression in preventing 'money trusts' by means of branching restrictions and limitations upon bank shareholdings. At the same time, a desire to avoid conflicts of interest sees constraints placed upon the range of activities of financial firms. Fourth, governments have sought to implement various social objectives through the financial system in the form of, for instance, finance for housing and agriculture. Finally, the central role of the payments system in facilitating production and exchange has given governments a particular interest in ensuring its smooth and efficient operation.

On a number of these grounds, one can point to a special interest in institutions called banks. But the major difficulty in actually differentiating some special 'banking' activities from other aspects of financial intermediation is that they all involve shades of grey. Characteristics of liabilities such as term to maturity, capital certainty, and default risk all lie along a spectrum with no obvious dividing line. Ambiguities can surround an apparently clear-cut difference such as whether or not an intermediary's liabilities serve as payments media. Call deposits which are non-transferable may be so readily accessible for conversion into payments media that a distinction between the store of value and means of payment is of limited relevance. Credit cards enable a further divorce between the medium of exchange (the card) and the means of payment (which could be funded monthly from a deposit with a non-bank financial institution).

For these sorts of reasons, we would argue that there is no natural dividing line between banking and non-banking financial institutions. Indeed, in earlier chapters, we have traced common threads running through many intermediation functions in terms of the guarantees and options provided to customers. Because intermediaries span a wide range of these functions, the possibility of finding a natural *institutional* distinction seems remote.

That need not prevent governments from trying to create legal distinctions. Just as the most practical means of legislating against noise pollution may simply be to prohibit noise in excess of some decibel level, so might a need for government involvement in the financial sector be most practicably achieved by creating clear-cut distinctions between, and regulations applying to, certain activities. Here we shall focus first upon actions to improve macroeconomic stability and then upon those to prevent crises.

While the activities of any class of intermediary can have macroeconomic consequences, some activities, and especially the provision of payments services, are generally thought to be of greater significance than others. The convention has been to regard deposits usable in the payments system as 'money' and accord them special significance. Two attributes of deposits have given them this importance. First, because of their high liquidity and thus acceptability, creation of an excess supply can occur more easily than for other assets. Second, because they had no 'own price' (deposits had a fixed value in terms of the unit of account and bore no market interest rate), the excess supply or demand spilled over into other markets (bond, foreign exchange, commodities) with macroeconomic consequences.

Recent developments in the financial sector have altered those characteristics. Some assets now used for transactions have an uncertain price in terms of the unit of account (such as money market mutual funds). A growing proportion of transactions accounts bears variable interest rates, altering responses to policy actions.[7] Taking these factors into account has led some to suggest that, on macroeconomic grounds, official interference can be limited to regulation of the supply of base money (note issue and central bank deposits). Base money still has a fixed price in terms of the unit of account, and the need for financial institutions to acquire reserve assets acts as a constraint upon the profitable expansion of deposits. Given this demand, and the continued use of currency for hand-to-hand transactions, control of the supply of base money is, at least in principle, sufficient for monetary control.[8]

In practice, a number of considerations lead central banks, concerned with control of the amount of liquid assets over relatively short periods of time, to continue to pay attention to the supply of transactions media (or 'narrow' money). The substitutability of non-cash payments media for cash is one. Also, potential elasticity of the demand for cash as a reserve asset by banks introduces variability into the link between base money and macroeconomic variables.[9] Legal reserve requirements on deposits are often imposed (or retained) to enhance control over the supply of transactions media. Constant reserve ratio requirements can create a more reliable link between base money and other payments assets, while variable ratios serve as an additional method of monetary control.[10]

Variations can still occur in the *demand* for transactions media due to alterations in the relative attractiveness of non-transactions deposits, and these have been of such a magnitude in the 1980s as to give rise to growing doubts about the wisdom of adhering to strict money supply targets.[11] Nevertheless, the supply of payments media remains an important indicator of monetary conditions, while for others it continues to have a social significance sufficient to prompt regulation of the suppliers.

Governments also provide a 'safety net' to reduce financial instability and protect depositors (Chapter 5). Exactly which set of deposits and balances held at particular institutions warrants safety-proofing (and how) is a question which different governments have answered in a number of ways. But the importance of getting the answer right is illustrated by the fact that the Federal Reserve banks felt constrained from acting more forcefully as lenders of last resort in the US banking crisis of the 1930s because most of the troubled banks were not members of the Federal Reserve System.[12]

Transactions accounts provide a natural starting point for safety-proofing of assets on functional grounds, and such an approach can overcome regulatory duplication and inaction. That is the current procedure for determining lender-of-last-resort coverage in the USA, and it enabled the Federal Reserve to come to the aid of the Ohio thrift institutions in 1985, despite the fact that the institutions were chartered, insured and regulated under state laws.[13] The Bank of England placed under its aegis (since confirmed by legislation) all institutions taking deposits of any kind from the public with its intervention in the secondary 'banking' crisis of 1974, even though many were not regarded by it as banks and *ipso facto* not subject to its supervision. How far safety-proofing should go is an issue which is obviously strongly country- and institution-specific.[14]

The preceding arguments suggest that regulatory distinctions between financial institutions might be warranted on these two grounds, namely, the provision of payments services and safety-proofing of deposits. Indeed, the functions of providing transactions services and a safe haven for funds are the ones most commonly thought of as *banking* functions. But in drawing *institutional* distinctions the problem still arises that financial institutions tend, where allowed, to undertake a diversified group of activities. It is thus of interest to ask whether functional specialisation can be expected. If not, the problem arises of how to limit costs and benefits of regulatory intervention to the activities concerned, rather than having them spread across all activities of the institution concerned. It is also of interest to ask whether economies of scale and scope exist which promote concentration, since this may induce a different regulatory interest in the financial sector. These matters are taken up in the remainder of this chapter.

7.4 The Nature of Financial Services

This chapter began by noting differences between national banking and financial markets. Behind those differences lie distinctive customs and regulations and (not to be underrated) the luck and foresight of particular individuals whose successes influenced subsequent institutional developments in those markets. But there are some common elements in the markets for financial services and these can be expected to encourage similarities in market organisation.

Demand for Services

On one side of the market, the demand for financial services reflects a set of basic needs. Individuals and businesses demand financial services to satisfy three needs:

(a) Transactions facilities, providing means of paying for and acquiring goods and services.
(b) Wealth accumulation, enabling individuals to rearrange the holding of wealth over time by means of saving and borrowing.
(c) Financial security, ensuring the continuance of spending in the face of changed economic circumstances.

These needs provide the 'building blocks' for most financial packages. Most financial institutions offer a range of services which encompass at least two of these needs. For illustrative purposes, Figures 7.2 and 7.3 identify some major financial product lines in retail financing with these needs. Banks in both the USA and the UK have traditionally combined facilities for payment services (e.g. a cheque account), facilities for borrowing (e.g. personal loans), and a means of holding wealth (e.g. savings accounts). Life insurance offices have traditionally offered financial security in the form of, say, life cover with wealth accumulation which amounts to a long-term savings deposit. These and the basic product lines of other institutional groups are shown by the circles in the figures. Some of the international differences in financial markets simply reflect the different ways in which these three needs can be met by various service packages. Within nations, competition between intermediaries often takes the form of the adaptation of particular services to meet a slightly different need.

Considering the retail sector alone, a feature of developments in the UK over the last decade or so has been a broadening of the range of financial products offered by institutional groups. Life insurance offices have expanded into a variety of investment products based around unit trusts and managed portfolios. Banks have moved into life insurance and other protection products. They sell unit trusts and shares, offer money market accounts which are better vehicles for longer-term savings, and have moved into housing finance. Building societies now offer transactions services and, under new legislation passed in 1986, are able to offer insurance products and consumer finance to their customers. Figure 7.2 illustrates the directions of change.

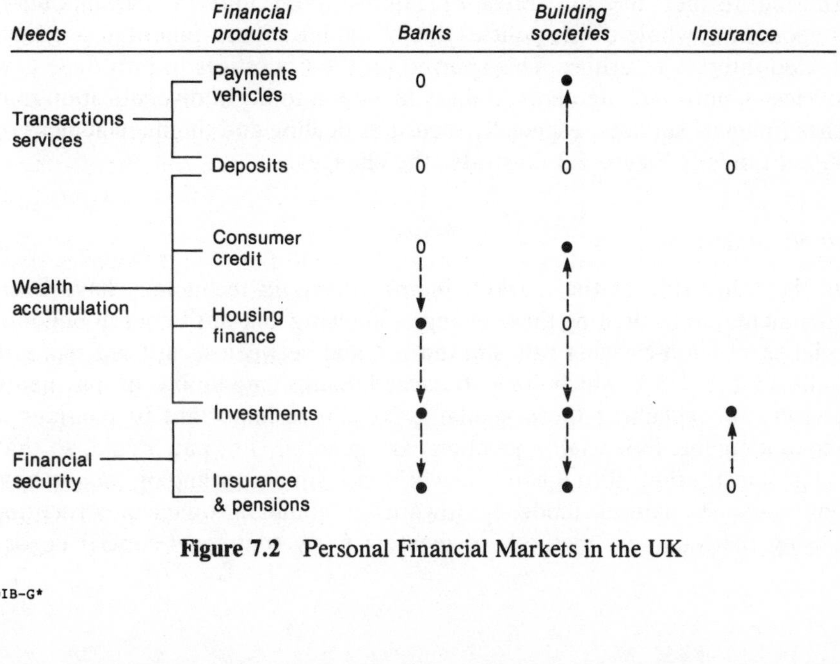

Figure 7.2 Personal Financial Markets in the UK

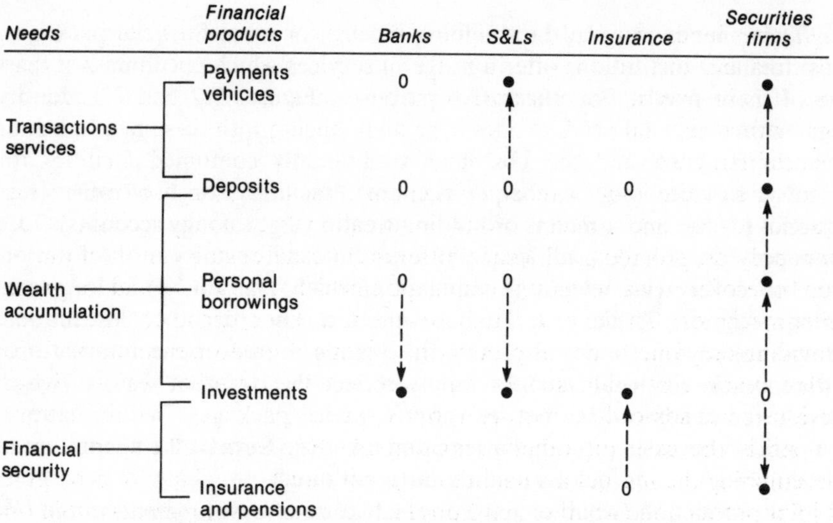

Figure 7.3 Personal Financial Markets in the USA

In the USA, the process of change in the 1980s has been rapid. Securities companies, which sold vehicles for longer-term savings, found that one of their basic products, the mutual fund, could be modified, repriced and allied to payments services via cheque-writing facilities. Legislation was rushed through in 1980 and 1982 which then allowed banks and savings institutions to offer new instruments such as money market deposit accounts and super-NOWs in competition to the money market funds. These new deposit instruments overlapped into the 'investment sector' of financial markets, exposing further the low rates of interest built into the accumulation component of whole-of-life policies due to the life offices' inherited portfolio of fixed-interest securities. This spurred on the life offices to introduce new policies — universal life and variable life — and to begin diversification into other financial services, especially securities dealing and the management of mutual funds.[15] Figure 7.3 illustrates the changes.

Supply of Services

On the other side of the market, improvements in technology have been instrumental in facilitating these changes, allowing link-ups between building societies and non-clearing banks in the UK and between securities firms and banks in the USA which have breached banks' monopoly of payments services. In explaining these similar trends, it is important to consider a second element. Financial innovations are generally not patentable, so that financial institutions throughout the world face similar technological and cost conditions. A natural tendency towards a common financial structure, utilising the least-cost methods of meeting fairly common financial needs, might thus be expected. In the light of financial deregulation, technological advances and the cross-fertilisation flowing from multinational bank expansion, it is interesting to speculate on the extent to which national customs, legal structures, taxation systems, and so on, will sustain differences in financial structures.

Some of the issues can be crystallised by considering two hypothetical situations. At one extreme, one multinational company could have a monopoly on providing all financial services to all customers in all nations from one office (via telephone banking, electronic networks and automatic teller machines). At the other, there could be a host of small companies each providing only one financial product to a group of customers in competition with a number of other suppliers in each small geographic region. Reality obviously lies somewhere between, but where?

As is the case for other commodities, the impact of transport costs (determining the market available to an institution), possible cost economies of joint production (whether joint production of several products within one firm is more efficient than separate production), and possible economies of scale (whether average costs of providing particular services decrease with the scale of production) are relevant. On all these counts a relatively concentrated structure seems feasible. Finance is often described as the most fungible of all commodities. Financial services seem ideally suited to the application of information technology, employing large multi-purpose capital equipment. To what extent this gives rise to economies of scale and scope is taken up in the next section.

Market structures are governed by many other dimensions, however, and we want to know whether there are characteristics of financial products which distinguish them from other traded goods and services. It is our contention that there are some differences. Market characteristics need to be seen as a continuum, with financial services most usually marked by a preponderance of certain features at one end of a spectrum. Financial markets are those which are perhaps most conditioned by time, information characteristics, confidence and trust.[16]

Service Characteristics

Firms operating in financial markets produce services rather than goods. The essence of a service is that it is performed on a particular person's, or firm's, behalf and brings about a change in the condition of an individual or organisation. Given the nature of a service, it cannot be regarded as existing until it is exchanged and, consequently, it cannot be produced in advance and stored on the shelf awaiting sale. Nor can services be ordered from stocks kept elsewhere. Thus, a service is basically intangible and non-storable whereas physical products have tangibility and can be stored and inventoried.

This dichotomy between goods and services can be overstated: after all, goods are required for the services they render and the needs they satisfy. The provision of financial services often requires considerable investment in plant, buildings, computer equipment, staff, and so on. All goods and services thus have some 'physical' and 'service' attributes. But the point remains that for financial services, the customer–firm interaction is at the forefront. For banks, which provide services jointly to customers on both sides of the balance sheet, there is a need to interface with different types of customers whose transactions vary in size and frequency and for whom transactions costs play differing roles. In retail business, the location of depositors (whose transactions are smaller and more frequent than borrowers') used to dictate the physical location. Technological advances have diminished the importance of location for deposit-gathering, and arrangements which enable access to cash and payments at, for example, supermarkets via electronic networks threaten to reduce the significance of location even more.

Information

Financial services take the form of a contract between two parties in which the identity and reputation of the parties is a key determinant of its worth. A two-way flow of information is entailed which is not common for many consumer goods. Continuing business dealings can lead to a 'banker–customer relationship' in which knowledge acquired by each about the other makes the costs of dealing with each other less than with some competitor. Two implications follow from this. First, where an important business firm diversifies geographically, there may be an incentive for its banker to follow. This has been an important factor in the growth of multinational banking (see Chapter 8). Second, entry into new markets (geographical, product) will be easier if information built up in existing markets can be utilised in those new markets, and if new contracts forged there flow back to existing lines (for example, bank holding companies' involvement in mortgage banking and consumer instalment credit).

Confidence and Trust

The need for confidence and trust is apparent from the intertemporal character of financial contracts, in which future obligations are traded against current receipts. Purchase of a financial contract requires an act of considerable trust in the stewardship of the institution concerned. Quality is hard to verify, standards are difficult to enforce, and the service is often irreversible. In these circumstances *reputation* will act as a powerful device in avoiding risks.

Once reputation is established, it becomes a sunk cost which can be spread across other product lines (with the firm seeking to trade on its good name by 'branding' other services, so reducing customers' search costs). The latter seems to apply particularly to Sears Roebuck (the retailer) and

American Express (the credit card issuer) in the USA. Both firms have an established reputation and are trusted. These characteristics have enabled them to climb over an important barrier to entry into financial services. In the UK, the entry of Lloyds Bank into the broking of real estate provides an example of 'branding' to enhance the perceived quality of this service. Of course, economies of marketing and advertising (e.g. Lloyds' Black Horse logo or the Citicorp logo) may be realised as well when offering a set of related services to actual and potential customers.

Without confidence, fractional reserve banking is difficult to sustain. In the absence of government guarantees, customers would most likely look for safety in terms of indicators such as the size of the institution ('safety in numbers'), its longevity (past survival being used as a guide to future survival), and its inherited reputation in other activities. In this respect, an explicit and generous scheme of deposit insurance, as in the USA, which reduces the significance of a bank's 'name' to potential depositors, can lower entry barriers and ensure survival to large numbers of small banks, as compared with the unstated guarantees common in many other countries. This difference has an important bearing on the industrial structure of banking in the USA compared with elsewhere.

Expansion Paths

When examining the activities of banks in previous chapters, we gave emphasis to their role as information producers and as providers of risk-bearing services. By acting as processors of information, banks enable individuals and firms to delegate to them the job of evaluating the creditworthiness of borrowers, monitoring their performance, and arranging 'workouts' when borrowers fall into arrears. As providers of risk-bearing services, banks pool customers' liquidity and credit risks, acting either by themselves (as is typical in retail banking), or in conjunction with other banks (as in wholesale banking). They also help customers gain access to securities markets by organising backup credit support and guaranteeing their performance (as in off-balance sheet banking).

Taking into account the additional factors mentioned in this section, we may be entitled to think of banks as **marketing intermediaries**, providing a range of distributive services to consumers.[17] In retail merchandising, the importance of the depth of the product range and the ambience of the shopping environment has long been recognised.[18] Financial markets, we have argued, are significantly conditioned by time, search costs and the attributes of quality and repute. There are also important **implicit contracts** in financial services deriving from the longer-term relationships involved. Banks' marketing services are bundled together with, indeed form part of, the financial products offered, so allowing customers to save on the access and search costs which they would otherwise incur.

Bearing these various characteristics of financial production in mind, we can identify four avenues for expansion, as relevant for financial as for non-financial firms:

(i) The simplest case, corresponding to traditional ideas of large-scale operations, is where more of the same activities are conducted from the same location in a concentration of activities in a **large-scale plant**.

(ii) In the second method of expansion, the services are provided from the same location to a **new market** (such as an institution serving the wholesale market moving into retail activities, or vice versa).

(iii) A third mode of expansion involves the establishment of activities in multiple locations, thus 'bringing the services to the customer', rather than vice versa. By establishing **branches and outlets** the firm reduces the 'access costs' (transport, time, effort) and search costs incurred by the customer in obtaining services. Location increases in importance as the frequency of transactions increases and the average size of transaction decreases. Day-to-day payment functions fall into this category, making physical proximity of importance for depository institutions. Clearly, changes in technology and the growth of Automatic Teller Machines, point-of-sale terminals and home banking, have important implications for the form in which the customer–firm interaction occurs, and the level of representation of the institution.

(iv) A fourth form of expansion involves the extension of the range of services provided (or activities conducted) by the firm. **Diversification of services** stems from customers' demands for a 'cluster' of services, embracing various combinations of transactions, wealth accumulation and financial security needs. To them, the relevant commodity is the group of services which is purchased jointly and at less cost and inconvenience than would occur had separate suppliers been used.[19] This is due to the saving on access costs and search time afforded by the convenience of 'one-stop shopping'. Here we have the basis of banks' provision of agencies for insurance. Alternatively, skills developed in providing particular services may be well suited to use in other activities, such as insurance companies using their investment skills to manage mutual funds. Diversification can take various forms: within the firm, as in 'universal banking' in Germany or Switzerland; in multifirm activities, as in the holding company form of organisation; or in other ways, like franchising or networking.

As compared with the situation in the UK, expansion of financial firms in the USA by the third and fourth routes listed above has been restricted by regulations compartmentalising firms by product and geography.[20] As the population has become more mobile geographically, both intra- and interstate, the potential has increased too for *existing* producers of the services to lower customers' external costs. Simultaneously, improved technology has made it cheaper for firms to expand by these routes, and thus to find ways around geographical and product barriers. But because the barriers continue to restrict banks, those firms with existing non-financial geographical distribution channels (Sears Roebuck) or with a widely distributed financial product line (Prudential, Merrill Lynch, American Express) have been able to enter consumer banking and develop as broadly-based financial conglomerates. Table 7.1 shows that these firms are able to offer their customers (albeit by different ways) a product line nearly as wide as that offered by UK banks, and certainly much broader than the services provided by US banks.

With various regulatory and technological barriers to expansion becoming less significant, it is important to ask what underlying cost conditions dictate the shape of expansion. (Unfortunately, though, technological changes may be reducing the relevance of the empirical record in providing an answer to this question.) Two aspects warrant attention: the extent of economies of scale and of economies of scope.

7.5 Economies of Scale and Scope[21]

Economies of scale in financial institutions are normally thought of in accounting terms as a decline in unit costs as output increases, without considering the production function which underlies the cost figures. But the strict definition is in terms of the production function. A cost saving resulting from economies of scale is said to exist when a proportional increase in all inputs used in production leads to a greater-than-proportional increase in output of the good being produced. For several reasons this strict definition is unduly constraining, if not irrelevant, for assessing the implications of size differences between financial institutions.

First among these reasons, we note that size differences between financial firms rarely (if ever) involve purely a scaling factor. Rather, they involve different characteristics in the firms' activities which may often be predicted on the basis of a priori reasoning. Second, financial firms generally engage in multiproduct operations. When a collection of inputs contributes to several outputs, problems are created for a strict definition of scale economies unless outputs are produced by completely independent processes or are perfectly joined products. Third, the standard approach focuses upon the internal production activities of the firm and largely ignores issues relating to the interface between customer and firm, and is obviously unsatisfactory when the products under consideration are services.

Various sources of scale (or size) economies can be identified for financial firms, most of which have been outlined in earlier chapters of this

Table 7.1 Comparison of Product Lines of Selected Financial Institutions in the USA and UK

	National Bank (USA)	*Federal Savings and Loan*	*Merrill Lynch*	*Prudential Bache*	*Sears*	*American Express*	*Clearing bank (UK)*	*Trustee Savings Bank*	*Large building society*
Cheque book/transactions account	Yes	Yes	Yes	Yes	Yes	Yes	Yes	Yes	Yes
Savings account	Yes	Yes	Yes	Yes	Yes	—	Yes	Yes	Yes
Certificate of deposit	Yes	Yes	Yes	Yes	Yes	Yes	Yes	Yes	Yes
Government insurance	Yes	Yes	Yes	Yes	Yes	—	Yes	Yes	—
Credit cards	Yes	Yes	Yes	Yes	Yes	Yes	Yes	Yes	Yes
Home mortgages	Yes	Yes	Yes	—	Yes	Yes	Yes	Yes	Yes
Consumer credit loans	Yes	Yes	—	—	Yes	—	Yes	Yes	Yes
Commercial loans	Yes	Yes	Yes	Yes	Yes	Yes	Yes	Yes	—
Investment Banking	—	—	Yes	Yes	Yes	Yes	Yes	Yes	—
General insurance broking	—	—	Yes	Yes	Yes	Yes	Yes	Yes	Yes
Life insurance broking	—	—	Yes	Yes	Yes	Yes	Yes	Yes	—
Insurance underwriting	—	—	Yes	Yes	Yes	Yes	Yes	Yes	—
Mutual funds management	—	—	Yes	Yes	Yes	Yes	Yes	Yes	—
Discount stock broking	Yes	Yes	Yes	Yes	Yes	Yes	Yes	Yes	—
Investment management/advisor	Yes	Yes	Yes	Yes	Yes	Yes	Yes	Yes	—
Real estate broking	—	—	Yes	—	Yes	Yes	Yes	—	Yes
Offshore services	Yes	—	Yes	Yes	—	Yes	Yes	Yes	—
Travel agency	—	—	—	—	—	Yes	Yes	Yes	—
Data processing services	—	Yes	—	—	Yes	—	Yes	Yes	—

Source: Committee on Banking, Finance and Urban Affairs, House of Representatives and Annual Reports.

book. To examine them, it is useful to set out a stylized set of accounts for the financial firm (Table 7.2). From the viewpoint of the firm, economies of size may be said to exist if increases in size lead, in the absence of reductions in its fee scale, to an increase in the rate of return on shareholders' funds. This definition, if unfamiliar, includes the standard one as a special case. Its advantage is in highlighting the three ways in which size economies can occur. (There is another advantage. Financial firms can substitute implicit interest — involving higher operating expenses — for explicit interest so that a focus solely upon operating costs can ignore any substitutions which are related to scale.)

Table 7.2

Profit and Loss Account

Income	*Expenditure*
Fees and charges	Operating expenses
Interest earnings on assets	Interest paid on liabilities
	Profit (transferred to shareholders' funds)

Balance Sheet

Assets		*Liabilities*	
Financial assets	A_1 ⋮ A_N	Deposits and other liabilities	D_1 ⋮ D_M
Capital assets	K	Shareholders' equity	E

The first source of scale economies is what we term 'real resource' savings, where physical inputs and thus operating expenses grow less rapidly than the scale of activities. Interpreting scale (for the moment) as being reflected in the size of balance sheet items, and assuming that all other items in the profit and loss account move proportionally to scale, profits will increase more than proportionally. Consequently, the rate of return on shareholders' funds will be increased.

Secondly, there is the possibility that increases in size lead to an ability to rearrange the asset portfolio so that interest earnings on assets grow faster than interest paid. Prominent is the scope to diversify across uncertain maturities of liabilities (and assets) as size increases and operate with a lower ratio of low-yielding reserve assets (see Chapter 3, section 4).

Third, the income earned on assets is stochastic. Variations in earnings in any period could lead to losses which reduce the firm's net worth. If increases in size lead to lower variability in profits, around the same expected level of profits, the firm may be able to operate with a higher degree of leverage and thus raise the rate of return on shareholders' funds for a given degree of risk (see Chapter 3, section 5).

General studies of portfolio management suggest that most of the benefits of diversification can be captured by a relatively small amount of diversification. In this respect, the 'pecuniary economies' outlined above (the second and third sources) should tend to diminish in importance as size increases,[22] and careful portfolio management should prevent lack of diversification from being a major drawback for all but very small institutions. However, experience indicates that diversification by banks need not be so effective. Agricultural banks and those with loans primarily to a particular industry or region (e.g. Texas oil, California real estate) may, because of loans to many customers, have an apparently diversified portfolio, but the common factor (of industry or region) behind those loans makes that diversification illusory. Expansion overseas by widening the market provides scope for gains from diversification, but lending risks have been concentrated there as well (see Chapter 10).

Some of the possible size disabilities facing small institutions have been greatly reduced by developments in market organisation and information technology. Futures and options markets enable small institutions to shift financial exposures onto specialised risk bearers, rather than rely on portfolio diversification. Markets in which mortgage, automobile and credit card loans are collaterised and 'securitised' enable a small firm to acquire participations in a wide range of financial assets. Interbank funding markets enable a pooling of reserve asset positions to occur outside the firm and they serve as an alternative to pooling within an organisation by means of the 'intra-bank market' which a branch network permits. With the development of micro-electronics, desk-top computers are able to equal or even outperform old-generation mainframe hardware. Time sharing and computer bureaux have further reduced the advantage of the large firm.[23]

Table 7.3 summarises the results of a number of empirical studies of scale economies in banking[24] for the United States (16), the UK (1) and Australia (2). The results for the USA display an interesting trend. While earlier studies pointed to the existence of scale economies, more recent results suggest a 'u-shaped' average cost curve wherein scale economies peter out at some moderate-size level.

Several reasons can be advanced to explain this change in the results. One possibility is that technological change has altered the cost conditions associated with banking. While this does, undoubtedly, occur (reducing the policy relevance of such studies), it does not explain the change recorded. The more recent studies often cover the same time period as earlier ones and we must thus look to differences in the methodology adopted and data used pertaining to the measurement of bank output, the measurement of costs, the statistical cost function adopted, the treatment of within-branch versus multibranch economies, and the role of joint products.

Table 7.3 Studies of Economies of Scale in Banking

Study	*Country and data*	*Approach*	*Results*
(1) ALHADEFF, D.A. *Monopoly and Competition in Banking*, 1954.	USA. Cross-section of California banks, 1938–1950.	Tabulation of operating expenses per unit of earning assets (loans + investment) by deposit size.	Unit costs (operating expenses per unit of earning assets) '. . . decline fairly sharply in the early ranges [up to perhaps $5 million in total deposits], remain fairly constant over a wide intermediate range [up to $50 million or more in total deposits], and then decline again in the range of the largest banks [over $275 million in total deposits].' (p. 83)
(2) HORVITZ, P.M. 'Economies of Scale in Banking', in Commission on Money and Credit, *Private Financial Institutions*, 1963.	USA. Cross-section of member banks, 1949–1960. Banks range in deposit size from less than $1 m. to over $500 m.	Tabulation of operating expenses per unit of earning assets (loans + investment) by deposit size.	Substantially in agreement with Alhadeff. 'The largest size group [deposits greater than $500 m] had the lowest costs and . . . the next largest group [$100–$500 m in deposits] was second lowest. The declines were usually sizeable from the smallest to the third smallest group [up to $5 m of deposits], but over the middle range of bank sizes [from $5 m to $100 m] there was virtually no decline.' (p. 14)
(3) SCHWEIGER, I. and McGEE, J.S. 'Chicago Banking', *Journal of Business*, July 1961.	USA. Cross-section of all member banks and Chicago banks for 1959. Banks range in deposit size from less than $2 m. to over $500 m.	Regression of operating expenses per unit of total assets on deposit size.	'Banks of less than $50m in deposits can realize marked cost savings by growing. Cost savings from larger size are very sharply reduced for banks larger than $50 m in deposits . . .' (p. 215)
(4) GRAMLEY, L.E. *A Study of Scale Economies in Banking* for Federal Reserve Bank of Kansas City, 1962.	USA. Cross-section of 270 Kansas City member banks for 1956–1959. Banks range in deposit size from $2 m. to $50 m.	Regression of operating expenses per unit of assets on total assets.	Unit costs decline continuously with bank size, but at a diminishing rate. (The largest size banks in Gramley's sample are much smaller than those in Horvitz's study).

Table 7.3 (continued)

Study	Country and data	Approach	Results
(5) GREENBAUM, S.I. 'Costs and Production in Commercial Banking', *Monthly Review*, (Federal Reserve Bank of Kansas City), 1966.	USA. Cross-section of 1,158 member banks for Kansas City and Richmond.	Regression of operating expenses on an adjusted measure of revenue.	Unit costs decline to a minimum for banks with about $300 m. deposits, and afterwards rise.
(6) BENSTON, G.J. 'Economies of Scale and Marginal Costs in Banking Operations', *National Banking Review*, June 1965.	USA. Cross-section of 80 member banks for 1959–1961. Banks range in deposit size from $3.4 m. to $55 m., and from 900 to 21,707 chequing accounts.	Separate studies made of six forms of 'output': demand deposits, time deposits, mortgage loans, instalment loans, business loans, securities. Costs of operating related individually to *numbers* of loans, deposits, etc. and to the average value of transactions (size of loans etc.).	'. . . there are economies of direct cost with respect to the number of deposit accounts or loans; but these are not great: efficiency of operations is not largely a function of bank size.' (p. 541)
(7) BELL, F.W. and MURPHY, N.B. 'Economies of Scale and Division of Labour in Commercial Banking', *Southern Economic Journal*, October 1968.	USA. Cross-section of 283 member banks, 1963–1965. Banks range in deposit size from $2.8 m. to $801 m. and from 1,000 to 57,000 chequing accounts.	Similar to Benston in study (6) above.	'Demand deposits, installment loans, business loans and real estate loans showed economies of scale' [with respect to direct cost].' (p. 133) They calculate an overall elasticity of operating costs with respect to output of 0.93.
(8) HASLEM, J.A. 'A Statistical Analysis of the Relative Profitability of Commercial Banks', *Journal of Finance*, March 1968.	USA. Cross-section of member banks, 1963 and 1964. Banks range in deposit size from less than $1 m. to $100 m.	Correlation between measures of bank profitability and deposit size.	'The results indicated that the most favourable size category (in terms of net return on capital) is neither the largest nor the smallest. Of the eight size [groupings] the seventh largest — $50 m to $100 m — is most favourable to high profitability . . . the least profitable size is that

Table 7.3 (continued)

Study	Country and data	Approach	Results
(9) THE MONOPOLIES COMMISSION Barclays Bank Ltd, Lloyds Bank Ltd, and Martins Bank Ltd, *A Report on the Proposed Merger*, HMSO, 1968.	UK. Cross-section of 6 clearing banks, 1967. Banks range in deposit size from $500 m. to $2,500 m. (dollar equivalents).	Tabulation of operating costs per unit of output by bank size.	'Using the value of deposits as a measure of output it was found that the larger banks had lower unit costs than the smaller banks.' (para. 162) 'Using clearing as a measure of bank output, no relationship could be found between unit costs and bank size.' (para. 163)
(10) EDGAR, R.J., HATCH, J.H. & LEWIS, M.K. 'Economies of Scale in Australian Banking, 1947–1968', *Economic Record*, March 1971.	Australia. Time series of 8 major trading banks, 1947–1968. Banks range in size from $144m. to $2,270m.	Regression of operating costs relative to deposits and loans, adjusted for account turnover.	'Seven of the eight banks have experienced scale economies in their commercial bank operations . . . but we have been unable to determine how important technical progress has been over the period.' (p. 36)
(11) SCHWEITZER, S.A. 'Economies of Scale and Holding Company Affiliation in Banking', *Southern Economic Journal*, October 1972.	USA. Cross-section of Minneapolis district banks, 1964. Banks range in asset size up to $100 m.	Regression of total operating expenses on output, measured by revenue from loans and investments.	'. . . the existence of scale economies for banks with total assets under $3.5 m., constant returns to scale between $3.5 m. and $25 m., and decreasing returns for larger banks. Banks in the $3.5 m. to $25 m. interval, while not subject to scale economies, are subject to economies of holding company affiliation.' (p. 265)
(12) DANIEL, D.L., LONGBRAKE, W.A. and MURPHY, N.B. 'The Effect of Technology on Bank Economies of Scale for Demand Deposits', *Journal of, Finance*, March 1973.	USA. Cross-section of 967 member banks for 1968. The largest bank processed over 100,000 chequing accounts.	Regression of operating costs of demand deposits on the number of demand deposits and the average value of transactions. Also examine response of operating costs to the type of technology used by banks (book-keeping machines, computers, etc.).	'The coefficient of the number of accounts is the scale parameter, indicating that there are some scale economies.' (p. 136) 'Banks using conventional technology with fewer than 10,600 accounts have lower average costs than banks of similar size which have used computers. . . . After a certain size has been attained, computer technology is far more efficient.' (p. 138)

Table 7.3 (continued)

Study	Country and data	Approach	Results
(13) LONGBRAKE, W.A. and J.A. HASLEM 'Productive Efficiency in Commercial Banking', *Journal of Money, Credit and Banking*, August 1975.	USA. Data sample as in (12) above.	Regression of operating costs on demand deposits on measures of plant size, branch expansion and form of organisation.	'Within the number of demand deposit accounts [per office] increases, average costs decline in all banks except unit banks which are not affiliated with holding companies '(p. 330) 'The number of offices operated by a branch bank has little effect on average operating costs per dollar of demand deposits.' (p. 329)
(14) MULLINEAUX, D.J. 'Economies of Scale and Organisational Efficiency in Banking: A Proft-Function Approach', *Journal of Finance*, March 1978.	USA. Cross-section of 951 member banks for 1971 and 1972.	Regression of profit (operating revenue minus operating costs) on measures of the number of banking offices (and prices of productive factors).	'The production function for all banks is characterized by increasing returns to scale. The magnitude of scale economies indicated by profit function estimates exceeds that of most cost function estimates.' (p. 278)
(15) VALENTINE, T.J. and WILLIAMSON, P.J. 'A Note on Economies of Scale in Australian Banking', *Australian Financial System Inquiry*, 1981.	Australia. Time series and cross-section of 7 major trading banks, 1970–1979.	Pooled regressions of operating costs relative to local assets and debits to accounts with other explanatory variables.	'There appear to be economies (of scale) to be achieved in the administration of the payments mechanism — represented here by a variable which is a proxy for the number of transactions per account. There is no evidence of economies with respect to the sheer size of a bank.' (p. 11)
(16) BENSTON, G., HANWECK, G., and HUMPHREY, D. 'Scale Economies in Banking: A Restructuring and Reassessment', *Journal of Money, Credit and Banking*, November 1982, Pt 1.	USA. 4 cross-sections of banks numbering between 747 and 852 for 1975–1978. Sizes ranged up to $1 b. (deposits).	Translog regression of total operating costs for five deposit and loan functions: input prices of labour and capital, number of banking offices, average account size, holding company affiliation variable, total bank output (various measures)	Branch and unit banks possess different cost functions. Perhaps the most dramatic finding is that economies of scale are experienced by the branch state banks and diseconomies of scale by the unit state banks.' (p. 443) '. . . for branch state banks, scale economies at the "plant" level change to scale diseconomies at the "firm" level.' (p. 446) 'Average operating costs for both branch and unit state banks are U-shaped or upward sloping.' (p. 452)

Study	Country and data	Approach	Results
(17) FLANNERY, M.J. 'Correspondent Services and Cost Economies in Commercial Banking', *Journal of Banking and Finance*, March 1983.	USA. Cross-section of 737 banks for 1978. Size ranged from $4m. to $1.5b. in assets.	Translog regression of operating costs on the prices of labour and physical capital, an account activity measure, number of branches, several (alternative) weighted average measures of bank outputs. Includes in the cost measures or estimate of 'omitted' costs in the form of interest foregone on correspondent balances.	Branch and unit banks have different cost functions due to 'significance of branches as relatively fixed-cost factors of production'. (p. 96) Little difference in results for various output measures. 'The average branch bank's explicit costs are characterized by significant scale economies.' (p. 94)
(18) CLARK, J.A. 'Estimation of Economies of Scale in Banking Using a Generalized Functional Form', *Journal of Money, Credit and Banking*, Feb. 1984.	USA. Cross-section of 1,205 metropolitan area unit banks for 1972–1977. Banks ranged in size from $7m. to $425m.	Generalized functional form regression of total operating costs on the prices of labour, real capital inputs and loanable funds and various (alternative) output measures.	'Economies of scale in the banking industry appear to be small.' (p. 67) 'The estimates . . . appear to be rather insensitive to the choice of a measure of bank output.' (p. 67) NB: Doesn't reject Cobb–Douglass although greater evidence of scale economies with generalized form. But even generalized form imposes always increasing or decreasing returns.
(19) GILLIGAN, T., SMIRLOCK, M., and MARSHALL, W. 'Scale and Scope Economies in the Multi-Product Banking Firm', *Journal of Monetary Economics*, May 1984.	USA. Cross-section for 1978 of 714 banks of size less than $1 b.	Translog regression of non-interest expenses on input prices of labour and capital, average loan and deposit sizes, output as measured by deposits and loans entered as separate variables to examine existence of economies of scope.	'Significant cost complementarities exist across the balance sheets of banks . . . we find product specific diseconomies of scale.' (p. 404)

The problems of defining bank output have been discussed earlier (pp.20–21) and the variety of measures used in the studies surveyed in Table 7.3 attests to those conceptual problems. Humphrey (1984) identifies two general classes of approach: the production approach (which focuses upon the number of accounts and transactions on accounts) and the intermediation approach (one version of which is the Sealey–Lindley view of loan volume as a measure of output, as discussed in Chapter 3). Paralleling these different interpretations of bank functions are different measures of costs. In the latter case, operating *and* interest costs appear to be the more appropriate measure of the costs of producing loans, while for the former (production) approach, operating costs alone seem more appropriate.

That choice between bank output and cost measures reflects a more general problem of the multiproduct nature of bank activities and the role of bank–customer interaction. On the latter score banks can incur explicit costs which reduce the transactions costs sustained by bank customers in consuming bank services. This is relevant to the role of costs in single versus multibranch retail institutions. A multibranch institution may incur greater operating costs than a single branch institution of the same aggregate size (if operating scale economies exist at the branch level), but may incur lower interest costs in attracting deposits because of the greater locational convenience to customers of multibranch operations. In fact, Humphrey (1984, Table 10) presents 1981 US data showing a u-shaped average operating-cost curve with a minimum cost per account for unit banks at a size range of \$25–50m. of deposits. Although the operating costs of branch banks of equivalent total size were significantly greater, their total (i.e. including interest) average costs per dollar of deposits were slightly lower. This is consistent with the argument advanced above regarding interest savings from locational advantages, but could also be explained by multibranch banks having larger average account size.

The multiproduct nature of bank output raises problems of statistical methodology since the possibility exists of joint costs yielding economies of scope. Formally, the problem can be interpreted as asking whether

$$C(X, Y) = C(X) + C(Y)$$

where $C(X, Y)$ is the cost of simultaneously producing X and Y while $C(X)$ and $C(Y)$ are the costs of independently producing X and Y. Where the equality holds, separate cost functions for each product (X and Y) can be estimated, but otherwise the interdependency needs to be recognised. Economies of scope exist when the two or more goods can be produced jointly for a total cost which is less than the combined cost of producing the same amount of each good separately.

Because of economies of joint production, standardised depository, loan, brokerage and insurance products may be produced in combination more cheaply than a number of specialised producers could produce the same products on a stand-alone basis. In addition, there are special factors arising from the nature of financial services. Among these we again note that:

- Offering a range of services in one office may provide the convenience of one-stop shopping to customers and reduce travelling costs when acquiring a package of services.
- By branding, a known and trusted supplier can reduce consumers' search costs.
- Dealing with a large and diversified firm provides safety in numbers and continuity of supply.
- The information flow to the financial firm from a customer's dealings in diverse financial services may reduce the costs of tailoring new services to meet that customer's needs.

An inability to cope adequately with multiproduct activities was one of the problems of the statistical methodology used in early studies. There, the common approach was to estimate a log linear cost relationship of the form (or some variant of it):

$$\log C = a + \beta \log Y$$

where C is total costs and Y is an output measure.[25] The estimated value of β indicated the nature of scale economies, a value in excess of one signifying decreasing returns to scale and a value below one signifying increasing returns. Attempts to generalise this approach to allow for multiple outputs (by adding extra output measures as explanatory variables) create severe problems of interpretation.[26]

A more fundamental problem with the log linear (or Cobb–Douglas) specification of the cost function lies in the strong assumption it makes about the shape of the cost function. Returns to scale are assumed to be increasing everywhere ($\beta<1$), constant everywhere ($\beta=1$) or decreasing everywhere ($\beta>1$). The possibility of a u-shaped curve is not permitted. Partly for this reason, more recent studies have focused upon cost functions such as the translog function which, in simplest form, could be written as

$$\log C = a + \beta \log Y + \delta \tfrac{1}{2} (\log Y)^2$$

Since the log linear function is a special case of the translog function (when $\delta=0$ in this simple version) researchers have been able to test (and generally reject) the assumption of unchanging scale economies over the entire range of output.[27] Moreover, the translog function enables the introduction of several output measures and thus provides for the possibility of discovering joint costs. To this date, however, the results on this score have not been definitive, although some evidence of joint costs has been presented.[28]

7.6 Diversification and Organisation of Financial Firms

The absence of definitive statistical evidence on economies of scope should not be taken to indicate that gains from diversification in the provision of financial services are not to be had. Various arguments outlined earlier suggest reasons. First, banker–customer relationships may create in customers a preference for purchasing additional financial products from a familiar supplier rather than from a separate producer. Second, savings on customer transactions costs from one-stop shopping may also bias demand in favour of diversified producers. Third, regulations have often prevented financiers from exploiting possible cost-reducing diversification strategies. Fourth, advances in technology raise doubts about the relevance of evidence from years past to more recent developments.

Taken at face value, recent experience (summarised in Figures 7.2 and 7.3) would tend to point to a trend in diversification and a move towards financial supermarkets and conglomeration. Nonetheless, that experience needs to be interpreted with caution. Some part of the recent growth in diversification needs to be seen as reflecting 'defensive positioning' by intermediaries as yet unsure of the path which the financial structure will take. Also, while many financial products can be mass-produced as homogeneous services (transactions accounts for example), many others need to be tailormade to reflect customers' individual needs. The ability of financial supermarkets to perform that latter role better than specialists is clearly open to doubt, although recent advances in information technology may enable an increased 'customisation' of financial services to accompany a widened product range.[29]

What also needs to be considered is the question of whether financial institutions can arrange to satisfy the range of their customers' needs by means other than in-house production. One possibility is that of joint ventures, cooperative arrangements and agency arrangements whereby links are created between independent financial institutions spanning a range of products. Customers of each are given access to a desired product range without the need for individual institutions to diversify into production of that product. Examples of such 'bought' diversification can be found in the UK building societies' provision of chequing facilities to their customers via agency arrangements with Scottish banks. Merrill Lynch provides transactions facilities on its cash management account by cooperation with Bank One, Ohio and VISA. Depository institutions in a number of countries offer agency facilities to insurance institutions. Such arrangements can also be used to overcome any disadvantages which might arise from being small. Shared automatic teller machines are an obvious way in which small retail institutions can overcome locational handicaps as compared with multibranch giants.

In all such joint venture arrangements, a problem which arises is that of 'guilt by association'. Inefficient service or the failure of an associated institution can rebound upon the institution whose customers have been steered in that direction. Service contracts normally have a short time horizon, raising doubts about the continuity of supply. Thus the willingness of institutions to pursue such links very far without some degree of ownership or control over their affiliates may be limited.

One way in which institutions can specialise but be a part of a diversified whole is via the holding company route. Indeed, banking groups in many nations frequently take this form, largely as a result of regulations which limit the direct involvement of banks in other financial services. In the USA, the number of bank holding companies has increased significantly from the 121 companies in 1970, when amendments were made to the Bank Holding Company Act of 1956, which brought companies owning one, as well as more than one, bank under the auspices of the Act, and established a more flexible standard for defining permissible non-bank activities. By 1985, the number of such companies had grown to 6,453, and they controlled 92 per cent of all commercial bank assets. The largest 248 companies, which are the large regional and multinational companies with consolidated assets in excess of $1 billion, controlled 82 per cent of aggregate holding company assets (and thus 75 per cent of all commercial bank assets).[30] Table 7.4 gives data for 1984 of the 10 largest US bank holding companies. Holding companies have allowed geographical diversification to owners in the face of restrictions on branching, and operation by means of non-bank offices into certain other financial activities. Table 7.5 indicates the most popular non-bank activities of bank holding company subsidiaries for 1982.[31] In the UK and Australia, bank holding companies have interests in finance companies, merchant banking,

Table 7.4 Ten Largest US Bank Holding Companies

	Domestic assets 1984 ($)	*Domestic deposits 1984 ($)*	*Banks*	*Branches*	*Non-bank offices*
Citicorp	106.0	42.7	42	375	525
Bank America Corp.	92.1	65.0	22	1,224	238
Chase Manhattan Corp.	49.6	28.9	15	373	240
Manufacturers Hanover Corp.	54.1	22.1	16	236	126
Chemical New York Corp.	38.4	22.1	11	310	177
J.P. Morgan & Co.	44.9	14.9	10	12	51
First Interstate Bancorp.	42.5	31.3	34	995	54
Security Pacific Corp.	40.0	23.6	12	666	583
Bankers Trust NY Corp.	34.9	9.1	10	14	88
First Chicago Corp.	31.8	14.5	15	24	80

Source: Information provided by Federal Reserve Bank of Chicago.

Note: Banks and branches are as of year-end 1984; non-bank offices are as of year-end 1983.

securities firms, travel agencies, and so on. (Table 7.1 shows the range of activities undertaken by UK banks.)

The expansion of bank activities via holding company arrangements is a cause of concern for regulators. At one level, fears about anti-competitive behaviour have arisen, as the non-bank subsidiaries may use the benefits of bank affiliation. At another, the possibility that bank stability might be threatened by the collapse of a non-bank affiliate has also been a worry. In Australia, the only modern example of a bank's position inducing official intervention (when the takeover of the Bank of Adelaide by the ANZ Bank was arranged) occurred as a result of losses sustained by its finance company subsidiary. Recently the Bank of England announced that it is moving the focus of its depositor protection and supervisory interests from the banks to the entire holding company or group activities.[32] At a third level, the problem arises of the potential for conflicts of interest, as information gained confidentially in one area of operations may enable unfair, profitable dealings in other areas. In this respect, the holding company structure may be perceived to have advantages over diversification within a firm and the need to erect 'Chinese Walls' to prevent the abuse of privileged information. Regulators and legislators in the USA have prevented banks and bank holding companies from undertaking activities where the potential conflicts and risks are acute. The Glass–Steagall Act prohibits banks from underwriting or purchasing securities for their own account, except for government and certain other investments, and bans affiliations and interlocks between member banks and securities companies. In addition, the Federal Reserve Bank specifies other non-permitted activities for bank holding companies (such as underwriting general life insurance, providing credit ratings on bonds, or acting as a specialist in foreign currency options). Finally, dislike of concentrations of economic and financial power has also played a role in regulatory concern about holding company expansions, especially in the USA where limitations have also been placed upon the ownership of banks by

Table 7.5 Non-Bank Financial Services Provided by US Bank Holding Companies, 1982

Finance company services	4,613
Insurance agent	2,440
Underwriting credit life	1,118
Loan servicing	995
Mortgage banking	623
Leasing	580
Issuing money orders and travellers cheques	177
Industrial banking	125
Financial adviser	92
Trust activities	68

Source: Federal Reserve Bank of Atlanta, *Economic Review*, May 1983.

other financial and non-financial groups (hence the concern about the 'non-bank bank' loophole noted earlier).[33]

In this last respect, concern about increased concentration in financial markets via the growth of giant financial conglomerates needs to be tempered by one observation. The deregulation of worldwide financial markets in the past decade has generally opened up domestic markets to giant *foreign* financial conglomerates. To the extent that they are able to compete effectively in domestic markets with local entities, the degree of concentration need not be increased. That feature, of foreign banks penetrating local markets, is but one aspect of a major trend in banking — its internationalisation — which we shall examine in the remaining chapters of this book.

Notes

1. Foreign banks which are recognised as DTIs can use the word 'bank' in their title so long as it is followed by 'licensed deposit taker'. The two-tiered structure is planned to be abolished in amendments to the Banking Act, expected to be placed before Parliament in 1987.
2. *United Dominions Trust* v. *Kirkwood* (1966).
3. Thus banks and savings institutions in the USA have separate charters and supervisory authorities, although there is some overlap in deposit insurance, since 357 institutions (just over half of mutual savings banks) amongst the 3,903 savings institutions in 1985 were insured by the FDIC. In the UK, the supervisory framework is meant to be based on function, not institutional form, yet banks and building societies have different regulatory authorities.
4. Thus a commercial bank acquired by an institution, normally prevented from engaging in banking under the holding company provisions, can forswear one of these activities – say, the making of commercial loans. The acquired 'non-bank bank' then becomes a 'consumer' bank exempt from the Act, yet is still able to obtain federal insurance and in every other respect act as a fully-fledged bank. This loophole has enabled retailers and securities firms to enter banking. See Lewis (1986) and Federal Reserve Bank Bulletin, June 1985, pp. 424–427.
5. For example, Guttentag–Lindsay showed that, if equal-sized changes in α and β were to have the same effect on C_t, the size of NFIs relative to banks needed is given by $K^* = 1/(\beta - \alpha)$. For 1965 US data they estimated a value of $K^* = 16$.
6. Two examples may illustrate this. First, the layering and fixed-ratios approach yields a money multiplier-type relationship between base money and NFI liabilities. Provided the multiplier is stable, broader aggregates incorporating NFI liabilities will move in line with base money and conventional money supply measures. Alternatively, the source of any NFI offset to policy can be determined by examining movements in the multiplier's components. A second example concerns the effect of banking deregulation. Enhanced competitiveness of banks carries with it a need for faster money supply and base money growth if growth in broad aggregates is not to be choked back. See Davis (1985) and Valentine (1985) for discussions of this in an Australian context.
7. Exactly how those responses differ depends on what is assumed about the behaviour of deposit rates. If they respond directly to the excess supply or demand for deposits, the impact of monetary policy is reduced (see Tobin 1969). If deposit rates vary with earnings on bank assets, the impact is increased (see Davis and Lewis 1982a).

8. For a recent interchange on these points, see Havrilesky (1986) and Niehans (1986).
9. That is, in terms of the standard textbook analysis of money supply determination, which gives:

$$M = \frac{1 + d}{d + r} B$$

where M is the money supply (cash and deposits) and B is base money, there is short-run variability in d, the public's cash-to-deposits holdings, and in r, the depository institutions' reserve ratio.
10. Constant reserve ratios are retained in the USA, although the rationale for their introduction earlier this century was more in terms of bank safety; see Goodfriend and Hargraves (1983). Variable reserve ratios featured prominently for many years in the UK (special accounts) and Australia (statutory reserve deposits) as levers upon bank lending, but they have been little used in the 1980s. Their original uses are described in Artis and Lewis (1981) and Davis and Lewis (1980).
11. For a recent survey of the predictability of the demand for money see Roley (1985). The impact of deregulatory changes upon the demand for narrow money is examined by Keeley and Zimmerman (1986), while Taylor (1986) examines changes in the GDP–narrow money relationship.
12. Working Group of the Cabinet Council on Economic Affairs (1985), Chapter 1.
13. Before passage of the Monetary Control Act of 1980, only banks that were members of the Federal Reserve System had regular access to the discount window. The act extended reserve requirements to non-member institutions and at the same time provided that any such institution having deposits reservable under the act (transaction accounts and nonpersonal time deposits) would have access to the discount window on the same basis as member institutions. These institutions include domestic non-member commercial banks, US branches and agencies of foreign banks, savings banks, savings and loan associations, and credit unions. Reservable transaction accounts are demand deposits, NOW accounts, automatic transfer accounts, share draft accounts, and any other account at a depository institution on which the account holder is permitted to make withdrawals by negotiable or transferable instruments, payment orders of withdrawal, and telephone and preauthorised transfers (in excess of three per month) for the purposes of making payments to third persons or others. See Board of Governors of the Federal Reserve System (1984).
14. Recent proposals by Karen Horn, President of the Federal Reserve Bank of Cleveland, and Gerald Corrigan, President of the Federal Reserve Bank of New York, indicate some of the difficulties in determining precise boundaries, even within one country. Both agree that 'transactions deposits' should be insured, but they disagree as to whether all institutions offering them should be called banks, with Corrigan looking to a return to a distinction between 'banks' and 'thrifts' on the basis of housing loans. Both also disagree on whether all deposits withdrawable by ATM should be insured, as well as money market mutual funds. Horn would include both, but Corrigan recommends that transactions balances must be payable to third parties (excluding ATM cash withdrawals) and at par (excluding money market funds). See Horn (1986) and Corrigan (1986) for their proposals.
15. Lewis (1986).
16. These characteristics are examined in greater detail in Carter, Chiplin and Lewis (1986).
17. Lewis (1987a).
18. But it is only recently that these factors have been formally incorporated into retailing models. See Betancourt and Gautschi (1986).

19. The concept of a 'cluster of services' in banking has long been recognised by US courts. In the antitrust decision in 1963 of *United States v. Philadelphia National Bank and Trust Co.*, the Supreme Court held that the relevant product line is the 'cluster' of banking products, making banking a distinct line of commerce. For discussion, see Rosenblum, Di Clemente, and O'Brien (1985) and a special issue of *The Antitrust Bulletin*, Vol. XXX, No. 3, Fall, 1985.
20. The regulations are outlined in Benston (1984).
21. This section draws upon earlier work by us (Davis and Lewis 1982b).
22. This can be seen from equation (3.9) in Chapter 3 above. Risk, measured as the standard deviation of the return on assets, is related to size, given by the number of independent loans, in the following way:

$$\sigma_{\omega} = \frac{cA}{\sqrt{m}}$$

A one-hundredfold increase in the number of loans is needed to reduce the standard deviation tenfold.
23. Chiplin (1986).
24. For a listing of other studies and further discussion, see Gilbert (1984) and Mester (1987).
25. Other explanatory variables such as factor input prices would be included where appropriate data were available.
26. See Davis and Lewis (1982b, p.670).
27. See Benston, Hanweck and Humphrey (1982).
28. See Gilbert (1984) for a survey.
29. See Lewis (1987a). Examples of financial products which can offer increased customisation due to improvements in computer technology are cash management systems pre-programmed to individual risk-return preferences, and 'universal' life insurance policies giving policyholders the choice of a number of investment vehicles and allowing them the flexibility to speed up or remit premium payments at will.
30. Information is from the Appendices to the Statement by the Chairman of the Board of Governors of the Federal Reserve System before the Subcommittee on Commerce, Consumer and Monetary Affairs of the Committee on Government Operations of the United States House of Representatives, June 1986.
31. Other activities include the provision of data processing services for the holding company, courier services, appraising real estate, and engaging in futures trading. Some of the activities permitted to bank holding companies can now be carried out by bank service corporations. Advantages of the holding company formula are the acquisition of banks and thrifts in certain other states and the undertaking of most permitted activities, except for retail deposit taking, across all geographic regions. Note, however, that the existence of many of the holding companies has nothing to do with geographic or product diversification, for they are single subsidiary companies. Rather, the one-bank holding company form of organisation offers tax advantages, because the two organisations can file a consolidated tax return, with the income of the bank reduced for tax purposes by the holding company's interest on its debt (Huggins 1986). Assets of the 'non-bank' subsidiaries of bank holding companies represent a modest percentage (6.4 per cent) of aggregate holding company assets.
32. 'Consolidated supervision of institutions authorised under the Banking Act 1979', *Bank of England Quarterly Bulletin*, March 1986.
33. Proposals for reform of US banking by Horn (1986) and Corrigan (1986), referred to earlier, envisage repealing all or some of the Glass–Steagall Act, enabling bank holding companies to undertake a full or fuller range of 'non-bank' services, but they wish to retain the separation of 'banking' from 'commerce'.

8

International Banking

8.1 Characteristics of International Banking

It is often said that there is 'nothing new under the sun' and the long and chequered history of international banking supports that adage. International lending by means of letters of credit and bills of exchange can be traced back as far as the twenty-first century BC (Walter 1985a). In more recent history, the Florentine banking houses of the fourteenth and fifteenth centuries — the Bardi, Peruzzi and the Medici — rose on the back of the growth of international trade in wool cloth and silks, and at the height of their influence had branches, subsidiaries and offices throughout Europe. Ominously, in view of present-day concerns about country indebtedness, the merchant bank empires declined just as rapidly as loans to sovereigns and princes assumed ever greater importance in their balance sheets, exposing their capital resources to the impact of tardy repayments and periodic defaults. Medici's London operation lent four times its capital resources to Edward IV, the successor of Edward III who had ruined earlier Florentine bankers (de Roover 1963).

During the nineteenth century, British and European bankers lent to the 'new world'. The economic development of the United States, from the colonial period through the nineteenth century, was financed in large part by capital from London and European centres. Not all of the capital flowing across international borders passed through the banks' balance sheets. British merchant banking houses — notably Barings, Hambro, Rothschild — sponsored, underwrote and held issues of foreign bonds. Many of the foreign bonds issued were acquired in the traditional way, by private investors through the London Stock Exchange. Others were issued 'internationally', much like Eurobonds are placed nowadays. The bonds were issued simultaneously by a number of issuing houses in several markets, each house specialising in selling the bonds to investors in their geographical region.

Yet much British foreign investment in the nineteenth century was carried out by banks, in particular the 'overseas' banks like Standard of South Africa, Hong Kong and Shanghai, London and River Plate, which were founded in London for the express purpose of funnelling funds to the Empire and other countries. In France and Germany, it was almost exclusively the banks which undertook foreign investment (Born 1983). Deutsche Bank was established expressly to challenge British domination of foreign finance (Kindleberger 1984). Many of the overseas banks undertaking foreign lending ran into difficulties, as did those underwriting and acquiring foreign bond issues. Davis (1976) notes that, in 1873–4 alone, the governments of Honduras, Costa Rica, Santo Domingo, Paraguay, Spain, Egypt, Turkey, Peru, Uraguay, Liberia, Guatemala and Bolivia defaulted on bond interest and repayments.

Throughout most of the first half of the twentieth century, the United States was a major source of net capital for Latin America, Canada and Europe, especially Germany, in interwar years. Most of the German borrowings were short-term, and US banks became heavily involved in extending loans during the 1920s. At the onset of the Great Depression, 90 US banks between them held two thirds of Germany's outstanding short-term debt, much of which was locked up in standstill agreements during the 1930s.[1]

What, then, is there about the growth of international banking in postwar years that is new? One difference is simply that of scale. In 1470 , the entire European network of branches and subsidiaries of the Medici empire employed in total 57 individuals spread over eight offices. This operation contrasts with Citicorp's 2,000 or so offices or 'money shops' in 90-odd countries, or Barclay's 2,000 branches, offices and finance houses in 75 countries. Yet such extensive networks are not a particularly new phenomenon. In 1910, there were 32 British colonial banks headquartered in London with a total of 2,104 branches in the colonies. Other London-based banks had branches in Latin America and the Middle East. Banks headquartered in France and Germany together had about 500 overseas branches at that time. In earlier years, British banks had opened branches in the United States.

Perhaps the outstanding feature of modern international banking is the extent of business carried out in so-called 'offshore' centres. These are locales where the conduct of banking is facilitated by favourable and/or flexibly administered banking laws, exchange control and tax structures, and in which the volume of business is unrelated to the size and needs of the domestic market. Offshore banking was not unknown in earlier times. For example, many Paris bankers took themselves and their funds to Geneva during the French Revolution and the Terror, and then conducted banking for Frenchmen away from French political influence: an idea copied by Russian and other banks in Paris and London with US dollars in post-World War II years.

Before the war, banks in London had taken deposits in US dollars and other foreign currencies from both resident and non-resident customers. During the 1920s there was an active business in US dollar and sterling deposits in Berlin and Vienna. The really crucial difference which distinguishes modern international banking came when banks operating in London and elsewhere began making loans in US dollars and in a wide variety of currencies. Previously, the location of a bank's operations determined the currency in which it would make loans; thus banks in London made loans primarily in sterling, New York was for dollar loans, Paris for the French franc, and so on. Such 'traditional' international banking still occurs. But, in addition, banks in each of the major European centres now take deposits and lend in US dollars (the Eurodollar market), or in Japanese Yen (Euro-yen), or in Deutschmarks (Euromarks), etc. As a consequence the nexus has been severed between the location of financial centres and currency of lending. Before, the major centre (London, New York) was determined primarily by which country had the largest amount of capital for export. London was able to survive the 'dollar hegemony' due to the innovation of the Eurodollar market. In much the same way, London is surviving the growth of Japanese and German capital exports during the 1980s because of the rapid expansion of the Eurobond market and because of new instruments which have blurred the traditional distinctions between international banking and bond markets. These developments are considered in Chapter 10.

Despite the continued use of the prefix 'Euro', the business is no longer confined to European centres. As of September 1986, 57 per cent of Eurocurrency claims were held at the European centres. The remaining transactions take place in locations as diverse as the USA, Canada, Japan, Bahamas, Hong Kong, Singapore, Bahrain and the Netherlands Antilles. A eurocurrency deposit may be held or a loan made in any part of the world where such transactions are permitted, which is normally outside the country that issues the currency in which the deposit or loan is denominated. Thus a Deutschmark deposit with a bank in Singapore is just as much a Euromark deposit as is a Deutschmark deposit with a bank in Brussels. In consequence, the branch and agency networks of major banks are no longer confined to ex-colonies or to countries with which major trade links exist: the networks are truly global or 'multinational'.

The types of activities undertaken by international banks are also diverse, namely:

a. taking deposits and making loans in domestic currency to foreign governments, enterprises and individuals;
b. taking deposits and lending in foreign currencies to domestic and foreign entitites;
c. managing and acting as agents for syndicated loans; designing special financing requirements for international trade and projects;
d. foreign exchange transactions, dealing in gold and precious metals, international money transfers;
e. providing documentary letters of credit, standby letters of credit, multiple currency credit lines, bank acceptances, Euronote issuance facilities;

f. trading in currency futures and options, financial futures and options, interest rate and asset swaps; writing interest rate caps;
g. underwriting and placement of Eurobond issues, distribution of Eurocommercial paper, assisting cross-border mergers, acquisitions and sales, financial advisory and investment services.

The first two are on-balance sheet business. The last four are off-balance sheet activities, while the third straddles the two.

We use the term 'international banking' to refer to the cross-border and cross-currency facets of banking business. For example, cross-border lending can occur in the traditional manner of taking deposits from foreigners and making loans to foreigners in the currency of the country where the bank is located. Lending by banks in New York to foreigners in US dollars is an example of this traditional activity. Until the 1960s, banks conducted the great bulk of their international banking transactions from offices in the home country. But now loans in US dollars may be made by banks located in London (some of which, we note, are branches of US banks). If the foreign currency loans by UK-based banks are to foreigners (i.e. non-residents of the UK), they are cross-border (i.e. external) claims and come under our definition of international banking. When such loans are made in US dollars (or other non-sterling currencies) to UK residents, they are cross-currency claims and are also included in our definition of international banking, in line with the Bank of England and Morgan Guaranty measures. Only the two cross-border categories are included in the IMF's measure of international (or external) banking.[2]

By the term 'multinational banking' we refer to the location and ownership of banking facilities in a large number of countries and geographic regions; that is, we focus upon the global nature and ownership characteristics of banking operations. Frequently the term 'foreign banking' is used to refer to the ownership of banking facilities located in one country by citizens of another. We prefer the term 'multinational banking' to signify the more global character of banking ownership and financial activities today. Multinational banking is distinguished from international banking to signify also that some different questions are posed by its existence. Before examining these we shall look at some more precise definitions of various aspects of international operations.

8.2 Some Definitions

Table 8.1 classifies the possible range of banking activities connected with a particular country, *A*, which for expositional purposes we shall take to be the UK. In the top panel are set out the activities undertaken in country *A*, where:

a. the activities of the banks are initially divided into domestic and

Table 8.1 Classification of Activities of Banks Operating in Country *A*

DENOMINATED IN	TRANSACTED BY	WITH	AT SCALE OF
1. BUSINESS LOCATED IN COUNTRY *A*			
Domestic currency (onshore)	1. Indigenous (*A*-owned) banks 2. Foreign banks	(i) Residents of *A* (ii) Non-residents	(a) Retail (b) Wholesale
Foreign currencies (Euromarket)	3. Indigenous (*A*-owned) banks 4. Foreign banks	(i) Residents of *A* (ii) Non-residents	Wholesale
2. BUSINESS LOCATED ABROAD			
Local currencies (onshore)	5. *A*-owned banks 6. Other banks	(i) Residents of *A* (ii) Others	(a) Retail (b) Wholesale
Other currencies (incl. Euromarket)	7. *A*-owned banks 8. Other banks	(i) Residents of *A* (ii) Others	Wholesale
Local currencies (onshore offshore)	9. International banking facilities	Residents of other than local country	Wholesale

Definitions:

Domestic banking	: 1(i) + 2(i)
International banking in *A*	: 1(ii) + 2(ii) [Traditional] + 3 + 4 [Eurocurrency]
Traditional international banking	: 1(ii) + 2(ii) + 6(i)
Eurocurrency banking	: 3 + 4 + 7 + 8 + 9
Offshore banking in *A*	: 3(ii) + 4(ii)
Wholesale banking in *A*	: 1(b) + 2(b) + 3 + 4
Domestic (*A*) currency wholesale banking	: 1(b) + 2(b) + 7 + 8
Multinational banking in *A*	: 2 + 4
Multinational banking by *A*-owned banks	: 5 + 7

foreign currency operations, both undertaken in the particular country;
b. the banks are divided into those indigenous to the country (locally owned and incorporated) and those owned and controlled by foreigners (primarily foreign-based financial institutions);
c. the nature of business is subdivided into business with residents or non-residents and also by scale, that is, whether retail or wholesale.

Both UK banks and the foreign banks operating there also transact business abroad. This is set out in the lower panel of the table. Here the major classification is between banking business conducted in the currency (dollars) of the host country (USA, for example) and business denominated in other currencies (including perhaps pounds).

International banking embraces two conceptually distinct types of operation. **Traditional foreign banking** operations involve transactions in sterling with non-residents (either banks or non-banks) who maintain balances with UK-based banks or borrow sterling from them for the purpose of effecting international payments or obtaining capital funds. These activities correspond to categories 1(ii) and 2(ii) in Table 8.1. In addition, though, UK-based banks (and some UK business firms) maintain foreign currency balances with banks abroad (such as US$ deposits with New York banks). Thus traditional foreign banking also includes 6(i).

The second category is **Eurocurrency banking** business, which in the UK comprises the operations of UK-based banks in currencies other than sterling with both residents and non-residents (who may be either banks or non-banks). Eurocurrency business conducted in the UK thus encompasses points 3 and 4 in Table 8.1, although the UK banks may engage in Eurocurrency business through branches in other countries. As noted, the name 'Eurocurrency' is somewhat inaccurate, since not all such markets are located in Europe. Nor is the acceptance of foreign currency deposits sufficient to distinguish Eurocurrency from traditional banking business, for banks in New York have long accepted sterling deposits, as have London banks accepted US dollar deposits. What is distinctive about Eurocurrency banking is the intermediation involved in foreign currencies and the relative freedom from local reserve requirements and monetary regulation.

The preceding components of banking business in the UK constitute international banking and incorporate 1(ii), 2(ii), 3 and 4. The remaining elements in the top panel of Table 8.1, 1(i) and 2(i), refer to transactions between UK-based banks and UK residents in sterling, and coincide with what has traditionally been viewed as **domestic banking**. In addition, some non-resident business is not for the purpose of effecting international payments, but represents the domestic transactions of non-residents based in the UK. As a consequence, some parts of 1(i) and 2(ii) may constitute domestic banking.

Offshore banking can be defined in two different ways. The first concentrates on the distinction between location and currency denomination of business. Defined as banking carried out in one country but denominated in foreign currencies, offshore banking in the UK comprises items 3 and 4 in Table 8.1 and is the same as Eurocurrency business. Alternatively, residency may be emphasised, so that instead offshore banking in the UK is business carried out there, denominated in currencies other than sterling, with non-UK residents. Defined this way, the business has normally been free of reserve requirements and monetary controls by the domestic authorities (of all countries). We shall adopt this latter definition which thus corresponds to items 3(ii) and 4(ii). This category is sometimes called 'entrepôt' or 'turntable' business.

Freedom from domestic monetary regulation is the basis of **onshore offshore banking**. This is business conducted by International Banking Facilities (IBFs), essentially onshore 'duty-free' zones, which operate in the USA and, since December 1986, in Tokyo. The idea originated in the United States in 1981 so that banks operating in the US could transact in US dollars with non-resident bank and non-bank customers along similar lines to the overseas branches of US banks. Other restrictions ensure that the business is 'wholesale' and not related to activities which would likely be conducted onshore. Although called a 'facility', there is no office or physical identity in the United States other than a separate set of books within existing bank institutions. IBFs are directly equivalent to the operations of US banks with 'booking', 'shell' or 'brassplate' offshore centres located in the Bahamas and Cayman Islands, as we shall explain in the next section. So we argue that onshore offshore banking should be included in the statistics along with 'conventional' Eurocurrency operations. From a global viewpoint, Eurocurrency banking comprises categories 3, 4, 7, 8 and 9.

Multinational banking has been defined as 'operating a bank in, and conducting banking operations that derive from, many different countries and national systems' (Robinson 1972, p. 4). Since 'conducting banking operations' embraces traditional foreign banking and Eurocurrency banking, while 'operating a bank in' picks up domestic wholesale and retail operations, this definition effectively encapsulates the whole of banking operations. In order to focus upon the issues of ownership and geographical expansion, we define multinational banking more narrowly (see p. 219). Multinational banking of British banks refers to categories 5 and 7, being the activities of British banks which operate branches and subsidiaries overseas. In the UK, multinational banking refers to categories 2 and 4, being the activities of foreign banks which operate in the UK.

By defining multinational banking in the UK in this way we exclude indigenous banks, but encompass both onshore and offshore activities. This classification frames the major questions to be asked of multinational banking. One question involves the motives that make foreign banks want to enter a country. Another question concerns the success of the operation. That is, having made the decision, what special characteristics enable foreign banks to compete successfully with local institutions in both offshore and onshore operations? These questions are discussed in section 8.5, which focuses upon the operations of multinational banks. For the moment, we return to international banking and Eurocurrency operations.

Another classification in Table 8.1 refers to the scale of business transacted. **Wholesale banking** refers to the type of banking business, and not the residency of the customer. As explained in Chapter 4, its main distinguishing characteristic, compared with retail banking, is the size of the units in which business is transacted, for wholesale bankers typically have a small number of large customers (on both sides of the balance sheet). Wholesale banking has some other features: bankers provide few payments services to customers; there is a large amount of interbank transactions; and much lending is by term loans. Since Eurocurrency business is characterised by these features (there is no Eurocurrency retail business), wholesale banking located in the UK comprises 1(b), 2(b), 3 and 4. The first two of these categories represent the UK market for sterling wholesale business, but may not constitute the *whole* market for sterling wholesale business. Exchange controls (or more particularly the lack of them) allow the development abroad of a Euromarket in sterling, in which both British and other businesses, and British and other banks, participate. This market, together with the domestic market, may effectively constitute a single market.

Two further points then follow. First, if a Euromarket in a particular currency exists, access of foreign banks to this market is in a real sense an alternative to entry into the domestic economy (although it is an alternative which the authorities may well not prefer). Second, if (i) the Euromarkets and the domestic markets in particular currencies are interconnected, and if (ii) the various Euromarkets are linked (in practice, very closely), it follows that the various onshore markets, along with the Euromarkets, will also be linked in all countries, albeit indirectly, and will possibly also constitute part of the one market.

There may exist various links between the onshore market and the Euromarket in any country. First, individual banks engaged in the two may (in response to market conditions) alter their mixture of activities between domestic and foreign currency business. Second, banks may adopt various covered or uncovered positions in foreign currencies, for example, borrowing in foreign currencies which are sold for domestic currency to make domestic currency loans. Third, for some firms loans in foreign currencies may be a substitute for loans in domestic currency. These links increase the complexity of monetary policy and the problems of defining money.

Because individual banks are engaged in both onshore wholesale banking (some to non-residents in the form of traditional foreign banking) and Eurocurrency banking (which is also wholesale), much of the earlier analysis in Chapter 4 applies. Thus, when we examine the nature of international banking in the next two chapters we focus most upon the differences which arise from the earlier analysis because the claims are cross-border and cross-currency. We shall now document the cross-border and cross-currency facets of international banking.

8.3 Measuring International and Eurocurrency Banking

Table 8.2 provides some measures of international bank lending and the Eurocurrency market for the years 1977 to 1986, based on data which banks in various countries report to the Bank for International Settlements (BIS).[3] We divide international lending by banks into three categories. First, there is *traditional foreign lending*. As at September 1986, outstanding loans made in domestic currency by European, US, Japanese and Canadian located banks amounted to $620 billion (valued in terms of US dollars), and were 17 per cent of the total. Second, there is *cross-border* (or external) lending by banks operating in the various Eurocurrency centres including the IBFs in the USA. At September 1986 outstanding claims totalled $2,380 billion, or 64 per cent of the total. Third, there are the *cross-currency* loans made by banks in foreign currencies to residents of the countries in which the Eurocentres are located. At September 1986, claims totalled $736 billion, or 19 per cent of the total. Together, the three categories sum to $3,736 billion. This figure corresponds to the Bank of England's measure of gross international bank lending. Except for a different treatment of IBFs since 1983, it tallies with the international bank lending figure produced by Morgan Guaranty Trust Company.[4]

Clearly, an outstanding feature of international lending is the extent to which the lending occurs out of Eurocurrency centres rather than from the domestic location of the currency employed. Thus, for example, Japanese and British banks make loans in US dollars from London rather than having the loan originate in New York. At September 1986, 83 per cent of lending occurred in this fashion rather than in the traditional way. These figures are 'gross' of interbank transactions and likely overstate the Eurocurrency contribution because of the extent of bank to bank loans included in the figures. At the foot of the table are appended estimates by the BIS of international bank lending net of double-counting which results from the redepositing of funds between related offices and other reporting banks within the reporting area. This leaves claims on non-bank entities, central banks and banks outside of the reporting area, along with the conversions of Eurocurrencies into domestic currencies (switching).[5] Net international bank lending so calculated is an amount totalling $1,710 billion at September 1986. Similar adjustments made by Morgan Guaranty Trust give a net Eurocurrency market figure. Even if we treat all traditional foreign bank claims as being on a net basis, it is apparent that about two thirds of net international bank lending (excluding cross-currency loans) is made by means of Eurocurrency credits.

Obviously, it is important to ascertain why so much of international bank lending is sourced from the Eurocurrency market. A parallel trend in the 1980s has seen issues of Eurocurrency bonds increase greatly relative to traditional foreign bond issues. During 1986, 83 per cent of international bonds issued were Eurobonds. Chapter 10 examines the reason for this trend in the international capital markets. We argue that it derives largely, as is also the case with international bank lending, from the benefits of 'globalisation' and the ability of banks to operate simultaneously and with an increased freedom of movement in a number of financial markets. Chapter 9 focuses upon Eurocurrency banking and the various explanations which have been offered by economists as to the functions of Eurocurrency banking operations. In the remainder of this section we give a broad outline of the structure of the Eurocurrency banking markets.

Prior to the formation of the international banking facilities (IBFs) in the USA and Tokyo, the Eurocurrency banking market could be defined as an international banking market dealing in deposits and loans and off-balance sheet business denominated in 'Eurocurrencies', i.e., currencies other than that of the country where the participating bank is located — for example, US dollar transactions made by banking offices in London. Being in US dollars, the business is not subject to any reserve requirements and any money supply controls applied by the Bank of England to sterling currency business. Since the banking is done offshore in London, or Paris, or Singapore, it falls outside the Federal Reserve's sphere of monetary controls. It was always open for a country to exempt certain kinds of transactions carried out at home in the domestic currency, namely those with non-residents, from reserve requirements and other controls, and that is the basis of the IBFs in the USA and their Japanese equivalents. Since 'the IBFs operate in an environment broadly similar to that in eurobanking centres' (Lamb 1986), we have included them in our definition of the Eurocurrency market in Table 8.2.

But political, rather than economic, considerations seem to have been instrumental in the origins of Eurocurrency business. After the Second World War, Russia and the new government of China wanted to hold US dollars for the financing of foreign trade, but not in New York where they would (like Iranian balances during the hostage crisis of 1979) be subject to US political control. Holding US dollars in Europe met their requirement. Some confirmation of this account comes from the name of the Soviet-owned trade bank in Paris, the Banque Commerciale de l'Europe du Nord. Its cable address is 'Eurobank', and it is believed that this telegraphic address was the original reason for the US dollars on deposit at that bank being called 'Euro'-dollars.[6]

Once it was appreciated that Eurodollars — dollars held outside the United States — were free of US political control, it did not take bankers long to recognise that the dollar balances were also free of US banking laws governing the holding of required reserves and controls upon the payment of

Table 8.2 Measures of International[1] Bank Lending and the Eurocurrency Market as at End of Year, 1977–1986 ($ billion)

	1977	1978	1979	1980	1981	1982	1983	1984	1985	1986[2]
I. EXTERNAL LENDING IN EUROCURRENCIES BY BANKS IN:										
1. European centres	384.9	501.9	639.8	751.3	846.6	866.8	903.4	921.4	1,119.5	1,308.1
2. Canada	17.8	21.9	25.0	34.9	36.9	37.0	39.5	39.7	42.8	44.9
3. Japan	18.2	25.7	34.0	48.7	63.6	65.6	78.3	86.9	120.9	163.5
4. United States[3]	—	—	—	—	63.4	144.6	172.4	188.6	201.7	230.2
5. Other offshore centres	174.1	214.5	262.2	318.0	411.0	426.9	501.1	519.9	587.6	633.3
6. Total external lending in Eurocurrencies	595.0	764.0	961.4	1,152.9	1,421.5	1,540.9	1,694.7	1,756.5	2,072.5	2,380.0
II. FOREIGN CURRENCY LENDING TO RESIDENTS IN:										
7. Europe, Canada and Japan	153.5	191.0	242.0	319.0	382.9	429.3	450.6	459.9	561.1	736.5
8. **Bank of England/Morgan measure of gross Eurocurrency market**	748.5	955.0	1,203.4	1,471.9	1,804.4	1,970.2	2,145.3	2,216.4	2,633.6	3,116.5

III. DOMESTIC CURRENCY LENDING TO FOREIGNERS BY BANKS IN:										
9. European centres	81.4	109.5	136.2	151.7	151.6	156.2	145.8	141.6	209.4	276.6
10. Canada	0.4	0.5	0.6	0.6	1.3	1.8	2.4	3.6	2.9	3.1
11. Japan	3.5	8.0	11.4	17.0	21.0	25.3	30.8	40.0	73.8	129.1
12. United States	90.2	115.5	133.9	172.6	188.2	211.1	216.9	210.1	210.3	211.0
13. **Bank of England measure of gross international bank lending**	924.0	1,188.5	1,485.5	1,813.8	2,166.5	2,364.6	2,541.2	2,611.7	3,130.0	3,736.3
14. **IMF measure of gross international bank lending** (= 13−7) (= 6+9+10+11+12)	770.5	997.5	1,243.5	1,494.8	1,783.6	1,935.3	2,090.6	2,151.8	2,568.9	2,999.8
Memo: Net international bank lending (BIS)	435	530	665	810	945	1,020	1,240	1,280	1,485.0	1,710
Net size of Eurocurrency market (Morgan Guaranty)	390	495	590	750	890	960	985	n.a.	n.a.	n.a.

Sources: BIS, *International Banking Developments* First Quarter 1984, First Quarter 1985, First Quarter 1986, Third Quarter 1987. Morgan Guaranty Trust Co., *World Financial Markets* (various).

Notes: 1. All cross-border and cross-currency business of BIS reporting banks. See text.
2. End of September 1986 figures.
3. Mainly IBFs.

interest. Freedom from such controls has given Eurobanking a competitive advantage which is still able to attract customers away from traditional foreign banking. This is especially the case for the currencies of those countries (United States, West Germany) which continue to apply reserve requirements on domestic banking transactions or which exempt overseas subsidiaries of banks from domestic capital adequacy requirements (e.g. West Germany) or which restrict the range of activities that banks undertake (United States, Japan).

For other countries, where banking activities are treated differently, the sharp distinctions between traditional foreign banking and Eurobanking are increasingly being blurred, since the two are carried out under much the same set of rules. Thus in the UK there are no reserve requirements, interest rate restrictions or maturity controls upon either domestic currency or foreign currency banking by banks in the UK. Both categories of banking are subject to a uniform climate of prudential oversight governing holdings of capital and liquidity. We consider the supervision over international banking on prudential grounds in Chapter 11. Despite recent moves to harmonise prudential regulation, considerable differences remain in how foreign currency business is treated in different countries, and the extent to which banking authorities supervise the operations of their own banks in overseas locales.

Eurocurrency market activities have also greatly outpaced banks' domestic currency banking business because world trade has grown faster than domestic economic activity. Some offshore financial centres are also tax havens, and transactions occur there for this reason. Freedom from taxation and banking controls is not the whole story. London remains the largest offshore centre, despite being located in what is in comparison with the tax havens a heavily taxed country. Some (but not much) Eurobanking is transacted in Germany, although that country imposes reserve requirements on Eurocurrency liabilities of banks located within its borders. Other relevant factors are the range of money markets available, commercial laws, exchange controls, communication facilities, the country's time zone, its language, and political and social stability.

Because of some of these factors, Eurocurrency activities are now conducted on a large scale in certain locations outside Europe. Customers of the markets are located in almost all countries of the world, and include central banks and official monetary institutions, and also non-bank customers, as well as other commercial banks. The US dollar is the main currency of denomination of banking, but other currencies are used and they have altered in importance in recent years. Much of the first great wave of growth in the late 1950s was due to the influx of US bankers to Europe, but the relative importance of US banks has declined over the years. The major centres have different financial characteristics. Tables 8.3–8.5 examine the Eurocurrency market in terms of the first four factors: location of centres, currency composition, type of customer, country of source of participating banks. The characteristics of the major financial centres for international banking are surveyed in the following section.

Location of Operations

Part A of Table 8.3 divides gross Eurocurrency claims into the geographical regions of operation at various dates from 1977 to 1985. Banks in Western Europe constituted the largest single area of operations in the world, with London having a share of just under 30 per cent of overall Eurocurrency business at the end of 1985. Banks in the United States (by means of IBFs), Japan and Canada together held claims of $537 billion. The remaining $552 billion of claims was held in seven offshore centres: the Bahamas, Singapore, Bahrain, Hong Kong, Cayman Islands, Panama and Netherlands Antilles.[7]

Since 1977, London's relative position as the largest centre for Eurocurrency operations has declined somewhat with the rise of New York and Tokyo. The United States captured second place amongst host countries soon after the establishment of the IBFs in 1981, but has since been displaced by Japan. Expansion also in Singapore and Hong Kong has seen the Far East assume greater importance in the 1980s.

Currency Composition

The US dollar has always been the most widely used currency for the denomination of Eurocurrency transactions. Dollar denominated Eurocurrency claims (i.e. Eurodollar claims) as at December 1985 amounted to 78 per cent of total Eurocurrency claims. After the US dollar, the most widely used currencies are the German mark, Swiss franc, and the Japanese yen. Relative usage of the dollar in Eurocurrency transactions has changed little over the years, and the same is true of the Swiss franc. Increased usage of the yen since 1977 has coincided with a declining relative use of the German mark in the denomination of Eurocurrency transactions.

A survey by Grassman (1975) found the US dollar and German mark to be the most widely used currencies for the invoicing of foreign trade. The United States and Germany also levy relatively high reserve requirements upon domestic banks, encouraging the development of Euromarkets in these currencies.

Type of Customer

Banks in the Eurocurrency market have three types of customers: non-banks, central banks, and other commercial banks. Table 8.3 shows the distribution of claims between these groups from 1977 to 1983. Interbank positions include *intra*-bank transactions; that is, transactions between offices of the

Table 8.3 Location of Eurocurrency Centres and Distribution of Claims by Currency and Type of Customer, 1977–1985

	December 1977		*December 1980*		*June 1983*		*December 1985*	
	Total	*%*	*Total*	*%*	*Total*	*%*	*Total*	*%*
A. MARKET CENTRES								
(a) *European centres:*								
United Kingdom	232	(31.4)	485	(31.8)	635	(30.9)	764	(29.2)
France	64	(8.6)	124	(8.1)	127	(6.2)	190	(7.3)
Luxembourg	46	(6.2)	84	(5.5)	79	(3.8)	121	(4.6)
Belgium	22	(3.0)	62	(4.1)	74	(3.6)	116	(4.4)
Netherlands	27	(3.6)	55	(3.6)	52		65	(4.4)
Italy	23	(3.1)	46	(3.0)	37		63	
Switzerland	20		35		34		46	
Austria	10		23		25		45	
W. Germany	16		25		23		30	
Spain	9		21		17		22	
Sweden	4		11		14		20	
Denmark	2		3		4		11	
Ireland	2		4		4		5	
Unallocated	34		67		114		26	
(b) *Other centres*								
United States[1]	—		—		171	(8.3)	192	(7.3)
Japan	36	(4.9)	100	(6.6)	126	(6.1)	273	(10.4)
Canada	25	(3.4)	54	(3.6)	67	(3.3)	72	(2.8)

(c) *Other offshore centres*								
Bahamas	90	(12.2)	126	(8.3)	137	(6.7)	143	(5.5)
Singapore	21	(2.8)	54	(3.6)	105	(5.1)	130	(5.0)
Bahrain	16		38		57	(2.8)	52	
Hong Kong	8		32		54		101	(3.9)
Cayman Islands[2]	16		33		46		86	(3.3)
Panama	15		35		43		33	
Netherlands Antilles	2		7		11		7	
B. CURRENCY								
US dollar	562	(75.9)	1138	(74.7)	1641	(79.8)	2031	(77.7)
German mark	104	(14.1)	190	(12.5)	175	(8.5)	202	(7.7)
Swiss franc	35	(4.7)	83	(5.4)	98	(4.8)	117	(4.5)
Japanese yen	4		17		29	(1.4)	68	(2.6)
British pound	10	(1.4)	36	(2.4)	25	(1.2)	32	(1.2)
French franc	7		22	(1.4)	20			
Dutch guilder	8	(1.1)	12		20			
Others (inc. ECU)	10		26		48			
C. CUSTOMER								
Interbank	505	(68.2)	1047	(68.7)	1483	(72.1)		
Official monetary insts.	100	(13.5)	150	(9.8)	84	(4.1)	n.a.	n.a.
Non-banks	135	(18.3)	327	(21.5)	489	(23.8)		
GROSS MARKET SIZE[3]	740	(100)	1524	(100)	2056	(100)	2615	(100)

Sources: Morgan Guaranty Trust Co., *World Financial Markets*, January 1984. BIS, *International Banking Developments*, July 1986. IMF, *International Financial Statistics*, December 1986.

Notes: 1. IBFs only.
2. US branches only.
3. Due to data revisions, figures for gross market size reported here for 1977, 1980 and 1985 differ slightly from those calculated in column 8 of Table 8.2.

same banking groups located in different countries. Data recently released by the BIS enable us to distinguish such intra-bank positions from inter-bank transactions from 1984 to 1986. These data are shown in Table 8.4. As at September 1986, loans to related offices amounted to $730 billion (23 per cent of total claims), loans to other banks were $1,477 billion (46 per cent), loans to non-bank entitites amounted to $971 billion (30 per cent), and claims on central banks and CDs held were $52 billion (1.6 per cent). Non-banks are much more important as borrowing customers than as suppliers of funds. By contrast, central banks are larger depositors than borrowers from the market. In rough terms, around 70 per cent of transactions are either intra- or inter-bank.

Eurocurrency bank lending to non-banks can be split into two broad categories. One is short-term bank lending which is not publicised, and the other is syndicated credits of which three quarters are to public sector borrowers. Syndicated lending by Eurocurrency banks is examined in Chapter 10.

Table 8.4 International[1] Assets and Liabilities of BIS Reporting Banks[2] by Type of Customer as at September, 1984–1986 (%)

	ASSETS			*LIABILITIES*		
	1984	*1985*	*1986*	*1984*	*1985*	*1986*
Related offices[3]	22.6	22.2	22.6	23.1	22.8	24.5
Other reporting banks	43.5	44.6	45.7	45.9	46.8	46.5
Non-bank entities	32.3	31.5	30.1	19.9	20.0	19.5
Official monetary institutions	1.0	1.1	1.0	5.8	6.0	5.0
Certificates of deposit	0.6	0.6	0.6	5.3	4.4	4.5
TOTAL	100.0	100.0	100.0	100.0	100.0	100.0
$ billion	2,235.9	2,486.2	3,228.9	2,131.0	2,397.1	3,092.7

Source: BIS, *International Banking Developments*, Third Quarter 1986.

Notes: 1. 'International' consists of all cross-border business, plus local business in foreign currency with non-banks and non-affiliated banks.

2. Banks in European reporting countries, Canada, Japan, United States and the cross-border operations of the branches of US banks in Bahamas, Cayman Islands, Panama, Hong Kong and Singapore.

3. Cross-border transactions with related offices. Positions on related offices are not reported by banks operating in Canada, Germany and Italy.

Participation by Banks

Banks which operate in the Eurocurrency market, which is largely but not exclusively a market in US dollars, are of a wide variety. Some are branches and subsidiaries of US banks operating in London and other Eurocentres, such as Chase Manhattan's branches in London or Paris. Others are large banks with a strong multinational presence domiciled in the United Kingdom, Japan, or France, for example, such as Barclays, Fuji Bank or Banque Nationale de Paris which may transact at head office or at an overseas branch. Some are smaller banks specialised in international trade and finance, like the British merchant banks. Others are just ordinary local commercial banks with some borrowing and lending in Eurocurrencies. In some cases, banks may be established specifically to transact in Eurocurrencies. Such consortia banks allow groups of banks to pool their individual resources. However, consortia banks hold only about 2 per cent of total international bank claims.[8] Noting this exception, it can be said that participation in Eurocurrency lending or international lending generally is *not* carried out by special 'Eurobanks'. Eurobanking is part of ordinary banks' overall balance sheet, and the risks of international lending are borne along with the risks of domestic banking.

Growth of international bank lending, and the Eurocurrency markets, has been sustained by successive waves of participation by banks of different countries. Each wave has been marked by rate cutting by the banks concerned to gain a presence, after which follows a period of consolidation. There was first the migration of US banks to the European centres. Then

Table 8.5 International[1] Bank Lending by Source Country[2] of Parent Bank, September 1986

	Total claims		*Non-bank claims*	
Source of parent bank	*\$ billion*	*% of total*	*\$ billion*	*% of total*
Japan	1,019.4	31.6	286.2	29.5
United States	601.2	18.6	162.5	16.7
France	264.5	8.2	76.2	7.9
West Germany	250.5	7.8	77.9	8.0
United Kingdom	213.1	6.6	73.0	7.5
Switzerland	145.3	4.5	36.5	3.8
Italy	120.9	3.7	33.0	3.4
Canada	90.2	2.8	33.6	3.5
Netherlands	89.1	2.7	31.1	3.2
Belgium	65.7	2.0	26.2	2.7
Austria	55.8	1.7	13.0	1.3
Consortia	44.4	1.4	19.6	2.0
Other developed countries	171.6	5.3	68.6	7.1
Middle East	26.5	0.8	6.4	0.7
Others	70.7	2.3	26.9	2.7
TOTAL	3,228.9	100.0	970.7	100.0

Source: BIS, *International Banking Developments*, January 1987.

Notes: 1. 'International' is defined as in Table 8.4.
2. Country of incorporation or charter of the parent bank.

came the large scale participation by European banks. After 1974 Japanese banks entered international banking in a very large way. The final wave in the late 1970s and 1980s has seen the entry of Middle Eastern and Antipodean banks to the Eurocurrency markets.

Table 8.5 classifies international bank assets as at September 1986 according to the nationality of the parent bank. Japanese and US banks dominate. Together, banks sourced in the two countries account for nearly 50 per cent of outstanding claims. French, German and British banks, in that order, have the next largest shares. North American, European and Japanese banks together account for 94 per cent of international bank lending.

8.4 The Major International Centres

Since banking taxes, levies, licence fees, exchange controls, chartering and other conditions differ between centres, and change over time, almost every financial centre has its own special characteristics and balance of business. Our discussion must necessarily be selective and we focus upon the four major areas for international banking, namely London, Tokyo, New York and the 'offshore centres', which we divide into the Caribbean and Hong Kong and Singapore. Panel A of Figure 8.1 shows, as at September 1986, the shares of international bank lending, which we define as before as traditional foreign lending and Eurocurrency bank lending. Since the latter dominates, our examination naturally concentrates most upon Eurocurrency operations.

Financing generally is moving increasingly to a New York–London–Tokyo axis, and the other panels of Figure 8.1 present for information other comparisons across centres. Panel B shows the results of a survey of foreign exchange dealing in London, New York and Tokyo undertaken by central banks in those three countries during March 1986 (reported in Comotto, 1986). The other panel gives a comparison of stock markets around the world as at the end of 1985 in terms of the market capitalisation of both equities and bonds.

London

London is far more of an international centre than either New York or Tokyo. While its stock market is far smaller than the other two, 20 per cent of the listed companies in London are foreign as compared with 3.5 per cent in New York, 6.5 per cent in both NASDAQ and the American exchanges, and 1.4 per cent on the Tokyo exchange. Turnover of foreign exchange in London is nearly as large as that of New York and Tokyo combined. Such are the centripetal forces in modern-day computerised and telephone markets that many dealers in London report that even the vast New York market is to some extent a derivative of London when their trading hours overlap, in the sense that the largest deals in New York are routed through London.[9]

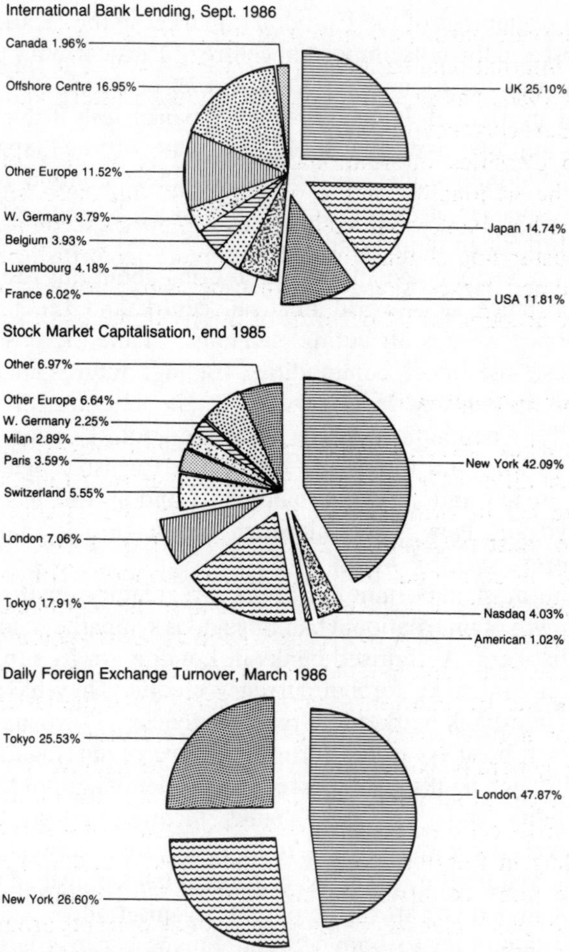

Sources: International Bank Lending: as per Table 8.2.
Stock Markets: London Stock Exchange.
Foreign Exchange: see *Bank of England Quarterly Bulletin*, Sept. 1986.

Figure 8.1 Comparisons of International Financial Centres

At this juncture we note that a distinction needs to be made between foreign exchange transactions, entailing the buying and selling of foreign exchange, and Eurocurrency transactions, involving banks in the borrowing and lending of foreign exchange. In the former, a switch of currency must occur, while in the latter the borrowing and lending can all be in the one currency. Nevertheless, as we explain in the next chapter, much foreign exchange trading is covered by means of borrowing and lending, and here foreign exchange and the Eurocurrency activities overlap, reinforcing the position of London relative to other centres.

From the beginnings of the Eurodollar market in the 1950s, London has been the largest and the most important centre of Eurocurrency operations. It has sustained this position even though the position of UK banks is overshadowed by that of Japanese and US banks (see Table 8.5 above). Lamb (1986) reports that almost 40 per cent of the Japanese banks' international banking business is booked by their London branches and subsidiaries. A quarter of the international banking business of US banks is also conducted through their London offices.

A number of factors have interacted to bring about this result. London's historical importance as a world financial centre and the financial skills thereby developed were contributing elements. Unlike the position in some other countries, insurance, commodities trading, futures markets, stock-broking, bond trading and legal services in the UK are all concentrated around the City. Communications facilities are good, London is a pleasant city in which to live, and the ability to use the English language is clearly advantageous to US and Japanese bankers. London also has a time zone between Tokyo and New York, although this feature is shared by other European centres.

One of the most important factors is a regulatory environment which favours the growth of international banking and is sympathetic to the needs of international bankers. Authorised banks in London are free to take foreign currency deposits or make foreign currency credits. They have access to a deep domestic interbank market in foreign currencies. There are no obstacles placed upon such business in the form of reserve requirements or maturity constraints, although banks are expected, on prudential grounds, to maintain adequate liquidity and, for those banks incorporated in the UK, an appropriate level of capital funds. Unlike some other centres, no separate capitalisation is required of branches of foreign banks; instead, their capital adequacy is evaluated as part of the parent organisation.

Especially important to both US and Japanese banks is the ability to operate in London as 'universal' banks, for London is the focal point of the Eurobond market: some traders suggest that as much as 80 per cent of issues are organised in London. As one indicator of the significance of this market, in both 1983 and 1984 the volume of US dollar Eurobonds issued actually exceeded the total issues of corporate bonds in US domestic markets. Involvement in the arranging of Eurobond issues is important to banks because of the business which carries through to interest rate and currency swaps, since a large proportion of fixed rate Eurobond issues is swap-related. US banks are no longer debarred from engaging in securities business, despite the constraints of the Glass-Steagall Act. Through affiliates, they are in fact able to underwrite or distribute 80 per cent of domestic securities issues, including commercial paper. But underwriting of corporate bonds and equities is still prohibited, and this applies also to the foreign branches of US banks. But the ownership of foreign subsidiaries enables the banking organisations to conduct a broad range of financial activities, and most of the large US banks have merchant or investment banks in London underwriting corporate debt and equity securities.[10] These subsidiaries frequently syndicate placements of both Eurobonds and international loans.

The Japanese equivalent of the Glass-Steagall Act, dating back to the US military occupation in early post-war years, constrains Japanese banks and their branches from engaging in a full range of securities activities. A London location offers to them much the same advantages as it offers to US banks, namely the freedom to combine banking and securities business. The same is true for Nomura Securities, the largest Japanese securities firm, which is able to operate also as a bank in London, which is denied to it in Tokyo or New York. All 13 of the Japanese City banks operate in London, as do the three Long Term Credit banks and six of the seven Trust banks. The Japanese banks use the London market extensively to borrow foreign currency, especially US dollar, funds for on-lending at their head offices and other overseas branches.

When examining the other Eurocentres, a distinction needs to be made between fully operational centres, booking centres and IBFs. London, Paris and Brussels are prime examples of *fully operational centres* (or *functional centres*). Actual deals are struck there with customers in respect of the obtaining of deposits and the negotiating of loans. Markets exist for banks to borrow and lend deposits to other banks, and (in the case of London) to issue certificates of deposits. Bankers there arrange syndicates for lending and have lawyers prepare documentation. They arrange facilities for the underwriting and/or placement of notes and commercial paper.

Caribbean Centres

By contrast, the Bahamas and the Cayman Islands are examples of *booking centres*, or 'shell' or 'brassplate' centres. These centres are essentially booking agencies where deposits and loans are legally placed, but no transactions are physically made there. Often the only material evidence of a bank's 'presence' is a brassplate screwed onto the outside of the office of a lawyer or agent in Nassau or Grand Cayman. More than 90 per cent of the business of these offshore centres is in US dollars and two thirds is with US banks. Virtually all the US branches in the Bahamas and Cayman Islands are 'shell' branches: that is, a place where a set of ledgers is managed and kept by the agent, representative or bank officers, rather than a location where business is transacted. All the records are maintained at the head offices of the banks in the United States. Because Nassau and Grand Cayman are in the same time zone as New York, head office staff of the banks are able to interact with the 'branches' during normal working hours.

Unlike the Bahamas and Caymans, Panama does not permit the establishment of shell branches, but in common with those centres has strict regulations about the secrecy of bank accounts. That feature, together with the longstanding US military presence and the use of the US dollar as legal tender, makes it a haven for 'secret money' from both Latin America and the United States arising from illegal operations.[11] The Netherlands Antilles has been more important for Eurobond operations due to a 1948 tax treaty with the USA whereby its 'residents' were exempted from most of the 30 per cent US withholding tax which US entities were required to deduct on interest income paid to foreigners. Thus, prior to the repeal of the withholding tax in 1984, US borrowers were able to avoid the tax by issuing Eurobonds through a subsidiary located in the Netherlands Antilles with a parent-company guarantee. The affiliates borrowed the funds from abroad and then re-lent them to the US parents. Bermuda is important as an offshore centre, but for insurance, trust operations and investment management rather than for banking.

The 'paper' arrangements in the Bahamas and Cayman Islands offer advantages to the banks, their customers and the countries concerned. For many customers of banks the booking centres are valued as tax havens, while for others secrecy laws influence their decisions to place funds. Booking centres give many small banks a low-cost access to the Eurocurrency markets. Local capital requirements are negligible, licensing fees are low, entry is easy and taxes and levies on offshore (*entrepôt*) business are non-existent. Hence funds for international lending can be raised (i.e. booked) through these centres free of domestic reserve requirements. The centres are also used by banks operating internationally to minimise overall taxes and levies. A large amount of purely interbank activity in the Eurocurrency market area is booked in these branches, and some of it represents a diversion of funds within a bank's organisation to minimise taxes at a global level and to escape regulation. This is one explanation why interbank activity is much larger in the Eurocurrency wholesale business than in domestic wholesale business. (Other explanations for interbank dealings revolve around the role of banks in Eurocurrency markets as participants in a global funds market. Another explanation sees the banks as participants in borrowing and lending operations associated with foreign exchange trading. These are examined in Chapter 9.)

Banks which book transactions through the offshore centres incur various local expenditures (salaries, fees) which, while small in relation to the value of assets on the books and low relative to the costs of a London branch, nevertheless contribute to income in the countries concerned. For the Bahamas, expenditure of offshore banks contributes about 15 per cent of GDP and employs nearly 2,000 locals, making it second only to tourism (about 70 per cent of GDP) in economic importance (McCarthy 1979, Walter 1985b). Competition for this business amongst offshore centres has led to competition in regulatory and tax laxity, not unlike that which breaks out occasionally between state banking authorities in the United States.

Since all the records of US 'shell' branches are maintained also at head offices in the United States, they are available for inspection by US banking supervisors. Business in the Bahamas and Caymans, like all international and Eurocurrency activity of US banks, is not free of prudential regulation, despite being exempted from US reserve requirements and interest rate controls (e.g. the inability to pay interest on demand deposits). When granting approval for member banks to establish branches in the booking centres, the Federal Reserve Board has made its approval conditional upon full records being kept at head office. Another condition has been that the branches may not be used to shift deposits and other banking business from the United States. That is, they can be used for business that has already shifted offshore, but not for the shifting offshore of new business. It was a short step from these 'shell' branches of US banks in the Caribbean to the establishment of 'duty-free zones' for banking, called *International Banking Facilities*, at the head offices themselves.

New York

Traditional foreign lending from the United States represented 5.6 per cent of international bank loans as at September 1986, and such lending has historically been made by the large New York money market banks. But New York has an importance in international banking which far transcends this activity for three reasons. First, New York is the nerve centre of the worldwide operations of those US banks with the largest presence in the Eurocurrency markets. The Euromarkets are mainly dollar markets: about 60 per cent of Eurobonds are now issued in US dollars (see Table 10.3) and 90 per cent of syndicated bank loans are denominated in US dollars (Table 10.10). New York commercial and investment bankers are prominent as lead managers of both Eurobond and Euroloan syndicates. They also dominate the arrangement of Euronote facilities, Eurocommercial paper distribution and trading in swaps.[12] Second, US banks use their overseas branches to switch US dollar funds between the Euro and domestic deposit markets according to the relative cost of funding. These operations help to tie Eurodollar interest rates to domestic money markets which revolve around New York. Finally, New York is the location for the majority of IBFs, accounting for the great bulk of funds in these facilities (see Table 8.6).

IBFs are 'onshore offshore' centres which consist merely of a separate set of books maintained within existing banking institutions operating in the United States. Conditions attached to the business are:

(i) Dealing must be only with non-residents. This is to ensure that the business is of an offshore character.
(ii) Deposit and loan transactions have a minimum size of \$100,000. The requirement is to make the business 'wholesale', leaving the 'retail' end of international banking to traditional foreign banking.

Table 8.6 Location and Ownership of International Banking Facilities, September 1983

Location	*Total IBFs*	*US chartered banks*	*Edge Act Corporations*	*Agencies, branches of foreign banks*	*Liabilities of reporting IBFs ($ billion)*
Total USA	477	144	69	264	173.4
of which:					
New York	208	38	16	154	133.8
California	84	16	11	57	20.1
Florida	79	27	27	25	3.3
Illinois	30	6	7	17	13.1
Others	76	57	8	11	3.1

Source: Chrystal (1984b)

(iii) Banks operating IBFs undertake that the deposits and loans are not to be related to a non-resident's business in the USA. Like the condition attached to 'shell' branches in the Caribbean, this is ostensibly to stop the IBFs from competing directly with domestic banking business.

(iv) IBFs are not allowed to issue negotiable instruments, such as CDs. Because such instruments could be sold readily in the United States for domestic business, this requirement further separates the IBFs from onshore activities.

(v) The deposits must have an initial maturity of at least two working days. This provision, along with others above, has its origins in the Federal Reserve Board's discovery around 1979 that US banks and corporations were transferring ownership of call deposits at offshore branches in settlement of debts. That is, the offshore deposits were serving as a substitute for domestic payment facilities. The two-day restriction tries to ensure that IBFs do not provide a close substitute for cheque accounts in the USA.

Table 8.6 shows that at September 1983 there were 477 IBFs in the United States, operating in 17 states plus Washington DC, of which 208 were located in New York, holding 77 per cent of liabilities. Of the 477, 264 were operated by branches and agencies of foreign banks based in the USA, 144 by US chartered banks, and 60 by Edge Act Corporations. Formation of an Edge Corporation is to allow US commercial banks to conduct an international banking business outside their home state and thus avoid interstate banking restrictions. Agencies and branches of foreign banks feature prominently amongst the owners of IBFs because Japanese banks are not permitted by their Ministry of Finance to establish 'shell' branches in the Caribbean, so that the IBFs give them low-cost access to offshore dollar banking in US time zones. Separate data of the assets and liabilities of the IBFs reveal that 98 per cent of liabilities were denominated in US dollars. Only about 16 per cent of liabilities and about 30 per cent of assets were due to non-banks. Interbank activity dominates. Further details can be obtained from Key (1982) and Chrystal (1984b).

Formation of the IBFs was meant to see dollar banking business return from London and the shell locations to New York. By the end of 1985, 540 IBFs had been established,[13] but the growth of claims held, after the initial growth in 1981 and 1982, has been modest as, indeed, has been the impact upon London and the offshore centres (see Tables 8.2 and 8.3). Restrictions imposed upon the IBFs but not upon the overseas branches and subsidiaries of US banks provide an explanation. Multinational enterprises are unwilling to have two-day notice accounts in New York when they can receive interest on call deposits in London. The importance of this factor, incidentally, casts doubt upon many explanations of Eurocurrency banking which describe it as 'time deposit' banking.

Increasingly, also, Eurocurrency banking is 'universal' and involves the combining of traditional deposit taking and lending with various forms of investment banking and off-balance sheet business related to securities issues. London remains the centre where these activities can most readily be undertaken.

Hong Kong and Singapore

Amongst the 'functional', or fully operational, centres a distinction exists between 'international' and 'regional' financial centres. *International centres* cater to regions extending far beyond the boundaries of the country or area in which the centre is located, and they cater to the financial needs of customers worldwide. On the other hand, *regional financial centres*:

> . . . derive their role primarily from a combination of geographical proximity to the countries in which customers operate and the safety and ease of operation of subsidiaries, branches and agencies of foreign banks whose head offices lie in international financial centres, rather than generating customers in other parts of the region through their own national size and international power and the competence of their own national banks in international financial business. In other words, they are largely hosts of foreign financial institutions that find it convenient to locate offices there rather than magnets of financial power in their own right, attracting foreign enterprises to establish subsidiaries in order to obtain a piece of the action. (Johnson 1976, pp. 261–2)

Although the distinction is now far less clear-cut, London, New York and Paris are truly international centres and 'magnets', whereas Singapore and Hong Kong began as regional financial centres. Banks operating Asian Currency Units (Eurobanking facilities) in Singapore still act as intermediaries between Asian countries and the rest of the Eurocurrency markets, and operate a substantial network within the Asian region for mobilising surplus funds and channelling them into development projects. Details can be obtained from Hodjera (1978).

Hewson (1981) suggests a further distinction within the more regionally based centres between 'funding' and 'arranging' centres. The latter specialise in arranging or syndicating loans, with a large portion of the funding coming from other functional centres. Banks in the former specialise on the funding side and, for a variety of reasons, do not act so much as lead managers or arrangers of loan syndicates. Hewson suggests that Singapore is more of a funding centre and Hong Kong more of an arranging centre for loans, as is Bahrain. In fact both Hong Kong and Singapore tend to be net takers of funds from other centres, especially London, and following the lifting of withholding taxes on foreign currency deposits in Hong Kong in 1982, the imbalance of functions has been redressed to some extent. This brings out the point that for 'host' centres, the allocation of business is highly sensitive to cross-centre differences in the regulatory environment and conceptions of political and economic stability.

Because of their time zones, Singapore and Hong Kong are important for enabling deposits, loans and position taking in the Eurocurrencies to continue uninterrupted 24 hours a day worldwide. For the same reason, these centres are also involved in foreign exchange dealing. Recent rapid growth of Eurocurrency business in Hong Kong and Singapore owes much to the rapid growth of the new industrialised countries in the Asian region, and to the freedom of those countries from international indebtedness problems. Because Japanese banks' international lending operations are naturally focused in the Asian region, those banks have benefited accordingly. Because Japanese banks have such a prominent presence in international lending and the Eurocurrency markets, the position of Tokyo warrants an extended comment. In doing so we overlap to some extent with the next section on multinational banking.

Tokyo

In one respect Tokyo is an international financial centre of the 'traditional' type, owing its status to Japan's trading strength and Japanese savings and capital exports. But whereas London and New York have a history of international financing, Tokyo has had a mainly domestic orientation. It is only since the early 1970s that Japanese banks have made a concerted move into international banking. Yet this internationalisation of Japanese banking was not accompanied by the internationalisation of the yen nor of the Japanese money and capital markets. Relative to Japan's importance in world trade, the yen has been little used as a reserve currency: at the end of 1982, only 3.7 per cent of world official foreign exchange reserves were held in yen.

In 1984, only 40 per cent of Japanese exports were denominated in yen, while only 3 per cent of imports were in yen; the latter reflecting that the markets for the fuel and raw materials which make up the bulk of Japanese imports use dollar pricing. The yen has been more important as a borrowing currency, and in 1986, 10 per cent of international bonds were issued in yen, while yen lending as at September 1986 accounted for just over 6 per cent of total international bank loans.

Tokyo is now the world's second largest stock market (in terms of either market capitalisation or turnover), but at the end of 1985 only 20 listed companies, out of a total of 1,497 listings, were foreign. Japan's traditional fear of potential foreign dominance has also prevented large foreign bank participation in Japan itself. Japan stands out from the data presented in Table 8.7 in comparison with a number of selected countries, and especially the UK and USA, in terms of the relatively small number of foreign banking institutions operating in Japan (76 in 1985) and their low share of banking business domiciled in Japan. This is in line with the small amount of direct foreign investment generally in Japan: cumulated direct investment liabilities at the end of 1983 were 0.4 per cent of GDP as compared with 3.4 and 3 per cent respectively in the United States and Germany.[14]

While there were more than 5,300 banking-type institutions operating in Japan at the end of 1985 if we include the postal savings network and the over 5,000 agricultural and fishery cooperative financial institutions, the principal components of the system are the 13 city banks (based in Tokyo, Osaka, Nagoya and Kobe and restricted to offering deposits with maturities of two

Table 8.7 Foreign Banking Presence in Selected Countries, June 1985

Host country	*Number of banking institutions*	*Assets of foreign banks relative to bank assets in country (%)*
United Kingdom	472	63.1
United States	348	17.0
France	147[1]	18.2[2]
Switzerland	119	12.2
West Germany	95	2.4
Japan	76	3.6
Belgium	57	51.0
Canada	57	6.3
Netherlands	40	23.6
Italy	36	2.4

Sources: Bank for International Settlements (1986b); Lamb (1986); 72nd Annual Report of the Board of Governors of the Federal Reserve System.

Notes: 1. Number of banking offices.
2. End 1984.

years or less), three long-term credit banks (specialising in long-term financing for industry and obtaining funds by the issue of three- and five-year debentures), seven trust banks (operating trust accounts and fund management along with commercial banking), 64 regional banks (private locally-oriented banks) and 69 sogo or mutual loan banks (which concentrate on lending to small and medium-sized business enterprises). The other major financial institutions are the 43 insurance institutions and the 255 securities companies.

Some of these institutions are amongst the largest in the world. Eight of the city banks (DKB, Fuji, Sumitomo, Mitsubishi, Sanwa, Tokai, Mitsui, Taiyo), two of the long-term credit banks (IBJ, LTCB), two of the trust banks (Mitsubishi, Sumitomo) and the central clearing house for the 4,530 agriculture and forestry credit cooperatives (Norinchukin Bank), making 13 banks in total, were amongst the largest 25 banks in the world in 1985 in terms of assets. The four largest securities houses (Nomura, Daiwa, Nikko and Yamaichi), which dominate the securities business in Japan, all feature in the 12 leading arrangers of Eurobond issues in 1986 (see Table 10.7).

Table 8.8 gives details of the consolidated group assets, shareholders' capital funds (excluding subordinated debt, loan losses and minority interests), net income after expenses and tax (but before allocation to reserves), and the number of employees of the 25 largest banks in the world. It reveals some differences between the Japanese and other banks. First, the Japanese banks have few employees for their size, reflecting a large wholesale business resulting from their role as bankers to large corporations and trading companies. Second, in comparison with other privately-owned banks, the Japanese banks have low published holdings of capital relative to assets. Their high gearing is a source of friction in banking circles. However, Japanese banks keep large 'hidden reserves' in the form of marketable securities and real estate entered in the accounts at historical cost or less, rather than at market value. Inclusion of these stocks at current values would likely raise capital ratios from around 3 per cent to between 7–8 per cent, although the ability of the banks to actually realise the values quickly in the face of large losses might be limited. Because of their large holdings of equities and property, the Japanese banks are a hybrid of commercial banks and investment trusts, making it difficult to compare their capital position with US and UK banks. Third, Japanese banks' earnings on assets employed are low. In contrast to banks from most other countries, they are apparently willing to forgo profitability in the short term in order to promote 'group' relationships and the longer term national interest. In order to explain why, we need to consider two characteristics of the Japanese financial and economic system.

Japanese banks, like many Japanese firms, cannot be considered in isolation from the industrial groups, originally in the form of 'Zaibatsu' (roughly 'property groups' or 'plutocracy') and more recently as 'Keiretsu' (or 'linked groups'). Before the war, four large family-owned Zaibatsu (Mitsui,

Table 8.8 25 Largest Banks in the World, 1985

Asset ranking	*Bank*	*Head office*	*Total assets ($bn)*	*Shareholders' funds ($bn)*	*Net income ($mn)*	*Total number of employees*
1.	Citicorp	New York, USA	167.2	6.55	998.0	81,300
2.	Dai-Ichi Kangyo Bank	Tokyo, Japan	157.6	3.75	304.8	21,125
3.	Fuji Bank	Tokyo, Japan	142.1	4.01	340.9	15,836
4.	Sumitomo Bank	Osaka, Japan	135.4	3.85	367.7	14,486
5.	Mitsubishi Bank	Tokyo, Japan	132.9	3.83	333.6	15,075
6.	Banque Nationale de Paris	Paris, France	123.1	2.31	302.2	59,294
7.	Sanwa Bank	Osaka, Japan	123.0	3.32	298.6	15,766
8.	Crédit Agricole	Paris, France	123.0	5.22	145.5	74,900
9.	BankAmerica Corp.	San Francisco, USA	114.8	3.84	337.2	83,299
10.	Crédit Lyonnais	Paris, France	111.5	1.37	167.3	54,870
11.	National Westminster Bank	London, UK	104.7	4.29	639.9	92,000
12.	Industrial Bank of Japan	Tokyo, Japan	102.8	2.92	219.6	5,601
13.	Société Générale	Paris, France	97.6	1.67	214.3	44,172
14.	Deutsche Bank	Frankfurt, W. Germany	95.8	3.91	354.0	48,851
15.	Barclays Bank	London, UK	94.1	4.78	648.6	105,900
16.	Tokai Bank	Nagoya, Japan	90.4	2.40	171.6	13,748
17.	Mitsui Bank	Tokyo, Japan	88.5	2.09	166.9	11,331
18.	Chase Manhattan Corp.	New York, USA	87.7	3.79	564.8	46,500
19.	Norinchukin Bank	Tokyo, Japan	85.2	0.50	96.9	3,143
20.	Midland Bank	London, UK	83.9	2.67	176.2	78,590
21.	Mitsubishi Trust and Banking Corp.	Tokyo, Japan	80.5	1.66	104.6	6,313
22.	Sumitomo Trust and Banking Co.	Osaka, Japan	79.2	1.71	105.4	5,937
23.	Dresdner Bank	Frankfurt, W. Germany	76.4	2.26	180.3	33,098
24.	Long-term Credit Bank of Japan	Tokyo Japan	78.8	1.62	130.6	3,447
25.	Taiyo Kobe Bank	Kobe, Japan	74.5	1.35	99.4	14,773

Source: Euromoney, June 1986.

Mitsubishi, Sumitomo and Yasuda), along with some smaller ones, developed an immense concentration of interests and controlled virtually the whole economy. Each of these conglomerate oligopolies combined manufacturing, mining, trading companies and banks. The four largest Zaibatsu banks made about three quarters of the loans of all Japanese banks (Buckley and Mirza 1985).

After the war the Zaibatsu were prohibited under antitrust laws introduced by the Allied occupying forces, but financial combines re-emerged after 1954 when rules governing bank directorships and bank holdings of securities were liberalised (Wilson 1986). These Keiretsu consist of businesses with close ties to one another and to the banks, and some of them are the old Zaibatsu still carrying the original family names. Six of the city banks (DKB, Fuji-Yasuda, Sumitomo, Mitsubishi, Sanwa, and Mitsui) are members of linked groups, as are a number of the trust banks. The typical bank-centred group embraces a city bank, a trust bank, an insurance company, a trading company, and a variety of manufacturing and service firms (Coulbeck 1984).

Participation in the groupings provides the 'main banks' with ready access to domestic and foreign lending business largely free of moral hazards and information asymmetries, and with credit risks effectively diffused across the combine. About 20–30 per cent of group bank lending is to affiliated companies. Banks also gain deposit business from the group companies and their employees, while the companies in which banks hold equity gain some protection from takeover bids. Membership of the group enables Japanese banks to evade some of the barriers of 'Article 65' of the Securities and Exchange Act, the Japanese variant of the Glass-Steagall Act, in a number of ways. They can effectively expand their equity interest in securities houses beyond the maximum allowable level of 5 per cent by letting industrial companies allied to the bank acquire equity capital. Another method involves acquiring the whole of an issue of securities and selling it off to other members of the group; in effect, underwriting and placing the issue.

A second feature of the Japanese financial system is the close liaison between industry, finance and government, achieved partly through the Keiretsu but also through administrative 'guidance' in the national interest from the Japanese authorities, in particular the Ministry of International Trade and Industry (MITI) which coordinates Japanese strategies in export and overseas markets, and the Ministry of Finance (MOF) which has a Banking Bureau.[15] In the 1950s and 1960s, the overriding objective was to rebuild an economy shattered by the war, and the banking and financial system was fashioned to channel the savings of consumers stimulated by various tax exemptions into long term industrial investment and the working capital needs of exporters. Foreign involvement in the financial system might have interrupted this process, and thus Tokyo's possible role as an international financial centre was deliberately retarded.

During the 1970s this emphasis changed. As Japanese manufacturing firms began to locate production overseas, the demand arose for Japanese banks to meet their foreign exchange and financing needs in foreign locales. In addition, the authorities perceived that a situation was arising in which Japanese banks were falling behind their Western counterparts in sophisticated financial techniques, and that the Japanese economy was becoming increasingly dependent upon overseas financiers for banking and insurance services. Japan's deficit on the invisibles account of the balance of payments had widened and in 1981, for example, the trading surplus of $11 billion was offset by its deficit in services (Buckley and Mirza 1985).

From the early 1970s, the national financial strategy changed with the promotion of two additional objectives. The first was for Japanese banks to acquire expertise in international banking and to gain access to the dollars needed to finance Japanese overseas investments and those overseas firms wanting to buy Japanese goods. The second allowed for a gradual widening of the use of the yen as a major international currency. Since the second objective would eventually expose Japanese banks to foreign competition in their domestic currency and in local markets, this reinforced the need for Japanese banks to 'go multinational' and acquire the necessary skills to meet this potential competition.

With the active encouragement of the authorities, the Japanese banks have worked since the early 1970s to a concerted long-term four-stage programme of internationalisation. In the first stage, they entered into correspondent links with banks overseas. Second, correspondent relationships were replaced by branches and representative offices based around the international business of Japanese multinational corporations. In the third phase, foreign as well as Japanese companies became customers of Japanese banks, and merchant banking and underwriting activities grew. The fourth phase involves expansion into retail banking overseas. Ishigaki and Fujita (1981) found that, by 1978, most Japanese banks had reached the third stage, with loans to non-Japanese firms accounting for 55 per cent of the business of their overseas branches. Joint ventures with indigenous institutions have aided this process and helped the banks to acquire financing skills. Their participation in syndicated loans, especially to third world countries, has however been subject to periodic guidance from the Ministry of Finance. Few Japanese banks have as yet made major inroads into overseas markets for personal financial services, but they have established a significant presence in markets previously dominated by local banks, such as the US bankers' acceptance market (Jensen and Parkinson 1986).

Unlike British or French banks which syndicate international bank loans in foreign currencies domestically, the Japanese banks' syndicated loan business is conducted from their foreign branches. Following the liberalisation of exchange control regulations in 1980, there has been a rapid growth of foreign currency business in Japan itself, and Tokyo is now the second largest centre. While the principle embodied in the 1980 overhaul of the Foreign

Exchange and Foreign Trade Control Law was that external transactions should be free, 'emergency' provisions existed for its application to be suspended while monitoring and screening procedures continued along with administrative guidance over foreign currency operations (Horne 1985). Over half of the foreign currency lending by Japanese banks in Japan (most of which is in US dollars) is to Japanese enterprises for the financing of imports and other such purposes (i.e. cross-currency loans). Japanese banks also lend to overseas affiliates of Japanese firms and trading companies with funds tapped from London and other centres, and the Eurocurrency positions in Japan are the statistical counterparts of these transactions. Finally, foreign currency positions of banks in Japan have grown strongly since September 1985 when central banks began to encourage a fall in the value of the US dollar. Banks in Japan have made foreign currency loans to Japanese savers and institutions which have acquired large holdings of long-term US Treasury bonds and other foreign currency securities, so enabling them to put a short-term hedge on their foreign exchange position risk in the face of appreciations in the value of the yen.

Data reported in Tables 8.2 and 8.3 predate the offshore banking market established in Tokyo in December 1986. The offshore accounts are modelled on the IBFs in the United States and constitute an 'onshore offshore' (*entrepôt*) market in loans and deposits mainly for non-residents, free of most domestic banking regulations and the withholding tax on deposit interest. They allow the regional and other small banks previously prohibited from international banking to engage in Eurocurrency transactions. Altogether 181 banks applied for offshore licences, and on the opening day the equivalent of \$55 billion was placed on deposit. By March 1987, that figure had increased to \$131 billion.[16] Most of the deposits in the Japan Offshore Market come from overseas financial institutions operating in the Asia–Pacific region. Unlike the IBFs in the USA, the majority of the business (80 per cent at the end of December 1986) is in foreign currencies rather than in domestic currency. But in common with the IBFs, banks operating the offshore accounts cannot engage in securities transactions, which is an important reason why the leading Japanese banks will continue their operations overseas.

8.5 Multinational Banking[17]

Multinational banking embraces both the Eurocurrency banking activities of foreign banks and their banking in host country currencies. Aliber (1977) argues that the latter was the sole activity of US banks' foreign branches prior to 1960 and is still the principal activity of most branches. In terms of assets, however, it is the offshore business which predominates. He estimates that in 1976 as much as 85 per cent of the foreign business may have been offshore. An explanation of the nature of this business is needed, along with the links to onshore markets.

We shall focus upon the precise nature of banks' Eurocurrency operations in Chapter 9. Here we note that as with other externalised activities (e.g. duty-free products), differences in taxes and regulations along with costs of transport, which make it profitable to produce in one location and consume in another, are relevant. Banks' securities business and their international lending is the subject matter of Chapter 10. An important factor prompting banks' move to international lending is risk diversification: reducing the variability of returns by spreading lending business across loans with different risk characteristics, different interest rate adjustment factors and having different funding requirements. Banks' desire for diversification means, at the global level, that loan risks are transferred to those who are most willing to bear them, reducing the cost of providing risk-bearing services. Generally the wider risks are spread, the lower is the cost. Loan syndications and more informal interconnections through the interbank market can be seen as devices for selling shares of international bank lending to banks not originally holding a share. It is estimated that during the 1970s about 60 new banks a year became active in international financing (Teeters 1983). By drawing in successive waves of new banks, risks of international lending have been spread worldwide.

While the growth of multinational banking has paralleled the growth of international banking and Eurocurrency banking, banks have also located themselves abroad in cities and countries where Eurocurrency centres do not exist. Table 8.9 sets out the 'top 40' world financial centres, ranked in terms of banking offices of various kinds (branches, agencies, subsidiaries, representative and other offices). Featuring high up in the listing are cities such as Sao Paulo and Sydney in which banks do not conduct Eurocurrency or entrepôt business, but have representative offices or affiliates which liaise with local businesses and solicit custom for head office or for branches located in the Eurocurrency centres. Table 8.10 classifies 4,300 overseas banking offices by region of operation and country of the parent bank.[18] What is readily apparent is that banks operating out of most countries have a global sphere of operations; that is, banking is truly multinational. We want to establish what economic factors have prompted this global coverage.

At one level the explanation for why banks enter overseas markets is obvious: they anticipate making greater profits (or satisfying growth objectives) by moving to multinational status than can be obtained from alternative forms of expansion. Here we seek to pinpoint the sources of the extra profitability (or potential for growth) anticipated. Another question concerns the success of the operation. That is, having made the decision, what special characteristics enable foreign banks to compete successfully with local institutions in *both* offshore and onshore operations?

In addressing these two questions we draw upon earlier analyses of multinational banking, based on theories of direct foreign investment, developed by Grubel (1977) and Caves (1977) along with recent surveys by Niehans (1983), Aliber (1984) and Walter (1985a). This area of economics

Table 8.9 Number of Banks Represented at Various Financial Centres, as at 1981

Ranking	*Centre*	*Branches*	*Representative offices*	*Subsidiaries*	*Multinational consortium*	*Other offices*	*Total*
1	London	209	121	39	66	28	463
2	New York	97	58	36	9	41	241
3	Hong Kong	69	61	66	24	14	234
4	Singapore	44	52	12	22	53	183
5	Frankfurt	44	106	14	6	2	172
6	Paris	50	56	32	26	7	171
7	Luxembourg	14	—	72	35	34	155
8	Manama (Bahrain)	24	40	3	8	63	138
9	Sao Paulo	9	89	16	16	7	137
10	Tokyo	55	65	2	2	9	133
11	Sydney	5	69	18	16	21	129
12	Grand Cayman	68	1	37	2	1	109
13	Nassau (Bahamas)	65	—	33	4	3	105
14	Jakarta	14	58	1	28	4	105
15	Los Angeles	25	14	13	3	33	88
16	Beirut	24	41	17	3	2	87
17	Toronto	3	51	30	1	2	87
18	Rio de Janeiro	9	49	17	9	—	84
19	Caracas	5	70	2	2	3	82

20	Zurich	16	21	31	7	6	81
21	Brussels	24	19	20	12	5	80
22	Buenos Aires	14	52	7	5	2	80
23	Mexico City	2	68	1	2	1	74
24	Manila	4	28	1	3	27	63
25	Melbourne	4	20	17	18	3	62
26	Chicago	33	20	3	5	—	61
27	Cairo	19	28	5	3	4	59
28	San Francisco	19	6	12	3	16	56
29	Madrid	5	38	8	3	2	56
30	Tehran	2	46	4	2	1	55
31	Geneva	7	6	30	9	2	54
32	Johannesburg	3	35	12	2	2	54
33	Panama City	20	9	17	6	2	54
34	Kuala Lumpur	14	15	5	12	7	53
35	Hamburg	24	12	11	5	—	52
36	Seoul	31	17	—	2	1	51
37	Amsterdam	18	8	15	7	2	50
38	Milan	16	19	10	—	1	46
39	Bangkok	12	15	8	7	4	46
40	Düsseldorf	27	9	9	—	—	45

Source: Compiled from *Who is Where*, 1981/82, published by the Banker Research Unit.

Table 8.10 Location of Overseas Offices* of Banks of Various Nationalities, as at 1981

Source country of bank	*Europe*	*North America*	*Caribbean*	*Central/Latin America*	*Middle/Near East*	*Asia*	*Oceania*	*Africa*	*Centrally planned economies*	*Total*
US	361	31	102	169	74	251	45	19	3	1,055
UK	197	74	13	58	62	101	47	34	7	593
Japan	108	112	9	47	31	131	30	3	—	471
France	127	40	8	55	38	62	11	21	5	367
West Germany	96	28	7	47	17	40	9	12	3	259
Italy	117	36	7	36	18	27	4	6	4	255
Canada	47	37	19	22	14	38	7	—	—	184
Switzerland	39	29	14	31	18	22	13	6	1	173
Spain	68	20	4	43	6	5	2	1	1	150
Netherlands	48	16	1	23	12	23	4	4	1	132
Scandinavia	39	9	2	5	7	28	3	—	2	95
Belgium	39	9	1	8	11	14	6	5	—	93
Brazil	32	24	3	14	5	4	1	1	—	84
South Korea	16	20	—	3	9	22	1	1	—	72
Hong Kong	16	13	—	1	11	17	3	—	—	61
India	22	7	2	1	8	16	1	3	1	61
Israel	17	21	5	9	—	1	—	4	—	57
Australia	14	10	2	—	3	17	10	—	—	56
Pakistan	19	6	2	—	13	5	—	—	—	46
Iran	25	6	—	—	11	2	—	—	1	45
Subtotal	1,447	548	201	572	368	826	197	121	29	4,309

Other Europe	87	29	3	6	16	23	4	11	3	182
Caribbean	8	2	2	3	—	3	—	—	—	18
Central/Latin America	26	14	—	14	—	3	—	—	—	57
Middle/Near East	54	4	—	—	31	4	—	3	—	96
Asia	23	19	—	—	1	55	—	—	—	98
Oceania	2	2	—	—	—	3	2	—	—	9
Africa	13	—	—	—	—	—	—	4	3	20
Centrally planned economies	52	10	—	2	5	1	2	2	—	74
Other (various)	52	12	8	33	19	24	4	3	—	155
Subtotal	317	92	13	58	72	11	12	23	6	709
Grand Total	1,764	640	214	630	440	942	209	144	35	5,018

Source: Compiled from *Who is Where*, 1981/82, published by the Banker Research Unit.

Note: *Overseas Offices is the sum of branches, agencies, subsidiaries and other banking offices *excluding those in the home country*.

remains relatively undeveloped in part because the data remain sketchy and the multi-faceted nature of operations does not lend itself to precise modelling. As we noted in Chapter 7, an adequate framework to study the banking firm must take account of multi-service, multi-plant operations, even in the (presumably) simpler context of domestic banking. Multinational banking involves an increased variety of products (services), operation in a larger number of markets, and a variety of regulatory constraints.

The theory of foreign direct investment itself has not stood still since the original contributions.[19] In terms of the ownership-locational-internalisation (OLI) paradigm developed by Dunning (1981), any theory of multinational enterprise — including banking organisations — must identify some specific firm assets, such as a patent technology or special know-how or certain organisational skills, and explain why these special factors are exploited within the organisation rather than by licensing, franchises, etc. Once this is done, location theory is left to determine the worldwide distribution of production and the form of local representation (e.g. branch, regional office, subsidiary representative, agent etc.). It must be explained why firms do not concentrate all of their operations in one country and export to other locations. Relevant considerations in banking are the costs of production in various countries, the cost of transporting information and people, country regulations and taxes, and the marketing and other characteristics of the various types of international financial services.

There is a growing appreciation (Rugman 1986; Ethier 1986; Horstmann and Markusen 1986) that the major issue to be addressed in this paradigm is that of internalisation — why activities occur within the firm rather than by means of market exchanges. Multinational banks compete not only with domestic financial institutions and other multinational banks, but also with market-based transactions, as the worldwide trend to 'securitisation' indicates. Thus we need to examine a third question: what governs the boundaries between multinational banking firms and financial markets? In doing so we link up with the theory of domestic banking developed in earlier chapters.

Growth of Multinational Banking

Four factors in particular seem to have sparked the moves amongst banks to 'go multinational'. First, there was the discovery that some banking services can be produced externally to the home market. International banking services can be provided in two ways: on an 'establishment' basis or on a 'trade' (in services) basis. Since banks produce services rather than goods, there is, by definition, necessarily communication between a bank and its customers in order that banking output be produced. But a physical presence of customers at the bank's offices is not needed. Certain banking activities can be conducted externally to the domestic economy, and when this occurs banking services are provided to local residents on a *trade* basis from an overseas location. Alternatively, if proximity matters, bank services can be provided to locals on an *establishment* basis, involving indigenous and foreign-owned banks producing non-traded service flows.

An ever-increasing number of international banking services probably falls into the category of what Bhagwati (1986) calls 'long-distance' services, capable of being supplied by means of modern micro-electronic technology and telecommunications equipment without there being physical proximity between the user and provider. Other banking services require physical contact, but the interaction can be achieved by some low-level presence such as an agent or representative office, allowing the productive facilities to be located externally. Low comparative production costs, low transportation costs and less costly regulatory requirements in other nations encourage the production of banking services to be shifted overseas. Thus branches of US banks conduct US dollar business from London which is a substitute for traditional foreign banking which could be undertaken in the USA. Also, branches of German banks undertake business in Deutschmarks from Luxembourg for residents of West Germany which could be undertaken domestically. It is estimated that one third of all Euromark assets consists of claims on West German residents, the great bulk of these being held by the Luxembourg branches of German banks (Dale 1984). By routing domestic or international lending through their Luxembourg subsidiaries, German banks avoid the reserve requirements which the Bundesbank applies to both mark and other currency deposits, while the 33:1 gearing ratio imposed by the authorities in Luxembourg enables the banks to expand their balance sheets faster than would occur domestically.[20] Because the regulatory environment can alter, multinational banking may also be motivated by a desire to diversify production across various 'plants'. Some US banks are said to be unwilling to unwind their 'shell' branches in the Caribbean in favour of IBFs, since the latter are artificial constructions which could be altered by regulatory changes.

Second, for many banks the opportunities to engage in this external production arose out of the traditional system of international correspondent banking. Banks which conduct international transactions for their customers in the traditional fashion maintain balances with correspondent banks in a number of centres. They may also open a branch in one or two of the centres to service resident tourists and assist with trade advice. Balances maintained with indigenous banks can perform a dual function. As well as acting as working balances for receipts and payments in a given currency, they can serve as a base for intermediation in that currency. For example, dollar balances in New York can serve as a base for offshore dollar operations based in London: a classic 'economy of scope'. Deposits received can be on-lent to other banks or 'swapped' into other currency loans. Although the margins are fine, the business is profitable because it is additional to existing facilities. Because of the number of banks (and now non-bank intermediaries) operating in the major centres (650 in London alone) and because foreign currency business can often be transacted in the bank's domestic economy (e.g. Canada), this 'marginal business' is of significance.

To digress for a moment, there is an important implication from the observations in the preceding paragraph for the idea of a Eurocurrency multiplier. As regards non-US banks conducting Eurodollar business, reserves for offshore business are indistinguishable from the reserves for traditional foreign banking. As regards US banks, reserves for the US dollar business of offshore branches cannot be distinguished from the reserves of their parents. As Aliber (1980) has noted, the search for a separate Eurocurrency multiplier relating Eurocurrency deposits to Eurocurrency reserves is not just unmeasurable, it is meaningless. There is no separate multiplier because there is no separate system as such; there are merely separate balance sheet categories. This point was made perceptively by Friedman back in 1969. We examine his analysis in the next chapter.

Third, expansion overseas can present opportunities for profit making which differ from those available from expansion in the home market. Many US banks saw this to be the case during the 1970s when expansion both geographically and into related services was hampered by branching and product restrictions. Some US regional banks shifted back to the home market in the 1980s as the erosion of branching laws and product barriers encouraged greater expansion in domestic markets, and international debt problems mounted. Other US banks altered the focus of their international operations to conduct securities and investment banking business which they are precluded from undertaking domestically due to the Glass–Steagall Act.

Finally, a major factor prompting multinational banking has been the growth of multinational trading companies and the pursuit of these companies abroad by banks from their home country. For example, in 1957, investment by US multinational companies abroad was 9 per cent of that in the US. At that time, foreign deposits of the largest US banks were about 8.5 per cent of domestic balances. By 1972, investment abroad by US multinational corporations had grown to 28 per cent of home investment. As production has spread abroad, banks have followed their customers. 'Cross-hauling' by European companies into US product markets has been accompanied by the 'cross-hauling' of European banks into US financial markets.

The initial aim of the banks concerned was probably to provide banking services to these firms abroad, and meet their borrowing demands in local markets. Later the banks may have aimed to lead their customers abroad, providing economic intelligence and advice to firms considering overseas expansion. Provision of financial services overseas may thus serve as a lever to attract (or retain) business in the home market. This interactive process seems likely to result in links between the worldwide pattern of trade in products and that of trade in services.

But it would seem that the internationalisation of banking may have greatly outstripped that of production. In 1972, foreign deposits of the 20 largest US banks were 43 per cent of their domestic deposits (Brimmer 1973). By 1977, international earnings accounted for as much as 70 per cent of the largest US banks' earnings (Wallich 1977).

Table 8.11 presents some measures of the involvement of US banks overseas from 1960 to 1985. Between 1960 and 1985, the number of foreign branches of US banks has increased nearly eight-fold. Assets of those branches increased nearly ten-fold between 1970 and 1985. In addition to branches located overseas, US banks have expanded offshore by means of foreign incorporated subsidiaries, either wholly or partly owned. These subsidiaries enable US banking organisations to underwrite securities issues, to benefit from local tax laws and regulations and, in some cases, to gain entry into countries that prohibit branches of foreign banks. At the end of December 1985 there were almost 900 foreign subsidiaries with assets of about $100 billion: a five-fold increase since 1973. While a broad range of activities is undertaken including real estate, insurance, import-export and shipping, it is the case that investment in banking activities, especially merchant and investment banking, accounted for 94 per cent of all investment in subsidiaries.[21]

In seeking to explain the continued growth of multinational banking we

Table 8.11 Measures of Foreign Involvement of US Banks, 1960–1985

	1960	*1965*	*1970*	*1975*	*1980*	*1985*
1. Number of US banks operating foreign branches	8	13	79	126	159	163
2. Number of foreign branches of US banks	124	211	532	762	799	967
3. Total assets of foreign branches of US banks ($bn)	n.a.	8.9	46.5	176.5	397.5	458.0
4. Total assets of all US banks ($bn)	257.6	377.3	576.2	965.2	1,703.7	2,301.6
5. Percent of row 3 to row 4	n.a.	2.4	8.1	18.3	23.3	19.9
6. Claims of US banks on foreigners ($bn)	4.5	9.8	11.8	54.7	176.9	419.4
7. Claims of US banks on foreign banks ($bn)	1.4	3.1	5.1	33.8	119.6	309.0
8. Claims of US banks on foreign non-banks ($bn)	3.1	6.7	6.7	20.9	57.3	110.4
9. Claims of foreigners on US banks ($bn)	9.7	17.3	31.3	62.7	151.4	381.2

Sources: 1960–1980: Darby (1985); 1985: 72nd *Annual Report of the Board of Governors of the Federal Reserve System*, 1985; *Federal Reserve Bulletin*, September 1986, Tables A18, A55; IMF *International Financial Statistics*, June 1986.

suggest some additional factors under two headings: one deals with the possible competitive advantages of multinational banks as compared with national banks, the other looks at the competitive position of foreign multinational banks *vis-à-vis* domestic multinational banks.

Multinational Versus Domestic Banks

Traditional foreign banking is capable of being explained readily in terms of standard theories of international trade. Unequal distribution of the supply of loanable funds via capital exports corresponds to the theory of relative factor endowments. As a consequence, international banking emerged in traditional foreign banking as a natural monopoly of banks located in the major surplus nations. At the same time, the need for some physical link connecting the end-user and the producer explains the correspondent relationship which existed in traditional foreign banking between the local banker, retailing to the customer, and the international banker, wholesaling on a trade-in-services basis. Much of the 'cross-hauling' by European and US banks, however, seems to be between countries with relatively similar factor endowments, and with the replacement of correspondents by branches and subsidiaries, it seems natural to adapt to banking the theories of foreign direct investment by multinational enterprises.

Market imperfections: Kindleberger (1969) saw international trade in goods and services as the natural outcome of the standard neoclassical trade theories when it is assumed that information is costless and there are no barriers to trade and impediments to competition. It follows that market imperfections of various kinds can act as a spur to foreign direct investment. Applied to banking, services provided on an establishment basis substitute for trade in services. In particular, where exchange control regulations prevent foreign banks from competing on a trade basis, acting like a tariff wall as a form of protection, penetration of the domestic market becomes necessary, where allowed, if foreign banks are to provide banking services to locally operating firms.

Because banking is frequently heavily regulated for monetary policy purposes, the domestic banking market prior to foreign bank entry has frequently been characterised by a lack of competition, cartel arrangements and excess profits. Entry of foreign banks has often been the vehicle for breaking down these local monopolies. Even without exchange controls, economic factors may limit the scale of such activities and thus the share of the market which is achievable. Banking involves a 'package' of services and, while offshore activity may attract some business, the lack of a full range of services makes it an imperfect substitute for domestic operations, especially at the retail end. In addition, deposits offshore may be seen as more risky than those in locally operating banks which are subject to regulation and support by the local authorities, thereby increasing the cost of funds. (In practice, the different regulations applied to offshore markets enable these difficulties to be offset, and at the same time provide multinational corporations with protection against political interference.)

Here, then, the *existence* of exchange control regulations can provide inducement for foreigners to establish branches or subsidiaries in the overseas country. Of course, the *absence* of exchange controls can also encourage establishment, not to service the local market but to provide a base from which to conduct international banking business on a trade basis to customers located in other countries.

In the case under consideration, in which exchange controls are in place to ensure that locals are supplied by domestic producers of financial services, the second 'market imperfection' needed to explain foreign bank entry is the existence of barriers to entry which preclude new domestic entrants. Legal barriers to entry are frequently little more than a formalising of commercial realities, one of which is the large scale of activity needed for operations to be viable. Other barriers depend on the nature of the activity and the type of entrant. For domestic 'near banks', such as savings institutions, access to retail markets which rely on local appeal and convenience is often easier than entry to wholesale/international financing. For foreign banks, barriers to entry are low for the latter but not for retail activities, where their 'foreignness' is a disadvantage.

Companies operating in overseas markets balance up three factors when choosing a bank for domestic and international transactions: the convenience of having a bank with branches in various countries; knowledge of local conditions; and the cost and efficiency of service. The first favours the multinational bank, the second the local bank, while the third may favour multinational banks if they have an overall lower level of costs sufficient to offset any disadvantage from a lack of local knowledge. The advantages considered here are the same as for any multinational versus a national enterprise. Caves (1971) distinguished vertical from horizontal integration as a source of advantage for multinational enterprise.

Vertical integration occurs when a firm covers all stages of production and distribution, thus internalising market transactions. The possible advantages are most clearly perceived in the case of foreign exchange. Some countries limit foreign exchange dealing to banks, but even where this is not the case, banks still dominate the market. In New York, for example, interbank turnover is eight times larger than turnover by non-bank institutions (in April 1983). Banks' competitive advantage over other traders comes from their worldwide network of banking correspondents. Amongst banks the large multinational organisations are the leaders in trading worldwide. Table 8.12 gives the market shares of the 20 largest foreign exchange dealers from 1980 to 1986. Some larger banks generate as much as 5 per cent of total revenue from foreign exchange-related trading. Multinational banks' advantage over other banks is their network of branches. Compared to

Table 8.12 Largest Foreign Exchange Dealers

Rank	Bank	*1986*	*Estimated market share (%)* *1984*	*1980*
1.	Citibank	6.5	4.8	11.4
2.	Barclays Bank	5.5	2.8	0.6
3.	Chemical Bank	3.7	4.3	0.9
4.	Chase Manhattan	3.5	2.8	4.5
5.	Bank of America	2.5	4.4	6.1
6.	Bank of Montreal	1.9	2.1	—
7.	Morgan Guaranty	1.6	2.6	5.2
8.	Bankers Trust	1.5	3.3	3.8
9.	First Chicago	1.4	1.4	—
10.	Standard Chartered	1.1	1.5	—
11.	Australia and New Zealand	1.0	—	—
12.	Royal Bank of Canada	0.9	4.1	0.5
13.	Midland Bank	0.8	—	—
14.	Swiss Bank Corp.	0.8	2.2	4.5
15.	Lloyds	0.8	2.2	—
16.	Goldman Sachs	0.7	—	—
17.	Skandinaviska Enskilda Banken	0.7	2.1	0.7
18.	Société Générale	0.6	—	—
19.	Manufacturers Hanover	0.6	2.3	—
20.	Algemene Bank Nederland	0.5	—	—
Market share of largest dealers		36.6	50.9	51.7

Source: Euromoney, May 1986.

operating via correspondent banks, funds used in effecting transactions are held in the multinational's 'float' for a longer time. (This is one reason why branch banks have an advantage over correspondent banking for domestic payments systems.) Banks may also marry up forward sales against forward purchases by their customers, netting out transactions before they reach the market and so providing a cheaper and faster service. Finally, the continuous trading permitted by a branch network straddling the various time zones enables banks to make a more intensive use of market intelligence and to avoid having to carry overnight positions, lowering risks for a given amount of position taking (Callier 1986).

Some financing activities may be internalised. Banks may be able to provide trade finance at both ends, facilitating the contract. Frequently, assistance with financing is a crucial factor clinching the deal for an exporter. Niehans (1983) argues that interbranch costs are significantly lower than interbank costs. Instead of dealing with another bank through an interbank broker, a branch in need of loanable funds may be able to obtain some of them from a branch elsewhere. By transacting with each other, they can avoid the chain of interbank transactions.

These benefits of an intrabank market are also apparent in some of the new off-balance sheet activities. With interest rate and currency swaps, banks often act as counterparties when arbitrage opportunities arise, or guarantee the performance of counterparties (see Chapter 10, section 2). A multinational bank seems likely to be better able to cover these risk exposures and, by central coordination of funds, it may be better able to take advantage of arbitrage opportunities. Kogut (1982) and Kindleberger (1983) argue that the great advantage possessed by multinationals, both financial and non-financial, is the ability to arbitrage daily on a world basis. Banks differ greatly in the extent to which they decentralise or centrally coordinate treasury operations. Bankers Trust, Manufacturers Hanover and Midland Bank, for example, are moving towards greater centralisation of the global Treasury function.

Horizontal integration occurs when technology and know-how can be transferred to new locations at little cost. Financial technology is a combination of process technology, products, management and marketing skills, and it is inviting to apply to the case of financial services the theories which see multinationals as transferers of production technology. But there are differences between financial and other products. New products and services in banking cannot be patented, thereby encouraging expansion by 'internalisation'. Process technologies can be copied and sometimes can be bought 'off the shelf' (for instance option pricing programmes and dealing equipment). Multinational expansion rarely involves exact replication of activities in the home market, thereby necessitating a change in product mix as well as scale. Nevertheless, with experience of operation, it may be cheaper to adapt tried and tested ideas than to start afresh.

Multinational banks may develop skills in corporate financing, project evaluation, arranging mergers and acquisitions etc., which can be readily transferred into domestic markets at little cost. Non-indigenous multinational banks may do this less well than indigenous multinational banks, but both may have a competitive edge over small-scale local banks. Frequently the skills may be in terms of the human characteristics of encouraging 'intrapreneurship', and agility of mind under competitive pressures. Marketing know-how may be valuable. Citibank, Chase Manhattan and Crédit Lyonnais have a substantial share of wholesale (corporate) banking business in Brazil. Citibank alone has 6,000 employees in Brazil, 19 offices in 18 cities, and about 3,300 corporate customers. Activities extend also to the retail arena, conducted in 11 cities, with about 600 employees servicing more than 100,000 accounts. Their VISA/Credicard operation has 400,000 accounts in Brazil. Citibank are a prime example of what Porter (1985) calls a global, as opposed to multinational, company. Products are devised, produced and marketed globally. One advertisement in *Newsweek* or *The Economist* serves many locations.

Foreign Versus Domestic Multinational Banks

So far we have looked at the possible competitive advantages that multinational banks have over banks confined to local activities. Foreign banks have not been able (nor have they generally tried) to capture a large market share of all banking operations. Rather, their penetration has been limited to particular sub-markets, like international trade financing, foreign currency operations, wholesale lending, which could be undertaken by domestic multinational banks. What is the competitive advantage of foreign multinational banks over them? The answer cannot be that, say, US banks have developed skills in lending compared with other countries' banks, for this cannot explain the phenomenon of 'cross-hauling' (foreign banks also entering the US market). We must ask what makes cross-hauling a characteristic of international banking.

Any competitive superiority lies not so much in technical innovations (data collection, handling, processing, etc.) as in the skills and knowledge possessed by bank staff and the private information held in bank records, which are less easily replicated, and for which markets to transfer property rights across national boundaries operate poorly. Grubel (1977), Caves (1977), and Niehans (1983), emphasise the specific 'knowledge capital' of foreign banks which can be utilised at low marginal cost in alien markets and offsets their general knowledge disadvantage in some segments of the alien markets. This knowledge (or more generally, 'asset specificity') which the foreign bank possesses takes several forms.

First, there is the banker–customer relationship established with companies in the home market which have become multinational. This knowledge and goodwill is of importance for obtaining access to business connected with international trade. (It has been estimated that US multinationals accounted for about 60 per cent of US international trade in 1983. Nearly 77 per cent of US exports and 46 per cent of US imports are transactions between the domestic and foreign subsidiaries of the same parent multinational conglomerates.)[22] Access to proprietary information is clearly valuable for securities underwriting, arranging mergers and acquisitions and writing standby letters of credit.

Second, competition for the business of multinational corporations, as in domestic markets, takes non-price forms, and here we recall the argument of Chapter 7 which envisaged banks as 'marketing intermediaries', reducing customers' access and search costs. Completing and accentuating the value of knowledge asset, there is the physical asset of a worldwide network of branches and agencies enabling coordinated financial services to be offered globally to firms whose activities straddle several countries. These services may be based around a worldwide management team for each client headed by a relationship manager (coordinating activities) with account managers located in the customer's major areas of business and product managers specialising in merchant banking, foreign exchange, project financing, etc. The team is likely to develop systems for monitoring foreign exchange exposures and provide worldwide cash management and fund transfers.

Such multinational servicing via a worldwide network is a competitive weapon to attract new customers, to enhance existing customers' relationships, and to solicit fee-generating activities. Other motives for the network are prestige ('to complete the system'), establishing a 'beachhead' before (or when) foreign entry is limited, and establishing a presence ('strategic positioning') to take advantage of future developments (see Phalen 1977).

Third, some multinational banks benefit because their home currency is used in international trade and finance. Firms engaged in international trade, with receipts and payments in these currencies, can reduce transactions costs and eliminate exchange risks by maintaining deposits and borrowing in a major currency. Banks whose source country operations are in that currency have cheaper funding by virtue of having better access to domestic retail deposits. Goodman (1984) argues that they also have a risk advantage, by virtue of access to the lender of last resort in that currency. Accordingly, they can counteract their inherent disadvantages in host country operations by lending to residents in their own currency. Thus, US banks have a cost advantage in dollar transactions whereas German banks have an advantage in mark transactions. Aliber (1984) calls this the 'currency clientele' effect.

In support of this argument, it was indeed the case in 1986 that 51 per cent of Eurodollar bonds issued were lead managed by US banks, 86 per cent of Euromark bonds issued were managed by German banks, 91 per cent of Euroyen bonds issued were managed by Japanese banks, and 57 per cent of Eurosterling bonds issued were managed by British banks. In interpreting these observations, it must be noted that until May 1984, foreign banks were not allowed to lead manage Euroyen bond issues, and it is only since May 1985 that non-German banks have been able to lead manage Euro-DM bond issues. A major counter-example to the hypothesis is provided by the Japanese banks. Some years ago it was thought that they were at a competitive disadvantage in international lending as compared with American banks, since the latter could transact internationally in their domestic currency. However, the success of the Japanese banks has demonstrated that the internationalisation of the yen cannot be regarded as a prerequisite for the internationalisation of Japanese banking. Rather, 'traditional' explanations based on Japanese savings and current account surplus seem pertinent.

The 'currency clientele' hypothesis can be interpreted as part of a more general position which seeks to attribute the pattern of multinational banking to inter-country differences in the cost of capital. Thus firms are able to expand their market share relative to that of competitors when their cost of inputs (as above in terms of deposits) or their cost of capital is lower (Callier 1986). Capital requirements play an important role in international banking due to the high leverage in the banking industry. The recent rise of

Japanese banks to their pre-eminent position in international banking has partly been attributed to a relaxed attitude of the Japanese authorities to capital requirements.[23] In addition, the Japanese banks have benefited in recent years by virtue of having their capital base in yen, with the strong appreciation of that currency enabling them to expand their Eurodollar book. Since much of their international business is denominated in yen, the appreciation has also entailed an automatic increase in the dollar value of their asset base.

When examining the motives for multinational banking, it must also be remembered that some of the banks involved, like participants in the international airline business, are state-owned, and their motives for seeking multinational status may not be as amenable to conventional economic reasoning. To some extent this may be true of the Japanese banks. They are neither state-owned nor are they state-directed. But neither can the corporate vision and national consensus discussed earlier be overlooked.

Why Multinational Banks?

The theories examined above, adapted for banking from the standard analyses of foreign direct investment, account for the involvement of existing banking firms in multinational production, but do not examine the alternatives to international banking and thus the rationale for the multinational banking firm. International financing may take place in the internal capital market of a non-financial multinational enterprise. A number of multinationals (for example BP, Volvo, Swedish Match, Scania, GEC) have established what amounts to 'in-house banks' coordinating Treasury operations and managing risks in a variety of currencies on a global basis, as we noted in Chapter 4. Others have established separate legal identities to perform this finance function. The central finance staff often operate like an intercompany bank, and subsidiaries of the multinational enterprise deal with them only if deposit rates and foreign exchange quotations are more advantageous than those on offer outside the company (Andersson and Engrall 1984). In the face of this competition banks have broadened their multinational customer base and reorganised their world corporate operations to service smaller international accounts. Citicorp, for example, has expanded the 450 global multinational corporate accounts handled by its World Corporation Group in 1974 to 2,500 accounts in 1980 which constituted the bulk of its corporate loan portfolio (Channon 1986).

A major trend in international financing in the 1980s is the decline of bank lending and the concomitant rise of securities issues. An alternative to the production of financial services by banking firms is for the financial exchanges to occur through markets. Thus the choice betwen hierarchical structures and markets, as means for organising financial exchanges internationally, needs to be considered. Since a multinational bank is merely a particular class of firm, the issue of why multinational banks exist is another way of asking why banks exist as firms: this echoes the question, originally posed by Coase (1937) in a different context, of whether transactions can be internalised more cheaply than they can be marketised.

In domestic markets we traced the basis of banking to three factors: first, banks produce and process information; second, banks act as marketing intermediaries; third, they are able to achieve economies of size, especially in risk-bearing services. These all apply in international banking.

As 'information processors', banks acquire and use proprietary information. Some borrowers prefer to establish relationships with a selected group of institutions and in doing so avoid the costs involved in providing information publicly to market participants. Others need the assistance of banks when they transact in securities markets in the form of credit lines and performance guarantees. Economies of scope may be realised by banks when combining lending with the provision of international payments services, enabling them to select better investments and monitor their performance at lower costs than would be the case if lenders did so themselves or sought to use other information provision and credit rating agencies. Bank loan contracts are more flexible than market instruments, and banks specialise in work-out solutions with problem borrowers.

Convenience of location and a reputation for reliable service and advice are as important for international banking as they are domestically, and in their role as 'marketing intermediaries' banks reduce the search and access costs of companies trading and locating abroad. In comparison with the standardised financial products such as futures and options contracts traded on international marketplaces, banks are able to offer financial packages tailor-made to customers' specific needs. These packages may also be tax and regulation efficient, with multinational banks arbitraging between various regulatory and tax structures.

Banking firms also owe their existence in part to economies of size. Size may be important in a number of respects in international operations. Success in arbitrage, options and futures dealings depends much on being able to assimilate, monitor, forecast and act faster on market developments than one's rivals. Volume business may allow the development of support facilities for the gathering of information and its retrieval, and the hiring of skilled staff for forecasting market trends. Or, scale may simply permit internal specialisation in particular functions, so that 'going multinational' allows institutions to break out of the confines of small local markets. When acting as an investment banker, size may enable a firm to act as a manager as well as a placer of securities. Customers are thought to peruse the 'tombstone' notices recording institutions which have managed issues of international securities and to be influenced by them when selecting arrangers themselves.

More generally, multinational banks coordinate the production of financial services to customers domiciled in a number of countries by employing capital, materials and labour located in one or more countries. Scale economies can arise from the technological production function, relating inputs of the factors of production to the output of services, as they can in other industries. But a peculiarity of banking, as a financial industry, is the importance of stochastic elements governing the ratio of inputs of reserves of base money to deposits and the extent of financial leverage in terms of the ratio of equity capital to loans. In both cases banks are able to employ the insurance principle of the law of large numbers to reduce the size of these ratios. In the first case the risks arise because of uncertain withdrawals of demand deposits and the utilisation of loans where there are open credit lines and various facilities backing up customers' issuance of securities. In the second case, the bank maintains equity capital to protect the banks' creditors from the risk of default on loans and failure of a customer whose performance is guaranteed by the bank, so maintaining the necessary confidence of depositors needed for fractional reserve banking to succeed.

Thus in earlier chapters we saw banks in a third role: that of providers or organisers of risk bearing services. The importance of this function in international banking depends on the nature of international banking, which we examine in following chapters. For example, deposits could be gathered from lenders in one part of the world and lent on by banks to borrowers elsewhere without any essential alteration to the characteristics of the claims involved, other than the substitution of the bank's name for that of the borrower. But we argue that this is not the case, and that there is a degree of 'liquidity creation' which parallels that in domestic banking. In addition, the 'wholesale' character of deposits, loans and off-balance sheet activities adds additional hazards and the role of central bank assistance is more ambiguous.

When outlining the theory of wholesale banking in Chapter 4, we emphasised that domestic wholesale and international banking should be looked upon as parts of a whole — literally, separate compartments of bank consolidated balance sheets. Nevertheless, there are differences arising from the cross-border, cross-currency nature of international banking which will be considered in the following chapters. Most attention is given to Eurocurrency operations: this is mainly because it is the largest component of international bank lending, partly because it is the most distinctive and intriguing, but also because it is the area of international banking about which outside observers have the most statistical information.

Notes

1. This paragraph and the next draw heavily upon information in Davis (1976).
2. The various statistical sources are compared by Mills (1986) and in the *Bank of England Quarterly Bulletin*, March 1985, p.64.
3. The reporting area includes banks in the Group of Ten countries (Belgium, Canada, France, West Germany, Italy, Japan, Netherlands, Sweden, United

Kingdom, Unites States) plus Luxembourg, Austria, Denmark, Finland, Ireland, Norway and Spain, as well as banks engaged in international business in the Bahamas, the Cayman Islands, Hong Kong and Singapore, all offshore banking units in Bahrain, all offshore banks operating in the Netherlands Antilles and the branches of US banks in Panama.

4. The BIS, which compiles the data upon which all calculations are based, and the Bank of England treat IBFs as part of the parent bank's external lending in domestic currency. Morgan Guaranty has, since 1983, treated the IBFs as a separate unit apart from the parent bank operation. Morgan figures can be approximated roughly by adding IBFs to row 13 of Table 8.2.
5. The principles used for calculating the net figures are described and analysed by Dennis (1984).
6. Robinson (1972, p. 164).
7. Other offshore (non-reporting) centres are located in Barbados, Bermuda, Lebanon, Liberia, Vanuatu and the British West Indies. All are smaller than the Netherlands Antilles and in total hold about one half of one per cent of gross Eurocurrency claims.
8. One reason for the relative decline of the consortium banks is the natural tendency of the parent banks to keep the best deals for themselves.
9. During March 1986, daily dollar–yen trading in London at \$12.6 billion, for example, exceeded that in New York at \$11.5 billion.
10. The major merchant or investment banking subsidiaries of US banking organisations operating in the United Kingdom are:

    Bank of America International Limited
    Bankers Trust International
    Carolina Bank Limited
    Chase Manhattan Limited
    Chemical Bank International Limited
    Citicorp International Bank Limited
    First Chicago Limited
    First Interstate Capital Markets Limited
    Irving Trust International Limited
    Manufacturers Hanover Limited
    Morgan Guaranty Limited
    Wells Fargo Limited

11. Havens for 'secret money' are examined in Walter (1985b).
12. The shares of New York-based commercial and investment banks and other US banks in these activities for 1986 were:

	Syndicated loans lead managers	*Note issuance facilities arrangers*	*Euro-commercial paper arrangers*	*Arrangers of swaps*
New York banks	52%	65%	62%	67%
Other US banks	4%	3%	5%	16%

Source: Euromoney, Annual Financial Report, March 1987.

13. 72nd Annual Report of the Board of Governors of the Federal Reserve System, 1985, p. 179.
14. *World Financial Markets*, June 1984. See also Wathen (1986).
15. Japanese policy making is examined in Horne (1985).

16. *Financial Times*, 1 May 1987.
17. This section draws upon earlier work by us (Davis and Lewis 1982c).
18. Since the data are of 'banking' offices, more general financial activities are excluded. Thus the 400 outlets in the USA of Barclays American Corporation are excluded, as are Citicorp's 'money shops' and finance company affiliates.
19. For recent surveys of multinational enterprise, see Larsson (1985), Sugden (1985), Dunning and Norman (1986), Galbraith and Kay (1986) and Rugman (1986).
20. See Dale (1984). Revisions to the West German Banking Act, which came into force in 1985, require the banks to consolidate their Luxembourg banking subsidiaries with the parent for the purpose of assessing capital adequacy.
21. Federal Reserve Board Staff (1986).
22. Federal Reserve Bank of Chicago, *International Letter*, No. 561, August 1986.
23. In response to pressures to conform to the capital requirements proposed by the Bank of England and the Federal Reserve Board, the Ministry of Finance published revised guidelines on capital ratios for Japanese banks in May 1986. For banks with overseas branches, a target capital ratio of 6% of average outstanding assets was set, to be implemented in April 1987. The banks will be able to comply with this ratio by adding up to 70% of unrealised gains on their securities portfolio. Capital is defined as including tax adjustments but excluding existing special reserves against bad loans.

9

Eurocurrency Banking Operations

9.1 An Outline of the Functions

Sir Roy Harrod in 1969 described the formation of the Eurocurrency market as 'a great landmark in monetary history'.[1] While national governments were fumbling with plans to create a new international money, private enterprise had created an international market in money. While economists and officials were discussing how to distribute the 'seigniorage' which came from governments and international traders having to hold dollar reserves in New York at low, regulated rates of interest, private enterprise had established a system which effectively eliminated the 'seigniorage' by allowing dollar balances to be invested in Europe, and borrowed in Europe, at competitive market rates of interest.[2] While finance ministers debated how to adjust payments imbalances between countries, private enterprise had formed a banking system which would play a major role in financing payment imbalances in the decade ahead. While governments and international economic institutions were worrying about how to divert capital resources to the newly industrialising and developing countries, private enterprise had established a banking market which was to assume this function in the 1970s.

Until the 1960s, banks conducted international banking from their home bases. With only minor exceptions, the location of banking and the currency of denomination were inseparable: banking was a natural monopoly of the banks located in the country issuing the currency used for borrowing and lending. Deposits were taken from foreigners, and lending to foreigners occurred, in the currency of the country in which the main offices of banks were located. Much international bank lending is still carried out in this traditional way. Thus, Deutsche Bank, say, lends marks to foreign borrowers from Frankfurt, and Chase Manhattan lends to foreigners in US dollars from New York. However, at September 1986, only 17 per cent of gross international bank lending outstanding was 'booked out' in this traditional fashion (see Table 8.2 in the previous chapter). Most international lending is instead *externalised* in the Eurocurrency centres.

By separating the location of banking from the currency used for borrowing and lending, the Eurocurrency system also separated currency (exchange rate) risk from political risk. A depositor holding dollar balances in a country other than the United States combines the currency risk of holding US dollars with the political risk of the particular country (Britain, Belgium, Singapore, etc.) which is host to the dollar operations. This 'essential feature', as Niehans (1984) calls it, was instrumental in the origins of Eurocurrency operations. With the advent of the Cold War, Russian and other holders of dollars had a desire to conduct dollar banking business in locales where their balances could not be impounded as they had been in the USA during World War II by the alien property custodian.

But growth during the 1960s owed more to economic blockages. Since the US dollar was the 'intervention' currency in the Bretton Woods system, there was a worldwide demand to hold dollar balances in the United States to serve as a means of effecting international payments and as a store of value for future international transactions. Because the US dollar was the preferred medium for deferred payments, there was a demand also to borrow dollars. This demand had been met by borrowings from banks and securities markets in New York and from other capital flows in the form of official aid and direct foreign investment by US corporations. Measures were then introduced in the mid-1960s by the US authorities, worried about the US balance of payments deficit, to control outflows. At the same time, domestic reserve requirements and ceilings which limited the interest rates that US-based banks could offer on deposits provided a continuing incentive for recipients of dollars to place deposits, still in dollars, with banks operating in Europe, free of these US controls. Banking had also been separated from the economic risk of taxes and duties levied by the country issuing the currency of denomination.

Banking transactions in US dollars outside the United States expanded rapidly. By dealing in dollars, British and other European merchant and international banks were able to put their expertise to work in international trade financing, despite being restricted from lending overseas in their domestic currencies. Banks in Europe were thus able to survive, and may have even encouraged, increased use of the dollar in world trade. In the late 1940s perhaps nearly 50 per cent of world trade was in sterling. Now the position is markedly different. Almost all trade in primary commodities is invoiced in US dollars. The US dollar is also the vehicle currency in foreign exchange trading, perhaps in over 90 per cent of transactions (Kenen 1983). In London, which is the largest foreign exchange market (see Figure 8.1), trading which does *not* involve the US dollar is 3 per cent of total business (Comotto 1986). A bank buying sterling with marks will typically buy dollars with marks, and then sterling with dollars (McKinnon 1979).

Not all the original Eurobanks were European: US banks were prominent in developing branch networks overseas to accept dollar deposits and to make dollar loans. While originally confined to Europe — hence the prefix 'Euro' — Eurocurrency borrowings and lendings are now conducted on a large scale in a number of other locations as well (see Table 8.3). Customers of the banks are located in almost all countries of the world, yet the great bulk of total gross Eurocurrency business is business of one bank with another (Table 8.3). Some Eurocurrency activity is not international at all and occurs within a country's domestic banking market: deposits are taken from residents and loans made to residents denominated in non-local currencies. Although the US dollar is the main currency of denomination, other currencies account for 20 per cent of operations (Table 8.3). US banks are no longer the largest national grouping of participants: Japanese banks hold more international loans. But major banks from virtually all countries conduct Eurocurrency business (Table 8.5). There are few Eurobanks as such: most are merely branches, subsidiaries or departments of 'domestic' banks, with Eurocurrency operations being a compartment of an overall banking balance sheet. Nor is there a Euromarket as such. Although it is located in terms of book transactions in various Eurocentres, the worldwide market physically consists of networks of telephones, telexes and monitor screens around the world – communications equipment which might be used for purposes other than Eurocurrency transactions.

From an estimated $20 billion in 1964, the gross size of the Eurocurrency market has grown to $3,117 billion at September 1986, details of which are given in Table 9.1. This is in terms of Eurocurrency lending to both non-residents and residents of the countries concerned, that is, both cross-border and cross-currency lending. Table 9.1 also gives estimates which exclude foreign currency lending to residents, and hence focus upon the cross-border aspect alone. Also included in the table, where available, are various measures of the size of the Eurocurrency market net of interbank redepositing.

When we seek to explain why international bank lending has occurred in 'offshore' locations rather than in the traditional fashion, the factors which are relevant are, to a large extent, the same ones which would be invoked to explain why any production might be externalised. Like other duty-free products, these factors are differences in taxes, differences in regulation, costs of transport and communications, political and economic stability, time zones, and so forth. What we wish to focus upon here is the nature of the 'product' which is being externalised in the Eurocurrency markets.

Experts have come up with different explanations for the rise of offshore international bank lending, six of which we itemise here. Some have emphasised the offshore element, so that the operations in the Eurocurrency markets are seen to be providing *substitutes for domestic intermediation* — like the branches of the German banks in Luxembourg. Where the transactions are between banks, Eurocurrency operations act as an *alternative interbank market*. Others have concentrated on the currency aspect, looking upon the Eurobanks as adjuncts to the *wholesale foreign exchange markets*. Yet others have focused upon the cross-border characteristics, seeing the banks' operations as part of a *global funds market*. There is also the role of

Table 9.1 Measures of Gross and Net Size of Eurocurrency Markets in Terms of Claims Outstanding ($ billion)

	Cross-border and cross-currency claims		*Cross-border (external) claims*	
	Gross	*Net*	*Gross*	*Net*
1964	20	14	12	9
1965	24	17	14	12
1966	29	21	18	15
1967	36	25	23	18
1968	50	34	34	25
1969	85	50	57	44
1970	115	65	78/93	57
1971	150	85	114	71
1972	210	110	150	92
1973	315	160	248	132
1974	395	220	293	177
1975	485	255	343	205
1976	595	320	418	247
1977	748	390	514/595	300
1978	955	495	764	377
1979	1,203	590	961	475
1980	1,472	750	1,153	575
1981	1,804	890	1,421	665
1982	1,970	960	1,541	702
1983	2,145	985	1,695	n.a.
1984	2,216	n.a.	1,757	n.a.
1985	2,634	n.a.	2,073	n.a.
1986 (Sept.)	3,117	n.a.	2,380	n.a.

Sources: as for Table 8.2.

Note: Differences between the measures were explained in the text of Chapter 8 and in the construction of Table 8.2.

In this table, the external claims measure from 1964 to 1970 is for the narrow Eurocurrency market (i.e. European reporting areas) alone (in liabilities). The measure was widened progressively after 1970 to include banks in other reporting areas. In 1977, the measure was widened to incorporate non-reporting banks in certain offshore centres.

some offshore centres as *tax havens* to be taken into account, for 23 per cent of assets and liabilities are inter-office transactions (Table 8.4), some of which may be transfer pricing activities undertaken by multinational banks to reduce taxation and evade regulations. We see all these activities as parts of an even larger whole, in which the Eurobanks are also involved as *wholesale intermediaries* in the cross-border, cross-currency production of liquidity services.

These different explanations reflect not only the multidimensional characteristics of Eurocurrency operations, but also changes over time in the functions of the market. For much of the 1960s, Eurodollar lending was to companies, mainly but not solely American, and by single banks in amounts ranging from $1 million to $50 million (Donaldson 1979, Chapter 1). One indicator of the extent of non-bank participation is the difference between 'net' and 'gross' measures of the Eurocurrency markets shown in Table 9.1. In the years 1964 to 1969, the net figure was around 75 per cent of the gross. It was natural to see the Eurodollar market as an alternative to domestic intermediation; hence the first explanation. During the so-called 'credit crunches' of 1966 and 1969–70, when US monetary policy was tightened sharply, US banks borrowed dollars from other banks and their own branches overseas to shore up their liquidity domestically. The banks came to look on the Eurodollar market as an alternative to the Federal Funds market for liability management, and by 1978 the net figure was around half of the gross. This is the second explanation. Since banks in the offshore (Euro)centres are active in foreign exchange dealing, much of the interbank activity came to be seen as part of hedging and covering transactions in the forward exchange markets. This is the third explanation.

Table 9.2 sets out the sources and uses of funds to the narrowly-defined Eurocurrency market (i.e. the European Eurocentres) net of interbank redepositing within that area. In 1970, the US was a net user of funds; this is consistent with much market activity being a substitute for intermediation and traditional foreign banking which could have been conducted in the US, as in the explanations so far. But because the dollars came in part from non-US banks and from non-US deposits, the idea arose of the Eurodollar market serving not so much as an offshoot of the US markets, but as a global funds market, transferring idle balances between different parts of the world — the fourth explanation. Transactions with offshore banking centres feature prominently in the sources and uses of funds, leading to the fifth explanation that many transactions are for tax and regulatory avoidance. Finally, as is apparent from Table 9.2, growth of Eurocurrency activities in the 1970s was particularly stimulated by the emergence of oil-producing (OPEC) countries as suppliers of funds, and oil-importing countries as borrowers of funds. There was a role for the Eurobanks to act as intermediaries of balance of payments deficits and of long-term capital exports to developing countries; this is the basis of the sixth explanation.

A common thread running through the various explanations, which we survey below, comes from the absence of regulations of various kinds. In the Eurocurrency 'compartment' of their balance sheet, banks are normally free of reserve requirements and deposit insurance premiums, and usually have greater freedom to determine the holding of bank capital and to select the quality of their loan and investment portfolio. They are, as a result, able to transact more cheaply than from their home bases. International traders are thus able to hold balances of the major currencies used in international trade, and to cover forward foreign exchange commitments, more cheaply and more

Table 9.2 Distribution of Net Size of the Narrowly Defined Eurocurrency Market. Estimated Uses and Sources of Eurocurrency Funds

	Reporting European area	*United States*	*Canada & Japan*	*Other developed countries*	*Eastern Europe*	*Offshore banking*	*OPEC countries*	*Other developing countries*	*Unallocated*	*Total*
USES										
1983 (March)	280.0	53.6	56.5	67.8	31.6	79.5	35.5	84.7	11.8	701
1982	275.5	53.5	55.5	68.5	33.4	81.5	36.9	85.0	12.2	702
1981	247.0	51.1	52.2	61.7	39.9	83.1	35.7	83.3	6.0	665
1980	216.5	39.7	45.1	52.3	38.9	74.0	33.8	69.8	4.9	575
1979	171.6	36.7	33.0	40.5	36.0	68.7	30.4	54.1	4.0	475
1978	139.5	24.6	24.6	34.7	31.4	55.0	24.3	40.1	2.8	377
1977	110.4	21.3	18.7	30.8	25.7	43.9	15.7	30.3	3.2	300
1976	75.1	18.3	21.6	33.0	20.8	40.7	9.6	24.7	3.2	247
1975	63.0	16.6	20.2	25.8	15.9	35.5	5.3	19.5	3.2	205
1974	61.5	18.2	18.2	20.4	10.1	26.7	3.5	15.7	2.7	177
1973	49.0	13.5	12.7	14.7	7.4	18.7	3.3	11.0	1.7	132
1972	38.9	9.6	—	—	43.1	—	—	—	0.4	92
1971	32.8	8.3	—	—	28.9	—	—	—	1.0	71
1970	24.0	13.1	—	—	19.0	—	—	—	0.9	57

SOURCES

1983 (March)	262.0	121.5	32.0	31.8	13.9	91.0	82.2	45.7	20.9	701
1982	265.0	114.5	31.5	32.6	13.8	87.0	89.2	45.9	22.5	702
1981	253.5	84.5	27.9	34.7	12.3	77.9	110.3	46.3	17.6	665
1980	211.0	59.7	22.1	33.6	12.8	69.3	110.7	45.1	10.7	575
1979	174.0	50.5	15.2	31.8	13.0	54.0	81.1	46.9	8.5	475
1978	144.5	37.0	13.0	26.2	8.8	45.5	54.7	39.8	7.6	377
1977	117.3	25.4	8.4	18.8	7.0	33.4	54.5	29.6	5.6	300
1976	87.6	18.8	10.5	21.3	6.4	30.1	45.2	21.3	5.8	247
1975	79.5	15.4	8.3	19.9	5.4	21.8	34.6	16.2	3.9	205
1974	67.8	11.9	8.7	18.5	5.1	17.6	29.1	15.5	2.6	177
1973	60.8	9.5	9.8	17.7	3.7	12.5	10.0	14.6	3.4	132
1972	35.2	6.9			47.9				2.0	92
1971	32.4	6.1			1.4				1.1	71
1970	27.7	4.5			24.0				0.8	57

Source: Bank for International Settlements, *International Banking Developments*, July 1983 (after which the series was discontinued).

effectively than by means of traditional foreign banking. Clearly, this particular competitive advantage of Eurocurrency business would be lost if the domestic rules and regulations were removed. In that respect the markets are creations of regulations.

But Eurobanks, like all banks, act as financial intermediaries. They activate balances which would otherwise have been idle and put them to use financing projects which might otherwise not have taken place. As compared with domestic banking, the funds are collected across national boundaries. Much of the Eurocurrency banking activity may therefore transcend what banks would carry out in traditional banking. Central to the global funds market theory, interbank markets in centres such as London are seen as efficient allocators of funds on a worldwide basis. The Eurocurrency markets might conceivably retain this advantage even if the cost advantage of the regulatory environment were removed by deregulation in domestic markets.

When examining domestic banking we drew a distinction between banks as processors of information and their role as asset transformers and bearers of risk. More emphasis is placed upon the information and brokerage function of banks in the explanations canvassed above of Eurocurrency operations. In interbank operations particularly, banks are seen as distributors of liquidity across countries and across currencies. We argued in Chapter 4 that wholesale banks do more than just distribute liquidity and that interbank markets in wholesale intermediation do more than just rearrange funds. It is our contention that the same holds for Eurocurrency banking: that banks undertake considerable liquidity production in Eurobanking and that the interbank markets, like the reinsurance markets in international insurance business, play a major role in sharing among groups of banks the risks of international lending operations.

9.2 Duty-Free Banking

Until Milton Friedman's 1969 paper, analysis of the growth of the Eurodollar market had tended to focus upon the US balance of payments position and especially on the contribution of the US balance of payments deficit in pumping out a flow of dollars to overseas holders (under fixed exchange rates). Friedman's analysis made clear that the Eurodollar market was a monetary and banking phenomenon. He showed that Eurodollars could be 'created' with an unchanged balance of payments position. Friedman's hypothesis was that the Eurodollar market should be seen as part of the US banking system and that Eurodollars are created, like domestic deposits, by the portfolio decisions of banks and depositors.

Like Friedman, we focus on the Eurodollar market. Because banks operating externally are not subject to reserve ratios and other regulatory constraints, they are able to offer depositors a *higher* return than is obtainable from deposits held with US banks operating domestically. At the same time, they are able to lend to borrowers at rates *lower* than charged domestically. That is, they are able to operate with a lower spread than domestic US banks. Deposits held offshore are subject to less political risk for those holders whose domestic deposits are susceptible to blockage or expropriation. These benefits of a higher return and lower political risk must be balanced against a greater default risk, since the deposits do not have *de jure* deposit insurance, although, as noted in Chapter 5, they may enjoy *de facto* insurance. We shall assume, as did Friedman, that the balance of these factors favours a shift from domestic banking to the external markets in order to provide an illustration of the workings of the market.

Let one depositor contemplating a switch to the Eurodollar market be company *X*, which may be a US resident or non-resident corporation. Let us suppose the latter, and that company *X* has a demand deposit for $10 million with US Bank, a domestic US bank, which represents the proceeds of a maturing CD. This is the first position shown in panel A of Table 9.3.

Panel B of the table shows the initial impact of a transfer of the deposit from the US bank to Eurobank *A* operating in London. Eurobank *A* may be a branch of US Bank, or the branch of another US bank, or the branch of a Japanese or European or Australian bank, or a British bank. Whatever the case, we assume that Eurobank *A* holds its reserves in the form of deposits with US Bank, which is Eurobank *A*'s New York correspondent. Consequently, the transfer of $10 million initially merely rearranges the ownership of deposits at US Bank, with deposits of company *X* falling and being replaced by the deposit of Eurobank *A*.

Eurobank *A* now has funds to lend out. Following Friedman's illustration, we suppose that the Eurobank wants to hold, on prudential grounds, 10 per cent of its deposit base in the form of reserves — which are deposits held with US Bank. Accordingly, the Eurobank has $9 million available to add to its loans and investments. It makes a loan of $9 million to company *Y*, also a non-resident of the US. The loan is effected by Eurobank *A* writing a cheque drawn on US Bank in New York. This brings out the point that Eurodollars are merely deposits, or claims against deposits, at commercial banks located in the United States. They are thus indirect claims against US currency issue. Company *Y*, we assume, wants to build up its working balances or precautionary balances held for international trading. By coincidence, it also banks with US Bank and thus adds the cheque from Eurobank *A* to its bank balance at US Bank.[3] At this juncture, the deposits 'leave' the Eurodollar 'system' and the process is truncated. These transactions are shown in panel C of the table.

Considering panels A–C, a number of features stand out. First, the position of US Bank is unchanged. It began with $10 million of deposits and assets and finished with the same balance sheet aggregates. There may be some rearrangement as between CDs, demand and time deposits, and thus required reserves (which differ as between demand deposits and other

Table 9.3

Assets ($ million)		**Liabilities** ($ million)	
PANEL A			
		US Bank	
Various	10	Deposit of company *X*	10
PANEL B			
		US Bank	
Various	10	Deposit of Eurobank A	10
		Eurobank A	
Deposit at US Bank	10	Deposit of company *X*	10
PANEL C			
		US Bank	
Various	10	Deposit of Eurobank A	1
		Deposit of company *Y*	9
		Eurobank A	
Deposit at US Bank	1	Deposit of company *X*	10
Loan to company *Y*	9		
PANEL D			
		US Bank	
Various	10	Deposit of Eurobank A	1
		Deposit of company *Y*	9
		Eurobank A	
Deposit at US Bank	1	Deposit of company *X*	10
Loan to Eurobank B	9		
		Eurobank B	
Loan to company *Y*	9	Deposit of Eurobank A	9
PANEL E			
		US Bank	
Various	10	Deposit of Eurobank A	1.0
		Deposit of Eurobank B	0.9
		Deposit of Eurobank C	8.1
		Eurobank A	
Deposit at US Bank	1	Deposit of company *X*	10
Loan to company *Y*	9		
		Eurobank B	
Deposit at US Bank	0.9	Deposit of company *Z*	9
Loan to company *V*	8.1		
		Eurobank C	
Deposit at US Bank	8.1	Deposit of company *W*	8.1

categories) but that depends on the assumptions made.

Second, since only the ownership of non-resident deposits with US Bank has altered, there is no change to the US money supply. Third, there is no change to the US balance of payments position. The reduction of $10 million in short-term claims on the US by company *X* is matched by increased deposits of Eurobank *A* and company *Y*.

Nevertheless — fourth — Eurodollars of $10 million have been 'created' by the transactions. For every dollar held as a cash reserve by Eurobanks in New York there are in existence 10 Eurodollars. As the holder is a non-resident of the US, there has been an increase in the worldwide holdings of US dollars.

If company *X* and company *Y* were resident corporations of the US, the position with respect to the US money supply would be different. Deposits held by domestic and foreign banks are excluded from the money supply, but the Eurodollar holdings of US residents with foreign branches of US banks are included. Accordingly, the US money supply is decreased by the amount of Eurobank *A*'s deposits with US Bank. If Eurobank *A* is not a branch of a US bank, then company *X*'s deposit is excluded; and the money supply falls overall. But if Eurobank *A* is a branch of a US bank, company *X*'s deposit is counted in the money supply which, overall, increases. Irrespective of the treatment statistically, however, in all cases there is an increase in US dollar denominated deposits and claims, because the process of converting claims on the US banking system into claims on Eurobanks increases Eurodollar deposits by $10 million without reducing the assets and liabilities of US banks. There is an additional layering of deposits on the base of US currency issue.

Many variants on this basic story are possible, and we examine two in panels D and E. In panel D, Eurobank *B* which also operates in London is approached instead by company *Y* for the loan of $9 million. Not wishing to turn away the loan business it bids interbank for deposits, 'taking' them (as interbank borrowings are frequently called) from Eurobank *A*, the recipient of the Eurodollar deposits. As before, company *Y* deposits the loan proceeds with US Bank, truncating the process of Eurodollar creation. In this case, $19 million of Eurodollars have been created. The *gross size* of the Eurodollar market is the total deposits in Eurobanks of $19 million. But $9 million of this amount is contributed by interbank depositing. If we subtract the interbank deposit, we are left with the *net size* of the Eurodollar market of $10 million, represented by the liabilities held by non-bank customers. In the first example, there was no difference between the gross and net size of the market since all deposits were held by non-banks.

In reality, as we have shown above, there is a considerable difference between the gross and net size of the market. What needs to be explained is why Eurobanks 'place' funds with each other (as interbank depositing is often described). In panel D, the interbank activity came from a division of labour between the banks. Eurobank *B* had the established contact with the customer and specialised in lending intermediation. Eurobank *A* concentrated on deposit intermediation, leaving the final on-lending to another bank. Some examples of such specialisation can be observed within Eurocentres, as in London, where US banks have usually been net suppliers of dollar funds to other banks. There are substantial flows of interbank funds between Eurocentres, with banks in Hong Kong and Japan using funds collected from non-banks in London and the Caribbean. This, and other explanations of interbank activity, are considered later.

In the examples above, credit creation amongst the Eurobanks was truncated when company *Y*'s loan proceeds of $9 million left the Eurobanking system. Suppose instead that in the first example company *Y* uses its balance at US Bank to buy goods from company *Z* which takes advantage of the higher interest rates available on Eurodollar deposits to lodge the proceeds with Eurobank *B*. Eurobank *B* holds 10 per cent of $9 million, that is, $0.9 million, in the form of reserves at US Bank and lends out $8.1 million to company *V*. It, in turn, uses the finance to buy goods from company *W*, which also redeposits the proceeds, in this case with Eurobank *C*. For the purpose of the illustration, we truncate the process at this point. So long as interest rates and other portfolio preferences continue to favour depositing with the Eurobanks, the process could conceivably continue. If each Eurobank held reserves of 10 per cent, and loan proceeds were redeposited with Eurobanks, deposit expansion would be:

$$\$10 \text{ m.} + \$9 \text{ m.} + \$8.1 \text{ m.} + \$7.3 \text{ m.} + \ldots = \$100 \text{ m.}$$

relative to deposits of the Eurobanks with US Bank of $10 million, the original 'primary' deposit. Friedman termed this the Eurodollar multiplier.

In the wake of Friedman's analysis, a long debate ensued to ascertain whether in actual practice growth of deposits in the Euromarket could be expected to resemble the situation in panel E, of multiple Eurodollar deposit expansion, or that in panels A–C, of Eurodollar creation. This debate will be examined in the following section. We may note, however, that in both cases Eurodollar creation occurs in so far as Eurodollar deposits are a multiple of the cash base held at US banks. In both instances, the expansion of deposits at Eurobanks is a layering upon US bank deposits much like the domestic layering of claims examined in Chapter 7. Finally, the growth of Eurodollar deposit liabilities in both cases depends on the willingness of recipients of the loan proceeds to place the funds on deposit with the Eurobanks: that is, on the public's portfolio preferences.

Friedman demonstrated that none of the transactions need be allied to the US balance of payments position. Current account deficits place US dollar claims at the disposal of non-resident holders. These claims can be placed in a large variety of assets and need not be held with Eurobanks. Also, rearrangement of existing outstanding claims can occur independently of the concurrent balance of payments position. Yet, as Johnston (1983) notes, the view that a link *need not* exist does not preclude the possibility that a link *can* exist. There is little evidence linking the US balance of payments position with market growth, but nonetheless it remains a potential source of growth.

9.3 Eurodollar Credit Creation

Friedman's analysis of Eurodollar credit creation invited a direct comparison between the Eurodollar market and domestic banking systems. Indeed, at one juncture Friedman likened the Eurodollar institutions to 'Chicago banks'. Since Eurobanks were seen as maintaining working balances of at most 2 per cent and probably much less, this conjured up the image of an almost limitless expansion, deriving from an initial primary deposit, based on the reciprocal of the market's low reserve ratio. Friedman is often attributed with the view that the Euromultiplier must be 'extremely high'.[4] In fact, Friedman's original piece contained almost all the points raised by later critics and clearly stated that the actual multiplier would be low. Nevertheless, it may be helpful to readers to try to sort out the issues.

Returning to the example of the previous section, an initial deposit in the Eurodollar market was seen to lead to a multiple increase in Eurodollar deposits. The 'worst case' scenario was that of panel C, where no return flow of deposits to the Eurodollar market occurred after the lending generated by the initial deposit. Here, the deposit multiplier was unity, and two points warrant elaboration. First, because of the layering of claims, even this worst case scenario saw an expansion overall in bank lending and in dollar denominated deposits. The only effect upon the US banking system was a change in the ownership of its deposits, and the loans made by the Eurobank constituted an extra layer of credit creation upon that of domestic banks. Even a deposit multiplier of one thus appears to be of significance.

It is here that a second point needs spelling out. For any bank in a multibank system, its deposit multiplier following an autonomous initial increase in its deposits is approximately unity. Very few, if any, of the loans made by a single bank expanding independently will result in a return flow of deposits to that bank. Exactly what the multiplier for the system as a whole will be depends very much upon the source of the initial deposit. Where it reflects a portfolio shift which transfers a deposit from another bank, the system-wide multiplier will be zero: the new loans and subsequent deposits generated at other banks will be offset by the calling in of loans and subsequent deposit contraction of the bank losing the initial deposit. Where, however, the initial deposit is new into the system resulting from (say) an expansion in base money, the system-wide multiplier can exceed unity.

This discussion should make clear the basis for Friedman's drawing of a parallel between Eurobanks and Chicago banks. Any bank or group of banks forming a part of a wider whole has little independent capacity to create credit. Loans made by Chicago banks leak to other parts of the US monetary system, with little in the way of redeposits at Chicago banks. By the same token, however, loans made by other banks flow to Chicago banks enabling them to participate in the multiple expansion of credit and deposits which follows an increase in reserves. Similarly, Eurobanks are part of a system so that they may share in a generalised process of multiple credit and deposit creation, but correspondingly have little independent credit-creating ability.

Nevertheless, Eurobanks are part of the system in ways which are different from Chicago banks. Whereas transfers of deposits between Chicago and other US banks involve no overall deposit or loan expansion, transfers from US banks to Eurobanks do bring about an overall increase in deposits and lending. In this respect, then, it is important to distinguish between two sources of Eurobank expansion, the first arising from a system-wide expansion (following an increase in reserves) and the second from a portfolio shift from US bank deposits to Eurodollar deposits. Some simple algebra will help to make the points precisely.

For the moment, we shall ignore the existence of deposit and loan markets in currencies other than US dollars and focus upon the Eurodollar market as a part of the US dollar financial system. Moreover, for simplicity, we shall assume that all holders of Eurodollar deposits are US citizens so that (ignoring currency holdings) the US money supply (M) consists of bank deposits (D) plus Eurodollar deposits (E) held by the non-bank US private sector,[5] namely:

$$M = D + E \tag{9.1}$$

Fundamental to understanding the role of the Eurobanks in the credit creation system is recognition of the fact that they keep their reserves (R_E) in the form of deposits at US banks. The latter, in turn, hold Federal Reserve Bank liabilities (B, for base money) as reserves, so that there is a three-tiered system or 'pyramid of credit', with the Federal Reserve at the apex and the Eurobanks at the base. Denoting the reserve ratios of Eurobanks and US banks respectively as q and r, we have:

$$q = R_E/E \tag{9.2a}$$
$$r = B/(D+R_E) \tag{9.2b}$$

Finally, we denote by p the proportion of the non-bank sector's total money holdings held in Eurodollar deposits, namely:

$$E = pM \tag{9.2c}$$

Manipulating the various equations above it is easy to obtain expressions for D, E and M as multiples of base money, B:

$$M = \frac{1}{r[1-(1-q)p]}\,B \tag{9.3}$$

$$E = \frac{p}{r[1-(1-q)p]} B = \frac{1}{[1-(1-q)p]} \frac{pB}{r} \tag{9.4}$$

$$D = \frac{1-p}{r[1-(1-q)p]} B \tag{9.5a}$$

Equation 9.4 illustrates the two main ways in which growth in Eurodollar deposits can arise: via increases in B or in p. The former case involves a generalised deposit expansion as increases in base money injected at the apex of the credit pyramid spread through the entire structure. The latter involves shifts in portfolio preferences (from D to E) and the difference *vis-à-vis* the former is best seen by assuming $q=0$, that is, the Eurobanks hold zero reserves. Then,

$$D = B/r \tag{9.5b}$$

and the expansion in Eurodollar deposits involves no decline in the non-bank sector's US bank deposits and thereby constitutes a net addition to the money stock. (When $q \neq 0$, this result regarding the money stock does not hold, but total US bank deposits ($D+R_E$) are not affected by the portfolio shift.) Effectively, the base of the credit pyramid is widened without any alteration to the size of the upper tiers.

An intuitive feel for the basis of the formula for Eurodollar creation in equation 9.4 can be gained from the following example. Suppose Eurobanks receive a \$1 million dollar initial deposit of which \$(1–q) million is lent out and \$$q$ million kept as reserves. The loan recipient spends the loan proceeds and thus transfers ownership of the deposit at a New York bank (which the lending bank has made available to it) to another corporation. A proportion (p) of the \$(1–q) million is redeposited with Eurobanks and the remainder is held as other assets. The Eurobanks receiving the \$$p(1-q)$ million redeposit are then able to lend a fraction (1–q) of it, and a fraction (p) of this sum equalling \$$p^2(1-q)^2$ million is further redeposited with Eurobanks. Continuing the process leads to a total increase in deposits at Eurobanks of:

$$1 + p(1-q) + p^2(1-q)^2 + p^3(1-q)^3 + \ldots = \frac{1}{1-p(1-q)} \tag{9.6}$$

Comparing equation 9.4 with 9.6, the term pB/r, which corresponds to the initial deposit at Eurobanks, represents the claims on base money (in the form of US bank deposits) which flow to the Eurobanks following from an expansion of base money.[6]

Considerable interest has attached to what formulæ such as (9.4) and (9.6) might imply for the total increase in Eurodollar deposits following from an autonomous initial deposit. Referring to equation 9.6, values of 0 and 0.2 for q and p respectively seem perhaps not greatly wide of the mark,[7] giving a multiplier of 1.25. In fact, although empirically estimated multipliers have ranged from 0.63 to 18.45, the consensus view nowadays puts this multiplier slightly in excess of one.[8] This accords with Friedman's own early assessment. The openness of the system seems likely to limit severely Eurobanks' independent credit-creating ability, but even a multiplier of one means that, because of layering, the Eurobank deposits and loans are additional to, rather than in place of, those of domestic US banks.

In terms of the arguments we advanced in Chapter 7, the existence of layering should warn us as to differences in the character of the intermediation of Eurobanks. They do not participate in retail activities. Their balances are not commonly used as payment media. Those Eurobanks which are not branches of US banks conduct traditional foreign banking at the retail level as well as operating a Eurocurrency book. There is a difficulty in distinguishing balances held with correspondent US banks for traditional foreign banking from reserves against Eurocurrency operations. Indeed, we suggested that many banks may initially enter Eurobanking so as better to utilise balances held with US banking correspondents (see Chapter 8, section 5). These banks' dollar deposits and loans are also part of an overall balance sheet involving non-dollar currencies. Some part of a dollar deposit may be 'switched' into local currency for the purpose of lending locally. Recipients of dollar loans may themselves convert dollar loan proceeds into other currencies. Both involve sale of dollars for other currencies. In order to make the multipliers operational, assumptions must be made about the willingness of the buyers (whether they be central banks or other parties) to redeposit the dollars bought with the Eurodollar segment of the system.[9] Whether banks and others want to make currency switches depends on the juxtaposition of interest rates and exchange rates, and we shall examine this behaviour later.

Whatever the category of Eurobank under consideration, it is important to remind ourselves that there is not a separate Eurocurrency banking system 'which is segmented from the several domestic banking systems in the same way that the dollar banking system is segmented from the sterling banking system' (Aliber 1980). Friedman argued that Eurodollars are a segment of the dollar banking system. By similar reasoning, Euromarks are part of the Mark banking system, and so on. Where the Eurodollar banks are branches of US banks there is not even a different currency involved (as is also the case with branches of German banks in Luxembourg). Reserves held by the foreign branches of US banks against Eurodollars are not segmented from those of domestic offices. In the same way, reserves of domestic branches are not separated from those at head or regional offices. Banks pool reserves against domestic and offshore deposits, just as they pool reserves against time, demand and other deposit categories, and thus hold few, if any, additional reserves against offshore deposits. Consequently, efforts to compute a fractional credit multiplier for the offshore system are complicated by the difficulty of distinguishing the reserves of offshore banks (and this factor perhaps accounts for the wide range of the estimates made).

Most Eurodollar liabilities, moreover, like most domestic bank liabilities nowadays, are dated contingent liabilities. They are promises to be ready to deliver dollars when the liability falls due, the 'dollars' in this case being deposits at New York banks, which themselves can be converted into Federal Reserve funds. But the Eurobanks need not actually hold dollar balances in New York awaiting the contingency. They may hold bills and securities or certificates of deposit which can be converted at short notice into demand deposits at New York banks. Or, the Eurobanks may hold an 'option' of borrowing interbank should depositors exercise their option of not renewing the deposits. Thus the 'backing' for Eurodollars is 'command' over dollars from the wholesale funds markets. In this respect, wholesale banking generally, of which Eurocurrency banking is one part, can be seen as layering upon the reserve base. It is a layering that rests upon confidence on the part of banks that the funds can be commanded, and upon confidence by depositors that the funds will be commanded.

Layering of Eurocurrency claims also has implications for monetary control. Analogously to the extension of multiplier analysis to non-bank intermediaries (Chapter 7), the presence of Eurodollars can increase the leverage of monetary policy. That is, the existence of the Eurodollar system (i.e. a non-zero value for p) increases the value of the multiplier linking the money stock (M) to base money (B). Both parts of the dollar banking system participate in the changes in credit following a change in base money and smaller changes in base money are needed to achieve a given change in the volume of total credit. In practice, though, this effect may not be great. Taking $q=0$, $r=2$, an increase in p from 0 to 0.1, for example, increases the multiplier in equation 9.3 from 5 to 5.56, a 10 per cent saving in the use of base money due to the layering effect. A further implication of equations 9.3–9.5 is that, in the absence of changes in p or q (or r), both Euro- and domestic markets expand or contract in harmony. Of course, the attention paid to the Euromarkets reflects precisely the fact that they have grown more rapidly than the domestic markets. For this reason there have from time to time been calls to control the expansion of Eurocurrency lending by the application of reserve requirements on non-bank business. This issue is discussed in Chapter 11 in a broader context.

Both of the points raised in the preceding paragraph come from assuming constant values of p and q. The possibility of countervailing changes in p and/or q which offset monetary policy must be acknowledged along with secular changes in portfolio preferences which seem likely to have led to growth over time of Eurodollar banking. In practice, the portfolio preferences summarised by the ratio p cannot be expected to be a constant, but will depend upon interest rates and other relevant economic variables which seem likely to be affected by Euromarket expansion. Current portfolio ratios would then be of limited relevance to determining multipliers at the margin. This is the principal message of the portfolio approach to which we now turn.

9.4 Eurocurrency Interest Rates and Portfolio Preferences

Figure 9.1, based on Dufey and Giddy (1978), Argy (1981) and Johnston (1983), depicts the simultaneous equilibrium in the Eurodollar and domestic US bank deposit and bank loan markets. Because of the absence of reserve requirements, or because some costs are borne by other areas of business, banks in external markets are able to intermediate between borrowers and lenders with a lower spread than (often the same) banks domestically.

If Eurobanks offered the same deposit rate as in domestic business, it is assumed that some depositors, on political grounds, would prefer to hold dollars externally. This is indicated by the quantity Q'. As the Eurodollar deposit rate increases relative to the domestic CD rate, so does the supply of dollar deposits to the market. Some borrowers may prefer, also on political grounds, to borrow externally even if the loan rate is the same as the US prime, and their numbers will be increased as Euroloan rates fall below domestic levels. Should Eurobanks be able to operate with a spread of *cd*, as compared with a domestic spread of *ab*, the quantity of Eurodollar loans and deposits is Q_E, with a loan rate of *c* and deposit rate of *d*.

Interest rates on the figure are those ruling during February 1985. The domestic deposit rate is the issue rate of 3-month negotiable certificates of deposit by Morgan Guaranty Trust Company. For the Eurodollar deposit rate, we use the 3-month interbank bid rate. The Eurodollar loan rate is LIBOR (i.e. interbank offer rate) plus a spread of 60 basis points (the average during 1985 on syndicated loans). The domestic loan rate is the weighted average rate on long-term commercial and industrial loans of $1 million or more revealed by the Federal Reserve Board's survey of commercial banks' terms of lending as at February 1985. For many loans the actual rate, and thus the domestic spread, would be higher due to interest-free compensating balances maintained on deposit.

It is apparent from these figures that Eurobanks can simultaneously offer depositors a higher deposit rate than domestically and a lower loan rate than on domestic business. To some extent Eurocurrency business is of a larger size, with lower spreads to match. Perhaps loans are made to less risky borrowers, and competition is keener than domestically. But the Eurobanks are also free of some domestic costs. One cost is federal deposit insurance. The basic assessment is 0.083 per cent, but banks have usually received a credit based on the FDIC's net income which has typically reduced premiums to around 0.037 per cent. Banks must also recover the cost of 3 per cent reserve requirements which, with a CD issue rate of, say, 9.22 per cent, raises the cost of domestic issues of CDs to 9.54 per cent, and widens the required spread between borrowing and lending rates on domestic intermediation. US banks and other participants in the dollar banking system have responded by intermediating externally where there is an initial cost advantage due to the absence of these taxes and duties. Because they share this cost advantage,

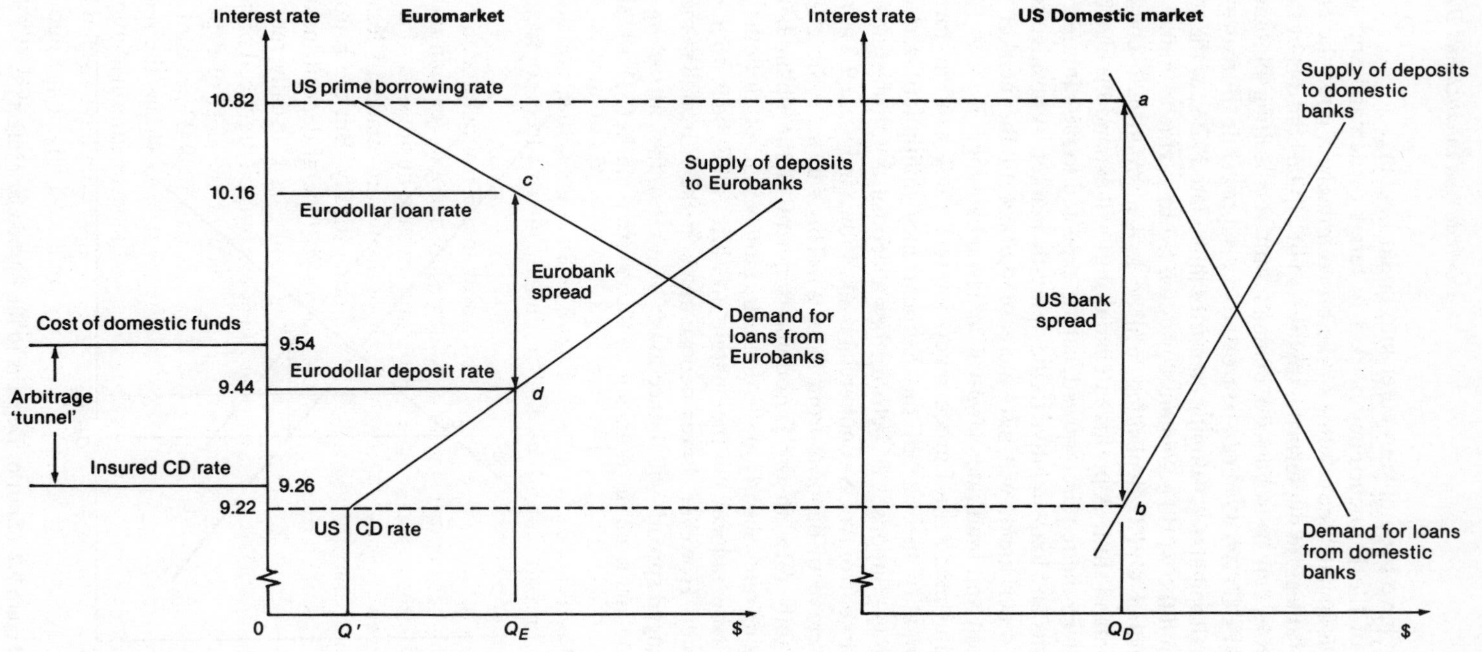

Figure 9.1 Eurodollar and Domestic Banking Markets

non-US banks have been able to enter into dollar banking.

Analysis of the Eurocurrency market in terms of demand and supply enables us to assimilate better some of the broad influences upon the growth of the market (at least in net terms). Application of capital controls by the US in the mid-1960s can be seen as a demand shift. Depositing of funds by members of OPEC after 1974 can be treated as a supply shift. Borrowings by newly industrialising and developing countries in the late 1970s, as the second oil price rise and the world economic slowdown led to payments imbalances, along with further OPEC depositing, can be looked upon as a combined supply and demand shift. A positive demand shift will expand the size of the market and, given the required spread, can be expected to raise interest rates on both deposits and loans relative to the domestic market. A positive supply shift, on the other hand, will also increase the size of the market while lowering deposit and loan rates *vis-à-vis* domestic banking.

These adjustments in Eurocurrency interest rates can, in turn, be expected to modify the size of the Eurocurrency multipliers derived in previous sections. Suppose, as before, that a deposit is transferred to the Eurodollar market from a US commercial bank, shown in Figure 9.2 as a shift in the supply curve of deposits from S_0 to S_1. This will have the effect of depressing slightly rates in the Eurodollar segment of the dollar banking system, or raising rates slightly in the domestic money market, or both. Some depositors will be induced at the margin to shift funds back to the US domestic market. However, lower deposit rates in the Eurodollar market, with an unchanged spread, will induce lower loan rates, thus attracting some borrowers of dollars from the domestic to the external market. This is shown

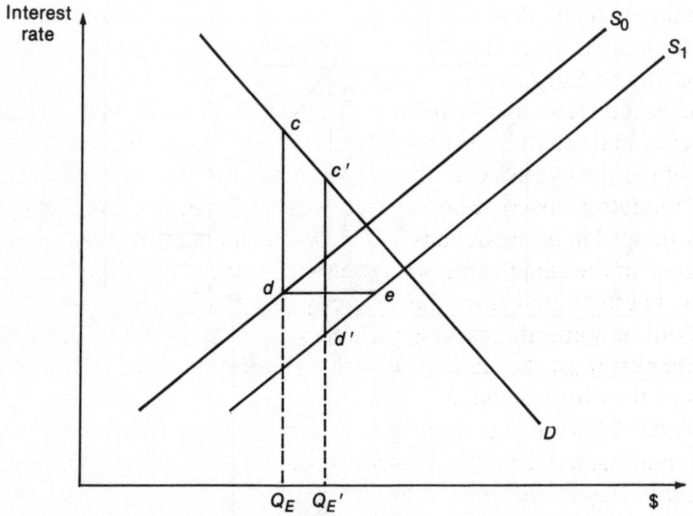

Figure 9.2 Shift of Deposits to the Eurodollar Market

in Figure 9.2 as the movement down the demand curve for loans from c to c'. Overall, there is an expansion of the Eurocurrency market from Q_E to Q_E', but it is less than the initial shift, *de*. The Eurodollar multiplier is necessarily less than unity.[10] Niehans and Hewson (1976) draw a parallel between the relationship of the Eurodollar system and US domestic markets and any other two substitute products, such as butter and margarine. 'If there is a spontaneous shift in preferences from butter to margarine, the ultimate increase in the quantity of margarine will be less than the spontaneous shift, because the relative increase in the price of margarine will induce some former users to shift to butter. The 'margarine multiplier' would thus be less than unity.'

This result raises the question of how the portfolio analysis can be reconciled with the multiplier analysis given earlier, and with the empirical estimates of multipliers slightly in excess of unity. Here it is necessary to remember the precise definitions of the elements of the multiplier formula, and thus the appropriate interpretation of the magnitude *de* in Figure 9.2. The appendix to this chapter provides a detailed analysis. In terms of equation 9.6, the easiest approach is to assume that, *at the margin*, $p=0$ at existing interest rates. Thus the multiplier in equation 9.6 is unity, because the redeposit ratio is zero, and *de* then represents both the size of the initial autonomous deposit and the final outcome of the multiplier process.[11] However, once interest rates are allowed to vary as they can be expected to, the public's portfolio preferences and the redeposit ratio will vary. In particular, expansion of the Eurodollar market (following an autonomous increase in deposits) will depress Eurocurrency rates relative to domestic rates. This will reduce p, meaning, in the current example, that Eurobanks not only receive zero redeposits but also lose some other deposits in response to the lower yields. The 'multiplier' is clearly reduced (to below unity in this example) but, because it is necessary to examine the cause and extent of interest rate variations, the multiplier approach apparently loses much of its appeal.

At a practical level, however, use of the multiplier analysis (other than as a conceptual exercise to show the similarity of Eurodollar and domestic banking) rests on factors which render Eurocurrency interest rates insensitive, in the short run, to portfolio shifts of the type illustrated in Figure 9.2. As Johnston (1983) notes: 'it is very difficult to find evidence that short-term Eurocurrency interest rates adjust to non-bank deposit flows' (p.239). A number of reasons can be offered. First, the multiplier approach is often criticised for assuming that banks can make loans and expand dollar assets without major repercussions on loan yields. Yet for marginal variations, Eurobanks even as a group may face an elastic supply of dollar-earning assets in the form of CDs and other short-term securities which they can hold. Second, on the deposit side there may be disequilibria resulting from any 'moneyness' characteristics of Eurodollar deposits. While not serving as a means of payments, they may serve as temporary abodes of purchasing power. To the extent that holders add temporarily to Eurodollar deposits funds intended for later spending or investment, the Eurobanks may share in the process of money creation.

Johnston's own explanation for the apparent insensitivity of Eurocurrency interest rates to customers' deposit flows comes from the *arbitrage activities* of US domestic banks (in many cases head offices of the Eurobanks). If the Eurocurrency deposit rate exceeds the effective cost of domestic funds, which allows for deposit insurance premium payments and reserve requirement on domestic time deposits and CDs, then US domestic banks will find it profitable to conduct *outward arbitrage*. That is, US domestic banks will issue deposit liabilities domestically and place the funds interbank in the Eurocurrency market driving down the interbank rate.[12] Thus *outward arbitrage* will take place until:

return from interbank deposits ⩽ domestic cost of funding

that is,

$$i_{ED} \leqslant \frac{i_{CD} + I}{(1-r_d)} \tag{9.7}$$

where i_{ED} = Eurocurrency deposit rate
i_{CD} = domestic certificate of deposit rate
I = FDIC insurance premium, per cent
r_d = reserve requirement applicable to CDs and time deposits.

This gives the 'ceiling' to the arbitrage tunnel. Arbitrage should keep Eurodollar deposit rates below this level.

On the other hand, if the Eurodollar deposit rate falls below the insured domestic CD rate, it will pay US banks to fund domestic lending externally. This is known as *inward arbitrage*, and involves US banks borrowing interbank on Eurocurrency markets and replacing the domestic issue of liabilities. Such arbitrage will be profitable when the external funding cost, given by the Eurodollar deposit rate adjusted for reserve requirements on Eurodollar liabilities, is less than the domestic funding cost and will cease when:

external funding cost ⩾ domestic funding cost

that is,

$$\frac{i_{ED}}{(1-r_{ed})} \geqslant \frac{i_{CD}+I}{(1-r_d)} \tag{9.8}$$

where r_{ed} = domestic reserve requirement which applies to US banks' net Eurodollar liabilities. Since, as a result of the amendments to reserve requirements in 1980, reserve requirements on Eurodollar liabilities are the same as on short-term CDs and time deposits, i.e. $r_{ed} = r_d$, (9.8) becomes:

$$i_{ED} \geqslant i_{CD} + I \tag{9.9}$$

This is the 'floor' to the arbitrage tunnel, and arbitrage by banks should prevent Eurodollar deposit rates from falling for long below this level.

In practice, the arbitrage tunnel illustrated in Figure 9.1 will be widened by the bid/offer spread on CDs and the bid/offer spread on interbank funds in the Eurocurrency market. In the past, potential for arbitrage by US banks has come from differences in the reserve requirements on Eurocurrency and domestic deposit liabilities, widening or narrowing the arbitrage tunnel. Nevertheless, if arbitrage is effective, the Eurodollar deposit rate (and, with competition, the loan rate also) will vary within or closely around the arbitrage tunnel. Kreicher (1982) and Johnston (1983) present evidence which shows that such has been the case during the 1970s and the early 1980s.

A number of implications follow from the existence of arbitrage between the domestic and Eurocurrency interest rates. First, arbitraging by both banks and non-banks means that Eurodollar interest rates closely follow movements in interest rates in the USA. Any rise in domestic interest rates will see non-bank borrowers shift to the Eurodollar market and depositors shift back to US domestic banks. As banks' domestic funding costs rise relative to Eurodollar rates, the US banks will enter as borrowers from the market and be net takers of funds. With the demand for Eurodollars increasing and the supply falling, Eurocurrency rates will follow the rise in US interest rates. By similar reasoning, Euromark interest rates will closely track German interest rates, and so on.[13] Evidence presented by Kneeshaw and Van den Bergh (1985) supports this expectation.[14]

Second, when the Eurocurrency markets were small relative to the domestic market, it made sense to think of Eurocurrency interest rates as primarily determined by domestic interest rates. As the external markets have grown relative to domestic rates, reverse causation has assumed greater importance. It now makes more sense to think of the two sets of interest rates as being jointly determined by the overall demands and supplies for dollar funds. Thus an increase in dollar loan demands, domestically or externally, will raise dollar interest rates in both external and domestic banking markets.

Third, Johnston argues that, in the short term, interbank arbitrage between the two segments of the dollar banking system dominates the non-bank arbitrage. Consequently, inflows and outflows of funds by non-banks can occur without the alterations to Eurocurrency interest rates implied by the portfolio analysis outlined earlier. To this extent, the prediction of that analysis — that the Eurocurrency multiplier must necessarily be less than unity — is invalidated. But the corollary is that a multiplier for non-bank deposits makes less sense in an environment in which interbank transactions are of such importance. A bank's decision to lend to a non-bank customer is effectively divorced from the deposit inflow. Analysis of lending decisions needs to take into account the role of the interbank market. This is true of wholesale banking in general, as we noted in Chapter 4.

Fourth, arbitrage by banks between the domestic and Eurocurrency markets provides one explanation for the extent of interbank activity in Eurocurrency business. At times, the movement of funds to and fro by US banks has been considerable. In 1979 the Eurocurrency markets received a flow of net deposits in the wake of the second oil price rise and Eurodollar rates fell relative to the arbitrage 'floor'. As the effective cost of external funds fell below that of domestic funds, US banks shifted from being net suppliers of funds to the market to being net takers, reversing their net position by about $30 billion. During 1980, US interest rates declined sharply relative to Eurodollar rates and the cost of domestic funds — the tunnel ceiling — fell below Eurodollar deposit bid rates. US banks effectively reversed the position of the year before and became net lenders to the market to the extent of $15 billion (see Kreicher 1982).

Such arbitrage transactions, while important for tying together the Eurocurrency and domestic markets, do not go far towards accounting for the large and persistent gap between the gross and net size of the market due to interbank redepositing (see Table 9.1). Accordingly, other explanations have been offered for the vast amount of interbank activity, and these will be examined in the following sections.

9.5 Eurobanks and Foreign Exchange

Eurocurrency transactions are not the same as foreign exchange dealings and need have nothing to do with them, as we observed in the previous chapter. Dealings in foreign exchange consist of purchases and sales. Eurocurrency operations, by contrast, consist of loans and repayments. Eurodollar IOUs are claims against 'ordinary' dollars; Euromarks are claims against ordinary Marks, and so on. Whereas the 'price' of currency dealings is in terms of the exchange rate, the 'price' of Eurocurrency deals is an interest rate. Conceptually, then, the Eurocurrency market is completely different from the foreign exchange market.

In practice, the two markets are closely connected. Partly this is because both are banking markets. One party to a Eurocurrency transaction must be a bank (or financial institution); more often than not, both parties are banks. One of the parties to a foreign exchange transaction is invariably a bank, and again it is the case that both counterparties are usually banks (Comotto 1986). Most of the Eurocurrency centres are prominent in foreign exchange trading. In the early days of the market, Eurocurrency operations used to be conducted out of the foreign exchange department; some small banks still do so. This interconnection between the two forms the basis of McKinnon's (1977) explanation for the extent of interbank dealing in Eurocurrency business. In order to explain why the interconnection exists, we must first examine some of the day-to-day workings of foreign exchange markets. In doing so, we shall complete the analysis of Eurocurrency interest rates in the previous sections.

The close connection we have noted between foreign exchange and Eurocurrency operations is a more general one, for the foreign exchange market in every country either forms part of, or is closely related to, the national short-term money market. Also, because a foreign exchange deal must involve at least two currencies, every foreign exchange market, no matter how small, is inevitably international in character. Even in the major centres, the main trades occur without a formal meeting place. Trading is by computer terminals or telephone, and transactions, even into many millions of dollars or pounds, are concluded 'on screen' or orally. Each market is linked by modern telecommunications with markets abroad and, with trading 24 hours a day, there is a single worldwide market in foreign exchange.

Nevertheless, it is usual to make a distinction between the retail and wholesale foreign exchange markets. In the retail market, trading is almost entirely between banks and individual customers. The wholesale market is largely but not exclusively an interbank market. Some large multinationals, like BP, buy and sell in such large quantities that they deal, and run a 'book', more or less as equals with banks. In some cases these corporations are more than equals, since they are largely free of worries about adequate capital cover for risks borne, which cannot be said of banks in the 1980s. However, it is still the case that because of their worldwide branch networks and the arbitrage opportunities which are presented between retail and wholesale markets, the large multinational banks still dominate overall (see Chapter 8). As in banking markets, retail and wholesale differ because of the scale of transactions, with spreads between bid and offer (ask) prices commensurately very much narrower in wholesale deals.

A further distinction is made in terms of delivery, with spot markets and forward markets and also markets for futures, and options on spot, forwards and futures. Spot contracts involve the simultaneous delivery, or at least within two working days, of one currency for another. About 60 per cent of the foreign exchange transactions passing through the banks are for spot delivery. The remainder are forward transactions, consisting of contracts for the delivery of one currency for another in the future, most commonly for periods up to one year. As we shall see, a further distinction exists within the forward market between outright forwards and swaps; the former are retail transactions between banks and customers, while the latter are largely interbank, wholesale deals.

While forward contracts are futures contracts, broadly interpreted, the description 'currency futures' has a specific meaning. It refers to futures contracts which are traded in standardised quantities with specified regular maturities on organised exchanges, such as those operated in Chicago by the Chicago Mercantile Exchange, in London by the London International Financial Futures Exchange and in Sydney by the Sydney Futures Exchange.

While the contract is a legally binding agreement to buy or sell a set quantity of a particular currency at an agreed price at some specific date in the future, actual delivery is rare; most contracts are closed out by an offsetting transaction in the other direction. With a foreign exchange option, by contrast, there is the option but *not* the obligation to buy or sell a designated quantity of a currency at a specified price on or before a certain date. Once forward and futures contracts are made they must be fulfilled (or closed out), whether or not prices have moved unfavourably or not. Options need not be exercised and thus separate a buyer's 'upside' and 'downside' risk.[15]

While banks are involved in the spot, forward and options markets, we shall focus upon their forward transactions. These are 'futures contracts' which are tailor-made in terms of amount and date of delivery, in contrast to the trading in standardised currency futures. The distinction between forward and futures markets is accordingly one of the degree of informality in the market's organisation. This 'informality' does not extend to pricing. When a forward contract is negotiated, no actual cash changes hands (although sometimes the customer may have to put up a margin). There is an exchange of IOUs for one currency in terms of another currency. Niehans (1984) notes that a simple implication should follow from this fact. The 'price' of the contract (i.e. the forward rate) ought to be calculable from knowledge of the spot exchange rate of the two currencies involved and the interest rates on the IOUs. It is here that Eurocurrency banking operations and foreign exchange markets overlap.

Suppose that a bank's customer buys forward Deutschmarks against the sale of US $1 million for settlement in six months' time. This could be a speculative transaction, but forward markets also enable firms involved in international trading to hedge their future commitments. The customer may be a US firm buying goods from Germany and having to pay for them six months hence. By contracting now to buy marks at the agreed exchange rate, the customer covers the risk that the mark may appreciate against the dollar in the interim.

From the viewpoint of the bank, it has agreed now that in six months' time it will sell marks and buy US dollars. How does the bank respond? It has three alternatives.[16] One is to do nothing: the bank then has a mismatched position, long in US dollars, short in marks. In six months the bank must carry out the spot transaction, at an uncertain profit, or even a loss. While banks do take considerable positions themselves on currency movements, their speculation is usually not long-term — most is on within-day movements in exchange rates. Thus they will seek to make an offsetting forward transaction.

An offsetting forward transaction might be with a customer. But it would be entirely fortuitous if an exactly opposite deal in currency and amount happened along, and in the meantime the forward exchange rate might change, eroding the profitability of the transaction. Having a worldwide branch network increases the possibility of offsets, but there would still likely be some net position to be covered. An opposing forward transaction could be with another bank, but banks do not normally write outright forwards with each other. This is because there is a cheaper option available, namely to make a forward transaction via the 'swap' market. The swap market is a largely interbank market in which banks swap, for a price, their different maturities of currency exposure on a sell now — repurchase later basis. In this instance, the bank would cover the foreign exchange position by (i) using US dollars to buy marks in the spot market, and then alter the cash timing by (ii) selling spot against US dollars the marks which it has just bought (so cancelling out the initial spot purchase) and simultaneously buying marks six months forward against US dollars. Via the swap transaction (ii) the bank is left with a contract to buy marks forward which offsets the commitment to sell marks forward left from the contract with the customer. At the same time, the US dollars which the bank has agreed to purchase would restore its dollar balances. The cost is the 'swap margin'.

A third alternative is for the bank to use the money market. Immediately the outright forward contract is written for the customer, the bank would (a) borrow US $1 million for six months. It would then (b) sell the dollars in the spot market for marks. These marks would (c) be put on deposit or invested for six months. By this means the bank will also have exactly offset its original commitment. Proceeds from the maturing investment provide the Deutschmarks needed to meet the sale to the customer. Dollars bought from the customer pay off the outstanding loan. All outstanding contingent liabilities are thus unwound. For the bank the cost (approximately) is the interest rate difference between its Deutschmark deposit and its dollar loan.

In both cases, then, the bank's expected profit from the deal with the customer is the difference between the forward and spot rate embodied in its contract with the customer. When the bank covers via the swap market, its cost is the swap margin. When it covers via the money market, the cost is the interest rate differential. The bank can be expected to choose the least cost route of covering. Some customers have the choice between negotiating a forward contract with a bank or hedging themselves via the money market. Given competition and low transactions costs, arbitrage by banks and customers would lead one to expect the forward premium/discount quoted to customers to be driven to approximate equality with both the swap margin and the interest rate differential. That is, interest rate parity would be achieved. McKinnon (1979) argues that such arbitrage is the dominant force in forward foreign exchange markets, so that this result is the norm.

So far we have made no mention of Eurobanks, and indeed they are in no way necessary to the story. However, when the bank is seeking to make a competitive quotation to the customer, it will seek out the cheapest source of borrowing dollars and the highest return from depositing Deutschmarks. These come from the Eurocurrency market. Hence the McKinnon thesis: a major function of the Euromarkets is to provide facilities for the covering of foreign exchange transactions. With the transition from fixed to floating exchange rates around 1973, the need for the covering of foreign exchange risks on a regular basis grew rapidly; so did the Eurocurrency markets. Most Eurocurrency transactions are interbank; the same is true of foreign exchange markets. Most forward contracts are for less than six months; so too are most Eurocurrency deposits.

Consequently, McKinnon's argument does fit in with some major facts about Eurocurrency banking. Moreover, his emphasis upon the interest arbitrage activities is reinforced by the multicurrency operations of many banks in the Eurocurrency markets. Suppose that a Eurobank receives a deposit in dollars. Suppose further that it does not have a sufficient demand for dollar loans to use the funds profitably, but at the same time is experiencing a heavy demand for loans in Deutschmarks. Accordingly the bank will investigate 'switching' the dollar deposits into mark loans. The first step involves selling dollars for marks on the spot market. Although banks will usually have a 'view' about exchange rates, most switching will occur on a covered basis, in the form of a swap operation involving, as before, a combination of a spot sale and a forward repurchase. A covering transaction involves buying dollars forward at the same time as selling dollars in the spot market. The bank's willingness to undertake this transaction clearly depends on the relative interest rates concerned, and on spot and forward rates. Placing \$1 in Eurodollars earns $\$(1+i_d)$. Exchanging \$1 into DM buys $1/R_s$. This earns $DM(1+i_f)/R_s$. In \$, this converts to $\$R_F(1+i_f)/R_s$. The transaction is profitable so long as:

$$R_F(1+i_f)/R_s > (1+i_d) \tag{9.10}$$

Undertaking such arbitrage will cause at least one of: R_F to fall, R_s to increase, i_f to fall, and i_d to increase until interest parity is attained, namely:

$$R_F(1+i_f)/R_s = (1+i_d) \tag{9.11}$$

Rearranging and deducting 1 from both sides, we obtain:

$$\frac{R_F - R_s}{R_s} = \frac{i_d - i_f}{1 + i_f} \tag{9.12}$$

where the interest rate differential expression and the spot-forward differential are equal to each other.

In this schema, one economic function of the Eurosystem is to undertake covered interest arbitrage, align interest rate differentials with forward rates and reduce private transactors' costs of hedging. The other is to undertake currency transformation. By intermediating between currencies, the Eurobank matches demands for DM loans, say, with dollar deposits.

Some Eurocurrency markets are essentially 'satellite' markets with a shortage of market-makers in the particular currency. Eurosterling is an example. A bank in Paris or Brussels receiving a Eurosterling deposit has usually not sought to find a sterling borrower, nor to increase working balances in London. Rather it has sold pounds spot, held the funds in US dollars and covered forward. Similarly, a bank which is requested to supply a Eurosterling loan would 'manufacture' the currency by borrowing US dollars and 'swapping', that is, buying pounds spot and selling forward. Eurosterling can always be created in this way independently of funds from the domestic market. As Stigum (1983) puts it: 'to any funding officer, every Eurocurrency deposit is nothing but a Eurodollar deposit with a swap tagged on' (p.168). For this reason, currency deposits in the satellite markets are simply quoted as Eurodollar deposit rates adjusted as via equation (9.12) for the forward discount or premium relative to the US dollar.

These close links between the Eurocurrency interest rates enable us to flesh out the relationship we suggested earlier between Eurocurrency and domestic interest rates (again due to interbank arbitrage). The links are depicted in Figure 9.3, following Dufey and Giddy (1978). It follows that, if there is a close relationship between Eurodollar and Euromark interest rates due to interest arbitrage by banks, and if at the same time both of the Eurocurrency interest rates are tied also to the respective domestic interest rates, the US and German capital markets are linked, even if few direct transactions occur between the two. In practice, the indirect links are reinforced by direct arbitrage between the two, so there is effectively one world capital market for short-term funds. This is the message also in Niehans and Hewson's (1976) theory of a global funds market due to Eurocurrency operations.

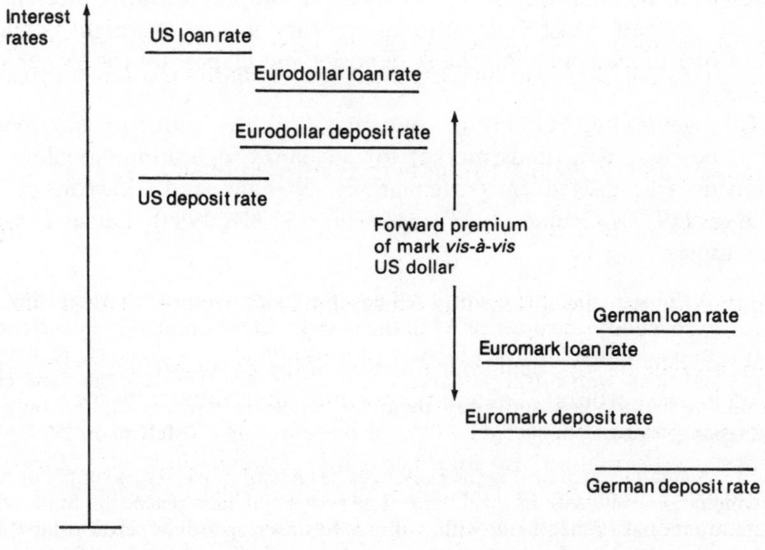

Figure 9.3 Interest Rate Links in the Eurocurrency Markets

9.6 A Global Funds Market

In earlier sections we envisaged a new Eurodollar deposit of a non-bank customer at a particular bank in London and the various ways in which the funds can be disposed of:

(i) The dollars can be kept on deposit with a New York bank, building up the bank's liquid assets.
(ii) The deposits can be lent to another non-bank customer in London.
(iii) The funds can be redeposited with another bank in London which lends to the non-bank customer.
(iv) The bank may sell the dollars in the foreign exchange market and lend in another currency to a non-bank customer.
(v) The dollars can be lent back to the head office of a US bank.
(vi) The funds can be lent, or channelled via interbank redepositing, to a bank in another centre.

Our discussion of Eurocurrency credit creation focused on outcomes (i)–(iii); (iv) was considered in the last section; and (v) was implicit in the arbitrage activities of banks. When economists were searching for appropriate analogies to describe the workings of the Eurocurrency market, the importance of outcome (v) on occasions led to the suggestion that the market was an annex of the Federal funds market (Lutz 1974). A US bank seeking to increase its reserves with the Federal Reserve Bank can either bid for Federal funds locally or borrow dollars from its overseas branches or from any bank in London (or Paris or . . .). By either means the borrowing bank acquires reserves from another US bank, but there are important differences in the length of the loan. Most Federal funds transactions are overnight, while 80 per cent of Eurocurrency interbank deposits and claims are for longer than seven days.

More generally, building on outcome (vi), the Eurocurrency market came to be seen as a funds market for all banks, operating globally. This function is emphasised in particular by Niehans and Hewson (1976), McKinnon (1977), Grubel (1977), and Thore (1984, 1986). Let us consider two examples:

> A domestic bank in country A finds itself with a reserve shortage, and bids for Eurodeposits in currency A. In the absence of a Euromarket in currency A (or an undeveloped market in A, eg Eurosterling) or if domestic regulations prevent deals with offshore markets in the domestic currency, the bank could bid for Eurodollars and swap them for domestic reserves (at the on-going exchange rate). (McKinnon 1977, p. 26)

> A small French firm in the provinces has a temporary excess supply of funds which it deposits with its local bank. The provincial bank places the funds with a multinational French bank with whom it has correspondent relationships. This bank may lend the funds to an overseas branch of US multinational bank, which may transfer the funds to London for on-lending. Going through a number of

> banks, the funds may eventually end up as a loan to a small Japanese borrower dealing with a small Japanese provincial bank. As an alternative the funds could finish up as a loan to a small French firm in the same province or town in which the original lender resides. (Grubel 1977, p. 357)

By such means the Eurocurrency system 'serves as a medium for world-wide redistribution of short-term funds from surplus units and surplus regions to deficit units and deficit regions' (Thore 1984).

Niehans and Hewson proposed a network theory in which funds flow from ultimate depositor to ultimate borrower via a network of interbank transactions, illustrated in Figure 9.4. Four requirements are listed for such a network to arise:

1. There are large excess demands or excess supplies of funds in local areas, arising from differences in savings and investment propensities, liquidity preferences, interest rates, and from balance of payments disequilibria.
2. Transactions costs between non-banks are very high. (This prevents direct financing from a non-bank in one country to another. However, the requirement is less applicable to foreign trade where trade credit is well developed.)
3. Transactions costs between banks and non-banks vary widely. (This prevents each bank from balancing its non-bank business.)
4. The costs of peripheral banks dealing with each other are greater than deals between peripheral banks and 'centre' banks. (For this to result in a Eurosystem, there must be relatively undeveloped interbank markets in the various countries, unless the excess demand and excess supply of funds originates simultaneously across borders from a foreign trade transaction.)

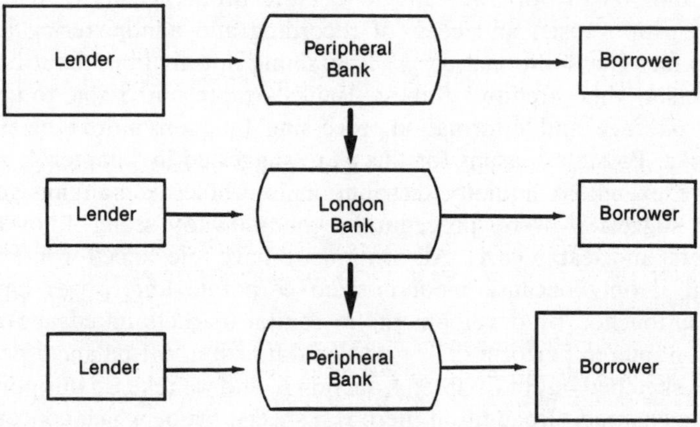

Figure 9.4

As an historical description of the development of the Eurocurrency market during the 1970s, it is readily apparent that some of these conditions have been met. Large excess supplies and demands for funds have arisen at a world level from factors such as oil price shocks. Since payment imbalances are symmetric, with the surplus of one country matched by deficits elsewhere, excess supplies and demands for funds can originate simultaneously across borders. These imbalances, moreover, were intermediated through the offshore and domestic banking systems rather than via the capital market. We shall examine these factors in the next chapter.

Conditions in the 1980s, however, would seem to fit in less happily with the model. Large payments imbalances have again occurred, but these have not been intermediated through banks' balance sheets to anything like the same extent. 'In-house' banking by multinationals and the trend to 'securitisation' point to a reduction in the costs of transacting between non-bank entities. Indeed, the Cross Report (BIS 1986b) wonders whether banks may be losing their comparative advantage in favour of direct financing through capital markets. This trend finds reflection in, and may have been facilitated by, an increase in credit-rating agencies. There are now 17 agencies operating internationally, seven of which were established since 1981.[17] They disseminate to institutional savers, especially insurance companies and pension funds, information which previously gave banks some of their advantages in credit evaluation.

In this respect, we note that the examples quoted above assume implicitly (it is explicit in Niehans and Hewson) the absence of maturity transformation by the banking system. Thus lenders, borrowers, and banks all deal in securities of the same type and term to maturity, and the function of banks is one of spreading more evenly a given amount of liquidity. Transaction and information costs are the basis of banks' existence. In the absence of banks, firms would solicit loans from each other and face various costs. Common to borrower and lender are brokerage fees, search costs, communication costs, and costs of recording and administering accounts. Lenders face the additional costs of obtaining information about borrowers and assessing their creditworthiness. Banks are presumed able to undertake these 'brokerage' and 'information processing' functions more efficiently than non-banks. Possible reasons for this were suggested in Chapter 4, section 2 when we examined liquidity distribution in wholesale banking generally. Factors suggested were procedural economies of scale, knowledge of customers, and search costs. All continue to have relevance for international banking, if only because medium-sized corporate enterprises have been largely untouched by developments in capital markets noted above. Also, banks continue to perform their traditional functions off-balance sheet along the lines sketched out in Chapter 4, section 6, and we take up this point in the following chapters. In addition there is a special factor which concerns costs of transportation.

When discussing why production of any product, including banking, might be externalised, we said that differences in taxes and regulations, along with costs of transport, must make it feasible to produce in one location and consume in another. So far we have emphasised the importance of reserve requirements and regulations such as interest rate ceilings and asset quality requirements, but have ignored costs of transportation. For a US resident obtaining a dollar loan from an overseas branch of a US bank, or a German resident borrowing in marks from the branch of a German bank in Luxembourg, it is less convenient to obtain a loan externally than domestically but, given the negligible 'transport costs' (for the funds do not actually have to be shipped), there is no great inconvenience for wholesale amounts. Suppose, however, that a UK resident is obtaining the dollar loan. In the past, the firm would have had to approach or be introduced to a New York bank. If the firm is a customer of Midland Bank, it could deal with European American Bank (linked with Midland) but it is surely more convenient all round to obtain a dollar loan from Midland Bank itself in London.

Given the existence of inherited banker–customer relationships and other factors leading to information and transaction costs, the worldwide demand for currencies such as the dollar, mark and yen will encourage the development and continuance of offshore banking markets. So long as there are enough customers, it is cheaper for the bank to take the production of banking services to the customer than for the customer to transact at a distance. As in retail banking, a desire to achieve proximity to the customers and lower their costs of acquiring banking services is an important determinant of the location of banking offices.

These arguments go a long way to explaining why Eurocurrency centres exist in Singapore and Bahrain to act as feeders to peripheral banks in the region and why it is that some European centres like London and Paris serve as global centres, intermediating between the regional markets. But there is no large number of customers or regional banks in the Caribbean, and some special factors are relevant when we consider the role of these centres.

9.7 Offshore Tax Havens and Regulatory Arbitrage

While proximity to the customer and the presence of specialised markets influence the location of banking, substantial freedom from taxes, duties, regulation and operating restrictions of one kind or another is the impetus for most Eurocurrency operations. Thus, for example, a US bank making a dollar loan to a German firm will not wish to make the loan in either New York or Frankfurt, where funding attracts reserve requirements and other costs, but will aim to book the loan in London, Luxembourg, or Brussels. But the financial environment and operating costs differ greatly between centres, and it would hardly be surprising if multinational banks, like other transnational corporations, sought to arrange their affairs so as to minimise the impact of the residual charges and controls. A bank is to a large extent an accounting arrangement which can be reorganised and restructured readily, while modern communications facilities enable there to be a divergence between the legal and actual location of banking activities.

In Chapter 8 we drew a distinction between functional centres and paper centres. A functional centre is one in which deposit taking, final lending and actual intermediation occur. Paper centres, otherwise known as 'booking', 'shell', 'brass-plate', 'routing', or 'suitcase' centres, are locations where transactions are legally booked, but they are really a set of ledgers maintained by an agent: the intermediation occurs elsewhere. Branches of US banks in the Caribbean are a prominent example. For many US banks without full-service branches in London and other functional centres, such locales offer low-cost access to the Eurocurrency system. But much of the motivation for transacting through them is different.

Eurobanks, we have emphasised, are not separate institutions. Most Eurobanks in London, for instance, are branches of US, continental European, Japanese, Canadian, Middle Eastern or Australian banks. Many British Eurobanks in London have branches in other centres. Flows of funds between branches or between head office and branches get picked up in some interbank statistics. As a result, interbank transactions often include positions that really are 'intrabank' (see Table 8.4). Some transactions between related offices may be to fund cross-currency or external lending in other centres, such as the transfers between London and Tokyo. Others may rather be designed to minimise global tax payments, to undertake 'transfer pricing' and to avoid regulatory restrictions upon profit making.

Consider first the role of paper centres as tax havens. US branches prefer to operate abroad as branches. Income earned overseas is immediately subject to US income tax, after allowable credits for foreign income tax paid. Use of the Bahamas and Cayman Islands does not enable avoidance of US federal tax. But their use can avoid double taxation when no double taxation agreement exists. Also, when the foreign tax rate is higher than the US rate, there are benefits in shifting income from the foreign country to tax-free locations to avoid what is known as the 'tax cushion problem' (Stigum 1983). This occurs when the bank has excess foreign tax credits to put against US federal taxes, so that it needs to earn foreign profits without at the same time increasing foreign taxes paid. It can do this by routing business through a tax haven, such as the Bahamas or Cayman Islands, which does not levy profits tax. US banks in the Caribbean 'make' far more loans to non-bank customers than the deposits which they 'collect' from non-banks. The banks issue deposits in London and other centres and book out loans in the Caribbean, so lowering taxable income in London.[18]

Banks also use the paper centres to undertake what Dale (1984) calls 'regulatory arbitrage', that is, transactions with the explicit purpose of circumventing national regulations and concealing actual exposures from bank regulators. Evidence comes from a Securities and Exchange Commission investigation into the international activities of Citibank over the period 1973–1980: activities which one of the bank's officers described as 'rinky dink deals'. Our account of them below relies upon Dale's summary of the evidence.

Citibank employed two well-known techniques. One is 'garaging' or 'parking', whereby a branch in one country trades an exposure, say, in foreign currency, with a branch in another country. Dale gives an example involving Citibank's London branch. During some of the period examined by the SEC, the Bank of England limited Citibank's overnight currency position against sterling to $1 million. In order to avoid this restriction, Citibank transferred its much larger exposure to Nassau by undertaking an offsetting transaction with its Nassau branch. With all parking transactions the reverse transaction can be written at non-market rates which ensure that the profit or loss from the exposure goes to the location which enables the bank to maximise global income. Dale cites other examples involving Citibank's Swiss and Frankfurt branches.

The other well-known technique used by Citibank was 'back-to-back' or 'round-tripping' or 'counter' loans, which involves funds being deposited with one or more branches which then redeposit with the first branch. The Bank of England examines the balance sheets of UK-based banks to monitor, amongst many other things, the extent of maturity mismatching or 'interest rate gapping' by banks, because of the possible losses should interest rates rise sharply between interest rate adjustment periods. During the period 1975–77, Citibank's London branch was apparently mismatching to the maximum extent possible under flexi-rate lending: borrowing dollars at call and lending them back interbank for six months. In order to conceal this exposure from the Bank's regulators (who, unlike US regulators, do not examine the dealing records or operating departments), Citibank London round-tripped with Citibank Nassau. London borrowed from Nassau at six months and re-lent to Nassau at call, so 'snugging up' its London book, shifting not only the mismatched exposure but also most of the profits (averaging $1 million per month over 2½ years) from London to Nassau.

Round-tripping by Citibank was not limited to transactions with the Caribbean. Dale summarises many transactions involving the European branches of Citibank. Consider one example. French banking authorities require that short-term deposits have a 60 per cent covering of liquid assets. Citibank undertook a series of transactions to boost its cover. Citibank Paris placed deposits at call with its London branch, which in turn deposited call with Amsterdam, which then deposited call with Paris. Each transaction added one-for-one to short-term deposits and assets, thus 'improving' the liquid position.

Of course, we do not know to what extent such transactions, documented in detail by Dale, are peculiar to Citibank or are generic to multinational banks. Certainly, 'snugging up', and various ways of artifncially inflating balance sheets, are examined by Stigum and Branch (1983) as strategies for banks to employ in their overall management of assets and liabilities.

9.8 International Wholesale Intermediation

Eurocurrency banking operations are complex, and it is not surprising that attempts to explain the nature of a bank's business are numerous. Some see Eurobanking activities as international in location only, arguing that Eurobanks provide facilities which merely replicate offshore the functions of domestic banks and domestic interbank markets. According to this view, they are essentially externally transplanted non-banking intermediaries and substitutes for the Federal funds market. Others see the Eurobanks as supplanting traditional foreign banking, providing international trade financing and forward foreign exchange covering free of regulations which hamper the domestic production of these services. Another view sees Eurobanks as truly international in their operations, collecting idle funds from one region of the world and channelling them via interbank and intrabank networks to other regions of the world.

We agree with all these views: Eurobanking is multidimensional and serves a number of ends. What appears to be disagreement amongst economists is more a reflection of the passage of time. As the market has grown, so it has taken on more functions and has progressively become more global.

But we want to take the above arguments one step further. The basic point of contention is the view (expressed by Niehans and Hewson, and McKinnon) that little maturity transformation occurs and that the liabilities of Eurobanks are as liquid as their claims — in other words, that there is a substantial extent of matching in the market as a whole. Their argument is that in Eurocurrency operations the 'brokerage' function dominates that of 'liquidity production', so that Eurobanks distribute liquidity but do not create it. If this were so, we find it hard to explain the known role of the Eurocurrency markets of matching OPEC preferences for short-term deposits with the developing countries' demand for long-term loans. The observations made in the preceding section suggest that some special factors like 'regulatory arbitrage' can influence the pattern of interbank transactions. At least one example suggested that the extent of maturity mismatching may exceed that which is reflected in aggregate balance sheet data. Accordingly, examination of non-bank business may provide a more reliable guide to the extent of maturity transformation. We reach the same conclusion, but for different reasons. The preceding views have either treated interbank activity as distinct from non-bank, or have allowed Eurobanks to be mere feeders for domestic banks. Our own views integrate both the interbank and non-bank activities of Eurobanks, and the offshore and onshore activities.

Following the analysis in Chapter 4, we see the Eurobanks as wholesale intermediaries, undertaking as a byproduct of their intermediation considerable maturity transformation and liquidity production. Interbank markets do provide facilities for forward foreign exchange covering and do distribute short-term funds between banks and across countries. But interbank markets are also a vital part of banks' management of the liquidity needs and risks of international lending. Interbank markets both widen the balance sheet options open to the banks and make for informal risk-sharing arrangements. We see them, along with loan syndications, as performing much the same role in banking markets as reinsurance markets play in the international insurance business. Both are institutional devices which have developed for the purpose of spreading liquidity needs across the whole 'industry'. Both are institutional responses to risk: large risks are broken up or subcontracted into shares or participations which are, in the end, individually small enough to be encompassed and pooled with other participations in an individual firm's portfolio. In the case of international banking via the Eurocurrency markets, these mechanisms allow liquidity production to occur.

Banks in Eurocurrency operations, we contend, transform customers' short-term funds into long-term loans. In doing so, Eurobanks create liquidity by virtue of the 'insurance policies' which they write. They give the majority of depositors the assurance that deposits can be withdrawn at short notice, despite holding assets of much longer maturity. They give their customers the assurance that sums deposited with them can be redeemed at full value, while themselves holding assets which fluctuate in redemption value. They assure borrowers that loans will not have to be repaid within the period over which the funds are committed. Borrowers are insured against interest rates on their loans fluctuating daily, despite variations each day in the banks' cost of funds. We now look at some evidence as to the extent of maturity transformation carried out in the Eurocurrency market.

Niehans and Hewson advanced their theory of the distributive role of the Eurocurrency market after observing (i) the extent of interbank activity in the market and (ii) the overall extent to which maturities are matched. The data on which the latter observation is based was for 1973, for UK-based banks, and is reproduced in both Niehans and Hewson and in McKinnon. McKinnon concentrates on the same two points, but with somewhat different emphasis. He argues, in effect, that since the 'liquidity distribution' function of banking is carried out in domestic markets without such extensive interbank activity, the Eurobanks must be doing something different. That difference he attributes to forward exchange.

Data after 1973 indicate more extensive maturity transformation for both total and non-bank business. Table 9.4 shows that, for total business in January 1987, claims one year or longer represented 24.8 per cent of banks' assets, while liabilities of this term represented only 9.4 per cent of the total. But much more of maturity transformation is indicated by non-bank liabilities

Table 9.4 Maturity Structure of Liabilities and Claims of all UK-Based Eurobanks (% of total)

	CLAIMS					LIABILITIES				
	March 1974	*Feb. 1977*	*Feb. 1980*	*Feb. 1984*	*Jan. 1987*	*March 1974*	*Feb. 1977*	*Feb. 1980*	*Feb. 1984*	*Jan. 1987*
TOTAL BUSINESS										
Less than 8 days	18.3	17.0	16.9	16.5	18.3	21.5	22.6	21.9	22.8	24.0
8 days to 1 month	19.6	13.2	16.0	15.7	17.5	21.0	17.0	19.4	20.1	22.3
1 month to 3 months	22.6	22.0	23.0	23.4	21.9	26.4	26.9	28.1	28.1	25.7
3 months to 6 months	16.9	15.8	15.8	14.0	12.1	19.7	18.7	18.4	17.7	13.8
6 months to 1 year	7.7	8.0	7.0	6.4	5.4	7.6	8.1	7.3	6.2	4.8
1 year to 3 years	5.0	9.8	6.7	7.2	5.9	2.2	4.8	3.2	2.6	2.9
3 years and over	9.9	14.2	14.6	16.8	18.9	3.4	1.9	1.7	2.5	6.5
NON-BANK BUSINESS										
Less than 8 days	8.2	4.5	8.9	7.1	12.0	31.7	35.8	31.7	35.1	38.2
8 days to 1 month	13.0	5.7	8.6	9.0	11.0	19.7	22.1	21.6	21.2	24.0
1 month to 3 months	19.7	11.4	11.2	12.2	13.7	20.8	21.4	23.9	21.7	18.2
3 months to 6 months	14.9	9.4	8.2	8.0	9.3	13.3	12.1	12.9	12.3	6.9
6 months to 1 year	6.3	8.3	6.0	6.5	6.1	7.7	4.9	5.7	4.9	2.7
1 year to 3 years	10.7	20.5	13.4	16.5	13.1	2.7	1.7	2.0	1.5	2.0
3 years and over	27.2	40.2	43.7	40.7	34.8	4.1	2.0	2.2	3.3	8.0

Sources: Bank of England, *Sterling Business Analysed by Maturity and Sector*, March 1987; Bank of England, *Maturity Analysis by Sector of Liabilities and Claims in Foreign Currencies*, March 1987.

and assets. Not only is the transformation considerable, but it has increased greatly since 1973. With non-bank business, in 1973, 0–7-day liabilities were 28.4 per cent of total, while assets three years plus were 20 per cent of total. In 1987, the respective figure for 0–7-day liabilities was 38.2 per cent and for assets three years plus it was 34.8 per cent.

In Chapter 4 we showed a very close similarity between the maturity mismatching by British banks in Eurocurrency operations and in sterling business. This led us to the suggestion that we may be entitled to speak of characteristics of 'wholesale intermediation', whether carried out in Eurocurrencies or in domestic currencies. This is hardly surprising when we remember that Eurobanks are not a special category of institution, but ordinary banks using common techniques to produce banking services.

Others have been led to emphasise the differences between international and domestic banking operations by observations like the one by McKinnon, quoted above, comparing interbank transactions in Eurocurrency and domestic operations. A certain amount of churning of transactions at wholesale level is perhaps necessary to match lenders with ultimate borrowers, but the vast amount of interbank transactions within the Eurocurrency system seems disproportionate if the system is to be treated merely as a substitute for domestic financial intermediation within the confines of a single currency. How disproportionate the interbank activity in Eurocurrency business is depends on the basis of comparison. In Eurocurrency operations, interbank liabilities are about 70 per cent of total liabilities (see Table 8.3). This is indeed striking when compared with estimates of interbank liabilities relative to the US banks' domestic liabilities of around 12 per cent (embracing correspondent balances and other funds)[19] since the US financial market is not unlike a vast 'intercontinental' market in certain respects (distance, number of centres, time zones). But Eurocurrency statistics include positions amongst related offices which are generally netted out in local markets. Also, US data relate to retail as well as wholesale banking. Given our contention that interbank markets are part of the production process in wholesale banking, the comparison should be made with domestic wholesale banks. Our sample of such banks in Britain embracing accepting houses, British overseas banks, other British banks and consortium banks (but excluding clearers and subsidiaries) shows their interbank liabilities in sterling to be 46 per cent of total sterling liabilities. This indicates the importance of interbank transactions to wholesale banking. While interbank activity is clearly much larger in international business, the difference seems readily explicable in terms of intrabank positions, forward exchange covering and a certain amount of extra 'churning' without having to put Eurocurrency banking practices into a separate category.

In fact, the major explanations (global funds market, wholesale foreign exchange, wholesale intermediation) can be readily integrated. International banks can be regarded as having a balance sheet comprising a variety of currencies and maturities and with end-users located in different countries. The economic function of banks is to undertake three different kinds of transformation:

(1) Mismatching across currencies: the mix of currency assets desired by lenders may differ from the mix of currencies preferred by borrowers. By undertaking covered interest arbitrage, banks' intermediation permits the menu of currency obligations of final borrowers to differ from the menu held by ultimate lenders.
(2) Mismatching across countries: because capital can be readily transported, dollar deposits by oil exporters can be readily transformed into loans to, say, Swedish importers.
(3) Mismatching by maturity: banks can transform short-term deposits by, say, oil exporters into longer-term loans to borrowers like the developing countries.

We now shall go on to examine the special techniques followed by the banks in carrying out such lending.

Notes

1. Harrod (1969), Chapter 12.
2. Seigniorage refers to the above-normal profits which accrue to the producers of money (currency plus bank deposits) when, because of interest rate ceilings or other controls, balances earn less than the competitive return on earning assets.
3. Had Company *Y* banked with another bank in the USA, the Eurodollar transactions would have given rise to an interbank clearance in the USA. Since the transactions involve large sums, and usually give rise to transfers between New York banks, it is customary for settlements to be made through CHIPS (see Chapter 6).
4. See Niehans (1984, p. 186).
5. For simplicity we ignore the existence of the interbank market; thus E corresponds to the *net* size of the Eurodollar market.
6. If we were considering a shift from cash into 'money' (instead of a shift from one class of deposit into another deposit), (9.6) could be written in perhaps more familiar ways. The redeposit ratio p would then be $(1–c)$ where c is the ratio of currency to money holdings. Denoting the reserve ratio as r, instead of q, the multiplier (9.6) becomes:

$$\frac{1}{c + r(1-c)} \tag{9.6a}$$

Sometimes it is preferred to work with d, the ratio of currency holdings to deposits (instead of money) where $d{=}c/1{-}c$. Substituting into (9.3a), we have:

$$\frac{1 + d}{d + r} \tag{9.6b}$$

which is the familiar money-base multiplier.
7. Reasons for supposing the 'reserve ratio' (q) for Eurobanks to be zero are given in

the next paragraph. Non-bank holdings of Eurodollar deposits as at December 1985 were approximately 0.3 of the US money supply M1 and approximately 0.1 of the money supply M2, and we have chosen the average of these values for illustrative purposes.

8. Estimates are given in Carli (1971), Fratianni and Savona (1971), Lee (1972), Makin (1972), and Owens (1974). Recent surveys and assessments are contained in Swoboda (1980) Johnston (1983) and Kane (1983).
9. It is possible to conceive of an almost limitless Eurodollar multiplier based on central bank redepositing of loan proceeds to the market. Many earlier analyses supposed that recipients of dollar loan proceeds would convert all amounts not redeposited with the Eurobanks into local currencies. Foreign central banks were then assumed to buy the dollars and supply local currencies to support the ruling exchange rate, and then deposit the dollars with the Eurobanks. As Swoboda (1980) observes, this is merely assuming an infinite thirst for Eurodollar deposits. Applying this assumption in the standard analysis would, equally unrealistically, give a nearly infinite Eurodollar multiplier.
10. See Argy (1981), on which Figure 9.2 is based.
11. Assuming $p>0$ at the margin implies that, if de is the initial autonomous deposit, redeposit at Eurobanks as part of the credit creation process would involve subsequent shifts of the supply curve to the right. See the appendix to this chapter.
12. Since the transaction expands the bank's consolidated balance sheet, it has the disadvantage of bringing about a deterioration in its capital ratio.
13. The arbitrage tunnel for the Deutschmark is, however, different from that for the dollar. No reserve requirements apply to interbank deposits in Germany, but borrowing by German banks in the Euromarket is subject to the requirements, so that domestic interbank interest rates are lower in the Euromarkets than in Germany. We are indebted to Mr J.S. Alworth for this point.
14. These authors examined the correlation between monthly changes in Euro- and domestic interest rates in the case of the United States, Canada, Japan, United Kingdom, Germany, France, Italy, Netherlands and Belgium, for the period 1979 to 1984. Only in the case of Italy and France do exchange controls and other obstacles to the movement of funds seem to inhibit integration of the home and offshore money markets effectively, a finding which receives clear visual support from graphs of comparable domestic and Eurocurrency interest rates from 1970 to 1986 by Fukao and Hanazaki (1986). This separation has been in evidence in recent years on a number of occasions shortly before realignments of exchange rates under the European Monetary System. Devaluations of the French franc and Italian lira have been expected, and overnight Eurorates have risen to very high levels relative to domestic interest rates.
15. The organisation of the US spot and forward markets is described in Revey (1981). the UK equivalents are examined in Bank of England (1980b). A recent account embracing spot, forward, futures and options markets is in Chrystal (1984a). For an examination of the workings of spot, forward and futures markets in the Australian environment, see Polasek and Lewis (1985a). An excellent exposition, which looks as well at the strategies open to firms, is given by Buckley (1986).
16. Our analysis has benefited considerably from reading the excellent account by Hudson (1981).
17. *Banker International*, April 1987, pp. 21–23.
18. The British Inland Revenue requires that a bank's London branch makes some small taxable profit on such transactions, by means of a markup of around 5/64 per cent. See Stigum (1983).
19. Estimates by the Federal Reserve Bank of New York cited in Dale (1984).

APPENDIX
Multipliers and the Portfolio Approach: A Geometric Exposition

For this analysis we assume that $R_E/E=q=0$: in other words, Eurobanks hold no reserves (except perhaps temporarily in the interim between receiving deposits and making loans). The public's preferences are represented by:

$$E/(E+D)=p(i_e, X) \tag{9.13}$$

where E is Eurodollar deposits, D is US bank deposits, i_e is the interest rate on E and X stands for other relevant variables such as other interest rates. Then, p lies between 0 and 1. The US money supply is given by $M=E+D$, and $D=B/r$ where B is the stock of base money and r the reserve ratio of US banks. Consequently

$$M=\frac{1}{1-p}\ \frac{B}{r}$$

We are considering two specific situations: in the first the authorities peg B so that M varies directly with p; in the second M is assumed constant, an expository device for deriving the results of this analysis.

In the north-west quadrant of Figure 9.5 is shown the relationship between i_e and p, that is, the portfolio preferences of depositors for some given set of values of the X variables. The south-east quadrant is simply a construction line. The south-west quadrant is based upon the relationship:

$$E=pM=\frac{p}{1-p}\ \frac{B}{r} \tag{9.14}$$

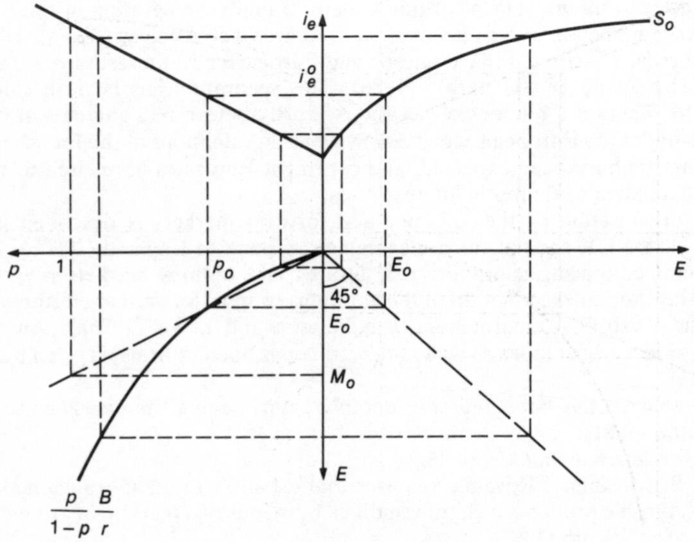

Figure 9.5

Two lines are shown. The curved line, which shifts only if B/r changes, shows the relationship between E and p when B/r is held constant and M is allowed to vary. The straight (broken) line is drawn for a particular initial value of $M=M_o$ and initial value of $p=p_o$ and assumes M constant at M_o. It has a slope of M_o and intersects the other line at $p=p_o$. The line thus represents positions of disequilibrium immediately following changes in p from $p=p_o$ such as in the first step of the multiplier process when the private sector converts US bank deposits into Eurodollar deposits. Initially no change in M occurs, but once loans are made by Eurobanks, M will increase (and the line rotate until it intersects the other at the new value of p).

The supply curve of Eurodollar deposits in the north-east quadrant is derived using the construct line shown by starting at particular i_e values in the north-west quadrant and tracing through the figure counter-clockwise, using the solid (curved) line in the south-west quadrant. The straight line in the south-west quadrant is not at this stage relevant to the analysis but is drawn assuming a current interest rate of $i_E{}^{\circ}$, portfolio ratio of p_o and money stock of M_o.

Figure 9.6 illustrates the effects of an autonomous shift in portfolio preferences towards Eurodollars, depicted by a leftward shift of the line in the north-west quadrant. Here, the two lines in the south-west quadrant come into play. At the initial interest rate of $i_e{}^{\circ}$ which we temporarily hold constant, the immediate effect on Eurodollar deposits (before any credit creation) is determined from the broken line in the south-west quadrant as an increase from E_o to E_p corresponding to the increase in p from p_o to p_1. (US

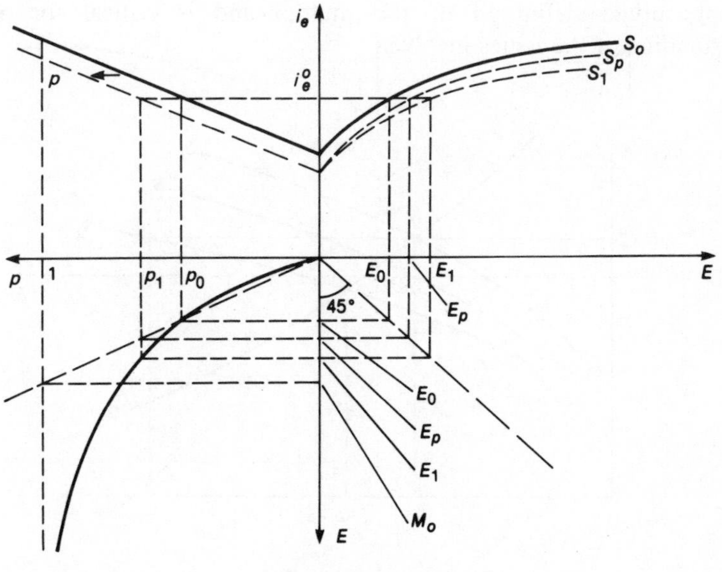

Figure 9.6

deposits have fallen correspondingly so that M is constant.)[1] This initial shift is depicted by the movement from S_o to S_p in the north-east quadrant. However, the process of credit creation by Eurobanks leads to an increase in M (as described in the text) until, at the initial interest rate $i_e°$, equilibrium is achieved at p_1 with $E=E_1$. The supply curve thus shifts to S_1.

In the context of the formula used in the text, $(E_1-E_o)/(E_p-E_o)$ corresponds to the multiplier $\frac{1}{1-p(1-q)}$ of equation 9.6 and (E_p-E_o) to the initial autonomous deposit. The analysis of a change in base money and US bank deposits involving a shift in the solid line in the south-west quadrant is left as an exercise to the reader.

Figure 9.7 takes the north-east quadrant of Figure 9.6 and augments it by a curve representing the demand for loans from Eurobanks. To do this, it is assumed that a fixed spread exists between Eurodollar loan and deposit rates, enabling us to depict the demand for loans against the deposit interest rate. Initial equilibrium is thus at point A, after the shift in portfolio preferences, interest rates change, leading to a moderation of that shift and to equilibrium at E_2 rather than at E_1.

As drawn, the ultimate change in E is(E_2-E_o) which is less than the initial change (E_p-E_o), but this need not necessarily be the case. Thus, the initial deposit multiplier *could* be less than unity if interest rate changes were sufficiently large. But this is not the appropriate analogue of the 'margarine multiplier' referred to by Niehans and Hewson and discussed in the text. That example and multiplier is more appropriately interpreted as referring to $(E_2-E_o)/(E_1-E_o)$ which *must* be less than unity. As emphasised in the text, the appropriate definition of the multiplicand is critical for a clear understanding of the issues involved.

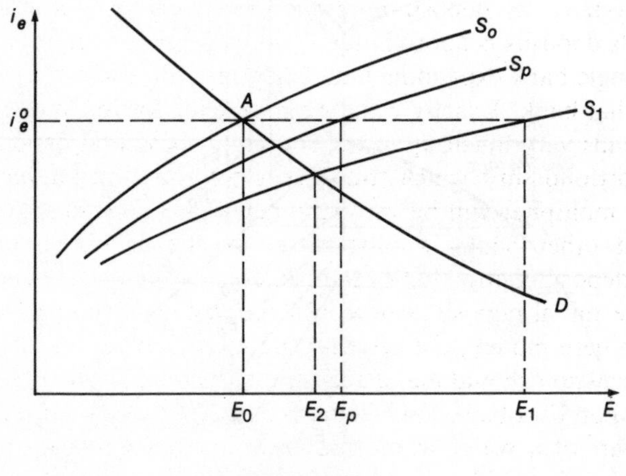

Figure 9.7

Note

1. While, for reasons listed later in the paragraph, the result is an analytical device, it can be assumed that this is brought about by US depositors withdrawing cash from US banks which is redeposited with Eurobanks. The initial impact, prior to Eurobanks expanding their loans, is a reduction in D and an increase in E, with M constant.

10

International Financing and Bank Lending

10.1 Financing of World Payments Imbalances

During the decade after 1973, international bank lending in net terms — net of interbank redepositing — increased at an average rate of 22 per cent per annum. One of the distinctive features of many international loans during this period has been their connection with the financing of current account deficits in the balance of payments. Countries have used external borrowings on a scale unknown for decades to finance programmes of industrialisation and development, and also to cushion the impact of adverse changes occurring in the world economy upon their international trading positions.

Statistics of international bank lending were presented and explained in Chapter 8. It was shown that by far the greater part (in 1986 nearly 80 per cent) of external lending[1] consisted of lending sourced from the various Eurocurrency centres. Eurocurrency banking operations were examined in Chapter 9. While recognising that such operations are multifaceted, we concluded that Eurobanks, like banks anywhere, collect idle funds on a short-term basis from one region and activate them by lending to other regions, often for much longer terms. As compared with domestic banks, special problems may arise because the lending is across countries and across currencies, and also because the banking is 'wholesale' with individual loans ranging from millions up to billions of dollars. In this chapter we examine some of the mechanisms which banks have developed to cope with these characteristics.

First, however, we shall comment on the financing of imbalances, domestically and internationally. Then we shall look at the major types of international finance provided by private markets, in particular distinguishing between the role of banks as underwriters or placers of bond and note issues and their role as deposit takers and lenders. It is a feature of international banking that there is an overlap between commercial banking and investment banking activities.

In international economic parlance, intermediation by banks which results in funds flowing from surplus to deficit regions is referred to as 'recycling'. Recycling attracted attention because of the vast size of the sums which were directed through the banks' balance sheets from members of OPEC to the group of countries known as the non-oil exporting developing countries. But the position has been much more general. In the early 1980s, the USA was also a large net supplier of funds to the Eurocurrency banking markets. Canada and Japan have also been net users of funds along with Eastern European countries (see Table 9.2).

Recycling, that is, international financial intermediation, is in fact little different from the inter-regional financing which banks carry out domestically. Some regions of a country have investment projects which exceed local savings, others have a savings capacity in excess of investment. Partly for this reason, but for many other reasons also, areas within a country have a payments imbalance, deficit or surplus, with other areas. Banks play a major part in facilitating the adjustment of regions to these imbalances domestically, and it should not be surprising to find them assuming similar functions in the international economy.

Consider first the nature of inter-regional adjustment. In response to a payments deficit, members of a region within a country must issue liabilities, that is, borrow, or draw down assets, or do both, in order to finance the imbalance. Liabilities could be issued to banks by means of bank borrowing or be sold in local or national capital markets. Alternatively, members of the region can run down bank balances or sell other assets. In a branch banking system, local loans will grow relative to local deposits, funnelling funds from the surplus regions to the deficit region. In a system of unit banks, local banks will call upon correspondent balances and sell off assets as they lose reserves to other banks in the system. Again, funds flow from surplus to the deficit region, financing the imbalance. This process can continue until national banks and lenders in other regions are unwilling to lend further or members of the region run out of assets which can be sold off or borrowed against. More likely, as the repayment burden grows and net assets and wealth decline, members of the region will revise plans, cut wages and lower prices, so adjusting expenditures and tending to correct the imbalance of payments. These mechanisms are reinforced by income effects and expenditure 'multipliers'. Alternatively, private finance may be supplemented by transfer payments from the national government.[2]

We do not know the relative importance of these various channels domestically since inter-regional adjustments are largely concealed in aggregate statistics. However, from the fact that 'recycling' is not a major domestic concern, it can be presumed that the financing is handled efficaciously. This probably owes much to the role of asset markets and banks. Members of a region may hold large stocks of nationally saleable assets. If so, these can be sold off to finance a deficit with little variation in yields as between surplus and deficit regions. Banks hold large stocks of nationally marketable assets, but their importance in inter-regional finance comes also from the branch banking network and from correspondent and interbank relationships which link the various regional banking markets.

In the international economy, the trend toward bank and other private financing of imbalances can be seen as taking modes of international adjustment some way towards domestic conditions. Development of Eurocurrency banking and the parallel growth of Eurobonds (i.e. bonds issued internationally mainly in markets other than those of its currency of denomination), have greatly widened the extent of internationally transferable assets. Funds flow from one region to another through a network of interbank markets which effectively link up to form a global funds market. It has been estimated that as many as 1,350 banks in over 50 countries have some regular involvement in the international interbank market (Clarke 1983).[3] Such a network forms a large catchment area for the collection of short-term funds. But perhaps the major change has been the willingness of international banks to undertake voluntarily (at least partially) medium-term financing of regional imbalances.

By way of an aside, we note that these developments in private international finance seem likely to have altered, in a fundamental way, modes of exchange rate behaviour. Trade surpluses and deficits are being balanced now to a large degree by flows of private capital. To that extent, the need for movements in exchange rates to bring about short-run adjustments to trade flows is largely obviated. Instead, exchange rates will be responding to lenders' preferences for assets denominated in the various currencies. Here we have the basis for the asset theory of exchange rate determination.[4]

A study by the Bank of England (Stanyer and Whitley 1981) showed that payment imbalances at a world level, measured absolutely, without regard to sign and expressed relative to the gross national product of market economies, approximately doubled after the first oil price shock of 1973–74. The pattern of imbalances changed markedly at the same time. Table 10.1 shows world current account imbalances from 1978 to 1986 for industrial countries (divided into USA, Japan, Germany and others), oil exporting developing countries, non-oil developing countries, and centrally planned economies. During the 1950s and 1960s the pattern of imbalances as between these groups remained fairly constant. After 1973–74, and again in the late 1970s and early 1980s, the pattern of imbalances was marked by the surplus of the oil exporters and the deficit of the non-oil developing countries. This type of comparison ignores surpluses and deficits within each grouping and the financing opportunities which these present for bank intermediation. But for the moment we shall concentrate on the financing of the developing countries' deficits in the 1970s.

Prior to the 1970s, the current account deficits of the non-oil developing countries were financed in the main by official transfers (government-to-government aid) and flows of direct investment. Table 10.2 takes up the story after 1970.[5] Borrowings from banks and from other private sources (including

Table 10.1 World Current Account Balances[1], 1978–1986 ($ billion)

Countries	*1978*	*1979*	*1980*	*1981*	*1982*	*1983*	*1984*	*1985*	*1986*
Industrial countries	14.5	−25.5	−61.8	−18.9	−22.2	−23.0	−64.1	−54.2	−9.3
United States	−15.4	−1.0	1.9	6.3	−8.1	−46.0	−107.4	−117.7	−140.6
Other industrial countries	30.0	−24.6	−63.7	−25.2	−14.1	23.0	43.2	63.4	131.3
of which:									
Japan	16.5	−8.8	−10.7	4.8	6.9	20.8	35.0	49.7	86.0
Federal Republic of Germany	9.0	−6.1	−15.8	−5.5	3.4	4.1	6.8	13.2	36.0
Developing countries	−34.5	7.1	27.9	−49.2	−90.9	−58.9	−35.1	−34.1	−47.6
By region:									
Africa	−12.8	−3.4	−1.6	−21.9	−21.3	−11.6	−6.7	−1.4	−7.0
Asia	−6.8	−12.6	−19.3	−20.7	−17.3	−14.3	−4.8	−15.4	2.1
Europe	−7.1	−10.0	−12.3	−9.9	−6.1	−4.2	−1.9	−2.3	−1.7
Middle East	11.2	54.2	90.7	45.8	−5.1	−18.5	−18.1	−10.7	−24.9
Western Hemisphere	−19.0	−21.1	−29.5	−42.6	−41.1	−10.3	−3.6	−4.3	−16.1
By analytical criteria:									
Fuel exporters	−6.1	51.4	95.1	31.0	−25.6	−14.8	−8.6	−6.5	−35.7
Nonfuel exporters	−28.4	−44.3	−67.1	−80.2	−65.3	−44.1	−26.5	−27.6	−11.9
Eastern European countries	−9.5	−6.5	−4.6	−3.3	−0.5	1.1	2.3	−2.4	0.7
Total[2]	−29.5	−24.9	−38.5	−71.5	−113.5	−80.8	−96.9	−90.8	−56.2

Source: International Monetary Fund, *World Economic Outlook*, April 1986 and April 1987, Table A30.

Notes: 1. On goods, services, and private and official transfers.

2. Reflects errors, omissions, and symmetries in reported balance-of-payments statistics on current account, plus balance of listed groups with countries not included.

Table 10.2 Current Account Deficits of Non-Oil Developing Countries, Financing Transactions and Some Major Components, 1973–1982 ($ billion)

	1973	*1974*	*1975*	*1976*	*1977*	*1978*	*1979*	*1980*	*1981*	*1982*
Current account deficits	11.3	37.0	46.3	32.6	28.9	41.3	61.0	89.0	107.7	86.8
Financing transactions:										
Official transfers	6.1	9.3	6.5	7.6	9.0	10.5	15.0	13.9	14.1	13.7
Direct investment flows	4.2	5.3	5.3	5.0	5.4	7.3	8.9	10.1	13.9	11.4
Borrowings from private banks	9.8	18.6	23.2	21.5	14.7	25.6	35.9	53.3	52.5	21.4
Other borrowings	1.6	6.5	9.7	11.5	12.3	15.2	13.8	16.0	29.3	33.2
Reduction in reserve assets (accumulation −)	−10.4	−2.7	1.6	−13.0	−12.5	−17.4	−12.6	−4.5	−2.1	7.1
Some components of current account deficits:										
Oil trade deficit	3.8	13.9	13.9	17.1	18.4	18.6	25.2	38.7	37.3	30.0
Non-oil trade deficit	6.5	19.4	26.9	10.0	6.8	18.0	26.1	35.6	42.3	22.2
Interest payments	6.9	9.3	10.5	10.9	13.6	19.4	28.0	40.5	55.1	59.2

Source: IMF, *World Economic Outlook*, Occasional Paper 21, 1983.

the bond markets) took over from official aid and direct investment as the financing vehicles of the current account deficits of the developing countries. Indeed, for most years shown, borrowings were large enough to 'over-finance' the deficits and allow large additions to international reserves.

Disentangling cause and effect is difficult.[6] Because the intermediation by international banks has been discussed in the context of 'recycling' there has been a tendency to interpret the current account deficits as giving rise to oil-induced borrowings. From the balance of payments accounts with payments overall in balance we define capital account financing, K, as:

$$K = Im - X + F \tag{10.1}$$

where Im is imports of goods and services, X is exports of goods and services, and F is net factor income and assorted transfers paid to foreigners (including interest payments). The right-hand side is the current account deficit. Components of the current account deficits of the non-oil exporting developing countries are shown in Table 10.2. Adverse changes in oil imports and other components are seen on this interpretation as leading to borrowing to sustain expenditures and living standards.

But there is another interpretation, in which borrowing from overseas gives rise to claims over foreign resources. In the developing countries, the capital programmes of private and public sector investors are greater than the extent to which the countries are prepared to abstain from currently consuming their national production. Inflows of capital borrowed from abroad augment domestic savings, providing claims upon additional resources. Utilisation of these claims on resources is equal to the value of imports of goods and services and interest payments on debt not paid for from proceeds of exports and goods and services. In national accounting terms, this is measured by the current account deficit of the balance of payments, namely:

$$[I - S] + [I_G - (T - G_C)] = Im - X + F \tag{10.2}$$

where $[I - S]$ is the excess of private sector investment over private sector saving, $[I_G - (T - G_C)]$ is the excess of public sector investment over public sector saving (which equals taxation receipts less current government spending), and the expression on the right hand side is, as before, the current account deficit.[7]

Borrowings in the immediate aftermath of the first oil price rise are generally thought to favour the first interpretation. 'Over-financing' in the years 1976–1978 may point to the second interpretation. Most writers look to the first explanation again to account for increased borrowings from 1979, as the second round of oil price rises worsened the oil-importing countries' oil trade deficit, as the world downturn widened the non-oil trade deficit, and as sharp increases in interest rates added to these countries' interest payments.

OPEC current account surpluses and the developing countries' current account deficits were tailor-made for financing by intermediation through the banking system rather than by direct means. Many of the developing countries did not have the credit standing to issue internationally marketable securities and bonds. OPEC countries had an underlying preference for the holding of bank deposits. A marrying of the two groups occurred most readily across the banks' balance sheet. While it is the case that Brazil, Mexico and Israel together raised $12 billion through international bond issues over the years 1973–1981, it is mainly for the developed countries that bond issues offer an alternative to financing by bank borrowing. Industrial countries accounted for over three quarters of issues over the years 1977–1986 (see Table 10.5 below) and most of the remaining issues were made by international economic institutions (such as the World Bank).

As is the case with international banking, the market for international bonds has its 'Euro' and domestic components. International banks are actively involved in the Eurobond market and, where permitted to do so, in domestic issues of foreign bonds. Before going on to look at bank lending and the special techniques developed by banks for making loans in the Eurocurrency markets, we must distinguish between the banks' bond and loan activities.

10.2 Eurobonds and Euronotes

Whereas the Eurocurrency market is a largely unregulated international banking market, the Eurobond market is a largely unregulated international capital market. Funds flow directly from surplus regions to deficit regions without involving banks and other institutions as financial intermediaries. Banks are often middlemen, organising and underwriting the exchanges, but the lender of funds holds the security issued by the borrower and not a claim against the bank. With Euroloans, the bank interposes itself between the borrower and lender, collecting deposits from the lender and on-lending them, usually on different terms and conditions, to borrowers.

When examining Eurobanking operations, we distinguished between 'domestic', 'international', 'traditional foreign' and 'Euro' activities. These appellatives have their counterparts in the capital markets. A **domestic bond** is one issued in a country by a resident borrower of that country. An **international bond** is issued by a borrower in a country outside of that in which the borrower is domiciled. Data on international bond issues include all public issues with an original maturity of one year or more either by foreign borrowers on national markets (foreign bonds) or on the international market (Eurobonds).

Thus a **foreign bond** is one issued by a non-resident borrower on the market of a single country and denominated in that country's currency (e.g. a US dollar bond issued by a Canadian company and sold in New York, or a Swiss franc bond issued by a Japanese company and sold in Zurich). In New York, Tokyo and London such issues are known respectively as yankee, samurai and bulldog issues. Foreign bonds issues are underwritten and sold by a group of banks or issuing houses of the market country. In contrast, a **Eurobond** is underwritten and sold in various national markets simultaneously, usually through international syndicates (e.g. an issue of US dollar denominated bonds by a German company through a syndicate of banks in different countries arranged in London).

Nature of Eurobonds

Being 'external' means that placements of Eurobonds are not subject to the rules and regulations which govern issues of foreign bonds in that currency. For Eurodollar bonds, chief amongst the regulations avoided is the registration with the Securities and Exchange Commission needed for US domestic issues and sales, and interest-withholding tax which is deducted at source before interest is paid for non-resident holders of bonds. So as to avoid SEC registration, US dollar Eurobonds are not issued new in the US but they enter after issue in the secondary market, in which existing bonds are traded. For this reason, some would add to our definition above a rider that a Eurobond is sold outside the country of the currency in which the issue is denominated. Indeed, this addition is the most commonly used description of a Eurobond, although for non-dollar issues the condition has not always been met. Purchasers of Euro-yen bonds are mostly Japanese investors. Issues of Eurobonds in Deutschmarks have been placed in Germany so long as they meet the conditions which are imposed by the German government.

This is one of a number of respects in which it is not entirely accurate to describe the Eurobond market as one free of regulation and government control. As Dufey and Giddy (1978) note, 'the issuing techniques for Eurobonds take the form of "placing" rather than formal issuing, to avoid national regulations on new issues' (p. 19), but there are rules governing the conduct of securities business in centres such as London where the syndicate members operate. There is self-regulation of market practices by the Association of International Bond Dealers (AIBD). It has always been desirable for the bonds to be listed on one or more Stock Exchanges, which requires compliance with listing requirements. In addition, governments have exercised considerable influence over issues denominated in their own currency. Thus, Germany has required that Eurobonds issued in Deutschmarks be lead managed by German banks (lifted in May 1985) and conform to a calendar organised by a government committee (now notification to the Bundesbank). Japan has also exercised 'guidance' over lead management of Euro-yen bond issues (lifted in April 1985). Switzerland has prevented the emergence of a Eurobond market in Swiss francs. In all cases the aim has largely been one of controlling the international use of a country's currencies. Legally it would seem that the countries concerned could not prevent foreign banks outside their borders from organising the issue of Eurobonds in the various currencies. But their wishes are made known to placing banks and to the central banks in the banks' source and host countries, with the desired effects achieved.

Characteristics of Issues

Tables 10.3 and 10.4 give details of international bonds issued in 1986, classified according to type of bond (Euro and foreign), currency of denomination, and the country of the borrower. Issues of Eurobonds greatly exceeded issues of traditional foreign bonds in all currencies with the notable exception of the Swiss franc for reasons explained above. Nearly 94 per cent of bonds issued internationally were by borrowers from industrial countries, and over half of the issues were in US dollars.

Table 10.5 provides a classification of international bonds, again by type, currency and country, but this time for the years 1977–1986 (so covering the same period as the data presented in Chapter 8 for Eurobanking). Bonds are denominated in currencies important for international trade and upon which no restrictions are placed when third parties use them for capital transactions. Both considerations underscore the use of the US dollar. Yet it is apparent that in the Eurobond market, and this is a contrast with Eurobanking transactions, non-US dollar issues, especially in the Swiss franc, Deutschmark and yen, are of considerable importance. These countries have high savings propensities as compared with other industrial countries which borrowers wish to tap, while many investors have a preference for securities issued in strong currencies.

Most developing countries currently have limited access to international bond markets, and this has to a large degree always been the case. Partly in consequence, national governments and public utilities account for a quarter or less of total issues as shown in Table 10.6. This is in further contrast to

Table 10.3 Issues of International Bonds by Currency, 1986 ($ billion)

Currency of denomination	*Eurobonds*	*Foreign bonds*	*Total*	*Per cent*
US dollar	118.2	6.0	124.2	54.9
Japanese yen	18.7	4.8	23.5	10.4
Swiss franc	—	23.4	23.4	10.3
Deutschmark	16.9	—	16.9	7.5
Sterling	10.5	0.3	10.8	4.8
ECU	7.0	—	7.0	3.1
Other	16.7	3.9	20.6	9.0
TOTAL	188.0	38.4	226.4	100.0

Source: Morgan Guaranty Trust Co., *World Financial Markets*, February/March 1987.

Table 10.4 Issues of International Bonds by Country of Borrower, 1986 ($ billion)

Country of borrower	*Eurobonds*	*Foreign bonds*	*Total*	*Per cent*
1. Industrial countries				
USA	38.6	5.0	43.6	19.3
Japan	25.4	9.0	34.4	15.2
Canada	13.6	2.8	16.4	7.2
UK	18.5	0.9	19.4	8.6
France	12.5	0.9	13.4	5.9
W. Germany	10.2	1.0	11.2	4.9
Denmark	8.5	0.5	9.0	4.0
Sweden	4.9	0.9	5.8	2.6
Norway	5.2	0.4	5.6	2.5
Other Europe	24.8	4.1	28.9	12.8
European institutions	6.5	3.1	9.6	4.2
Australia	7.8	2.5	10.3	4.5
New Zealand	3.3	1.5	4.8	2.1
2. Developing countries				
China	0.5	0.9	1.4	0.6
South Korea	0.4	0.3	0.7	0.3
Hong Kong	0.5	—	0.5	0.2
Singapore	0.3	—	0.3	0.1
Oil exporters	0.4	—	0.4	0.2
Other developing	0.8	0.3	1.1	0.5
3. Eastern European countries	0.3	—	0.3	0.1
4. International institutions				
World Bank	2.9	2.3	5.2	2.3
Other	1.1	2.0	3.1	1.3
5. Other	0.9	0.1	1.0	0.5
TOTAL	188.0	38.4	226.4	100.0

Source: OECD, *Financial Statistics Monthly*, March 1987.

Eurobanking. Large banks and financial institutions (such as savings institutions and finance companies) are the most important category of issuer. Many banks are believed to hold Eurobonds as investments, financed by bank deposits.

Growth of Eurobonds

A striking similarity exists in the importance of 'Euro' transactions in the international banking and capital markets: 83 per cent of international bank loans outstanding at September 1986 were Eurocurrency loans, while 83 per cent of international bonds issued in 1986 were Eurobonds. Table 10.5 shows

Table 10.5 Issues of International Bonds Classified by Type, Currency and Borrower, 1977–1986

	1977	*1978*	*1979*	*1980*	*1981*	*1982*	*1983*	*1984*	*1985*	*1986*
Total international bonds issued, $ billion	36.1	37.5	39.0	38.3	51.8	75.5	77.1	109.5	167.7	226.4
By type (%):										
Eurobonds	54.0	42.5	47.9	53.2	60.4	66.6	64.9	74.6	81.5	83.0
Foreign bonds	46.0	57.5	52.1	46.8	39.6	33.4	35.1	25.4	18.5	17.0
By currency (%):										
US dollar	55.5	37.4	37.8	42.7	63.0	63.9	57.0	63.5	61.1	54.9
Japanese yen	4.2	12.7	7.3	4.9	6.0	5.2	5.3	5.5	7.7	10.4
Swiss franc	13.7	20.2	24.9	19.5	15.7	15.0	17.5	12.0	8.9	10.3
Deutschmark	18.6	21.9	22.0	21.9	5.0	7.1	8.6	6.2	6.7	7.5
Sterling	0.6	0.9	0.7	3.0	2.8	2.6	3.9	5.1	4.1	4.8
ECUs	0.1	0.5	0.8	0.2	0.8	2.6	2.6	2.8	4.2	3.1
Other	7.3	6.4	6.5	7.8	6.7	3.6	5.1	4.9	7.3	9.0
By borrower (%):										
Industrial countries	64.7	61.1	70.9	74.5	75.9	79.0	77.4	83.5	87.5	93.8
Developing countries (inc. OPEC)	11.7	15.4	8.5	5.6	8.5	6.2	4.2	4.8	4.8	2.0
Eastern European	0.7	0.1	0.1	—	0.1	—	—	—	0.2	0.1
International institutions	19.8	22.5	19.2	19.4	14.5	14.2	17.3	10.8	6.6	3.6
Other	3.1	0.9	1.3	0.5	1.0	0.6	1.1	0.9	0.9	0.5

Source: OECD, *Financial Statistics Monthly* (various issues).

that this is far from being the usual pattern. When the international bond market was relatively small, and very much in the shadow of the syndicated loan market, Eurobonds and traditional foreign bonds were roughly of equal significance. As issues of international bonds have increased sharply, and the syndicated loan market has declined, it is apparent that most of the growth has been concentrated in the Eurobond sector. These events — the decline of syndicated loans, the growth of international bonds, and the prominence of Eurobonds — are certainly not unrelated. They illustrate again the adaptability of banking, financial techniques and the costs of financial operations to changes in the economic environment. A number of factors have interacted here: changes in the world economy and the balance of payments, the loan problems of banks, pressures to de-regulate capital markets, declining transactions costs and the 'globalisation' of national capital markets. We shall attempt to draw these together in the final chapter. For the moment we focus on the growth of Eurobonds relative to foreign bonds.

Eurobonds have traditionally maintained a cost advantage over foreign bonds due to the ability of buyers to evade withholding and income tax on interest receipts. In order that Eurobonds gain exemption from withholding tax they are frequently issued in the name of special subsidiaries, registered in Luxembourg and other locations, which do not levy tax on non-residents' interest income. Holders of Eurobonds are attracted by this favourable tax status. Eurobonds are issued in bearer form so as to give the holders anonymity and thus the potential to avoid the tax liabilities from interest payments and capital gains. Issuers benefit from the lower yields which follow. These advantages might well have been expected to diminish following regulatory changes in recent years. In 1984, the USA repealed the 30 per cent withholding tax deducted from interest paid to foreign purchasers of domestic bonds, and the US Treasury established procedures enabling US corporations to issue bearer bonds directly to foreign investors. Repeal was designed to put the US capital market on a par with foreign markets by allowing foreigners to issue bonds in New York and sell them to either residents (subject to withholding tax) or non-residents (without deduction of tax).[8] The Japanese government has favoured the samurai market over the Euro-yen market, yet the distribution of activity has swung (as is the case with Deutschmarks and sterling) to the Eurobond market.[9]

Five factors seem likely to be of significance in explaining this trend. First, Eurobonds can be arranged more speedily since they bypass the official registration procedures which must be followed with domestic issues. This is an important consideration in a climate of interest rate and exchange rate volatility, where borrowing cost 'windows' (i.e. opportunities) often arise fleetingly. Second, foreign borrowers may prefer to draw upon the established distribution channels and banking relationships in their own countries by having their own bankers lead manage 'Euro' issues. Third, the regulatory changes which have taken place in New York, Tokyo and Germany governing

Table 10.6 Issues of Eurobonds and International Bonds by Sector, 1982–1986 (percentage of total issues)

	Eurobonds					*International bonds*	
	1982	*1983*	*1984*	*1985*	*1986*	*1985*	*1986*
Mining, exploitation of hydrocarbon deposits	7.2	2.2	5.8	4.3	3.0	3.9	3.0
Manufacturing	24.9	12.4	14.8	14.8	19.7	14.0	18.7
Commerce	2.0	1.6	1.5	1.7	1.4	1.7	1.3
Transport and communication	5.8	3.0	3.3	4.1	4.0	3.9	4.3
Public utilities (electricity, gas, water)	8.8	5.8	3.5	5.2	3.7	5.4	4.0
Financial institutions	26.8	40.4	42.6	47.7	44.5	43.9	41.2
National government, provincial and local authorities	16.2	18.1	20.2	14.4	17.2	15.1	17.7
International organisations	7.6	15.7	6.4	6.0	5.6	10.3	8.8
Miscellaneous	0.7	0.8	1.9	1.8	0.9	1.8	1.0
	100.0	100.0	100.0	100.0	100.0	100.0	100.0

Source: European Investment Bank, *EIB Papers*, February 1986 and March 1987.

capital markets have enhanced the access of resident borrowers to the international capital markets. For example, issues of Eurobonds by US firms represented 21 per cent of all issues in 1983; in 1986 they were 42 per cent of the total. At the same time, the deregulatory changes have enabled more institutional investors to buy Eurobonds. Fourth, with the 'globalisation' of capital markets and the broad placing power of the international syndicates, borrowers have turned away from national capital markets. Fifth, these developments have been facilitated by streamlining of the original cumbersome Eurobond syndication procedures and by alterations to the composition of the underwriting groups.

Syndication Methods and Fees

There are some similarities in the way Eurobonds have traditionally been placed and the methods used for organising large Euroloans. A group of institutions or banks, called co-managers, organise the issue of Eurobonds under the direction of a lead manager and then underwrite it in conjunction with a number of underwriters. With large-sized Euroloans, a group of banks, called managers, and again under the direction of a lead manager, organises and underwrites the loan. With Eurobonds, the managers and underwriters combine with selling institutions to sell the bonds throughout the world to individual investors, investment accounts and financial institutions. In the case of Euroloans, the managing banks sell shares or certificates of participation (some transferable) in the loan throughout the world to other banks.

Placement fees and commissions for the issue of Eurobonds are structured according to the distinctive roles of the syndicate members:[10]

Lead managers organise and administer the syndicate, determine the price and support it during the distribution process.

Co-managers perform much the same functions as the lead manager, but in a subsidiary capacity.

Underwriters, chosen because of their placing power, are committed to purchase a certain number of bonds, but not to support the issue price.

Selling institutions are smaller members which do not agree to a specific commitment, but contribute their placing ability.

Management fees (0.375–0.5%) are divided equally between managers, after the lead managers have taken a 'praecipium' for themselves. The underwriting fee (0.375–0.5%) is shared between managers and underwriters in proportion to their commitment. Finally, the selling commission (1.25–1.5%) is split between all those placing the securities — managers, underwriters and selling institutions.

Thus total fees for bond issues arranged in the conventional fashion have generally been around 2–2.5%, varying with the initial maturity of the bonds, although reallowances or discounts might reduce the figure by 1 per cent. This is in excess of gross underwriter spreads of about 0.75 per cent on a comparable US domestic issue, a factor which in combination with other weaknesses led to new distribution procedures. Under the traditional method the pricing occurs after the issue is announced and the syndicate is organised, a period of about seven days. With demand thus established, market conditions are reviewed and pricing and allotment occurs. After the issue has been made there is a pre-market or stabilisation period during which bond prices are supported in pre-market trading to ensure that a smooth placement takes place.[11]

This procedure was ill-suited to handle the financing needs which were presented in the 1980s, and the 'bought deal' has come to the fore. A small number of managers (or perhaps only one) bids for a mandate at a fixed price and amount. If accepted, the small group buys the entire issue and then either sells off parts to other banks and investment houses or preplaces them with institutional investors. The procedure is faster, reduces the uncertainty about final issue price, and bypasses the large underwriting and selling syndicates designed to reach many small investors. It is thus more appropriate for the growing number of institutional buyers of international bonds, and better suited to a market environment in which precise pricing and speed of issue is of importance. A hybrid procedure has also developed in which a 'pre-priced offer' is made by a lead manager which is conditional upon the formation of a management group within a short space of time, say two to four days. When the group is formed, it buys the bonds and proceeds as in a bought issue. These deals call for managing banks with large capital resources and placing power, able to sell securities quickly and in large amounts to major buyers in the USA, Japan, Germany, Switzerland and other markets of importance. Instead of one broad syndicate to cover many geographical areas, Courtadon (1985) notes that managing groups are being broken down into several regional groups, each with a strong set of managers at its head.

Comparisons with Eurocurrency Loans

Like much of Eurocurrency banking operations, the Eurobond market operates worldwide by telephone and telex, with trading details supplied to the electronic information services like Reuters. A further similarity with Eurobanking comes from the pre-eminence of London as the centre of operations.

> London is by far the largest centre of its operations both in relation to the issue of primary securities and to dealings in the secondary markets.
>
> (Gower Report 1984)

As this quotation makes apparent (and in sharp contrast to Euroloans), there is an active and well-organised secondary market for Eurobonds, facilitated by the international securities clearing houses Euroclear in Brussels and CEDEL in Luxembourg which allow transfers of securities by means of book entries.

Further similarities between Eurobonds and Euroloans come about from the nature of the instruments issued. In the case of the basic 'straight' bond, the contrast could hardly be greater. Whereas Euroloans are flexi-rate and largely non-marketable, the basic Eurobond is highly marketable and issued at a fixed rate of interest, sometimes for as long as 20 years, although the weighted average is about 10 years. 'Straights' represented 76 per cent of Eurobonds and foreign bonds issued in 1986. Convertibles, which constituted 3 per cent of issues, carry the option of conversion into shares at a future date. They also differ markedly from Euroloans. But the remaining 21 per cent of bonds are 'floating rate notes' (FRNs). These are bonds (normally medium-term in length) issued with an interest coupon which consists of a margin over a reference rate, such as LIBOR, LIBID or LIMEAN, plus a 'spread'. The coupon is paid at the end of each interest period, normally 3 or 6 months, and is revised in line with current market rates, represented by the reference rate, for the next interest period.[12] This pricing arrangement is directly equivalent to that employed on Euroloans, and has the same objective of shifting most of the risk of variable interest rates from the lender of funds to the borrower. Floating rate notes are the direct counterpart in the bond market of the rollover technique pioneered with Eurocurrency lending. More precisely, since floating rate notes are normally amortised at maturity, they resemble a rollover loan which has a grace period that extends to the maturity date (i.e. a 'bullet' loan).

Despite these parallels, there is one fundamental difference between Eurobonds and Euroloans. When banks arrange Eurobond placements, they are acting in the capacity of investment bankers. Indeed, as Table 10.7 shows, the major organisers of the placements are securities houses (such as Merrill Lynch, Salomon Brothers) or 'universal banks' (such as Deutsche Bank, Union Bank of Switzerland). The leading arranger was Crédit Suisse/First Boston, a joint venture of a Swiss universal bank and a US investment bank. However, commercial banks like Morgan Guaranty, Bankers Trust, and Chase Manhattan feature amongst the leading firms. As we have said, one of the attractions of Euromarkets comes from the ability of commercial banks (and especially those from the USA and Japan) to be also investment banks, free of the lines of demarcation which exist in domestic markets, arising from legislation like the Glass–Steagall Act which prevents commercial banks in the USA from underwriting public issues of corporate bonds.

Since the banks in the Eurobond market are acting as investment bankers, their risk is limited to that of underwriters of the issue. There is no other obligation upon the banks to take up the bonds. Default risks, illiquidity risks and capital gains and losses from premature disposal are borne by those acquiring the bonds, not the arranging banks. With loan syndicates,

Table 10.7 Arrangers of Eurobond Issues, 1986

Rank	*Bank*	*Number of issues*	*Amount ($m.)*	*Share (%)*
1.	Crédit Suisse–First Boston	108	20,428.10	11.20
2.	Nomura Securities	129	14,321.60	7.85
3.	Deutsche Bank	92	12,156.10	6.66
4.	Morgan Guaranty	64	9,821.74	5.38
5.	Daiwa Securities	87	8,779.09	4.81
6.	Morgan Stanley International	73	8,764.36	4.80
7.	Salomon Brothers	55	8,362.25	4.58
8.	Banque Paribas	67	6,779.81	3.72
9.	Merrill Lynch Capital Markets	40	5,945.45	3.26
10.	Nikko Securities	54	5,085.18	2.79
11.	Union Bank of Switzerland	46	4,811.71	2.64
12.	Yamaichi Securities	59	4,358.39	2.39
13.	Shearson Lehman Bros International	23	4,122.48	2.25
14.	Goldman Sachs International	23	3,654.68	2.00
15.	Société Générale	27	3,090.89	1.69
16.	Long Term Credit Bank of Japan	26	2,941.90	1.63
17.	Swiss Bank Corp. International	24	2,877.99	1.60
18.	Industrial Bank of Japan	25	2,771.99	1.54
19.	S.G. Warburg	24	2,734.39	1.52
20.	Commerzbank	39	2,695.37	1.50
21.	Bankers Trust	20	2,546.33	1.41
22.	Midland Montagu	10	2,459.36	1.37
23.	Chase Manhattan	15	2,124.29	1.18
24.	Westdeutsche Landesbank	21	2,109.56	1.17
25.	Banque Nationale de Paris	25	2,080.96	1.16

Source: Annual Financing Report, *Euromoney*, March 1987.

the managers and other participating banks must contribute to the funding when the loan is drawn down. They must continue that funding at each rollover date. Finally, they acquire a share of the default risk. This fundamental distinction between the functions of an investment bank and those of a commercial bank separates the two markets.

In practice, this difference is blurred by three developments: the involvement of banks in the floating rate notes market, the interest rate swap market, and note issuance facilities. The floating rate notes market is dominated by banks as both issuers and buyers, and developments in it are closely related to banking markets. Interest rate 'swaps' arbitrage risk differences embodied in the pricing of Eurobonds and bank loan instruments, and allow borrowers from banks to have *indirect* access to the securities market. Euronote facilities provided by banks bridge maturity differences between bank loan and short-term securities markets, and back-up their bank customers' *direct* access to securities markets.

Floating Rate Notes Market

Banks take part on both sides of the market for floating rate notes. Over one half of the funds raised in the floating rate market from 1975 to 1983 was due to bank issues (Ramsden 1984). During 1984 and 1985 banks were also the largest issuers of floating rate notes: in 1986, bank issues were 41 per cent of the total. Banking regulations in some countries (e.g. France, Japan) require banks to match up part of their medium-term Eurocurrency lending with liabilities of equivalent terms. Floating rate notes are a medium-term liability but have costing characteristics which resemble short-term liabilities. Other countries allow floating rate notes issued in the form of subordinated debt (see Chapter 5) to be counted as part of capital, allowing banks to gear up additional lending. British banks are large issuers of perpetual FRNs, i.e. notes issued without a maturity, which the Bank of England allows to be ranked as primary capital (up to a maximum of 50 per cent). On the other side of the market, it seems that about 75 per cent of bank issues of floating rate notes are bought by other banks (Gluck 1987). Japanese banks in particular have acquired them because they fall outside certain domestic regulatory and capital guidelines applied to loans. The market for floating rate notes has thus acquired some of the characteristics of an international interbank market for long-term funds.[13]

'Swap' Markets

A second link between the markets for bonds and bank lending comes from the very extensive 'swap' market. Swaps enable a borrower to raise funds in the market to which it has the best access yet to make the interest or principal payments in its preferred form or currency.[14] An *interest rate swap* is an exchange of interest payments of different character at regular intervals between those participating in the transaction. A classic 'coupon' or 'plain vanilla' swap, in particular, is a financial transaction in which a stream of fixed interest payments is exchanged for a stream of floating rate interest payments in the same currency. It effectively arbitrages differences which exist between the assessment of risk in the bond and loan markets, so that two borrowers divide up, in a mutually beneficial way, any comparative advantage which each might have in one of the markets. The working of a fixed/floating interest rate swap is probably best explained by an illustration, given below and summarised in Figure 10.1. While the numbers chosen are hypothetical, we note that in 1983 and 1984, for example, quality spreads between Aaa-rated borrowers (highest quality) and Baa-rated borrowers (medium quality) averaged 1.50 per cent in the US corporate fixed rate bond market, yet the equivalent quality spread differential for floating rate borrowing was around 0.50 per cent. We also assume in the illustration, as is now usual, that the swap occurs through an intermediary bank, and in practice fees of from 0.05

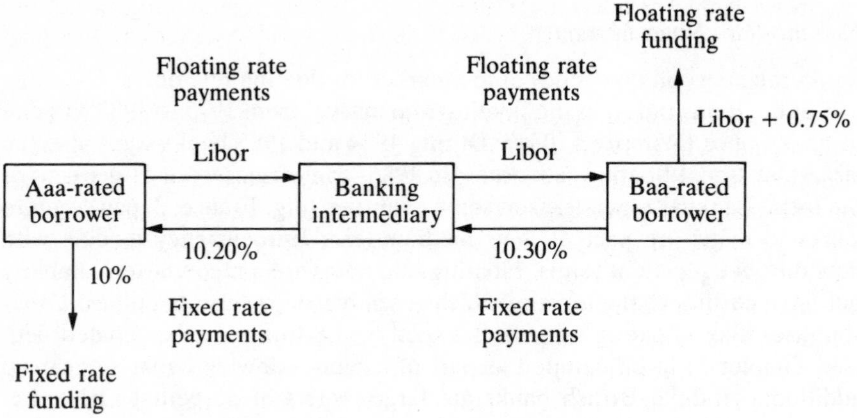

Figure 10.1 Illustration of a Fixed/Floating Interest Rate Swap

to 0.12 per cent per annum (5 to 12 basis points) are common for a transaction of this type.

Company *B* (a Baa-rated company by Moody's) wants a fixed interest rate on borrowings, yet has a low credit rating on bond markets, and would have to pay 11.5 per cent p.a. Nevertheless, it can obtain a floating rate rollover credit from a syndicate of banks on reasonable terms (LIBOR + 0.75 per cent p.a.). It enters into a swap with company *A* (an Aaa-rated borrower), which could be a bank, wanting floating rate funding, and able to borrow at LIBOR + 0.25 but having a good bond rating and able to issue a bond at a fixed rate of 10 per cent p.a. A swap can be beneficial to both, since *B*'s disadvantage is less in the loan market. Company *B* pays the fixed coupon rate of 10 per cent for *A*'s bonds plus an additional margin of 0.20 per cent to induce *A* to enter the transaction, along with the intermediary bank's fee of 0.10 per cent levied to cover the costs and risks assumed. Nevertheless, company *B* can gain. Company *B* will achieve a cost of funds to it of 11.05 per cent per annum, i.e. 10+0.75+0.20+0.10, which is below the 11.5 per cent p.a. it would have had to pay.

Both borrowers take out debt in the respective markets, company *A* in the bond market and company *B* in the loan market, and remain responsible for the debt. *A* contracts to pay LIBOR to *B* in return for 10.20 per cent. *A* uses the 10.20 per cent income stream to service its 10 per cent obligation, gaining 20 basis points *below* LIBOR on its floating rate funds. *B*, we have shown, uses the LIBOR payments to pay for its LIBOR + 0.75 debt, with the 0.75 difference creating 11.05 per cent p.a. No actual interest payments need be paid by one party to the other, since a net amount can be calculated and paid from *B* to *A*.

Although the Aaa borrower enjoys an absolute cost advantage in both the fixed rate and floating rate markets, the combined interest rate differential between the two borrowers on the two markets provides a potential which makes the swap profitable to all three parties. There is a 100 basis point difference in *A* and *B*'s relative risk assessment which is divided up in this instance with 45 basis points to *A* (LIBOR − 0.20 versus LIBOR + 0.25), 45 basis points to *B* (11.05 versus 11.5 per cent p.a.) with 10 basis points going to the intermediary. The equal division of the combined interest rate differential between the borrowers in this illustration is entirely arbitrary. In practice, the division of the differential between the firms could occur in any way they wished.

Although no accurate figures are available, it is estimated (Gilibert, Lygum and Wartz 1986) that 70–80 per cent of Eurobond issues were 'swapped' in 1985. Because swap business is similar in some respects to conventional lending operations this overlap provides banks with an incentive to engage in the arranging of Eurobonds. Swaps along the lines sketched out above effectively arbitrage the risk spread differential which exists between capital markets and the bank credit markets. Each party raises funds on the market where it has a comparative advantage, and then trades with the assistance of the intermediary bank.[15] Any differences reflect a number of informational and institutional characteristics which distinguish the markets. While banks are holders of Eurobonds, other groups are involved:

> Market operators believe that around 40 per cent of orders from final buyers reach the market via Switzerland and many of these are probably on behalf of wealthy private clients of Swiss banks . . . Another source of demand is from offshore insurance markets such as Bermuda, which need dollar-denominated fixed interest securities; and central banks are believed to hold relatively modest amounts. (Economists Advisory Group 1984)

Securities have long been sold solely on the issuer's reputation (bond ratings were not introduced until 1982), limiting the market to well-known international borrowers with a very high credit rating. By contrast, banks are able to use proprietary information in their international loans, so that banking markets are open to borrowers without international repute. Presumably, also, differences in the pricing of risk between bond and loan markets reflect the banks' greater willingness or capacity to bear the riskiness of non-prime borrowers, due to arrangements for risk-sharing described in following sections. But the effect of swaps is apparent. Since the higher-rated firm acts as a surrogate borrower for the lower-rated borrower, middle-ranking firms thereby gain an access to the international capital markets.

Information asymmetries, we may note, are also important in *cross-currency swaps*. In a cross-currency swap (frequently referred to simply as a 'currency swap') the counter-parties exchange interest payments in one currency for interest payments in another currency. In contrast to interest rate swaps, where interest is calculated on the basis of a notional principal amount but no exchange of principal actually takes place, cross-currency swaps usually involve a final exchange of principal and sometimes also an initial exchange of principal (although the spot foreign exchange market might be used instead). Liabilities can be swapped on a fixed/fixed basis or on a floating/floating basis. The former especially can exploit differences in borrowers' risk assessment in markets for fund raising in different currencies. For example, a US firm seeking expansion in Germany may be wanting DM funding, but it is unknown in the German capital market. Correspondingly, a German firm seeking US dollar borrowings may be well known in Germany, but little known in the USA. By each borrowing in their home currency and 'swapping' the interest and principal at an agreed exchange rate, both parties can lower funding costs. This type of 'currency swap' is to be distinguished from that discussed in Chapter 9 which related to the foreign exchange market and involves a spot sale and forward repurchase of an amount of currency. It also needs distinguishing from the 'currency swaps' from which the swap market evolved, being a contractual commitment entered into by two parties to exchange currencies while simultaneously agreeing to reverse the exchange at the same rate on a specified date in the future, usually three or more years hence, making it in essence a long term foreign exchange transaction. In fact, there is a common thread through the three meanings of 'currency swap' since in all cases there is a spot exchange of currencies (either through the foreign exchange market or in the swap transaction) which is accompanied by a future reversal of the exchange at a rate agreed upon in advance. Because of this similarity, cross-currency swaps can be seen to allow longer maturities, larger transaction size and greater flexibility than is customary in the foreign exchange markets.[16]

From a very low level in 1981, the world-wide swap market has grown to between $350 and $400 billion at the end of 1986, valued in terms of notional principal amounts (Hammond 1987; Whittaker 1987). As in any arbitrage activity, one would expect exploitation of the opportunities for profit to erode the arbitrage margin. Thus in examples like that given above of fixed/floating coupon swaps, we might expect over time lower-rating firms' fixed rate borrowing costs to fall and their floating rate costs to rise, while higher-quality firms' fixed rate borrowing costs should rise and their floating rate costs decrease, so narrowing the combined interest rate differentials. Continued growth of the swap market can be attributed in part to a broadening of the market, and to changes in the behaviour of banks.

In addition to interest rate and cross-currency swaps, there are also *basis swaps*, which swap floating interest rate payments priced on one basis (e.g. LIBOR) with another (e.g. US prime or commercial paper rates), and *cross-currency interest rate swaps*, which are a combination of an interest rate and a cross-currency swap. Even more complex forms have evolved such as amortising swaps, zero-coupon swaps, forward swaps, callable and index swaps (see Hammond 1987). Transformation of the market has come with the introduction of swaps on *existing* liabilities, as well as new ones, and with *asset swaps*, which transform the currency or interest rate of existing assets. Consequently, swaps have become an instrument for asset and liability management. All of these developments have been aided by the changing role of banks in the market.

Banks are involved in swaps in one of three capacities: as an agent, intermediary, or principal. When the market began, banks acted as agents or brokers, advising the parties involved, bringing them together and organising the transaction for an arrangement fee. Reliance on a 'double coincidence of wants' arising clearly limited the size of the market, as did the need for each counter-party to bear the risk of the other's default. The opportunity arose for banks to intermediate between the end-users, guaranteeing the payments of both parties, and acting as market-makers. Anonymity of the two borrowers could be preserved by the bank writing separate contracts with each on a matched basis, incorporating an intermediation margin to cover costs and the risks of providing 'insurance' against counterparty default, as in the example above. As the market developed and the need for speed of operation grew, banks began to 'warehouse' swaps. This means contracting into a swap agreement on their own account with one counter-party, while either carrying an open swap position or taking out a temporary hedge in the bond or futures market until offsetting swap agreements are written. Swap operations may incorporate several currencies and several counterparties each contracting different forms of debt in different countries. As many as six banks may stand between two ultimate end-users, and in this respect the distinction between the 'gross' and 'net' size of the market is as relevant for swaps as for other international banking transactions.

When running a 'book' on swaps, banks are able to accommodate customers' individual needs and widen the choices open to customers. Banks are reluctant to make fixed rate loans when their liability base is floating rate, but a floating rate loan provided to a borrower with a warehoused swap creates the equivalent of a fixed rate loan. Conversely, by entering into swaps themselves, banks are able to hedge fixed/floating mismatches resulting from customers' own hedging responses. Thus, in the face of an expectation of rising interest rates, banks' customers will seek to borrow fixed rate long-term and deposit funds short-term. With an expectation of falling interest rates, customers will borrow floating rate short-term and buy long-term CDs and time deposits at fixed rates. In the latter case, say, the bank may be able to engage in a swap itself, receiving fixed rate payments in exchange for disbursing LIBOR-related floating rate payments. This converts the banks' fixed rate funding to variable rate funding, effectively 'size intermediating' the hedge for customers, and complements other vehicles for hedging interest rate risk.

These 'intermediary' activities of banks in the swap market are not dissimilar to those in traditional intermediation, and involve risk taking by banks. Warehousing of swaps and the size intermediation conducted when combining a number of smaller risk exposures involves the banks in *position risk* should interest or exchange rates move adversely once the deals are struck. Evaluating and guaranteeing the creditworthiness of counter-parties opens a bank to *credit risk* should a party default. This risk, however, is not always the same as that on a straight loan. With an interest rate swap, for example, the bank guarantees payment of interest under the swap contract, not the original loan or debt instrument itself. Thus a bank is faced with the cost of entering into a new set of transactions which offsets the contract which it has with the non-defaulting party: a cost which depends on interest rates at the time of default. Proposals to measure this risk for the assessment of capital adequacy feature in UK–US regulatory agencies' 'convergence accord' discussed in Chapters 5 and 11.

Note Issuance Facilities

A third development which blurs the sharp distinctions between bond and bank markets is the emergence since 1978 of a market for Euronotes, based around committed note issuance facilities provided by the banks. This development has bridged the gap between the bond and loan markets in terms of maturity and risk transformation. With bonds, the holding preferences of buyers must coincide with sellers, unless the securities are prematurely disposed of, whereas banks reconcile differences in holding patterns, borrowing short and lending long. While banks arranging security flotations underwrite the issue, banks making loans assume default and illiquidity risks on behalf of customers. Those sharp differences have been reduced.

Euronotes are similar to US commercial paper, and are bearer debt in the form of short-term, unsecured promissory notes. Underwritten note issuance facilities (NIFs) formalise the credit lines which normally back up issues of commercial paper in the US, and allow the borrower the opportunity to raise long-term funds while issuing a stream of short-term notes. They embrace an underwriting commitment and a placing arrangement, and they operate in the following way. A facility is arranged with a bank or a syndicate of banks, under a lead bank or arranger. Facilities are normally medium-term, say 7–10 years, much the same length as Euroloans. Funding over those years is by means of successive issues of notes at set maturities of one, three or six months, normally in units of $500,000. In contrast with a loan, the participating banks in the syndicate are not necessarily obliged to fund or rollover the maturing notes. Instead, they guarantee the continuance of the funding to the issuers of the notes. Thus the banks stand ready over periods as long as 10 years to buy the notes which remain unsold; 'unsold' meaning those which cannot be placed at the interest cost specified in the underwriting contract (the interest rate 'cap').

When the facility is activated, the notes are placed by a tender panel which bids for the notes issued. This is the method used in about three quarters of the underwritten facilities. In the remaining cases, the notes are placed by a single bank as the sole placing agent (normally called a RUF, i.e. revolving underwriting facility). Although the tender panel very likely includes many of the underwriting banks, they are not required to take up and dispose of the notes unless the cost to the borrower exceeds the cap rate.

From the viewpoint of borrowers, Euronotes have characteristics which make them essentially equivalent to Eurocurrency loans: they are medium-term, flexi-rate and have guaranteed renewal. Since placement is handled by the arranging and underwriting institutions, transactions costs are relatively low. Yet holders (including banks) of the notes have an investment avenue which is more flexible and more liquid than loans, more akin to certificates of deposit. The underwriting banks gain fee income and, so long as the notes are placed at each maturity date without difficulty, off-balance sheet business.

This potential transformation of short-term funds into long-term lending is not unlike that which occurs on banks' balance sheets. Indeed, the parallel is almost complete if we return to the idea of banks as insurers, for banks are providing in two different ways much the same insurance-type service to borrowers. With conventional loans, a bank can be visualised as accepting liquid deposits from lenders and offering them to borrowers with an insurance policy added. That policy, in effect, is a guarantee that the bank stands ready over a number of years to provide substitute deposits, on agreed terms, should lenders be unwilling to continue with their funding. This guarantee is explicit with NIFs. With flexi-rate loans, the costs of servicing the 'policy' are recovered from the spread over funding costs and in service charges; again, this is much as with note issuance facilities.

Only a minority of facilities have in fact been used in place of syndicated loans, partly because of the standing of the borrowers and because actions by some central banks (such as the Bank of England) to have banks maintain capital backing for the facilities has resulted in alterations to market techniques. With issuers of low credit standing, the banks could be faced with very large and unpredictable purchases of unplaced notes: they would have a large contingent liabilities risk, against which capital would need to be held. For this reason, note issuance facilities are presently limited to borrowers of high credit standing, and as of 1986 few commitments have been drawn down. Instead, the facilities have been used mainly as a standby line of credit, and this feature has prompted a change in practices.

Initially, Euronote facilities were negotiated mainly for banks and other borrowers from small industrial countries such as Australia, New Zealand and Sweden. Growth from 1985 of a Euro-commercial paper market has seen facilities arranged for borrowers from the USA, France, UK and other large industrial countries along different lines, some of which have been heavily drawn down. Unlike the original type of facilities which are underwritten, many of the new programmes do not have specific commitments, so avoiding costly underwriting fees. Also notes are distributed via dealerships rather than by tender panel or sole placement arrangements. In essence, there has been a separation of the underwriting and placement functions, which are combined in traditional facilities. Whereas the original Euronotes are surrogates for medium-term loans, the uncommitted notes are more akin to commercial paper: indeed, the new note programmes are known generally as Euro-commercial paper programmes.

Euro-Commercial Paper

The Euro-commercial paper market is almost entirely centred around London, as is the case with Euronotes generally. Amounts of Euro-commercial paper outstanding at the end of 1986 are estimated at about $30 billion, as compared with around $5 billion outstanding under the old Euronote tender panel system. The US dollar is the most used currency of denomination and in a number of respects the market seems to be converging on the model of the US commercial paper market (Jensen 1986; Topping 1987; Gilibert, Lygum and Wartz 1987). In addition to the dealership distribution methods, those features which are becoming common in Euro-commercial paper are: shorter and more flexible issues tailored to buyers' preferences, continuous issues, setting of rates on an absolute basis rather than by reference to LIBOR, LIBID or LIMEAN. As in the USA, dealers impart marketability to the notes by agreeing to repurchase them from holders before maturity, but in addition some dealers make a secondary market by quoting two-way prices for outstanding issues, which is uncommon for US commercial paper. A further difference is that Euro-commercial paper is normally offered without ratings from the credit agencies and without direct back-up lines of credit, although issuers may acquire bank credit lines separately or, in the case of US borrowers, rely on domestic credit lines. US borrowers accounted for about 20 per cent of outstandings at 1986, the other borrowers being highly rated governments, corporations and financial institutions (such as Japanese banks) from the other OECD countries.

At the time of writing it is difficult to judge whether, in retrospect, the original note issuance facilities will be seen merely as a transition phase in the development of an international commercial paper market, much along US lines, or whether the Euronote markets will continue to exhibit different characteristics. In this respect we note that some Euro-commercial paper is beginning to be issued with 18-month to two-year maturities, whereas maturities in the US commercial paper market are invariably 30 days or less. These longer-term issues of Euro-medium term notes bridge the gap for savers and prime borrowers between the short-term instruments and Eurobonds.

Eurocurrency Loans

Borrowers of lower credit standing in international capital markets are confined to Eurocurrency loans. Standards of creditworthiness tend to be higher on Eurobonds and notes, as we observed above, which has excluded most of the developing countries as borrowers from the international capital markets. But Euroloans also appeal to those borrowing enterprises which find the prospectuses and other capital market requirements both onerous and intrusive. As we will see in section 4, syndicated loan contracts are flexible, and give the borrower choice of when to draw down the loan or repay the funds, and to select the interest rate basis and currency of interest and principal. By contrast, proceeds of capital market issues are paid out upon placement of the securities, while to alter the interest rate basis or currency of the liability requires the writing of a separate swap contract. Syndicated loans also enable vast sums of money to be raised in a very short interval of time, as was illustrated by a syndicated loan for BP in March 1987 to finance that company's offer to acquire the remainder of Standard Oil. In the space of five working days, a syndicate of 64 banks led by Morgan Guaranty agreed to commit more than $15 billion to the financing of the tender. This is the largest commitment of funds ever made in the Euromarkets and exceeded the amount sought by BP by $10 billion.[17] However, this scale of borrowing has not been typical of recent activity in the syndicated loan market.

A comparison of the magnitudes of the three basic types of international financing instruments[18] is provided in Table 10.8 which compares announced issues of Eurobonds (straights, FRNs and convertibles), Euronotes (facilities arranged), and syndicated Eurocurrency bank loans for the years 1981 to 1986. During 1986, Eurobond issues totalled $226.4 billion and Euronote facilities arranged amounted to $90.6 billion, whereas new syndicated Eurocurrency loans amounted to only $44.1 billion. By contrast, in 1981 syndicated bank loans ($131.5 billion) were nearly three times greater than issues of Eurobonds and Euronotes ($45 billion). This was the relative position which had ruled for the previous decade. One has to go back to 1972 to find a year in which Eurobond issues roughly equalled in amount new syndicated lending by Eurobanks.

This switch in the 1980s from international bank lending to issues of bonds and notes means that the role of the banks is changing away from lending business to investment banking or underwriting business, and to activities which straddle the two. In order to explain why this is so we shall now look at the nature of banks' international lending during the past decade and the difficulties — some would say crises — which have emerged.

10.3 Nature of International Bank Intermediation

Deposits could be gathered from surplus regions of the world and lent on by banks to the deficit regions without any essential alteration to the characteristics of the claims involved, other than that of the substitution of the bank's name for that of the borrower. Banks and other intermediaries would be acting as brokers or distributors of funds. Most intermediation by banks, however, involves some transformation to the claims, and this is true of the intermediation of international banks. On the liability side, OPEC depositors have generally preferred to hold short-term liabilities, and this has been true also of other non-bank depositors. As of January 1987, 87 per cent of deposits by non-banks were for maturities of less than 6 months and 38 per

Table 10.8 Measures of International Bond and Loan Activity, 1981–1986 ($ bn)

	1981	*1982*	*1983*	*1984*	*1985*	*1986*
SECURITIES MARKET INSTRUMENTS:						
Fixed rate bonds ('straights')	32.1	56.4	50.0	65.5	100.4	172.6
Floating rate bonds (FRNs)[1]	7.8	12.6	15.3	34.1	55.9	47.8
Convertible bonds[1]	4.1	2.7	6.8	8.5	7.3	6.0
Backup facilities:						
Note issuance facilities[2]	1.0	2.3	3.5	17.4	36.3	21.4
Other back-up lines[3]	—	—	6.0	11.4	10.5	5.6
Euro-commercial paper programmes	—	—	—	—	11.2	55.6
Other non-underwritten facilities	—	—	—	—	10.6	8.0
TOTAL	45.0	74.0	75.4	136.9	232.2	317.0
SYNDICATED BANK LOANS:						
Eurocurrency new voluntary lending[4]	128.1	93.1	44.8	33.7	24.9	35.7
Traditional foreign lending	3.4	7.4	7.0	8.8	6.6	8.4
TOTAL	131.5	100.5	51.8	42.5	31.5	44.1

Sources: BIS Annual Report 1986; OECD, *Financial Market Trends*, February 1987.

Notes: 1. Eurobond issues and foreign bond issues in domestic capital markets.
2. Underwritten facilities for the issue of Euronotes and multiple component facilities (which allow either the issue of Euronotes or use of a short-term bank advance).
3. Back-up lines for commercial paper and bank acceptances.
4. New Euroloans *minus* re-negotiations, refinancing and new loans extended in the context of restructuring agreements. These data are estimates of the OECD based on loan completions and differ from the Bank of England series of announced loans reported in Table 10.9, col. 2.

cent of total deposits matured within one week. On the asset side, at January 1987, 54 per cent of claims outstanding of non-banks had a maturity of 6 months and more, and 35 per cent had a remaining maturity of three or more years.

More generally, we argued both in Chapter 4 and in the last chapter that the characteristics of the contracts which international banks make with their customers do not differ in their essentials from the contracts issued by retail banks. Hence they must, like all banks, manage asset risk, liquidity risk, interest rate risk, and contingent liabilities risk. Because their operations are international, which we define as cross-border, cross-currency business, they must also manage country risk and currency risk. Before examining how international banks do this, we summarise the implications of being 'wholesale' bankers.

The major theme of this book is the essential similarity of financial services. Most financial firms — whether called banks, insurance houses, savings institutions, securities firms — are trading in information and dealing in, underwriting and managing risks. In terms of their risk processing, we have found it helpful to use the language of insurance. Accordingly, we visualise banks in both retail and wholesale business, and in both on– and off-balance sheet operations, as providing customers with 'insurance' against various portfolio risks and issuing to customers options which can be exercised in various circumstances. It is a special form of insurance and the peculiarity comes about because confidence, as well as natural hazards, governs the banking firms' exposure. Nevertheless, a bank's liquidity production is defined by the nature of the contracts it writes with lenders and borrowers. Since the contracts are much the same in retail, domestic wholesale and international business, liquidity creation occurs in all three types of banking. The contrast comes about from the manner in which the liquidity creation occurs.

In retail markets, institutions themselves provide for their own safety by pooling risks on their own balance sheets. Wholesale banks cannot operate on the same principles so readily and accordingly rely on the banking equivalent of 'reinsurance' arrangements to share among a group of participating banks some of the risks of international banking. By virtue of these collective devices, no one bank is left with a large share of the maturity transformation and liquidity creation process.

US banks engaged in banking in foreign currencies are cut off from their usual liquidity support arrangements. The same is true of French or German banks engaged in dollar banking. One response of banks to this mutuality of interests is to adopt cooperative solutions. These take a variety of forms, both formal and informal. One formal arrangement is in the terms of reciprocal deposit agreements,[19] by which banks agree to lend funds to one another for long periods, perhaps 7–10 years. Thus a US bank operating in Paris will extend dollar funds in return for French francs from a French bank with US branches. Such deposit agreements might be written with a number of local banks, so that both sets of banks have assured long-term funds for their offshore operations. They also negotiate formal standby credit lines on a reciprocal basis, enabling them to borrow from each other when in extreme need. Since the deposit agreements are fully drawn and the standby lines are for emergency use, banks also need more flexible funding on an informal basis which is satisfied through the interbank market.

Interbank markets have featured prominently in most explanations of Eurocurrency business: accounting as they do for around 70 per cent of transactions they could hardly fail to do so. In keeping with this attention, the international interbank market performs many functions. It ties regions together much as money markets do domestically, at the same time linking interest rates across markets. By standing between end suppliers in one location and end users elsewhere, the market performs an intermediary function in the global flow of funds. It provides facilities for forward exchange covering and enables banks to take speculative or hedging positions against interest rate and exchange rate movements. Many transactions are not interbank at all, but are statistical images of intrabank arbitrage and transfer pricing motivated by banks' avoidance of tax and banking regulations. These aspects were discussed in the previous chapter.

In addition, the interbank market aids liquidity and risk management in a number of ways. A major function of interbank funds is to enable banks to cope with the lumpiness of wholesale-sized deposits and loans, and plug up holes in the balance sheet. Unwanted deposits can be laid off to other banks, funds needed to support lending can be bid for interbank. In this way, the need for reserves as such is largely obviated: interbank and related funds markets give banks confidence that funds to meet balance sheet contingencies will be available. This confidence underpins banks' willingness to issue standby credit lines in off-balance sheet business. Banks go to considerable length to maintain a market presence and to keep open interbank credit lines, for unlike formal standby lines of credit interbank borrowing is never assured: 'the market lives on lunchtime gossip' (Clarke 1983). Banks adopt the habit of redepositing: a practice which incidentally inflates the statistics of market size. Trading on both sides of the interbank market prevents a bank from being seen as a perpetual taker of funds, so enhancing its repute. It also enables reciprocal relationships with other banks to be formed. Most banks immediately redeposit with other banks over 40 per cent of funds obtained in the market.[20]

Interbank markets break up the maturity transformation process. In retail banking, maturity transformation is normally undertaken fully by the bank which accepts the deposit. On their way from end suppliers like OPEC countries, to end users like the developing countries, funds in international banking may pass through several chains of banks, and maturity transformation can take place in any one of the chains. While the bank making the end placement is likely to carry the largest share, each bank is still left with some share of the transformation process (Ellis 1981, Bergendahl 1985). Taking positions in the interbank market 'masks' and thus facilitates the overall degree of maturity transformation inherent in non-bank business. By their addition, greatly mismatched non-bank business is 'padded out' or diluted in the total balance sheet. Each bank's total balance sheet is mismatched, but not to a great extent.

Finally, the interbank market enables the risks of lending to be spread amongst many different institutions. Loan risks are backed not just by the capital of the lending bank, but also indirectly by the capital of the banks which agree to lend to it. This risk sharing is known to participating banks and finds reflection in the practices of interest rate 'tiers' and lending limits. Banks are classified into interest rate tiers according to perceived risk. The margin levied by the lending bank is in effect a premium paid by the borrowing bank for 'insurance' against the default risk shared. In normal times, the range of rates for most banks is around ¼ of 1 per cent. But at times some banks have paid as much as 2 per cent above LIBOR to get funds. Nearly all banks set overall and daily limits on interbank placement of funds. Factors governing the size of limits are: the size and profitability of the institution, quality of management, evidence of overtrading in the market, and its access to lender of last resort funds in its national market.

Whereas interbank dealings can be looked upon as in part an informal means of risk-sharing, banks do seek to protect themselves against loan risks in more formal ways. These include co-financing with official lending institutions, credit insurance schemes with public agencies, and securing home government guarantees with national export banks or agencies. But by far the most important risk-sharing device is the syndication of large loans.

Loan syndicates are a formal subcontracting of lending risks, precisely equivalent to co-insurance and re-insurance arrangements in international insurance markets. Their purpose is the same: they enable the individual institutions to spread risks, avoiding too much exposure to individual cases. Because of the arrangements, institutions both individually and collectively take on greater risks than would otherwise be the case. We now examine syndication procedures.

10.4 Syndicated Lending

Not all Eurocurrency loans to non-bank borrowers are syndicated. Even in 1981, at what seems to be the high water mark of bank lending, syndicated loans outstanding represented only 55 per cent of net loans outstanding. The remaining, unpublicised, credits are connected with shorter-term trade financing by means of documentary letters of credit, the discounting of bills of exchange, and forfaiting (the discounting of promissory notes and bills with medium-term maturities that are used to finance the export of capital goods). Unlike syndicated loans which have extensive documentation, circulated amongst possible participating banks in the syndicate, the unpublicised loans are normally handled without extensive documentation. Direct negotiations between the customer and the bank result in the establishment, say, of a letter of credit against which the borrower can draw upon for some maximum amount and for some maximum period. Alternatively, the borrower may issue notes or paper, sold to the lending bank. This method allows for informal participations, since the lending bank can sell some or part of the notes or paper to other banks. Liquidity is also aided, since the bank is able at a later date to 'securitise' or 'marketise' part of its loan portfolio.

Some overall details about syndicated Eurocurrency lending over the period 1972–1986 are set out in Table 10.9. In this instance we use data collected by the Bank of England. They relate to announced syndicated loans

Table 10.9 Details of Syndicated Eurocurrency Lending, 1972–1986

Year	Number of syndicated loans announced	Value of syndicated loans announced[1]	'Unspontaneous lending' Rescheduling[6]	'New money' loans[5]	Gross syndicated lending	Estimated drawdown of new loans[2]	Estimated scheduled repayment of new loans[3]	Estimated net new loans	Stock of syndicated loans, excluding rescheduling[4]	Stock of syndicated loans, including rescheduling[6]	Average size of syndicated loans	Mean spreads	Mean final maturities
		($bn)	($bn)	($bn)	($bn)	($bn)	($bn)	($bn)	($bn)	($bn)	($mn)	(%)	(years)
	1	2	3	4	5	6	7	8	9	10	11	12	13
					=2+3+4			=6−7	=Σ8	=Σ8+3	=2÷1		
1972	226	7.4			7.4	5.4	0.3	5.1	5.1	5.1	32.9	1.01	6.57
1973	261	21.7			21.7	18.6	1.3	17.3	22.4	22.4	83.0	0.80	9.12
1974	409	29.4			29.4	30.4	4.4	26.0	48.4	48.4	71.9	0.89	8.17
1975	345	19.6			19.6	19.6	7.9	11.7	60.1	60.1	56.8	1.56	5.67
1976	376	27.5			27.5	26.6	11.7	14.9	75.1	75.1	73.1	1.52	5.76
1977	481	38.9			38.9	32.8	16.1	16.7	91.8	91.8	81.0	1.28	6.80
1978	653	64.8			64.8	65.3	20.6	44.7	136.5	136.5	99.2	0.98	8.54
1979	873	77.6			77.6	72.7	26.3	46.4	183.0	183.0	88.9	0.77	8.71
1980	957	82.9			82.9	80.5	32.9	47.6	230.5	230.5	86.6	0.73	7.37
1981	1,070	131.5			131.5	101.7	41.1	60.6	291.1	291.1	122.9	0.71	7.51

1982	960	89.2	16.4	11.2	116.8	97.2	50.9	46.3	337.4	353.8	93.0	0.82	6.78
1983	484	38.1	47.0	13.7	98.6	42.5	58.2	−15.7	321.7	385.1	78.8	0.75	6.91
1984	376	28.5	40.2	6.5	74.9	27.9	53.7	−25.8	295.9	399.5	75.7	0.67	6.98
1985	266	19.0	n.a.	2.3	n.a.	21.8	55.3	−33.5	262.4	n.a.	71.4	0.59	6.82
1986	304	29.8	n.a.	—	n.a.	23.1	56.9	−33.8	228.6	n.a.	98.0	0.42	7.16

Source: Bank of England.

Notes: 1. Based on information publicly announced when the loan mandate is awarded preparatory to the completion of the loan when the deal is signed.

2. Estimated by assuming that the loan is drawndown one month after completion or, where completion date is not known, four months after announcement. The large discrepancy between drawdowns and completions in 1981 is due to the exclusion of large merger-related standby loans which were negotiated and announced but not used.

3. Based on a hypothetical repayment schedule for each loan derived from the announced grace period, final maturity and the frequency of amortisation payments.

4. The cumulated excess of estimated drawdowns over repayments.

5. 'New money loans' are new syndicated loan packages for troubled debtors made in the framework of officially sponsored new credit packages, and thus result in both gross and net new lending.

6. Rescheduling of loans does not result in any new net lending but simply postpones the repayment of existing loans. To the extent that existing, announced syndicated loans are those which are rescheduled, the estimated repayments shown in column 7, based on the hypothetical repayment schedule for each loan, will not actually have taken place. Accordingly, rescheduled loans are cumulated in column 10 to give an estimate additional to that in column 9 of the total stock of syndicated credits outstanding.

For further information about the nature of the data used see Bond, *The Syndicated Credits Market*, Bank of England Discussion Paper No. 33, March 1985.

with an original maturity greater than one year. They differ from the OECD data of Table 10.8 which are based on completions, not announcements. They differ from the BIS data in Chapter 8 which include also unannounced and shorter-term credits.

The table gives figures of the number and value of new loans announced, both spontaneous and involuntary (due to rescheduling); estimates of the drawdown, repayment and outstanding stock of loans;[21] and some average data relating to the size, interest rates and length of loan. Syndicated lending in the Eurocurrency markets began in 1968 and the estimated value outstanding at the end of 1971 was $8.6 billion. But the first reliable data collection began in 1972 and the table starts at that date. We note, however, that the institution of syndicated lending predates the first oil price increase of 1973/74. Thereafter, we observe, lending did increase sharply, as did the size of individual loans. The first billion dollar syndication was made in 1973, the first $3 billion syndication occurred in 1978, and 1981 saw two $6 billion syndications put together, both for US private corporations.

Tables 10.10 and 10.11 classify the loans according to four characteristics: currency, country grouping, type of borrower and geographic region. The market is predominantly, and in some years almost entirely, based on the US dollar, which is a contrast with the Eurobond market. Perhaps surprisingly, in every year except one, Western industrialised countries were the largest borrowers, although since 1978 non-oil producing developing countries have grown in importance as borrowers. Borrowings in 1980 and 1981 were inflated by loans related to mergers, takeovers and management buyout attempts in the USA, and many of the loans announced were not subsequently used. For this reason they have been excluded from the drawdown and repayment series in Table 10.9. In most years sovereign borrowers and public sector borrowers dominated, which further contrasts with Eurobonds. Whereas European countries were the largest borrowers in the first half of the period covered, there was a switch to North and South American countries in the second half.

Syndications bring benefits to both banks and customers. They are an institutional device for spreading around the loan business of entities whose demand for funds makes them too large to be safe borrowers from single banks. If syndicates were not formed, individual banks might face bankruptcy from a number of defaults, or illiquidity in the case of deferred repayments. Borrowers would have to compensate the banks generously for taking these risks. Customers would probably aim instead to negotiate much smaller loans with a number of different banks. The mechanisms developed by banks enable this task to be carried out more conveniently and cheaply. Banks are thus organisers of risk-bearing services.

Procedures for arranging and managing participations are complex. Since an excellent account of them (McDonald 1982) ran to 264 pages, we can present here only the salient features.

Table 10.10 Syndicated Lending Classified by Currency and Borrowing Country, 1972–1986

	1972	*1973*	*1974*	*1975*	*1976*	*1977*	*1978*	*1979*	*1980*	*1981*	*1982*	*1983*	*1984*	*1985*	*1986*
CURRENCY OF DENOMINATION (%)															
US dollar	90.1	99.2	98.3	96.7	97.0	96.9	98.0	96.6	96.5	95.1	94.3	90.6	86.0	81.9	83.5
Sterling	6.3	—	—	0.2	—	—	—	—	0.2	0.8	1.3	4.9	3.1	2.1	5.1
Deutschmark	1.4	0.6	1.3	2.4	2.8	2.4	1.4	2.6	1.5	1.2	0.6	1.0	1.6	2.2	3.6
Swiss franc	1.6	0.2	0.1	—	0.2	0.3	—	0.1	0.5	0.3	0.4	0.6	0.5	0.9	1.6
Japanese yen	—	—	—	—	—	0.1	0.3	0.3	0.2	0.3	1.7	0.2	—	4.0	2.2
Composite currency units	—	—	—	—	—	—	—	—	—	1.1	0.4	2.1	7.9	6.8	1.8
Other	0.6	—	0.3	0.7	—	0.3	0.3	0.4	1.1	1.2	1.3	0.6	0.9	2.1	2.2
COUNTRY OF BORROWER (%)															
Industrialised countries	59.2	52.4	67.0	30.9	33.8	40.5	41.0	35.1	48.2	60.5	47.1	57.0	52.3	49.9	60.8
Oil exporting countries	11.8	19.2	4.2	14.5	15.1	21.0	14.8	14.6	15.7	9.8	15.5	14.5	12.3	6.6	11.1
Non-oil exporting developing countries	21.8	17.2	21.4	41.7	35.4	29.3	38.6	40.1	31.3	28.3	35.2	22.7	24.7	23.0	15.1
Eastern European countries	1.3	4.5	4.1	10.4	5.8	5.6	4.4	5.4	3.4	0.8	0.6	1.4	7.5	19.0	7.9
Other countries[1]	4.4	2.1	2.8	2.2	3.9	0.1	0.2	4.3	0.7	0.3	1.6	1.1	2.8	1.5	3.8
International institutions[2]	1.5	4.6	0.5	0.3	6.0	3.5	1.0	0.5	0.7	0.3	—	3.3	0.4	—	1.3
Total	100.0	100.0	100.0	100.0	100.0	100.0	100.0	100.0	100.0	100.0	100.0	100.0	100.0	100.0	100.0
$ Million	7,433	21,660	29,427	19,605	27,486	38,945	64,787	77,599	82,856	131,499	89,261	38,120	28,471	18,961	29,763

Source: Bank of England.

Notes: 1. South Africa and China.
2. EEC, International Investment Bank and African Development Bank.

Table 10.11 Largest 20 Syndicated Loans Classified by Type of Borrower and Geographic Region, 1972–1982

	1972	*1973*	*1974*	*1975*	*1976*	*1977*	*1978*	*1979*	*1980*	*1981*	*1982*
TYPE OF BORROWER (%)											
Sovereign	33.6	19.7	70.1	63.7	62.7	76.9	65.5	58.9	37.2	11.0	72.9
Public sector	20.1	61.8	24.6	30.6	30.3	20.6	29.9	38.6	37.9	13.7	8.8
Private sector	46.3	18.5	5.3	5.7	7.0	2.5	4.6	2.5	24.9	75.3	18.3
GEOGRAPHIC REGION (%)											
Europe, Middle East and Africa	71.1	88.6	81.7	50.7	56.5	60.8	35.9	40.5	31.5	12.3	38.9
North and South America	27.0	9.9	5.0	23.5	39.5	36.1	57.2	34.4	68.5	84.9	51.9
Far East	1.9	1.5	13.3	25.8	4.0	3.1	6.9	25.1	—	2.8	9.2
MEMO:											
20 largest loans as at per cent of total syndicated loans	54.4	45.2	40.6	40.5	32.3	38.0	40.6	43.1	34.1	48.8	51.9

Source: Compiled using information from *Euromoney*, recorded in McDonald (1982).

Characteristics of the Loans

Several aspects are common. All loans are syndicated amongst many, sometimes over 100, banks. They are medium-term, with maturities ranging from 3–15 years, with 6–8 years being about average. Virtually all loans are on a rollover basis, with interest rates adjusted regularly several times a year. Thereafter differences abound. It is usual to give the borrower the choice of currency in which the loan is granted and in which interest is payable. Most choose to denominate their loans in US dollars, although some borrowers choose a composite currency unit such as the ECU or SRD. Amounts borrowed range from about $10 million up to a massive $6 billion. As is apparent in Table 10.9, column 10, even the average size of loan fluctuates widely over time. In 1981, loans averaged $123 million, by 1985 that figure had shrunk to $71 million.

Once loan negotiations are concluded, the borrower is normally permitted up to one year to draw the full amount of the loan. A variety of options are available for repayment. There may be one lump sum at maturity date (a bullet loan), several instalments at maturity dates fixed in the contract, or an option to repay the whole or part of the principal after some minimum time has elapsed. Repayments can be tailored to projected cash flows on project loans. Normally, however, repayments of principal are required on a regular semi-annual basis, although usually after a grace period of normally 3 to 5 years. During the grace period, the borrower pays only interest on the loan without making any amortisation payments.

A secondary market exists in participation certificates. Informal interbank trading in participations has existed for as long as syndications have been arranged. In 1983, the volume of trading was estimated at $15 billion (Hurn 1985). Negotiability is aided when loans are issued with transferable participation certificates by which lenders can sell and totally transfer their share in a debt, and the change of ownership can be registered. Without such certificates, a sub-participant has no direct claim in law and must rely on the original participant to act on his behalf. Nearly 20 per cent of syndicated loans made in 1985 and 1986 were transferable.

Syndicate Participants

As in Eurobond syndicates, members of the group can be put into a number of categories, according to the roles they perform:

(i) **Lead manager.** This bank is responsible for conducting the loan negotiations with the customer and organising the syndication.

(ii) **Managers.** Along with the lead manager, they organise the syndicate participants and underwrite fully or partially the amount of the loan.

(iii) **Participants.** These are normally smaller banks, without the expertise or size to perform one of the above functions. By means of the formal placing memorandum, they purchase a share or participation of the loan and thus the non-underwriting risks.

(iv) **Agent.** In US domestic syndications the agent has always been the lead manager. But in the Euromarkets, this function is sometimes delegated to another bank. The agent carries out the mechanical tasks of running the loans, collecting the funds from the syndicate members once the notice of drawdown is given, and calculating and collecting the interest and repayment of principal for distribution to members.

Fees and charges connected with the loan are distributed amongst the banks according to these functions.

Fees and Charges

Costs of the loan to the borrower encompass five basic charges: expenses, management fees, agency fee, commitment fee, and interest cost:

(i) **Expenses.** A borrower must reimburse the lead manager for all out-of-pocket expenses connected with the loan negotiations and organising and executing the syndicate. These embrace legal, printing and telex costs, and travel and entertainment. Clearly, these costs depend on the size and complexity of the loan and the number of potential and actual participants approached. A syndicate for $800 million arranged in 1981, for example, embraced eventually 89 banks but there were approaches to nearly 300 banks with 4-foot long offers transmitted by telex and lengthy international phone calls.[22] Expenses have been known to run to $400,000 on 'jumbo' loans.

(ii) **Management fee.** This is normally a front-end flat fee ranging from ½ to 1 per cent of the total principal amount of the loan, divided amongst the syndicate members according to their functions and the size of the participation. There is always a 'praecipium' on the whole amount for the lead manager, a larger share for all co-managers due to underwriting risks, and a 'pool' which is shared amongst the managers for the role in organising the participants. Donaldson (1979) suggests for illustration that a 1 per cent fee might be divided up as follows:

> ⅛ per cent praecipium to the lead manager on the whole amount
> ⅞ per cent to each manager pro-rata on the amount taken, say $20 million
> ⅝ per cent to participants taking $10 million or more, on amount taken
> ½ per cent to participants taking $7–10 million, on amount taken
> ⅜ per cent to participants taking $4–7 million, on amount taken

¼ per cent to participants taking $2–4 million on amount taken.

For a management fee of ½ per cent, these figures would be halved. But in the case above, if the whole loan were taken up by the underwriters, i.e. managers, the full fee would be absorbed by the praecipium of ⅛ and the ⅞ divided pro-rata between all managers. However, if the loan were taken up by participants each contributing $15 million, there would be a 'pool' of ¼ (= 1 − ⅛ − ⅝) left over to be shared between the managers. Had smaller participants contributed, there would have been an even larger pool. Thus the pricing is an incentive to widen the participation and thus spread the risks.

(iii) **Agency fee.** This is paid to the agent or to the lead manager when performing this function. Since the agent's job is to organise the loan after it is signed, the fee is normally charged as a flat per annum cost (say $500) per bank in the syndicate (say 40), giving a charge in this case of $20,000 per annum. Sometimes, for small syndicates, there is a once-only fee levied.

(iv) **Commitment fee** (for example, ⅜ per cent per annum). Levied on the undrawn portion of the credit facility, and calculated on the basis of the actual number of days elapsing. This is analogous to fees levied by US banks on unused loan commitments and by British and other banks on the unused overdraft limit.

(v) **Interest cost**. Consists of two parts, base plus margin, most often calculated as follows:

Interest cost = LIBOR + spread

although pricing is frequently in terms of the US Prime or CD rates as the basis. Sometimes the borrower is given a choice of the base or an option to change the basis during the course of a loan. LIBOR (London interbank offer rate) is the rate at which banks offer to place deposits interbank with other prime Eurobanks. For the purpose of calculating the interest cost to the borrower, a reference weighted average rate for participating banks is used. It corresponds to the term of the *interest period* in the contract when interest is paid. Because of end-of-month bunching of interest periods, the calculation is sometimes spread over several days. Note that the rate which leading banks are prepared to pay for Eurodeposits is LIBID (the London interbank bid rate). There is normally a margin of ⅛ per cent between LIBOR and LIBID, and so the pricing arrangement has built into it a funding or Treasury profit for major banks.

Whereas LIBOR is usually different at each interest period in line with market forces, the spread which is added is pre-set for the length of the loan. Often the spread is split according to the term of the loan. In the circumstances of 1984, for example, the typical spread was ⅝ per cent (62.5 basis points) for years one to four, say, and ¾ per cent (75 basis points) for later periods. The slightly higher return compensates the banks for the continued exposure to loan and funding risks beyond the fifth year. It is a practice which belies the notion that banks treat a seven-year rollover loan as a commitment which extends merely to the next interest rate adjustment period.

Overall, then, the interest costing formula is one which means that the interest cost to the borrower varies over the length of the loan in line with the lending banks' funding costs at each interest rate period, related to LIBOR, plus the 'spread'.

Determination of the Spread

Out-of-pocket expenses associated with the negotiation and organisation of the syndicate, costs of underwriting the issue, and costs of collecting repayments are, as we have seen, generally collected separately from the borrower. As a first approximation it might be thought that the spread is independent of these factors, and is determined by the strength of the demand for loans from borrowers (such as arising from world payments imbalances) and the willingness of banks to supply funds. This is the basis of the analysis in Goodman (1980), Johnston (1980) and Fleming and Howson (1980). But the revenue to banks and the cost to the borrower is given by the spread *plus* fees, and neither banks nor their customers are indifferent to the mix between the two components. There is evidence that banks do not treat spread income and potential fees as independent, because of their different timing characteristics (a dollar in the hand . . .), and vary spread and fees charged according to circumstances. Also, because the spread is announced (in the tombstone notice) but the fees are not publicised, borrowers with an interest in concealing their true borrowing costs are prepared to trade increased fees for a lower announced spread. Thus, in the general case, both the spread and the fees should be treated as determined by the demand for and supply of funds (Mills and Terrell 1984). It is convenient, however, to go along with the fiction that fees just cover costs, and focus upon the determination of the spread.

From the viewpoint of a participating bank, the spread along with the funding profit constitutes the (or one part of the) anticipated return from the loan, available to pay wages and 'overheads' and to earn profits for shareholders. These costs plus the extent of competition amongst banks (i.e. whether it is a lenders' or borrowers' market) will govern the margin which banks seek. But part of the margin must also be seen as the 'insurance premium' which banks levy to cover the risk of default and the funding risk.

Funding risk comes about because borrowers are provided with the assurance that, barring extreme circumstances, the loan will be rolled over, so exposing the bank to difficulties should interbank funds markets dry up. The longer the term of the loan, the longer are these risks being carried.

In assessing the 'insurance premium' levied to cover these risks, banks can be expected to look at the totality of their operations. In the theory of finance, it has long been appreciated that the appropriate measure of an asset's riskiness is its perceived contribution to the risk of the investor's portfolio rather than its objective risk considered in isolation. Since Eurobanks are almost all domestic banks as well, the risk premium demanded will depend on the extent to which banks already have an internationally diversified portfolio, and whether international risks have characteristics which offset or magnify domestic banking risks.

Empirical studies of the spread by Goodman, Johnston and Fleming and Hewson found evidence of most of the factors suggested above. Table 10.9 reveals cyclical variations in the spread which seem readily explicable at least in terms of supply characteristics. Spreads rose sharply in 1974 following the Herstatt, Franklin National and British secondary banking crises, as banks became aware of risks of interbank funding. The decline afterwards through the rest of the decade may reflect the success of syndicate managers in drawing in ever larger numbers of banks seeking international portfolio diversification. New entrants' assessment of international lending risks would seem likely to be lower than that made by the existing lenders (Snowden 1985). Surprisingly, spreads have not widened in the 1980s in the face of mounting debt repayment difficulties. This is largely a statistical illusion because of the exclusion of rescheduled loans from the spread calculations. Because of the risks, some of those involuntary loans have been negotiated at spreads of up to 2 per cent above LIBOR.

10.5 Risks of International Lending

Banks in international lending face the risks common to all banks: liquidity risk, interest rate risk, credit (asset) risk, and contingent liabilities risk. There are some further risks particular to cross-border and cross-currency transactions. We now examine how banks seek to avert these risks.

Currency Risk

Banks face losses from three sources: their own position if short or long in a particular currency; dealing positions taken by employees who gamble with the bank's money; and defaults by counter-parties to forward exchange contracts and covering transactions. These risks were well illustrated by events in 1974: Bankhaus Herstatt, Cologne, collapsed due largely to losses on its foreign exchange exposures; Lloyds Bank, Lugano, lost $77 million due to unauthorised trading by staff. Herstatt's closure by the Bundesbank during working hours left many banks with unfulfilled foreign exchange transactions. Since then banks and authorities have tightened their control. Banks still take a position on foreign currencies and put traders on commission to speculate on their behalf, but mainly on within-day trading or on overnight positions (often concealed by 'regulatory arbitrage', see Chapter 9, section 7 above). On longer-term positions banks aim to match liabilities and claims in a particular currency or cover the difference in the swap market.

Regulatory Risk

Regulatory risk can take a variety of forms in cross-border and Eurocurrency operations. Pricing of loans relies on the absence of reserve requirements and regulations by the host country. Imposition of these would most likely remove the profitability in the spread. Loan contracts normally include clauses to cover this contingency, forcing the borrower to bear the extra cost. Repayment of a loan often relies on foreign exchange being made available to the borrower by the central or monetary authority in the country concerned. An undertaking to this effect is usually required prior to a signing of the syndication. Permission may be required of governments to allow drawdowns, and a letter to this effect is also sought.

Contingent Liabilities Risk

In lending related activities, risks derive from the underwriting of loan syndicates, the granting of loan commitments, and the provision of informal bill and note acceptance facilities. Banks also underwrite bond issues and provide revolving underwriting facilities (note issuance facilities) with commitments stretching over periods as long as ten years. They guarantee the performance of counterparties and take positions in a variety of 'swap' transactions. Banks bear the default and liquidity risks which these facilities entail. They can shift the interest rate risk of loan commitments (where drawdowns are predictable) onto future markets, although with rollover loan contracts, rather than fixed rate loans, the need to do so is largely obviated.

Liquidity Risk

In the Eurocurrency markets, banks have generated a number of balance sheet options to cope with the uncertain demand for funds arising from short-term deposits, drawdowns of lines and loan commitments, and variations in loan repayments. Some are bilateral in the form of standby credit lines negotiated with banks which enjoy favoured access to funding in particular currencies. A number of markets exist in which individual banks are effectively price-takers, able to obtain whatever volume is required at the market rate without, individually, exerting a significant effect on the rate. This is especially so in the interbank markets in London, and in major centres such as Singapore, and the banks have come to regard liability raising in the markets as a major line of defence.

Banks have also institutionalised options on the assets side of the balance sheet matching the options which are held against them. The contingencies are referred to as 'securitisation' or 'marketisation' of assets, especially loans. For example, participation certificates issued as part of a syndicate can often be resold to the issuing banks; or a managing bank retaining participation certificates may issue them subsequent to the granting of the credit, thus carrying a smaller part of the loan to maturity. Details of these activities are given in Bond (1985).

Interest-Rate Risk

In the Eurocurrency markets, bankers pioneered arrangements by which interest rate risks are passed on fully to borrowers at rollover dates, since pricing is based directly upon representative funding costs. In between the dates when interest rates are adjusted, an interest rate risk is borne since banks generally rely on borrowings much shorter than the rollover period (see Table 9.4). Consequently, they face a profits squeeze over the intervening period until loan rates are renegotiated. If customers opt for loan pricing off US prime, while banks are funding relative to LIBOR, banks can face a 'basis risk' (which provides an impetus for 'basis swaps' so that banks can lock into a fixed spread). There can be an 'earnings risk' over the period of the loan if increases in operating costs erode the fixed margin above LIBOR or whatever basis the bank is charging for loans. But the most important risk facing the bank is a 'funding risk', i.e. that a bank may be unable to tap sufficient resources to meet its continuing obligations. Interbank credit lines may dry up if the bank is perceived to be unsafe, or to have exceeded its daily overall credit limit.

Credit Risk and Country Risk

Credit risk refers to the ability of an entity to repay its debts, country risk to the ability and willingness of borrowers within a country to meet their obligations. Risk-sharing arrangements are adopted by banks to spread loan risks, avoid too much exposure to individual borrowers and accordingly undertake lending to a wider range of entities than they would consider prudent to do individually. Syndicates divide up loan risks in formal and identifiable ways, making explicit each bank's contribution to the total risk. Interbank markets do so in less formal ways, as we have noted above. To the extent that multilateral development banks and official institutions co-finance with banks or guarantee bank loans, the risk to commercial banks is partly underwritten. Finally, 'cross default' clauses in syndication contracts give any bank the right to accelerate a loan should the borrower default on any other loan.

These various arrangements were developed and legally refined so that banks undertaking international lending would be largely protected from the risks that participating banks would otherwise face. They are summarised in Table 10.12.

10.6 What Went Wrong?

To pose this question presupposes that something is awry with banks' international financial intermediation. Although we will address this point further in the next chapter, for the moment we probably need look no further than to the $135 billion of involuntary lending by the banks in the years 1982 to 1984, and to the sharp cutback in new voluntary loans negotiated from $132 billion in 1981 to $30 billion in 1986 (Table 10.9). Even when rescheduling and other involuntary lending is included, lending in recent years has been well below levels of earlier years. Growth of Eurobond issues and Euronote

Table 10.12 International Lending Risks

Risk	*Source of risk*	*Risk reduction strategy*
Currency risk	Mismatched assets and liabilities in a particular currency.	Currency matching.
Regulatory risk	Imposition of reserve requirement or taxes on the banks.	A clause in the loan contract which forces the borrowers to bear this risk.
Contingent liabilities risk	Options of borrowers to drawdown lending commitments. Underwriting of syndicates.	Liability management. Marketing of assets. (applies to contingent liabilities risk and liquidity risk)
Liquidity risk	Options of depositors to withdraw deposits.	
Interest rate risk	Mismatched maturities unpredictable movements in interest rates.	Pricing of credits on a rollover basis.
Credit risk	The ability of an entity to repay its debts.	Syndication of loans. Risk-sharing via interbank market. Diversified loan portfolio. (applies to credit risk and country risk)
Country risk	The ability and willingness of borrowers within a country to meet their obligations.	

Source: See text.

facilities is symptomatic of a changed market for international loans.

In any account, the altered circumstances of the non-oil developing countries must serve as a backdrop. They were major borrowers, and have featured most amongst the rescheduling and involuntary lending (accounting for two thirds of amounts renegotiated in 1983). A conjunction of three interrelated events, the impact of which is summarised at the bottom of Table 10.2, has led to the changed environment. One event is the second oil price cycle beginning in 1979/80. Higher prices increased the value of oil imports. A second factor is the world recession and the consequences it has had for world trade. After expanding steadily for nearly three decades, world trade stopped growing in 1981 and actually declined by 2 per cent in 1982. The potential for the developing countries to expand exports and generate a current account surplus to repay debt and interest declined commensurately. Finally, interest rates in the US increased sharply in the late 1970s and early 1980s. They dragged up Eurocurrency rates along with them and raised sharply the interest payments of those borrowers with floating rate debt to service. Perhaps 80 per cent of the increased indebtedness of the non-oil exporting developing countries in the late 1970s and early 1980s can be attributed to these three 'external' circumstances (Cline 1983).

In the face of such a marked revision in the underlying environment, it is inevitable that loans made in earlier circumstances will take on a different complexion. And it is easy to be wise after the event. But looked at coldly in terms of the principles of banking there were three 'problems' with the way banks handled international lending.

Banks pool risks on both sides of their balance sheet, but there was not independence between the two sides. Following the increases in oil prices, lending opportunities were presented on both sides of the balance sheet. Bankers were able to take funds from the present oil producing countries and lend them to countries financing projects which would make them either future producers of oil or producers of alternative energy resources, made viable by currently high oil prices. Both sides of the balance sheet rested to some extent on the continuance of high oil prices. When the impact of rises in oil prices lessened and prices actually began to fall, both sides of the balance sheet experienced deterioration. Deposit growth from the oil exporters slowed down. The drop in oil prices posed a major problem for some of the borrowing countries; for others it eased their debt position, but overall borrowers fell behind in repayments.[23]

Second, in terms of the objective of risk-spreading, syndication had in fact created a fiction. Loans were syndicated, and participations spread across many banks. Each bank may have had a diversified portfolio of participations. But risk is not in terms of loans. It is in terms of independent fates. With rollover credits, risk is best measured by the amount of outstanding debt of countries on floating rate terms, net of bank claims held by those countries. The pattern of drawdowns and repayments meant that by 1982, 75 per cent of the net floating rate syndicated debt was held by four countries alone: Mexico, Brazil, Argentina and South Korea. Table 10.13 gives details.

Syndication is meant to be an anti-accumulation device, to use a term common in insurance, preventing too much of an accumulation of risk in individual portfolios. But there was clearly accumulation in the aggregate loan portfolio: in a sense there was one risk. Adding interdependent participations does not improve the spread of risks in a bank's balance sheet. In insurance terms, it was as if each insurer had a diversified portfolio of houses insured for earthquake damage, but it just happened that each lay along the San Andreas fault.

For many banks in the USA the position was compounded by the interrelationship between their international and domestic loan book in the 1980s. Energy prices generally fell along with those of many farm commodities so that those banks with loan concentrations to the developing countries and to domestic energy industries were doubly blighted. Banks were attracted into international banking because it seemed to present lending returns and risks dissimilar to those domestically, but there was strong positive covariation between the two in the particular circumstances.

Third, bankers did not appreciate the difference, well known to students of taxation, between initial and final incidence. International bankers pioneered the now almost universal arrangements by which interest rate risks are passed on fully to borrowers at rollover dates. Pricing at the rollover period is based directly upon funding costs (e.g. LIBOR, CD rates) making it a cost-plus contract, like those employed for military purchases of new technology, when the government compensates the supplier for all costs plus an agreed profit margin. Such an arrangement can be visualised as a fixed-price (i.e. rate) contract combined with an 'insurance' contract by which the purchaser takes on the insurance function and reimburses the supplier for unexpected costs. In the case of military purchases, it is thought to be an appropriate distribution of risk bearing: risk is shifted to the agency best able to bear it.

For borrowers with low risk tolerance and incomes which decline when interest rates rise, the appropriateness of such insurance arrangements for loans can be questioned. As noted in Chapter 4, the nature of the risk to a

Table 10.13 Floating Rate Debt — Major Debtors, 1982

	$ billion	*Per cent*
Mexico	59	31.6
Brazil	46	24.6
Argentina	21	11.2
South Korea	16	8.5
Other net debtors	45	24.1
Total	187	100.0

Source: Bank of England Quarterly Bulletin, March 1983.

bank is changed more than shifted, since loan default risks are increased and, moreover, no longer have independent fates, rebounding onto the banks. Banks thought that they had shifted the refinancing and interest rate risk of lending onto borrowers, but it is the banks which bear the ultimate credit risk should the borrower be unable to pay the higher interest costs. Because so many loans are to public sector or sovereign borrowers, credit risk became synonymous with country risk. Due to the small number of really large borrowers and the size of the amounts involved, an uneasy interdependence exists between the fates of the borrowers and the banks.

So far, the banks have fared much better than might have been expected in 1982 when it seemed that a collapse of the world banking system was in the offing. As we have seen, banks have cut back on much new lending while shortening the maturities on those loans, and have shifted some new loans to other customers off-balance sheet by means of note issuance facilities. They have extended new loans to the debtor countries as part of lending packages and have agreed to reschedule a substantial amount of existing debts, but have continued to receive interest servicing from most of the debtors. In some years after 1982 banks have been able to reverse the flows to the developing countries and reduce their exposures to them by repayment of existing loans, many from private sector borrowers, and reductions in trade finance and interbank lines. Governments of the major industrial countries have assisted this process by extending new direct loans, guaranteeing some of the credits extended by the commercial banks, and by rescheduling official debt through the 'Paris Club' framework.

In their dealings with the borrower countries, banks have not agreed to forgive debt nor in any way reduce the value of their contractual obligations. They have been aided in this stand by domestic regulatory agencies which have allowed banks to keep loans on their balance sheets at face value, despite trading on secondary markets at much discounted values.[24] Loan renegotiations have generally been contingent upon the country's acceptance of an IMF adjustment programme designed to improve resource allocation, reduce inflation, increase exports and domestic savings. Maturities on rescheduled loans have gradually lengthened, but the principle that interest payments must not be rescheduled has been upheld. Banks have insisted on commercial terms to compensate for commercial risks, with spreads above LIBOR sometimes well in excess of those which ruled when the original loan was negotiated in headier times. Commenting on the position in 1982, a study group of the Group of Thirty (1982) observed as follows:

> Creditors have so far emerged relatively undamaged from rescheduling . . .
>
> From the borrowers' perspective, however, the terms have been quite onerous, failing to reflect their likely cash flows and essential adjustment plans.

That conclusion seems not inappropriate as of 1986.

Any discussion of the appropriateness of rescheduling arrangements, and of bank intermediation generally, soon leads us into the wider issues of the consequence of borrower default and of the alternatives to bank intermediation. We take up these issues in the next chapter.

Notes

1. In Table 8.2, external lending corresponds to the IMF measure of gross international bank lending.
2. Excellent accounts of inter-regional adjustment mechanisms are given in Scitovsky (1969) and Goodhart (1975).
3. Some estimates put the number of banks participating in the international interbank market as high as 2,000. See Llewellyn (1985b).
4. See Branson (1977).
5. Due to data revisions between 1983 and 1986, the figures in this table differ from those in Table 10.1. The large overall balancing item, approaching $100 billion in some years, casts doubt on the reliability of the figures for any of the categories.
6. This discussion has benefited greatly from reading Argy (1983).
7. This identity follows from the standard definition:

$$GNP = GDP - F$$
$$GDP = C + I + G + X - Im$$
$$GNP = C + S + T$$

   where $G = I_G + G_C$.
8. See Walter (1985b, p. 120). Fears on this score were expressed in the Economists Advisory Group (1984).
9. A detailed discussion of recent regulatory and structural changes in capital markets is contained in Watson, Mathieson, Kincaid, and Kalter (1986) and Gilibert, Lygum and Wartz (1986, 1987).
10. Information about commissions and the syndication process is based on Fisher (1979), Courtadon (1985) and Kidwell, Marr and Thompson (1985).
11. Trading occurs in the so-called 'gray market' and managers buy 'loose' bonds frequently from syndicate underwriters who have overestimated demand, in order to keep the price falling far below the issue price during the placement process.
12. FRNs have usually embodied a minimum interest rate clause. However, the fall in interest rates in 1986 saw a number of outstanding FRNs with such clauses begin to act like fixed rate bonds. They were withdrawn from the market and newly issued FRNs carried no minimum rate protection. See Gilibert, Lygum and Wartz (1987).
13. Developments in 1986, when foreshadowed regulatory developments created the expectation that Japanese banks would withdraw as buyers, and prices of perpetual FRNs in the market fell sharply, showed that conditions are closely linked with developments in banking. See *Bank of England Quarterly Bulletin*, February 1987, p. 41.
14. Hammond (1987). Swap transactions in the international capital market are examined also in BIS (1986b) and Das (1986).
15. In this respect, swaps are the financial equivalent of the Ricardian principle of comparative advantage well known in international trade theory. This interpretation is questioned by Wall and Pringle (1987), especially in domestic markets, and they wonder why existing arbitrage instruments have not worked to eliminate the comparative advantage. In international markets the quality spread differences seem more readily explicable.
16. The similarities and differences between the three 'currency swaps' are examined

in Henderson and Price (1986) and Redhead (1986). In the foreign exchange swaps considered in chapter 9, the forward and spot exchange rates will usually differ. For cross-currency swaps the exchange rates are normally the same for the initial and final exchanges of principal, with the forward premium or discount finding reflection in the periodic interest rate flows.

17. *Financial Times*, 30 March, 1987, p. 21.
18. The broad categories employed conceal the great variety of instruments within each category. Floating rate notes are issued with 'caps', 'mismatches', 'flip-flops', 'mini-max' formulae etc. See Vittas (1986).
19. These are described in Stigum and Branch (1983) and our discussion draws upon their first-hand knowledge.
20. Group of Thirty (1982).
21. Notes at the foot of the table explain how some of the series are calculated. It needs to be emphasised that the repayment of the loans, and thus the outstanding stock in column 9, is estimated on the basis of a hypothetical profile for each loan derived from information provided when the loan was announced. It thus makes no allowance for either premature or tardy repayment. The latter is provided for in the table by data on rescheduled loans. Due to lack of reliable information, the former is not, although some Eurobond flotations in recent years have replaced or accelerated repayment of syndicated loans by means of a fixed rate bond issue combined with an interest rate swap.
22. McDonald (1982, pp. 9 –17).
23. A number of papers in the Winter 1985 issue of the *Oxford Review of Economic Policy* address this issue.
24. The regulatory treatment of international loans in the United States is examined by Guttentag and Herring (1985), while Bell and Rutledge (1984) compare the treatment in different countries.

11

Some Issues in International Banking

Few of those concerned about the 'dollar shortage' in the 1950s foresaw the rise of the Eurodollar and other external currency markets after 1957. Hardly any observers of the international scene predicted the oil price rise of October 1973 and the dramatic impact that it was to have upon world payments imbalances and flows of international finance. Very few of the many who congratulated private enterprise in general, and the international banking system in particular, on the success of recycling OPEC surpluses to the developing countries gave warnings of the international debt problems of the 1980s. Chastened by these reminders, we shall not risk our names being added to a future list by trying to put a crystal ball to the future. Instead, we shall look briefly at some contemporary issues of international banking. Since some of them have merited full-length book treatment in their own right, our account must necessarily be more circumspect.

11.1 Controlling the Euromarkets[1]

Calls for regulating the Eurocurrency markets have arisen in the context of three alleged consequences. First, it has been argued that the markets increase the degree of capital mobility, giving rise to undesirable flows of capital and instability of exchange rates. Second, there is concern on prudential grounds that losses from exposures in Eurocurrency market operations may spread to domestic markets. Third, the growth of an unregulated banking system offshore is thought to hamper control of money and/or inflation.

Capital Mobility

Most concern about capital mobility has arisen in the context of relatively fixed exchange rates. At the risk of some simplification of present thinking, the effects of increased capital mobility are well known. Under relatively fixed exchange rates, domestic interest rates are tied more closely to world levels (via interest parity); sterilisation of international influences upon the money supply is more difficult; and the impact of monetary policy upon domestic variables is diluted. In the limiting case of perfect capital mobility, loss of monetary sovereignty is complete. Under flexible exchange rates, asset market considerations dominate trade effects in the short-run determination of exchange rates.

International banking, and the development of more open financial systems, carries implications for the degree of mobility of capital. Table 11.1 sets out a simplified balance sheet for an 'open' banking system. As compared with a 'closed' banking system, foreigners hold deposits and borrow in the local currency (external liabilities and loans). Domestic residents, for their part, hold foreign currency deposits and borrow in foreign currency in addition to their usual local currency banking business.

Banks' activities can lead to an increase in the magnitude and/or interest rate sensitivity of financial flows in a number of ways. In the first place, banks' intermediation is likely to lower the transactions costs involved in utilising foreign currency facilities and widen the appeal of them amongst residents. More medium-sized companies might wish to borrow in foreign currencies and maintain deposits in foreign currencies. When a large amount of business is conducted internationally and denominated in foreign currencies, residents' holdings of foreign currency deposits, and especially those held with a local bank, are a substitute for domestic money balances (convertible into foreign currencies). Also, banks' balance sheets are likely to exhibit a greater responsiveness to interest rate differentials than are the positions of those involved in direct financing. Banks are aware of the possibilities for interest rate arbitrage and are better placed to take advantage of them. The Eurobanks arbitrage freely between the various Eurocurrencies, 'manufacturing' the currency as required by covered transactions.[2]

For these reasons we would expect international banking to facilitate international capital movements and increase the extent of capital mobility by speeding the movement of funds in and out of domestic currency in response to variations in domestic and foreign interest rates. But 'high' capital mobility does not mean 'perfect' mobility and need not preclude a measure of independence in the conduct of monetary policies, as is evidenced by studies of the experiences of Canada and West Germany in the 1960s under fixed exchange rates.[3] While these findings are in dispute, several other factors point to the same conclusion.

Table 11.1 Balance Sheet of an 'Open' Banking Sector

Assets	*Liabilities*
Domestic currency loans to:	Domestic currency deposits:
Residents	Residents' holdings
Overseas entities	Overseas holdings
Foreign currency assets	Foreign currency deposits

First, transactions costs limit the extent to which assets of different currencies are perfect substitutes from the supply side. Branson (1969) estimated that the minimum covered interest differential necessary to induce covered forward arbitrage is 0.18 per cent per annum. Later estimates for Eurodeposits in the same geographic location suggest 0.25 per cent per annum, with possibly wider margins when the assets are Treasury bills (Frankel and Levich 1977).

Second, foreign securities held overseas are subject to different risks merely because they are domiciled under another legal jurisdiction and regulatory environment. New rules about capital controls may be instituted after the securities have been purchased, and new tax arrangements may be introduced which alter the rate of return from the assets. This political risk is less for short-term than for long-term securities. For longer term securities interest arbitrage is more likely between assets denominated in currencies of countries which have low perceived risks (USA, Switzerland).

Third, the return on a foreign currency asset depends not only upon the yield in that currency but also upon the exchange rate which applies when the funds are repatriated, and this may change from that ruling at the time the funds were invested. Forward cover provides an incomplete hedge. It does not exist for all maturities, especially those in excess of six or nine months. It cannot cover all risks: the investor may desire to switch out of the security before maturity in order to take advantage of more profitable opportunities elsewhere; or unexpectedly early transactions may force premature repatriation. Interest parity is likely to be approximated only for short-term securities.

These three factors (transactions costs, political risk and exchange risk) make for imperfect substitutability between foreign and domestic securities and allow for some deviations from interest rate parity, especially for long-term securities, even when there is high capital mobility. A fourth factor depends upon the way in which interest parity is achieved. For short-term (90-day) securities, interest parity is:

$$\frac{R_F - R_S}{R_S} = \frac{(\mathrm{i_d} - i_f)/(1 + i_f)}{4.055}$$

where the interest rates on 90-day domestic (i_d) and foreign (i_f) securities are expressed as per cent per annum and the left-hand side is the 90-day forward premium on foreign currency (forward discount on domestic currency) expressed as a per cent of the spot rate. The left side of the equation shows the gain made on purchasing a unit of foreign currency today and selling it forward (for delivery in 90 days). The right side shows the cost of that strategy where ($i_d - i_f$) represents the interest earnings foregone by holding foreign rather than domestic assets and the term $1/(1 + i_f)$ indicates the number of units of foreign currency assets needed today to yield one unit in 90 days.

By itself, the equation is an equilibrium condition and does not tell us whether it is maintained by adjustments in interest rates, the spot rate or the forward premium. Interest parity need not be a complete obstacle to monetary independence, as shown by Herring and Marston (1977), to the extent that the shift in the forward premium insulates domestic interest rates from, say, movements in overseas interest rates. It can be shown further that this partial insulation of the money market exists even when arbitrage activities of multinational banks link the markets in the various Eurocurrencies.[4] However, if either (i) securities denominated in different currencies or (ii) domestic and Eurocurrency assets in the same currency are very close substitutes, the insulation would be lost. Domestic interest rates would then be maintained at parity with foreign (Eurodollar) rates, as if there were perfect capital mobility.

With the abolition of exchange controls in a number of countries, we are much closer to conditions of perfect capital mobility than during the era of relatively fixed exchange rates in the 1960s and early 1970s. Even so, experience in those years points to a failure to take account of international monetary interdependence when framing domestic policies. In 1972, for example, the coincidence of tight monetary policy in Germany and expansionary domestic policy in the USA saw a flood of dollars flow from the USA to Germany and other European countries, expanding international reserves and the world money supply.[5] World commodity price rises, and thus indirectly the rise in oil prices in 1973, have been attributed to this monetary expansion. But note that the Eurocurrency markets were merely the conduit: the same transactions between the USA and Europe could have taken place (albeit less expeditiously) through traditional channels. The role of the Euromarkets was to bypass capital controls, lower transactions costs considerably, and thus link up domestic markets indirectly via Euromarket transactions. In this environment, those countries like Australia which sought to persist with controls and managed exchange rates found their freedom of movement increasingly restricted (see Polasek and Lewis 1985b).

While some economists (such as Tobin 1978) have advocated taxes on capital movements to raise transactions costs, enabling some monetary independence under fixed rates, most major countries have moved to floating exchange rates. Indeed, in terms of Mundell's (1963) analysis the classic prescription for a small open economy wanting an independent monetary policy under conditions of high capital mobility is to float its exchange rate. The core of the argument for floating exchange rates is that the monetary base and hence the money supply can be insulated from monetary flows from abroad and can be allowed to respond to domestic influences. An inflow of capital, say, induces an adjustment to the exchange rate so as to maintain an overall balance of international payments without reserve flows and without any impact upon the money supply. Conversely, an alteration to domestic credit can impact upon the money supply without inducing offsetting capital flows. Monetary autonomy in this sense is not destroyed by high capital mobility. Mundell's analysis, we may note, did not incorporate the forward market or expectations about exchange rates, and Argy and Porter (1972) argued that, when allowance for these is made in the model, the movement of the forward rate may be such that the domestic money market is not fully insulated from external monetary disturbances. Their analysis is based on the role of speculators in the forward market. But the activities of international banks in arbitraging freely between different Eurocurrencies, covering forward against exchange risks, seem likely to have reduced the impact of speculation on the forward rate, as McKinnon (1979) argues. In this respect the growth of Eurocurrency banking should improve the efficiency of floating exchange rates in achieving monetary independence.

If there is, in consequence, a high degree of substitutability between securities denominated in different currencies, and in the limit effectively one world capital market, this independence afforded by floating exchange rates may not allow monetary policy to exert much impact upon real interest rates and domestic output. Under conditions of 'super neutrality', for instance, domestic real interest rates would tend to equality with foreign real interest rates. Nominal interest rates would then differ between countries in terms of interest rate parity by the expected change in the spot exchange rate (which in turn would tend to equal the expected difference in inflation rates, under purchasing power parity, and the premium of the forward rate relative to the spot rate, under an appropriate set of expectations.)[6]

But even in this event monetary policy should still be able, via impacts upon inflation expectations, anticipated exchange rate changes and other channels, to alter the domestic rate of inflation. Indeed, this link might be commensurately closer as a consequence, and this could be seen to be a good thing from the viewpoint of inflation control. In consequence, a country's inflation rate would be governed by domestic monetary policy, whereas greater financial integration under fixed exchange rates makes domestic inflation depend on the inflation performance of all countries whose monetary policies are linked together.

Actual experience, however, has shown that the switch to floating exchange rates has been far from a panacea. Evidence presented by Fukao and Hanazaki (1986) suggests that inter-country differences in real interest rates have on average narrowed considerably in the 1980s; nevertheless, differentials have often been large. A number of considerations suggest that, even in the most propitious of circumstances, floating exchange rates may provide only limited insulation against real disturbances if world economies are highly integrated. They do not prevent external flows from influencing the money stock (defined as private residents' holdings of cash and deposits denominated in the domestic currency). In terms of Table 11.1, a balance of payment surplus, for example, can be financed by non-residents drawing down their deposits in the local currency or by banks switching foreign currency positions into domestic currency, so that the money supply increases although there is no change in reserve flows across the exchanges. A freely floating exchange rate, which reduces to zero the official financing of the balance of payments, isolates the money supply from reserve flows, but does not eliminate the influence of net external flows upon the money supply. The net external effects can be shut off only when the exchange rate is driven to a level where the balance of payments surplus becomes zero (Goodhart 1984, Chapter 8).

Variable exchange rates render currencies less perfect substitutes in terms of their supply, but not necessarily non-substitutes in terms of demand. Without exchange controls, residents hold (larger) money balances in other currencies so as to facilitate transactions in those currencies (which are made more costly at present by frequent conversions) and to diversify their portfolio. More flexible exchange rates make national currencies less good substitutes for the key currencies in the financing of international trade and raise the returns to be had from currency diversification. Or, it may be that savers want to hold bonds and other assets denominated in 'strong' currencies as an inflation hedge. Such international portfolio diversification lessens the extent of monetary independence which can be gained from exchange rate flexibility (Miles 1978). As currency diversification increases, control of a volume of liquid assets denominated in a particular currency becomes of lesser relevance to the control of macroeconomic conditions in the country that issues the currency. In the limiting case, inflation in any country becomes as under fixed exchange rates the joint outcome of monetary policies of all countries (Niehans 1984, Chapter 15).

Finally, the theoretical case for floating rates presented by Friedman (1953) and Johnson (1972) focused around the trade account of the balance of payments. Stability came from the activities of traders and other operators taking up long-run speculative positions. In practice, as we have noted, foreign exchange transactions are dominated by banks' arbitrage and short-run asset holding positions. It is estimated that trade-related positions account for less than 5 per cent of total transactions; most are connected with lending and borrowing across currencies and asset holding positions. Asset markets, like commodity markets for wool or gold, can exhibit 'bootstrap' behaviour. Exchange rates, like other commodity prices, equalise expected returns from assets in different currency, but these returns include expected appreciation and depreciation. In the short run, there can be a direct feedback as those currencies which attract an inflow of funds rise in value and, by rising, become more attractive. Such extrapolative expectations cannot continue indefinitely, but reinforce tendencies to 'overshooting'. When interest parity operates, variations in market conditions can give rise to pronounced 'overshooting' due to divergencies in the speed of adjustment of asset markets relative to the prices of industrial products and labour markets. There is a growing literature on these topics, to which the reader is referred.[7]

Prudential Regulation

Prudential regulation refers to actions by the central bank to ensure that banks and other financial institutions maintain adequate capital reserves and adequate liquid resources to meet their obligations. These obligations come about because banks in Eurocurrency operations are issuing promises to pay in the future, and are writing options and contingent contracts of various kinds, much as occurs domestically. What differs is the scale of the business transacted and the collective mechanisms by which banks share globally among a group of banks the risks of international intermediation and provide jointly for liquidity needs. We have likened these arrangements to the coinsurance and reinsurance treaties which exist in the international insurance business. But more so than in insurance markets, confidence is a major factor because of the informality of the links which connect banks via the inter-bank market and in off-balance sheet business. These links have, if anything, added to the potential instabilities, for a number of reasons. Runs on banks are more likely to begin with wholesale depositors who are the first to hear rumours of impending trouble. This is well illustrated by the run on the Continental Illinois Bank, which began overnight in the interbank markets in Hong Kong and Singapore. Second, the interbank markets associated with wholesale banks institutionalise the 'chain risk'. If one bank defaults, the losses are not confined initially to its own customers. Third, interbank markets conceal and thus may encourage extra risk taking. A bank located at one end of an on-lending chain has difficulty in ascertaining to whom the funds will ultimately be lent. The same is true of many off-balance sheet activities. Swaps and options draw in extra risk-bearers and thus work to unbundle and diffuse risk, but the long chains of bank and non-banking counterparties could act in adverse circumstances to widen the spread of defaults. Further, when the process of liquidity creation is shared out informally across a large number of counterparties the extent of risk-bearing in the system as a whole may be concealed. The very novelty of many of the new financial instruments which feature off-balance sheet makes an informed assessment of the risks difficult.

Chapter 5 discussed various means by which banks and banking supervisors might implement collectively means of averting the risks which are being undertaken and avoid contagion should confidence falter. Insofar as special issues are posed by international banking, they come from (i) the magnitude of the risks of international lending and their potential to generate a global shock to the system, which we shall take up in section 11.3; (ii) the division of authority between host and source authorities; and (iii) the layering of intermediation.

We noted in the previous chapter that international banks took over from official aid and development bodies much of the task of financing world payments imbalances. This meant not only that the creation of international liquidity passed from official bodies to private ones, but also that the ultimate responsibility for supervision was transferred from international authorities to national ones, whose surveillance had previously been confined mainly to national boundaries. Eurobanks are, for the most part, not separate institutions, but branches, subsidiaries and affiliates or divisions of domestic banks. They consequently have potential access to lender of last resort facilities in their home base and are also subject to potential prudential supervision from that source. But ambiguities arise due to the different methods of incorporation in overseas operations.[8] From the viewpoint of the host country, the legal status of a foreign bank's branch as integral to, and indistinguishable from, its parent organisation reduces the risk of insolvency, as compared with other ways of operating overseas. The activities of the branch are backed by the full resources and stature of the bank. By contrast, possible failure of a subsidiary does not legally require the parent to extend support facilities over and above those encaptured in the shareholder's funds. It may be argued that large multinational banks would feel it necessary to rescue a subsidiary, especially a fully-owned one, to protect the parent's good name. But, as Aronson (1976) points out, support by the parent of a subsidiary in excess of that required by law may invoke legal action from shareholders of the parent company. To this extent, we are left with the Bank of England's view, expressed by the head of Banking Supervision, that although the legal position of foreign subsidiaries and joint ventures is different from that of foreign branches, the parent authorities cannot be indifferent to the 'moral responsibilities' of parent institutions for seeing that their offshoots do not default on their commitments.[9]

A major issue, then, is the question of how the onus for depositor protection is divided between the monetary authorities in the host country and in the parent's home country. Where the host country's authorities take responsibility for protecting depositors with the branch, the host country is indirectly providing support facilities to the parent bank. Since the host country's authorities have no control over the parent's extraterritorial activities (which could endanger the branch's solvency) an asymmetry exists.

It was in order to clarify such matters that a Committee of Group of Ten countries (Belgium, Canada, France, Germany, Italy, Japan, Netherlands, Sweden, United Kingdom, United States) plus Switzerland met in Basle in 1975 under the auspices of the BIS to identify areas of responsibility amongst themselves. Their recommendations have become known as the Basle Concordat.[10] Supervision of liquidity of both forms of foreign offshoot were thought to be the case of the host authority. To the extent that a branch's liquidity cannot be judged in isolation from the whole bank, it was also considered to come within the source authority's sphere of interest. The demarcation for supervision of solvency fell upon the host authorities for subsidiaries and the source authority for branches, as we suggested above.

Some of the ambiguities which remained were revealed all too clearly in 1982 by the strange case of Banco Ambrosiano and its chairman, Mr Robert

Calvi.[11] Banco Ambrosiano was then Italy's eleventh largest bank and the largest private bank and in addition was a multinational banking group with a complex structure. The bank's collapse was precipitated by doubtful loans that its 70 per cent owned subsidiary, Banco Ambrosiano Holdings SA which was a Luxembourg financial holding company, had routed through its Latin American subsidiaries to various Panama companies. The Bank of Italy disclaimed responsibility because BAH was a Luxembourg holding company, not Italian. Luxembourg banking authorities argued that Ambrosiano's holding company was exempt from supervision because it was a non-bank corporation. In 1978 the principle of supervision of a bank's international business on a consolidated basis by source country authorities had been recommended by governors of the G10 central banks. But this was not part of the 1975 Concordat and in any case consolidated supervision could not take place because of secrecy laws in the offshore centres where the holding companies' subsidiaries were located. In the event the Bank of Italy and major Italian banks put together an aid package enabling a new consortium to assume and later liquidate Ambrosiano's assets.

This regulatory mix-up stimulated the revised Concordat of 1983.[12] The revised guidelines are set out in Table 11.2. Whereas under the 1975 Concordat primary responsibility for supervising the solvency of foreign subsidiaries was vested in the host authorities, it became a joint obligation of host and source authorities in the revised format. Subsidiaries thus need to be financially sound in their own right, but by involving the parental authority as well, the Concordat embraced the principle of consolidated supervision. Following the lead from Basle, and also doubtless with the Ambrosiano affair in mind, the Council of the EEC in the same year adopted a Directive on the supervision of banks on a consolidated group basis.

The Netherlands, Switzerland and the UK presently base their prudential supervision on banking groups' consolidated world-wide operations, and all BIS reporting countries supply consolidated statistics for their external position semi-annually to the BIS. But it is probably fair to say that the United States has been the most active in this area: it has developed a

Table 11.2 Areas of Primary Responsibility Recommended by the Basle Committee of Banking Supervisors, 1983

Form of foreign establishment	*Supervision of liquidity*	*Supervision of solvency*
Branch	Host + source authority	Source authority
Subsidiary	Host authority	Host + source authority
Joint venture	Authority in country of incorporation	Authority in country of incorporation

Source: Committee on Banking Regulations and Supervisory Practices (1983).

comprehensive reporting system. The overseas branches of US banks are examined by the Comptroller of the Currency in much the same way as domestic offices (the Comptroller maintains an office in London, with bank examiners). The Federal Reserve Board gathers data and other information about the foreign activities of US banks. Various regulations have restricted member banks' borrowings from foreign branches and lendings by branches to US residents. Applications for the establishment of foreign branches and affiliates are reviewed to ensure that the bank has the managerial resources to carry the risks.

Many important issues were not resolved in the 1983 Concordat. First, secrecy laws in the offshore centres inhibit the application of consolidated supervision. To this end, international banking supervisory conferences are held biennially with over 90 countries attending, including the offshore countries. Second, some institutions continue to fall outside the regulatory net by virtue of being treated as non-banks. Third, actions taken by one authority to tighten the supervisory regime in response to market innovations, like that by the Bank of England to include off-balance sheet exposures from note issuance facilities in capital adequacy assessments (see Chapter 5), may lead to 'regulatory arbitrage'. That is, the provision of the services may be shifted to locations where capital requirements are more lax and to institutions which are less closely monitored.

It was recognition of the need for international harmonisation when bringing about any changes in the regulatory environment which prompted US and British regulators to seek a uniform approach to the treatment of bank capital adequacy in 1986. It happened that the US authorities were in the process of devising a risk-weighted approach to capital requirements at the same time as the Bank of England was discussing with UK banks its proposals of March 1986 about off-balance sheet business.[13] The possibility of convergence was raised in mid-1986 in discussions between the Chairman of the Board of Governors and the Governor of the Bank of England and the idea appealed to both. Officials of the Bank of England then worked with officers of the Federal Reserve, the Office of the Comptroller of the Currency and the FDIC. Despite the different financial systems and regulatory philosophies, a uniform approach was worked out and released for discussion in January 1987.[14]

Basically, as described in Chapter 5 above, the proposal embraces an agreed definition of capital assets, and the use for supervisory purposes of a ratio of capital to assets and off-balance sheet activities both weighted according to a set hierarchy of risks. Risk weights range in five categories from 0–100 per cent. Assets are classified according to maturity and the character of the claim or collateral. Each class of off-balance sheet business is to be marked-to-market, converted into a credit equivalent and then classified according to the maturity and identity of the obligor. No separate distinction is made for country risk which it is proposed will be done on a judgemental basis for each bank. A common minimum ratio so calculated is planned to apply in both the US and UK. However, it is hoped that the proposal will be followed by other countries.

Despite these various initiatives, differences in regulatory treatment across countries are considerable (see Dale 1984, Pecchioli 1983) and seem likely to persist. Even in the case of the United States, where supervision of international banking business is extensive, it is apparent that the supervision is (naturally) affected by the source country's and the parent banks' intersts. For example, Federal Deposit Insurance Corporation premiums need not be paid by US banks on deposits in their branches abroad since these deposits are not insured.[15] Fortunately, because of the close interconnection between external and domestic banking markets, international and national interests often coincide.

A special responsibility rests on the United States because the dollar remains the most important reserve and intervention currency, and is the major currency for trade invoicing and for the international financial market. The great bulk of Eurocurrency business is in US dollars and the Eurodollar market is effectively part of the US banking system, despite the different regulatory treatment. Due to the layering of intermediation, the reserves of the Eurobanks are just deposits at large commercial banks in the US. Minsky (1984) explores the implications:

> The fact that US bank deposits are high powered money for the Eurodollar market makes the banks in which these deposits are held of particular importance for the stability of the world financial structure. The Continental Illinois collapse was triggered when 'withdrawals' of offshore deposits took place. The deposits that 'ran' were de facto reserve deposits of offshore banks that manage a dollar book. The offshore dollar system was at stake in the Federal Reserve intervention in the Continental Illinois case; if the $7 billion of refinancing that Fed provided was not forthcoming the ability to deliver New York dollars for all of the offshore dollar banking system would have been in doubt — and such doubt triggers runs.
>
> Thus the Continental Illinois case shows that in the current structure of financial relations the Federal Reserve is the 'de facto' lender of last resort not for just the United States chartered organisations but for all banks that run dollar denominated books. The Federal Reserve therefore has responsibilities where it does not have control.

For this reason, as well as those noted in Chapter 5, large banks are able to gain *de facto* insurance on the uninsured portion of their deposit structure. In this respect, also, the Eurocurrency system as a whole, or more particularly those banks involved in Eurocurrency operations, are 'free-riding' upon domestic deposit insurance and national 'safety nets'.

Monetary Control

In contrast to some other studies, we argue that Eurobanks do create liquidity when they intermediate between end-suppliers and end-users of funds, providing the former with assets which are much more liquid than those issued by the ultimate borrowers. They intermediate at a global level and thus do so also with respect to liquidity creation, facilitating the process of saving, investment and spending internationally. Under fixed exchange rates, this was thought to expand the 'world money supply' (or its velocity) and increase 'world inflation'. But under floating exchange rates, these concepts have little meaning, yet the connection between Eurocurrencies and national money and inflation is far from simple. Our comments focus upon Eurodollars.

Banks which form the Eurodollar system have only a small independent ability to expand the supply of Eurodollars. It is better to think of them adding, like domestic non-banking intermediaries, an extra layering of intermediation upon the domestic monetary base. Their lending activities absorb little, if any, of the monetary reserves held by domestic banks, so that demand shifts to the market add to the total supply of dollar deposits without contracting domestic deposits. There is not a domestic and external market, but a world dollar banking system. The potential leverage of an expansion of base money is enhanced as a flow of reserves spills over to add to the supply of dollars both domestically and externally. These interconnections were explained in Chapter 9.

However, the extra layering of intermediation which is added by the Eurodollar market has characteristics which make it less amenable to conventional 'money multiplier' analysis. Banks hold 'reserves' against 'deposits', but the reserves are not cash and the deposits are not chequing accounts. Rather, reserves consist of funding options in the interbank and wholesale markets which are held by the banks against the funding options which they themselves issue to depositors. The Eurobanks, like wholesale bankers generally, must have confidence that funds can be commanded, while customers for their part must have confidence that the funds will be commanded. Eurodollars may not be transactions balances themselves, but their ready access via the banking system, high yields and low transactions costs, obviate many of the reasons for holding (as opposed to using) payments media. Balances can be held idle in call or short maturity deposits as a temporary abode of purchasing power until the actual moment that payment is made. Eurodollar deposits are also ideal repositories for the precautionary or speculative balances of corporations.

In terms of the opportunities presented for economising on holdings of the means of payment and for the spreading of liquidity services across a broad spectrum of assets and markets, the Eurocurrency system goes some way towards the hypothetical *laissez-faire* banking world which a number of writers[16] have sketched out. Exactly how the volume of dollar claims represented by the Eurodollar markets is connected to expenditures is to that extent as yet unresolved, but the answer would seem to lie more in the Radcliffe concept of 'general liquidity' than in a transactions-based quantity equation. The Radcliffe Committee in 1959, undoubtedly ahead of its time, emphasised that decisions to spend were influenced not by 'immediately transferable purchasing power' but 'liquidity in the broad sense', that is, the 'amount of money people think they can get hold of'.[17]

There are also ambiguities in determining what part of Eurodollar claims is of importance for domestic as opposed to international spending. The rationale for controlling the money supply lies in the presumption of a close linkage between the aggregate and domestic macroeconomic variables. It is usually thought that Eurodollars due to US residents are unambiguously a substitute for domestic deposits and that they conceptually belong in the monetary aggregate. Not all of those dollars are spent in the US, however. Some will be spent elsewhere reflecting the use of the dollar as the main means of international payment. Foreigners hold US dollars because they wish to buy goods from US firms. They also acquire dollars in an environment in which there is currency substitution for speculative reasons — to diversify portfolios or to take advantage of interest rates or exchange rate developments. A study of the characteristics of the deposits is needed before a decision can be made.

Residents' deposits in foreign currencies could be held for international trade or international investment, with little relationship to developments domestically, or they could be a substitute for domestic currency balances. A Deutschmark deposit and a forward contract to convert that deposit back into dollars is equivalent to a dollar time deposit. A mark deposit held by a US firm, uncovered because the firm is confident that the mark appreciation will exceed the dollar–DM interest rate differential, might also be considered equivalent in terms of the impact upon the firm's spending plans (Goodman 1980). The same questions arise about foreign currency loans to domestic residents. They are, of course, merely implications of increased international integration *per se* which the Eurocurrency markets have enhanced rather than brought about.[18]

Because of these ambiguities, monetary authorities have come to focus more upon interest rates as monetary policy indicators with their control device being open market operations in the domestic currency. In Chapter 9 we explained why arbitrage by both banks and non-banks would keep Eurodollar interest rates closely tied to interest rates in the US for comparable deposits and loans. When interest rates in the US rise, depositors will tend to switch back from Eurocurrency to domestic deposits; borrowers will switch to Eurocurrency loans. Banks themselves will borrow interbank externally to lend domestically. This arbitraging will quickly raise Eurodollar rates until the normal relationship with domestic interest rates is restored. In this way the domestic credit restraint is paralleled in the external markets.

Despite the apparently fast transmission of policy via interest rates, there is still concern about the Eurocurrency markets on the grounds of credit control. The Eurodollar market has some scope for independent credit creation, and links from base money to Eurodollar deposits may be less direct than those to domestic bank deposits. As the Eurodollar segment of the world dollar market grows in size relative to the domestic segment, its contribution to the overall determination of interest rates can be expected to grow commensurately. Evidence has suggested that monetary restraint pinches disproportionately upon domestic dollars *vis-à-vis* Eurodollars and small, local banks *vis-à-vis* large banks involved in Euromarket business.[19]

For these reasons there have been calls from time to time for the imposition of reserve requirements on Eurocurrency deposits. Reserve requirements apply to the net Euro-liability position of banks in the United States, but it has been suggested that they should apply also to non-bank deposits by US residents abroad. In 1979 the Board of Governors of the Federal Reserve System issued a discussion paper[20] to this effect, and in conjunction with the Bundesbank sought the cooperation of other central banks, particularly the Bank of England, for the more general application of reserve requirements. Grounds given for applying controls were the 'misleading signals' induced into monetary aggregates, 'undesired speculative switches between currencies', 'unsound banking practices' due to lesser supervision, and the competitive disadvantage of domestic banks. These have been discussed above. It was recognised that application to Eurodollars alone, or differential rates for different currencies, would be ineffective and would only offer customers a Eurosterling deposit and an accompanying forward exchange contract. Instead, the proposal was for a minimum reserve ratio uniform for Eurocurrency deposits of all denominations, with reserves held in the same currency, encompassing liabilities held at branches, subsidiaries and affiliates wherever located.

This US–German proposal failed to gain support from central banks of other major countries, and especially from the Bank of England. There were a number of reasons. First, the Bank of England argued that the scheme embraced only reserve requirements and ignored other regulatory differences (e.g. interest rate controls) which gave rise to incentives to external intermediation. Second, the scheme was suggested for G10 countries. To the extent that business shifted from London to non-G10 Eurocentres, even more 'unsound banking practices' would occur. Third, there was presumably a measure of national self-interest involved, caused by worries that world financing would shift from London back to New York. Lastly, the Bank was able to argue persuasively that the correct solution was for the US and Germany to reduce the 'heavy-handedness' of their regulation, rather than extend it internationally and interrupt the process of international financial intermediation.

The Bank of England's solution, by and large, is what has occurred. While the US authorities responded to their own bankers' interests by establishing International Banking Facilities, domestic regulation in the US has been lightened. It thus seems appropriate to examine the impact upon the external markets of reduced domestic regulation.

11.2 Future of the Eurocurrency Markets

What might have happened had the Eurocurrency markets not developed? For some transactions, the answer is that there would have been little difference. International trade financing would still have taken place, but at a higher cost and lower volume. Forward covering of foreign exchange transactions can be made in domestic markets, but the cost of forward cover would have been higher, so impeding world trade. To the extent that the markets are substitutes for domestic intermediation, the story is the same as the one which would have been told had domestic non-bank financial intermediaries failed to develop in the early post-war years when banking intermediation was restrained. Presumably, some forms of financing would have been less plentiful and capital formation would have been impeded. Euromarkets also gave US banks a mechanism for indirectly swapping excess reserves. By being deprived of an efficient substitute for the Federal Funds market, US banks would have held larger cash reserves on average, and the money supply and domestic financing supported by the monetary base would have been less.

In the case of the international intermediation carried out by the Eurocurrency markets, the answer is more problematical. Banks have developed a distinctive form of intermediation — wholesale banking — which has been able to respond flexibly to changing financing needs.[21] At the same time, banks subcontract, formally and informally, across the more than 1,000 banks participating in international interbank markets, the liquidity risks and lending risks of massive-sized deposits and loans. We simply do not know whether individual syndications of over 100 banks, individual loans of $6 billion and interbank markets of such breadth and depth would have developed in the context of traditional foreign banking. Rollover credits, flexi-rate lending, wholesale funds markets, floating rate notes, multiple currency loans are examples of innovations which could have occurred domestically, but did not, and are now part of the nuts and bolts of modern banking. Eurobanking gave banks the freedom to innovate and try out new ideas. Yet, given the record of adaptability of banks internationally, there is nothing to suggest that such innovative techniques might not have taken place eventually in New York.

The fact is that the Eurocurrency markets did develop, and their existence puts a different slant upon the question of what might happen if domestic banking in the US, Germany and elsewhere were deregulated further and reserve requirements and other restrictions lifted. Presence of the markets currently provides banks with 'insurance' against (what are to them) excessively harsh economic regulations. Indeed, migration of banking business to the markets has exerted a continuous pressure on authorities to lighten the controls over domestic intermediation. Banks can be expected to maintain a pattern of production internationally which provides them with protection against future, unknown regulatory developments, and this is one reason to expect a continuance of Eurocurrency operations (Niehans 1983). In a similar vein, some Eurocurrency operations can be seen as a form of vertical integration by multinational banks, with the banks ensuring that they are not cut off from future supplies of funds and lending opportunities (Kindleberger 1983a). This is especially the case where markets such as Singapore and Hong Kong give access to regional funding and loan business.

Eurocurrency banking, we have suggested, can also be likened to duty-free shopping. Are duty-free shops located at airports or in city centres? Without freedom from imposts would there be shops at airports? The answer depends on customer convenience and consumer tastes. One of the outstanding achievements of the development of the Eurocurrency markets has been to bring about a separation of currency and location. Prior to their growth, the holdings of a US dollar deposit or the obtaining of a US dollar loan meant, with only minor exceptions, New York or Chicago or another US centre. Getting the currency meant a domestic transaction, and with it US political risk. Now the inconvenience to some customers of a US location has been conquered. A dollar loan can be obtained in London or a dollar deposit held in Singapore, and the convenience and political risk of those places are bought also. In modern banking, then, it is often cheaper to take the service to the customer than the reverse, with the bank bringing about a lowering of customers' access and search costs. A British firm will likely continue to find a dollar loan from London more convenient than one from New York.

European and other centres have already been affected by the development of International Banking Facilities in the United States. In the first six weeks of their operation, IBFs in New York attracted about 5 per cent of the total Eurocurrency business, and all IBFs now account for about 7 per cent of the business. Much international deposit business has shifted back to New York following the reduction in domestic reserve requirements. London is no longer predominant. To give one example, until 1980 banks in Australia arbitraged in terms of Eurodollar deposits in Singapore or London. They are now using US domestic deposits, bills and securities, and a further deregulation in US banking would hasten that transfer. To an increasing extent, London competes for the title of the world's financial capital with Tokyo, as well as New York.

New York and Tokyo are mainly domestic currency 'traditional' centres, gaining much from the strength of their currencies and the financial power of their banks. London is a Eurocentre: a home for banks of all countries. While Eurocurrency centres are located worldwide, redrawing the map of international finance, it is still the case that 'its heart . . . beats . . . in London',[22] which accounts for nearly one third of Eurocurrency business. So far, the return to New York and the rise of Tokyo have bitten more sharply into the business of the 'offshore' centres and other European centres. What is the special attraction of London? Would London survive domestic US and

Japanese deregulation? Again, this is a case where the present siting of business puts a different complexion upon the answer. Banks in international banking provide for liquidity risks by developing 'balance sheet options', relying upon interbank and other wholesale funding specialist markets to raise liquidity when needed. London has the 'deepest' interbank markets and its money market brokers perform an essential role in matching sources and uses of funds. Competition and the size of the London funds markets lead the brokers to quote margins which are competitive by international standards, and this has been one stimulus to the growth of London as a financial centre. Interestingly, the London brokers now play a large role in New York.

Eurocurrency banking is complementary to foreign exchange dealing, spot and forward. London is pre-eminent in foreign exchange, with estimated daily turnover of $90 billion in March 1986, compared with turnover in New York of $50 billion and in Tokyo of $48 billion per day (see Figure 8.1). London is the main centre for international loan syndications, although loans are negotiated also in New York and some other centres. For many borrowers it is the case that Eurobonds, Euronotes and syndicated loans are financing alternatives, and most international banks act as underwriters, arrangers and placers of securities issues as well as providers of Euroloans. Increasingly, US and other firms are issuing commercial paper in the Euromarkets, and secondary markets are developing internationally for mortgage-backed securities and securitised automobile loans. London is the main base for arranging Eurobond placements, organising Euronote facilities, and distributing Eurocommercial paper.

Formation of syndicates — whether for Euroloans, Euronote issuance facilities or the underwriting of Eurobonds — is a business which calls for speed of operation, good legal services, and a combination of face-to-face, telephone and telex contact. London still has the greatest number of overseas banks represented. Legal services are good, and so are communication facilities. Communications must also be simultaneous so as to avoid disrupting the working day of other parties. London's location at zero hours GMT means that its banks are able to communicate with the Far East at the close of the Asian working day and yet overlap for nearly half of a working day with New York. It is one of the most convenient locations for international business. Markets also enable operators to swap opinions and serve an important function in disseminating information about lending risks, evidence of over-trading and other irregularities. But this is a derivative characteristic, where success breeds success. Information will be traded most quickly and efficiently in the centre where the most action takes place.

The 'Euro' securities markets are also to a considerable degree creations of domestic regulation. Cumbersome registration procedures and issuing queues and calendars applied to domestic issues of foreign securities can be avoided, along with withholding taxes on interest receipts. While many of these requirements have been lifted, restrictions still exist on the trading of options and futures in many domestic markets and barriers prevent a full merging of commercial and investment banking in a number of countries. To this extent, the question arises as to the future of these Euromarkets in the face of further domestic de-regulation.

This question has in many ways already been answered, for the removal of restrictions upon domestic capital markets has seen a marked growth of Eurobond activity (see Table 10.5). The reasons are similar to those which continue to propel Eurobanking transactions and stem from the advantages of an international market for finance over domestic ones. Table 10.1 shows marked changes in the current account balances of various countries over the years 1978 to 1986. Even within this short space of time, neither the US, Japan, nor Germany has remained a consistent exporter or importer of capital. Eurobonds, having a truly international market, can be placed in the countries which at the time have the capital to spare. Borrowers can use the currency which suits them best for the purposes of the transactions, and deal with the banks which are the most familiar with their creditworthiness. So long as their choices are valued, there is likely to be a continuing demand for the markets for international finance.

Indeed, it is in the context of the growth of international securities markets that most questions are posed about the future of Eurocurrency and international banking in view of the trend away from traditional bank intermediation towards financing via securities markets. Many wonder whether banks have permanently lost their comparative advantage in financing in favour of direct capital market exchanges (e.g. BIS 1986, p. 237). But some special factors are at work and we look now at the 'securitisation' of bank lending and international finance.

Discussion of the fate of Eurocurrency business, indeed international banking in general, cannot be divorced from current conditions in the markets. Two engines of growth of international banking in the 1970s have gone, and the weight of past behaviour continues to cloud the market's future. Demand for the intermediation services of banks depends both on the underlying distribution of wealth and the liquidity and risk preferences of the wealthholders. During the 1970s both factors favoured bank intermediation. Many commentators (such as Frydl 1982) have depicted the financial behaviour of OPEC countries, especially in the initial years of high surplus, as cautious, with a desire to hold funds in instruments having a high degree of liquidity. Even by 1985, 41 per cent of OPEC countries' stock of overseas investments were held in bank deposits, and only 10 per cent in bonds.[23] At the same time, the desire of developing countries to continue investment programmes by medium-term funding presented the banks with a tailor-made opportunity to intermediate the wealth transfer process.

The pattern of current account deficits and surpluses has altered dramatically in the mid-1980s. For 1986, the US had the largest current account deficit ($141 billion) and the other industrialised countries had in total current account surpluses of $131 billion (see Table 10.1). With Japanese and German lenders preferring to acquire securities and other claims issued directly by the United States, the wealth transfer process has reverted to more 'traditional' channels. Capital flows are running in the main amongst the industrial countries.

Banks were able to sustain international lending during the 1970s by pulling in a steady stream of banks fresh to the international scene. On average about 60 new banks entered international banking every year. The opportunity which was thereby presented for risk spreading kept the margins for risk low. The average spread added to LIBOR in loan costing declined each year from 1975 through 1981. Here again, matters have changed. Bankers have learnt, through experience, the high positive co-variation between some international and domestic loan risks. For the moment, at least, it would seem that the process of international portfolio diversification by banks has run its course. The world has run out of additional banks willing to enter into international loan syndicates. By contrast, there seems to be no shortage of institutional and other investors seeking an internationally-diversified portfolio of good quality bonds and notes. Removal of exchange controls and the liberalisation of capital markets in the UK, Japan and Europe has widened demand, while US corporations and financial institutions have looked to market issues of securities internationally.

Banks' activities may have unwittingly contributed to this trend in a number of ways. As processors of information and organisers of risk-bearing services, banks are vulnerable to developments which lower the costs of transacting and acquiring information. These can erode the boundaries between those activities which are profitably 'internalised' by intermediation as opposed to those which can be 'marketised' by exchanges of securities. There is nothing new in this. Financial intermediaries rely on transactions costs for their existence, yet historically have improved the workings of markets for primary securities. Banking supports an infrastructure of security exchanges, dealers and brokers which reduce the operating costs and risk of banks' portfolios. More so than in domestic intermediation, banks in their international operations have relied upon money and securities markets to develop balance sheet and funding options matching those issued by them to deposit-holders. The switch from official financing to bank and other private financing of balance of payments imbalances has undoubtedly widened the range of internationally transferable private assets. In these ways, international banking has worked against the fragmentation of security markets. Those markets are continuing the process of 'globalisation' begun by the banks 20 or so years ago. By making themselves market-reliant, banks may have rendered themselves market-substitutable.

But it is wrong to see a sharp division between banking and securities markets, for banks complement and assist the workings of securities markets in a number of ways. They provide markets with transactions services and provide loans to the dealers in securities. Markets are ill equipped to handle liquidity strains and much issue of marketable paper is backed by credit lines or back-up liquidity facilities provided by banks. Many firms do not have stand-alone access to securities markets and banks assist them when borrowing from markets by adding their name to the firm's paper. As noted in the previous chapter, a number of innovations in financial instruments have seen securities markets take on some of the character of banking markets.

Indeed, in a number of respects it is a mistake to equate 'securitisation' with 'disintermediation'. Many of the banks' activities allied with securities issues merely shift off-balance sheet the 'insurance' of liquidity needs and credit risks handled before on-balance sheet. Note issuance facilities and discount commitments insure against liquidity risks with the banks agreeing to accept short-term paper from their customers and manage the funding through their ability to rediscount the paper in the market. Banks insure against credit risks by means of bank acceptances and letters of credit. In both cases, banks guarantee payment of a customer's liability to a holder of its debt should the customer default. Interest rate risks can be handled now by interest rate caps and collars rather than by loan contracts.

Use of markets is also a means of separating operations which were previously fully vertically integrated within particular banks, and dividing them up amongst a number of different institutions. Most Euronotes are purchased by banks, although they are often not the underwriting banks. Banks are involved as both issuers and holders of floating rate notes, so that the market for this type of Eurobond has acquired some of the characteristics of an international interbank market. Risks of fixed interest loans can be shifted to other parties by combining a floating rate bank loan with one or more fixed-floating 'swaps'. Accordingly, by means of securitised lending, activities are unbundled, allowing individual banking institutions a better balance of risks, even if they are not disintermediated.

Access to proprietary information and skills in making informed credit judgments are clearly as valuable for securities underwriting, arranging mergers and acquisitions and issuing guarantees as for conventional lending. With interest rate and currency swaps banks often act as counterparties, when arbitrage opportunities arise, or guarantee the performance of other counterparties. Futures and options markets, whether for interest rates or currencies, deal in standardised parcels, often for specified maturities. Banks tailor-make contracts to match customers' own requirements and also perform a size intermediation between retail and wholesale transactions, as in traditional banking.

While the implications of the 'globalisation' of securities market trading are indeed profound, it is also the case that, from a number of viewpoints discussed above, the switch to securitisation has involved less of a change and more of an adaptation by banks to prevailing market conditions. Banks are thus continuing their record of innovation in international finance, noted above, by devising instruments which blur the distinctions between traditional intermediation and securities dealing.

While one might be sanguine about the future of international banking on the score of the banks' adaptability to change, the banks continue to be dogged by the inheritance of their past lending activities. As loan maturities lengthen in consequence of the rescheduling of existing debt, banks have sought to undertake less maturity transformation in new business — making shorter loans and, wherever possible, taking longer deposits. Banking authorities have also been raising capital requirements, further reducing the scope for new lending. The banks' search for off-balance sheet activities has coincided with many customers' preferences. Depositors have undoubtedly revised their perceptions of the relative quality of bank-issued liabilities *vis-à-vis* bonds and notes issued by highly rated government and corporate borrowers. Because of lenders' changed preferences, the banks' best borrowers have found that they can issue bonds, floating rate notes and commercial paper in the international capital markets on better terms than they are able to obtain by bank loans. Table 11.3 shows that, on the BIS measure, new net issues of Eurobonds and traditional foreign bonds during 1984 caught up with new net international bank lending (syndicated and 'unpublicised' credits). During 1985, net bond issues exceeded bank loans; while in 1986, there was approximate equality between the two. In terms of outstanding stocks, however, bank loans are much larger. Because of the longer maturity of syndicated loans, outstanding stocks include a hard core of loans to their 'old' clients, the non-oil exporting developing countries. Thus the immediate future of international banking rests with how banks will be able to handle their existing debt, and we shall now turn to this issue.

11.3 Problems of International Debt

In their international bank operations during the 1970s and early 1980s banks played a major role in on-lending (i.e. 'recycling') the short-term deposits of the oil exporting countries to borrowers around the world. A substantial amount of these funds was lent to developing countries, allowing them to sustain economic development programmes in the face of depressed trading conditions and to purchase imports of oil and other goods well in excess of current export receipts. This was seen as a triumph for the world economy and economic development, as this quotation in 1977 from Mr Witteveen, managing director of the IMF, makes clear:

> By and large these banking systems have done a commendable job in recycling the surpluses of the OPEC countries in a manner which has helped to sustain world trade and economic activity.[24]

But as the debts have accumulated and the difficulties which the countries face in servicing the debts have become evident, opinions have altered.

Table 11.3 Estimated Net Lending in International Markets: Changes in External Claims of Banks and International Bond Issues

	Flows excluding exchange rate effects (US$ bn.)									
	1978	*1979*	*1980*	*1981*	*1982*	*1983*	*1984*	*1985*	*1986*	*Stocks end-1986*
Total international lending of reporting banks	179.7	205.5	241.1	264.8	180.3	105.2	125.4	221.5	476.6	3,221.1
minus : double counting due to redepositing among the reporting banks	89.7	80.5	81.1	99.8	85.3	20.2	40.4	121.5	316.6	1,451.1
A = Net international bank lending	90.0	125.0	160.0	165.0	95.0	85.0	85.0	100.0	160.0	1,770.0
Eurobond and foreign bond issues	37.5	37.3	39.4	49.0	71.7	73.5	107.7	163.6	226.4	n.a.
minus : redemptions and repurchases	8.5	9.3	11.4	12.5	13.2	14.5	23.7	38.6	70.4	n.a.
B = Net international bond financing	29.0	28.0	28.0	36.5	58.5	59.0	84.0	125.0	156.0	700.0
A + B = Total bank and bond financing	119.0	153.0	188.0	201.5	153.5	144.0	169.0	225.0	316.0	2,470.0
minus : double counting	6.0	8.0	8.0	6.5	8.5	14.0	24.0	55.0	76.0	190.0
	113.0	145.0	180.0	195.0	145.0	130.0	145.0	170.0	240.0	2,280.0

Source: Bank for International Settlements, *Annual Report* (various).

Instead, the prospect of endless rescheduling seems to hang like a cloud over the world banking system.

Table 11.4 shows that the problem goes far beyond that of the negotiations between the commercial banks (the so-called 'London club' of banks) and the developing countries. Bank claims and bond holdings, shown in row 1, account for just over half of the outstanding debt at the end of December 1985. Debt owed to the 'Paris club' in the form of official development aid loans and insured or guaranteed export credits, given in rows 2 and 3 of the table, constitutes 25 per cent of total debt. Use of IMF credit and borrowings from the World Bank and other multilateral development banks, shown in rows 4 and 5, represent 13 per cent of indebtedness. These are priority claims which must be met in full. Finally, the remaining 11 per cent of debt comprises other private lending, such as inter-company loans, along with lending by non-Paris club governments sharing the burden of the rescheduling of official debt. Given this distribution of indebtedness, it is not surprising that the official lending bodies, banks and the debtor countries have worked within a cooperative framework to improve the prospects for repayment.

A second feature of the indebtedness of the developing countries is documented in Table 11.5. While the flow of funds to the developing countries is intermediated by banks chartered in many countries, the large commercial banks in the major industrial countries, especially the USA and UK, constitute the prime channel. Banks in the USA, UK, and Germany hold more than 50 per cent of the bank loans of the 25 developing countries shown in the table.[25] Because of this fact, and the extent of official lending, decision-making by parties to the 'London club' negotiations is inevitably fashioned by the wider context. A country contemplating repudiation of bank debt risks having its links severed with the rest of the international financial system. A

Table 11.4 International Debt of Developing and Eastern European Countries, December 1985 ($ billion)

	Developing countries	*Eastern European countries*	*Total*
1. Commercial bank debt	546.3	41.4	587.8
2. Official development assistance debt	74.6	—	74.6
3. Insured or guaranteed export credits	180.7	37.2	217.9
4. IMF loans	34.4	1.8	36.2
5. Loans by multilateral development banks	107.0	1.7	108.7
6. Other government and private lending	111.1	14.6	125.7
TOTAL DEBT	1,054.1	96.7	1,150.8

Source: OECD, *External Debt Statistics,* 1987.

Table 11.5 International Bank Claims on Selected Debtor Countries, End of 1984 (based on residence of borrower, in $bn.)

	BIS reporting banks	*of which:*			
		US banks	*UK banks*	*German banks*	*Other banks*
Argentina	26	8.0 (31)	3.4 (13)	2.4 (9)	12.2 (47)
Brazil	76	23.9 (32)	9.3 (12)	4.8 (6)	37.7 (50)
Chile	14	6.7 (49)	2.1 (15)	0.8 (6)	4.0 (30)
Columbia	7	3.0 (43)	0.8 (11)	0.3 (5)	2.9 (42)
Ecuador	5	2.1 (45)	0.7 (15)	0.3 (6)	1.6 (34)
Mexico	73	26.5 (37)	8.8 (12)	3.5 (5)	34.0 (47)
Peru	6	2.4 (41)	0.7 (12)	0.3 (6)	2.4 (42)
Venezuela	26	10.8 (41)	2.8 (11)	1.9 (7)	10.7 (41)
Subtotal	232	83.4 (36)	28.6 (12)	14.3 (6)	105.5 (46)
Indonesia	14	3.4 (24)	1.5 (11)	1.9 (13)	7.4 (52)
Korea	31	10.0 (32)	2.8 (9)	1.0 (3)	17.1 (56)
Malaysia	11	1.7 (16)	1.7 (15)	0.6 (5)	7.2 (65)
Philippines	14	5.5 (40)	1.7 (12)	0.5 (4)	6.0 (44)
Taiwan	6	2.8 (48)	0.5 (9)	0.5 (8)	2.1 (35)
Thailand	7	2.2 (30)	0.4 (6)	0.4 (6)	4.4 (59)
Subtotal	83	25.6 (31)	8.5 (10)	4.9 (6)	44.2 (53)
Algeria	8	1.0 (13)	0.7 (8)	0.8 (10)	5.6 (70)
Egypt	7	1.3 (18)	0.8 (11)	1.0 (14)	4.0 (57)
Israel	6	2.1 (33)	0.5 (7)	1.6 (26)	2.1 (34)
Morocco	4	0.9 (20)	0.4 (8)	0.5 (10)	2.7 (60)
Nigeria	8	1.5 (19)	2.4 (29)	1.5 (18)	2.7 (33)
Turkey	5	2.1 (40)	0.4 (8)	1.7 (33)	1.0 (20)
Subtotal	39	8.8 (23)	5.0 (13)	7.1 (18)	18.0 (46)
Hungary	7	0.8 (11)	0.8 (12)	1.1 (16)	4.1 (61)
Poland	9	0.7 (8)	1.2 (13)	2.3 (26)	4.9 (54)
Romania	4	0.2 (5)	0.6 (16)	0.3 (9)	2.7 (70)
Soviet Union	16	0.1 (1)	2.3 (14)	3.2 (20)	10.8 (66)
Yugoslavia	10	2.4 (25)	1.7 (18)	1.6 (17)	4.0 (42)
Subtotal	46	4.2 (9)	6.6 (15)	8.5 (19)	26.4 (58)
25 countries	400	121.9 (31)	48.7 (12)	34.9 (9)	194.0 (49)
Other developing and East European countries	99	14.8 (15)	10.8 (11)	7.8 (8)	65.2 (68)
TOTAL	498	136.7 (27)	56.9 (12)	42.7 (9)	259.2 (52)

Source: Morgan Guaranty Trust Co., *World Financial Markets*, July 1985.
Note: Figures in parentheses are the percentage of BIS-reporting banks.

decision about whether to concur with the 'cooperative strategy' necessarily overlaps with those about development assistance, trade policy, technology licensing and military aid. As Sachs (1986) observes: 'a decision by a country unilaterally to suspend its debt repayments is as much a foreign policy decision as a financial one' (p. 411).

With hundreds of banks taking part (600 with Mexico, 800 with Brazil, 450 with Venezuela) negotiations are long, complex and costly. Cooperation of the many different banks has been facilitated by the negotiations of an 'advisory committee' of about 12 leading banks and the IMF, which is stage-managing the debt-adjustment process. Under its Articles of Agreement, the IMF is required to exercise firm surveillance over the exchange rate policies of its members. Since 1977 this surveillance has been based 'against the background of its (a member's) reserve position and its external indebtedness' (Hooke 1982). Almost all commercial bank reschedulings are in conjunction with a programme of economic stabilisation concluded by the IMF with the countries on a case-by-case basis. The IMF assists the debtor countries in preparing the data required for the negotiations, and provides information to both the Paris club and London club creditors. Much of the fresh money provided by commercial banks in the context of rescheduling packages has come about from IMF pressure (Buttner 1985).

Most of the rescheduling which took place in the 1981–1983 period tended to proceed on largely *ad hoc* principles, and was of a bridging form which left both parties in a state of uncertainty. Rescheduling since then has been for longer maturities (10–12 years) with grace periods of up to five years, some in the form of multi-year restructuring agreements (MYRAs).[26] For example, Mexico in 1985 negotiated a settlement which saw loans due 1985–1990 restructured up to the end of the century. Banks have charged a rescheduling fee and market rates of interest to cover the increased risks involved, and spreads over LIBOR or US prime have narrowed considerably from those levied in the initial agreements. For example, rescheduling for Chile in 1983 was at 2⅛ per cent over LIBOR (or 2¼ per cent above US prime), but the arrangement in 1985 was at 1⅜ per cent over LIBOR. The early loans were premised in the hope that three or four years' funding might see the IMF's adjustment programme accomplished and voluntary lending through the bank loan markets recommence. Clearly, the later loans are an admission that a much longer period of adjustment is needed.

It is too early yet to speak of a further phase, but there seems to be increasing doubt expressed about the adequacy of the cooperative strategy. The Chairman of the Board of Governors of the Federal Reserve System gave voice to the unease in June 1986 when he referred to the 'sense of frustration' and the 'sense of fatigue among borrowing countries', and queried the adequacy of the flow of new lending from the private banks. His assessment of the situation echoed that of US Secretary of the Treasury, Mr Baker, whose 1985 'plan' called for an intensification of the existing strategy and a step up in the flow of both private and official lending. Outside of banking and official circles there are many who call for alternative approaches.

Proposals to solve the debt crisis abound, and we cannot survey the literature in full.[27] Table 11.6 summarises some of the ideas, and we focus upon those elements which touch on the themes of bank intermediation with which this book has been concerned. From this perspective we place the various proposals into two groups. First, there are those which focus upon the character of the banks' intermediation and suggest ways to alter it. Banks' intermediation of the development process supplanted 'traditional' channels, namely official aid, lending by the IMF and the World Bank, direct investment and bond issues, and unfavourable comparisons are made with them. At the second level, it might be argued that the scale of lending and the inherent risks are so large — essentially 'uninsurable' — that there is private market failure and a case for intervention by governments. Certainly a number of proposals have envisaged some form of debt forgiveness under government auspices. In 1983, Kenen proposed the establishment of a new public institution which would purchase developing country debt at a discount from the banks, and manage repayment at the written down value. The

Table 11.6 Various Proposals for Aiding the International Debt Problem

I. MULTILATERAL GOVERNMENT ACTION
International organisation to buy bank debt
Establish international lender of last resort
II. CREDITOR GOVERNMENT ACTIONS
Reduce trade barriers
Reduce market interest rates
Insulate debtor nations from interest rate increases
Give financial aid
III. DEBTOR GOVERNMENT ACTIONS
Implement IMF adjustment programme
Reduce restrictions on direct investment
IV. BANKS' ACCEPTANCE OF OR PREPARATION FOR LOSS
Reduce interest rates or cancel part of principal
Write off debt or add to loan loss reserves to reduce dividends
V. DEBT RESTRUCTURING
Interest rate caps
Multi-year rescheduling
More generous repayment stretchouts and grace periods
Graduated repayments
Repayment based on export earnings
Convert debt to long-term bonds
VI. DEBT CONVERSION
Convert debt to equity

Source: Based on Anderson (1985)

Bradley plan of 1986 envisaged debt relief allied with economic policy reforms on a case-by-case basis.[28]

Looking first at bank intermediation, one set of arguments views it as inappropriate to the financing needs of developing countries because of the *way* intermediation occurs, the other because it *is* intermediated. Banks' loan contracts are seen to be of an insufficiently long maturity. Many of the suggestions noted in Table 11.6 such as multi-year scheduling, more generous repayment stretchouts and grace periods, and graduated repayment have now been encompassed in recent restructuring packages. These packages still incorporate risk-sharing features which many consider to be unfavourable to the borrowing countries,[29] especially the shifting of interest rate risks by the banks to the borrowing countries. Not all risks are transferred: banks bear interest cost increases within interest rate adjustment periods; they bear the risk of funding markets drying up at rollover dates; and they bear the ultimate credit risk should the borrower be unable to pay the interest cost which is passed on. Lessard (1983) argues that debt service patterns vary perversely with developing countries' foreign exchange earnings, increases in interest rates coinciding with reduced export prospects. Loan contracts with interest rate caps are widely used domestically in the US. These are employed to insure mortgage borrowers against large interest rate changes: the usual arrangement is to limit interest rate adjustments to 5 percentage points over the lifetime of a loan and to one adjustment of no more than 2 percentage points in any year. Such contracts have not been written for the foreign loans taken out by the developing countries. Most observers in any case see interest rate caps as merely a palliative. What is really needed are repayment schedules (interest plus principal) tied to national wealth or export earnings. This is the basis of the unilateral action taken by Peru in 1986 to limit its debt servicing to 10 per cent of exports.

Intermediation *per se* is thought to be inappropriate because of the risk of default by one or more countries and the concentration of that risk in a few key large banks. At the end of 1982, loans to Argentina, Brazil, Mexico, Venezuela and Chile stood at 175 per cent of Citibank's capital, 158 per cent of Bank of America's capital, 154 per cent of Chase Manhattan's capital and 263 per cent of Manufacturers Hanover's capital base (Cline 1983). Bank capital positions have strengthened considerably since then, and at September 1986, the outstanding loans to those countries range from 80 to 126 per cent of capital for the four banks mentioned. Exposures of this magnitude could still lead to instability and deposit runs should there be even a rumour of a default. Accordingly, there have been calls to establish an international lender of last resort or to form an international deposit insurance system[30] to shore up the international banking system.

Much of this argument overlooks that the world financial system has changed greatly since 1971. There is no longer a gold standard and the risk of a multiple contraction of bank deposits. Rather, the present international monetary 'non-system', as Williamson (1983) calls it, is one of inconvertible money balances, made so by the removal of gold convertibility. A switch to gold can no longer destroy bank deposits; it alters the price of gold instead. Nor is it likely that depositors would want to shift into non-interest-bearing cash. If they did so, the Federal Reserve or any other central bank could offset the reserve loss by expanding the supply of currency. A switch from Eurobanks to domestic banks would also achieve little, since the two classes of bank are most often the same institution. In that respect the Eurobanks are already backed, albeit indirectly, by central banks: although if liquidity support is provided in foreign currency there would be exchange rate problems for the central banks concerned. There might be a switch from 'risky' to 'safe' banks, but the ensuing deposit switches could, in principle at least, be recycled as in the British 'lifeboat' of 1974. This is not to say that a run provoked by international lending risks would not lead to substantial problems. But the consequences are most likely to be a write-down of banks' equity capital; a higher risk premium on banking intermediation; and 'adverse selection' as the best lending risks shift away from banks to bond and securities markets, leaving banks holding the worst loans. These are consequences which already confront the banks.

A switch from bank loans to financing via bond markets merely worsens the position of banks without improving that of the developing countries, since the problem debtors do not have access to the Eurobond markets and are no longer issuers of international bonds. An unfavourable comparison is often made between bank intermediation and bond financing by reference to the nineteenth century. It is said that delayed interest payments merely resulted in the write-down of bond prices, and that losses from debt repudiation wiped out many individual private investors without endangering the system as a whole. In fact, as Arndt and Drake (1985) document, the nineteenth century experience shows a mixture of outcomes. Bonds from colonies or Dominions were issued with explicit mother country government protection, while others had performance guaranteed by British 'gunboat' diplomacy. Interest and principal were sometimes rescheduled ('deferred' in the parlance of the time), while new loans were occasionally floated to allow interest servicing to continue. Generally it was the case that losses were borne by bondholders and not by banks nor the community at large, although the Baring crisis of 1890 and the Bank of England's lifeboat rescue at that time of several merchant banks provide a counter-example.

In terms of the capacity to bear risks, it is difficult, also, to accept the idea that the world financial system would have been better off had development programmes and payments imbalances of the scale experienced in the 1970s been financed by bond issues rather than by bank loans. Syndication of loans, formally and informally, spread across more than 1,000 banks, would seem to offer a more than adequate potential for risk sharing. If there are unexploited avenues for further risk spreading from portfolio diversification, the answer would lie in the repackaging and resale of loan participations for other institutions to hold: an idea which so far has failed to attract much interest.

How matters would have fared had there been direct investment by multinationals instead of bank financing of the investment programmes seems a more appealing line of enquiry. The case would rest in part on the allocative superiority of the internal capital markets operated by multinationals over those operated externally by banks and other institutions: markets which are perhaps less prone to the 'herd instinct' which seems to grip bankers. But the case rests mainly on the opportunity which would have been presented for risk sharing by means of equity participations instead of loans. Equity claims allow the possibility for repayments to be accelerated and deferred in line with earnings and other such variables directly related to the countries' capacity to repay. With bank loans, repayments have depended more upon variations in US monetary policy which raise LIBOR and thus the interest cost.

Nor is the possible superiority of equity finance over bank loans purely a matter for conjecture. A number of schemes are being implemented to convert foreign currency debt of the developing countries into local equity capital.[31] But these programmes are still in their infancy and, for better or worse, the developing countries chose bank financing in the 1970s. They did so because they wanted to retain nominal autonomy over their own development programmes. Whether in retrospect those countries would prefer management by multinationals to orchestration by the IMF is a question that others might want to ponder.

Also interesting is the idea that lending to the developing countries is an activity inappropriate to the private sector. The banks' method of handling the loan risks essentially followed the method used in international insurance markets, involving the equivalent of reinsurance arrangements to spread the risks as widely as possible around the globe amongst participating firms. But risk spreading only works for risks which are capable of being diversified. From the viewpoint of society, these are small, independent risks. Even if risks are somewhat interdependent, having a large number buy shares of the risk is usually adequate. But for 'social risks', risks which derive from a change in the state of nature or state of the world, these risk-spreading techniques do not help. They do not help because losses are interdependent: there is a large, undiversifiable background risk common to all participations which cannot be diversified away.[32]

Such risks are well known to insurers. Economic depression, unemployment, natural disasters and war are examples of cases where risks have a large accumulation hazard, and insurers refuse to underwrite many such risks. Take the case of insuring against the effect of economic depressions. The onset of a depression would see a conjunction of large, persistent losses. Insurance cover provided by means of the 'reserves principle' would require a thick reserve holding by the underwriting companies. Once losses were paid out, attempts to rebuild reserves by raising premiums would see 'adverse selection' set in, that is, the good 'depression risks' would leave the pool and self-insure. Attempts to insure by means of the 'mutuality principle' (Marshall 1974) by writing indemnity contracts, whereby the gainer compensates the loser, would be confounded by moral hazard (individuals putting themselves into the position of being losers).

All these hazards of insuring social risks may be seen to apply to loans made by banks by developing countries. Problems arose because of a change in the 'state of the world' as the worldwide economic decline took hold and the non-oil developing countries were affected most by the oil price movements and rising interest rates. While in principle the existence of mutual indemnity contracts ought to be possible (oil importers and oil exporters agreeing to share losses and gains from oil prices and changes in economic fortunes), the costs involved in designing contracts and policing the extensive potential to 'moral hazards' make it unlikely that they would actually be written.

The banks' holdings of capital reserves have not been 'thick' in comparison with exposures. (Loans outstanding to oil importing developing countries by the 204 US banks substantially involved in international lending represented over 200 per cent of lending banks' capital at the end of 1981.)[33] International banking has tended to be carried out under conditions of 'utmost faith', and the many small banks needed for enhanced risk spreading tended, when buying participations, to rely on the country risk assessment of the syndicate leaders and correspondent banks. As concern about capital adequacy and perceived credit risks has grown, many banks (US-owned banks in particular) have curtailed the extent of their interbank activity and are monitoring ongoing exposures more carefully, adding to costs of 'traditional' international bank deposit and lending business. Banks' move off-balance sheet has matched in with many customers' preferences, and prime banking business has returned to securities markets. 'Adverse selection' has occurred.

The analogy with insurance is an apt one in another respect. Insurers *do* underwrite natural disasters. They face swingeing losses should there be a repetition of the San Francisco earthquake of 1906 or the Tokyo earthquake of 1923. In such events there is the expectation of supportive action and responsibility for compensation by governments, acting as insurers of last resort. Insurers anticipate that, in the event of an occurrence or series of occurrences of great devastation, bringing about the financial ruin of many national and international insurers, it would be socially and economically necessary for governments to provide support for reconstruction by means of standby loans. Solvency requirements might need to be waived temporarily. Governments might need to help insurers to dispose of their assets at reasonable prices.[34]

As we have noted, many argue that the same is true of banking today: that one answer is for governments and multilateral organisations such as the World Bank and IMF to step in and, by cofinancing with the banks and refinancing their loans, give more aid in the reconstruction process. There is undoubtedly much potential for 'moral hazards' in such a course. Future borrowers may be induced to undertake policies which lead to debt relief. Banks may interpret assistance as an underwriting of future loan risks. But there are risks in present arrangements: that the rush into prime paper internationally will continue and that banks will be more cautious in new loans and less generous in repayment provisions than is desirable for world development and political stability.

Continuing the analogy with insurance, the insurance industry has experienced difficulties in handling 'wholesale' insurance, and underwriting results in the 1980s have greatly deteriorated, especially in reinsurance. Insurers have not found it easy to determine the premia appropriate when providing insurance cover for large aeroplanes, supertankers, space satellites, advanced medical and bio-technology. They have learnt from experience that the reinsurance arrangements needed for the underwriting of large risks give rise to problems of collective risk. When risks are shared and subcontracted, overall exposure for the system as a whole is not easy to assess for an individual underwriter or reinsurance participant. Risk limits and exposure limits, like credit limits in interbank markets, are a help, yet international insurance has been prone to cycles of competitive rate cutting and of optimism and pessimism.

Such 'professional sinning' was also rife in international banking. Bankers undoubtedly overlent and followed the herd. Many banks failed to apply to participations the standards followed for ordinary loans, and risks were underrated. Information transmission in international banking was poor, and many of the participating banks ignored the evidence of a growing overall loan exposure to the developing countries. Why they did so remains an open question. Perhaps the passage of time had dulled bankers to the possibility of a worldwide financial disaster, or they thought themselves to be adequately diversified against risks, or they were driven on by competitive pressures, or they believed that the IMF or central banks would ultimately bale them out, or they simply thought that lending to governments must be secure.[35] Perhaps some mixture of all of these played a part.

Whatever the explanation, bankers did fill a void in international financing by lending to developed countries on scales which were beyond the capacity of the official institutions and the willingness of national governments to undertake. 'Recycling' was a considerable achievement. Continuance of lending to the developing countries into the early 1980s sustained growth in the world economy (Houthakker 1984). However, recovery, and thus repayment of the debt, is not just a matter between banks and the borrower countries under the aegis of the IMF. It rests much on the achievement of sustained and non-inflationary economic growth in the industrial countries, and to actions taken by governments to reduce protectionism and expand trading opportunities for developing countries.

Unwillingly, perhaps, banks both individually and collectively now have a direct pecuniary stake in the economic viability of the developing countries. By proxy, so do the citizens of their home countries as depositors, shareholders of banks, or taxpayers. That is a new development, and a not unencouraging one for world progress.

Notes

1. For a fuller examination of many of the issues discussed here the reader is referred to Davis and Lewis (1982c).
2. See Chapter 9 section 5 for a discussion of the 'satellite' Eurocurrency banking markets.
3. Kouri and Porter (1974), Kouri (1976), and especially Herring and Marston (1977).
4. This conclusion is based upon research work undertaken by the International Division, Bank of England. Aspects are reported in Johnston (1979) and in an unpublished paper by Howson (1980). See also Davis and Lewis (1982c).
5. See McKinnon (1979, Chapter 11) and Tew (1977, Chapter 15).
6. The fourway equivalence 'theorems' are set out in Buckley (1986, Ch. 5).
7. Dornbusch (1976) argued that exchange rates overshoot to compensate for sluggish domestic wage and price movements. McKinnon (1984b) argues that exchange rates overshoot also to compensate for inflexible domestic interest rates.
8. The different forms of incorporation and the extent of prudential supervision over foreign establishments are examined in Pecchioli (1983).
9. *Bank of England Quarterly Bulletin*, 1977, p. 325.
10. Committee on Banking Regulations and Supervisory Practices (1975).
11. Mr Calvi was known as 'God's banker' because of connections between Ambrosiano and the Vatican bank, and he was found dead hanging from a London bridge, apparently due to foul play. See Branch and Stigum (1983) for an account.
12. Committee on Banking Regulations and Supervisory Practices (1983).
13. This paragraph relies heavily upon Coppel (1987).
14. Agreed proposal of the United States Federal Banking Supervisory Authorities and the Bank of England on primary capital and capital adequacy assessment, *Bank of England Quarterly Bulletin,* February 1987.
15. In view of the *de facto* insurance provided, this policy is under review.
16. For example, Black (1970).
17. Radcliffe Committee (1959), para. 390.
18. Implications of international integration are examined in Lindbeck (1978). The problems of defining money in an open economy are covered in Bryant (1980).
19. Brimmer (1973) and Wallich (1979).
20. Federal Reserve Board Staff (1979).
21. The inherent adaptability of international intermediation is stressed by Llewellyn (1985b).
22. Kindleberger (1974) p. 4.
23. *Amex Bank Review*, Vol. 13, No. 4. April 1986, p. 3.
24. Quoted in Lever and Huhne (1985).

25. Japanese banks do not provide details publicly as to their country exposure in lending.
26. Rescheduling and restructuring packages from 1978 to 1985 are documented and reviewed in Watson, Mathieson, Kincaid and Kalter (1986).
27. For recent surveys of the major issues, see Cline (1983), and Guttentag and Herring (1985).
28. This proposal by Senator Bradley of New Jersey is discussed by Sachs (1986) and Dornbusch (1987).
29. See Lessard (1983), and Colaco (1985).
30. Grubel (1979) and Guttentag and Herring (1983). There is an excellent balanced survey of the major issues in Cline (1983).
31. These schemes allow multinational companies to purchase debt from the banks at a discount which can then be swapped, at terms favourable to the debtor country, into equity investments in the country concerned. See *Euromoney*, August 1986, pp. 67–75.
32. Brainard and Dolbear (1971).
33. Brimmer (1985).
34. The expectation of government support is clearly expressed by Allison (1983) and Berliner (1982).
35. Disaster myopia is argued by Guttentag and Herring (1986), competitive pressures by Emminger (1985). The adequacy of diversification and the idea that sovereign lending must be safe is associated with Walter Wriston of Citicorp, cited in Sampson (1981) and Lever and Huhne (1985).

Bibliography

Aliber, R.Z. (1977) 'Discussion' in *Key Issues in International Banking*, Proceedings of a Conference, Federal Reserve Bank of Boston Conference Series No. 18: 45–50.

Aliber, R.Z. (1980) 'The integration of the offshore and domestic banking system', *Journal of Monetary Economics*, October: 509–526.

Aliber, R.Z. (1984) 'International banking: a survey', *Journal of Money Credit and Banking*, November, 16(4) Pt 2: 661–678.

Allen, L. and Saunders, A. (1986) 'The large–small bank dichotomy in the Federal Funds market', *Journal of Banking and Finance,* Vol. 10, No. 2, June: 169–325.

Allison, J. (1983) 'Catastrophes and their insurability', *Insurance and Natural Disaster Management*, Centre for Disaster Studies, James Cook University, Queensland: 12–48.

Anderson, G.H. (1985) 'Solutions to the international debt problem', *Economic Commentary*, Federal Reserve Bank of Cleveland, August.

Andersson, B.C. and Engrall, C. (1984) 'Financial planning and control in some Swedish multinational corporations', Stockholm School of Economics, Research Paper 6289, June.

Andrews, M.D. (1984) 'Recent trends in the US foreign exchange market', Federal Reserve Bank of New York, *Quarterly Review*, Summer, 9(2): 38–47.

Argy, V. (1981) *The Postwar International Money Crisis — An Analysis*, George Allen & Unwin.

Argy, V. (1983) 'The growth of international debt (1973–1982): a review of the issues', Centre for Studies in Money, Banking and Finance, Working Paper 8312, October.

Argy, V. and Porter, M.G. (1972) 'The forward exchange market and the effects of domestic and external disturbances under alternative exchange rate systems', *International Monetary Fund Staff Papers*, November.

Arndt, H.W. (1984) 'Measuring trade in financial services', *Banca Nazionale del Lavoro Quarterly Review*, June, 149: 197–213.

Arndt, H.W. and Drake, P.J. (1985) 'Bank loans or bonds: some lessons of historical experience', *Banca Nazionale del Lavoro Quarterly Review*, June, 155: 373–392.

Aronson, J.D. (1976) 'Politics and the international consortium banks', *Stanford Journal of International Studies*, Spring.

Arrow, K.J. (1970) *Essays in the Theory of Risk-Bearing*, North-Holland.

Arrow, K.J. and Debreu, G. (1954) 'Existence of equilibrium for a competitive economy', *Econometrica*, 22: 265–290.

Arrow, K.J. and Hahn, F.H. (1971) *General Competitive Analysis*, Holden Day Inc., San Francisco.

Artis, M.J. and Lewis, M.K. (1981) *Monetary Control in the United Kingdom*, Philip Allan.

Arvan, L. and Brueckner, J.K. (1985) 'Efficient contracts in credit markets subject to interest rate risk: an application of Raviv's Insurance Model', BEBR Working Paper 1136, University of Illinois, Urbana-Champaign.

Bain, A.D. (1981) *The Economics of the Financial System*, Martin Robertson.

Baltensperger, E. (1972) 'Economies of scale, firm size and concentration in banking', *Journal of Money, Credit and Banking*, 4(3): 467–488.

Baltensperger, E. (1980) 'Alternative approaches to the theory of the banking firm', *Journal of Monetary Economics*, January, 6: 1–37.

Bank for International Settlements (1986a) 'The management of banks' off-balance sheet exposures: a supervisory perspective', Committee on Banking Regulations and Supervisory Practices, March.

Bank for International Settlements (1986b) *Recent Innovations in International Banking*, Basle.

Bank of England (1980a) 'The measurement of capital', *Bank of England Quarterly Bulletin*, September, 20(3): 324–330.

Bank of England (1980b) 'The foreign exchange market in London', *Bank of England Quarterly Bulletin*, December, 20(4): 437–444.

Bank of England (1986) 'Consolidated supervision of institutions authorised under the Banking Act, 1979', *Quarterly Bulletin*, March, 26(1): 85–90.

Bankers Clearing House (1984) *Payment Clearing Systems: Review of Organisation, Membership and Control*, Banking Information Service, London.

Bell, G. and Rutledge, G. (1984) 'How to account for problem loans', *Euromoney*, January: 43–46.

Benston, G.J. (1983) 'Deposit insurance and bank failures', Federal Reserve Bank of Atlanta, *Economic Review*, March.

Benston, G.J. (1984) *Financial Services: The Changing Institutions and Government Policy*, American Assembly, Prentice-Hall.

Benston, G.J., Hanweck, G.A. and Humphrey, D.B. (1982) 'Scale economies in banking: a restructuring and reassessment', *Journal of Money, Credit and Banking*, November, 14: 435–456.

Benston, G.J. and Kaufman, G.C. (1986) 'Risks and failures in banking: overview, history and evaluation', *Staff Memoranda* 86–1, Federal Reserve Bank of Chicago.

Benston, G.J. and Smith, C.W. (1976) 'A transactions cost approach to theory of financial intermediation', *Journal of Finance*, May, 31: 215–231.

Bergendahl, G. (1985) *The Euromarket and OPEC Oil Revenues: A Study of Banking Intermediation*, Oxford Institute for Energy Studies.

Berliner, B. (1982) *Limits of Insurability of Risks*, Prentice-Hall.

Bernanke, B.S. (1983) 'Nonmonetary effects of the financial crisis in the propagation of the Great Depression', *American Economic Review*, June, 73(3): 257–276.

Bernanke, B. and Gertler, M. (1986) 'Banking and general equilibrium', Discussion Paper No. 108, Woodrow Wilson School of Public and International Affairs, Princeton University.

Betancourt, R. and Gautschi, D. (1986) 'The economics of retail firms', Working Research Paper No. 86/12, European Institute of Business Administration, Fontainebleau.

Bhagwati, J. (1986) 'Trade in services and developing countries', Discussion Paper No. 307, Columbia University.

Binks, M.R. and Coyne, J. (1986) 'Entrepreneurial finance for small business', Ch. 9 in R.L. Carter, B. Chiplin and M.K. Lewis (eds) *Personal Financial Markets*, Philip Allan.

Black, F. (1970) 'Banking and interest rates in a world without money', *Journal of Bank Research*, Autumn, 1(3): 8–28.

Black, F. (1975) 'Bank funds management in an efficient market', *Journal of Financial Economics*, 2: 323–339.

Board of Governors of the Federal Reserve System (1984) *The Federal Reserve System: Purpose and Functions*, Seventh Edition, Washington D.C.

Bond, I.D. (1985) 'The syndicated credits market', Bank of England Discussion Paper 22, March.

Born, K.E. (1983) *International Banking in the 19th and 20th Centuries*, Berg Publishers, Leamington Spa.

Brainard, W. and Dolbear, F.T. (1971) 'Social risk and financial markets', *American Economic Review*, May: 360–370.

Branson, W.H. (1969) 'The minimum covered interest differential needed for international arbitrage activity', *Journal of Political Economy*, December, 77(6): 1028–1035.

Branson, W.H. (1977) 'Asset markets and relative prices in exchange rate determination', *Sozialwissenschaftliche Annalen*, Vol. 1.

Brimmer, A.F. (1973) 'Multinational banks and the management of monetary policy in the United States', *Journal of Finance*, March: 439–462.

Brimmer, A.F. (1985) *The World Banking System: Outlook in a Context of Crisis*, New York University Press.

Bryant, R.C. (1980) *Money and Monetary Policy in Interdependent Nations*, The Brookings Institution, Washington, D.C.

Bryant, R.C. (1981) 'Bank collapse and depression', *Journal of Money, Credit and Banking*, November, 13(4): 454–464.

Buckley, A. (1986) *Multinational Finance*, Philip Allan.

Buckley, P.J. and Mirza, H. (1985) 'The wit and wisdom of Japanese management: an iconoclastic analysis', *Management International Review*, Vol. 25, No. 3: 16–32.

Budzeika, G. (1980) 'The effect of liability management by banks on their lending policies', 'Federal Reserve Bank of New York Research Paper 8007.

Burns, J.M. (1971) 'On the effects of financial innovations', *Quarterly Review of Economics and Business*, 11(2): 83–95.

Burns, J.M. (1979) *A Treatise on Markets*, American Enterprise Institute Studies in Economic Policy, Washington, D.C.

Buser, S.A., Chen, A.H. and Kane, E.J. (1981) 'Federal deposit insurance, regulation policy, and optimal bank capital', *Journal of Finance*, March, 36: 51–60.

Buttner, V. (1985) 'The IMF's adjustment concept — a strategy for a permanent solution in the debt crisis?' *Intereconomics*, Vol. 20, No. 4: 168–173.

Callier, P. (1986) '"Professional Trading", exchange rate risk and the growth of international banking: a note', *Banca Nazionale del Lavoro Quarterly Review*, December, 159: 423–428.

Carli, G. (1971) 'Eurodollars: a paper pyramid', *Banca Nazionale del Lavoro Quarterly Review*, June, 97: 95–109.

Carroll, E., Kalambokidis, N.A. and Kise, J.A.G. (1986) 'Deposit insurance, capital regulation, and bank risk', *Proceedings of a Conference on Bank Structure and Competition*, Federal Reserve Bank of Chicago: 287–310.

Carron, A.S. (1982) *The Plight of the Thrift Institutions*, The Brookings Institution, Washington, D.C.

Carron, A.S. (1984) 'The structure of financial regulation', *Proceedings of a Conference on Bank Structure and Competition*, Federal Reserve Bank of Chicago.

Carter, R.L. (1979) *Reinsurance*, Kluwer Publishing.

Carter, R.L., Chiplin, B. and Lewis, M.K. (1986) *Personal Financial Markets*, Philip Allan.

Caves, R.E. (1977) 'Discussion' in *Key Issues in International Banking*, Proceedings of a Conference, Federal Reserve Bank of Boston, Conference Series No. 18.

Channon, D.F (1986) *Bank Strategic Management and Marketing*, John Wiley.

Chessen, J. (1986) 'Off-balance sheet activity: a growing concern?' *Proceedings of a Conference on Bank Structure and Competition*, Federal Reserve Bank of Chicago.

Chiplin, B. (1986) 'Information technology and personal financial services',

Ch. 4 in R.L. Carter, B. Chiplin and M.K. Lewis (eds) *Personal Financial Markets*, Philip Allan.

Chrystal, A. (1984a) 'A guide to foreign exchange markets', Federal Reserve Bank of St Louis, *Review*, March, 66(3): 5–18.

Chrystal, A. (1984b) 'International Banking Facilities', *Federal Reserve Bank of St Louis Review*, April, 66(4): 5–11.

Clarke, S.V.O. (1983) *American Banks in the International Interbank Market*, Salomon Brothers Center for the Study of Financial Institutions, Monograph Series in Finance and Economics, No. 4.

Cleveland, H. van B. and Huertas, T.F. (1985) *Citibank 1918–1970,* Harvard University Press.

Cline, W.R. (1983) *International Debt and the Stability of the World Economy*, Institute for International Economics, MIT Press.

Close, R.O. (1987) 'Some aspects of the Treasury function in a UK clearing bank', in J.S.G. Wilson (ed.) *The Management of Bank Assets and Liabilities*, Euromoney Publications, London.

Coase, R.H. (1937) 'The nature of the firm', *Economica*, New Series 4: 386–405.

Colaco, F. (1985) 'International capital flows and economic development', *Finance and Development*, September, 22(3): 2–6.

Committee on Banking Regulations and Supervisory Practices (1975) 'Principles for the supervision of banks' foreign establishments' (The Basle Concordat), Basle, February.

Committee on Banking Regulations and Supervisory Practices (1983) 'Principles for the supervision of banks' foreign establishments' (The Revised Basle Concordat), Basle, May.

Comotto, R.D. (1986) 'The market in foreign exchange in London', *Bank of England Quarterly Bulletin*, September: 379–382.

Cook, C. and Wroughton, J. (1980) *English Historical Facts 1603–1688*, Macmillan.

Cooper, J. (1984) *The Management and Regulation of Banks*, Macmillan.

Coppel, J.V. (1987) 'The international harmonisation of banking supervision', LSE Seminar on Regulation of Financial Services, February.

Corrigan. E.G. (1982) 'Are banks special?' *Annual Report*, Federal Reserve Bank of Minneapolis.

Corrigan, E.G. (1986) 'Financial market structure: a longer view', *Seventy-second Annual Report*, Federal Reserve Bank of New York.

Coulbeck, N. (1984) *The Multinational Banking Industry*, Croom Helm.

Courtadon, C.L. (1985) 'The competitive structure of the Eurobond underwriting industry', Monograph Series in Finance and Economics, No. 1, New York University.

Covick, O.E. and Lewis, M.K. (1985) 'Insurance institutions' in M.K. Lewis and R.H. Wallace (eds.) *Australia's Financial Institutions and Markets*, Longman Cheshire, Melbourne: 187–246.

Crouhy, M. and Galai, D. (1986) 'An economic assessment of capital requirements in the banking industry', *Journal of Banking and Finance*, June, 10(2): 231–241.

Dacey, W. Manning (1951) *The British Banking Mechanism*, Hutchinson.

Dale, R. (1984) *The Regulation of International Banking*, Woodhead-Faulkner.

Darby, M.R. (1985) 'The internationalization of American banking and finance: structure, risk, and world interest rates', Discussion Paper No. 62, University of Hong Kong.

Das, S. (1986) 'The evolution of swp financing as an instrument of international finance', *Bulletin of Money, Banking and Finance*, No. 2, Macquarie University: 1–68.

Davis, K.T. (1985) 'Australian monetary policy: recent experience and some current issues', *Australian Economic Review*, 4:37–50.

Davis, K.T. (1986) 'Financial deregulation and the measurement of bank output', University of Virginia, mimeo.

Davis, K.T. and Lewis, M.K. (1980) *Monetary Policy in Australia*, Longman Cheshire, Melbourne.

Davis, K.T. and Lewis, M.K. (1982a) 'Can monetary policy work in a deregulated capital market?', *The Australian Economic Review*, 57, First Quarter: 9–21.

Davis, K.T. and Lewis, M.K. (1982b) 'Economies of scale in financial institutions', *Australian Financial System Inquiry, Commissioned Studies and Selected Papers, Part I*, Australian Government Publishing Service, Canberra.

Davis, K.T. and Lewis, M.K. (1982c) 'Foreign banks and the financial system', *Australian Financial System Inquiry, Commissioned Studies and Selected Papers, Part I*, Australian Government Publishing Service, Canberra.

Davis, S.J. (1976) *The Euro-bank*, Macmillan.

Dennis, G.E.J. (1984) *International Financial Flows: A Statistical Handbook*, Graham and Trotman Ltd, London.

de Roover, R. (1963) *The Rise and Decline of the Medici Bank 1397–1494*, Harvard University Press.

DeVany, A.S. (1984) 'Comment', *Journal of Money, Credit and Banking*, November, 16(4), Pt. 2: 603–609.

Deshmukh, S.D., Greenbaum, S.I. and Kanatas, G. (1983) 'Banks' forward lending in alternative funding environments', *The Journal of Finance*, September, 37(4): 925–940.

Diamond, D. (1984) 'Financial intermediation and delegated monitoring', *Review of Economic Studies*, July, 51: 393–414.

Diamond, D.W. and Dybvig, P.H. (1983) 'Bank runs, deposit insurance and liquidity', *Journal of Political Economy*, 91(3): 401–419.

Donaldson, T.H. (1979) *Lending in International Commercial Banking*, Macmillan.

Dornbusch, R. (1976) 'Expectations and exchange rate dynamics', *Journal of Political Economy*, December, 84(6): 1161–1176.

Dornbusch, R. (1987); 'International debt and economic stability', *Economic Review*, Federal Reserve Bank of Kansas City, January: 15–32.

Dothen, U. and Williams, J. (1980) 'Banks, bankruptcy, and public regulation', *Journal of Banking and Finance*, March, 4: 65–87.

Dufey, G. and Giddy, I.H. (1978) *The International Money Market*, Prentice-Hall.

Dunning, J.H. (1981) *International Production and the Multinational Enterprise*, Allen and Unwin.

Dunning, J.H. and Norman, G. (1986) 'The location choice of offices of international companies', Discussion Paper No. 53, University of Leicester.

Economists Advisory Group (1984) *City 2000: The Future of London as an International Financial Centre*, Lafferty Publications, London.

Edgeworth, F.V. (1888) 'The mathematical theory of banking', *Journal of the Royal Statistical Society*, 51: 113–127.

Edmister, R.O. (1986) *Financial Institutions: Markets and Management*, Second Edition, McGraw-Hill.

Eichengreen, B. and Portes, R. (1987) 'The anatomy of financial crises', Institute for International Economic Studies, University of Stockholm, Seminar Paper No. 375.

Einzig, P. (1971) *Parallel Money Markets*, Macmillan.

Einzig, P. (1973) *Rollover Credits*, Macmillan.

Ellis, J.G. (1981) 'Eurobanks and the interbank market', *Bank of England Quarterly Bulletin*, September, 21(3): 351–364.

Ely, B. (1985) 'Yes — Private Sector Depositor Protection is a Viable Alternative to Federal Deposit Insurance', *Proceedings of a Conference on Bank Structure and Competition*, Federal Reserve Bank of Chicago: 338–353.

Emminger, O. (1985) 'The international debt crisis and the banks', *Intereconomics*, Vol. 20 No. 3: 107–113.

Ethier, W.J. (1986) 'The multinational firm', *Quarterly Journal of Economics*, Vol. 101, November: 805–833.

Fama, E.F. (1980) 'Banking in the theory of finance', *Journal of Monetary Economics*, January, 6: 39–57.

Fama, E.F. (1983) 'Financial intermediation and price level control', *Journal of Monetary Economics*, 12: 7–28.

Fama, E.F. (1985) 'What's different about banks?', *Journal of Monetary Economics*, 15: 29–39.

Federal Reserve Board Staff (1979) 'A discussion paper concerning reserve requirements on Eurocurrency deposits', April, mimeo.

Federal Reserve Board Staff (1986) Appendices to the Statement by the Chairman of the Board of Governors of the Federal Reserve System before the Subcommittee on Commerce, Consumer and Monetary Affairs of the Committee on Government Operations of the US House of Representatives, Washington DC, June.

Feeney, P. (1986) 'Sterling commercial paper: the banker's dilemma, Research Papers in Banking and Finance 86/14, Institute of European Finance.

Felgran, S.D. and Ferguson, R.E. (1986) 'The evolution of retail EFT networks', *New England Economic Review*, Federal Reserve Bank of Boston: 42–56.

Fischer, S. (1983) 'A framework for monetary and banking analysis', *Economic Journal*, 93 (supplement): 1–16.

Fisher, F.G. (1979) *The Eurodollar Bond Market*, Euromoney Publications, Chapters 5–7.

Flannery, M.J. (1985) 'A portfolio view of loan selection and pricing' in R. Aspinwall and R. Eisenbeis (eds.) *Handbook for Banking Strategy*, John Wiley.

Fleming, A.S. and Howson, S.K. (1980) 'Conditions in the syndicated medium-term Euro-credit market', *Bank of England Quarterly Bulletin*, September, 20(3): 311–318.

Frankel, J.A. and Levich, R.M. (1977) 'Transaction costs and interest arbitrage: tranquil versus turbulent periods', *Journal of Political Economy*, December, 85: 1209–1226.

Fratianni, M. and Savona, P. (1971) 'Eurodollar creation: comments on Prof. Machlup's propositions and developments', *Banca Nazionale del Lavoro Quarterly Review*, June, 97: 110–125.

Freedman, C. (1977) 'Micro theory of international financial intermediation, *American Economic Review*, February, 66(1): 172–179.

Friedman, B.M. (1984) 'Financial intermediation in the United States', National Bureau of Economic Research, Working Paper 1451, Cambridge, Mass.

Friedman, M. (1953) 'The case for flexible exchange rates', in his *Essays in Positive Economics*, University of Chicago Press.

Friedman, M. (1960) *A Program for Monetary Stability*, Fordham University Press.

Friedman, M. (1969) 'The Eurodollar market: some first principles', *Morgan Guaranty Survey*, October: 4–14.

Friedman, M. (1986) 'The resource costs of irredeemable paper money', *Journal of Political Economy*, Vol. 94, No.3, Part 1, June: 642–647.

Friedman, M. and Schwartz, A.J. (1963) *A Monetary History of the United States, 1867–1960*, Princeton University Press.

Friedman, M. and Schwartz, A.J. (1970) *Monetary Statistics of the United States*, National Bureau of Economic Research, New York.

Frydl, E.J. (1982) 'The Eurodollar conundrum', *Federal Reserve Bank of New York Quarterly Review*, Spring: 11–19.

Fukao, M. and Hanazaki, M. (1986) 'Internationalization of financial markets: some implications for macroeconomic policy and for the allocation of capital', OECD Department of Economics and Statistics Working Paper No.37, November.

Galbraith, C.S. and Kay, N.M. (1986) 'Towards a theory of multinational enterprise', *Journal of Economic Behaviour and Organization*, March, 7: 3–19.

Gardener, E.P.M.(1986) 'Securitisation and the banking firm', Research Papers in Banking and Finance, 86/15, Institute of European Finance, Bangor.

Giddy, I.H. (1985) 'Regulation of off-balance sheet banking', in *The Search for Financial Stability: The Past Fifty Years*, Federal Reserve Bank of San Francisco.

Gilibert, R.A. (1984) 'Bank market structure and competition: a survey', *Journal of Money, Credit and Banking*, November, 16(4), Pt 2: 617–645.

Gilibert, P.L., Lygum, B. and Wartz, F. (1986) 'The international capital market in 1985', *EIB Papers*, February.

Gilibert, P.L., Lygum, B. and Wartz, F. (1987) 'The international capital market in 1986', *EIB Papers*, March.

Gluck, J. (1987) 'International "middle-market" borrowing', *Federal Reserve Bank of New York Quarterly Review*, Vol. 11, No. 4: 46–52.

Goldsmith, R.W. (1968) *Financial Institutions*, Random House.

Goodfriend, M. and Hargraves, M. (1983) 'A historical assessment of the rationales and functions of reserve requirements', *Federal Reserve Bank of Richmond Review*, March/April.

Goodhart, C.A.E. (1975) *Money, Information and Uncertainty*, Macmillan.

Goodhart, C.A.E. (1984) *Monetary Theory and Practice*, Macmillan.

Goodhart, C.A.E. (1985) *The Evolution of Central Banks*, Suntory–Toyota International Centre for Economics and Related Disciplines, London.

Goodman, L.S. (1980) 'The pricing of syndicated Eurocurrency credits', *Federal Reserve Bank of New York Quarterly Review*, Summer: 39–49.

Goodman, L.S. (1984) 'Comment', *Journal of Money, Credit and Banking*, November, 16(4), Pt 2: 678–684.

Goodman, L.S. and Santomero, A.M. (1986) 'Variable-rate deposit insurance: a re-examination', *Journal of Banking and Finance*, June: 203–218.

Goodman, L.S. and Shaffer, S. (1983) 'The economics of deposit insurance: a critical evaluation of proposed reforms', Federal Reserve Bank of New York Research Paper No. 8308.

Gorton, G. (1984) 'Private clearing houses and the origins of central banking', Federal Reserve Bank of Philadelphia Business Review, January/February.

Gower, L.C.B. (1984) *Review of Investor Protection*, Cmnd. 9125, HMSO.

Grassman, S. (1976) 'Currency distribution and forward cover in foreign trade', *Journal of International Economics*, May, 16: 215–222.

Greenbaum, S.I. and Higgins, B. (1983) 'Financial innovation' in G.J. Benston (ed.) *Financial Services*, Prentice-Hall.

Greenfield, R.L. and Yeager, L.B. (1983) 'A laissez-faire approach to monetary stability', *Journal of Money, Credit and Banking*, August: 302–315.

Group of Thirty (1982) *Risks in International Bank Lending*, First Report of the International Banking Study Group of the Group of Thirty, New York.

Grubel, H.G. (1977) 'A theory of multinational banking', *Banca Nazionale del Lavoro Quarterly Review*, December, 123: 349–363.

Grubel, H.G. (1979) 'A proposal for the establishment of an international deposit insurance corporation', *Essays in International Finance*, No. 133, July.

Grunewald, A.E. and Pollock, A.J. (1985) 'Money managers and bank liquidity', *Proceedings of a Conference on Bank Structure and Competition*, Federal Reserve Bank of Chicago.

Gurley, J.G. (1961) 'Financial institutions in the saving–investment process' in L.S. Ritter (ed.) *Money and Economic Activity*, Houghton Mifflin.

Guttentag, J.M. and Herring, R. (1983) 'The lender-of-last-resort function in an international context', *Essays in International Finance*, No.151, Princeton University, May.

Guttentag, J.M. and Herring, R. (1985) 'The Current Crisis in International Lending', *Studies in International Economics*, The Brookings Institution, Washington.

Guttentag, J.M. and Herring, R.J. (1986) 'Disaster myopia in international banking', *Essays in International Finance*, 164, September.

Guttentag, J.M. and Lindsay, R. (1968) 'The uniqueness of commercial banks', *Journal of Political Economy*, August/September, 76(5): 991–1014.

Hadjimichalakis, M.G. (1982) *Monetary Policy and Modern Money Markets*, Lexington Books.

Hahn, F.H. (1982) *Money and Inflation*, Basil Blackwell.

Hall, R.E. (1982) *Inflation: Causes and Effects*, University of Chicago Press, for the National Bureau of Economic Research.

Hammond, G.M.S. (1987) 'Recent developments in the swap market', *Bank of England Quarterly Bulletin*, February: 66–79.

Harrington, R. (1987) *Asset and Liability Management of Banks*, OECD, Paris.

Harrod, R. (1969) *Money*, Macmillan.

Hart, A.G. (1935) 'The Chicago plan of banking reform', *Review of Economic Studies*, 2: 104–116.

Haubrich, J.G. (1986) 'Financial intermediation: delegated monitoring and long-term relationships', Rodney L. White Center for Financial

Research, Wharton School of the University of Pennsylvania.

Havrilesky, T. (1986) 'A comment on Niehans: Innovation in Monetary Policy', *Journal of Banking and Finance*, 10: 611–613.

Henderson, S.K. and Price, J.A.M. (1986) *Currency and Interest Rate Swaps*, Butterworth.

Herring, R.J. and Marston, R.C. (1977) *National Monetary Policies and International Financial Markets*, North–Holland.

Hess, A.C. (1984) 'Variable rate mortgages: confusion of means and ends', *Financial Analysts Journal*, Jan–Feb: 67–70.

Hewson, J.R. (1981) 'Offshore banking in Australia' in Australian Financial System Inquiry, *Commissioned Studies and Selected Papers, Part 2*, AGPS, Canberra.

Hicks, J.R. (1946) *Value and Capital*, The Clarendon Press.

Hirschhorn, E. (1986) 'Developing a Risk-Related Premium Structure', *Proceedings of a Conference on Bank Structure and Competition*, Federal Reserve Bank of Chicago.

Hodjera, Z. (1978) 'The Asian currency market: Singapore as a regional financial center', *IMF Staff Papers*, 25(2): 221–253.

Hooke, A.W. (1982) *The International Monetary Fund: Evolution, Organization and Activities*, IMF Pamphlet Series, Washington DC.

Hopton, D. (1983) *Payments Systems: A Case for Consensus*, Bank for International Settlements, Basle.

Horn, K.N. (1986) 'The changing nature of our financial structure: where are we headed? Where do we want to go?' *Economic Commentary*, Federal Reserve Bank of Cleveland, 15 December.

Horne, J. (1985) *Japan's Financial Market*, Allen and Unwin, Sydney.

Horstmann, I. and Markusen, J.R. (1986) 'Licensing versus direct investment: a model of internalisation by the multinational enterprise', Centre for the Study of International Economic Relations, Working Paper No. 8611C, University of Western Ontario.

Houthakker, H.S. (1984) 'Comment on international banking', *Journal of Money, Credit and Banking*, November, 16(4), Pt. 2: 684–690.

Howson, S.K. (1980) 'External financial markets and capital mobility, Paper presented to Macroeconomic Policy Group, Economics Division, Bank of England.

Hudson, N.R.L. (1981) *Money Exchange Dealing in International Banking*, Macmillan.

Huggins, S.M. (1986) 'Effective utilization of a bank holding company', *Proceedings of a Conference on Bank Structure and Competition*, Federal Reserve Bank of Chicago, pp. 488–504.

Humphrey, D.B. (1984) 'The US Payments System: Costs, Pricing, Competition and Risk', *Monograph Series in Finance and Economics*, Salomon Brothers Center for the Study of Financial Institutions, New York.

Hurn, S. (1985) 'The advantages of transferable loans', *Euromoney*,January: 27–31.

Ishigaki, K. and Fujita, M. (1981) 'The internationalisation of Japanese banking', Committee for Japanese Studies, Australian National University, mimeo.

Jensen, F.H. (1986) 'Recent developments in corporate finance', *Federal Reserve Bulletin*, November, pp. 745–756.

Jensen, F.H. and Parkinson, P.M. (1986) 'Recent developments in the bankers acceptance market', *Federal Reserve Bulletin*, January: 1–12.

Johnson, H.G. (1968) 'Problems of efficiency in monetary management', *Journal of Political Economy*, September/October, 76(5): 971–980.

Johnson, H.G. (1972) 'The case for flexible exchange rates, 1969' in his *Further Essays in Monetary Economics*, Allen and Unwin.

Johnson, H.G. (1976) 'Panama as a regional financial centre: a preliminary analysis of development contribution', *Economic Development and Cultural Change*, January, 24: 261–262.

Johnston, R.B. (1979) 'Some aspects of the determination of Eurocurrency interest rates', *Bank of England Quarterly Bulletin*, March, 19(1): 35–46.

Johnston, R.B. (1980) 'Banks' international lending decisions and the determination of spreads on syndicated medium-term Eurocredits', Bank of England Discussion Paper No. 12, September.

Johnston, R.B. (1983) *The Economics of the Euromarket: History, Theory and Policy*, Macmillan.

Kane, D.R. (1983) *The Eurodollar Market and the Years of Crisis*, St Martin's Press.

Kane, E.J. (1984) 'Technology and regulatory forces in the developing fusion of financial services competition', *Journal of Finance*, July, 39(3): 759–771.

Kareken, J.H. (1983) 'The first step in bank deregulation: what about the FDIC?', *American Economic Review*, May, 73(2): 198–204.

Kareken, J.H. (1986) 'Federal bank regulatory policy: a description and some observations', *The Journal of Business*, January, 59 (1): 3–48.

Kareken, J.H. and Wallace, N. (1978) 'Deposit insurance and bank regulation: a partial equilibrium exposition', *Journal of Business*, July, 51: 413–438.

Kaufman, H. (1983) 'Financial institutions in ferment', *Challenge*, May–June: 20–25.

Keeley, M.C. and Zimmerman, G.C. (1986) 'Deposit rate deregulation and the demand for transactions media', *Economic Review,* Federal Reserve Bank of San Francisco, No. 3, Summer: 57–62.

Kenen, P.B. (1983) 'The role of the dollar as an international currency', *Occasional Papers*, No. 13, Group of Thirty, New York.

Key, S.J. (1982) 'International banking facilities', *Federal Reserve Bulletin*, October, 68(10): 565–577.

Keynes, J.M. (1936) *General Theory of Employment, Interest and Money*, Macmillan.

Kidwell, D.S., Marr, W.M. and Thompson, G.R. (1985) 'Eurodollar bonds: alternative financing for US companies', *Financial Management*, Winter.

Kindleberger, C.P. (1969) *American Business Abroad: Six Lectures on Direct Investment*, Yale University Press.

Kindleberger, C.P. (1974) 'The Formation of Financial Centers: A Study in Comparative Economic History', *Princeton Studies in International Finance* 36, November.

Kindleberger, C.P. (1978) *Manias, Panics and Crashes: A History of Financial Crises*, Basic Books, New York.

Kindleberger, C.P. (1983a) 'International banks as leaders or followers of international business: an historical perspective', *Journal of Banking and Finance*, December, 7(4): 583–596.

Kindleberger, C.P. (1983b) 'Financial institutions and economic development: a comparison of Great Britain and France in the eighteenth and nineteenth centuries', Institute for International Economic Studies, Seminar Paper No. 234.

Kindleberger, C.P. (1984) *A Financial History of Western Europe*, George Allen and Unwin.

Klein, M.A. (1971) 'A theory of the banking firm', *Journal of Money, Credit and Banking*, May, 3: 205–218.

Kneeshaw, J.T. and Van den Bergh, P. (1985) 'International interest rate relationships: policy choices and constraints', *BIS Economic Papers*, 13.

Kogut, B. (1982) 'Foreign direct investment as a sequential process', in D. Audretch and C.P. Kindleberger (eds) *The Multinational Corporation in the 1980s*, MIT Press.

Konstas, P. (1986) 'Brokered deposits', *Banking and Economic Review*, Federal Deposit Insurance Corporation, May: 4–5.

Kouri, P.J.K. (1976) 'The exchange rate and the balance of payments in the short run and the long run: a monetary approach', *Scandinavian Journal of Economics*, 78(2): 280–304.

Kouri, P.J.K. and Porter, M.G. (1974) 'International capital flows and portfolio equilibrium', *Journal of Political Economy*, May/June, 82: 443–467.

Kreicher, L.R. (1982) 'Eurodollar Arbitrage', *Federal Reserve Bank of New York Review*, Summer, 7: 10–22.

Laidler, D. (1984) 'The buffer stock notion in monetary economics', *The Economic Journal*, 94: 17–34.

Lamb, A. (1986) 'International banking in London, 1975–1985', *Bank of England Quarterly Bulletin*, September: 367–378.

Larsson, A. (1985) 'Causes and consequences of foreign direct investment — a review and an empirical inquiry', Working Paper 4, University of Uppsala.

Lee, B.E. (1972) *The Euro-dollar Market* (unpublished Ph.D. thesis, Manchester).

Leland, H.E. and Pyle, D.H. (1977) 'Information asymmetries, financial structure and financial intermediation', *Journal of Finance*, 32: 371–387.

Lessard, D. (1983) 'North–South: the implications for multinational banking', *Journal of Banking and Finance*, December, 7(4): 521–536.

Lever, H. and Huhne, C. (1985) *Debt and Danger: The World Financial Crisis*, Penguin.

Lewis, M.K. (1980a) 'Theories of banking and the implications for monetary controls in Britain', *SSRC Money Study Group Discussion Papers in Monetary Economics*, New Series No. 7.

Lewis, M.K. (1980b) 'Is monetary base control just interest rate control in disguise?', *The Banker*, 130: 35–38.

Lewis, M.K. (1986) 'Financial services in the United States' in R.L. Carter, B. Chiplin and M.K. Lewis (eds) *Personal Financial Markets*, Philip Allan.

Lewis, M.K. (1987a) 'The provision of retail financial services', *International Journal of Bank Marketing*, Vol. 5, No. 2, pp. 33–46.

Lewis, M.K. (1987b) 'Off-balance sheet banking', in J.S.G. Wilson (ed.) *Asset and Liability Management*, Euromoney Publications, London.

Lewis, M.K. and Chiplin, B. (1985) 'Deregulation and the competitive pressures upon British banks', in *Proceedings of a Conference on Bank Structure and Competition*, Federal Reserve Bank of Chicago.

Lewis, M.K. and Wallace, R.H. (1985) *Australia's Financial Institutions and Markets*, Longman Cheshire, Melbourne.

Lindbeck, A. (1978) 'Economic dependence and interdependence in the industrialized world' in OECD, *From Marshall Plan to Global Interdependence*, Paris.

Llewellyn, D.T. (1985a) 'The evolution of the British banking system', *Gilbart Lectures on Banking*, Institute of Bankers, London.

Llewellyn, D.T. (1985b) *International Financial Intermediation and the International Role of Banks*, World Bank, World Development Report.

Lutz, F.A. (1974) 'The Euro-currency system', *Banca Nazionale del Lavoro Quarterly Review*, September, 114: 183–200.

Madden, C.H. (1959) *The Money Side of The Street*, Federal Reserve Bank of New York.

Makin, J.H. (1972) 'Demand and supply functions for stocks of eurodollar deposits: an empirical study', *The Review of Economics and Statistics*, November, 54(2): 381–391.

Markowitz, H.M. (1959) *Portfolio Selection: Efficient Diversification of Investments*, Wiley.

Marshall, J.M. (1974) 'Insurance theory: reserves versus mutuality', *Economic Inquiry*, December, 12(4): 476–492.

Mayer, T. (1986) 'Regulating banks, a comment on Kareken', *The Journal of Business*, January, 59(1): 87–96.

Mayers, D. and Smith, C.W. Jr (1982) 'Toward a positive theory of insurance', *Monograph Series in Finance and Economics*, Salomon Brothers Center for the Study of Financial Institutions, New York.

McCarthy, J. (1979) 'Offshore banking centres: benefits and costs', *Finance and Development*, 16(4): 45–48.

McCarthy, J. (1980) 'Deposit insurance: theory and practice', *IMF Staff Papers*, September, 27(3): 578–600.

McCulloch, J.H. (1981) 'Misintermediation and macroeconomic fluctuations', *Journal of Monetary Economics*, 8: 103–115.

McCulloch, J.H. (1986) 'Bank regulation and deposit insurance', *The Journal of Business*, January, 59(1): 79–85.

McDonald, R.P. (1982) *International Syndicated Loans*, Euromoney Publications, London.

McKinnon, R.I. (1977) 'The Euro-currency market', *Essays in International Finance*, No. 125, Princeton University.

McKinnon, R.I. (1979) *Money in International Exchange, The Convertible Currency System*, Oxford University Press, New York.

McKinnon, R.I. (1984a) *An International Standard for Monetary Stabilization,* Institute for International Economics, MIT Press.

McKinnon, R.I. (1984b) 'Why floating exchange rates fail', *Servizio Studi della Banca d'Italia*, 42, November.

Melton, W.C. (1985) *Inside the Fed: Making Monetary Policy*, Dow Jones–Irwin, Homewood, Ill.

Mester, L.J. (1987) 'Efficient production of financial services: scale and scope economies', *Business Review*, Federal Reserve Bank of Philadelphia, January–February: 15–25.

Miles, M.A. (1978) 'Currency substitution, flexible exchange rates, and monetary independence', *American Economic Review*, 68: 428–436.

Mills, R.E. (1986) 'Foreign lending by banks: a guide to international and US statistics', *Federal Reserve Bulletin*, October: 683–694.

Mills, R.H. and Terrell, H.S. (1984) 'The determination of front-end fees on syndicated Eurocurrency credits', *International Finance Discussion Paper*, No. 250, Board of Governors of Federal Reserve System, Washington D.C.

Minsky, H.P. (1975) *John Maynard Keynes*, Columbia University Press.

Minsky, H.P. (1984) 'Central banking and money market changes: a reprise', Working Paper 72, Dept. of Economics, Washington University.

Mitchell, G.W. (1986) 'Similarities and contrast in payment systems', *Journal of Bank Research*, 16(4): 175–177.

Modigliani, F. and Miller, M.H. (1985) 'The cost of capital, corporation finance and the theory of investment, *American Economic Review*, 48: 261–297.

Moore, B.J. (1968) *Theory of Finance*, Free Press, Glencoe.

Mundell, R.A. (1963) 'Capital mobility and stabilization policy under fixed and flexible exchange rates', *Canadian Journal of Economics and Political Science*, November.

Murton, A.J. (1986) 'A survey of the issues and the literature concerning risk-related deposit insurance', *Banking and Economic Review*, Federal Deposit Insurance Corporation, Vol. 4, No. 6, September/October: 11–20.

Myers, S.D. (1977) 'The determinants of corporate borrowing', *Journal of Financial Economics*, 4: 147–175.

Newlyn, W.T. and Bootle, R. (1978) *The Theory of Money*, Oxford University Press.

Niehans, J. (1978) *The Theory of Money*, The John Hopkins University Press.

Niehans, J. (1983) 'Financial innovation, multinational banking and monetary policy', *Journal of Banking and Finance*, December, 7(4): 537–552.

Niehans, J. (1984) *International Monetary Economics*, The John Hopkins University Press.

Niehans, J. (1986) 'Further comment on financial innovation', *Journal of Banking and Finance*, 10: 615–616.

Niehans, J. and Hewson, J.R. (1976) 'The Eurodollar market and monetary theory', *Journal of Money, Credit and Banking*, 5(1) Pt. 2: 465–504.

Owens, J.P. (1974) 'Growth of the Euro-dollar Market', Bangor Occasional Papers in Economics No. 4, University of Wales Press.

Pavel, C. (1986) 'Securitization', *Economic Perspectives*, Federal Reserve Bank of Chicago, July/August, 10(4): 16–31.

Pecchioli, R.M. (1983) *The Internationalisation of Banking*, OECD, Paris.

Pesek, B.P. (1970) 'Banks' supply function and the equilibrium quantity of money', *Canadian Journal of Economics*, III: 3, August: 357–383.

Pesek, B.P. and Saving, T.R. (1967) *Money, Wealth and Economic Theory*, Macmillan, New York.

Phalen, G.E. (1977) 'Discussion' in *Key Issues in International Banking*, Proceedings of a Conference, Federal Reserve Bank of Boston, Conference Series No. 18.

Polasek, M. and Lewis, M.K. (1985a) 'Foreign exchange markets and capital inflow' in M.K. Lewis and R.H. Wallace (eds) *Australia's Financial Institutions and Markets*, Longman Cheshire, Melbourne.

Polasek, M. and Lewis, M.K. (1985b) 'Australia's transition from crawling peg to floating exchange rate', *Banca Nazionale del Lavoro Quarterly Review*, June, 153: 187–203.

Porter, M.E. (1985) *Competitive Advantage: Creating and Sustaining Superior Performance*, Free Press, Glencoe.

Pyle, D.H. (1971) 'On the theory of financial intermediation', *Journal of Finance*, June, 26: 737–747.

Radcliffe Committee (1959) *Committee on the Working of the Monetary System Report*, Cmnd 827, HMSO.

Ramsden, N.F.E. (1984) 'The international market in floating rate instruments', *Bank of England Quarterly Bulletin*, September, 24(3): 337–345.
Raviv, A. (1979) 'The design of an optimal insurance policy', *American Economic Review*, March, 69: 84–96.
Redhead, K. (1986) 'Swaps', Coventry Lanchester Polytechnic Staff Discussion Paper No. 71, May.
Reid, M. (1982) *The Secondary Banking Crisis 1973–1975*, Macmillan.
Revell, J.R.S. (1968) 'Changes in british banking: the growth of a secondary banking system', Hill Samuel, Occasional Paper No. 3, London. Reprinted in H.G. Johnson (ed.) (1972) *Readings in British Monetary Economics*, The Clarendon Press.
Revell, J.R.S. (1978) 'Competition and regulation of banks', Bangor Occasional Papers in Economics, 14, University of Wales Press.
Revell, J.R.S. (1983) *Banking and Electronic Fund Transfers*, OECD, Paris.
Revey, P.A. (1981) 'Evolution and growth of the United States foreign exchange market', *Federal Reserve Bank of New York Quarterly Review*, Autumn, 6(3): 32–44.
Robinson, J.S. (1972) *Multinational Banking*, A.W. Sijthoff, Leiden.
Roley, V.V. (1985) 'Money demand unpredictability', *Journal of Money, Credit and Banking*, Vol. XVII, No. 4, Part 2, November, 511–641.
Rolnick, A.J. and Weber, W.E. (1985) 'Banking instability and regulation in the US free banking era', *Federal Reserve Bank of Minneapolis Quarterly Review*, Summer, 9(3): 2–9.
Rosenblum, H. Di Clemente, J. and O'Brien, K. (1985) 'The product market in commercial banking: Cluster's last stand?' in *Economic Perspectives*, Federal Reserve Bank of Chicago, January/February, pp. 21–34.
Rugman, A.M. (1986) 'New theories of the multinational enterprise: an assessment of internalization theory', *Bulletin of Economic Research*, May: 101–118.
Sachs, J. (1986) 'Managing the LDC debt crisis', *Brookings Papers on Economic Activity*, 2: 397–431.
Sampson, A. (1981) *The Moneylenders*, Viking Press.
Santomero, A.M. (1983) 'Fixed versus variable rate loans', *The Journal of Finance*, December, 38(5): 1363–1380.
Saunders, A. (1986) 'The interbank market, contagion effects and international financial crises', Working Paper No. 385, Salomon Brothers Center for the Study of Financial Institutions, New York University, June.
Sayers, R.S. (1967) *Modern Banking*, 7th edn, The Clarendon Press.
Scitovsky, T. (1969) *Money and the Balance of Payments*, Rand McNally.
Scott, G. McL. and Wallace, R.H. (1985) 'Business financiers' in M.K. Lewis and R.H. Wallace (eds) *Australia's Financial Institutions and Markets*, Longman Cheshire, Melbourne.
Sealey, C.W. and Lindley, J.T. (1977) 'Inputs, outputs and a theory of

production and cost at depository financial institutions', *Journal of Finance*, September, 32: 1251–1266.

Selden, R.T. (1963) 'Trends and cycles in the commercial paper market', Occasional Paper 85, National Bureau of Economic Research, New York.

Shaw, E.R. (1978) *The London Money Market*, 2nd edn, Heinemann.

Shea, E.P. (1979) *Large Bank Liability Management Behaviour and the Market for Immediately Available Funds* (unpublished Ph.D. thesis, Boston College Graduate School).

Sheppard, D.K. (1971) *The Growth and Role of UK Financial Institutions, 1800–1962*, Methuen.

Smith, P.F. (1982) 'Structural disequilibrium and the Banking Act of 1980', *Journal of Finance*, May, 37(2): 385–397.

Smoot, R.L. (1985) 'Billion dollar overdrafts: a payments risk challenge', *Business Review*, Federal Reserve Bank of Philadelphia, January–February: 3–13.

Snowden, N. (1985) 'International reserves and indebtedness: legacy of bankers' greed or official policy failure?', University of Lancaster Discussion Paper 83/5.

Sofianos, G. (1985) 'Lending with default: a model of intermediation' Working Paper No. 341, Salomon Brothers Center for the Study of Financial Institutions, New York University.

Spero, J. (1980) *The Failure of the Franklin National Bank*, Columbia University Press.

Stanyer, P.W. and Whitley, J.A. (1981) 'Financing world payments balances', *Bank of England Quarterly Bulletin*, June, 21(2): 187–199.

Startz, R. (1979) 'Implicit interest on demand deposits', *Journal of Monetary Economics*, October, 5: 515–534.

Stevens, E.J. (1984) 'Risk in large dollar transfer systems', *Economic Review*, Federal Reserve Bank of Cleveland, Fall: 2–16.

Stigler, G. (1967) 'Imperfections in the capital market', *Journal of Political Economy*, June: 287–292.

Stigum, M. (1983) *The Money Market*, Dow Jones–Irwin, Homewood, Ill.

Stigum, M. and Branch Jr, R.O. (1983) *Managing Bank Assets and Liabilities*, Dow Jones–Irwin, Homewood, Illinois.

Stutchbury, O.P. (1964) *The Management of Unit Trusts*, Thomas Skinner & Co.

Sugden, R. (1985) *Why Transnational Corporations*? Discussion Paper IX, University of Edinburgh.

Swary, I. (1985) 'Continental Illinois crisis: an empirical analysis of regulatory behaviour', Working Paper No. 335, Salomon Brothers Center for the Study of Financial Institutions, New York University.

Swary, I. and Udell, G.F. (1985) 'The role of collateral in commercial lending', Working Paper No. 359, Salomon Brothers Center for the Study of Financial Institutions, New York University.

Swoboda, A.K. (1980) 'Credit creation in the Euromarket: alternative theories and implications for control', Group of Thirty, Occasional Paper No. 2, New York.

Taylor, H. (1986) 'What has happened to MI?' *Business Review*, Federal Reserve Bank of Philadelphia, September–October: 3–14.

Taylor, L. and O'Connell, S. (1985) 'A Minsky crisis', *Quarterly Journal of Economics*, Vol. 100 Supplement.

Teeters, N. (1983) 'The role of banks in the international financial system', *Journal of Banking and Finance*, December, 7(4): 453–464.

Temin, P. (1976) *Did Monetary Forces Cause the Great Depression?*, W.W. Norton.

Tew, B. (1977) *The Evolution of the International Monetary System, 1945–1977*, Hutchinson.

Thore, S. (1984) 'Spatial models of the Eurodollar market', *Journal of Banking and Finance*, March, 8(1): 51–66.

Thore, S. (1986) 'Regional lending risk in Eurodollar markets', *Scandinavian Journal of Economics*, 88(2): 437–451.

Timberlake, Jr, R. (1984) 'The central banking role of the clearing house associations', *Journal of Money, Credit and Banking*, February.

Tobin, J. (1963) 'Commercial banks as creators of money' in D. Carson (ed) *Banking and Monetary Studies*, Richard D. Irwin Inc.

Tobin, J. (1969) 'A general equilibrium approach to monetary theory', *Journal of Money, Credit and Banking*, February, 1(1): 15–29.

Tobin, J. (1978) 'A proposal for international monetary reform', *Eastern Economic Journal*, 4: 153–159.

Tobin, J. (1984) 'On the efficiency of the financial system', *Lloyds Bank Review*, July, 153: 1–15.

Tobin, J. (1985) 'Financial innovation and deregulation in perspective', *Bank of Japan Monetary and Economic Studies*, September.

Topping, S.L. (1987) 'Commercial paper markets: an international survey', *Bank of England Quarterly Bulletin*, February: 46–53.

Towey, R.E. (1974) 'Money creation and the theory of the banking firm', *Journal of Finance*, 39, March: 57–72.

Trundle, J.M. (1982) 'Recent changes in the use of cash', *Bank of England Quarterly Bulletin*, December: 519–519.

Valentine, T.J. (1985) 'The effect of deregulation on M3 growth: a note', *Bulletin of Money, Banking and Finance*, 1984–5, 3: 42–48.

Vaubel, R. (1984) 'Private competitive note issue in monetary history', in P. Salin (ed.) *Currency Competition and Monetary Union*, Martinus Nijhoff Publishers, Kluwer, The Hague.

Vittas, D. (1986) 'The new market menagerie', *The Banker*, June: 16–27.

Volcker, P.A. (1985) 'Statement to Congress, September 11, 1985', *Federal Reserve Bulletin*, November, 71(11): 866–873.

Wall, L.D. and Pringle, J.J. (1987) 'Alternative explanations of interest rate

swaps', 'Federal Reserve Bank of Atlanta, Working Paper 87–2, April.
Wallich, H.C. (1977) 'Statement to Subcommittee on Financial Institution Supervision of Committee on Banking, Finance and Urban Affairs of the US House of Representatives', *Federal Reserve Bulletin*, 65(4): 362–366.
Wallich, H.C. (1979) 'Statement before the Subcommittee on Domestic Monetary Policy and the Subcommittee on International Trade, *Federal Reserve Bulletin*, August 67(8): 611–617.
Walter, I. (1985a) *Barriers to Trade in Banking and Financial Services*, Thames Essay No. 41, Trade Policy Research Centre, London.
Walter, I. (1985b) *Secret Money. The World of International Financial Secrecy*, Allen and Unwin.
Wathen, J.C. (1986) 'Towards the year 2000 — Japan's emerging role in world finance', *Midland Bank Review*, Summer.
Watson, M., Mathieson, D., Kincaid, R. and Kalter, E. (1986) *International Capital Markets, Developments and Prospects*, IMF Occasional Paper No. 43, Washington DC.
Wesson, B. (1985) *Bank Capital and Risk*, The Institute of Bankers, London.
Weston, R. (1980) *Domestic and Multinational Banking*, Croom Helm.
White, L.H. (1984) *Free Banking in Britain*, Cambridge University Press.
Whittaker, J.G. (1987), 'Interest rate swaps: risk and regulation', *Economic Review*, Federal Reserve Bank of Kansas City, March: 3–13.
Williamson, J.R. (1983) *The Open Economy and the World Economy*, Basic Books Inc.
Wilson, J.S.G. (1986) *Banking Policy and Structure, A Comparative Analysis*, Croom Helm.
Working Group of the Cabinet Council on Economic Affairs (1985) 'Recommendations for changes in the US federal deposit insurance system', *International Currency Review*, October, 17(1): 109–160.
Wright, D.M. (1986) 'Housing finance and consumer credit', Chapter 7 in R.L. Carter, B. Chiplin and M.K. Lewis (eds) *Personal Financial Markets*, Philip Allan.
Wriston, W. (1986) 'Maintaining comparative advantage in an information society', *Proceedings of a Conference on Bank Structure and Competition*, Federal Reserve Bank of Chicago: 9–18.

Glossary of Selected Terms

NB: See also Table 4.6 on pp.117–8 for Glossary of some 'off'-balance sheet activites

AAA (Aaa)	Highest rating for bonds given by the US rating agencies, Standard and Poor's and Moody's.
ACH	Automated Clearing House: US term for computer clearing and settlement system, often under the aegis of the Federal Reserve Bank.
Arbitrage	A purchase of foreign exchange, securities, or commodities in one market coupled with immediate resale in another market in order to profit risklessly from price discrepancies. The effect of arbitrageurs' actions is to equate prices in all markets for the same commodity.
ATM	Automated teller machine: unmanned terminal, usually activated by a magnetically coded card, which can be used to dispense cash, take instructions on fund transfers and summarise information on the state of the account, etc.
Balance of Payments	A summary of the flow of goods, services and funds between the residents of a country and the residents of the rest of the world during a particular period.
Banker's Acceptance	A bill of exchange that has been endorsed by a bank — i.e. the bank has given its guarantee that payment will be forthcoming from it, if not from the buyer: a popular way of financing trade. The merchant who gets his bills accepted by a first-class bank can then sell the bills at a discount and get immediate payment for the goods he has exported.

Bank Holding Company — US term for a holding company that owns one or more banks and comes within the supervisory ambit of the Federal Reserve Board.

Base Money — Total reserves plus currency in the hands of the public. Known also as high-powered money, or the monetary base.

Base Rate — Interest rate such as LIBOR or prime used for pricing variable rate loans (floating rate loans, rollover credits).

Basis — The spread or difference between two market prices or two interest rates. For example, the spread between commercial paper and Eurodollar rates, or the spread between a futures price and the price of the underlying asset.

Basis Point — One one hundredth of 1 per cent.

Bearer Bond — A bond held by whoever is in possession. With no registration of ownership, it has the advantage of anonymity.

Best Efforts Basis — A securities issue which is not fully underwritten, but sold on the basis of what the market will stand.

Bid — The price offered for securities or foreign exchange.

Billion — Billion in this book follows American usage and means one thousand million.

Bill of Exchange — A written order telling one person to pay a certain sum of money to a named person on demand or at a certain time in the future. Formerly much used as a means of payment in home trade, bills of exchange; now used mainly in foreign trade.

BIS, Bank for International Settlements — An international bank established in 1930 to assist in transferring German reparations which has developed into a bank for European central banks and a major source of data on the Eurocurrency markets.

Bond — A document issued by a government or a company borrowing money from the public, stating the existence of a debt and the amount owing to the holder of the document, called a bondholder, who must use the document to obtain repayment of the loan.

Book Entry Securities — In the USA, securities which are maintained as computerised records at the Federal Reserve in the name of member banks rather than as engraved pieces of paper.

Bought Deal — A bond issue that is completely bought up by a bank or syndicate on fixed terms.

Broker — A broker brings buyers and sellers together for a commission paid by the initiator of the transaction or by both sides; he does not position. In the money market, brokers are active in markets in which banks buy and sell money, and in interdealer markets.

Brokerage — Fee or commission charged by broker.

Building Society — Financial organisation which issues shares (i.e. accepts deposits), collecting money which it lends to borrowers predominantly for home mortgages. They operate in the UK and in Australia.

Bullet Loan — A bank term loan with no amortisation; it is repaid in one go at maturity.

Call Money — Interest-bearing bank deposits that can be withdrawn on 24 hours' notice. Many Euro-deposits take the form of call money.

Call Option — *See* Option.

Cash Management Account (CMA) — A system developed by Merrill Lynch which sweeps funds from a margin (brokerage) account to a selection of money market mutual funds, and allows cheque-writing and operation of a credit card.

CD (Certificate of Deposit) — A negotiable certificate issued by a bank as evidence of an interest-bearing time deposit.

CHAPS (Clearing House Automated Payments System) — UK equivalent of CHIPS for the electronic transfer in the UK of sterling payments between banks.

CHIPS (Clearing House Interbank Payments System) — An automated clearing facility set up in 1970 and operated by the New York Clearing House Association, which processes international money transfers for its membership and embraces over a hundred US financial institutions — mostly major US banks and branches of foreign banks.

Clearing — The process of cancelling offsetting evidences of indebtedness, such as cheques, notes, trade payments, etc., so as to economise on payments in money.

Clearing House	An institution through which clearings take place.
Co-financing	Loans to developing countries made by commercial banks or other lending institutions in association with the World Bank and other multilateral development banks.
CMO (Collaterised Mortgage Obligation)	Mortgage-backed bonds on which principal is repaid periodically. CMOs generally consist of several tranches or classes, with various classes receiving principal repayments in a prescribed order. Principal in the first class is retired before the mortgage amortisation and prepayments are used to pay down the principal in the second class, and so on.
Collateral	A security given for the repayment of a loan.
Commercial Paper	An unsecured promissory note with a fixed maturity of no more than 270 days. Commercial paper is normally sold at a discount from face value.
Commitment (Credit Line)	A legal commitment undertaken by a bank to lend to a customer.
Compensating Balances	In the USA, a deposit which a borrower must maintain with a bank, usually between 10 and 20 per cent of the line of credit extended.
Consolidated Supervision	Assessment as a group of parent institution and subsidiaries on prudential grounds.
Consortium Bank	A merchant banking subsidiary set up by several banks that may or may not be of the same nationality. Consortium banks are common in the Euromarket and are active in loan syndication.
Contingent Liability	Possible debt which will come into existence only on the occurrence of a contingency (uncertain event), e.g. when the liability of a guarantor is called on.
Convertible Bond	Bond giving the investor the option to convert the bond into equity at a fixed conversion price.
Counterparty	The party on the other side of a transaction; for instance, a swap transaction is undertaken between two agents with each being the counterparty of the other.
Country Risk	The risk that most, or all, economic agents (including the government) in a particular country will for some

	common reason become unable or unwilling to fulfil international financial obligations.
Coupon	A certificate attached to a bond evidencing interest due on a payment date.
Covered Interest Arbitrage	The act of investing, say, dollars in an instrument denominated in a foreign currency and hedging the resulting foreign exchange risk by selling the proceeds of the investment forward for dollars.
Credit Line	The amount of credit (upper limit) a bank promises to grant when and if it is needed.
Credit Risk	The likelihood, in lending operations, that a borrower will not be able to repay the principal or pay the interest.
Cross-currency Swap	Transfer of equivalent debt obligations in different currencies between two counterpart companies.
Cross-default Clause	A clause in a loan agreement that allows the lender to declare the loan immediately repayable and to terminate any further extension of credit if the borrower defaults on any other debt.
Current Account	In banking, UK and Australian term for demand deposit.
Daylight Overdraft	Indebtedness which arises in a clearing system when more funds are transferred out of an account than are transferred into the account.
Dealer	A dealer, as opposed to a broker, acts as a principal in all transactions, buying and selling for his own account.
Debt Rescheduling	Formal deferment of debt-service payments with new maturities applying to the deferred amounts.
Default	Failure to make timely payment of interest or principal on a debt security or otherwise to comply with the provisions of a bond indenture.
Demand Deposit	Deposit at a bank which can be withdrawn (e.g. by means of a cheque) at any time without having given prior notice.
Demand for Money	The functional relationship between some measure of money and other variables such as wealth, income, and interest rates.

Developing Countries	Classified by the World Bank (IBRD) as those countries which had an average income per head in 1984 of up to US$5,000.
Discount	A sum of money allowed for immediate payment of a sum due at a later date. If the sum is secured by a bill of exchange, the party who buys the bill and receives the discount is said to discount the bill (the discounting of bills).
Discount Window	Familiar term for the division of a Federal Reserve Bank that extends loans to banks and certain other financial institutions.
Diversification	Dividing investment funds among a variety of securities offering independent returns.
Draft	An order by a seller, directing the buyer to pay under certain (agreed) conditions. *See* Bill of exchange.
ECU	European currency unit, a composite currency made up of the currencies of the members of the EEC.
Edge Act Corporation	A subsidiary of a US commercial bank whose income arises from operating in foreign countries. It is given powers not held by domestic US banks to operate in ways similar to the practices of the foreign banks.
EFTPOS	Electronic Funds Transfer at Point of Sale: system which allows funds to be switched automatically as goods are bought in a store.
EFT System	Electronic Funds Transfer System: system which allows funds to be switched by electronic communication rather than paper.
Eligible Banker's Acceptance	In the USA, a banker's acceptance which is acceptable by the Federal Reserve as collateral at the discount window.
Equity	(a) That part of a company's capital belonging to its shareholders. In a company (quoted at the stock exchange) this is worth the price per share times the number of shares. On the company's balance sheet it is what is left over when all the company's liabilities have been deducted from its assets, except those liabilities due to shareholders.

	(b) In Britain, shares are themselves often referred to as equities.
Eurobank	Financial institutions that bid for deposits and make loans in currencies other than that of the country in which they are located.
Eurobond	A bond underwritten by an international syndicate of banks and placed internationally.
Eurocommercial Paper	Notes sold in London for same-day settlement in US dollars in New York. The maturities are more tailored to the needs of issuer and investor than the standard Euro-note terms of 1, 3, and 6 months.
Eurocurrency Credit	A loan denominated in a currency that is foreign to the country of the bank office extending the credit. Loans made in domestic currency from IBFs are sometimes also included.
Eurodollar	Originally, dollar deposits in banks in Europe, including the branches there of American banks. More recently, dollars anywhere in the world outside of the United States and, more generally, a term used for Eurocurrencies which are deposits in a given country denominated in any currency but that legally used there.
Euronote	Short-term notes issued on a one-, three- or six-month basis in the syndicated loan market, sometimes structured as a medium-term loan in which the underwriters agree to issue notes on request.
Excess Reserves	Reserves held by banks and certain other financial institutions in excess of their required reserves.
Exchange Controls	Restrictions imposed by the central bank or other government authorities on the convertibility of a currency or on the movement of funds in that currency.
Exchange Rate	The number of units of one currency expressed in terms of a unit of another currency.
FDIC (Federal Deposit Insurance Corporation)	A US federal institution that insures bank deposits, currently up to $100,000 per deposit.
Federal Funds Market	A market for unsecured loans between depository institutions in the United States in immediately available funds; essentially, reserves held at Federal

	Reserve Banks. Most activity is for next-day maturity.
Federal Reserve System	Central banking system in USA. Consists of the Board of Governors, Federal Reserve Banks (12 districts) and Federal Open Market Committee.
Fedwire	The Federal Reserve's electronic funds and securities transfer network.
Float	The difference between credits to a bank's reserve position on cheques cleared and debits made to a bank's reserve accounts on the same cheques.
Floating Rate Interest	Interest rate changed regularly, on a set formula, to reflect changes in market rates. Usually calculated at so many points above interbank rate; hence floating-rate CDs, floating-rate bonds, floating-rate notes (FRNs), etc.
Floating Rate Loan	A loan made with floating rate interest provisions.
Floating Rate Note (FRN)	A medium-term security carrying a floating rate of interest which is reset at regular intervals, typically quarterly or half-yearly, in relation to some predetermined reference rate, typically LIBOR (*See* LIBOR).
Foreign Bond	A long-term security issued by a borrower in the capital market of another country. Usually underwritten by a syndicate from one country and sold on that country's capital market, the bond is denominated in the currency of the country in which it is sold.
Forfaiting	Forfaiting means to buy a client's receivables *à forfait*, i.e. wholesale and without right of recourse (which is possible in the case of factoring). Factoring is designed for short-term receivables (rather under three months), whereas forfaiting has a long-term character.
Forward Contract	A contract for a financial instrument or commodity to be settled on a mutually agreed future date. Contrasts with futures contract in that it is not standardised.
Forward Premium (or discount when negative)	The difference between the forward and spot exchange rates, expressed either as an annualised percentage of the spot exchange rate or as so many cents or pfennigs. When forward currencies are worth more than the corresponding spot amount, the stronger currency is at a premium; the weaker currency is at a discount.

Free Reserves	In the US, excess reserves less member bank borrowings from the Federal Reserve System.
Futures Contract	A standardised contract covering the sale or purchase at a future date of a set quantity of commodity, financial instruments, cash, etc.
Giro Network	A payment system organised by banks and the postal authority which allows customers of one bank to make payments to customers in any other without the use of cash or cheques (central clearing system).
Grace Period	Period between issue and first repayment of principal in a syndicated loan.
Hedge	To reduce risk by taking a position which offsets existing or anticipated exposure to a change in market rates.
IBRD (International Bank for Reconstruction and Development)	The World Bank was established at Bretton Woods in 1944, and is located in Washington; it makes loans to assist developing countries.
IMF (International Monetary Fund)	An institution established at Bretton Woods in 1944, along with the IBRD also located in Washington, that assists countries in payments difficulties by furnishing credits.
Information Costs	The cost of acquiring information relevant to particular transactions.
Interest Rate Mismatch	The risk/opportunity banks face that a shift in interest rates will reduce/increase interest income. The mismatch arises out of the repricing schedule of assets and liabilities. The banks' traditional interest rate mismatch, lending long-term and borrowing in short-term markets, exposes them, for example, to the risk that rates will rise: as interest rates rise, low-yielding short-term liabilities will be replaced and repriced more rapidly than assets.
Interest Rate Parity	The condition that the interest differential should equal the forward differential between two currencies.
Interest Rate Swap	A transaction in which two counterparties exchange interest payment streams of differing characters based on an underlying notional principal amount. The three

main types are coupon swaps (fixed rate to floating rate in the same currency), basis swaps (one floating rate index to another floating rate index in the same currency), and cross-currency interest rate swaps (fixed rate in one currency to floating rate in another).

Intermediation — The process of standing between borrowers and lenders, by borrowing from the latter and lending to the former, for the purpose of bridging preferred habitats (the lenders want to lend short/borrow long), or risk (the lenders do not know or trust the credit of the borrower, preferring that of the intermediary).

International Banking Facilities (IBFs) — A means by which US banks may use their domestic offices to offer foreign customers deposit and loan services free of Federal Reserve requirements and interest rate regulations.

Investment Bank — A firm that engages in the origination, underwriting, and distribution of new issues.

Issue Price — The price at which securities are sold on issue.

Lead Manager — The managing bank in a new issue or loan, responsible for the co-ordination of the issue, selecting co-managers, 'running the book', and dealing with the borrower.

Lender of Last Resort — The institution, usually government or central bank, which stands ready in financial crisis to lend to banks, or occasionally business firms, that are in long-run sound condition, but are in immediate need of liquidity to meet their obligations.

Letter of Credit — In foreign trade, one that records a business arrangement between an importer and a bank by which the bank pays the seller of the goods in a foreign country as soon as certain stated conditions have been met. The bank is repaid by the importer. Such letters of credit are usually irrevocable, i.e. cannot be cancelled.

Liabilities — This means that one is liable to pay or do something; that one owes something to somebody.

LIBID — London Interbank Bid Rate. The rate which a bank is willing to pay for funds in the international interbank market.

LIBOR — London Interbank Offered Rate. The rate at which

banks offer to lend funds in the international interbank market.

LIMEAN	The mean (average) of LIBOR and LIBID.
Liquidity Risk	For banks, the risk that monies needed to fund assets may not be available in sufficient quantities at some future date. Implies an imbalance in committed maturities of assets and liabilities.
Loan	An agreed sum of money lent by a bank to a customer for a fixed period against an approved security.
Loan Sale	The sale, transfer or assignment of a loan or a loan participation to a third party with or without the knowledge of the borrower.
Long Position	To have greater inflows than outflows of a given currency.
Mandate	Borrower's authorisation to proceed with loan or bond issue on terms agreed with lead manager.
Margin	In bond markets, used to express the difference between bid and asked price. On loans, the rate of interest over and above reference price, e.g. LIBOR, expressed as a percentage. In commodity markets, a cash deposit with the broker for each contract as a guarantee of fulfilment of the futures contract. Also called the 'spread' in bond and loan markets and the 'security deposit' in futures markets.
Market-making	An institution that stands willing to buy or sell an asset, or an institution that deals so frequently and in such volume in an asset that it makes it possible for others to buy or sell that asset at almost any time.
Market Value	The price at which a security is trading and could, presumably, be purchased or sold.
Matching	A situation in which the distribution of maturities of a bank's liabilities equals that of its assets.
Maturity	The life expectancy of a loan. Original maturity is the length of time from the beginning of a loan to the date of the last repayment. Residual maturity is the time from today until the final repayment.
Member Bank	In the USA, national banks and state chartered banks which are members of the Federal Reserve System.

Merchant Bank	In the UK and Australia, a bank that specialises not in lending out its own funds, but in providing various financial services such as accepting bills arising out of trade, underwriting new issues, and providing advice on acquisitions, mergers, foreign exchange, portfolio management, etc.
Mismatch	A situation where assets and liabilities in a currency do not balance either in size or maturity.
Money Market	The market for short-term loans, in which the commodity is credit and the buyers and sellers are the banks, along with brokers, discount and acceptance houses (in Britain) and securities firms and fund managers (in the USA).
Money Market (Centre) Bank	A large US bank which operates in one of the major centres (typically New York) and plays a major role in the money market.
Money Market Mutual Fund	Mutual fund that invests solely in money market instruments.
Money Multiplier	In credit creation, the relationship which links the quantity of base money to the money supply.
Multi-currency Clause	Such a clause on a Euro-loan permits the borrower to switch from one currency to another on a rollover date.
Multiple Component Facility	Facility under which several different options for drawing funds are available to the borrower. These may include issuing notes, drawing on short-term or medium-term credits.
Multi-year Restructuring Agreement (MYRA)	Restructuring agreement where the consolidation period covers more than two years beyond the date of the signing of the agreement.
Mutual Fund	A pooled investment fund.
National Banks	National banks in the USA are federally chartered banks that are subject to supervision by the Comptroller of the Currency. State banks, in contrast, are state chartered and state regulated.
Note	A certificate of indebtedness like a bond, but used most frequently for short-term issues.

Note Issuance Facility (NIF)	A medium-term arrangement enabling borrowers to issue short-term paper, typically of three or six months' maturity, in their own names. Usually, a group of underwriting banks guarantees the availability of funds to the borrower by purchasing any unsold notes at each rollover date, or by providing a standby credit. Facilities produced by competing banks are called, variously, revolving underwriting facilities, note purchase facilities, and Euro-note facilities.
Notional Principal	A hypothetical amount on which swap payments are based. The notional principal in an interest rate swap is never paid or received.
OECD	Organisation for Economic Co-operation and Development. Its members are Australia, Austria, Belgium, Canada, Denmark, Finland, France, West Germany, Greece, Iceland, Ireland, Italy, Japan, Luxembourg, the Netherlands, New Zealand, Norway, Portugal, Spain, Sweden, Switzerland, Turkey, the United Kingdom and the United States. Yugoslavia takes part in certain work of the OECD and is included in statistics relating to OECD countries.
OPEC	Organisation of Petroleum Exporting Countries. An organisation of the major oil-exporting countries, originally formed to resist falling world prices of oil and, ultimately, in 1973 and 1979, pushing through major price increases.
Off-Balance Sheet Activities	Banks' business, often fee-based, that does not generally involve booking assets and taking deposits. Examples are trading of swaps, options, foreign exchange forwards, standby commitments and letters of credit.
Offshore Banking Facility	Bank subsidiary allowed to transact business, such as Eurocurrency dealing, that is normally prohibited to domestic banks.
Option	The contractual right, but not the obligation, to buy or sell a specified amount of a given financial instrument at a fixed price before or at a designated future date. A CALL OPTION confers on the holder the right to buy the financial instrument. A PUT OPTION involves the right to sell the financial instrument.

Overdraft Facility (Am. line of credit)	An agreed sum of money, by which amount a bank allows a customer to overdraw his account, i.e. to run into debt to the bank by drawing more than the amount standing to his credit in the account. The customer can make use of this money when he wishes, and for an agreed length of time. Interest is payable only on the amount overdrawn at the end of each day, but the bank may make an additional charge for agreeing to the arrangement.
Participation	The amount that a bank contributes to a syndicated loan.
Perpetual FRN	Floating rate note issued without a time limit.
Placing Power	A bank's ability to sell securities to investors, usually applied to new issues.
Praecipium	In the Euromarkets the manager of a bond or credit negotiates a fee payable by the borrower. From this the manager takes his own fee — the praecipium — before passing the remainder of the fee to the management group.
Prime Rate	US term for interest rate charged by banks to their most creditworthy customers.
Principal	1. The face amount or part value of a debt security. 2. One who acts as a dealer buying and selling for his own account.
Put Option	*See* Option.
Rating	A grading given by Moody's, Standard and Poor's, or other rating services as to the creditworthiness of an issuer of a security.
Registration	Requirement in the USA for a company to be registered under the Securities Exchange Act of 1934 before it can issue securities on the exchanges.
Repurchase Agreement	A holder of securities sells these securities to an investor with an agreement to repurchase them at a fixed price on a fixed date. The security 'buyer' in effect lends the 'seller' money for the period of the agreement, and the terms of the agreement are structured to compensate him for this.

Reserve Requirement	Fractional amount of a deposit or other liability that a bank or other depository institution is required to hold in eligible reserves.
Revolving Line of Credit	A bank line of credit on which the customer pays a commitment fee and can take down and repay funds according to his needs. Normally the line involves a firm commitment from the bank for a period of several years.
Risk	Chance of loss owing to accident, failure of a debtor, change of an exchange rate, etc.
Rollover Credit	A loan that is repriced ('rolled over') periodically at a predetermined spread or margin over the agreed upon, currently prevailing, base rate (such as LIBOR).
RUF	Revolving underwriting facility. *See* NIF.
Savings and Loan Association	In the USA, a federal- or state-chartered institution that accepts savings deposits and invests the bulk of the funds thus received in mortgages.
Secondary Market	The market in which previously issued securities are traded.
Securitisation	Narrowly used to refer to the process by which traditional bank or thrift institution assets, mainly loans or mortgages, are converted into marketable securities which may be purchased either by depository institutions or by non-bank investors. More broadly, the term refers to the development of markets for a variety of new negotiable instruments, such as NIFs and FRNs in the international markets and commercial paper in the United States, which replace bank loans as a means of borrowing.
Securities and Exchange Commission (SEC)	US agency created by Congress to protect investors in securities transactions by administering securities legislation.
Seigniorage	The difference between the value of coin, or other form of money, and its cost of production, including (in the case of coin) both metal and minting expense. When the mint privilege was limited to the lord or *seigneur*, seigniorage was a 'right of the *seigneur*'. Modern banks are said to earn seigniorage to the extent that interest on deposits and the costs of services rendered to

depositors fall short of interest on loans by more than the normal rate of profit.

'Shell' Branch — A foreign branch — usually in a tax haven — which engages in Eurocurrency business but is run out of a head office.

Spot Rate — The buying or selling price quoted for a transaction to be made on the spot (telegraphic transfers), usually referring to transactions in the foreign exchange markets. Spot prices for forward, futures or options contracts.

Spread — The same as margin. The rate of interest over the reference point in loans, the difference between bid and ask prices in the bond markets.

Standstill — An agreement between bank creditors and a government on a temporary deferment of amortisation payments on long-term debt and on a freezing or rollover of short-term debt.

Straight Bond — Fixed-rate bond without conversion.

Strips — (Separate Trading of Registered Principal of Securities) The US Treasury's acronym for zero coupon instruments derived from selected long-term notes and bonds. At a bondholder's request, the Federal Reserve, as the Treasury's fiscal agent, will separate a designated security into its individual coupon components and corpus or principal payment. The pieces may be traded separately and must be maintained on the treasury's book-entry system.

Subordinated Debt — Debt that can claim, in the event of liquidation, only after the claims of other debts have been met.

Swap — A given currency is simultaneously purchased and sold, but the maturity for each of the transactions is different.

Swap Rate — In the foreign exchange market, the difference between the spot and forward rates at which a currency is traded.

Syndicated Loan — The process by which a loan, arranged by one group of banks (i.e. the 'lead banks'), is funded by being sold to another group of banks.

Tax Haven	A country that imposes little or no tax on the profits from transactions carried on in, or routed through, that country, especially income from dividends and interest.
Tender Panel	A method for distributing notes issued under note issuance facilities. A group of financial institutions have the right to bid for the short-term notes issued under the facility on each issue date.
Tombstone	An advertisement giving, as a matter of record, the details of a new issue or loan and listing terms, the name of the issuer, the amount and the names of the managers and underwriters or syndicate members.
Transactions Costs	The cost of carrying out particular transactions.
Transfer Pricing	The pricing at which one affiliate in a group of companies sells goods or services to another affiliated unit.
Underwriting	An agreement in which a group of securities houses, banks or other financial concerns guarantees to subscribe to a set proportion of a new issue, at a specified price, to ensure the issue's full subscription.
Unit of Account	Function of money to serve as a yardstick for measuring prices, values and wealth.
Unit Trust	In Britain, an organisation that collects money from subscribers, called unitholders, usually small investors, and invests it in securities for their benefit. The securities bought are held, usually, by an important bank acting as custodian trustee.
Universal Bank	(All-purpose banks) Those banks (commonly found in Switzerland, West Germany and Austria) that are allowed to do almost anything financial, from lending other people's money to advising on investments, dealing in securities and valuable metals, etc.
Variable Rate Loan	Loan made at an interest rate that varies with base rate, prime or LIBOR.
Withholding Tax	Tax deducted at source on interest and dividend payments.

Author Index

Subject Index